MUSIC, MUSICIANS

AND THE

SAINT-SIMONIANS

Félicien David in Saint-Simonian costume—Ménilmontant, 1832. Oil painting by Raymond Bonheur (Musée municipal de Saint-Germain-en-Laye; photo Bibl. Nat., Paris).

MUSIC, MUSICIANS

AND THE

SAINT-SIMONIANS

RALPH P. LOCKE

THE UNIVERSITY OF CHICAGO PRESS · CHICAGO & LONDON

RALPH P. LOCKE is associate professor of musicology at the
Eastman School of Music, University of Rochester.

THE UNIVERSITY OF CHICAGO PRESS, CHICAGO 60637
THE UNIVERSITY OF CHICAGO PRESS, LTD., LONDON

© 1986 by The University of Chicago
All rights reserved. Published 1986
Printed in the United States of America
95 94 93 92 91 90 89 88 87 86 54321

Preparation for and publication of this volume have been assisted by the American
Musicological Society, the University of Rochester's Eastman School of Music,
and the Department of Music of the University of Chicago.

LIBRARY OF CONGRESS CATALOGING-IN-PUBLICATION DATA

Locke, Ralph P.
    Music, musicians, and the Saint-Simonians.

    Includes index.
    Bibliography: p.
    1. Music—France—19th century—History and criticism.
2. Saint-Simonianism.   3. Music and society.   I. Title.
ML270.4.L65   1985   780'.07'0944   85-20915
ISBN 0-226-48901-9
        0-226-48902-7 (pbk.)

For Lona, Martha, and Susannah

When will I hear the people sing the hymn of peace, more electrifying than the awesome "Marseillaise," more joyous than the simple "Parisienne"? . . .

Let him appear, too, the composer whose intoxicating and powerful music—richer than Rossini's and Beethoven's—will seize hold of the emotional power which music alone possesses (because of all its melodies and variations), in order to accompany the hymn of the future. . . .

Architects, where are your plans for the temple of peace?

Olinde Rodrigues
Chef du culte
27 November 1831

All social institutions must have as their aim the improvement of the moral, physical, and intellectual lot of the most numerous and poorest class.

All privileges of birth, without exception, will be abolished.

To each according to his capacity; to each capacity according to its works.

Slogans from the mastheads of
L'Organisateur and *Le Globe*
1830–31

CONTENTS

CONTENTS

CONTENTS

LIST OF PLATES

ACKNOWLEDGMENTS

Perhaps it is appropriate that a book about the Saint-Simonians be a collaborative effort. This one certainly is. I have profited and derived great pleasure from the contributions and support of many individuals and institutions during the twelve years that my labor has lasted.

Musicologists Philip Gossett and the late Dorothy V. Hagan and intellectual historian James B. Briscoe were there at the beginning and along the way, ready to read and willing to comment.

Other scholars kindly read chapters or offered assistance in areas of their special expertise. I must start with the Berliozians: John B. Ahouse, Peter A. Bloom, David Cairns, Nathalie Combase, Pierre Citron, D. Kern Holoman, Thérèse Husson, Hugh Macdonald, François Piatier, and Katherine Kolb Reeve. Then the Lisztians: Serge Gut, Maurice Hinson, Lorna D. Fraser Irwin, Alexander Main, Rena Mueller, Michael B. Saffle, Charles Suttoni, Edward N. Waters, and Sharon M. Winklhofer. The Mendelssohnians: Margaret B. Crum, Rudolf Elvers, Douglass M. Seaton and R. Larry Todd. Two fellow Davidians: Morton B. Achter and Mme A. Deniau-Treppo. Three experts on chansons and political music: Adrienne Fried Block, Dorothy S. Packer, and Frédéric Robert. Seven musicologists with wonderfully diverse eighteenth- and nineteenth-century interests: Jane Fulcher, Hans Lenneberg, David B. Levy, Rose R. Subotnik, Jurgen Thym, Gary Tomlinson, and Gretchen Wheelock. And eight no less varied historians, who helped set and keep me on the path: Keith M. Baker, Sanford H. Elwitt, Leonard Krieger, Frank E. Manuel, William McGrath, the late Gerhard Meyer, Edgar Leon Newman, Barrie M. Ratcliffe, David D. Roberts, William H. Sewell, Jr., and William Weber.

The French government gave me a crucial year-long *bourse* in 1974–75 and a *bourse d'été* in 1976. The inhabitants of Cadenet also helped in various ways, especially Mayor Jacques Kryn, the late Françoise Kryn, and Solange and Pierre Arnal.

The staff of the Music Division of the Bibliothèque nationale made me feel totally at home, notably François Lesure, Simone Wallon, and the tireless and devoted Jean-Michel Nectoux. Other habitués of 2 rue Louvois also offered helpful words: M. Elizabeth C. Bartlet, the late Rita Benton, H. Robert Cohen, Marie-Noëlle Colette, Robert Isherwood, Arnaud Laster, Mergier-Bordeix, Robert Orledge, and Lesley B. Wright. The Arsenal and Thiers libraries, the Bibliothèque historique de la ville de Paris, the Archives nationales, and the provincial libraries (Saint-Germain-en-Laye, Aix, Carpentras) were all enormously helpful, and so were (among others) the British, Newberry, New York Public, University of Chicago, and Harvard Business School libraries.

It gives me particular pleasure to thank everyone in and around the Eastman School of Music (University of Rochester) who supported, in various ways, my work on this project—especially Robert S. Freeman, Jon E. Engberg, the late Jerald C. Graue, Jurgen Thym (again), Aimée Israel-Pelletier, Ruth Kimmerer, Terry Adler, Chris McCormack, Fontaine McNamara, Shelley Gordon, Hali Fieldman, and the staffs of the Manuscript Center (Medical Center), Rush Rhees Library, and Sibley Music Library (notably, at Sibley, Iva Buff, Mary Wallace Davidson, Louise Goldberg, Jay Philip Lambert, Joan Swanekamp, Ruth Watanabe, and Ross Wood). Through Director Freeman's efforts, and with additional financial assistance from the Andrew W. Mellon Foundation and the University of Chicago's Department of Music, I was able to devote large blocks of time to revising the text (see Note on Sources) and producing a machine-readable version for the publisher.

In a more general sense, of course, any book is, however indirectly, the fruit of collaboration. The many devoted teachers and friends who have encouraged and guided me at different times in my life will find something of themselves in these pages. I will restrain myself and mention, of the many who have not yet been mentioned, only a few: Paul A. Bushkovitch, William B. Epstein, Robert E. Freeman, Herbert Fromm, Rabbi Roland B. Gittelsohn, Georg Knepler, Susan A. Kotlier, the late Edward E. Lowinsky, Joel Margolis, Leonard B. Meyer, Jessie Ann Owens, Ronald W. Takvorian—and the unforgettable Vita Zéphir.

I owe great thanks, too, to my sister Jean Locke Miller, my grandparents Bessie Blake and Lillian and Philip Locke, and my parents, Doris T. Schwartz and the late Merle I. Locke, who provided the indispensable basis: support, trust, and models of how to live and work.

And the three dedicatees have made it all worthwhile.

ABBREVIATIONS
AND SYMBOLS

Ars	Bibliothèque de l'Arsenal (Paris), manuscript no. . The numbers in the 7000s are part of the original Fonds Enfantin (the official archive of the Saint-Simonian movement, consisting of materials donated late in life by many members of the movement). Higher numbers (e.g., Ars 15032) indicate more recent acquisitions.
BHVP	Bibliothèque historique de la ville de Paris.
BNImp	Bibliothèque nationale, Département des imprimés. See Note on Sources
BNMus	Bibliothèque nationale, Département de la musique.
lettre autogr.	Bibliothèque nationale, Département de la musique, file of autograph letters by important musicians.
OSSE	*Oeuvres de Saint-Simon et d'Enfantin,* 47 vols. See Bibliography.
Thiers	Bibliothèque Thiers (Paris), Fonds d'Eichthal.
▽	In Chapters 8, 10, and 12 certain passages containing detailed musical discussion have been set in slightly smaller type, so that a reader who so wishes may easily bypass them. The beginning and ending of each such passage is further signaled by triangular "arrows" in the margin, as
△	at left.

Much of the material in Chapter 10 and Appendix D is drawn from six brochures published by the movement in 1832. These brochures will generally be referred to by the following short titles or descriptive phrases:

> *6 juin 1832*
> *Prise d'habit*
> *Travaux du Temple* (the "temple account")

Mort de Talabot ("account of Talabot's funeral")
Procès (août) and *Procès (octobre)* (the "trial accounts")
Full bibliographical data can be found in Chapter 10, note 20.

A number of Saint-Simonian songsters and collections of song sheets are listed with abbreviated titles in Appendix B. The abbreviated titles, like those of the brochures above, are used in the listings of Appendix D.

PART ONE
INTRODUCTION

1

MUSIC FOR
AN OLD TALE

A few years back, while reading a review of a book on Heine's social views, I was startled to come across the following grumpy words:

> [The author's] argument . . . will not quite do. It proceeds from an attempt to characterize Heine's modes of thought to an account of the influences on his thinking, especially one major influence. Hegel? Marx? Nothing so trendy. We are back with the old tale of the Saint Simonians.[1]

Historians political, economic, and literary—I have since come to realize—have reason to feel tired of "the old tale of the Saint-Simonians"; during the last century and a half, they have heard it many, perhaps too many times. The spreading of the story began with the Saint-Simonians themselves, who—in the late 1820s and early 1830s—put insistent claims on the public's attention through sermon and song, printed propaganda, and imaginative, appealing costumes and rituals. Furthermore, though the Saint-Simonian movement itself collapsed around 1835, its leading members carried important elements of the doctrine into their later work and teaching and, profoundly aware of the movement's contribution to history and social thought, preserved and gathered into a single mammoth archive tens of thousands of documents, including internal correspondence, financial records, and detailed bibliographies and collections of the movement's publications, whether books, brochures, or broadsheets.[2] In 1865–78 much of this material was reprinted, or (in the case of letters and memoranda) published for the first time, in an authorized forty-seven-volume edition, the first thirteen volumes of which comprise a minutely detailed history or—more accurately—chronicle. This imposing edition, partly through sheer bulk, has tended ever since to encourage writers to make a large place for the Saint-Simonian movement in their accounts of the age.[3] Much of what was not included in the forty-seven volumes has been published by later generations of scholars and has served to strengthen further the image of the Saint-Simonians as an all-pervading force.[4]

But all the propaganda in the world, and the collusion of all the world's historians, could not have created such a vast reputation out of thin air. The Saint-Simonians earned their reputation well, by their ideas and activities and by their direct and undeniable impact on their own and later generations, in France and elsewhere. And their particular influence just across the Rhine—on Heine and his fellow Young Germans, and on Marx and Engels—may now be an "old tale," but it is nonetheless a true one.

This is not to deny that—as the (anonymous) book reviewer implies—the Saint-Simonians and, of course, their revered precursor Henri Saint-Simon have at times been invoked rather sloppily in studies of nineteenth-century politics, economics, and literature. All too often they have been praised or blamed as the supposed originators and disseminators of ideas that were in fact common property of the age. This was perhaps unavoidable. The tendency to make exaggerated claims about the influence of any individual or movement of recognized importance is a natural one, and it leads just as naturally to an equal and opposite reaction: exaggerated attempts at deflation. Sooner or later, though, these one-sided views prove unsatisfying and are replaced by a more balanced assessment, a portrait that is true—warts and all. And often this portrait, despite differences in detail, confirms the initial judgement of history about the subject. In the present case, the hundreds of books and articles listed in Walch's *Bibliographie saint-simonienne* attest to a reputation that, despite the swings of intellectual fashion, stubbornly refuses to fade.

There remain of course many yet unwritten chapters in "the old tale of the Saint-Simonians." Musical matters—to come to our subject—have been almost completely neglected by historians interested in the movement; few musicologists have done anything to help fill the gap. The reasons are probably simple. Historians often do not have the expertise needed to treat musical questions. And we musicologists, members of a much younger discipline, are still heavily occupied with tasks central to our own field, such as authenticating, dating, and publishing the works of the masters. This has left us little time until recently for matters that straddle the border of another discipline, even a relatively accessible one such as history.

Whatever the reasons, the gap clearly exists. Whereas such topics as "Balzac and Saint-Simonism," "Saint-Simonian Influence on the Rise of Free Trade," or "Saint-Simon, the Saint-Simonians, and the Concept of Authority" have been treated over and over from differing points of view, the many topics that might be included under the general heading "Saint-Simonism and Music" have been almost universally neglected. Occasional writers, it is true, have attempted to assess briefly the influence that the Saint-Simonian views on the social role of art exerted upon the music criticism and even the (non-Saint-Simonian) musical compositions of the day.[5] But the "influence" of a body of ideas is a notoriously slippery concept, especially when the ideas that are doing the "influencing" have themselves never been adequately studied.

I decided to start with matters more securely graspable, and therefore to focus the present work at least as much on (to make a somewhat artificial distinction) the Saint-Simon*ians* as on Saint-Simon*ism,* their enormously varied and at times elusive philosophy. The topic to be explored can be stated in the form of two questions: (1) To what extent did the Saint-Simonians (and Saint-Simon before them) discuss music in their writings and public lectures, incorporate music into their activities, and try to draw musicians into their circle; and (2) What were the most direct effects of these varied efforts on the movement itself and on the ideas, works, and lives of the musicians of the day?[26]

To answer these questions, I shall of necessity be examining in fair detail (especially in Chapters 2–7) certain aspects of the movement's history and philosophy. In particular, I shall be taking that long-needed close look at the Saint-Simonian pronouncements on the social role of art. Along the way, I shall have occasion to offer new interpretations on various matters of "ism" and even to correct some misunderstandings that one encounters frequently, even in the more specialized literature. And these explorations will, I hope, provide a more solid basis for future "influence" studies and the like.

Nonetheless, the primary focus of the present work is not on abstract ideas but on people. The main task at hand will be to establish with precision, and to set in context, the specifically musical views and activities of Saint-Simon and the Saint-Simonians, and the specifically Saint-Simonian involvement of a number of musicians of the period. These musicians were no mean lot, from the tangentially associated Liszt, Berlioz, Mendelssohn, Nourrit, Hiller, Halévy, and Henri Reber to the faithful Félicien David, Jules Vinçard, and Dominique Tajan-Rogé. It is their stories that are told here: what attracted them to the movement (emotionally as well as intellectually), how long they participated, what they gave, and what they got.

The verbs—giving and getting—should perhaps be stressed. It remains my feeling that the present study reveals a rich *mutual* interaction and influence typical of periods in which musicians consider all of society their province and responsibility and in which social thinkers regard music and the other arts as something other than harmless diversions or intellectual exercises. Since our own period (at least in the nonsocialist world) is most definitely not one of those, some may find it of interest to look back to the Paris of the not too distant past and see what it was like.

Some words about the past and the present. That an understanding of the past can help people overcome their troubles (which are themselves a legacy of that same past) has long been an article of the historian's faith, though some have recently called it naïve. Different readers will no doubt come to a wide variety of conclusions about the continuing relevance that this particular chunk of the past has had for succeeding generations, and has for our own. I reserve for the final chapter (and the final section of Chapter 9) most of my own thoughts on the matter. Elsewhere I have kept a lower profile, in part for fear of turning a complex story into something too neat: a cautionary tale, perhaps, or a glorious epic. This is not to say that I have refrained entirely from commenting, interpreting, or suggesting parallels. But my main concern has been to assemble, or when necessary reconstruct, what historians in more innocent days used to call "the facts"—including a number of revealing and effective musical works by David and others—and to indicate their immediate historical and (occasionally) psychological context. Surely the Saint-Simonians, and the musicians of their day, deserve at least that much.

2

MASTER AND
POSTHUMOUS
DISCIPLES

The Saint-Simonian movement is widely recognized—and has been recognized almost continuously since the mid-nineteenth century—as perhaps the most influential social movement of its day. The movement was founded in 1825 by the disciples of the recently deceased social philosopher Henri Saint-Simon. The Saint-Simonians intended to spread their master's ideas, but in doing so they also extended them, adapted them, added to them, even contradicted them at times. Furthermore, their own views on certain issues underwent some rather striking transformations during the ten or so years between the movement's founding and its decline around 1835. Nonetheless, the most fundamental concepts of Saint-Simonian doctrine were deeply indebted to those espoused by Saint-Simon, and they remained fairly constant, marking with a recognizable stamp the words and acts of the movement's members.

The uniqueness of the Saint-Simonians is perhaps best seen by comparing them to other prominent utopian socialist movements of the period. What the utopian socialists all had in common, the Saint-Simonians included, was a sense of distress at the present state of society—especially the increasing misery of the urban working and unemployed classes. The solutions proposed by the various movements overlapped at some points and at others veered in strikingly different directions. Both Robert Owen and Charles Fourier, for example, based their respective plans for social reform on small, decentralized, and largely self-sufficient communities. Fourier imagined (and his followers actually created) *phalanstères:* primarily agricultural settlements whose internal organization was rather loose. (The Fourierists felt that individuals work best and are most content if allowed to engage in work that suits their natural inclinations.) Owen, a British manufacturer, established a kind of benevolent mill town in New Lanark, Scotland, with nonprofit stores and good housing and schools. His profits increased, and Owenite communities spread to the United States (notably New Harmony, Indiana), much as Fourierist communities flourished for a time at the Transcendentalists' Brook Farm and other American sites. Even at their most numerous and successful, though, the Owenite and Fourierist settlements were guided by the principles of starting small and working from the ground up.[1]

The Saint-Simonians, by contrast, thought large and aimed high.[2] While sharing Fourier's concern for the emotional life of the individual and Owen's emphasis on industrial productivity, they hoped to reorganize society from the top down. They felt that if society could be placed under the direction of the most competent and "productive" individuals (the leading industrialists and scientists), the economy would prosper and the most serious social ills would be cured. This theory was not the whole of Saint-Simonism; as the movement grew and developed, its ideology expanded to include other issues, such as the need for a new social religion, the liberation of women, the rehabilitation of sensual pleasure, and the restoration of a priestly, "social" role for artists, a role that (they noted) had been practiced in ancient Greece and medieval Europe but neglected in recent centuries. Even in its later stages, though, the movement retained at its core the desire to shift power from the unproductive landed aristocracy to the enterprising men of talent then rising in the middle class.

This central concept came from Henri Saint-Simon (1760–1825), or, as he was known before he dropped his own aristocratic embellishments, Claude Henri de Rouvroy, count of Saint-Simon (see plate 1). A distant descendent of the duke of Saint-Simon, the celebrated courtier and memoirist of the time of Louis XIV, Henri Saint-Simon had led an erratic career in his early years. From the age of seventeen he had served as an officer in the army, fighting side by side with the American colonists during their Revolution, and then in the Caribbean. After returning to France, he became involved in his own nation's Revolution, although this time his role was more ambivalent. In the provincial towns near his family's estates he was an active and vocal proponent of the new order, but in Paris he began to buy at bargain prices a number of mansions whose noble owners had fled or been guillotined. Imprisoned for a time (apparently in error), he eventually regained his freedom and reclaimed his properties.

Around the beginning of the century, Saint-Simon's thoughts began to turn more and more toward plans for a grand reorganization of science and society, so much so that his partner in the real-estate schemes, the Prussian Count Redern, finally decided to dissolve their union. Saint-Simon, trustingly, took the share that Redern determined was his and entered upon a life of independence which he attempted to maintain for many years, even long after the inadequate sum from Redern had given out.[3] From 1802 to his death Saint-Simon devoted himself to writing a series of pamphlets, books, periodicals, open letters, and pleas in which he sketched his ideas about science, industry, and (especially in his last book, *Nouveau Christianisme*) religion and the arts.

In these writings, as in his life, Saint-Simon straddled two ages. His spirit was predominantly rationalistic, even mechanistic, like that of the Encyclopedists, yet his predominant concern—the reorganization of society to serve the interests of what he called "the poorest and most numerous class"—showed a deeply humane sensitivity to the suffering and social dislocation caused by the recent unbridled expansion of industry and commerce.

Saint-Simon's ideas were absorbed and developed by his pupils and disciples. The first of these were Augustin Thierry and Auguste Comte, both of whom left the master after several years. Comte went on to become one of France's most prominent social thinkers and the founder of sociology; he insisted to the end of his life that Saint-Simon had contributed almost nothing to his thought and that, if anything, the influence had been the other way around.

More appreciative were Saint-Simon's last two disciples, Léon Halévy and Olinde Rodrigues, and a circle of admirers whom they brought to Saint-Simon in his final months. After the master's death, Halévy, Rodrigues, and these admirers became the founders of a movement, and, thereby, the first Saint-Simonians. They started by publishing *Le Producteur,* a journal filled with wide-ranging essays. The first two volumes, edited by A. Cerclet, continued in many ways the positivistic emphases of Saint-Simon's early and middle periods.

The third and fourth volumes of *Le Producteur* (1826) show a very different spirit attributable in part to the growing (Marguerite Thibert calls it "insinuating") influence of the future "Père" Enfantin.[4] Barthélemy-Prosper Enfantin (1796–1864) had entered the Saint-Simon circle in early 1825 and in April of that year had heard Rodrigues read aloud, in Saint-Simon's presence, the unpublished text of *Nouveau Christianisme.* Less because of his financial connections—he was the son of a bankrupt banker and had been sporadically active in commerce and finance—than because of his expansive and commanding personality, Enfantin, soon after Saint-Simon's death, joined Rodrigues as copublisher of *Le Producteur.* At first he contributed only sporadically, but he became a prominent force when in April 1826 he and Philippe Buchez took over the editorship from Cerclet. The more strictly positivistic and liberal contributors—Allier, Blanqui, Carrel, Comte, and Halévy (Enfantin later called them "the eunuchs of Saint-Simonism")[5]—were similarly replaced by spirits—Bazard, Laurent, Rouen—more compatible with an emphasis on the late, religious elements of Saint-Simon's teaching.

Toward the end of 1826 the disciples ceased trying to reach the public but continued to meet and develop their ideas further. From time to time they solicited support from Béranger, Lafayette, and other political figures, but without success. Gradually more of the original disciples fell away, but they were replaced, in numbers and enthusiasm, by eager young recruits, many of them either recent students at the Ecole polytechnique or young men of a more religious or even mystical bent: Margerin, Transon, Jules Lechevalier, Michel Chevalier, Henri Fournel, Hippolyte Carnot, Charles Duveyrier. Many of them were suffering from the *mal du siècle* so well described by Musset: "Everything which was, is no longer; everything which will be, is not yet. Do not look elsewhere for the secret of our woes."[6] Saint-Simon's social philosophy encouraged them to think that the new golden age—"everything which will be"—was not far off and that it could be reached even sooner by collective action and persuasion. Their faith in heavenly paradise and the old aristocratic order shattered, they poured their plentiful energies into a new faith that promised something very like paradise on earth.[7]

Toward the end of 1828 the Saint-Simonians decided to undertake a series of biweekly lectures. Held at first in Rodrigues's bank, where Enfantin was employed and had his lodgings, the lectures were soon transferred to a larger hall in the rue Taranne. The texts of these lectures, written collectively by the older disciples, later were revised by more recent recruits[8] and published in a volume known as the *Doctrine of Saint-Simon: An Exposition (First Year).*[9]

The lectures were usually delivered by Saint-Amand Bazard (1791–1832), a dedicated and brilliantly logical left-liberal who, with his friend Buchez, had earlier helped found the French Charbonnerie, a movement based on the Italian Carbonari and dedicated to the overthrow of the Bourbons. Attracted by Saint-Simon's more constructive vision of the future, Bazard had joined the circle of disciples, had contributed to *Le Producteur,* and gradually had become one of the movement's leading figures.

The published versions of the *Doctrine* lectures and a briefer second set from 1829–30, more directly attributable to Bazard, were supplemented by a growing stream of related publications: the *Lettres sur la religion et la politique* (1828–29) of Olinde Rodrigues's brother Eugène, who was a seminal figure in the movement until his untimely death early in 1830; summaries and explanations of the *Doctrine* by Carnot and Transon; and *L'Organisateur* (1829–31), a weekly journal named after one of Saint-Simon's own major publications.

Less publicly, the disciples began to reconstitute the Saint-Simonian School ("Ecole saint-simonienne") as a Saint-Simonian Church or Family ("Eglise," "Religion," or "Famille saint-simonienne"). On Christmas Day, 1829—the choice of day was typically symbolic—the leading disciples, known as the members of the "Collège," decided to elect as "Pères suprêmes" Bazard and Enfantin; this choice received the authoritative benediction of Olinde Rodrigues, the only person still active in the movement who had known Saint-Simon well. The lesser disciples were divided into two classes (second- and third-degree members), and each *fils* or *fille* was responsible in hierarchical fashion to a *père* or *mère* in the next higher level. (The women members at this point were few in number.)

Enfantin, who was growing ever fonder of speaking in the Lord's name and comparing himself to Moses,[10] decided in early 1830 to rent a modest apartment at 6 rue Monsigny (the Hôtel de Gêvres) for himself and several disciples; it served the ever-growing Family as a regular location for communal meals, private discussions, writing sessions, and semipublic entertainments. In

April 1830 the Saint-Simonian Church began to confront the public in a series of sermons at the rue Monsigny.

When the July Revolution broke out, most of the members, adhering to the pacifist principles of Saint-Simon, refused to take part. Nonetheless, it is no exaggeration to say that the Revolution "made" the movement. The overthrow of the Bourbons encouraged Frenchmen to think about the many possible ways of reshaping society and permitted them to act on those thoughts; for those who hoped to see major changes instituted by the new government, though, disappointment quickly set in, for power was being shifted from hand to hand, not truly spread about. The Saint-Simonians, with their apolitical or even antipolitical plan of social reform, profited from both this new rush of interest in social issues and this frustration with conventional solutions. Ever larger numbers of curious and earnest visitors, including many women and more than a few prominent figures in letters, politics, and the arts, attended the Saint-Simonians' lectures and soirees; many more read their publications or learned about their ideas through the daily press. The movement also had some success spreading their doctrine in working-class neighborhoods, in the French provinces, even in surrounding countries.

The Saint-Simonians quickly expanded their propaganda network. In October 1830 they relocated the sermons to the more spacious Salle Taitbout. That same month they gained control of *Le Globe,* which in the late 1820s, under the editorship of Sainte-Beuve and Pierre Leroux, had been the leading newspaper of the liberals and the Romantics. For the next year and a half it served as the major Saint-Simonian propaganda organ; in its last months it was even distributed gratis to anyone who was interested (or whom the leaders wished to interest). Soon after acquiring the *Globe,* whose offices were located on the third floor of the Monsigny building, the Saint-Simonians took over the large apartment on the first floor as well, in part as a location for rather substantial soirees. The number of members who gathered regularly at the house must have been swelling around this time. A financial statement for the eleven months beginning 4 May 1830 shows thirty people living at the Monsigny address (ten of them domestics) and forty-five eating there.[11] Later the number of place settings rose to at least ninety-five.[12] 1828–31 were years of expansion for the movement, and in many ways its years of glory.

It was in the public lectures and books of this period that the Saint-Simonians propounded their grand social plan most clearly and fully. Restating and embellishing many ideas first introduced by Saint-Simon, they called on the leaders of government and industry to abolish "all privileges of birth, without exception"—most importantly the right of aristocrats to inherit rent-producing lands and thus live off the labor of their peasants—and to end competition (*antagonisme*) among and within the various sectors of the economy, replacing it with a new and more productive principle: cooperation or solidarity (*associ-*

ation). The most powerful concept in Saint-Simonian social theory, and the one that raised it above pure utopianism, was its insistence on the crucial role of industrial production in these transformations. The Saint-Simonians realized that France, in contrast to England, was hamstrung in its industrial development by such remnants of a feudal-aristocratic economy as an archaic banking system, one that was not geared toward providing the capital necessary for building factories and railroads. They reasoned that growth in industry, agriculture, and commerce would serve the interests of the working masses as well as of the factory owners, financiers, and technologists. And so they urged the workers to submit, in the spirit of association, to the greater wisdom of the industrial leaders and the industry-affiliated government—in other words, to refrain from organizing themselves politically and acting "antagonistically" on their own behalf through strikes and uprisings.

This plan can be seen as an early form of corporate or welfare-state liberalism. As such it was already far in advance of many contemporary political parties and schools of social thought. But it also presented the kernel from which more radical social schemes were to grow. Marx and Engels, notably, appropriated the Saint-Simonian view of industrial economy but strengthened it with a renewed appreciation of the necessary and positive role that class conflict and class consciousness play in the transformation of society. It was they indeed who coined the term "utopian socialism" in order to distinguish their own "scientific socialism" from the systems of those precursors whom they still honored but in significant respects had superseded.

The Saint-Simonians had their own rather naïve class analysis of society, one that resulted incidentally in a unique attitude toward the arts. Starting from the assumption that the interests of industrial workers and their bosses are essentially identical, the Saint-Simonians—following Saint-Simon—placed both groups in the class of "industrials." (This class also included farmers, transportation workers, artisans, merchants—anyone "who works to produce or to bring within the reach of the different members of society one or several material means of satisfying their needs or physical tastes.")[13] In their early writings the Saint-Simonians granted priority to the "industrial" sector of society, subordinating to its interest other, less "productive" groups, such as scientists, planners, and artists. Indeed, during this period they seldom discussed the arts at all; at most they stressed that "artists"—the term will often be used here, as it was by the Saint-Simonians, to include not only visual artists but also authors, actors, and musicians—must serve the needs of industry. A slogan of Saint-Simon's was their guide: "Since everything is done *by* industry, everything should be done *for* industry."[14]

Sometime around 1829, though, the disciples began to shift their attention from such practical goals as technological development and industrial productivity to the processes by which society could be inspired and persuaded to work toward those goals. (It is for this reason that, drawing on ideas that the dying Saint-Simon had drafted in his last work, *Nouveau Christianisme,* they transformed their movement into a religion and reorganized their membership hierarchically.) Increasingly they began to view history as an alternation of "critical" epochs and "organic" ones, the former marked by social strife and contending philosophies, the latter by peaceful acceptance of the prevailing social structure and of a single, coherent set of religious principles. Their own aim was now to lead a "critical" Europe to a new state of "organic" wholeness. And to artists—as we shall see in Chapters 5–7—they now assigned a crucial new task: that of persuading individuals, classes, and nations to abandon their traditional rivalries and to work together, in the spirit of *association universelle,* to bring nigh the *nouvelle époque organique.*

A world ruled by *association* was not, as one might at first think, a world ruled by egalitarianism. What *association* meant in practical terms to the Saint-Simonians was encapsulated in one of their slogans: "To each according to his calling [*vocation*]; to each according to his works."[15] The first phrase indicated that positions of responsibility should be given to those most gifted to fill them, rather than to people whose sole credential consisted of having been born into a certain social class. Gone forever the obscurity of the talented writer, scientist, manager, all those who in the past had not been granted the opportunity to exercise their native talents for the good of society or handed the capital or other means necessary to carry out their ideas. As for the second phrase, "to each according to his works," a comparison with Marx's revision of it, "to each according to his need," makes clear that the Saint-Simonians intended to reward more heavily those who contributed in greater degree to the productivity and the social and spiritual well-being of the nation. Taken together, the two phrases of the slogan explain why the movement held an attraction for students from the Ecole polytechnique: these were the very engineers- and technocrats-in-training who would find a position, and a profitable one, in a *nouveau monde saint-simonien* (much as they do in our world today). Still, this is not to suggest that the Saint-Simonians' orientation toward the working class and other disenfranchised groups (notably women) was insincere. They would prove their sincerity, if not always their efficacy or common sense, over and over again in the months and years to come.

The events and social doctrines just outlined carry the story of the Saint-Simonians through 1830 or so, enough to provide the necessary background for their specific ideas on art and music, to be discussed in Chapters 3–7. The rest of the story will be told later in the book. But a brief summary may be helpful at this point.

Around mid-1831 the religious and mystical elements triumphed conclusively, a development symbolized by the rise of Enfantin to the position of sole Supreme Father (see plate 3) and by a series of turbulent schisms in which the movement lost a number of its most solid thinkers, most dedicated proselytizers, and wealthiest supporters. Crisis compounded crisis when the press and the government began to suggest that these outspoken but peaceable supporters of the working-class were to blame for the violent uprising in Lyons and for other political demonstrations that flared up in the wake of the July Revolution. (The movement had already brought itself into some disrepute by examining publicly during 1831 and 1832 certain delicate questions in the areas of marriage reform and sexual psychology.) In 1832 Enfantin and a group of disciples formed a celibate and ascetic community at Ménilmontant, a financially necessary but short-lived project that did little to repair the damage, although it proved to be of crucial importance for the development of a characteristic Saint-Simonian musical life. Late that year Enfantin was tried on various charges—mostly trumped up—and sent to prison for close to a year. His disciples scattered. A number of them headed toward the Near and Middle East to search for the female messiah; with them they carried diagrams for another distant dream: a canal through Suez that they hoped would improve international relations. They were gratified on neither count, but in time many of those who returned to France found prominence in business, the professions, the arts, and even government. (The Suez Canal was finally constructed under international auspices in 1869.) Thus the Saint-Simonians and their ideas, considered outrageous, immoral, and subversive during the early years of the reign of Louis-Philippe, found a degree of acceptance in the 1850s and 1860s, in the Empire of Napoleon III.

PART TWO
THEORY

3

ART AS A MEANS OF SOCIAL CONTROL

SOCIAL ROLES FOR ART

Of the many ideas that the Saint-Simonians promulgated during the ten or so years in which they were most active, one of the most novel and challenging, though by no means the most threatening to the authorities and the solid burghers, concerned the role of art in society. Scholars are generally agreed that Saint-Simon and the Saint-Simonians were the first (or at least the first moderns) to advocate consistently and explicitly a "social role for art," or, as the French often put it, "un art social," "a social art."[1] Phrases such as these may confuse more than they enlighten; a reconsideration of their usefulness gives some insight into what made the aesthetic doctrines of Saint-Simon and the Saint-Simonians uniquely stimulating in their day.

The term "social art" should perhaps be examined first—and then disposed of. To speak of proposals for a "social art" can be terribly misleading, for it can be construed as implying that the normal condition of art is the opposite: "asocial," autonomous, independent of the society in which it is created, perhaps even independent of the social being who created it. Put this baldly, such a philosophy would attract few adherents. But there can be no denying that a relatively strong emphasis on "the isolated, self-contained work" (Dahlhaus's phrase) has been a hallmark of serious aesthetic thought during much of our own century, from Russian formalism to "New Criticism" and recent semiotic approaches, and from Stravinsky's anti-"expressive" pronouncements to the analytical methods of Heinrich Schenker and his (largely American) followers.[2] This belief in the essential autonomy of art has, perhaps inevitably, found its way as well into recent *historical* writings on aesthetics and the arts. During the past few decades historians have tended to dismiss as obviously false the "social" doctrines of art proposed by the Saint-Simonians and others,[3] or—at best—to treat them as a peripheral development.[4] (No doubt the historians have been pushed to such a negative evaluation not only by their own aesthetic views but also by the sometimes horrifying ways in which "social" views have been appropriated by ideologues and oppressive governments on both the left and right.[5]) Fortunately, the reabsorption of social considerations into discussions of the arts is well under way in many fields—thanks in part to growing interest in the undeniably "social" arts of the non-industrialized nations (e.g., African ritual dance and song) and in the no less obviously "social" arts of the "lower" strata of our own societies (e.g., children's games, inner-city wall paintings, rural folksong, or urban-commercial popular music). "High" art is naturally more resistant to such treatment, because its relationship to the prevailing social conditions is more indirect and sometimes more complex. But the relationship is there, and scholars are beginning to seek ways to explicate it.[6] In short, we are gradually learning (again) that all art is in fact social art.

The concept of a social *role* for art is more useful, but still insufficiently precise. It is often invoked by writers in such a way as to suggest that there is but one role that art can conceivably play in society and that all proponents of a social role for art, from Plato to Mao, have been aiming at much the same (perhaps regrettable) thing—what might be called not *a* but *the* social role of art.[7] But this is a purely intellectual construct—a straw man, set up in order to be demolished. In reality, the ways that art can be engaged actively in the life of a society are multifarious; the particular type of engagement a given writer or political figure assigns to art depends upon many factors, including the needs of the historical moment, his or her own personal predispositions, and the artistic repertoire that he or she knows best. It will prove helpful for our later discussions if we pause for a moment to examine three views of the matter that have been widely espoused since around 1800.

What we might call the "democratic" or "recreational" view sees in art a wholesome leisure-time activity for all the active, productive members of society, even the most humble. Saint-Simon's contemporary utopian, Robert Owen, employed music and dance in very much this manner at his benevolent factory town in Scotland,[8] and the principle recurs, with varying emphases, in socialist (and Nazi) writings, as well as in the theory and practice of the lay-choral-singing movement, from Wilhem's Orphéon to the early 20th-century German Jugendbewegung and beyond. This view of the social role of art often tends to place special value on the performing arts because of their strong communal aspect (for performers as well as audience).

Another view has it that the arts find meaning and indeed justification in supporting the essential life-sustaining activities of daily existence (rather than in promoting relaxation after day is done). This rather "utilitarian" view, which applies most naturally to architecture and the decorative arts, was central to the writings of Saint-Simon's contemporary Quatremère de Quincy, a renowned architect and member of the French Academy,[9] and it has reappeared with differing emphases in the form-and-function debates of sculptors, architects, and designers down to our own day (Horatio Greenough, Sullivan and Wright, the Bauhaus movement, the postmodernist Robert Venturi).

Still another frequently encountered approach—less prescriptive than the previous two—holds that works of art cannot help but express a society's aspirations and reveal its innermost conflicts and concerns. Elements of this so-called sociological view, which seems particularly well suited to discussions of the more personal arts such as lyric poetry, were voiced during the early nineteenth century by Bonald and de Maistre—prominent spokesmen for an ultraconservative Catholic revival—and taken up with different emphases by the Romantic authors Chateaubriand, Stendhal, and Hugo. Literary historians of the time, such as Villemain and Ampère, promoted a related view in their occasionally quite subtle attempts at placing medieval poetry, Dante, and more recent repertoires into the context of the society that gave birth to them. Literature, wrote Ampère, "expresses what is hidden . . . latent, suppressed. . . . It often shows not the dominance of a fact but the reaction against it . . . the last sigh of what is dying, the first cry of what will live."[10]

These and other then-current views of art's contribution to the life of society appear at least occasionally in the writings of Saint-Simon and his disciples. Barrault, for example, echoes the "utilitarian" view in his repeated insistence that art is healthiest when it has a clear social function or "*destination*" (intended purpose). Barrault also likes to point out, "sociologically," the ways in which the poetry of his day reflects, perhaps unconsciously, the moral crisis that is brewing. And Saint-Simon himself occasionally argues "democratically" that art should no longer be just a luxury item for the idle rich. But the predominant Saint-Simonian view of art focuses on yet another "social role": the power of art to influence the behavior of its audience in desirable ways, and especially to stir their enthusiasm for the work that needs to be done if society is to advance. We shall call this principle "art as a means of social control."

The phrase "social control" is intended here in a neutral or even positive sense. Unfortunately, it often carries sinister or at least cynical connotations, as when people use it to refer to "opiate" or "safety valve" phenomena, such as the Romans' policy of plying the lower classes with bread and circuses.[11] But sociologists and political scientists generally accept social control—whether openly administered by a recognized body of authority or subtly diffused throughout society at large—as a necessary component of social health and harmony; without firm restraints on certain kinds of behavior, a society would be in perpetual upheaval and its members forever prey to each other's most brutish impulses.[12] Another relevant phrase, "art as propaganda," overlaps in part with this concept of "social control," but its negative connotations are even harder to combat. Propaganda, our newspapers tell us, is what our enemies spread: self-serving claims and distortions of the truth.[13] If, though, we can imagine truth as something changeable rather than fixed and objective, if we can conceive of a propaganda effort that aims to replace outdated and harmful concepts of truth with ones more appropriate to the goals and needs of a society at a certain stage in its development (such as, in our own day, the need for racial harmony, sobriety behind the wheel, and peaceful resolution of international disputes), then we will come close to the progressive, optimistic, ennobling vision of artistic propaganda—and social control—that formed one of the most novel elements in Saint-Simon's social system.[14]

The principle of social control was present in Saint-Simon's first discourse on the role of art (1802), and it continued through to the last major aesthetic pronouncements of his disciples (1832). It was to form in many ways the basis for socialist (and, again, fascist) thinking about the arts during the succeeding century and a half, and it has even been credited with stimulating, by its very exaggerations, the growth of an entirely opposite aesthetic trend, that of *l'art pour l'art*—art for art's sake.[15] It is this principle of art as a means of social control, as a weapon in the struggle for a better society, that most writers have in mind when they refer to the theory of art's "social role." And this principle, as they so rightly state, was given its first full presentation in the writings of Saint-Simon and the writings of the Saint-Simonians.

There are differences, of course, between Saint-Simon's views and his disciples', not least as regards art. But the adjustments the disciples brought, though immensely significant, rarely went so far as to contradict the master's essential principles. Thus a discussion of his views on art, especially his concept of art's social role, presents at the same time some of *their* most basic ideas as well.

SAINT SIMON'S VIEWS AND THEIR ROOTS

Saint-Simon's view of art as a means of social control can be seen best in one passage each from his last work, *Nouveau Christianisme* (1825), and from his first, the *Lettres d'un habitant de Genève* (1802). A rather close examination of these two passages (in reverse order) will permit us to bring out the main features of that theory and, simultaneously, to stress its mixture of novelty and tradition. For, like most ideas of any importance, Saint-Simon's vision of art grew, unsteadily and over many years, from the decaying pulp and lingering seeds of earlier doctrines and practices.

The later of the two passages, from *Nouveau Christianisme*, deals with the role that the arts can play in the ceremonies of New Christianity, the religion of the new industrial society. Saint-Simon here uses the word *culte* to refer to the New Christian worship service and the word *dogme* to refer to the preaching of the New Christian priest. He argues that *culte* and *dogme* will be fashioned in such a way as to remind the faithful of the moral principles of the new religion, "to call . . . [their] attention to philanthropic feelings and considerations," and to indicate how these principles and feelings apply to grand affairs of state as well as to more personal day-to-day interactions.[16] Saint-Simon specifically criticizes Leo X, the great Medici pope, for having organized the entire papal artistic effort around his own person.[17] And he sketches, in enough detail to make the passage worth quoting in full, the roles that the various arts will play in the *culte* of New Christianity:

> There are two main ways of calling men's attention to ideas of whatever sort and of pushing them strongly in a [particular] direction. Fear must be roused in them by the sight of the terrible evils which would result for them if they departed from the behavior prescribed for them. Or else one must lure them [*leur présenter l'appât*] with the joys that will necessarily result from efforts made by them in the direction which one indicates to them.
>
> In both cases, the strongest and most useful effect will be produced by combining all the resources and all the means that the fine arts can offer.
>
> The preacher, called upon (by the very nature of things) to make use of eloquence, which is the first among the fine arts, should make his audience tremble by depicting the horrid state in which a man finds himself in this life when he has earned the condemnation of his fellow man. He should even show God's [punishing] arm raised above the man whose feelings are not dominated by love of mankind.
>
> Alternatively, he should develop in the soul of his listeners the most powerful and generous feelings by making them realize [*sentir*] that the happiness derived from being highly regarded by one's fellow men is greater than all other forms of happiness.
>
> The poets should assist [*seconder*] the efforts of the preachers. They should provide the *culte* with pieces of poetry suited to being recited in unison [*en choeur*], such that the faithful all become preachers to each other.
>
> The musicians should enrich the religious poems by their harmonies and give them a musical character which will penetrate to the depths of the soul of the faithful. [*Les musiciens doivent enrichir de leurs accords les poésies religieuses, et leur imprimer un caractère musical profondément pénétrant dans l'âme des fidèles.*]
>
> The painters and sculptors should in the temples direct the attention of Christians to acts which are most eminently Christian.
>
> The architects should construct temples in such a way that the preachers, the poets and musicians, and the painters and sculptors can bring forth in the soul of the faithful, at will, feelings of terror or feelings of joy and hope.
>
> These are obviously the bases which should be given to *culte* and the means which should be used to render it useful to society.[18]

The roots of Saint-Simon's thinking here may be sensed in the very manner in which he expresses himself. The prose is rather dry, the structure almost mathematical; the whole recalls the sententious and systematic maxims of the previous two centuries—those of Boileau or Batteux, for example—far more than it does the spontaneous, startling, erratic insights characteristic of the Romantics and other writers active in the mid-1820s, such as Hugo or Stendhal.

This spiritual distance between Saint-Simon and the new generation is even more deeply engraved in the passage's content. Most of the central concerns of Romanticism—such as the rejection of Neoclassic standards of beauty, or the fascination with myth, fantasy, and distant lands—find no echo in Saint-Simon's scheme. And the Romantics' most central item of faith—that a work of art is essentially an expression or outpouring of the artist's personal feelings—stands in striking contrast to Saint-Simon's most basic assumptions about art. Those assumptions were largely inherited from the world of his youth.

The link to eighteenth-century aesthetics is perhaps not immediately apparent; one is struck more forcefully by basic and incontrovertible dissimilarities. During the latter half of the eighteenth century, artists and aestheticians alike often stressed the value of pleasure for its own sake and found beauty in balanced proportions and clarity of design. Art was fashioned according to rules and conventions, and the audience, patron, or consumer was deemed the judge of art, the one whose demands the artist was expected to fulfill and whose tastes he or she sought to gratify. None of this so much as glimmers from Saint-Simon's description of New Christian art. He seems entirely indifferent to the issue of what "the beautiful" is, he is concerned not to bring pleasure but to incite people to action. His audience does not make demands of art or artist but rather receives the art that it needs, and that need—defined largely in sociopolitical terms—takes the place of purely aesthetic considerations in determining the most desirable form and content for a work of art.

Saint-Simon's frank appeal to extrinsic criteria is precisely what makes his view of art so novel (and also precisely what people have in mind when they treat his view of art as something of an anomaly in the history of aesthetics). In some ways it connects him less to his immediate predecessors than to other utopian thinkers throughout history, among them Plato, whose *Republic* and *Laws* offered the classic formulation of an ideal society in which the almost seductive powers of art are carefully regulated and selectively encouraged (and discouraged) with the aim of eliciting from the populace whatever feelings and actions will best promote social cohesion. Saint-Simon was perhaps aware of this particular connection to Plato; he certainly knew many of Plato's writings—at times even viewed himself as the proponent of a new quasi-Platonic age in philosophy, an age in which a great idea (rather than timid Aristotelian observation) would be the moving force behind all intellectual activity.[19]

But, as he may not have fully recognized, his views were also the continuation of more recent traditions. Despite the quite striking differences between the role of art in Saint-Simon's New Christianity and in late eighteenth-century aesthetics, there remained an even more fundamental similarity. Underlying both schools of thought was the often unspoken assumption that art is valuable to the extent that it affects its audience, engages with it (pleasure being of course one possible kind of effect). This view of art, which has been called the "pragmatic" by M. H. Abrams, had in fact dominated critical thought from the Renaissance until the arrival of Romanticism, with its new artist-centered ("expressive") rather than audience-centered philosophy.[20]

Furthermore, Saint-Simon's views bear a striking resemblance to one particular stream of this "pragmatic" tradition—the moralizing and didactic tradition associated with rhetoric and, more generally, with the various literary arts. Abrams notes that the moralizing trend was strongest at the beginning of the "pragmatic" period—during the Renaissance—and yielded more and more to the aforementioned "pleasure" principle at the end—in the late seventeenth and eighteenth centuries. But even in the Renaissance the desire to preach and the desire to please were intertwined. The art of rhetoric, in particular, depended on the speaker's or writer's knowing the ways in which an audience or a reader could be persuaded, not simply browbeaten. And effective persuasion required an understanding—provided in large part by Horace's rules for orators—of the qualities of speech that give pleasure: clear structure, carefully planned points of stress and articulation, varied repetition of the main thought, and so forth. A skilled Renaissance poet knew how to entice his readers into virtuous behavior—Sidney put it nicely—"as if they took a medicine of Cherries." A century later Molière wrote that "the duty of comedy is to correct men by diverting them," a view that many others echoed in the eighteenth century (Samuel Johnson: "the end of poetry is to instruct by pleasing"; Jean-Jacques Rousseau: theater should, by means of the "secret charm of patriotism," make people feel "content with their fatherland, their fellow citizens, and themselves"; lawyer and concert promoter Cavendish Weedon: through well-wrought sacred music, listeners will be "charmed into devotion by delight").[21] And another fifty years later, amid the first blossomings of Romantic ego worship, Saint-Simon was still demanding that rhetoric ("eloquence, the first among the fine arts"), poetry, and the other arts "develop in the soul of [the] listeners the most generous and powerful feelings [toward their fellow human beings]."

Saint-Simon would perhaps have denied that his thoughts on art bore a strong resemblance to those of aestheticians of the preceding two or three centuries, and he would have been partly justified. The increased emphasis that he gave to "instructing" (rather than to "diverting" or "delighting"), and the basic shift of moral authority that he proposed (from bodies of religion to the science-assisted industrial state), amounted in some sense to a difference in kind, not degree. What he surely would have admitted gladly was his indebtedness to one specific episode in eighteenth-century art and aesthetics, itself treated too often as a sport: the French Revolution.[22]

The link to the arts of the Revolution is based on a link to Revolutionary religion. Saint-Simon's desire to create a new industrial religion was clearly an offspring of the civic religions established by Hébert and Robespierre in 1793–94 (worship of the Goddess of Reason and of the Supreme Being), and the monuments and ceremonies he envisaged had their origin in the symbolic architecture and mass public gatherings of the Revolutionary period. This connection is particularly evident in the other of his major statements under discussion here: the passage in the *Lettres* of 1802 that proposes building a temple in honor of Sir Isaac Newton. Saint-Simon undoubtedly borrowed the general idea from the architect Boullée, whose Newton cenotaph of some twenty years earlier, though never constructed, was a serious attempt at symbolizing the replacement of the traditional divinity by something more suitable to a new society.[23] The choice of Newton clearly reflected Saint-Simon's (and Boullée's) attachment to the principles of Enlightenment science: empirical observation and—more generally—rational investigation.[24]

Even in its details, Saint-Simon's description of the new temple recalls Revolutionary (and, more generally, eighteenth-century) precedents. He states that the world's twenty-one most prominent artists (including musicians) and scientists will join forces in the design and construction of the temple, using "any and all means which the artists can invent." One-half of the temple, he states, will be a mausoleum for Newton—but a rather joyous one, it seems, for this mausoleum will be the scene of "majestic and brilliant spectacle[s]" celebrating "all distinguished services performed for humanity and all actions of great utility in the propagation of the faith." The other half of the temple will be decorated no less artfully but with the opposite aim: "to give men an idea of the eternal fate that awaits those who impede the progress of science and the arts."[25] This bifurcation of the temple is not necessarily Revolutionary in origin; as Iggers points out, it recalls the Deist position that, though heaven and hell may not exist, they remain useful doctrines for encouraging righteousness and discouraging evil.[26] But the idea of grand visual and musical ceremonies to celebrate the contributions of society's heroes surely derived from the Revolutionary festivals of mourning, organized with the full assistance of the painter Jacques-Louis David and immeasurably intensified by hymns, chansons, and marches written for the occasion by the nation's leading composers and performed by enormous choruses and military bands.[27]

The search for models could perhaps go on endlessly, but one last source for Saint-Simon's view of art, and especially music, must be mentioned. This can be extracted from a paragraph that follows the detailed description of New Christian worship (1825) cited earlier. Here Saint-Simon specifically attacks, as an example of what not to do, Luther's reform of the church service. Luther, he says, reduced *culte* to a bare sermon and removed everything poetic and inspirational: sacraments, painting and sculpture, impressive architecture, and even music.[28] His accusations here reveal clearly his unspoken ideal, namely the ritual and art of French Catholicism.

Clearly, that is, except in regard to music. Saint-Simon's statement that Luther "suppressed music" is almost baffling in its wrongheadedness and furthermore appears to contradict his earlier statement on music. Luther had indeed cast all grand and self-important forms of music making from his church, but what he retained—simple chorale tunes, some of them based on folk song— gave renewed strength to worship, and was strengthened (made necessary) by it in return. One might well argue that what Luther had created was exactly what Saint-Simon himself called for in his description of New Christian *culte:* inspirational hymns to be sung by the crowd, the music "enriching," inten- sifying the moralizing effect of the words. Why, then, did Saint-Simon not claim Luther as an ally instead of vilifying him?

Ignorance, surely. But there must have been a deeper reason as well. Saint- Simon could simply not see the advantage of limiting in any way the deploy- ment of music in religion. This is an important point, for his discussions of the arts in the long passage from *Nouveau Christianisme* cited earlier can be easily misunderstood as restricting all art to the production of what one scholar has called "dry works of propaganda."[29] His words about music in that passage, it is true, deal only with a limited, "propagandistic" (if one must) musical product: hymns to be sung by the crowd. But his declared larger aim was to enlist "all the resources and all the means that the fine arts can offer" in the cause of "pushing [men] in [the right] direction." Surely Saint-Simon would have welcomed grand means as well as modest, thrilling ceremonial music as well as simple hymns. His endorsement of "all the resources" of the various arts surely was intended to include not only oil paint, marble, gold brocade, and sonorous verse but also the sounds he had heard as a youth in the churches and royal chapels of Paris: the glory of trumpets and drums, grand Te Deum settings, expansive Lalande and Campra motets with their virtuosic passages for solo singers and obbligato instruments. These would indeed be the musical equivalents of his beloved statues and pomp; these luxuriant, intoxicating styles and genres, more than simple hymn tunes, would have helped create the sort of "spectacle majestueux et brillant" that he had called for in the *Lettres* of 1802 and clearly still wanted in the year of his death.

4

THE DEVELOPMENT OF
SAINT-SIMON'S VIEWS
ON ART, 1801–25

THREE PHASES

The common features of Saint-Simon's first and last pronouncements on art are so striking that they may lead to false impressions. One might easily conclude that there are no important differences between the two and that Saint-Simon's writings during the twenty-two years separating them consist mainly of continued reiteration of the call for a new religion and a new religious art. In fact, though, there are substantial differences between the mentality of the *Lettres* and of *Nouveau Christianisme,* and these differences affect the view of art presented in each. As for the intervening publications, these display a great variety of attitudes toward art (as also toward religion); some echo faintly the theme of art as a means of social control, others offer new, imaginative suggestions or subthemes that support or enrich the theme of social control, and yet others mention art only briefly, if at all. These shifting views and new themes can best be seen by studying Saint-Simon's major writings in rough chronological order, placing them in the context of his social thought at each stage.

Saint-Simon's writing career can be divided with fair ease into three periods. During the Consulate and the Napoleonic Empire he advocated reorganizing the natural sciences toward more productive social ends. In the early years of the Bourbon Restoration, beginning around 1816, he shifted his attention to the needs of industry (broadly defined to include commerce and other "productive" branches of the economy). Only during the two years before his death in 1825 did his mind turn in a major way toward the issues of religion and art.

Saint-Simon claimed that these shifts in focus were tactical, not essential—that a single, constant aim guided his thought at all time.[1] The *Lettres d'un habitant de Genève* (1802), a work that in a sense antedates even the first, "scientific" period, supports this claim, insofar as it propounds many of the leading ideas he was to develop and disseminate during all three periods, including, as we have seen, a clear (if curiously dispassionate) vision of the central role that art can play in an ideal society. Still, the division into three periods is a natural one, and it helps explain some of the shifts in Saint-Simon's views on art.

BEFORE THE "LETTRES"

When Saint-Simon began his career as a social reformer, he was, as he himself put it, "no longer young."[2] His first major publication, the *Lettres,* dates from his forty-third year. His ideas and his personality were no doubt fixed by this point—an explanation, if one is needed, for the richness and representativeness of the *Lettres.* This is no tentative *oeuvre de jeunesse* but rather a confident manifesto dating from Saint-Simon's first maturity.

One naturally wonders about the man who wrote this remarkable little book. How much did he know of literature and the arts? How much did he care about them? The published accounts of his early life indicate that he was fed heavy doses of ancient Roman history and modern political philosophy (Voltaire, Rousseau, Diderot).[3] Art, music, and literature of the "finer" sorts go unmentioned, as does science for the most part.

This pattern in his education must have been reinforced by his experiences during the last decades of the eighteenth century. He got to know first-hand the intersecting worlds of politics, arms, and finance (land speculation), but in the natural sciences he was at most a dabbler.[4] As for the arts, there is no evidence that during these years he was interested in them in any way.[5]

Around the turn of the century he developed a desire to correct this gap in his knowledge.[6] He wanted not so much to learn about the arts and sciences themselves as to become intimately acquainted with the ways in which artists and scientists thought and felt. He considered such knowledge crucial now that he had decided to begin a new career as social reformer; no doubt he was already formulating the plan, announced soon after in the *Lettres,* of raising scientists and artists to a new status in society.

With the funds he had received from Count Redern he purchased an elegant apartment in the rue Vivienne and invited to dine and converse with him a seemingly endless procession of leading figures in the arts and sciences. In October 1801 he even acquired a charming wife, Sophie de Champgrand, to organize these gatherings and do the honors. Saint-Simon himself, through his own contacts, easily arranged the invitations for scientists, but the artistic side fell to the countess. Though known to posterity mainly as a skilled and witty writer (especially under her later name, Mme de Bawr), Sophie de Champgrand was also an accomplished musician who had taken lessons from the singer Garat and the composers Grétry and Nicolas Roze. During her long life, she published a number of songs, wrote successful plays and *mélodrames* (with her own music), and even published a knowledgeable book on the history of music.[7] At her wedding to Saint-Simon her witnesses were Grétry and the dramatist Alexandre Duval, and it was with their assistance that she drew to Saint-Simon's salon the most distinguished musicians and literary figures of Paris. Though neither her memoirs nor the various biographies of Saint-Simon offer a list of guests, one may well assume that such prominent musicians as Boïeldieu, Rouget de Lisle, Cherubini, Sophie Gail, Garat, and the violinist Baillot were among those who received the count and countess's lavish hospitality. Alas, Saint-Simon soon noticed—as he recalled later in life—that "my scholars and my artists ate much and spoke little" and that what little they did say was more often than not "stale stuff." At times he even dozed off from boredom. After less than a year he terminated this experiment and (to use his own expression) "dismissed" both wife and apartment, having no further need of either.[8]

Marguerite Thibert argues valiantly that, if Saint-Simon did not appreciate the luminaries assembled in his salon, the fault was not his alone. French writers of around 1800, she notes, were trapped in a sterile use of traditional forms and themes and could therefore hardly have been expected to stir the sympathies of this ever-innovative thinker.[9] A somewhat different defense could be made regarding Grétry and the musical guests. The violent political, ideological, and social upheavals of the past dozen years had produced a continual disruption in their composing and performing careers. The concern of most musicians was now an essentially conservative one—to restore stability to the nation's musical institutions and profitability to its musical life. Such trade talk would surely have seemed petty and unadventurous to Saint-Simon, compared to the grand social philosophy that was brewing in his own head.

Rather than defend Saint-Simon, though, we would do better to try to understand him—his weaknesses as well as his strengths. The evidence is overwhelming that Saint-Simon's interest in the arts did not go very deep. As Thibert points out, he never once, in all his writings, used the term "le beau" (the beautiful).[10] For that matter, he rarely if ever referred to individual literary figures (other than political philosophers), musicians (other than Rouget de Lisle), or artists. And one cannot help wondering about the literary and artistic sensitivities of a man who could turn out volume after volume of contorted and utterly colorless prose and who drew his favorite reading matter, at least in his last years, from the sensationalist and pornographic novels of Mme de Genlis and Paul de Kock.[11]

Perhaps he, too, could not help wondering about his sensitivities in this area. Why else would he have submitted himself for a year, and at horrifying expense (a total of 300,000 francs),[12] to the chit-chat of men in the arts? Did he himself recognize that only total immersion had a chance of penetrating his hopelessly inartistic shell? Predictably, the expense went for naught. Saint-Simon remained impervious to the claims and charms of art, and his interest in it remained forever superficial and abstract.

THE "LETTRES D'UN HABITANT DE GENÈVE"

An abstract interest, though, is an interest nonetheless, which is why the arts do at times play an important role, if a shifting and contradictory one, in Saint-Simon's writings. The contradictions are apparent in his first major work, the *Lettres d'un habitant de Genève,* published less than a year after the last of his parties in the rue Vivienne.

Saint-Simon's aim in writing the *Lettres* was to call attention to the low esteem in which the arts and sciences were held by most of society and to devise a system which could allow the representatives of both fields to pursue their bold imaginations without ties to class or government, or to academic and occupational responsibilities. The brochure proposes that a Council of Newton be established, consisting of the world's twelve most prominent scientists and the nine leading artists (three writers [*littérateurs*], three painters, and three musicians). These twenty-one were to be chosen by general election and their activities supported by a voluntary worldwide subscription.[13]

Several important themes appear in the course of the *Lettres,* most of them quite favorable to the arts. The passage describing the decorated temple-cum-mausoleum, as we have seen in Chapter 3, vigorously launches the central doctrine of "social control" and even offers some guidelines for how the art of the future will carry out this vital task—by embellishing and intensifying the religion of science, by creating a grand and impressive spectacle, by assisting the world's citizens in their worship of the most talented and productive members of society, and by creating vivid inspirational images of the choice that lies before each of us: honored service to humanity, or the eternal night of isolation and uncooperativeness.

In another passage Saint-Simon presents one of his secondary themes on art, one sternly disapproving of the artworks, and perhaps the artists, of the past and present. Saint-Simon argues that the greatest artists have been "sold off to special interests which debase them and steer them away from their true functions." Art has thus been engaged in "directions harmful to ... [the] tranquillity [of mankind]." By this Saint-Simon seems to mean that literature, the plastic arts, and music have too long sung the praises of war and warriors (such as Alexander the Great), oppressive government, and no less oppressive religion. Art, the *Lettres* imply, has always had what one might call a "social role," in that it has always served a portion of society—but that portion has been small in numbers, selfish, bloodthirsty, oppressive, tyrannical. The time has come for art to serve, not what Saint-Simon calls "special interests," but society as a whole.[14]

Of the secondary themes touched on in the *Lettres,* the most crucial and problematic one concerns the relationship between the artists and the two other significant groups in society: the scientists (*savants,* a term that includes economists and other learned folk), and the *industriels* (people who produce or distribute goods or services). We might state this theme in the form of a question: What sort of responsibility and authority should artists have in the social hierarchy? Or, put a bit more crudely: Are the artists to lead or to follow; do they make, or even help make, grand societal decisions, or do they merely follow the dictates of the other two classes?

In answering this question, Saint-Simon clearly reveals the inconsistency in his attitude toward the arts. On the positive side, he treats artists with reverence—a strong word, but none too strong for the context. Though the artists are somewhat outnumbered in the Council of Newton (nine artists to twelve scientists), Saint-Simon clearly implies that all twenty-one geniuses, whether artistic or scientific, can contribute in equal degree to enlightenment and social progress, and that they deserve the same esteem, money, and freedom.[15] He offers fine words in praise of these geniuses and their like: "[They are] the torches which enlighten [*éclairent*] all humanity, including those who govern as well as those who are governed. . . . How lovely is the occupation of working for the good of humanity. What an awe-inspiring goal! Does man have any means of drawing closer to the Divinity [than this]?"[16] The artists (like the scientists) are thus credited with special powers; they can in some sense light the path for the nation's leaders, not just for the masses.

On the negative side, this seemingly glorious role for the artists is undercut at several points, although it is never straightforwardly contradicted. The artists, lauded at one moment for their awe-inspiring influence on the *gouvernants,* are excluded at another from participation in the actual governing process. Saint-Simon places the temporal power in the hands of the *propriétaires* (land and factory owners) and delegates the spiritual power to the *savants,* but rather startlingly assigns no social function whatever to the *artistes!*[17] Presumably their assisting role in the religion of science is enough.

Saint-Simon's inconsistent, even erratic response to the question of how artists would relate to the other groups in society might be explained in part by the peculiar orientation of his early writings (the *Lettres* and the "scientific" works). He was concerned that all people work and that they find a gratifying and socially useful outlet for their native predispositions: people with natural inclinations toward rational thinking should become scientists, people adept at fashioning things with their hands or at administering enterprises should become workers and managers, and people gifted with poetic skills and sensitivities should become artists. And he felt strongly that the most gifted people should be allowed to rise to the top of their respective category—that they be given the authority, recognition, and honor due them in proportion to their usefulness to what he liked to call the "public welfare."[18] A strict hierarchy among the three basic capacities or social groups, though, was not yet something that Saint-Simon was predominantly seeking to establish.

But the explanation falls short, for in this particular case he did establish something of a hierarchy. It can be no accident that, in distributing two social functions (temporal and spiritual) among three social groups, Saint-Simon decided simply to let one group go away empty-handed. Similarly, one cannot help ascribing significance to the fact that, throughout the *Lettres,* Saint-Simon drew his examples of genius solely from the realms of science and mathematics: Newton, the Royal Academy of Science, and so forth. "No more honors for the Alexanders [of this world]," he proclaimed. "Long live the Archimedeses!"[19] No mention of Sophocles, Praxiteles, or the (alas, nameless) composers of choral chants for the Attic tragedies. These lapses and inconsistencies can only be explained by Saint-Simon's lack of familiarity with, and lack of affinity for, the arts.

The "Scientific" and "Industrialist" Years

During the next fifteen years Saint-Simon shifted his attention—as one could almost have predicted—away from the arts and toward science and industry. The first of his three main (post-*Lettres*) phases—the "scientific" phase—continued one particular strand of thought from the *Lettres* but applied it to science alone: science as a latent force that needs to be harnessed to the general welfare of society. Saint-Simon turned out wordy tracts on this subject, but included what Manuel has described as "pathological attacks" on the scientific establishment, as if to ensure that his writings would either be ridiculed or go unread by the very people whom he urgently wished to convince.[20] The "scientific" phase ended around 1813 in a period of emotional crisis, which was intensified by the strain of (futile) legal proceedings against Count Redern.[21] The cure came with Saint-Simon's discovery of the last and largest of the three great social groups, the *industriels.*

The *industriels* were—as mentioned earlier—the members of what Saint-Simon considered the "productive" branches of society, notably industry and commerce. The term *industriel* was widely used in France as the equivalent of "manufacturer" or occasionally of its later derivative "industrialist." Saint-Simon, though, used it in a larger sense, to indicate not only the manufacturers but the major bankers, farmers, and merchants, as well as—most characteristically—all the people working under them.[22] (In this and many other respects his ideas and terminology were indebted to those of liberal economists such as Adam Smith and J. B. Say.) It may at first seem curious to us that Saint-Simon could define as a single coherent group what we are accustomed since Marx to viewing as two antagonistic social classes: bourgeoisie and proletariat. But it was axiomatic to Saint-Simon, and later to the Saint-Simonians, that society should promote the interests of all its productive members and—an important divergence from the classical liberal position—should oppose those of the *oisifs,* the "idlers."[23] From his middle writings on, Saint-Simon's constant aim was to increase the wealth and happiness of all productive members of society by promoting expansion in the industrial sector and the creation of jobs. Thus he now directed his message primarily at the *grands industriels* (what he formerly called the *propriétaires*), but with the larger aim of improving the condition of the other *industriels,* i.e., the working masses. During the first years of the Bourbon Restoration, Saint-Simon was in fact supported and read by some of the nation's leading bankers and industrialists, who perhaps saw in him a thought-provoking, if erratic, proponent of their own class interests against the reactionary regime of Louis XVIII.[24]

If his somewhat combative version of "industrialism" brought Saint-Simon a degree of public acceptance, it also had liberating, curative benefits for the man himself and his writings. The undeniable insights of his doctrine won him two devoted, brilliant, and literate disciples, Thierry and Comte, who became his surrogate sons and chief collaborators—at least for a few years each. More crucially, his decision to take the part of industry, to place the leading *industriels* plainly at the top of the social hierarchy, gave a clear focus to his thinking. Whereas in the pre-"industrial" writings artists and scientists were urged to place their gifts in the service of a rather mysterious entity called "the public welfare," Saint-Simon now made quite explicit who and what needed to be served: "The industrial class must occupy the first rank [in society], because it is the most important of all. . . . The other classes must work for it, because they are its creatures and it keeps them alive [*elle entretient leur existence*]."[25]

Science, of course, retained an important role in the "industrial" system, for it provided the basis for technology—a handmaiden role, perhaps, but an essential one nevertheless. Art, in contrast, was granted almost no role at all. The few references are but brief, pale reflections of the vision of "social control" proposed in the *Lettres.* Art, wrote the author in *L'Industrie* (1817), should "excite [*passionner*] men about the establishment of the scientific and industrial system."[26] No further details. The abstract enthusiasm of the *Lettres* has here turned into an unenthusiastic abstraction.

Toward the end of the "industrial" period, though, Saint-Simon more and more, if at times ambivalently and with interruptions for late spurts of pure "industrialism" (notably the *Catéchisme des industriels*), began to give expression to the hope, last heard in the *Lettres* of 1802, that the arts would take a leading role—or at least what we have called an "essential handmaiden" role—in society. In 1819, in his exceptionally vivid and well-written parable contrasting the idleness of France's aristocrats and clergymen with the productivity of members of the Third Estate, he included the various types of artists and scientists in the same category as the men of finance and industry (though the numbers are far from equal).

Let us suppose that France suddenly loses her fifty leading physicists, her fifty leading chemists, . . . her fifty leading sculptors, her fifty leading musicians, . . . her fifty leading bankers, her two hundred leading merchants, . . . her fifty leading masons. . . .

. . . The nation would become a body without a soul at the moment that she lost them . . . and she would continue to be subordinate [to other prominent nations] . . . until she could grow a new head.

One would have to go back to Saint-Simon's first treatise, the *Lettres,* to find a precedent for his view here that artists, too, produce works that are "of positive usefulness to society."[27]

That Saint-Simon was beginning to return to a higher regard for art in 1819 is further indicated by a passage he published around the same time in *L'Organisateur.* Here he protests that art objects have become luxury items and are far too heavily concentrated in the homes and châteaux of the wealthy and aristocratic few, and he argues that this is giving rise to a gap in "civilization" between two classes of men: those "whose intelligence is developed by the habitual sight of the products of the fine arts" and those "whose imaginative faculties receive no development, since the material labors with which they are exclusively occupied do not stimulate their intelligence at all." "Today," he concludes, "conditions are favorable for making luxury national."[28]

Saint-Simon is giving voice here to yet another related yet distinct opinion about art and society—the "democratic" view (discussed in Chapter 3) that art is inherently good for people, that it fulfills a human need and thus should be made generally available. There was, at the time, some novelty to this. As Frank Manuel notes, the artistic utopia predicted by Saint-Simon "became a partial reality under the self-consciously Saint-Simonian Empire [1851–70] of Napoleon III. It is now so generally diffused an aspect of all peacetime government that its originality in 1820 is hard to appreciate."[29]

But to understand the full implications—and the full originality—of this passage one must relate it back to the concept of social control, which is what Saint-Simon, in the very next sentence, goes on to do:

Luxury will become useful and moral when the entire nation enjoys it. Our century has been vouchsafed the honor and the advantage of employing in a direct fashion, in political combinations, the advances made by the exact sciences and those made by the fine arts since the brilliant epoch of their regeneration [the Renaissance].[30]

Wider distribution was thus for Saint-Simon not so much a goal in itself as an opportunity to transform the arts from an extravagance into a social tool.

This transformation meant one thing in particular for the "industrial" Saint-Simon: public works projects. In *L'Organisateur,* Saint-Simon grouped musicians and visual artists with engineers in the first of three equal governmental "chambers." Their task was to propose a series of public works projects valuable for their "utility or pleasurableness [*agréments*]." The other two chambers—the scientists and *industriels*—would, respectively, examine the projects and carry them out.[31]

The creation of public works projects may at first strike us as a limited, indeed stultifying chore for the arts, but it is a chore that the arts have often performed, at times with distinction. One need only think of some of the world's great architectural monuments: the temples and royal palaces of Athens and Nineveh, the great European cathedrals, or the finer office buildings, railroad stations, and war memorials of our modern metropolises. Fortunately, Saint-Simon, in two passages from this same treatise, offered some examples of public works projects that might effectively incorporate the skill of artists at creating "pleasurableness."

In one of these passages Saint-Simon proposed the creation of "public festivals" in which gifted orators would either stimulate the citizens to work diligently toward bringing about a limitless future ("festivals of *hope*") or remind the people how inferior and constricted the lives of their ancestors had been ("festivals of *remembrance*").[32] These two contrasting festivals clearly continued the secularized heaven-or-hell principle on which the temple of Newton was based (1802). And just as clearly they anticipated the New Christian ceremonies (1825), with their visions of the joy to be derived from loving and aiding one's brothers and of the horrid isolation that results from selfishness and greed. Though the passage on the two festivals is brief and makes no references to music, pageantry, or indeed any arts other than rhetoric, we can assume that Saint-Simon must have intended, as we know he did in 1802 and again in 1825, that they all would reinforce the message.

In the other passage from *L'Organisateur,* Saint-Simon described the enormous English-style parks that he would establish for the relaxation and pleasure of nearby inhabitants and sojourning travelers. Here we find a particularly blunt statement of the principle of social control through art, for it is uncolored by any reference to temples or quasi-religious ceremonies—just artists, or more specifically musicians (mostly singers, one must suppose), arousing with their words and tones the better instincts of the populace.

> These gardens ... will also contain housing for artists who wish to stay there, and a certain number of musicians will always be maintained there, for the purpose of igniting in the residents of the area the passion the development of which is required by circumstances, for the greatest benefit of the nation.[33]

This pointed mention of music is notable, for Saint-Simon was in general quite sparing with details about his artistic program. It suggests that, around 1819, music in particular was coming to seem to the social philosopher a promising tool for guiding the minds and feelings of the masses. It was not entirely coincidental, then, that only two years later he collaborated on his one and only propagandistic work of art and that it was a song.

A Song for Industry

The word "collaborated" is perhaps a bit misleading. Saint-Simon wrote neither the words nor the music; for these he had the able assistance of Claude-Joseph Rouget de Lisle (1760–1836), author and composer of the "Marseillaise." But the song, entitled "Premier Chant des industriels," was apparently written at Saint-Simon's instigation, its text praises his loyal supporter, the woolens manufacturer Guillaume Ternaux, it was first performed at Ternaux's estate in Saint-Ouen, and Saint-Simon published the tune and text, with some commentary of his own, in his *Du système industriel* (1821). Clearly the song would not have existed but for Saint-Simon, and thus he may rightly be said to have had a part in its creation. The song is included below in Appendix A, accompanied by a fuller discussion of the circumstances surrounding its composition and performance. But it must briefly retain our attention here, at least as regards two matters: the song's "message," and Saint-Simon's comments on that message.

The text of the song is completely consistent with Saint-Simon's few specific suggestions elsewhere about the art of the future. One stanza honors the prominent manufacturer Ternaux for publicly refusing the title of baron—a principled "industrialist" act. This recalls the praise of great individuals suggested in the *Lettres* of 1802. More generally, the song hails all "children of industry," down to the lowliest factory hands; in fact, Rouget de Lisle cunningly worded the song in the first-person plural, with the result that workers who sang it—as a number did at the premiere in 1821—thereby sang in praise of themselves and their fellows.

> Honor to us, children of industry.
> Honor, honor to our fortunate labors!
> Vanquishing our rivals, in all the arts,
> Let us be the hope and pride of the fatherland!

In this respect the song fulfills the more daring suggestion of 1819 that the arts—especially music—might engender in people good feelings about themselves and the important work they do. In some ways the song would even satisfy the requirements of the New Christian doctrine of four years later. It is thus as complete a practical embodiment of Saint-Simon's artistic vision as we will ever have.

Saint-Simon's comments on the song embellish a theme he had raised briefly in 1802: the need for art to abandon its bond to reactionary "special interests." Defending his and Rouget de Lisle's decision to create a hymn to a businessman, he argues that, whereas trumpets are sounded in wartime to celebrate victories (even minor ones) and courageous actions (or seemingly courageous actions, for many battles are in fact won by sheer luck), the trumpets go silent when it comes to acts of "civil courage." Yet these acts demonstrate true generosity and "give a powerful impulse to the changes in social organization demanded by the march of civilization and the progress of knowledge." It is precisely "civil courage" that "society must excite by all the means in its power" if the *industriels* are to attain their rightful place. Ternaux has set the example, Saint-Simon concludes, and the arts should render him honor. "The first *industriel* who has refused to deck himself out with a feudal nickname ought to be praised, painted, engraved, sculpted and sung. All the fine arts should join forces to immortalize his name."

Last Writings: Art and Religion

The "industrialist" position, vividly expressed in Rouget de Lisle's song, continued to dominate Saint-Simon's writings until close to his death. During his last two or three years, though, a major transformation began to take place in his thinking. A new sense of urgency now filled his proposals, though his prose style remained unpalatably flat. More than ever before, and certainly more than during the "industrialist" years, he saw the world as gripped by a major crisis that needed to be resolved "*brusquely* and by direct measures," although—as always—without violence.[34]

In part this new emphasis derived, as he himself admitted, from the frustration and failure of his past efforts.[35] In 1820 he had been brought to trial for insulting the royal family and threatening the social order, the chief document being the parable that he had published in late 1819. (The case against him was intensified when, in an unfortunate coincidence, one of the prominent drones whom he had named as expendable, the duke of Berry, was assassinated by a republican.) Saint-Simon neither won nor lost the court case—it simply petered out—but around this time he seems to have lost much of his "constituency."[36] Few of the wealthy businessmen who had once subscribed to his publications remained at all interested in this figure who dared to suggest in the parable that "present-day society is truly upside down."[37] Of course, as Dautry wryly notes, Saint-Simon never went so far as to propose turning this upside-down society right-side up—the solution favored by republicans and others in the radical left.[38] He did intend to eliminate the ruling *oisifs*, but his plan was to replace them, not with the lowly workers, but with the workers' bosses, thus leaving the social pyramid intact but improved.[39] Such an arrangement promised the *grands industriels*, such as Ternaux and the banker

Lafitte, enormous power and even wealth, but there were no assurances that it would ever come to pass; what was sure was that Saint-Simon's plan could easily undermine the passably profitable relationship that these entrepreneurs had worked out with the Bourbons.[40] As the government grew more repressive in the early 1820s, restoring censorship of all political and religious writings, Saint-Simon grew more isolated, more despairing, more willing to break with the system.

In 1823 the feelings of isolation and despair, intensified by the growing antagonism of his disciple Comte, led Saint-Simon to attempt suicide.[41] The attempt failed, and he lived another two years, supported emotionally, intellectually, and financially by two wealthy and ardent young disciples: the writer Léon Halévy, son of a prominent cantor, brother of the young composer Fromental Halévy, and future father of the librettist Ludovic Halévy; and Olinde Rodrigues, a gifted mathematician and son of a prominent banker. Both were of Jewish origin (the first of several important Jewish Saint-Simonians), both had been blocked in their academic careers by the religious intolerance of the Restoration, and both were passionately interested in the social function of literature.[42] Saint-Simon, Halévy, and Rodrigues comprised the core of a writing collective that envisioned founding a newspaper and even a new encyclopedia to complete in a constructive way the bold work that the *Encyclopédie* of the *philosophes* had begun with admirable destructiveness. (The disciples did eventually publish a journal, *Le Producteur*, after Saint-Simon's death, but the encyclopedia project, although belatedly undertaken in the 1860s by a consortium of former Saint-Simonians and leading scholars, never passed beyond the organizational stage. Halévy's brother, the composer, was chosen to write the music entry.) This writing collective produced the more copious of Saint-Simon's last two published works, *Opinions littéraires, philosophiques et industrielles*, which must be withheld for discussion until Chapter 5, for the artistic views in it are clearly not Saint-Simon's.

The slender *Nouveau Christianisme*, in contrast, was written by the master himself, with only an introduction and a bit of polishing by Rodrigues,[43] and it was to become—he soon realized—his final testament. The essay is, simply put, Saint-Simon's reworking of his whole industrial system as a new social religion. He had always felt that a system of moral instruction was essential to society, and he had at various times put the scientists or the artists, or both groups together, in charge of spreading enthusiasm for the goals and projects established by those who best understood the path of progress (e.g., the leading *industriels*). Now he went further and declared that the industrial society he envisioned could only be achieved by a moral transformation, by universal acceptance of the fraternal principle that was at the root of Christianity. He therefore enjoined the leading *artistes, savants,* and *industriels* to take on the task of founding and heading New Christianity, a religion dedicated to directing people's attention to the Golden Rule in its revised, "industrial" form: "All of society must work for the improvement of the moral and physical existence of the poorest class."[44]

Despite this overriding concern for the lot of the working masses, already suggested in *Du système industriel* but never before stated so clearly, Saint-Simon was in no way abandoning his former allies. On the contrary, he made it quite clear that he intended to continue addressing himself to the rich and the powerful, in order to reassure them of his peaceful intentions; he would still try to convince the prominent artists, scientists, and *industriels* to take their predestined role as the natural leaders of the other workers; and he would attempt as before to persuade enlightened monarchs to use their power to force the rich to help better the lot of the poor.[45] All of these groups, he reasoned, needed to be brought to see that the interests of the greatest number were also their own interests, for the poor could only be raised up—and discouraged from taking violent action—by the expansion of industry, production, and employment.

Saint-Simon's pamphlet devoted much space to passionate, lengthy condemnations of the heresies of the prevailing religions, their willing submission to reactionary temporal powers, their calcified insistence on dogma and ritual, and their neglect of the revolutionary moral principle of brotherly love. As for the new religion that Saint-Simon was proposing in their place, his intention was to draft "its morality, its *culte,* and its *dogme*" (including a new Credo) in a later treatise[46] that, unfortunately, he did not live to write.

Fortunately, what he did say in *Nouveau Christianisme* about at least one aspect of *culte*—the arts—was simple and clear. The passage in question, quoted and discussed at length in Chapter 3, presents art as a means of social control—nothing less, nothing more. Nothing less, that is, because it is the fullest such statement from Saint-Simon's pen, with unusually detailed references to the specific functions that the various arts (and branches of literature) might play in reinforcing socially desirable cooperative behavior and discouraging people's disruptive, selfish tendencies.

But also nothing more. The passage displays not a glimmer of enthusiasm for art, of knowledge about its past and present triumphs and failures, of concern for its future. In short, it contains nothing likely to attract the attention and sympathy of people in the arts. Some might think this inevitable, that a doctrine that saw art not as a goddess but as a handmaiden—however essential—could not prevent itself from losing regard for her beauty and dignity.

Saint-Simon's disciples thought otherwise.

5

THE EARLY SAINT-SIMONIANS ON MUSIC AND AESTHETICS, 1825–26

THE "DIALOGUE"

Léon Halévy was the first of the disciples to tackle the problem of enriching and aestheticizing Saint-Simon's view of the social role of art. His views are found in a lengthy section of the collectively written *Opinions littéraires, philosophiques et industrielles* called "The Artist, the Scientist, and the *Industriel*: A Dialogue."[1] The fact that Saint-Simon was still alive when this "Dialogue" was published has led some writers—even those who recognize its collective authorship—to treat it simply as an expression of Saint-Simon's own views just prior to the posthumously published *Nouveau Christianisme*. This creates unnecessary problems. Hunt, for example, is forced to conclude that Saint-Simon, after giving voice to great enthusiasm for the arts in the "Dialogue," made a "decided regression" in *Nouveau Christianisme*.[2] The problems disappear when one recognizes that the "Dialogue" is mainly the work of Halévy and that, in particular, the passages spoken by the "Artist" are almost surely his alone (or nearly so). Furthermore, the work probably was composed around the same time as Saint-Simon's religious tract, not earlier.[3] It should by rights be considered not the next-to-last essay by Saint-Simon but one of the first essays by the Saint-Simonians.

What distinguishes the "Dialogue" most from *Nouveau Christianisme*—and what links it most plainly to the other early writings of the disciples—is its emphasis on the sciences and industry and its only very muted concern for religion. In general, the Saint-Simonians were slow to take up the religious message of Saint-Simon's last essay, even after it was published. Enfantin later admitted that even he did not at first grasp the significance of *Nouveau Christianisme*; indeed, six months after Saint-Simon's death he—and no doubt most of the other disciples as well—still supported Comte's view of human development as a progress *away* from religion and toward "positivism": rational behavior and planning based on the verifiability of science.[4]

The struggle between positivism and the new religious gospel—between, as it were, the scientific-industrial Saint-Simon and the prophet of New Christianity—was to become the predominant theme of the disciples' first years as a movement.[5] It already left its mark on the "Dialogue", for, though the general message there is a decidedly positivistic one, the religious element also creeps in from time to time.

What is most astonishing about Halévy's view of art in the "Dialogue" is how distinct it is from the views of art in both the "positivist" and the "religious" writings of Saint-Simon himself. Nothing in the work of the master prepares us for the refreshingly high regard for art in this first work of the disciples—a regard clearly based on respect, knowledge, and love. This regard is particularly apparent in Halévy's admission that art fulfills a human need of its own, quite apart from its effect on behavior and attitudes in other areas. Saint-Simon had come close to suggesting something of the sort in his statement that art civilizes people (*L'Organisateur*, 1819). But in the "Dialogue" Halévy announces plainly that "man is still eager for the delights that the fine arts procure."[6] The words "eager" (*avide*) and "delights" (*jouissances*) speak volumes.

Halévy also took the bold step of placing the artists among the rulers of society. Saint-Simon had made hints in this direction in 1819—in the parable and in the three equal governmental chambers of *L'Organisateur*. In the "Dialogue," the Artist (speaking for Halévy) states forthrightly that artists, scientists, and *industriels,* the only productive groups in society, share a single goal, though they approach that goal by different means. In the next sentence Halévy even appears—at first glance—to place the artists above the other two groups. Artists, he states, will comprise the movement's "vanguard," since "the power of the arts is in fact the most immediate and the most rapid."[7] A careful reading of the entire passage, though, makes clear that Halévy did not attach to the word "vanguard" (*avant-garde*) any connotations of superiority, such as one finds in radical political and aesthetic writings of fifty or a hundred years later. A more appropriate interpretation is suggested by the term's military origin—the members of vanguard battalions are sent ahead of other troops to fulfill essential "front-line" tasks (converting or subduing the local population and conveying back to the commanding officers their impressions of what lies ahead), but they are not in any real sense leading the march or making tactical decisions. Thus it is with the artist: he goes ahead of the others, yet he is by no means choosing the goal, or even the route.

The image of the artist as leader does, it is true, occur several times in the "Dialogue." Artists should "*lead* the march of civilization"; "literature and the fine arts will place themselves *at the head* of the movement" and "*soar ahead* of all intellectual faculties" (emphases in the present paragraph are mine).[8] But this image is mixed with other conflicting images. Artists, one passage proclaims, should become "the *guides* and the moral expression" of society, as they once were in ancient Egypt and Greece, and in Renaissance Florence and Flanders; they should "*march along* with their time," and they should "*follow* the course that people's minds are taking."⁹ The message is ambivalent. The artists are expected to take the lead, to guide (which is perhaps not quite the same thing), to march in lockstep, and to follow—all at the same time.

Hunt's terminology may be helpful here. He isolates in the writings of Saint-Simon and the Saint-Simonians three distinct social roles for the artist—what he calls the *vulgarisateur,* the *instigateur,* and the *révélateur.* The first and lowest of these roles—*vulgarisateur* or popularizer—reduces the artist to a mouthpiece for socially progressive ideas that have been formulated by the leading scientists and *industriels.* At most the artist-popularizer is granted the power of stimulating in people socially useful impulses and desires, but the projects toward which all desires need to be directed are determined by others: the true leaders. The second role—*instigateur* or inciter—places the artists among the rulers of society; his function is, through his special sensitivity and imagination, to inspire the other leaders to formulate the decisions and make the discoveries that are needed to regenerate society.¹⁰

These two roles appear, separately or blended together, in many of the writings of Saint-Simon and his early disciples. Saint-Simon, for example, seems to have been thinking of a combined *vulgarisateur-instigateur* role for artists when, in 1821, he urged them to "suspend their labors relating to the perfecting ... of the individual fine arts, in order to devote themselves to organizing a moral and political system which is so clear and positive that those who govern, in the same way as those who are governed, find themselves forced to follow it."¹¹ The two roles are also blended by Halévy in the various images from the "Dialogue" cited previously.

Hunt goes on to propose a third, yet higher role for the artist: that of *révélateur*—discoverer or seer. The artist-seer divines the hidden truths himself, becoming thereby an almost messianic figure.¹² This revelatory role, which overlaps in many ways with the Romantic exaltation of the artistic genius, was glimpsed briefly by Saint-Simon in the *Lettres* of 1802 and seems also to have left some traces on Halévy's imagery in the "Dialogue" ("s'élancer en avant de toutes les facultés intellectuelles").¹³ But a full and unhesitant exposition of the *artiste-révélateur* had to await a fundamental transformation within the Saint-Simonian movement.

In the process of arguing for a new social commitment for art, the authors of the "Dialogue" revived some secondary themes and introduced new ones. Echoing the *Lettres* of 1802, they proclaimed that artists must work for society at large ("les masses") rather than for "a few men" and must abandon the use of reactionary themes.¹⁴ More novel was their distinctly positivistic insistence that artists abandon their habit of treating art as an activity of the "imagination" alone. Saint-Simon had hinted at this theme in 1819 (the glories of art must be used in "political combinations") and in 1821 (the passage just quoted, advocating a suspension of "labors relating to the perfecting ... of the individual fine arts"),¹⁵ but the "Dialogue" found words for it that were nothing short of thrilling and bespoke a real conviction about the value and the power of art:

> No doubt imagination will hold sway over men for a long time yet, but its exclusive reign is over. And though man is still as avid as ever for the delights that the fine arts procure, he demands that his reason also find profit in these delights. The arts would risk losing their importance forever, and, far from leading the march of civilization, they would no longer be ranked among the needs of society, were they to insist on following a direction in which they have little to gain: that of imagination without purpose [*objet*], and reactionary [*rétrograde*] imagination.
>
> But if, on the contrary, they promote the general movement of the human spirit; if they too wish to serve the common cause, to contribute to the growth of the general welfare, to produce such fruitful sensations in man as are appropriate for his developed intelligence to experience, and to propagate, by means of those sensations, generous ideas which are timely—immediately they will see an immensely glorious and successful future opening before them. They will be able to take possession of all their energy again and rise to the greatest height of dignity which they can attain. For the power of imagination is incalculable when it bounds ahead in a direction of public good.[16]

"L'imagination sans objet"—in this phrase lies the key to the whole passage. Maxime Leroy, seeking to deny the hostility toward art for art's sake latent in the thought of Saint-Simon and his disciples, claims that the phrase refers, like the immediately following phrase "l'imagination rétrograde," to art that praises war and religion (e.g., the medieval past) instead of the forces of life, production, and positive philosphy.[17] But if the words "without purpose" are read in the context of the passage, they seem rather to refer to works of art of a different sort: overly polished and academic, or else individualistic and out of touch with the concerns of society. In short, Halévy is here recommending a turn away from the lyric *moi* and toward social description and commentary. Leroy correctly points out how fruitful the social vein predicted by Halévy soon became in the hands of French poets and novelists (Balzac, Sue, Sand), and one might well add that the same is true for architects, painters (Daumier, Courbet, and the more sentimental Millet), and of course many musicians as well (e.g., Meyerbeer, Berlioz, F. Halévy, Félicien David). Here, too, lies the kernel of Barrault's critique of the Romantic lyric poets and of much subsequent leftist comment on established art forms and practices.

Though Halévy's call for social commitment elaborates on thoughts expressed earlier by Saint-Simon, it is enriched by a concern for the fate of art that is entirely foreign to the master's own preoccupations. Halévy sought an art that might propagate timely ideas of generosity, not only in order to promote generosity, but also in order to revive the flagging energies of art itself, to restore it to the glory and greatness that it held previous progressive societies, such as democratic Athens or the enlightened Italian merchant cities of the Renaissance. This new stress on what art can gain from society marks the first serious attempt in the Saint-Simonian tradition to appeal to the self-interest of the artist and to the love he feels for his art. And because Halévy knows whereof he writes, his message carries conviction.

Halévy's particular knowledge of and concern for two of the arts—literature (especially drama) and music—appear in a short but subtle passage on the various ways in which the arts can influence society.

> We [artists] have arms of all kinds. When we want to spread new ideas among men, we inscribe them on marble or canvas. We popularize them in poetry and song. We use by turns the lyre [for accompanying an epic poem] or the fife, the ode or the chanson, the history [book] or the novel. The dramatic stage is open to us, and it is there, above all, that we exert an electric and victorious influence.[18]

Halévy's emphatic espousal of the stage is hardly surprising considering his own literary interests and the fact that the 1820s were seeing the birth of the Romantic movement in France and the growth of bourgeois, nonclassical forms of theater. His words "la scène dramatique nous est ouverte" were intended literally; an "opposition" or "sectarian" playwright, who before the French Revolution would have been automatically excluded from consideration by theater directors, could now find a stage for at least the tamer of his creations.[19] Perhaps, too, Halévy felt that addressing a live audience, rather than isolated individual readers, permitted the artist to gauge his impact and to adapt his approach for the widest possible effect. His use of the word *électrique* suggests further that the emotional current would flow not only from speaker to listener but also, by means of collective enthusiasm, from listener to listener throughout the auditorium. Finally, he may have considered group situations conducive to the presentation of social issues. All of these reasons certainly played their part in assuring the stage and lectern a special place in Saint-Simonian theory and practice for years to come.

Equally revealing in this short passage is Halévy's treatment of music. Perhaps because of his family's rich musical background, he invokes instruments or genres no fewer than four times in the first two sentences: *le chant, la lyre, le galoubet,* and *la chanson.* He seems to have thought of music as a rather popular art form, for in his rhetorical pairings he generally places these musical terms second, a position reserved for the more accessible art forms, such as the chanson and novel (as opposed to more elitist or intellectual forms:

the epic, ode, and history). Indeed, three of the four types of music making that Halévy invokes share a common feature that would tend to render them accessible to a broad public: they combine music with words. The one exception is his reference to the *galoubet,* a three-holed flute or pipe, as in the Provençal pipe and tabor ensemble; yet *le galoubet,* too, suggests music of a simple, popular, functional cast: marches and dances, not richly complex (and non-functional) symphonies or string quartets.

The net effect of this passage is a hesitancy to endorse autonomous instrumental music. Such a hesitancy may be explained in several ways. To begin with, Halévy in this passage is invoking, as much as possible, the arts of the ancients, whereas independent instrumental music of great consequence did not blossom until the eighteenth century. Second, though the instrumental repertoire includes symphonic, chamber, and solo piano works of Haydn, Mozart, and Beethoven which today we take to be among the unquestioned highpoints of Western music, these works were not regarded so highly by the French of the 1820s, who put more stock in opera and religious music (the fields cultivated by Halévy's brother and father, respectively). Finally and most significantly, Halévy is arguing here that art can and should spread ideas, a task for which instrumental music is by common consent poorly equipped. The Saint-Simonian musicians will follow Halévy's implied suggestion and favor vocal music using texts of clear ideological content. In the process, they will add their efforts to a long tradition in Western culture, from the ritual and celebratory music of the ancients and of the Catholic and Protestant churches to such recent developments as the hymns and cantatas of the Masons and the French Revolution.

"LE PRODUCTEUR"

When the first disciples, within months of their master's death, began to publish a weekly journal, *Le Producteur,* they based their view of art on the ideas presented in the "Dialogue" rather than on the *culte* of New Christianity. In his introduction to the first issue, A. Cerclet, the first editor-in-chief, merely paraphrased some of Halévy's phrases critical of art "sans objet."[20] Halévy himself carried the idea a bit further, arguing that when society has finally attained its full moral and positivistic condition, when morality has become "a science like physics," the artist will possess "the power to please and move [people]" with the same certainty that the mathematician and chemist possess in their respective domains.[21]

Other passages in the early issues of the *Producteur* embroidered upon Halévy's critique of "reactionary" art in the "Dialogue." Halévy, for example, now castigated the Académie's insistence on subjects drawn from Greco-Roman history; Alexandre Soumet contributed a poem in praise of the Languedoc Canal; and Adolphe Garnier, perhaps thinking of theater's potential for reaching large audiences, spoke of the need for dramas that reproduce "the current tendency of our society."[22] Garnier's critique of the artificialities of French Restoration drama was widespread among liberal intellectuals and would soon find expression in Hugo's *Cromwell* and *Hernani*. Nonetheless, Garnier seems to be voicing here a characteristically Saint-Simonian attraction to the theatrical and the declamatory that we have already seen in the "Dialogue" and that will infuse the lectures of the Saint-Simonians in 1829–31, the ceremonies of Ménilmontant, and even the *odes-symphonies* of Félicien David in the 1840s.

Less characteristic, perhaps, but more striking is Garnier's attempt to sketch a whole series of possible functions for the arts to replace their traditional connection to war. Architecture, according to Garnier, should decorate "the useful edifices and the vast workshops of modern wealth" (e.g., banks and factories). Instrumental music, "which has until now served to make regiments march ... , will perhaps be able to stimulate them in moments of rest; or it may preside over work in a port, signaling the arrival and departure of ships and even accompanying them on their voyage."

The down-to-earth quality of these suggestions is certainly unusual; there is probably no other passage in Saint-Simon's or the Saint-Simonians' writings on art that considers so realistically the role of art in embellishing daily life and labor. Indeed, Garnier's concerns here have far more in common with the "utilitarian" view of art propounded by, among others, the architect Quatremère de Quincy.[23]

However uncharacteristic, though, these practical proposals—no doubt by their very concreteness—stirred up more response in the *milieux artistiques et littéraires* than had Saint-Simon's or Halévy's comparatively abstract pronouncements. Stendhal dashed off an entire pamphlet in opposition to the threat to art that he thought he sniffed in these early issues of the *Producteur,* and the prominent novelist and liberal publicist Benjamin Constant reproached Garnier: "Must one then sing only of [steam] engines?" Cerclet and "P.A.D." responded in the pages of the *Producteur* with a categorical negative.[24] It is clear today that they had been misunderstood, but the misunderstanding was a natural one, and would recur.

Indeed, one may suspect that, even if Garnier had not offered his perhaps ridiculous and certainly premature examples of new social functions for art, the underlying aesthetic views now set forth in the "Dialogue" and the early volumes of *Le Producteur* were almost doomed to be either ignored or misunderstood. This was an age of defiant individualism in literature and the arts. To stress, as Halévy did, the impotence of independent, purely "imaginative" artists, and the superiority of those who, following the dictates of "reason," put "their works in harmony with the needs of the time,"[25] was to render the whole appeal unpalatable to artists, the very people whom Halévy and his fellows were trying to persuade. The chore of finding an acceptable form for the movement's aesthetic doctrines remained for the moment unsolved.

The first steps in this direction were taken in later volumes of *Le Producteur*, beginning in April 1826 when Enfantin and Buchez took over the editorship. Enfantin had been looking into *Nouveau Christianisme*, under the repeated insistence of Olinde Rodrigues that "everything is there." In it (he later recalled) he discovered the clue to the future development of the movement.[26] The religious message, with its concomitant emphases on universal association and a priestly mission for art, quickly found expression in the issues of *Le Producteur*. Enfantin, in the article that introduced his editorship and that he later called the movement's "first credo,"[27] carried on the call for art tied to a hopeful, brilliant future but also suggested its religious transformation by calling it "the energetic expression of moral feelings."[28] *Nouveau Christianisme* had placed the highest value on these very feelings, and so the next logical step was to proclaim, as Buchez did four months later, that art must necessarily have the highest and noblest position in the social structure:

> To sense the illness of the age and express it, to conceive the future, to discover through inspiration what the sciences learn [more ploddingly?] and to indicate to the great number this path of happiness and immortality—these things fall only to great talents. The artistic genius ... is no slave destined to follow after society step by step. His function is to rush ahead of it, to serve as its guide. He must march, and it must follow.[29]

This passage was a landmark in the development of the Saint-Simonians' aesthetics. It gave a clear answer to questions that had received ambiguous or unpalatable treatment in their previous writings. By combining Halévy's high regard for art with Saint-Simon's late, religious-sentimental message, Buchez produced a new role for the artist: Hunt's *révélateur*.[30] But whether the Saint-Simonians were willing to accept the consequences of a society led by artists, whether—in theory and practice—the artist would be permitted to remain a *révélateur*, remained an open question.

6

THE ROLE OF THE ARTIST IN THE MATURE SAINT-SIMONIAN SOCIAL SCHEME, 1828–31

The new religious direction became increasingly apparent in many of the Saint-Simonians' letters and publications during the late 1820s.[1] It was summarized and elaborated most convincingly and influentially in the two year-long series of lectures that were given in 1828–30 and then published, with revisions, as the *Doctrine of Saint-Simon*. In these lectures the Saint-Simonians applied their basic principles to a wide range of subjects, from public health and education to commercial loans, international relations, and—treated in a few trenchant paragraphs—art.

These paragraphs were soon complemented by two extensive publications on the same subject, both from the pen of the movement's leading aesthetician, Emile Barrault. Before joining the Saint-Simonians, Barrault had been a professor of rhetoric at the Collège de Sorèze, and he quickly became one of the movement's most frequent and grandiloquent public speakers.[2] Of his two long publications on the arts, one—the brochure *Aux artistes*—was apparently written directly for publication but is nonetheless marked by his love of exalted language; the Saint-Simonian leaders considered it "a superb piece" and "the best brochure the doctrine has yet published."[3] His other pronouncement on art, a sermon read at the Salle Taitbout on 1 May 1831 and entitled "L'Art: Paganisme, Christianisme, Saint-Simonisme," is no less "superb," and it received particularly wide distribution.[4] The views on art expressed in Barrault's *Aux artistes* and "L'Art," and in the paragraphs of the *Doctrine* (which Barrault may also have written),[5] were often novel, were usually expressed with verve and captivating imagery, and certainly remain crucial to any understanding of the movement's relations with musicians and its own musical activities (discussed in Parts Three and Four).

Organic and Critical Ages

The basic conception of art and its social role found in these three publications derived from three basic principles of history and social organization, all of

45

them inherent in Saint-Simon's writings, especially *Nouveau Christianisme,* but nowhere so systematically developed.

The first was that history moves in cycles, alternating between organic (or religious) and critical (or irreligious) periods. In the organic periods, typified by ancient Greece and medieval Europe, all of society is unified by a single set of values (polytheism and patriotism in the case of the Greeks; Christianity, feudalism, and papal authority during the Middle Ages). In these periods,

> education and legislation cause all actions, thoughts, and feelings to converge toward the common good. The social hierarchy becomes the expression of this goal . . . [and the ruling class is characterized by] *sovereignty* and *legitimacy.* . . . Organic epochs, furthermore, show a general feature which dominates all these specific features: they are *religious.* Religion is then the synthesis of all human activity, both individual and social.

In contrast, critical periods, notably the Roman Empire and the period since Luther, are unstable and conflict-ridden. They begin with a concerted effort of destruction that results in "the downfall of the old moral and political order," and they end in a long period of rampant individualism or egoism.[6]

The second basic principle was that these historical peaks and valleys do not alternate in static repetition; each peak is higher than the previous one, as can be seen in the progression from cannibalism to slavery, serfdom, and free labor. The Saint-Simonians felt that this passing from *antagonisme* to *association* would be fulfilled by the imminent arrival of the next organic period, in which the principle of love would guide all people in their daily behavior and in their social organization.

The third principle, crucial for questions of art, amounted to a shift in the balance among the three basic human capacities—thinking, feeling, and acting. Whereas thinking and acting (science and industry) had held priority in the early writings of the disciples, feeling (*sentiment*) now was in the ascendant. This priority of feeling, so directly contrary to all but the last of Saint-Simon's writings and even more so to classical liberal and Utilitarian doctrine, was claimed by the Saint-Simonians on two levels. For the individual, feeling was the necessary and sufficient precondition for thought and action.

> It is feeling which brings man to inquire about his purpose [in living] [*sa destination*], and it is feeling which first reveals the answer to him. Then, doubtless, science has an important role to fulfill. It is called upon to *verify* these inspirations, revelations, and divinations of feeling, and to furnish man with the insights to make him move rapidly and securely toward the goal which has been disclosed to him. But it is again feeling which, by making him *desire* and *love* this goal, can alone give him the *will* and *strength* necessary to attain it.[7]

46

On the higher, societal level, it was equally axiomatic that the best path for mankind and for any individual would be determined not by the scientist but by the man of feeling. Science would, through facts and reasoning, be able "to describe the obligations which individuals have by reason of their proper place in the social hierarchy. But this place can only be assigned by love, which is to say by the men who are most strongly animated by the desire of improving the fate of mankind."[8] Since it was the men "whom nature has especially endowed with a capacity for sympathy" who could best determine the goal of society and the place of the individual, it followed that these exceptional men also had the "mission" of providing the "moral education" of the mass of individuals mentioned earlier, of producing in the general population feelings of love, and desire for the aims of society. "Science, as we have just said, is able to indicate the means to be used in order to attain a certain goal. But why one goal rather than another? Why not remain stationary? Why not even retrogress? Feeling—that is, strong sympathy for the disclosed goal—alone can cut through this difficulty."[9] The coming organic age would thus be religious and dominated by religious leaders—men of "sympathy" and "feeling"—capable of kindling the associative desires of the masses and drawing them away from "unworthy" (i.e., reactionary) beliefs and practices. "If we want to heal mankind of this wound [ignorance and superstition] . . . if we want it to leave the Church of the Middle Ages, let us open for it the Church of the future".[10]

Artist and Priest

Who were these new religious leaders to be? The artists, perhaps? Both Saint-Simon and Halévy had sketched the possibility that the artist would be, in some sense, priestly. But for them the role of priest was not identical to that of society's leader or ruler (*gouvernant*). To grant the artist a "divine mission" or "sacerdocy" was less weighty an assignment than might first appear. Now, though, the Saint-Simonians had clearly chosen to place the direction of society in the hands of new religious leaders; the role of priest became crucial and powerful. Who would be called to fill it?

The natural conclusion that readers must have drawn from the *Doctrine* was that "the artist" or—as the *Doctrine* called him—"the poet," would be the priest. The opening lecture expressly divided all human activity into three spheres—science, industry, and fine arts—and plainly defined the last as "the expression of feeling" and as what induces man to do "social acts" and to realize that "his private interest [is subsumed] in the general interest."[11]

The authors even hinted strongly that the poet would be lawgiver, *révélateur*, perhaps leader. "The poet is the divine singer [*chantre*], placed at the head of society to serve man as interpreter, to give him laws, to reveal to him the joys of the future, to sustain and stimulate his onward march."[12] But the choice of

47

words reveals some hesitation. In a church, the *chantre* is the "cantor" or "precentor." The poet is thus the chief singer of the new religion. Who is the priest?

The same question strikes us when reading the text of the tenth session of the *Doctrine*. Society, the text states with great clarity, "has never been directly stirred onward except by the various expressions of feeling. . . . [These are] called '*culte*' in organic epochs or 'fine arts' in critical epochs." But obscurity enters when the identity of the leader is discussed. "The direction of society has at all times and in all places belonged to the men who have spoken to the *heart*. . . . Reasoning and syllogisms have never been more than secondary and indirect means." The words have a familiar ring; Halévy had used similar ones to describe the work of the artists.[13] But are the artists intended here? One begins to suspect not, and to sense rather that the category of art or *culte* is being understood here in a very large sense. Indeed, the passage goes on to give as an example of medieval *culte* the Catholic practice of confession![14] This is hardly the right job for an artist or a poet, as these words are usually defined (and are generally used by the Saint-Simonians), though of course there can be "art" (of a different kind) in hearing confession.

We must conclude that in 1829 the Saint-Simonians were either divided, ambivalent, or confused about the desirability of creating a special priestly class. And so in the *Doctrine* the message was mixed, the vision cloudy.

Around this time Emile Barrault composed his brochure *Aux artistes*, in which he called on people in the arts to lend their services to the Saint-Simonian cause. It is the chief document of Saint-Simonian aesthetics and a few passages from it have been cited over and over again by scholars as proof positive that the Saint-Simonians wanted to make of the artist a new priest. In fact, though, its message is marked by the same ambivalence as the passages in the *Doctrine*, and occasionally by what appears to be intentional concealment, verbal sleight-of-hand.

Barrault appears to answer the question definitively in his concluding sentences, a typical Barraultian peroration and *appel*:

> Come, come to us all those [of you] whose heart knows how to love and whose forehead can burn with a noble hope! Let us join our efforts in order to speed humanity toward that future [of universal *association*]. United among ourselves, like the harmonious strings of a single lyre, let us begin today those sacred hymns which will be repeated by posterity. From now on the fine arts are the *culte* and the artist is the priest.[15]

Hunt calls this passage an "eloquent proclamation of the rights of the idea in poetry," which it clearly is, but he also implies that it is an unambiguous statement of the artist as révélateur, as mystically endowed leader of all other branches of society. Hunt is being misled—as perhaps Barrault intended—by the powerful word "priest." In fact Barrault sees the priest here as, at best, an equal of the true leaders of society; if one eliminates the rhetorical flourishes about "unity" and "harmonious strings," one can begin to see that the artist is still being called, not to discover ideas, but to spread them, not to lead humanity, but to "join efforts" with those who are already leading it in a chosen direction.

This conflict between the Saint-Simonians' actual program and Barrault's persuasive efforts is even more apparent in an earlier passage from *Aux artistes*. The middle third of it—the image of the artist soaring, eagle-like, between man and God and thus leading humanity onward—has frequently been quoted in the scholarly literature as representing the Saint-Simonians' view of the artist's glorious social role.[16] Indeed, it does convey more clearly than any other passage in the writings of Saint-Simon or the Saint-Simonians a sense of trust in the intuitions of the artist.

Read as a whole, though, the passage gives heavy clues that the artist of the future, while "leading" humanity, would simultaneously be following instructions: making propaganda for "our ideas" and stimulating people to move in the direction of the new world announced by "us," *les pères saint-simoniens*.

> To him [the forward-looking artist of today] belongs the task of propagating our ideas in a powerful manner, to assure their success and their gradual acceptance in the world. . . . A hundred times people have repeated that in looking at mankind we [Saint-Simonians] could only see science and industry, or that we placed the arts on a secondary level. . . . We firmly reject this doctrine. . . . No, we do not feel that the artist, in the scientist's hand, is like an insect in a child's, tied to a string which limits its flight. The artist is not a feeble bird repeating in its cage the tunes which its master has taught it. Rather, he soars aloft freely, he glides high above the earth, and, being close to the heavens, it is from there that his inspired and often prophetic voice makes itself heard. Not lightning is it which descends with him but a pure, peaceful, sacred fire capable of setting all hearts ablaze!
>
> In short, only the artist, through the force of that sympathy which allows him to embrace both God and society, is worthy of leading humanity. Is this what you call making the artist a slave to the scientist? Therefore we do extend our hand loyally to the artists, our natural allies. And when, by scientific means and rigorous calculations, we announce the advent of a new world, toward which we must all direct ourselves instead of drifting upwind and downwind in eternal timidity, will they not feel irrepressible forebodings in their heart, will they not

smell the perfumes of the approaching coastline, will they have no songs to revive half-hearted souls, to instill courage, to rouse us to spread open all our sails in the hope of reaching the glorious goal? Ah! before such a prospect who among them would not feel his imagination flare up, his ardor strengthen, who would not bewail the limits of his talent![17]

Barrault's imagery was felicitous, or at least clever. The soaring bird was a favorite Romantic figure, for it represented independence.[18] Yet Barrault's bird is also a messenger from the Almighty and is thus in a certain sense not an independent agent at all but a dedicated, serene servant of a truth beyond art. The bird brings down to mankind heavenly fire, an image invoking the shadow of Prometheus, another Romantic favorite.[19] But in purging the fire bringer of his rebellious thievery, and thus of both his heroism and his resultant suffering, Barrault has eliminated most of what made Prometheus attractive to the Romantics. What remains is a fire bringer who is valued for his one special skill: flight. This skill is valued highly by Barrault. He specifically credits his artist-bird with the ability to revive the courage of the leaders themselves, not only of the lower orders. But it is still the leaders who, through "scientific means," discover and "announce" the goal. Does this not make *them* the true "seers"?

It was suggested earlier that Barrault may have intended to mislead his readers, or at least to disguise the ambivalence underlying his message. He had good reason to do so. His aim in *Aux artistes* was to persuade, not to present an objective and balanced picture of Saint-Simonian doctrine. The brochure was a direct appeal to artists, a rebuttal—as Barrault himself stated—of claims that the Saint-Simonians wished to place the arts "in a secondary position." Barrault was trying to convince artists to join the movement and place their gifts in its service. No doubt his own prestige in the movement depended on his success in attracting converts from among *les artistes*. Perhaps he even hoped, as leader of the movement's artistic wing, eventually to be invited to be part of a ruling triumvirate with Bazard and Enfantin. (In 1833 he would challenge Enfantin's authority directly, publicly, and—it seems—unnecessarily.) And so, in his eagerness to persuade artists, he placed the emphasis where it suited his purpose, on the centrality of the artist's role, even to the point of proclaiming, as the rest of the Saint-Simonian leaders were not quite willing to do, that the artist was now the priest and the only one worthy of leading humanity.

Even this seemingly straightforward proclamation, though, cannot be taken literally. We should note that Barrault, though he was making artists (and himself, the movement's most notable public performer) appear important and powerful, took care in this passage not to challenge the authority of the *pères*. He could safely call the artist a priest because the priest was not, in his terms, the maker of decisions. Enfantin showed perfect understanding of this when he acclaimed Barrault's brochure, and we have seen that the ambivalence in it is also found in the authoritative first volume of the *Doctrine*. Indeed, as long as the Saint-Simonians continued to divide humanity into three groups (scientists, *industriels,* and a third and highest group) and continued to give the members of the third group—the "men of feeling"—the name "artists," they were almost bound to give the erroneous impression that the artists would be the leaders of society.

They seem to have become aware of this in 1829. In that year, Eugène Rodrigues, as Bénichou has noticed, made a clear typographical distinction between the religious and the secular representatives of the loving branch of society: the PRIEST and (subordinate to him) the ARTIST.[20] Bazard made explicit this clarification of policy in a remarkable and rarely cited passage from the second volume of the *Doctrine:*

> In the course of the exposition which we gave last year, as also in several writings which we have published, we have often chosen to designate ARTISTS as the only representatives of the SYMPATHETIC faculty to which we attribute the direction of societies. At times it has even happened that we used the word ARTIST and the word PRIEST interchangeably as if they were perfectly synonymous. This could happen because in fact the ARTIST and the PRIEST live in the same sphere and are of the same family. But there is nonetheless an important distinction between them, and—now that we have arrived at the present stage in the development of our ideas—we should establish it [this distinction].
>
> The PRIEST CONCEIVES the future and produces the RULE which LINKS humanity's *past* destinies to its *future* ones. In other words, the PRIEST GOVERNS. The artist grasps the thought of the priest, translates it into his [own] language, and makes it perceptible to everyone by allowing it to take the various shapes appropriate to it. He reflects in himself the world that the priest has created or discovered, reduces it to a symbol, and unveils it before the eyes of all. It is through the artist that the priest manifests himself. The *artist,* to put it simply, is the *word* [*verbe*] of the PRIEST.[21]

Thus, in a startling turnabout, the artist was reassigned to the dependent role of "popularizer" that he had held in most of Saint-Simon's writings. Enfantin, in October 1830, put his seal of approval on this reassignment when he mentioned that, though the Saint-Simonian doctrine would directly penetrate "the upper classes," it would need to be presented "through its *culte* . . . . to the lower classes."[22] Clearly, he imagined the arts and artists as providing the necessary sugar coating.

The following February the Saint-Simonians published a large poster containing a systematic overview of their major ideas. On it they explicitly divided the "social hierarchy" into three major groups: scientists, *industriels,* and—in central position—not "poets or artists" but "priests or governors." Only paragraphs later did they mention the artist and then merely as the "agent" of the priest, not as a ruling member of the hierarchy.[23] In an ironic recapitulation of Saint-Simon's insulting arithmetic in the *Lettres,* the Saint-Simonians were now dividing three social functions among four groups, and one of those groups—the same one—again got sent away empty-handed.

Thus, in the formulation of Saint-Simonian doctrine from late 1830 and 1831, the artist is emphatically not the priest, nor is he the leader of humanity. Nonetheless, the views presented a year or two earlier, in *Aux artistes* and the first volume of the *Doctrine,* were not obliterated by Bazard and Enfantin's revisions—Barrault, for one, refused to accept being anyone's agent—and continued to contribute promise and confusion to the movement's appeal to artists over the next few years.

7

ORGANIC ART AND
MUSIC, 1828–32

It is hard to know how much or how little attention prospective "artistic" converts paid to these rather theoretical arguments about the position of the artist in the social hierarchy. Some—Liszt, for example—may have followed the debate fairly closely. Others, no doubt, were primarily interested not in the movement's attitude toward art at all, but rather in its general social doctrines. (This was demonstrably the case with Berlioz.) Between these two extremes lay a number of people in the arts who were indeed greatly interested to learn the Saint-Simonians' view of art, but in its practical rather than theoretical ramifications. These artists—including, it seems, such dissimilar spirits as David and Mendelssohn—were particularly eager to learn in some detail what sort of art the Saint-Simonians envisioned for their *nouveau monde*. The key to this, of course, lay mainly in the Saint-Simonians' evaluation of specific authors, artists, and composers of the past and present. Fortunately, Barrault and certain other disciples—unlike Saint-Simon or Halévy—gave freely of their opinions in such matters, and they even threw in occasional hints about the art of the future as well.

ART AND HISTORY

In order to understand these specific commentaries, it is first important to realize that they are generally based on the assumption—stated most explicitly in the *Doctrine*—that great flowerings of art must coincide with organic periods in human history.[1] This assumption creates occasional problems for Barrault, notably when he comes to deal with the arts of the Renaissance. Halévy had praised Renaissance art as the natural product of thriving mercantile economies such as those in Florence and Flanders.[2] Barrault, in contrast, finds himself forced to reject the whole concept of a cultural Renaissance, because in his view the fifteenth and sixteenth centuries launched the "critical" modern epoch, with its religious schisms (the Reformation) and challenges to temporal authority as well. Barrault can hardly deny the greatness of the artistic monuments

53

from these two centuries: the works of Michaelangelo and Raphael, the epic poems of Tasso, what he calls the "noble and religious accents" of Palestrina, or the restoration (by the Council of Trent) of the "simple, grave, expressive" Gregorian chant, which was "so well matched to the severe majesty of the sacred words." He accepts them all and praises them mellifluously, yet argues that they comprised not a "rebirth" (*renaissance*) but rather the "last birth" (*dernier enfantement*) of the previous era, the "organic" Middle Ages.[3]

Barrault's analyses are rarely this forced, but they are often this categorical, as for example when he argues that the critical epoch beginning with the Renaissance and continuing into the present eventually brought with it a drastic artistic decline climaxing in the skepticism of modern art, its introspection, its exaggerated desire to divert or to present a refined and polished surface. Though there is a substantial kernel of truth in this, it is hardly a fair summary, especially as regards music. Barrault's musical readers may well have recoiled— as we do today—at this implied dismissal of such giants as Bach, Haydn, Mozart, and Beethoven. In fact, as we shall see in the next subchapter, when Barrault comes to talk about music he changes his tack completely.

Barrault's analysis of the art of organic societies—specifically ancient Greece and medieval Europe—is generally more convincing, perhaps because he finds such traits as social harmony and belief in the Fatherhood of God more to his taste. He does admit, in *Aux artistes,* that the arts of these early periods lacked "perfection of details," a necessary reflection of the inherent "primitiveness" (*rudesse*) of those of earlier societies, further emphasized by the undeveloped state of artistic technique. Nonetheless, he insists, "those imperfect forms are alive" (pp. 14, 33). He also states that these periods have the mistaken reputation of being dark, barbaric, and artistically sterile (p.13—one imagines he is referring here primarily to the Middle Ages and not to the glory that was Greece), and he sets out to show, art by art and with fair success, how both periods in fact produced works of unsurpassed simplicity, grandeur, and communal significance: "the most beautiful works of which the arts properly speaking can boast" (pp. 33–34).[4] His views on architecture, literature, and the theater are particularly detailed and persuasive (and they prepare the ground for his discussion of music).

In architecture he sees perhaps the clearest expression of these earlier religious ages; the "severe simplicity" of the Greek temples and the "high proportions" of the great cathedrals still can convey "the lively impression of a special intended purpose," in contrast to modern churches, which resemble secular palaces or stock exchange buildings in their "ostentatious ornamentation" and their excessive attention to "elegance, purity, grace . . . [and] attractive and elegant groupings [*combinaisons*]" (pp. 15–19).

Turning to literature he notes in the epics of Homer and Dante the same "imposing grandeur" and large-scale unity, elements that are no longer to be found when one reaches the more individualistic efforts of Milton and Bossuet (pp. 20–22). Barrault even sees a decline in works written toward the end of the two organic epochs: in the more refined but less forceful epics of Virgil and Tasso, and even in the Greek tragedies, which seem to him, in their focus on individual motivation divorced from the will of the gods, "a degeneration of the epic," leading to the representative products of the critical age, the drama and the novel (pp. 21, 23). Barrault does not completely reject the theater, though. He admires its connection with the Church during the Middle Ages and, while noting that the theater has gradually become "critical"—a great "engine of war" aimed at the Church and the entire system of the past organic age—he praises Beaumarchais's modest efforts at restoring comedy to its "original intended purpose" of correcting man's vices (pp. 51–54, 79–80). It is now, he feels, the mission of art to regain its former didactic power (pp. 75–76).

Barrault gives examples of subject matter that might be used in the theater of the new age. Let tragedy, he says, paint the sufferings of the oppressed classes; let comedy, instead of clinging to old themes, attack the hypocrisy of wealthy liberals who weigh on the backs of the workers (p. 80). But he holds out little hope for literature as practiced in recent years. Barrault forcefully opposes those writers who stress the corruption and baseness of human nature (as Lesage did in *Gil Blas*); what doctor, he asks, would cure a sick person by bringing him through a plague ward (p. 54)? Barrault and his fellows are also critical of the leading contemporary writers, of whatever school or inclination. Barrault takes Scott, Chateaubriand, and Byron to task for escaping into an idealized past or for adopting a tone of destructive irony; the authors of the *Doctrine* tackle the current fashion among poets for satire and elegy (presumably meaning Auguste Barbier, Lamartine, and Hugo); and, in his sermon on art, Barrault—perhaps fearful of seeming too negative—attempts to sift out of all this hopelessly "critical" literature a saving "organic remnant."[5]

Did the Saint-Simonians, in passages such as these, mean to blame the writers of their day for not being more "organic"? The *Doctrine* suggests that they did not. It takes something akin to the "sociological" view of contemporary literary historians (see Chapter 3) and concludes that during a "critical" epoch a poet cannot help but express for the most part the tensions of his age. Since associative feelings are lacking, the poet "can no longer find any but sinister songs." "The fine arts no longer have a voice when society no longer has love. Poetry is not the interpreter of *egoism*. To reveal himself, the true artist needs a chorus which will repeat his songs [*chants*] and be receptive to his soul when it pours out."[6]

Barrault's view is slightly different. Like Buchez in his statement of 1826, he holds artists responsible for transcending their age, for pointing the way to the coming organic era. Perhaps he does not actually blame his contemporaries, although later he will come irritatingly close to it, but he does consider them free agents, capable of rising out of their lethargy or shaking off their habitual snideness in order to help bring that new age by stirring people to action.

Barrault even offers a specific vision of what the art of the new organic age would be like. He finds the key to it in the writings of a somewhat older but still "critical" author: Jean-Jacques Rousseau. In the midst of a life dedicated to denigration of the present and flight into an imagined golden age before the beginning of civilization, Rousseau recognized—as Barrault rightly notes— that modern man has a need for public festivals that will be "more touching, more elevated, more worthy of humanity" (p. 58).[7] Barrault extols the wisdom in Rousseau's plan and expands on it. The theater, Barrault concludes, will eventually give way to a new religious epic, reconciling the beautiful and the true, based on "eloquence" (p. 83) (i.e., public rhetoric, Barrault's own specialty),[8] and this mammoth world epic will be performed in the new temple of the organic age (p. 84).

> Music, painting, and sculpture will lend their support to the efforts of eloquence and poetry, in temples which architecture will have renewed under the influence of a more complete inspiration. These are the delights in store for our descendants, when a new worship [culte], rallying all men to the foot of the same altars, will have appeared on earth.

This vision of the new universal *culte* is clearly adapted from Saint-Simon's (in *Nouveau Christianisme*). The individual arts are arrayed in the same hierarchical fashion: they "support" or literally "second" (*seconderont*) the efforts of the poet and orator. But Saint-Simon's coldly rational plan is enriched here by an almost tangible passion for *association universelle* and for the "delights" of art. In the process it has become Romantic, and undoubtedly more persuasive.

MUSIC PAST AND PRESENT

The hint of a future religious music in the passage just cited is certainly significant and will be discussed shortly. But, with music as with the other arts, the Saint-Simonians' vision of the future depended on and derived from their analysis of the past and present. That analysis, though, was quite different for music. To begin with, it was more tentative. Whereas Barrault could confidently tick off examples of organic art and poetry from Attic Greece and the Middle Ages (the latter defined *very* broadly), in music he made fewer claims for a glorious organic past. He never expanded on the brief references to Palestrina and chant reform cited earlier (nor did he—more curiously—ever allude to the prominent functions of the chorus in Greek drama). A major reason for this was no doubt that Barrault and his listeners, however well read in the literary classics, knew almost no "ancient" music, i.e., music before Haydn. Similarly, whereas he willingly identified by name numerous "critical" literary figures of the Enlightenment and the modern age, he seems to have been more hesitant about castigating the composers of his day, perhaps again because to disapprove of most contemporary music would be tantamount to opposing the entire familiar musical repertoire and thus the art of music itself.

But Barrault also had more positive reasons for judging contemporary music leniently. His main passage on music makes clear that he shared the Romantic view that music was the most communicative and universal of the arts because it was the least representational.[9] Furthermore, the passage reveals his awareness that in his own day music was attaining a prominent and "popular" status (his own word) that it had rarely known before. (The burgeoning worlds of opera, virtuoso recitals, and salon music must surely have been in his mind when he wrote these words, and perhaps the towering figure of Paganini in particular.)

> Only one art retains a true power: music. Perhaps the most popular artist of our day is a musician. But music does not owe this power to its belated perfection, the necessary result of the introduction of harmony, an element unknown to the ancients and which [gradually] built itself up. It owes it to its very nature. In an epoch in which the external symbol has perished—a symbol which gave expression to the feelings and needs of the human heart—yet has not dragged these [feelings and needs] down with it, this vague and mysterious language, which responds to all souls and receives a special translation according to each person's situation, cannot help being the only common language among men. In such a state of affairs, all poetry is in the music, and words remain legitimately subordinated, until [the day when] poetry, invested again with precision, establishes a powerful harmony [*accord*] between the verses and the music. But today, like Ossian's lyre, music evokes around us fantastic clouds that everyone peoples and enlivens with his [own] regrets and his [own] hopes. Thus, the pure and solemn religious expression which Haydn, Mozart, and Cherubini were able to give [to music], thanks to the suppleness of this marvelous language, is a sort of initiation into the religious thoughts of the future.

Barrault's passage continues and concludes by pointing out a few "critical" tendencies in contemporary musical life: the decline of true religious feeling, the emphasis on vocal and instrumental virtuosity for its own sake, and the patchwork programming of most concerts.

> Nonetheless the sacred music of several composers often is theatrical in character, and its profane [i.e., sacrilegious?] elegance becomes a scandal. Finally, concerts. These solemnities of critical times ... are intended almost uniquely to let the skill of the performers shine and ... never offer anything but a variety without unity.[10]

Barrault's distaste for "theatrical" church music may at first seem a pedantic overextension of his beloved antithesis of temple and theatre (i.e., "organic" and "critical" *culte*). But hidden behind the vague term "élégance profane" is a trenchant critique of a major feature of European musical life around 1830: the spreading influence of Italian operatic style. Even taken narrowly, Barrault's comment clearly refers to sacred works of a type that had its roots in the eighteenth century (e.g., Mozart) and that was to culminate in Rossini's exhibitionistically operatic *Stabat Mater* (1832, rev. 1842). In a larger sense, though, Barrault's comment implicates the entire Italian operatic enterprise and its stylistic offspring as well (such as the French operas of Auber). That Barrault did not come out and criticize the *dilettanti* (lovers of warbling) or in fact refer to opera at all suggests that he was hesitant to attack the genre that was (and to some extent still is) at the center of musical life in France. Perhaps he was afraid of antagonizing his audience and especially the potential recruits he might make among musicians associated with the operatic stage. Perhaps, too, Barrault wished here, as in his passages on modern poetry, to appear as constructive as possible.

But tactical considerations do not suffice to explain this antagonism toward the cult of virtuosity and toward Italian operatic style. It ran deep, and it found expression in the writings of other Saint-Simonians as well. An anonymous *Globe* contributor, admittedly more ambivalent than antagonistic, felt ashamed that he so liked hearing Rossini's *Tancredi*. "All the joy they give is spoiled, poisoned by the memory of the many who have no bread."[11] Enfantin, too, revealed—perhaps inadvertently—a prejudice against most opera in his proof that the greatest works of art are of religious inspiration: "What are the subjects that have inspired Handel, Mozart, Haydn, Cherubini, and even Rossini [an apparent reference to *Moïse* and to the *preghiera* scenes in other operas] when they composed their most beautiful works[?]"[12] His distaste was expressed more passionately in a subsequent, rather confused paragraph on the empty splendor of the Italian opera, a splendor that (he implied) might in other hands bring about great moral deeds. "Like your brother, I also weep—moved, trembling, and troubled—at the voices of Desdemona, Tancred, or Arsace [in Rossini's *Otello, Tancredi* and *Semiramide*]. But from my eyes tears are still flowing when your brother's eyes have dried...."[13] And several years later, in a letter to Duveyrier, Enfantin specifically praised Beethoven and Weber, and he contrasted the operas of Gluck with the (presumably Italian or Italianate) operas of the day, which were nothing but "a beautiful exercise" for the singers' voices.[14]

As these examples indicate, the anti-Italian bias (and often a distaste for opera in general) went hand in hand with a strong predisposition in favor of German church and concert music. Enfantin and Barrault repeatedly praised the Austro-German tradition (including its leading representative in France,

Luigi Cherubini) for its greater seriousness and its manifest or potential "religious" qualities. Mozart, in particular, they singled out as the highest creator. In one private letter Enfantin wrote jokingly but revealingly that God spreads harmony everywhere and uses dissonance rarely, "for he is an even better composer than Mozart." And in another he echoed Barrault's words on religious music by praising the Mozart Requiem as the "sublime summary and germ of old music and new."[15]

Beethoven, no doubt a more "critical," disturbing composer than Mozart, occasionally left the Saint-Simonians unsatisfied. *Le Globe,* reviewing a concert by Ferdinand Hiller in 1831, regretted Beethoven's "somber misanthropy" in the same sentence that called for something more substantial than the "satirical, insouciant verve" of Rossini.[16] But when we find the two composers coupled again in a letter that Enfantin wrote to his cousin Thérèse from prison in 1833, we realize as the passage progresses that opera and not symphony poses the greater threat to moral and emotional health.

> Write to me when the demons which reign there [in Paris] inspire you, when you have just heard Beethoven or Rossini, Giulia Grisi and Rubini [leading singers of the Théâtre italien], when you leave the Opéra, dazzled and a bit scandalized, and its ladies and its costumes, its noise and its lights pursue you right into your bedroom.[17]

A possible explanation for this leaning toward the Germans may be that the Saint-Simonians, far from following essentially aesthetic principles, were being guided by their own personal taste as formed in large part by their class background. The bourgeois elite in all of Europe was split into two camps, aptly called "the gay world" and "the serious world" by one perceptive Parisian (Mme Girardin). Those in the "gay" camp eagerly pursued privileges and adopted tastes formerly limited to the aristocracy; they attended the opera (a visible sign of prestige because of the reserved seats and boxes) and acclaimed the fashionable virtuosi, often inviting them to play to guests in their salons.[18] The "serious" camp, disdaining tasteless commercialism and status consciousness, cultivated a taste for the eternal verities, represented in music by Habeneck's Beethoven concerts at the Conservatoire. It was of course possible to partake of both musical worlds, more so perhaps in Paris (where the "classical music" concerts were particularly prestigious) than elsewhere in Europe. But it comes as no surprise that the Saint-Simonian leaders, many of whom came from upper-middle-class families active in finance and commerce (which tended as a group to be more "gay" than "serious," as opposed to families involved in the liberal professions) and had turned against the exclusiveness and class bias of their families and of the do-nothing aristocrats, would side instead with the professionals and other "serious" types who sought to trade what they viewed as degenerate amusements for a seemly sobriety imported from beyond the Rhine and who sternly rejected the display of wealth and privilege, only to replace it with the display of taste and profundity.[19]

RELIGIOUS MUSIC OF THE FUTURE

These opinions on past and current music and musical life seem today rather general and incomplete. Unfortunately, the Saint-Simonians gave still fewer details about the kind of music they wanted religious composers to write in the future. Nonetheless, even the vaguest passages on this subject are of some interest. Some of them may have helped to attract (or occasionally to repel) individual musicians, such as Liszt; and they certainly served as a partial model for the various and extensive forms of musical activity that blossomed within the movement in the years 1832–33.

The essential recurring element in the Saint-Simonian vision of a future music was that it would serve as an integral part of the new religious cere- monies. This principle had been stated explicitly by Saint-Simon himself in 1802, 1819, and 1825, and it was formulated again by Barrault in 1830. Not surprisingly, the same principle can be found at work, subliminally (through the repeated use of the word "hymn"), in the "call to artists" by Rodrigues, which is the movement's single most detailed proposal for a future religious music.

The passage in question appeared as part of Rodrigues's more general *Appel,* a call to all people, which he delivered at the turbulent ceremony of 27 No- vember 1831 (only eight days after the Bazard schism) and which the movement published in three different formats by the end of December. During this long speech Rodrigues announced the movement's need for financial assistance and invited contributions from the leaders of finance and industry. He then called on all artists to lend their services to the cause, and he did not hesitate to make specific suggestions about the type of art (and more specifically music) that would be appropriate.

> I call upon artists who love the people....
> Where is he, the poet who truly loves the people, who— proud of having sung [the praises of] Napoleon and the peo- ple's flag, will henceforth sing the hope of a hardworking people, a people which wishes no longer to make war? When will I hear the people sing the hymn of peace, more electrifying than the awesome "Marseillaise," more joyous than the simple "Parisienne" [battle song of the July Revolution of 1830]? Where is he, the Saint-Simonian Béranger, the Tyrtaeus of peace, whose accents will halt the horrid battle and will convert the masters and the workers to the new faith.

Let him appear, too, the musician whose intoxicating and powerful music—richer than that of Rossini and Beethoven—will seize hold of the emotional power unique to music (thanks to all its melodies and all its variations), in order to accompany the hymn of the future.

Painters, do not soil your brushes any longer by offering to our eyes a debauched and bleeding liberty. Worthy heirs of Raphael and David, be inspired by the sufferings of the daughters of the people, cause us to admire the woman of the future, throwing her life and her faith into the midst of the combatants in order to win them over to the love of God and humanity.

Sculptors, let the Moses of peace burst forth from the marble.

Architects, where are your plans for the temple of peace?[20]

Rodrigues prescribed here with unusual clarity the two types of music that the Saint-Simonians envisioned for the new religious age: (1) a new "Marseillaise" appropriate to an age of peace, and other simple, functional (but also artfully worded) chansons that might bring the Saint-Simonian message to the workers; (2) a more elaborate concert work (or works) that, through the full resources of musical art, could communicate to an assembled group not just the intellectual content but also the emotional force of the Saint-Simonian vision.

In both these categories Rodrigues was summing up ideas that had been presented in scattered form over the preceding years and that, even more strikingly, were soon to be carried out in practice. The need for a new "Marseillaise," for example, had already been stated by several other Saint-Simonians, notably Chevalier and Barrault, and beginning in late 1832 the creation of Saint-Simonian chansons (including a few "Marseillaises") was to become a major feature of the movement's musical life.[21]

Rodrigues's other suggestion—a grand "hymn of the future" surpassing Rossini and Beethoven—derived similarly from statements by Barrault and others quoted earlier. But, whereas the coupling "Rossini and Beethoven" had often been merely a stock phrase equivalent to "the leading composers of our day," Rodrigues succeeded in implying with it a good deal more. Through the use of three parallel word pairs—"enivrante et puissante," "Rossini et Beethoven," and "mélodies . . . variations"—he suggested an affinity among the first terms in the three pairs and also among the second terms. By thus associating Rossini with intoxication and melody, and Beethoven with power and "variations" (an apparent reference not just to variation technique but to all feats of musical imagination—harmonic, structural, textural, or whatever),[22] Rodrigues drew attention to the styles characteristic of the two most flourishing traditions in the music of his day. But whereas Enfantin and Barrault tended to set the two styles in opposition, to the inevitable detriment of Rossinian opera, Rodrigues proposed in this passage that the new music combine them—

the tuneful, appealing Italian style and the grander, more intellectually rigorous and forceful German style—and, by combining, transcend them both and create something as heady as the one, as stirring as the other, and richer than either. This desire for a synthesis of the two great national styles was in its own way a commonplace of music criticism in the early 1830s. Many praised Meyerbeer's *Robert le diable* (1831), in particular, for combining Italian melody and German harmony (to which they might with justice have added French declamation and stagecraft). Admittedly, Meyerbeer's music may seem today less a true synthesis of styles than a massive compromise, the result of a search for a marketably low common denominator. But in its own day it was viewed as a grand dialectical fusion, a quasi-Hegelian *Aufhebung* of the diverse and fragmentary traditions that had come before. It was in this same sense that Rodrigues invoked Rossini and Beethoven as composers to be surpassed; he flattered the future Saint-Simonian composer by speaking as if to improve on the past were as easy (or even as desirable) in music as in industry or science.

This casual dismissal of the giants may have appealed to some, but it certainly did not sit well with those who idolized their recent predecessors. Felix Mendelssohn took offense at this very passage by Rodrigues, and Berlioz mocked the *Globe's* Hiller review, with its similarly offhand attitude toward Rossini and Beethoven.[23] Perhaps Mendelssohn sensed an oblique reference to the Ninth Symphony of Beethoven in Rodrigues's call for a grand (choral and orchestral?) hymn of the future. (Beethoven's last movement of course has "variations" in both senses.) The Ninth had been unveiled to the French public by Habeneck earlier that year at the Conservatoire concerts, and it quickly became the model work for younger composers. "It is beauty, ideal beauty . . . ," wrote the young Félicien David to a friend. "Never was there a more sublime composition."[24] Rodrigues clearly shared this admiration for Beethoven. But to proclaim the desirability of surpassing Beethoven's nine symphonies at a time when talented musicians were anxiously trying to live up to the challenge that those works posed was to push flattery into insincerity. Perhaps Rodrigues never expected his words to be taken so literally; perhaps he meant them only in a visionary, utopian sense, much in the same way that Barrault, in the peroration of *Aux artistes,* had described the musical pageants of the new temple. If so, it was a mistake for him to become so specific. By inviting musicians to stand on the shoulders of the masters, he only made himself look foolish to those who knew the art better than he and who held it in greater respect.

However poorly phrased, though, Rodrigues's words in favor of a major concert work on Saint-Simonian themes did find an echo two months later when Félicien David, a recent recruit, provided the movement with its first authentic musical composition. (Rouget de Lisle's "Premier Chant des industriels" had preceded the founding of the movement, and the one or two chansons written in 1830–31 were set to preexistent tunes.) David's *Hymne à Saint-Simon* and the dozens of pieces that he continued to turn out over the next two years certainly did not even attempt to rival (much less surpass) Rossini and Beethoven, but they did draw effectively on the available melodic and harmonic resources of the day and thereby lent to the propagandistic texts something of the "emotional power unique to music" of which Rodrigues had spoken.

VIEWS ON ART AND MUSIC DURING A YEAR OF CRISIS (1831–32)

The ceremony at which Rodrigues presented his *Appel* should perhaps be viewed as part of a transitional phase for the movement, a phase that had begun the previous week when Bazard, his wife Claire, and many other prominent members withdrew from the movement in protest against certain ideas about women and free love that Enfantin had fostered for years and that, although they were frequently unrelated to basic tenets of Saint-Simonian doctrine, he was now pressing upon his followers with the insistence of a man who had gone nearly mad with power. In January 1832 the government took its first action against the movement, shutting down the Salle Taitbout and instituting proceedings that climaxed late that year in two trials and the imprisonment of Enfantin and Chevalier. In the meantime, in February 1832, the movement suffered a second and financially crippling schism—this time the dissident was Rodrigues himself—and Enfantin finally decided to make a virtue of necessity by forming an ascetic commune in suburban Ménilmontant with his forty most devoted disciples.

These drastic changes will be examined in greater detail in Chapters 8 and 10, where it will be seen that they stimulated the growth of a rich and characteristic musical life within the movement. These same changes, though, undermined another equally important aspect of the movement's musical mission: the attempt to forge good relations with a number of sympathetic "outsiders," including such prominent musicians as Liszt and Berlioz. Many, though not all, of these "fellow travelers" (as we might call them in the jargon of a later age) found the developments of late 1831 and 1832 bizarre or even repugnant. Details on this matter, too, must be delayed (see Chapter 9). What is of immediate interest to us in the rest of this chapter, though, is that, as the fish began to flee the pond, the fishermen became at once more relentless and more cajoling.

Hints of this new, more anxious tone had appeared in the movement's writings as early as 1 May 1831. Barrault, in his sermon on art that day, protested, "Artists, we do not accuse you!" and lavishly praised them as a group for steadily defending political and artistic freedom and for spreading the awareness that society was in need of a religious belief that could foster loving relations among the social classes. It appears that some prospective followers had taken offense at Barrault's windy moralizing about the failure of the leading artistic figures of the day (especially writers), for he went on to assure artists that "we do not intend to entomb . . . under the first stone of our monument all the glories of the present age, but rather to explain them, absolve them, and open to them a vaster and more majestic theater."[25]

It is hard to imagine these words calming doubts; what artist in that era of Romantic ego worship would have wished to be "absolved" of his own choice of style or subject matter? Even allowing for some rhetorical excess, the choice of word was precisely wrong, evoking visions of a Saint-Simonian art-pope (or even an art-god, since in Christian doctrine only God can absolve man of sin!) dictating the correct manner in which future art should develop. As early as 1826, we may recall, Cerclet felt impelled to defend the aesthetic ideas of Saint-Simon against the charge of vulgar utilitarianism, and ever since then the movement had attempted to tread a narrow line, pleading ever more strongly with artists to become involved while insisting that, to produce art that would be both great and socially useful, they must be inspired by the principles of social and historical development preached by the Saint-Simonians. Now, in 1831, Barrault, perhaps giddy with the adulation and large audiences he was attracting but also frantic because his proud plan of drawing artists into the movement was encountering resistance among the artists themselves, was beginning to lose control and to undercut his own message.

By 27 November, at the ceremony that followed Bazard's schism, Barrault was willing to admit publicly that artists had thus far been scared away by the authoritarian aura of the movement. He tried to reassure them that they would not need to sacrifice their individuality in joining the Saint-Simonians, and this time he even more explicitly turned their love of freedom (a trait that the *Doctrine* would perhaps have castigated as egoistic and "critical") into a glorious social virtue. But again he weakened his appeal by ridiculing the present options for poets, options in which some of those who heard or read his remarks were perhaps quite proudly and lucratively engaged.

> Artists and poets—you men of desire and independence— listen to us! . . . Come to us without mistrust. Outside of us what can you do today? Extol or repudiate the past, blaspheme or sing [the praises of] the present, repeat what Lamartine, Byron, and Béranger have done. What, when the people is suffering, becoming agitated, and pushing ahead to new destinies, do you not feel that a new task is calling you? Artists, whoever you are, you are of the people, for you love your liberty and you sympathize with all desires for emancipation![26]

The frustration and despair of these months showed up as well in writings specifically directed to musicians. The lapse of tone in Rodrigues's remarks on Rossini and Beethoven, cited in the previous section, certainly makes more sense when viewed against the unsettled background of power struggle, schism, and the movement's increasingly apparent failure to attract artists. And there can be no mistaking the historical context of the movement's last major *appel* to musicians, the *Globe* review (cited earlier) of a concert of Ferdinand Hiller's music, for it followed faithfully the tack that Barrault and Rodrigues had been charting for several months. The anonymous reviewer repeated and even expanded on Rodrigues's Rossini and Beethoven remarks; he may have felt that such comments were particularly appropriate in a review of musical works that derived so plainly from the Beethoven tradition, but the effect was no better and probably worse. And when, at the end of the passage cited below, the reviewer stressed the necessity for the artist to seek and find his way to a new role—yet another attempt, perhaps, to assure artists that the movement intended no threat to their autonomy—the tone, half naïvely hopeful, half either coy or condescending, could only suggest that the writer, while going through all the old motions and feigning an air of confidence, knew that nobody was likely to respond to his call, that in fact the artists were very well choosing their "way" and it was not that of the Saint-Simonians.

> [Hiller] is a man ready to do beautiful and great things if one day an inspirational thought fertilizes the capacities of his imagination. This thought will be neither the gloomy misanthropy nor the energetic heaving [*soulèvement*] which were the glory and misfortune of Beethoven. Neither will it be the satirical and carefree verve which was the main inspiration for the author of the *Barber* [*of Seville*]. This thought, which men of talent are calling for and which gives each of them his place, his role, and his name—this thought is for the artists to seek. Let them seek, and they shall find.[27]

The shrillness and hollow optimism of these last calls to artists stand in sad contrast to the overwhelming self-assurance that marked Barrault's brochure of 1830. There was not much further one could go down this road and still keep a movement alive and actively pursuing contacts with the public. Indeed, the very last of the movement's blueprints for a "social" art and music were not *appels* at all; they were drawn up in the relative isolation of the Ménilmontant retreat and they recapture and intensify the ecstatic, visionary tone of the last paragraph of Barrault's *Aux artistes*. Though written at the same time as the events to be discussed in Chapter 10, these late theoretical sources— the *Livre nouveau* and Duveyrier's article "La Ville nouvelle"—require treatment here, for they are the complement and (at least for the musical theories) the culmination of ideas presented in the earlier publications. It seems likely, in fact, that these two works represent the first systematic presentation of ideas and visions that had been developed over several years in private discussions and lectures and that had found their way only in sharply muted form into public lectures and writings. (Enfantin's ideas on women and on reincarnation had similarly been kept from the public for several years.[28]) Perhaps, having withdrawn from their proselytization efforts, the Saint-Simonian leaders felt free to let their imaginations soar and wheel.

The *Livre nouveau* was sketched out (it was never finished) during the month of July 1832, when activity in the retreat was at its height. In spite of the great excitement and some new anxieties (the death from cholera of an apostle, the impending trials), Enfantin met with seven of his leading disciples for four nights, and together they hammered out a number of theories and conjectures that were to form the core of a new religious testament. This *Livre nouveau* attempted to reexamine the essential nature of the physical world and human culture from a Saint-Simonian viewpoint. In among the abstruse metaphysical ponderings and presumptuous analogies to the Bible, the apostles scattered prophecies and visions of the new universal and sacerdotal language and music. The language will blend together the rhythm of poetry and the freedom of prose. (Good examples of this *verbe rythmé* were indeed already being provided by Barrault, as in the quotation on pp. 136–37. Indeed, the *Livre nouveau* points to the highly differentiated system of underlining words and phrases in Enfantin's writings [italics, small capitals, etc.] as indicative of the diversity of emphasis that will eventually enrich spoken language as well.) As for music, it too will unite tendencies and qualities previously thought to be irreconcilable: melody and harmony, active and meditative character, Italian and German style.[29] (This last point makes explicit a concern that was slightly veiled in Rodrigues's *appel* of the previous November.)

The authors of the *Livre nouveau* did not think it wise or even possible to predict in greater detail what the new arts would be—that, they now believed, artists would discover.[30] Instead, they focused on the ways in which the new arts would be used, and this they expressed in high-flown but often striking images. The remarks on music are often based on a rather passive-Romantic conception of its emotive and harmonizing powers. Thus Chevalier suggested that the temple of the future, built of iron tubes of different sizes, would also function as a sort of pipe organ—a "booming orchestra and gigantic thermometer," "a temple of melody and harmony" in which "the life of men [would be] manifested by music, by all the arts . . . by panoramas. . . . What an immense communion!"[31] Barrault—endowed with a better sense of how to make *culte* appealingly participatory—imagined solemn religious pageants combining music, stage design, declaimed text (*verbe rythmé*), and dance.[32]

Charles Duveyrier developed many of these ideas according to the journalistic norms of the day and presented the resulting fantasy to the literary public as an article: "La Ville nouvelle; ou, le Paris des Saint-Simoniens." In it he sketched, in occasionally ridiculous detail, the Saint-Simonians' plans to rebuild and reorganize the city of Paris. He proposed that the city be laid out in the shape of a man, and he placed the various activities and industries in appropriate parts of the "body." The muscular neck would give forth a musical accompaniment as the various members and bodily parts took their assigned places. He created the temple in the form of a woman, placed her in the middle of the city, and imagined an immense organ with pipes of precious metals sending torrents of harmony and melody out through the orifices of her head to the city below.

In the midst of these largely symbolic suggestions, he proffered at least one noble and rather prophetic vision regarding music in the new city of his dreams. He wanted to uproot the opera houses and theaters from the boulevards and send them through the city, spreading pleasure "to the very extremities of the body of my colossus."[33] The wish to sever the link between the performing arts and their steady patrons—the rich bourgeois and the aristocrats—echoed Saint-Simon's idea of creating art parks in the provinces. But the idea was no less significant for not being entirely original, and it remains relevant even a century and a half later, when—in spite of the salutary influence of government support and the broadcasting media—the decentralization of cultural life and the encouragement of high standards for local artistic activities remain hotly pursued goals in many of the world's biggest cities and especially in Paris.

Charléty dismisses all these fantasies of Enfantin, Chevalier, Barrault, and Duveyrier as "words, nothing but words," of interest only as evidence of the "the mental state of the apostles after three months' stay at Ménilmontant."[34] But they have claimed our attention here precisely because, as fantasies, they permit us to sense the profound hopes that the Saint-Simonians, formerly prophets of industry, were placing more and more in music and the arts. The apostles had come to view music as a constant, throbbing element in the life of a society, motivating its citizens to work and beautifying their existence and their surroundings. It was a vision that thrived especially in the atmosphere of Ménilmontant, where music was already mingling with the *verbe rythmé,* where the piano and chorus regularly embellished the natural beauty of the open-air temple, and where the bearded workers marched to their daily chores with a pageantry both ascetic and colorful.

Of course the idea of a ceremonial music presented by Barrault and Duveyrier in 1832 was also the culmination of several years' thinking, as they themselves knew. Charles Lambert, in fact, described the *Livre nouveau*—to which he had himself contributed—as "a last, magnificent gleam" of the movement's theoretical work.[35] Although the wisdom copiously set down in the *Livre nouveau* was plainly not the definitive statement that the writers wished it to be, these late echoes of the call for a social art and a social music are of importance in themselves and even more so as links between the years of theoretical activity and the two years (1832–33) in which the principle of a *musique sociale* moved from theory into practice with a success that exceeded anyone's reasonable expectations.

PART THREE
PRACTICE

8

THE RUE MONSIGNY AND SALLE TAITBOUT: MUSIC IN THE FORMATIVE YEARS

The story of the Saint-Simonians is a complex and detailed one at every turn, but perhaps most of all during the three years—1829 to early 1832—in which, after much preparatory work, the movement finally succeeded in drawing general attention to itself, became widely recognized as perhaps the most notable new school of social philosophy, and then, just as quickly, was torn apart by internal tensions and brought into disrepute by an irresponsible daily press and a repressive government. The basic events of these years have been presented very briefly in Chapters 2 and 7 as a context for the Saint-Simonians' contemporaneous writings on aesthetics and music. In the present chapter I shall return to this fascinating story, emphasizing its practical rather than theoretical ramifications. In particular, it is during these years that the movement first attempted to develop a musical life of its own and—as a means to that end—to attract into their ranks a musician of real promise. Indeed, toward the end of 1831 they finally found their man, Félicien David. But before broaching this subject, it will be helpful to examine some of the more general developments—and to examine them in rather close detail. For they form the crucial backdrop not only to the (still relatively limited) musical activities of these three years but also to the movement's complex relations with Liszt, Berlioz, and several other "outsider" musicians (discussed briefly in this chapter and more thoroughly in Chapter 9) as well as to the movement's later and more heavily musical phases: Ménilmontant, the dispersal, and the mission to the Orient.

THE MOVEMENT BECOMES A RELIGION: HIERARCHY AND RITUAL

The most basic trend during these few years of expansion and persecution was Enfantin's reconstitution of the movement as a religion.[1] To attribute this to Enfantin alone is admittedly an oversimplification; Bazard certainly pressed for a religious restructuring of society in the second year of the Doctrine (1829–30), and he took full part in the movement's own internal quasi-religious

71

practices—from costumes and rituals to the introduction of a rigid and authoritarian hierarchical structure. But the main role was clearly Enfantin's. Although originally ill disposed to the religious path set forth in Saint-Simon's *Nouveau Christianisme,* Enfantin was encouraged by Olinde Rodrigues to take the book more seriously and he soon developed, with Rodrigues's brother Eugène, the religious-philosophical principle of *association* that was to underlie the *Doctrine* and in fact all Saint-Simonian writings and enterprises from then on.

The term *association* was used by the Saint-Simonians to mean cooperative effort or solidarity. Individuals, communities, or nations, they insisted, can achieve far more when they join together "in association" than when their efforts are splintered by isolation or, worse, are mutually destructive through egoism, competition, and antagonism. Admittedly, the principle of *association* is not necessarily a religious one. We see it at work today in many of the rather mundane, secular institutions that surround us—from trade unions and pension plans to public works projects and international conferences on tariffs or technology. But the Saint-Simonians saw more in the word *association* than a series of practical projects for improving the quality of life. They stressed that such projects could not be successfully undertaken without a solid foundation of "love" and "passion," by which terms they meant a willingness to forgo immediate personal and class interests (whether expressed in workers' uprisings, the campaigns of traditional political parties, or territorial wars). It was this preconditional sentiment of brotherly love that, as early as 1828, Enfantin and Eugène Rodrigues began promoting both within their movement and in the outside world.

The message of Saint-Simonism thus became an ultimately religious one, modeled quite consciously on the Christian ideals of patience and loving one's neighbor. Since the disciples had constantly preached (as had Saint-Simon before them) the need for a new social hierarchy led by the most capable and socially useful individuals, it was natural that when Saint-Simonism became a religion it would rely not on individual conscience but on divine revelation, transmitted by a few leaders to the larger group. This necessitated the establishment of a strict hierarchy within the movement. The decision was made to organize the most prominent of the early disciples of Saint-Simon into a group called the "Collège"; soon a "second degree" was formed, a larger circle of more recent recruits who would accept the authority of the Collège and serve as its link to the outer world. By 1830 a "third degree" existed and even a fourth group, consisting of beginners (*néophytes* or *catéchumènes*) who had not yet accepted the full responsibility of discipleship. This responsibility was never precisely defined—and it probably varied according to the individual. Emile and Isaac Pereire, for example, almost certainly did not accept moral authority and guidance in the wholesale manner that certain less wealthy and prominent disciples did; yet they were members of the second degree and thus officially subordinate to the Collège and to its two members who, in late 1829, became "Pères suprêmes" over the entire movement: Bazard and Enfantin.

The obvious first requirement of discipleship was an enthusiastic acceptance of the Saint-Simonian doctrine. But Enfantin insisted equally on acceptance of the hierarchy, calling it "the final proof, the *touchstone* of Saint-Simonian faith."[2] The authority of the Pères could be invoked and applied in numerous ways: to encourage new members to contribute financially to the movement;[3] to justify Enfantin's use (and perhaps abuse) of information gathered during confessions;[4] to correct, encourage, reproach, even humiliate individual disciples on any and all matters, whether doctrinal or more strictly personal (such as the choice of a wife).[5]

As a sign of their intention to create a new religious order, the Saint-Simonians adopted a simple costume in graded shades of blue—from very light "Flora" blue for Bazard and Enfantin to royal blue for the lowest members.[6] Those disciples who still held jobs in banks or offices must rarely have donned their outfits. Bit by bit, though, the uniform established itself, at least at official gatherings, and no doubt certain of the younger members who had given their lives totally to the movement—those who lived at 6 rue Monsigny and who breathed and spoke doctrine all day long—wore their blue costumes on a regular basis. The outside world posed no complication for them; secure in the Saint-Simonian nest, they had found a world of their own.

The consequences of this preoccupation with hierarchy extended into every aspect of Saint-Simonian life and activity. Meals and meetings of the disciples became infused with the value of obedience to benevolent authority. When Edouard Charton, later one of the movement's Sunday preachers, first attended an intimate gathering at the house, he was struck by the overwhelming presence of Bazard and Enfantin and the rapt attention of the young listeners. Bazard held forth calmly, logically, and impersonally, his eyes lowered, while Enfantin cast "caressing glances" throughout the room, thereby establishing a personal bond, full of paternal (or priestly) solicitude, with each individual disciple.[7]

The hierarchical emphasis and the entire religious thrust were by no means intended just for internal consumption. Several of the movement's most prominent members attempted in 1831 to avoid service in the National Guard by claiming the immunity of clergy.[8] In addition, the Saint-Simonians began to organize proselytization efforts of various kinds—from public lectures to actual missions in the working-class *quartiers* of Paris.[9] Enfantin was particularly intent on developing Saint-Simonian centers in the provinces; by late 1829 Enfantin and his representatives had achieved an astonishing rate of conversions in the South, especially in the town of Castelnaudary, but also in Sorrèze, Montpellier, and Carcassonne. Though other communities (Lyons, Nantes, the Belgian cities) were initially less responsive, by late 1832—as James Briscoe has demonstrated—"every provincial city and many towns and villages as well had small but active sects of adherents and somewhat larger numbers of sympathetic readers and listeners." For the first few years, at least, these Parisian and provincial branches were organized hierarchically, in imitation of the rue Monsigny Church, with a member of the Collège or of the second degree acting as director and as *père* to the lower disciples and new recruits. There was never a pretense at equality. Enfantin put it plainly in a letter to Jules Rességuier: Christians may be satisfied with mere fraternity, but the New Christians of the Southern Church must accept being sons to their father (Rességuier), just as the latter is himself son to Enfantin and Bazard.[10]

Members were encouraged to contribute financially to the movement's coffers. Those who moved into the rue Monsigny lodgings brought their belongings with them and shared them as would members of a religious commune. The leaders did not profit from this financially; on the contrary, many of them gave immense sums of their own money—several of them more than 50,000 francs apiece—toward the continued functioning of the movement, its house, its proselytizing efforts, and its extensive publishing activities.[11] Though the cause assured neither leaders nor followers any financial return, they had faith that—as Enfantin and Olinde Rodrigues often stated it—money, placed in moral hands, would exercise a moral power.

The religious surge also brought an increasing emphasis on ritual. Saint-Simon had expressed rather ambivalent attitudes toward ritual in *Nouveau Christianisme*. On the one hand, he claimed that previous religions had given *culte* (ritualistic enactment) undue emphasis, at the expense of *morale* and *dogme* (ethics and theology); on the other, he criticized Luther for depriving his religion of the appealing features of art, music, and ceremony that can make *culte* effective. Enfantin must have been attracted by this latter point, for it fit well with the doctrine of the "rehabilitation of the flesh" which he loved to elaborate, a doctrine that argued for a new respect for labor, wealth, the senses—all those manifestations of matter that had become degraded or despised in European civilization through years of separation from the spirit.

The resulting Saint-Simonian love of ritual showed itself in ways small and large. The leaders had a habit of underlining the symbolic significance of a particular date by referring to its position in the traditional Christian calendar or to its association with some event in Saint-Simon's life or Saint-Simonian history; this finally resulted in a new Saint-Simonian calendar, which renamed the days of the week and the thirty-one days of the month.[12] Larger and more significant, though, was the leaders' quite conscious decision to introduce new rituals and new ways of celebrating traditional ones.

The first traditional ritual to come under scrutiny was the funeral. Saint-Simon himself had set the pattern, expressly requesting that his own funeral be conducted in the simplest manner possible, without participation of clergy.[13] His disciples inherited his critical attitude toward the Catholic Church and developed it further. Laurent de l'Ardèche wrote glowingly in *Le Producteur* of the civil funeral of the great actor and republican Talma (who had been excommunicated). The fact that a number of public officials attended the funeral was clear evidence (Laurent wrote) of the growing recognition that the Church was an outdated institution, no longer competent to judge social virtue.[14] Thus, when, during the heady days of the rue Monsigny, the occasion arose for a Saint-Simonian funeral (that of the young daughter of two second-degree members, Léon and Caroline Simon), it was only natural that the ceremony be conducted by a member of the Collège (Jules Lechevalier) and that the funeral train consist of the Saint-Simonians arranged in hierarchical order, with other friends and relatives picking up the rear. Lechevalier, speaking in the names of God, Saint-Simon, and Les Pères, stressed in his brief allocution that little Léontine lived on in the love of those who survived her and that she was passing to the next phase of her eternal life. The brief surviving account of this funeral service[15] does not indicate whether music and ritual were employed, but the very existence of this first Saint-Simonian funeral created a precedent and model for that of Talabot in 1832, sober yet highly embellished by David's music (see Chapter 10), and for the spare, clergyless burials of Enfantin, David, and others in later years. Perhaps, too, the Saint-Simonians helped set the pattern in this regard for certain liberal or renegade Catholics: Liszt, who wished to be buried with extreme simplicity, accompanied only by a Gregorian mass sung by the local priest; or Lamennais, who, after a lifetime of battle with the Church authorities, chose to be buried without benefit of clergy in a pauper's grave.

In October 1831 Enfantin officiated at the first Saint-Simonian wedding, an even more heavily doctrinal ceremony than the first funeral. The young man and woman (unnamed) declared that they accepted the authority of Les Pères to join together and to break asunder (a direct affront to the Catholic marriage ceremony) and vowed to obey the law of Saint-Simon, to be directed by the leaders of hierarchy, and to work toward the propagation of the new law among all men and women. A similar ceremony joined Alexandre Saint-Chéron and the eldest daughter of the Bazards.[16] (Bride and groom probably exchanged vows in a separate civil ceremony, since the movement was not recognized as a valid religion by the state.[17]) As with the first funeral, these weddings may have been rather simple, and bare of music. Still, the precedent of holding such ceremonies was an important one. Only months later—with the move to Ménilmontant—love of ritual was to blossom into a central feature of Saint-Simonian life. And then, of all the arts, it was music that was to hold pride of place.

PUBLIC LECTURES, INTERNAL GATHERINGS, AND SEMIPUBLIC SOIREES

The Saint-Simonians were inveterate organizers and proselytizers. In particular, their attempts at converting members of the working and artisan classes were of importance in the development of French socialism. These bold and original

75

activities had their eventual musical aspects as well. In 1833 the proselytization centers in the various working-class *quartiers* were to form the core of Vinçard's chanson-loving Famille de Paris (see Chapter 11), and the provincial churches would shelter a number of apostles in exile and spread the propagandistic songs of David, Vinçard, and others (Chapters 11 and 12).

Of greater immediate significance to the movement's musical development—to its contacts with various established musicians and to the growth of musical activities within the movement itself—were the various organized activities in the movement's own house at rue Monsigny and in various lecture halls in Paris, activities aimed primarily at building a sense of community and reaching the literate, the influential, and the "talented." Most of these meetings fell into one of three categories: (1) formal, public lectures or sermons (*enseignements, prédications*); (2) intimate gatherings of members or prospective members; and (3) an intermediate category: soirees at 6 rue Monsigny in which members and guests mingled in an informal, sociable atmosphere. Not surprisingly, these three very different sorts of meetings differed widely in the extent and nature of their involvement with musicians and artists.

The first sort of meetings, the public lectures, constituted, with the *Globe,* the most visible manifestations of the Saint-Simonian movement until the Ménilmontant retreat of 1832. Tens of thousands of people must have attended over the course of only two or three years. Though Bazard's presentations of the *Doctrine* in 1828–29 were at first rather small affairs held in Rodrigues's Caisse hypothécaire, they grew large enough to be moved to a true lecture hall in the rue Taranne. In April 1830 the Saint-Simonians instituted a series of Sunday afternoon "sermons" in their rue Monsigny lodgings, relocating them in October 1830 to the more spacious Salle Taitbout. These sermons continued on a regular basis until the hall was shut down by the police in January 1832. Of all the public lectures, the Sunday sermons were the most important and apparently the most heavily attended. (The audience for the first sermon in the new hall numbered between five and six hundred, including one hundred women. Within two weeks the hall was already too small, in part because the number of women had doubled.[18]) Barrault wrote and delivered almost half of the sermons (twenty-three out of fifty-one), including the important sermon on art.

The socialist Louis Blanc, although unsympathetic to the movement's hierarchical aspect, captured in words the appealing display of ritual at these events and the effectiveness of the "noisy sermons."[19]

> Seated in three rows, facing an auditorium whose red benches were covered, every Sunday from noon on, with a buzzing throng, were serious young men dressed in blue and a few ladies in white robes and violet scarves. Soon the two Supreme Fathers, MM Bazard and Enfantin, made their appearance, bringing in the preacher. At the sight of them, the disciples

rose with looks of tender veneration [*attendrissement*]; the spectators became silent in contemplation or irony, and the orator began. Many listened at first with a smile on their lips and mockery in their eyes. But when he was done speaking, all assembled were astonished and full of admiration; the most skeptical could not help themselves from remaining caught up in thought for a long while or from feeling a secret emotion.[20]

Of the movement's various preachers, it was Barrault who best knew the art of building speeches to a climax in which the audience shook with frenzy. "Sobs, tears, embraces, everyone deeply moved," noted Enfantin.[21] Barrault achieved this effect not only through an urgent and elegant prose style, but also through a performer's command of voice and gesture which increased with the passing months. At the impressive Sunday sermons he apparently read a prepared speech. On other occasions he delivered highly rhetorical and either spontaneous or extremely spontaneous-sounding speeches called *improvisations,* and the effect must have been overwhelming. Reading the published extract of one of them, one can easily see why the audience felt impelled at various points to interrupt with cries of support and "bursts of applause."[22]

No music was performed at these or any other of the movement's pre-Ménilmontant public lectures, even after David joined in December 1831. But the aesthetic element was not entirely lacking. The disciples were seated on benches by "degrees," thus taking full scenic advantage of the gradations of blue worn by the different levels. Perhaps typical was the arrangement at the "Communion générale" of 8 July 1831. Les Pères sat in the center of the platform, surrounded by the Collège and the second-degree members. The third-degree members, numbering some thirty-nine, were placed in the balconies; those in the preparatory degrees were located on the main floor.[23] One imagines that these last continued to serve as ushers, as they had done during the first Salle Taitbout sermons.[24]

The audience at the Salle Taitbout often included a wide range of prominent figures, and, although only one sermon (Barrault's on art, 1 May 1831) was directly aimed at what the movement called "artists" (i.e., people active in music, literature, or the visual arts), there is no doubt that some musicians attended frequently. In the case of Franz Liszt we have his own testimony, and Ferdinand Hiller—another prominent pianist-composer—seems to have been an avid follower through the very day that the hall was closed by government troops (see Chapter 9). Those who did not attend could read the sermons when they were published, usually the very next day, in the Saint-Simonians' first newspaper, *L'Organisateur,* or in *Le Globe.* In addition, the aforementioned sermon on art was published as a separate offprint, no doubt for use in approaching prospective "artist" converts.

Considering that the Salle Taitbout was already too small in October 1830, only months after the July Revolution had freed people to examine in safety various new philosophies of social reform and reorganization, it comes as no surprise that it became unbearably overcrowded as the movement's doctrine and notoriety spread. By December 1831 the young German critic Ludwig Börne reported that one was obliged to arrive two hours ahead of time in order to gain entrance. He remarked that the Saint-Simonians may have roguishly chosen such a small hall precisely in order to increase the frantic clamor for seats.[25] This quip, whose tone is typical of the smug irony with which journalists of the day treated the Saint-Simonians, was the exact opposite of the truth. Since mid-1830 the Saint-Simonians had been multiplying the number of their public lectures and spreading them about the city. At first they organized a series of small weekly *enseignements* in various halls on different days or evenings; next they established one larger but still general *enseignement,* then specialized series directed at different groups in the population—workers, scientists, artists. The format varied. Some sessions consisted solely of a formal lecture, others were built around questions from the audience; some adhered to a systematic syllabus, others treated topics of the day or subjects of special interest to those in attendance. By August 1831 there was at least one such gathering on every day of the week, and on Sunday there were two (in addition to the regular Sunday sermon in the Salle Taitbout and a meeting for workers in the "preparatory degree").[26]

One of the specialized gatherings was the *enseignement pour les artistes,* apparently established early in 1831. In August it was meeting Monday nights at eight in the Salle Taitbout (the movement's largest hall). The director was Henri, a young architect and second-degree member who was friendly with Olinde Rodrigues and an active proselytizer among "the artists" since 1830.[27] Henri was assisted by Henri Baud (soon to become Olinde's brother-in-law) and Edouard Charton. Contrary to what one might expect, the lectures did not attempt to develop in further detail the Saint-Simonian analysis of the current state of the various arts:

> This exposition is not at all specially devoted to the study of the fine arts, but its form is that which is most appropriate to men whose tastes and labors make them eminently receptive to sympathetic language. Since the fine arts are the expression of social life, we put great weight on showing them the new path that is open to them through a new order of feelings, thoughts, and actions.[28]

Just how successful this weekly *enseignement* was at drawing people in the arts (and especially musicians) we cannot say. But the fact that it existed means that some musicians, perhaps even some of those whom we shall be studying, may either have attended its sessions or been stimulated by conversation with someone else who had. We know, for example, that David was brought to the movement by the painter Justus; perhaps Justus, if not David himself, had first seen the light during a lecture—or a postlecture chat—at one of these Monday-night meetings. In any case, the *enseignement pour les artistes* testifies to the movement's strong desire to reach out in any way possible to musicians and others who might help it spread its social message in new and compelling forms.

The second category of Saint-Simonian meetings—the internal gatherings of the Family—are much less easy to classify. Some of the most crucial decisions were made in private session by the two Pères in consultation with members of the Collège; other meetings included the members of the second degree as well, or of the second and third. On certain occasions, even nonmembers—those in the preparatory degree and certain outsiders—were permitted to attend. Many meetings—such as the one described by Charton (cited earlier)—took place around the common dining table in an atmosphere of stern yet benevolent authority and fraternal supportiveness.[29]

Little evidence survives of any musical activity at these internal gatherings. (This does not necessarily mean that there was little such activity; these intimate and even secretive gatherings are less well documented than the gatherings in the other two categories.) We do know that one Saint-Simonian chanson, *La Loi de Dieu* by Lagache, dates from 1831; perhaps it and other songs now lost were sung in the rue Monsigny lodgings. But there is no sign that any other musician or songwriter was part of the central circle of disciples before the arrival of Félicien David in December 1831 and the subsequent move from rue Monsigny to Ménilmontant.

In contrast, the third category of meetings—the semipublic social gatherings—can be clearly shown to have featured substantial amounts of music making. The soirees became a prominent feature of the movement's life after April 1830, when the Saint-Simonians moved into 6 rue Monsigny. These gatherings took place on Thursdays and Sundays, and, as was also true of the public lectures, were frequently attended by leading writers, political figures, and other notables. Louis Blanc's summary is felicitous: "The family in the rue Monsigny was like a glowing hearth which had the double virtue of attracting and radiating."[30] Many memoirs and contemporary descriptions stress the special atmosphere that reigned there, an atmosphere in which music played a large part. Edouard Charton wrote of the Thursday soirees, the movement's "largest and most brilliant," that "no ball, no literary or diplomatic meeting can give a fair idea of these gatherings. People never gambled. They rarely danced; sometimes they waltzed. . . . From time to time a voice would be heard at the piano. All conversations would cease, people would form a semi-circle in the salon, and they found other means than applause for expressing what they felt."[31]

The aura of these soirees was caught particularly well by Ludwig Börne in his *Briefe aus Paris,* a running series of chatty and perceptive commentaries in the German press on French life and politics. Although he had long objected to specific items of the Saint-Simonians' doctrine and even more to their authoritarian hierarchy, he finally decided to attend one of their intimate gatherings. Almost in spite of himself, he became entranced by the friendliness and warmth; and he, too, noted the music and dancing.

> It was as if I had come out of the winter's cold of a snow-bound northern city into a hothouse where springtime breezes and the scents of flowers greeted me.... A spirit of happy peacefulness hovered over these people, a bond of fraternity embraced them all, and I felt embraced with them. A sadness crept over me, I sat down, and unknown feelings lulled me into an obliviousness that brought me close to slumber. Was it the magnetic spirit of belief, which seizes the unbeliever against his will? I do not know. But enthusiasm must certainly be more effective when silent than when spoken aloud; for the speeches of the Simonists have never stirred me. Yet everything was delight and joy, only calmer. People danced, made music, sang; they played Haydn quartets. The men had come with their wives! Admittedly one sees this elsewhere in Parisian society; but there the men *come* and *leave* with their wives; while they are gathered, a kind of divorce takes effect between them. Here I could tell which man belonged to which woman. In the anteroom sat a whole series of chambermaids and servant girls. They frequently came into the sole reception room in order to watch and listen through the open door of the salon as their masters and mistresses danced and sang. This equality pleased me greatly. Even as I walked home on the boulevards I felt warm inside, and I went to Tortoni's [ice-cream parlor] and ate a Plombières sundae....[32]

Börne's irony about "this equality" was perhaps directed at Paris society in general more than at the Saint-Simonians. The fact is that there was a greater social mixing of men and women, and perhaps also of social classes, at the rue Monsigny soirees than was common in most Parisian salons. The leaders may even have made conscious efforts to aid in creating a congenial atmosphere, less stuffy and pretentious than many of the "literary or diplomatic" gatherings referred to by Charton, yet also less wild than the evenings frequently spent by young (and not so young) men in the company of courtesans and prostitutes. Certainly the music seems to have been kept sober and proper. Haydn quartets (mentioned by Börne) are quite in line with the leaders' almost moral preference for serious German music (discussed in Chapter 7). Even the dances were apparently drawn from the gentler ballroom species, such as the waltz (mentioned by Charton). One caricaturist, indeed, found the dancing at the soirees disappointingly staid; he depicted the Supreme Father standing on a footstool (Plate 5) and instructing the young couples that the *galoppade* is too similar to the cancan and will henceforth be banned from "our temple."

"And," the caption snidely continued, "everyone proceeds to admire the wisdom of the Supreme Father." Perhaps the dancing at 6 rue Monsigny was in fact a bit bland for those who were accustomed to more raucous get-togethers. But it, too, must have contributed to the atmosphere of sweet restraint and mutual respect, in which—as Charton noted—women felt welcome to take an active, often dominant role in discussions of social questions.[33]

MUSICIAN VISITORS, MUSICIAN MEMBERS

The role of music in all this may seem marginal to us, but it was viewed as central by leading figures in the movement. Early on, at least, Olinde Rodrigues himself seems to have taken an active role in the musical activities, and Claire Bazard considered the resulting performances a significant contribution to the Saint-Simonian religion, both as a symbol of social and international harmony and as an expression of the members' beliefs.

> Our Sunday evenings [are] gayer and more full of song [than ever]. Our poor Prussian ... now sings with Me [Maître?] Olinde. ... The combination of these two voices is for us yet another mark of progress. ... Besides, our music is going to grow like all the rest, since we must of course sing the glories of God, we who feel them so deeply. So our musicians are planning to get together, and we will be able to celebrate your return with the joyous sound of three or four instruments.[34]

The hope of eventually producing a religious music specific to the Saint-Simonians, implicit in Claire's words, followed quite naturally from the little that Saint-Simon had said about music and from the elaborations of Léon Halévy, Barrault, and the authors of the *Doctrine*. Yet a Saint-Simonian music could not be made without Saint-Simonian musicians. (The "musicians" Claire referred to were clearly amateur performers, not the skilled composer and music director necessary for building a new and distinctive repertoire.) It was with this thought in mind—as well as the hope of gaining further eminent converts—that the Saint-Simonians openly invited professional musicians to join their ranks and welcomed them at their soirees.

Two musicians who definitely attended the soirees in the rue Monsigny were Franz Liszt, who was already at nineteen years of age one of the city's most prominent young piano virtuosos, and Adolphe Nourrit, who was the leading tenor at the Opéra and generally admired for his musical intelligence and humanitarian views. Hippolyte Carnot later recalled that at the soirees "Liszt used to take a seat at the piano and abandon himself to his fantasy, and Adolphe Nourrit was heavily surrounded [by admirers]."[35] It is characteristic of the movement's wide appeal in 1830–31 that it drew two of the age's greatest and most highly acclaimed musicians to its salon and that Liszt, at least, lent his pianistic and improvisatory genius to the occasion. (Carnot does not specifically say that Nourrit sang, but it certainly seems likely. There is no evidence, though, for the contention that Nourrit or the soprano Maria Malibran participated in supposed "concerts sponsored by the movement."[36])

Other musicians almost surely attended these evenings. Mendelssohn apparently visited, though rather late (in the winter of 1831–32); most likely his friend Ferdinand Hiller was there with him. There is even some possibility that Mendelssohn performed his B-minor Piano Quartet at one of these soirees. Berlioz may have come with Liszt and Nourrit, for Enfantin mentioned the three in a single breath in October 1830: "Some artists, Liszt, Berlioz, Nourrit, are approaching us."[37] (Yet another musician, the singer François Delsarte, is said to have passed through a Saint-Simonian phase on his route to an idiosyncratic brand of Catholic mysticism, but no further evidence has turned up.[38] Cherubini, too, is sometimes mentioned in this context, but erroneously.[39])

The soirees at 6 rue Monsigny, and contact with the Saint-Simonians generally, elicited a strong response from all five of these distinguished musicians, and in some cases left a major imprint on their social ideas and on their views of their own roles as artists in society. Each of these musicians' experiences and reactions—whether positive, negative, or mixed—is of great significance for his biography and for an understanding of the ways in which the Saint-Simonian movement was perceived by outsiders. But none of these prominent figures, however deeply influenced, was active enough in the movement to have exerted an influence upon it in return or to contribute to its musical growth. Most, in fact, began to distance themselves by late 1831 or early 1832, just before the Saint-Simonian movement began to develop a significant characteristic musical life of its own at Ménilmontant and elsewhere. The rather extensive details of their involvement will therefore be reserved for separate discussion (Chapter 9).

There were, however, three professionally trained musicians who did take an active role in the Saint-Simonian movement and who willingly and eagerly lent their talents to the cause. Napoléon-Henri Reber contributed briefly, but not until 1834 (see Chapter 12). Dominique Tajan-Rogé and Félicien David, in contrast, were drawn to the Saint-Simonians during the glorious days of the rue Monsigny. Together they became the musical spokesmen of a movement that had courted and lost many a more illustrious figure. Whereas an account of Nourrit's or Mendelssohn's or Hiller's involvement begins and ends with the soirees (and the lectures in the Salle Taitbout), the rue Monsigny was for Rogé and David just the beginning of a long adventure.

TAJAN-ROGÉ AND FÉLICIEN DAVID

Dominique Tajan-Rogé (1803?–80) is a misty figure in music history. A good but not great cellist, Tajan-Rogé might be no better known to us than many another orchestral musician of his day (indeed, we do not even know what he looked like), were it not for his "side" activities: organizational work for two important orchestras; journalism; a late, lengthy book of memoirs; and—what concerns us most—spirited participation in the Saint-Simonian movement. Rogé, as he was known to friends and colleagues,[40] studied cello under Baudiot at the Conservatoire[41] and served as cellist at the Théâtre du vaudeville and at the Opéra-comique.[42] He was also one of the founding members of Habeneck's Société des concerts du Conservatoire and in 1828 personally prepared the first draft of the orchestra's strongly democratic statutes.[43]

Rogé entered the Saint-Simonian movement in 1830, a few months after his marriage to Clorinde,[44] who herself later became an important Saint-Simonian organizer. In a letter of 1845 Clorinde Rogé described her husband's early devotion to the Saint-Simonians and her initial inability to share it. Rogé, "because of his kindness of heart," could not help being "moved and converted" by Enfantin's words at rue Monsigny, and he finally decided to follow the Saint-Simonians, in order to, as he himself expressed it to her, "work toward the enfranchisement of the people and of women."[45]

During the period of the rue Monsigny, Rogé seems to have taken little role in the musical life of the movement. (He may, or may not, have played cello in the Haydn quartets, or the Mendelssohn B-minor Piano Quartet.) Perhaps his general involvement was not deep until 1832, or perhaps he was alienated for a time by the movement's internal schisms. It certainly seems significant that in 1832, as we shall see, he hesitated to don the apostle's habit at Ménilmontant, explaining to Enfantin that he had only "recently arrived" in the movement.[46] But if Rogé was slow to give himself to the Saint-Simonians, he would soon give without restraint.

The other musician recruited during the days of rue Monsigny was Félicien David (1810–76).[47] Although later to win international recognition as an innovative exponent of musical exoticism (in such works as *Le Désert, La Perle du Brésil*, and *Lalla-Roukh*), he came to the movement as an unknown and barely trained musician, only twenty-one years of age. During his brief tenure as a composition student at the Conservatoire, living hand-to-mouth from occasional piano lessons, he had become friends with a painter, Pol Justus, who was four years older and whom he admired almost to the point of glorification.[48] According to Azevedo, a source of some authority,

> [Justus had little] trouble predisposing him in favor of the doctine whose aim was to place each according to his capacity and to reward each capacity according to its works.
>
> Prepared in this manner, our musician let himself be led gently to the meetings of the Saint-Simonians in the salons of the rue Monsigny, toward the end of 1831, and soon he adopted completely their doctrine, which had just been transformed into a religion.[49]

Azevedo goes on to cite the various attractions that the movement held for David: the doctrine itself, "broad, free, and generous"; constant encouragement from "an intelligent, sympathetic, passionate audience"; and the specific opportunity to create a liturgical music for the movement, "to be in a way the Saint Ambrose, Saint Gregory, Palestrina, or Luther of the chorales of Saint-Simonism."[50] David must also have been attracted to the relative financial and psychological security of membership. Some months back his uncle had discontinued his fifty-franc monthly allowance;[51] the movement now offered him food, clothing and, presumably, a modest bed at rue Monsigny.[52] His psychological needs were perhaps even greater. Born in the Provençal town of Cadenet (Vaucluse), he had been orphaned at six and brought to Aix, where he was raised by an elder sister and the Church. In Enfantin he must have found the father of his dreams.[53]

Exactly when David dropped out of the Conservatoire is not clear—he was still hoping in late October to compete for the Prix de Rome[54]—but by January he had officially joined the movement.[55] Justus seems to have retained some responsibility for David during the first year. In Chapter 10 we shall see him shepherding the musician through the ceremony of the Taking of the Habit at Ménilmontant (6 June), and the two friends will parade side by side at Talabot's funeral (18 July). Justus is also occasionally mentioned as singing in the Ménilmontant chorus. But the young painter, although admired as a person by Vinçard and others, never became a leading figure in the movement and—surprisingly—appears rarely to have been invited to use his artistic skills, perhaps because of resentment or disapproval on the part of the more established painter Raymond Bonheur.[56] Whatever the reason, after participating briefly and somewhat traumatically in the Compagnons de la femme and publishing a spirited pamphlet in support of the women's cause, Pol Justus appears only sporadically in the annals of the movement.[57]

David, in contrast, made his first artistic contribution to the movement quite early and quickly became one of its best-known and most prized disciples. And this despite the fact that his musical training had been brief and incomplete before he arrived at 6 rue Monsigny. In Aix he had been a cathedral choirboy, had spent some frustrating years in the Jesuit Collège de Saint-Louis, and had served briefly as assistant conductor of the vaudevilles, as an attorney's clerk, and finally as chapelmaster in the Cathedral where he had earlier sung. The Bibliothèque Méjanes in Aix preserves a number of his works from this period: anonymous-sounding motets tossed into a folder with snippets from works of Haydn and Sigismund Neukomm, some of these copied by David himself.[58] If we add the repertoire that David had played at the Jesuit school—Haydn again, the dignified and unsmiling works of Luigi Cherubini and Jean-François Lesueur, and (in great contrast) retexted opera arias of Mozart and the facile Henri Berton[59]—we quickly see the diverse stylistic roots of the young musician.

During his year or so at the Conservatoire, David studied harmony, improvisation, and fugue, but his true desire was to compose an opéra-comique. This was a pointless task given the system by which works were "received" in the French theaters. (First the libretto had to be approved, and then a composer was selected to set it.) David completed at least five numbers of an opera,[60] but the work was never performed and is now lost. In the fall of 1831 he took up a genre both more practical and more suited to his temperament: lyrical character pieces for solo piano.[61] But David was never to be satisfied even with solid achievements in a modest, intimate mode; throughout his life he would feel the need to make the grand gesture, the public statement, however far it might lie beyond his limited energies. Like Berlioz and others of David's generation, the young Aixois was almost dazed in admiration of the power of *Der Freischütz, Euryanthe,* and especially the Beethoven symphonies (recently revealed by Habeneck at the Conservatoire concerts).

> That is beauty, ideal beauty. . . . Never was there a more sublime composition than the Choral Symphony. It is a poem whose aim is to sing the grandeur and the goodness of the Eternal. It is of course true that the most beautiful music has always been inspired by this sublime goal.[62] So where is German music? Who will give us something solid, something beautiful? It is true that my desires are quite ambitious, and my taste may be mistaken. Who today would be interested in learned music which they do not understand at all and which they would need to hear several times in order to grasp its beauties?[63]

The tension between salon style and grand (Germanic) style carried over into David's music-making activities during his first months with Saint-Simonians. His salon side seems to have been more constantly on view. We know that he improvised, played, and sang piano pieces and romances of his own composing, producing "an irresistible sensation."[64] (Perhaps he even accompanied the dancing during the sometimes lavish parties that continued during these last months at rue Monsigny.[65]) Some ten years later David was to have similar success at the salons, again with his songs and lyrical piano pieces[66]—many of them steeped in an Egyptian musical sauce that certainly added to their appeal. But one has the sense that David's success as salon musician, whether at the rue Monsigny or later, flowed as much from his personality as from the quality of his music. Certainly the humor, the intelligence, the touching sincerity that we find in his letters must have been even more endearing in person. "Charmant" and "doux" are two words that people later used when describing David; sweet charm no doubt helped him find shelter and a foster family in the rue Monsigny.

At the same time that David was serenading members and visitors, he was working on a far grander piece, the *Hymne à Saint-Simon* (Appendix E.1). It is the only surviving Saint-Simonian piece of his that can definitely be dated to the months at the rue Monsigny. The specific date, January 1832, and the style suggests that it was a kind of initiation piece, an effort on the part of the newcomer to establish himself as a respected composer in a circle wider, more influential, and more demanding than the group of penniless *amis intimes* that had encouraged him during his months at the Conservatoire. David surely knew that he was not at all the composer the movement had been seeking; maybe he hoped that, even if his credentials were less glorious than those of Liszt or Berlioz, he could right matters to some extent with a large-scale *Hymne à Saint-Simon*.

▽   The piece impresses us immediately by the size and variety of its musical forces. It employs mixed chorus, divided SATB or, for long stretches, SSATTB (actually written in the following clefs: SSSATB),[67] and contains a passage for men's voices marked "Les Travailleurs," topped by a tenor solo (in alto clef) marked "Coryphée," a term originally meaning leader of the chorus, as in a Greek tragedy.[68] In addition, there are prominent melodic passages for the second tenor section of the chorus and for the soprano section (i.e., all the women?), and the aforementioned "Coryphée" line grows out of a recitative for first tenor. (Perhaps David intended the solo tenor parts for himself, just as a few months later he took the high tenor vocalise in *La Danse des astres*.)

The *Hymne à Saint-Simon* has the structure of a short oratorio, from the opening choral invocation to the recitative and arioso passages for various voices. In many ways (beyond the exceptionally full and varied scoring) this work differs from the less pretentious pieces that David wrote for the movement in the succeeding months. A glance at the music of the *Hymne* reveals these differences and, perhaps more important, permits us to judge the ability of the young composer at the point when he left the Conservatoire and joined the Saint-Simonians.

The most striking element of the piece is its sure harmonic language. (Tajan-Rogé was later to speak of David's strong training in harmony.) There is one awkward modulation from C minor to E-flat major (top of p. 3), in which David neglects to provide a common chord between the two areas. But this kind of grammatical slip is more than counterbalanced by sensitive and varied harmonic and modulatory touches throughout the work. "(Je m'enchaine) d'amour," for example, is given a Haydnesque setting, the harmonic contrast heightened by antiphony between men's and women's voices. The same harmonic sequence returns in the cadence to the sopranos' solo (p. 15). David's skillful use of inverted chords adds great variety, as in the opening or the passages of parallel sixth chords (top of p. 5, bottom of p. 14). David makes particularly frequent use of sudden Schubertian modulations by a third, as on pp. 12–13 (B-flat to F-sharp) and p. 19 (at "honneur," D to F-sharp). One wonders whether David was thinking of Beethoven's astonishing progression from A to F at "Vor Gott" (in the Ninth Symphony, which David so greatly admired) when he made a similar third modulation (only in reverse, C-flat to E-flat) at the analogous words "gloire à Dieu" (p. 10).

Throughout the work, in fact, David shows great concern for the text, reflecting it in music of Mendelssohnian pomp (as in the opening paean to an almost divine Saint-Simon), of tenderness, of discord, of resolution, all according to the changing moods of the text. The settings of "de la nuit de l'abyme où se perd un vieux monde" are appropriately dark, featuring open-fifth tremolos on p. 7 and a sinking modulation to the relative minor on p. 9. David's declamation is natural and effective, as in the dotted rhythm of "Saint-Simon sois béni" (p. 2), and the piano part is more elaborate than in most of his Ménilmontant choruses. In addition, he shows himself freer here than he will be at the Retreat to make use of such techniques as modulations to rather difficult keys and occasional passages of independent rhythm for the different choral voices.

In this first major public effort, David showed himself to be a talented composer indeed.[69] Clearly he had more to offer the movement than his skill at improvising waltzes. This must have become apparent to Enfantin, too, for within a few months he knew well how to put David's talents to use.

This is not to say that David's *Hymne* was a total success. If it was intended to be performed at all—presumably by the musically assorted residents of the rue Monsigny—then to that extent it probably was a failure. No performance is mentioned in the archives or histories of the movement, or even in the biographies of David. Presumably the choral writing proved too difficult; the eager student, just out of school, had expected too much of his performers. But the student was still young and, though eager to display his technique, even more eager to succeed and to please. At Ménilmontant David would go to school again and relearn the beauty—and the efficacy—of simple means.

"La Question de la Femme" and the Two Schisms

The musical activities at the Ménilmontant Retreat and during the subsequent dispersion (Chapters 10–12) form the core of our story of the Saint-Simonians' journey with music. The relations between the movement and various non-member musicians, such as Mendelssohn, Berlioz, and Liszt (Chapter 9) constitute a perhaps less central but no less important episode in that same story. But before we can continue with any of this, we must first examine, in the rest of this chapter, a number of (nonmusical) events and developments that changed the face of the movement and that made the move to Ménilmontant not only possible but a matter of desperate necessity. For Ménilmontant was not part of Enfantin's or any other Saint-Simonian's original plan but rather a kind of salvage operation following a massive wreck in late 1831 caused largely by Enfantin himself and by his peculiar attitudes toward women and marriage.

It is hard to know from what source this ever-surprising thinker derived his ideas about women or exactly how early he started expounding them confidentially to his fellow leaders or other members. Certainly Saint-Simon had shown no great concern about either the future place of women or the social function of marriage.[70] A more direct precursor of the Saint-Simonians in this regard was the founding father of a rival brand of utopian socialism, Charles Fourier. The latter had expressly designed his society of the future around the principle that the institution of the family is one of the banes of humanity, forcing both men and women into denying or hypocritically veiling the natural variety of their sexual desires. The Saint-Simonians did not hesitate to borrow openly this and other aspects of Fourierist thought congenial to their own philosophy. Fourier accused them of plagiarism and, with less justice, of lacking the understanding to transform his theories into practice.[71] The Saint-Simonians actually did end up carrying out in a small way Fourier's proudest invention, for their Retreat at Ménilmontant incorporated some aspects of the ideal cooperative community that Fourier called the *phalanstère*. Similarly, in the matter of sexuality and the status of women, the Saint-Simonians developed further certain ideas found in his publications (though never, even at their wildest, did they surpass the boldness with which Fourier himself treated the subject in his notebooks, many of which remained unpublished until 1967).[72]

The Saint-Simonians' essential and least controversial conclusion was that women, heretofore subordinated to men and regarded mainly as producers of children,[73] must achieve true equality, since any and all exploitation of human beings will "be incompatible with the social state of the future which we foresee."[74] The Saint-Simonians' concern here is similar to their long-held interest in the welfare of society's poorest: no longer shall a small group of individuals live in leisure, luxury, and privilege while the greater majority of people toil and hunger and (in the case of women) are often reduced to dependency on the privileged ones (the males).

Fine words, certainly. To put them into practice was something else. Arguments began about whether the Saint-Simonian movement itself should accept females into its ranks. Buchez, among others, was unwilling to break with the Catholic Church and so refused to consider the participation of women in either religion or politics. But Enfantin prevailed, and two of the leaders' wives, Cécile Fournel and Claire Bazard, were brought into the Collège in order to help organize a search for female converts.[75] Their efforts met with little direct success (except belatedly, in 1832–35), but the wider circle of interested observers at lectures and soirees did come to include progressively more and more women, to the point where the latter often formed an absolute majority.

On 1 October 1830 the Saint-Simonians found it necessary to defend themselves in a letter to the Chamber of Deputies against rumors that they were proposing "la communauté des femmes," i.e., the abolition of marriage and of all other traditional restrictions on free love.[76] The very existence of such rumors testifies to the widespread fear of any attempt to restore to women some basic human rights and a more valued place in the social structure. Perhaps, too, we already see here the country's ruling forces trying to blacken the public image of a movement that had announced some potentially threatening social reforms. (The caricaturists of the day reinforced the image of the Saint-Simonians as unbridled sensualists: womanizers, tipplers, and gluttons—see plate 6.)

In part, though, the rumors may have derived from reports of discussions among the movement's leaders. True, the movement had publicly defended the sanctity of marriage, but Enfantin had made it clear to his fellows, if not yet to the outside world, that he considered this stated position a temporary one. The Catholic Church, he felt, had lost touch with the realities of human nature by setting celibacy as the highest goal and by insisting on the absolute sanctity of the marriage bond. These narrow confines, he believed, forced many people to seek release in adultery and prostitution.

The consequences that Enfantin drew from these musings were various and perhaps inconsistent. He certainly saw in the Church's denigration of sex and physical attractiveness yet another symptom of the mortification of the flesh, analogous to society's low regard for labor and for productive individuals, most especially the poor. (Prostitution combines exploitation of women with exploitation of the lower classes: men of the bourgeoisie preserve their own daughters' chastity with puritanical zeal while purchasing sex for themselves from women too poor to resist.) By mid-1831, and probably long before, Enfantin was expounding a new religious view of sex and marriage that Bazard found entirely revolting and that Rodrigues could accept only with great hesitation. Monogamy, Enfantin claimed, should remain a valid solution for those whose true nature was monogamous ("immobile" or "constant"). People whose natures are "mobile," who feel affections that are strong but transitory, must be allowed to live free of bonds, so that they may pass on to the next mate when the old affection has expired. Early on, Enfantin granted that this freedom of the mobile ones would consist essentially of a series of marriages and divorces. He still expressed himself in these terms in a letter to his mother in August 1831. But another passage in the same letter gives evidence of his more radical view that all sorts of love relationships, if relieved of their social stigma, could be condoned and even encouraged, "provided that the *new* union results in progress for the two individuals and for society."[77]

Who would determine the point at which mobility spilled over into harmful debauchery? Enfantin's answer was simple, if not clear: the priestly couple. The priest and priestess, being of mixed nature (both mobile and immobile), could minister to the needs of their more confused "children" by bestowing on them the guidance and reassuring grace of their own physical beauty, personal charm, and what we might call charisma or animal magnetism.[78]

Enfantin justified this theory of marriage and especially of the guiding role of the priestly couple by alluding to the principle of the "rehabilitation of the flesh." This principle had its roots in Saint-Simon's attempts to integrate into religion, traditionally overweighted toward the "spiritual" side, a new regard for the productive classes in society (at first the scientists, later the *industriels*). In the preachings of the Saint-Simonians (diffusely in the *Doctrine* and in a more focused manner by 1831) this principle took on a wider meaning. Science (a merely intellectual activity) would be redeemed and transformed by being tied to the needs of industry; both religious doctrine and a desiccated artistic tradition would be revitalized by a new emphasis on *culte* (the concrete en-actment, appealing to the senses); and life in general would be enriched by an emphasis on the pleasures and activities of the here-and-now rather than on the dubious rewards of a Christian hereafter.

This doctrine of the "rehabilitation of the flesh" was not in and of itself a matter for great debate. In fact, certain members were particularly sympathetic to the principle (e.g., Duveyrier and David), and even a number of outsiders, notably Heine and Liszt, responded to it with special affinity.[79] But Enfantin mixed this doctrine with others that had sprung more from his own personal ambitions or obsessions. He exaggerated the role of priestess, turning her first into a prophetess and eventually into a *Femme-Messie:* a female Messiah.[80] He did not hesitate to stake claims for himself as the obvious candidate for grand priest and husband of the long-awaited Woman; after all, he stated, he had always been the initiator of all important ideas and developments in the move-ment, whereas the cautious Bazard had usually echoed him more reservedly.[81] In addition to these claims, Enfantin dropped remarks suggesting that the priest's and priestess's special sanctified "mobility" could extend to sexual relations with their Saint-Simonian followers.[82] To Bazard's and others' many objections—that Enfantin had no right to designate the priest or to speak for the priestess, that the theory of mobility would disrupt the social fabric by leaving a child ignorant of his own father, that the entire matter was premature or divisive, distracting attention from more urgent projects—Enfantin replied with simultaneous agreement and obstinacy. He agreed in theory that the matter was only speculative at this point and could not be resolved until La Femme arrived; in practice he refused to refrain from discussing the issue in all its fantastic ramifications, or even to let it rest for a time.

The debates between Bazard and Enfantin—the "conservative" and the "innovator"—went on for weeks in private or in the presence of members of the Collège. Rodrigues tried to offer a compromise interpretation of the matter, to no avail;[83] various individuals began to side with one or the other of the two Pères; the insecurity of the situation drove some to fits of ecstasy or fainting; others, including the very practical Michel Chevalier (editor of *Le Globe*), drafted a letter begging Bazard and Enfantin to cease their wrangling and to take up the task again of spreading the doctrine and improving the lot of the poorest and most numerous class. These last disciples pointed out the obvious, that the issue was becoming one of personal power and pride as much as of ideology; but they also indicated that, if they were forced to choose between the two leaders, it was the cajoling, self-aggrandizing Enfantin whom they loved more and would follow, rather than the cold, intimidating Bazard.[84] During public confessions in the following days and weeks, it became apparent that a clear majority of the members, too, whatever their doubts about the doctrine of mobility, felt Enfantin to be the true Saint-Simonian Father.[85]

On 8 November Bazard finally agreed to step down to a secondary position: *chef du dogme,* parallel to Rodrigues's position as *chef du culte.* Bazard's act of self-sacrifice was announced from the stage of the Salle Tailbout that night and greeted with relief and rejoicing by all the members. The very next day Bazard withdrew, denouncing the new arrangement as impossible and childish. On 19 and 21 November Enfantin convened meetings of the entire Saint-Simonian family, only to discover that a number of prominent disciples— including Lechevalier, Transon, Carnot, Leroux, Reynaud, Charton, and Gué-roult—were prepared to leave with Bazard, to search for a religion elsewhere, or at most to remain behind in order to denounce Enfantin's pretensions.

Rodrigues stayed by Enfantin, as did Barrault, Duveyrier, d'Eichthal, Chevalier, and many others (especially many younger and newer members). All efforts were now directed toward restoring unity among those who remained, gathering new members and sympathizers, and instituting the first of the movement's practical schemes for social reform: a Saint-Simonian bond drive. On 27 November the Family gathered at the Salle Taitbout; the hall was packed full, with people squeezed into the aisles and onto the stairs, for word had gotten around that something was up. (The songwriter Béranger was there, as were various members of the Chamber of Deputies.)

The audience got what it came for. First, an empty chair was set beside Enfantin, as a symbol of the movement's desire to be joined soon by a priestess, La Femme. (This had already been done less publicly on 21 November.[86]) Le Père suprême then spoke majestically of the necessity to pass from science to industry, from theory to practice, from doctrine to *culte.* And he announced that women would be excluded again from the movement, until La Femme arrived and made known the precise terms under which all women were to become the equals of men.[87]

Next Rodrigues pronounced his *Appel,* a call to all people to aid the Saint-Simonians by placing their talents and especially their money at its disposal. Barrault continued with a long "improvisation" in which he admitted that the movement had failed to attract artists in the past and stressed its urgent desire to involve artists in its current phase. (The "artists" sections of these two speeches have been discussed in Chapter 7.) The evening was about to end in a storm of applause when Jean Reynaud rose and attacked the morality of Enfantin's ideas on women. Over the next hour and a half Rodrigues, and then Henri Baud, attempted to calm Reynaud and to restate the movement's doctrines. After a number of other disciples had run up to Enfantin and embraced him, Reynaud, in a climax to the long drama, approached him and kissed him farewell.

Enfantin had been attacked, accused, and abandoned before, but in private sessions. Reynaud's fierce words were pronounced before a large, startled audience. There is evidence that the Saint-Simonians realized the harm this could do. *Le Globe*, in one of the few apparently willful misrepresentations in all the movement's publications, portrayed this kiss of separation as marking instead Reynaud's impulsive acceptance of *Le Père*. ("Reynaud lui-même, après un instant d'hésitation, s'est jeté à son cou avec transport."[88]) The Saint-Simonians had reason to fear. Soon the bitter critiques of former members, many of whom had access to the press, became a major force in turning public opinion away from the Saint-Simonians.

But Enfantin and the Enfantinists (as some tagged the remaining Saint-Simonians) had even worse things to fear. In the year and a half following the July Revolution small and large groups of workers took to the streets in hopes of attaining the political and economic goals for which they had fought the 1830 Revolution. The Saint-Simonians expressed particular sympathy for the most daring of these, the weavers of Lyons, and also proselytized heavily in Lyons itself.[89] Many people put these facts together and concluded that the Saint-Simonians were a seditious lot, to be suppressed at whatever cost. The government must have thought so, too; at the very least they decided to go along with the tide of "enlightened" opinion, perhaps as a means of intimidating other groups that were more violent but less easy to prosecute.

The Saint-Simonians were a handy target. No other "opposition" social or political organization was as visible. The movement's views were established on paper and its members always identified themselves openly and proudly. The government began building its case on 28 November 1831, at first seeking evidence that the movement had provoked people to hate the royal government and to revolt against it.[90] Frustrated, it soon redirected its inquiries, hoping to find evidence of immoral doctrines, financial irregularities (such as fraud), and illegal gatherings of more than twenty persons, under the repressive Article 291 of the penal code. (This article did not apply to religious groups, but the Saint-Simonians had never succeeded in gaining religious status.) On 22 January 1832 soldiers interrupted the Sunday lecture, locked the doors of the Salle Taitbout, and confiscated important papers from the rue Monsigny. (The procurator was particularly intent on finding evidence of fraud in the Saint-Simonian bond drive or in other transfers of money and inheritances from members to the movement.[91]) Over the following months some 140 witnesses were interrogated and most of the charges eventually thrown out. Unfortunately, two of them—outrage of public morals and disobedience of Article 291—were uncontestable.[92] The trial for those charges in August proved to be perhaps the single darkest moment in the movement's history, relieved only by the leaders' eventual acquittal of the charge of fraud.

As if the Bazard schism and the threats of prosecution were not enough, the movement was soon cleft by a second schism, that of Olinde Rodrigues. The tensions were again partly doctrinal. Olinde had always clung to the hope that Enfantin would put his theories to rest, at least temporarily. If anything, though, Enfantin had stepped up his preaching and that of his closest associates.[93] On 12 January 1832 *Le Globe* announced publicly the impending arrival of the Femme-Messie.[94] In the same issue Duveyrier published a rather too vivid vision of life in the future as a banquet of delights, including a free and unbinding choice of sexual partners.[95] Rodrigues must have realized the pointless risk of writing this kind of provocative material at a time when the movement was under heavy government surveillance. But his objections, like those of Bazard before him, were not purely doctrinal or even tactical. Rodrigues had always been proud of his status as the "héritier direct de Saint-Simon";[96] Enfantin's exercise of Supreme Fatherhood now seemed to be leaving Rodrigues with heavy responsibility for developing and administering the bond drive[97] but little influence on the movement's policies. Doctrinal and personal tensions joined forces when Enfantin, perhaps smugly or even viciously, chose to reveal to Rodrigues some details about the sexual life of Mme Rodrigues that she had confessed to him.[98] The *chef du culte* announced his withdrawal on 16 February 1832 in the first of a series of independent publications denouncing Enfantin and bolstering his own claim to be the true leader of the Saint-Simonians.[99]

His efforts were in vain. Unlike Bazard, this dissident was not joined by a throng of supporters. Nonetheless, the movement's loss was substantial, for the much-needed bond drive came to a sudden halt. In April the movement was forced to cease publishing *Le Globe*. Enfantin, driven by financial necessity and by a desire to disprove some of the worst rumors of libertinism engendered by his moral theories, selected forty male disciples to join him in an ascetic, celibate community at his house in Ménilmontant, which was at the time a suburb of Paris (it is now in the twentieth arrondissement). The Retreat proved to be an experiment that captured the attention and imagination of all Paris, not least for its bold and original uses of music to enhance the communal activities and to spread the Saint-Simonian message to the larger world. From the musical point of view, especially, Ménilmontant was a new beginning.

9

SIX MUSICIANS IN CONTACT WITH THE SAINT-SIMONIANS

In her recent biography of Franz Liszt, Eleanor Perényi has perceptively remarked that Enfantin's "attempt at apotheosis and subsequent disgrace" not only destroyed the movement but alienated and embarrassed many outsiders who had taken an active interest in the soirees of the rue Monsigny or the sermons in the Salle Taitbout. "After 1832," she writes, "most of them hastened to say that they had never joined his commune, which was true, and never really taken him seriously, which was not."[1] The result has been a gap in their biographies.

For the musicians this gap can now be filled. The fact is that Liszt, Berlioz, and the tenor Adolphe Nourrit were, at least for a time, deeply involved with the Saint-Simonians; Ferdinand Hiller and Fromental Halévy had Saint-Simonian experiences of perhaps lesser but nonetheless real significance; and even Felix Mendelssohn received some quite heavy indoctrination, although he reacted more negatively than did his Parisian confreres. Each of these six cases must be approached somewhat differently, depending on the quantity and nature of the evidence that has survived; and each resulting "case history" demonstrates, in its highly individual way, how successfully the Saint-Simonians struck resonant chords in the minds of distinguished and sensitive musicians of the day.

HALÉVY AND THE SAINT-SIMONIANS

Jacques-François-Fromental-Elias Halévy (1799–1862), best known today as the composer of the grand opera *La Juive* (1835) and several exquisitely wrought *opéras-comiques,* holds an entirely neglected place in the history of music among the Saint-Simonians. The neglect surely derives in part from the unusual pattern of his involvement. He appears to have been greatly intrigued by the ideas of some Saint-Simonian friends during the late 1820s, and late in life he drafted an article on music for a projected encyclopedia that several Saint-

Simonians were editing, but in between there is little evidence of involvement with the group.

Halévy's brother Léon was Saint-Simon's personal secretary from 1823 to 1825 and, as we have seen, was probably the main author of the striking pages on art in the "Dialogue" of 1825. It seems likely, then, that the musician Halévy was exposed through his brother to the thought of Saint-Simon several years before Enfantin, Bazard, or Duveyrier appeared on the scene. The exposure was supplemented a few years later—after Saint-Simon's death—by contacts with three other fervent disciples of what was quickly becoming a movement. Olinde Rodrigues's father, an old friend of Halévy *père,* moved into the apartment directly above that of the Halévys, and Emile and Isaac Pereire—and of course Olinde himself—frequently visited and talked doctrine. Emile in particular, Léon later recalled, proclaimed his visions of "man's absolute domination over nature," of "France transformed by railroads and steam power," and of "physical well-being and even luxury for everyone, especially for men of intellect." Fromental, according to Léon, "took pleasure in this intelligent and passionate company, in which his judgment and wit shined. But he did not forget that ... across from the Théâtre italien, at which he was helping to rehearse masterpieces, there was another theater [the Opéra] which was looking for some [masterpieces]. That's where he wished to strike."[2]

Whether or not Léon is right in implying that it was Fromental's desire to establish himself as a composer for the Opéra that prevented him from becoming deeply involved, it does seem to be true that the musician had little if anything to do with the movement during its years of greatest activity. Not until 1845 does his name turn up again, in a letter from Enfantin to Félicien David. In the flush of public enthusiasm for David's *Le Désert,* people had begun to mention David (quite prematurely) as a candidate for the Académie des beaux-arts. The Saint-Simonians—in particular Olinde Rodrigues—seem to have attempted to pressure Halévy into securing this honor for their protégé. (Halévy had been a member of the Académie since 1836 and was named president in 1845; also, he had married Olinde's cousin Léonie in 1842.[3]) Halévy may have even made a gesture of cooperating, for Enfantin's letter to David says that Halévy had told Rodrigues that "it is agreed at the Institut [de France—parent body of the Académie] that the first free seat at the Beaux-Arts is for [David]." But Halévy, even if he had wanted, could surely not have swung the necessary votes. David was not elected until twenty-four years later.[4]

The discussions that Fromental Halévy had with the Pereires in the late 1820s thus bore no fruit for the movement, but they were not necessarily without significance for Halévy himself. They may well have stimulated—although one cannot safely say to what degree—his social awareness and his interest in intellectual matters. Some of his operas, for example, deal with interest in intellectual matters. Some of his operas, for example, deal with serious social issues (notably religious intolerance, in *La Juive*), and during the last years of his life, as Secrétaire perpétuel of the Académie des beaux-arts, Halévy spoke and wrote with great relish on quite diverse subjects, including painting and architecture.[5] The mature Halévy was particularly well informed about music history and was actively involved in the movement to teach music to the masses. He composed choruses for the Orphéon in 1851 and 1860 and published a singing primer for use in the schools of Paris (*Leçons de lecture musicale,* 1857; expanded ed., 1859). In this primer Halévy took the opportunity to speak inspiringly to his young audience of music as a "noble relaxation . . . , a sweet and salutary exercise, a companion when one is at work, bringing charm and consolation to our lives."[6]

Whether or not the Saint-Simonians should be given much credit for inspiring any of this, it is certain that they provided the occasion for Halévy's last extensive pronouncement on the relationship between music and society. In the early 1860s Chevalier, Duveyrier, the Pereires, and some other people who had been active in the Saint-Simonian movement set out to organize what they called *L'Encyclopédie nouvelle.* (This project never reached publication, but it progressed a good deal further than a similar project, drafted nearly forty years earlier by Saint-Simon, Olinde Rodrigues, and Halévy's brother Léon.) The editorial committee commissioned Halévy to write the music article—an essay, really, touching on music's past and present, its "social role," and its "problems and applications."[7] No doubt Halévy's primary credentials for the task were his renown as a composer and his eminence as an academician. (Indeed, a number of other prominent writers and scholars were also slated for articles or editorial duties.[8]) But Halévy's well-known interest in the social aspects of music may also have seemed ideally suited to an encyclopedia that was setting out, not simply to present facts, but to "determine how best to use all of today's moral, intellectual, and material resources . . . [in the interests of] social and political progress."[9]

Halévy did not live to complete the article.[10] Fortunately, though, its extensive preface, written several months before his death, does survive. It begins with a brief discussion of the origin of music and quickly moves to a demonstration of music's great diversity. Halévy then reverses the argument, insisting that, despite these "modifications" which time, culture, and social function have made upon the surface aspects of music, the art still remains, at its core, nothing less than the basic, universal, invulnerable "poetic sentiment which God has put in our hearts." Though outside influences upon music continue to exist, he reasons, modern communications have made people more tolerant of them. "We may argue about them, but we admit their existence. . . . Ideas have constituted a free market, to their [mutual] profit." The preface concludes with a transition to a section, apparently never written, which was to examine the principal characteristics of the world's various musical dialects.[11]

Like the singing primer, this preface shows Halévy to be concerned with the relationship between the arts and society. But his concern is primarily directed toward one side of that relationship: the influence of society upon the arts. (This approach resembles what we have called the "sociological" one typical of literary historians at the time—see Chapter 3.) Halévy nowhere mentions—as the editors hoped their contributors would do—the reverse possibility: using the arts to influence society (a prescriptive rather than descriptive approach). Indeed, we may recall that when Halévy, in his primer, dealt specifically with music's effect upon those who make it, he focused on the individual's need for "consolation" rather than on the needs and goals of society as a whole. In this respect his ideas resemble Owen's or Wilhem's appreciation of music as a means of relaxation and renewal (see Chapter 3 again) more than Saint-Simon's and Barrault's advocacy of music as a means of social control.[12]

Of course by 1861—the date of Halévy's preface—the Saint-Simonians themselves would probably have not written very confidently about music's great potential contribution to social progress. Even Félicien David was now writing more or less conventional operas about princes in disguise and the like; his Saint-Simonian ideals, though as strong as ever, were finding expression mainly in his support of the Galinist singing school, a project of no wider social impact than Halévy's involvement with the Orphéon.

But the difference is that Halévy had apparently never espoused anything different. The Saint-Simonians had of necessity moved into the mainstream, a process that was facilitated by the fact that the mainstream had shifted more than a bit toward them. Halévy was part of that mainstream, and always had been. If his extensive early Saint-Simonian contacts did have an effect on him, it was apparently slight. In his thoughts about music, as in his own musical compositions, he was touched but lightly by the bolder ideas of the day, ideas that drove his more passionate contemporaries to fits of frenzy.

NOURRIT AND THE SAINT-SIMONIANS

The involvement of Adolphe Nourrit (1802–39) with the Saint-Simonians seems to have been more significant. Remembered today as the leading tenor of the Opéra, as creator of leading tenor roles in *Guillaume Tell, Robert le diable, Les Huguenots,* and *La Juive,* as a fine musician, gifted actor, and sensitive mind, and as the dedicated proponent in France of Schubert's lieder, Nourrit was also actively concerned with the social aspects of his art and with the lot of the working classes. In letters and in conversations he expressed his dissatisfaction with the economic and social structure of France, the death of religious belief, and the recent tendency for the theater to serve as a trivial diversion for "the rich and the idle"—"your handsome yellow-gloved ones . . . your

Stock Exchange aristocrats."[13] He joined forces with Liszt on 3 August 1837 for a recital in Lyons to benefit the unemployed workers,[14] and—during the few years before his suicide at age thirty-seven—he was dreaming of a way to organize fine, uplifting theater and music for the popular masses. Indeed, Berlioz noted that Nourrit's funeral drew large numbers of workers who had been touched by the "humanitarian daydreams" of "poor Adolphe."[15] What Berlioz did not note, and what has escaped mention in most biographies,[16] is that these dreams were an obvious expansion of the visions that Emile Barrault had offered during the years when Nourrit was most closely associated with the Saint-Simonian movement.

Nourrit's first contact with the Saint-Simonians is not known.[17] We may recall that the memoirs of Carnot placed Nourrit along with Liszt in the salons of the rue Monsigny in 1830–31.[18] Fortunately, a little-known letter of Enfantin's makes things a bit more precise. Dated 26 October 1830, it indicates that Nourrit, as well as his cohorts Liszt and Berlioz, responded eagerly to the movement's very effective propaganda efforts during the first months after the July Revolution. The letter is also of interest for its tone of gratification, hopefulness, and eager, bustling activity.

> Our women have not been able to get many recruits, but, since there are close to two hundred of them at our sermons and since everybody is interested in us, we should make a fine catch before too long.
>
> Several artists, Liszt, Berlioz, Nourrit, are approaching us. Sainte-Beuve is coming to us by way of *Le Globe;* he attends our Thursday soirees. Cazeaux has got his hand on a budding little poet (Buchey, nineteen years old) who will do us some good. You will see something of his in the *Organisateur.*[19]

Nourrit himself seems to have remained interested until at least the beginning of 1832, when he subscribed to the Saint-Simonian bond drive at the expense of 300 francs, an act that was less an investment than a contribution—a gesture of support for the Saint-Simonians' activities and ideas.[20] (The bankrupt movement eventually reimbursed half of the sum, and even that half with much difficulty and delay.[21]) It may also have been through Nourrit's good offices that, later in 1832, Duveyrier and some others made their ostentatious visit, in costume, to the Opéra to hear *Robert le diable.*

No doubt it was during these years (ca. 1830–32) that Nourrit picked up the Saint-Simonian ideas and expressions (such as *oisifs*) that showed up a few years later in his writings. The most important of these ideas for Nourrit was that the artist and performer had a great and sacred mission to carry out. Nourrit had presumably been feeling this mission for several years, at least on the "purely" operatic level. He had, for example, put his talents in the service of the greatest operas, especially those that (as in the case of Gluck's tragedies) emphasized dramatic truth and musical dignity rather than ear-tickling vocal display. Similarly, he objected vehemently—and no doubt had long done so—to the claque (people paid by singers to applaud them) and the intrusive practice of stopping the action to repeat a favored aria.[22] These positions, which seem modest and sensible to us, were quite bold at the time, especially coming from a "mere" singer. But far bolder, and more plainly indebted to the Saint-Simonians, were Nourrit's earnest and passionate reflections, more and more frequent in his last few years, on the *moral* power that an artist can have over his listeners. Nourrit rejected, with the authors of the *Doctrine,* the argument that the artist stands, must stand, "outside of society."[23] Indeed, he willingly confessed the debt in 1836 when writing to Edouard Charton (who had been one of the most successful Saint-Simonian preachers in 1830–31):

> Your words [in a recent article in *Le Temps*] ... express so well what I deeply feel and thought I was almost alone in understanding. Yes, the theater can and must be something other than a place for the idlers [*oisifs*] to divert themselves. Since an actor's effect is often powerful, it must become *useful*. To awake generous thoughts, to exalt the loving faculties—there's our mission! May God help us by giving us the support of men of good will!
>
> I thank you from the bottom of my heart. Continue to sustain us and to guide us.[24]

This closing sentence should be taken literally; Nourrit was groping for a solution to a dilemma that had been facing him for years, and he found sustenance and guidance in Charton's echo of the message of Saint-Simon and Barrault.

Nourrit's ideas took more specific form after he retired prematurely from the Opéra in April 1837. (The administration had decided to engage an additional first tenor, the young and more powerful—if less artful—Gilbert Duprez, and Nourrit resigned rather than share the roles he had created.) Free now to commit himself wherever he chose, he began to conceive of a popular theater, accessible to all, stimulating to its artists, and edifying to the audiences. Here Nourrit, who became strongly religious in his last years, took up Barrault's and Enfantin's idea that an actor-priest could turn the theater into a new church for the masses.

> What I want is perhaps not hard to obtain: art for the people and by the people, a theater with low prices, and a school in which young artists will be trained before a new public that is free of prejudices in questions of art.... Having been the leading performer at the topmost theater [in Paris], the greatest glory in my eyes is [now] to be at the head of the bottommost. I repeat: art for the people, but wholesome art, art which causes

people to love one another, religious art. Today it is through
the theater that the people must pass in order to return to the
Church.[25]

"Génie oblige," as Nourrit's friend Liszt often expressed it.

The details of Nourrit's plan were still vague at this point, in part because
the singer was not yet free financially to give up his profitable tours and
undertake a more speculative venture.[26] Shortly after his death in 1839, though,
the *Courrier de Lyon* printed an article that described Nourrit's scheme with
greater precision, the details drawn perhaps from recent conversations. The
article says that Nourrit intended his theater to be truly popular—built entirely
for the people and supported solely by the financial contributions of the people.
It would not lack in grandeur. "Tragedy, drama, comedy, and music would be
reinforced by the full glories of the art of decor and the most faithful production
techniques." Indeed, the main function of the attached school that Nourrit also
envisioned would be to provide his theater with the "great choral masses and
numerous performing artists" that it required.[27] One of Nourrit's biographers
reports that François Delsarte had agreed to take part and that both singers
planned to accept secondary roles in order to attract other outstanding artists
to the project.[28] Liszt's mistress Mme d'Agoult was overwhelmed with admiration and confided to her diary in 1837 the hope that Liszt would soon
respond to the call with an analogous project of his own. (She must have
associated the Saint-Simonians with this call for humanitarian art, for in the
very next sentence, without a word of transition, she entered into a long
discussion of the principles of Enfantin and Saint-Simon, noting especially her
own yearning to become "a member of a family, one of the thousand rays
that meet at a center."[29])

In 1839 Nourrit, acutely sensitive to the increasing harsh criticisms of his
singing and unable to believe any longer in his own talents, ended his life by
jumping out of a window after a benefit performance in Naples. From then
on, Berlioz and others, with the dubious benefit of hindsight, spoke conde-
scendingly of Nourrit's grandiose "humanitarian" visions as the fantasies or
illusions of a person gone mad.[30] But one should ponder a moment the influence
that Nourrit, had he lived past 1839, might have had on theatrical and musical
life in Paris and to recall that his efforts, even had they failed, would have
been the most serious attempt of his day at realizing certain ideas proposed
in the "Dialogue" of 1825 and in Barrault's *Aux artistes* of 1830.

It is also worth noting that many of Nourrit's ideas have, since that era,
been modified and put into widespread practice, in the form of municipal music
schools, lay choral societies (such as the Orphéon), and state-supported musical
and theatrical institutions (such as the world's great opera houses). But these
organizations have often downplayed or entirely eliminated precisely what
Nourrit wished most strongly to emphasize: "the moral and religious tenden-

cies of the works being performed." It was clearly this "humanitarian" concern of Nourrit's, as much as the impracticability of his specific projects, that led his contemporaries to regard him as mad. And this same concern shows how much he continued to be—in his own words—"sustained and guided" by the disciples of Saint-Simon.

LISZT AND THE SAINT-SIMONIANS

The relationship between Franz Liszt (1811–86) and the Saint-Simonians has long needed to be studied in detail. Of all the musicians active in France during the nineteenth century, Liszt was the most prominent one to devote himself at periods throughout his life to such social issues as the artist's role and the problem of music and religion. That he received his first impulses from the Saint-Simonian doctrine is well known, but the precise nature of his participation in the movement has never been discussed with any precision, nor have writers drawn adequate attention to his continuing interest in the doctrine during his later years.[31]

It is perhaps best to begin with the most familiar account of his association, the one that has served as the source for almost all other published versions, namely that of Lina Ramann. Ramann's account, to be found in a chapter of the biography of Liszt that she wrote with some help from him and under the watchful eye of his second great mistress, Princess Carolyne von Sayn-Wittgenstein,[32] can be summarized as follows:

Liszt was introduced to the movement by Emile Barrault soon after the July Revolution of 1830. Liszt was still attending meetings in late November 1831 (during the Bazard schism), for he heard Enfantin's "remarkable fantastic-mystical announcement of the *femme révélatrice*" and "he was in the assembly when, in expectation of the fulfillment of the prophecy, a chair was solemnly set next to that of Enfantin." Liszt was drawn to the Saint-Simonians by two major concepts from the doctrine: the vision of a divine community on earth, ruled by the dictates of brotherly love (the principle of *association*), and the idea of an artist-priest mediating between God and the people. His attraction to these concepts derived from the religious crisis he had undergone in 1828–30, and these ideas remained the touchstone of his own behavior: "He was a priest of art his whole life long." As for the extent of Liszt's participation during his "Saint-Simonian period," at the beginning "he not only was among the most ardent visitors to their meetings but also considered joining them as a member." In the end, though, he never did join but only "embraced their essential philosophical ideas."

It is remarkable, considering the poor reputation of Ramann as a biographer, that the essential accuracy of this account is supported by almost everything we can learn about Liszt's Saint-Simonian activity from memoirs, letters, and

Liszt's own writings. To begin with, the letter of Enfantin quoted in the preceding pages on Nourrit confirms that Liszt became interested in the movement soon after the July Revolution—more precisely, by the end of October. Ramann is surely right about his having been prepared for this contact by certain experiences in his own life, especially, one suspects, his feelings of isolation and rejection. (Around 1829 he had proposed to one of his aristocratic pupils, Caroline de Saint-Cricq, and been promptly shown to the door by her father, the minister of commerce.[33]) Ramann's statement that Liszt was drawn not only to the movement's humanitarian views in general but also to their specific vision of the artist's role is internally consistent with her statement that Liszt's main contact was Barrault, the movement's spokesman on the arts.[34] Also, various jottings in Liszt's datebook for 1832 demonstrate clearly that by January of that year (if not earlier) he had absorbed the Saint-Simonian conception of the modern artist as an inspired being who is unappreciated and even mistreated by the "critical" society in which he lives. (Liszt's own description is vivid: "a society without poetry, without dignity, without love!"[35]) As for Ramann's description of Liszt's eager attendance at the Saint-Simonians' lectures, that is confirmed by the memoirs of his first great mistress, Marie d'Agoult: "[Shortly before I met him] he had followed assiduously the sermons of the sects and schools which were announcing new revelations. He went often to the meetings of the disciples of Saint-Simon."[36] Finally, Liszt's own writings, to be examined shortly, give plentiful proof of his frequent attendance at the Saint-Simonians' gatherings and of his particular attraction to their views on art.

There are indeed only two serious criticisms one can level against Ramann's account of this episode. (Three, if one includes the unrelievedly adulatory tone of her tiresome prose.) First, she portrays Liszt as a young, impressionable, and inconspicuous figure. Young and impressionable he surely was, but hardly inconspicuous. As we have previously seen, the fashionable virtuoso was considered quite a "catch" by Enfantin, and he attracted plenty of attention during soirees in the rue Monsigny by "abandoning himself to his fantasy" at the keyboard.[37]

Second, and more significant, Ramann states that Liszt remained "naïve" and "passive" in the face of Enfantin's teachings regarding the relationship of the sexes and that, as the "dangerous sect . . . hurried to its destruction," Liszt moved on to other philosophical and musical interests. It does seem reasonable and even likely that he was disenchanted by the direction that the movement was taking in late 1831 and 1832. But that his disenchantment was neither as complete nor as permanent as his biographer implies is clear from various of his letters and articles written during the following few years.

In 1833, for example, when Enfantin was in prison and the Saint-Simonians were widely viewed as criminals or clowns, Liszt lent the countess one of the movement's books that had impressed him. She replied with enthusiasm: "I am struck by the power, the clarity, and the soundness of most of the ideas in the Saint-Simonian book that you lent me."[38] And a bit later he wrote to her: "I very, very much wish you would reread the *Letters* of Rodrigues. It is a great book."[39] Interestingly, this reference to Eugène Rodrigues's *Letters on Politics and Religion* gives further support to Ramann's perception that it was particularly the religious and artistic theories of the movement that attracted Liszt. Rodrigues's book, an extended treatise on the need for a new social religion, had given the movement a decided tug away from its earlier, predominantly "industrial" philosophy. Liszt must have noted Rodrigues's presentation of the great social trinity of science, industry, and art, in which art was explicitly linked to religion and love (as science was to wisdom, and industry to power);[40] he later quoted some of these very phrases in his articles and letters.

As Fraser has noted, Liszt's letter to d'Agoult clearly suggests that the countess did not at this point take the Saint-Simonians as seriously as he did. In fact, her letter to him about "the Saint-Simonian book" (presumably the same book: Rodrigues's *Letters*) continues with some rather snippy jokes about his attraction to the movement, as well as to the fair sex: "Really, I am often astonished that you have never donned the fraternal vest. And it seems to me that a trip to the Orient in search of Woman would also have suited you very well."[41]

For a year or two after this, Liszt turned toward a new mentor, Lamennais; indeed, in autumn 1834 Liszt lived for several weeks at Lamennais's secluded home in La Chênaie (Brittany). But the liberal religious and social ideas of Lamennais were not necessarily incompatible with those of other "opposition" thinkers, and in summer 1835 he began reading some Saint-Simonian books again. On 27 June he recommended to George Sand two books in particular—the sermons, and the second year of the *Doctrine*—as containing "things of very great significance, marvelously beautiful in movement and fervor."[42] And in a diary entry from the previous week he specifically noted one of Barrault's published sermons, "L'Incrédulité."[43] These writings, too, confirm Liszt's attraction to the religious and artistic theories of the movement. *The Doctrine, Second Year* presented one of the movement's strongest statements of the need for the leaders of society to be "priests" whose visions would be translated to the people by the artists (see Chapter 6). And "L'Incrédulité" was one of Barrault's most persuasive statements about how a new social religion would cure the present ills of art.[44] (If Liszt read further into the same volume of sermons, he must also have come across "L'Art," Barrault's more detailed treatment of the religious role of art, which we examined briefly in Chapter 7.)

A few months later Liszt wrote again to George Sand, declaring, "I am almost ashamed to admit that [this summer] I was even more struck by them [the Saint-Simonians' writings] and more deeply moved than in the past." He continued with an astonishing defense of the Saint-Simonians' views on the sexes that clearly contradicts Ramann's implication that these very views had caused him to break with the movement in late 1831.

> Père Enfantin is uncontestably a great man, in spite of all the jokes and choice remarks that you hear in good company and bad. Shall I tell you what surprised me most of all? It was the wise and dignified reserve which he maintained regarding the infamous *question de la femme*. I think I remember your criticizing heatedly certain *supposed* Saint-Simonian opinions about women. At this moment I am looking at the brochure *Réunion de la famille,* which ends with a note about marriage and divorce, and it seems to me that when the question is posed in these terms it is perfectly acceptable both to any serious minds and to the *chaste women*.[45] I doubt that you have read this note carefully, but it is important to know it if you wish to base your judgment of the matter on solid evidence.[46]

Liszt's resurgence of interest in the Saint-Simonians during the mid-1830s shows up in other ways as well. He had an "enormous conversation about Saint-Simonism" with Enfantin's close friend Arlès-Dufour in April 1836, and around the same time he renewed his friendship with Barrault.[47] (Before long the countess was herself having Barrault to dinner and confiding in her diary that "of all our modern social systems, the doctrine of Saint-Simon is the one which embraces most completely my sympathies."[48])

More significantly, because more publicly, in his lengthy essay of 1835, "On the Situation of Artists and on Their Condition in Society," Liszt gave plentiful evidence of his familiarity with Saint-Simonian doctrine. Not only his main arguments—e.g., the unhealthy isolation of artists—but even certain details—e.g., the image of the artist as bringer of heavenly fire, or the proposal that music leave the church and spread its new religious message in the theater—recall the writings of Barrault and his fellows. Indeed, in one passage of this essay Liszt acknowledged that the ideas on the social and religious power of art that he was now espousing had first been voiced by a certain (unnamed) "society of men" that preached "the new *trinity* of *science, industry,* and *art*" and that, certain people decided, "ought to be persecuted by calumny, ridicule and [petty] legality."[49] A bold confession of indebtedness to a movement then in disrepute.

Liszt, to be sure, was careful in his essay not to present himself as an apostle—of the Saint-Simonians, Lamennais, or anyone else. Two years later, though, this image of independence was shattered when Heinrich Heine, in a wittily indiscreet article, mentioned by name and gently mocked each of the philosophical "hobby-horses" that Liszt had recently ridden.[50] Liszt seems to have taken this as an attack. He defended himself (with help from the countess) in an open letter, admitting that he had admired the Saint-Simonians' ideas but insisting, with a touch of sarcasm, that he did not own a "Saint-Simonian costume." (He even attacked back, noting pointedly that Heine himself had been involved with the Saint-Simonians at the same period, and indeed more deeply.[51]) Similarly, in 1844 he felt compelled to defend himself in more or less the same terms to Gustav Schilling, who had written a biography of Liszt that spoke baldly of the latter's "period of membership in the movement."[52] And in 1853 he rephrased the same ideas yet again in a letter to the publisher Heinrich Brockhaus, objecting to an encyclopedia article on him containing the words "he became a Saint-Simonian."

One cannot help noticing, though, that in the last of these three more or less public responses, Liszt's touchy feelings about his former involvement are no longer quite so strongly in evidence. He speaks, strikingly, of never having "had the honor" of being part of the Saint-Simonian family, and he recalls having heard many of their "eloquent" sermons.[53] It seems that, as the years passed and the controversiality of the Saint-Simonians began to fade, Liszt felt free again to admit how much he had admired, and still did admire, those hardy, if extravagant, pioneers. In a letter to Agnes Street-Klindworth in 1863 he confessed that he still had "a better opinion of the practical utility of certain ideas that the disciples of Saint-Simon used to *preach* than it is customary to mention in the salons of 'statesmen.' "[54] And at the very end of his life, reading Ramann's chapter on his "Saint-Simonian period," Liszt filled the margins of one page with some of the movement's slogans and other relevant names and phrases—including "Félicien David (Voyage en Orient)." More significantly, he took pains to correct several of the standard calumnies about the Saint-Simonians that Ramann had absorbed from other writers. Where she had attributed to Enfantin the doctrine of the "emancipation of the flesh," Liszt changed "emancipation" to "rehabilitation," a change indicating his belief that the call for a healthier attitude toward sexuality had some merit and should never have been interpreted as an irresponsible proclamation of libertinism. Furthermore he marked large X's through the words *nichts gemein,* showing justified disapproval of Ramann's statement that Enfantin's ideas had "nothing in common" with the teachings of Saint-Simon.[55]

These and other indications of Liszt's continuing support of Saint-Simonian doctrine in his later years[56] clearly suggest that it would be wrong to try to define Liszt's "Saint-Simonian period" as a discrete episode, ending in 1832 (as Ramann has it) or even in 1837 (with the attack from Heine and the resulting string of public denials). This continuing fascination suggests that Saint-Simonian ideas may be credited with some direct influence not only on Liszt's writings of 1835 (an influence that, as we have seen, he admitted himself) but, even more significantly, on his career and his musical output. In the 1830s and 1840s he performed in (and even organized) major benefit concerts and festivals for needy groups and other worthy causes: Italian refugees, unemployed workers in Lyons, a proposed Beethoven monument in Bonn. During these same years he strove to raise the intellectual and spiritual tone of virtuoso piano music by basing pieces on historic or poetic "programs" (e.g., the powerful "Lyon"—inspired by the weavers' uprising—and "La Chapelle de Guillaume Tell," both from the *Album d'un voyageur*). Less well known are his secular male choruses, some of which advocate the dignity of labor and the need for the working class to "struggle" against the privileged and land-owning classes (e.g., the *Arbeiter-Chor,* written shortly before the revolutions of 1848, and especially *Le Forgeron,* to a text by Lamennais.[57]) In the 1860s and later he attempted to renovate the music of the Catholic Church by writing austere yet expressive oratorios and liturgical pieces, some of which are only today beginning to find the audience they deserve. And all the while he lent precious support to other composers and gave free lessons to hundreds of young pianists from across Europe and America.[58]

Liszt was filled with a sense of mission, an urge to find a fulfilling new role for the artist in a society that had come to treat art as a consumer good and status symbol. This mission had been first and most plainly articulated by the Saint-Simonians. One must conclude that, of the six musicians discussed in this chapter, it was Liszt in whom the ideas of the Saint-Simonians echoed loudest and longest.

HILLER AND THE SAINT-SIMONIANS

Ferdinand Hiller (1811–85) was an enthusiastic frequenter of the Saint-Simonian réunions. The young musician went to Paris in 1828 where he established himself as composer and pianist. He became a close friend of Liszt, Chopin, Berlioz, Nourrit, Heine, and others and took an active interest in the political and intellectual affairs of the day, to the detriment—he later claimed—of his creative work. Hiller's fascination with "the whole Parisian hustle-bustle, including politics, to which I surrendered passionately,"[59] included a little-known phase of involvement with the Saint-Simonians. This is apparent from a letter of Mendelssohn's discussed in the following section, suggesting that Hiller tried to interest him in the movement. (Hiller may also have brought the Young German writer Ludwig Börne to the Saint-Simonian soiree that Börne described in his *Briefe aus Paris*—see Chapter 8.[60])

The Saint-Simonians seem to have recognized in Hiller an important potential ally. In late 1831 the Saint-Simonian *Globe* devoted a substantial article to a concert of Hiller's works—a notable gesture, considering the paper's usual lack of interest in nonoperatic musical events. The review began by claiming (erroneously) that Hiller had recently graduated from the Paris Conservatoire, and went on to discuss his music as an extension of the Beethoven tradition. It ended with an *appel* to Hiller (and to artists generally), an invitation to ascend to a position of glory in the vanguard of humanity by standing on the shoulders of Rossini and Beethoven.[61]

Hiller never responded to the call and presumably ceased visiting the Saint-Simonians as they fell into disrepute in 1832–33. Nonetheless, he appears to have kept his affection for the Saint-Simonians for a number of years. When Félicien David made his tour of Germany with *Le Désert*, Hiller welcomed him warmly and recalled with apparent pleasure Enfantin and "the veterans of the rue Monsigny."[62] Hiller may, it is true, have finally changed his mind about the Saint-Simonians in the last years of his life. In 1884, more than fifty years after his own Saint-Simonian adventures, he wrote of Maxime du Camp's friendship with Enfantin that it gave du Camp opportunity to observe "the follies of the spiritists" with his own two eyes.[63] Yet we should notice that this quotation refers primarily to Enfantin, of whom du Camp became a very late admirer (1853).[64] (Hiller seems not to have realized that the Enfantin of the 1850s was a very different and saner fellow than the one who led the movement into the "follies" of the mid-1830s.) It may be that Hiller distinguished the "Enfantinist" stage of Saint-Simonism from the sound and exciting social philosophy of the rue Monsigny and the Salle Taitbout. Whatever he chose to think about it later, though, he certainly seems to have taken a passionate interest in it all in 1831 and early 1832, as becomes evident from his attempts to involve the next of our six musicians.

MENDELSSOHN AND THE SAINT-SIMONIANS

Felix Mendelssohn (1809–47) spent five months in Paris in 1831–32, and several friends—among them, Hiller and Gustave d'Eichthal—tried to interest him in the activities of the Saint-Simonians. Mendelssohn, unique among the musicians discussed here, soon took a negative attitude to the doctrine, but even he at first visited the rue Monsigny and let himself be bombarded with arguments and pamphlets. The story has never before appeared in full, because the principal documents, Mendelssohn's letters, were abridged and censored by his family (and some were never published at all). I have transcribed them all afresh and in full. The resulting texts provide us with a good deal of unsuspected information about Mendelssohn's encounter with the Saint-Simonian movement—an encounter that might better be termed a collision.[65] And when the evidence from the letters is then interpreted in light of the movement's history and certain of its publications, we can finally comprehend why neither of the parties involved in this brief encounter, though hurtling toward each other with too much momentum, showed the least inclination to yield the right of way.

It is best to begin with the documentary evidence, including two long passages from Mendelssohn's letters, before moving on to more extensive interpretation and to a brief coda dealing with Mendelssohn's relations with the Saint-Simonians later in life.

Mendelssohn had made two trips to Paris as a youth, in 1816 and 1825, both times accompanied by members of his family. On this third visit, in 1831, he was twenty-two years old and traveling alone. Paris was one of his final stops on a two-year tour of the main cultural centers of Europe; his aim on this journey was to make himself better known and to gather the information and the impressions that would help him select the country and city in which he (as he put it) "would like to live and work [*wohnen und wirken*]" as a composer, pianist, and conductor.[66] The French capital must not have seemed very promising in this regard. True, Mendelssohn arrived full of liberal, pro-French sentiments, at least as regarded politics.[67] But in the area that concerned him most—music—he harbored grave doubts, based on vivid memories of what he had heard in Paris when he was sixteen.[68]

Mendelssohn arrived on 9 December 1831, bearing instructions from his father to look up various people—friends in finance, musicians, publishers, writers. First of all, though, he renewed contact with two old friends who quickly became his frequent companions—Hiller, whom he had known intimately since childhood, and Gustave d'Eichthal, who had became acquainted with Felix in 1824–25 while serving an apprenticeship in Abraham Mendelssohn's banking house in Berlin.[69] Hiller immediately went about finding Mendelssohn an apartment, and Hiller's banker cousin Léo engaged Mendelssohn in that essential Parisian pastime, political discussion. Mendelssohn announced with mock seriousness that he was a "doctrinaire," and—as he reported with amusement to his family—everyone took him seriously. "I think it's the best joke I've made in my life."[70] Doctrinaire, he must have known, was the one thing it was not fashionable to be after 1830. (The doctrinaires, Guizot among them, had been moderate and constitutional royalists during the Bourbon Restoration—the mildest possible opposition. Their program was now corpulently embodied in France's bourgeois monarch, Louis-Philippe.)

D'Eichthal appears in this letter of 11 December as a friend (a companion of Léo and Hiller) rather than as a Saint-Simonian. The representative of the movement whom Mendelssohn does mention in those terms is none other than Olinde Rodrigues, who was one of the two *pères* of the movement (the other being Enfantin) now that Bazard had left. Olinde's father was apparently another of Abraham Mendelssohn's contacts in Paris, not suprisingly, since the Rodrigueses were friends of the d'Eichthals. In an unpublished letter of 11 December Mendelssohn wrote in some consternation to know whether he was really expected to meet the younger Rodrigues as well as the father.

> By the way, I wanted to ask you if you want me to visit Rodrigues. Olinde has become a raging Saint-Simonian [*ein wüthender Saint-Simonist*]; and his wife, too. They try in every way to convert anyone they run into, so I'm not too inclined [to call on them]. But I don't know if you are as friendly with

him as you are with his father and so I ask you to tell me what *you* want.[71]

During his first few weeks in Paris Mendelssohn seems to have felt resentful about being imprisoned all winter in the frivolous French capital,[72] and he also seems to have kept a certain distance from the Saint-Simonians. Only in January 1832 did he begin to loosen up and enjoy the city.[73] Around the same time, the Saint-Simonians began to take a central place in Mendelssohn's letters and apparently in his life. In a longish letter written on 14 January 1832, Mendelssohn reported that he had recently had discussions with Gustave d'Eichthal, had been given brochures by Olinde Rodrigues to distribute in Germany, and had attended a Saint-Simonian meeting at which Olinde presided in authoritarian manner. Mendelssohn responded to all this with very mixed emotions.

> Eichthal has moved out of his parents' house into the rue Monsigny, where he now lives body and soul. His entire household is unhappy about it, and rightly so, but I cannot see an end to it, for it is an *idée fixe* with him. I have an appeal to all people by Olinde Rodrigues, in which he presents his confession of faith and calls upon everyone to give a portion of his fortune, as small as he may wish, to the Saint-Simonians. The call also goes out to artists to devote their art henceforth to this religion: to make better music than Rossini and Beethoven, to build temples of peace, to paint like Raphael or [Jacques-Louis] David. I have twenty copies of this appeal, which I am supposed to send to you, dear Father (as Père Olinde instructed me). I will leave it at *one*, and you will find it quite enough; and that one only when the opportunity presents itself, of course.
>
> It is a bad sign of the state of the public mind here that such a monstrous idea, in such detestable prose, should ever have come into existence and that a good many of the pupils of the Ecole polytechnique have taken part. You would not believe how it can be possible, since they approach the matter in a purely external way, promising honor to some, fame to others, a public and applause to me, money to the poor; since, in short, they want to reward everyone according to what he deserves; since they [would] therefore destroy all striving and desire for advancement with their perpetual, cold estimation of capacity.
>
> But then from time to time certain ideas appear—e.g., ideas of universal brotherly love, of disbelief in Hell, the devil, and damnation, of the annihilation of egoism—all ideas which in our country spring from nature, and which prevail in every part of Christendom, ideas without which I should not wish to live, but which they regard as a new invention and discovery.

And when they constantly repeat that they seek to transform the world and to make men happy; when Eichthal tells me quite calmly that they do not need to improve themselves, but others only, for they are not at all imperfect but, on the contrary, perfect; when they do nothing but praise and compliment each other and anyone whom they wish to win over, when they admire the talent or capacity [which you possess] and lament that such great powers should be lost through adherence to all the worn-out notions of duty, vocation, and activity, as they were formerly interpreted—when I listen to all this, it does seem to me a sad mystification.

Last Sunday I attended a meeting at which the Fathers sat in a circle, high up [on the stage]. Then came the highest Father, Olinde Rodrigues, who called them to account, praised and blamed them, addressed the assembled people and issued commands—it was the first time that I have seen him since seven years ago, and to me it was almost ghastly [*schauerlich*]! He too has renounced his parents and lives with the Fathers, his subordinates, and is endeavoring to organize a loan for their benefit. Enough of this![74]

On 22 January, a week after writing this first long letter on the Saint-Simonians, Mendelssohn wrote a second one, this time directed mainly to his elder sister Fanny. The letter indicates that Hiller, d'Eichthal, and Olinde Rodrigues were in the custom of calling on him at his lodgings, that there was still much talking of things Saint-Simonian, and that Rodrigues had recently offered some shocking "disclosures" about the movement that now made it seem utterly repulsive to Mendelssohn. (Also, the reference to a copy of his Piano Quartet in B minor, op. 3, suggests that he had at some point attended at least one soiree at the Saint-Simonians' headquarters, 6 rue Monsigny, and perhaps taken part in a performance of the Quartet there.)

[I am always being invited here and there.] So when am I to compose? In the forenoon, perhaps! Yesterday, first Hiller came, then Kalkbrenner, then Habeneck. The day before that, Baillot came, then Eichthal, then Rodrigues. Perhaps early in the morning! Well, I do compose then—so you are wrong, you witch. . . .

Rodrigues was with me yesterday, talking Saint-Simonism, and because he thought I was either stupid enough or smart enough, he made disclosures that shocked me so much that I resolved never again to go to him or to the other accomplices. This morning Hiller rushed into the room and told me that he had just witnessed the arrest of the Saint-Simonians. He wanted to hear their sermon; the Popes do not arrive. All of a sudden soldiers make their way in and request everyone

Plate 1. Saint-Simon in the year of his death (1825). Contemporary lithograph (Bibl. de l'Arsenal, Paris).

Plate 2. Saint-Amand Bazard. Lithograph by [Auguste?] Lemoine, after Ary and Henri Scheffer (photo Bibl. Nat., Paris).

Plate 3. Barthélemy-Prosper Enfantin. Lithograph by Duriez, after Grévedon (photo Bibl. Nat., Paris).

Plate 4. Contemporary caricature: Ball at the Saint-Simonians'—Women Are Free (Bibl. de l'Arsenal, Paris).

Plate 5. Contemporary caricature: "I Seek the Free Woman" (Bibl. de l'Arsenal, Paris).

Plate 6. F. Halévy, 1850s? Lithograph by Auguste Lemoine, after Roller (from Léon Halévy, *F. Halévy*).

Plate 7. Adolphe Nourrit. Engraving, after Vigneron (photo Bibl. Nat., Paris).

Plate 8. Franz Liszt, 1838. Lithograph by Kriehuber (Sibley Music Library).

Plate 9. Ferdinand Hiller. Anonymous engraving, after Sohl (photo Bibl. Nat., Paris).

Plate 10. Felix Mendelssohn, 1840s? Lithograph by Auguste Lemoine (from H. Barbedette, *Felix Mendelssohn Bartholdy* [Paris, 1868]).

Plate 11. Hector Berlioz, 1845. Lithograph by Kriehuber (Sibley Music Library).

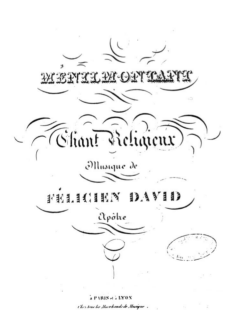

Plate 12. David's *Ménilmontant* series: unillustrated title page (Bibl. Nat., Paris).

Plate 13. Machereau's title page for the *Ménilmontant* series showing the taking of the habit (Bibl. Nat., Paris).

Plate 15. Le Père, 1832. Lithograph by Aglaé Saint-Hilaire, after Léon Cogniet (Bibl. de l'Arsenal, Paris).

Plate 14. Père Enfantin at Ménilmontant; *left,* the temple site; *right,* a tent and two apostles with shovel and wheelbarrow (Bibl. de l'Arsenal, Paris).

Plate 16. Emile Barrault, Michel Chevalier, and Charles Duveyrier, 1832. Lithograph by Cals, after L. Cogniet (Bibl. de l'Arsenal, Paris).

Plate 17. Illustration on Machereau's other title page for the *Ménilmontant* series, showing Barrault preaching from the temple (Bibl. Nat., Paris).

Plate 18. Key to plate 17: *a*, Raymond Bonheur; *b*, Achille Rousseau; *c*, Père Enfantin; *d*, Félicien David; *e*, Michel Chevalier; *f*, Emile Barrault; *g*, Charles Lambert; *h*, unidentified; *i*, Pol Justus; *j*, Gustave d'Eichthal; *k*, Edmond Talabot; *l*, Moïse Retouret; *m*, Victor Bertrand; *n*, [David's choir?].

Plate 20. Jules Mercier (from Vinçard, *Mémoires*).

Plate 19. Vinçard aîné (photo Bibl. Nat., Paris).

Plate 21. Julien Gallé, founder of mutual aid societies (from Vinçard, *Mémoires*).

L'HOMME NOUVEAU.

Air de la Marsillaise.

Apôtres de la foi nouvelle,
Que l'ignorance veut ternir,
Le Dieu dont la voix vous appelle
Vous garde un heureux avenir.   (bis)
Répandez toujours la lumière
Sur vos injustes détracteurs.
Des peuples zélés protecteurs,
Vous soulagerez la misère,

Enfans du même DIEU plus de servilité.
L'HOMME NOUVEAU chérit le PÈRE et sent sa dignité

Peuples qui cherchiez la victoire
Au milieu de sanglans hazards,
Non, non, la véritable gloire
N'est plus sur les pas des Césars.   (bis)
Celui qui désigne vos frères
A vos foudres, à vos fureurs,
Compte pour rien les mille pleurs
Qui coulent des yeux de vos mères.
Enfans du même DIEU, etc,

De l'homme compagne asservie,
Victime des mœurs et des lois,
Entre dans la nouvelle vie;
Tu retrouveras tous tes droits.   (bis)
Oui, ton sexe, dans quelques lustres,
Aura de la célébrité.
Déjà dans l'immortalité
Brillent mille femmes illlustres.
Enfans du même Dieu, etc.

Là-bas.... vainement une grille
LE sépare de ses enfans;
IL plane ici sur sa famille,
Il guide nos pas triomphans.   (bis)
Oui, nous finirons l'œuvre immense
Du plus généreux des mortels;
Nos fils un jour sur ses autels
Viendront bénir notre constance.
Enfans du même DIEU, etc.

Ennemis du SAINT-SIMONISME,
Vainement vos portez vos coups;
Il détruira le fanatisme :
DIEU l'inspire et sera pour nous.   (bis.
En dépit de la calomnie,
L'APÔTRE propage sa foi;
Le bonheur du PEUPLE est sa loi,
L'UNIVERS voilà sa patrie.

Enfans du même DIEU, plus de servilité.
L'HOMME NOUVEAU chérit le Père et sent sa dignité.

SALUT AU PÈRE ET GLOIRE 'A DIEU.

MORA.

Imprimerie de Sétier, rue de Grene lle-ll. 2

Plate 22. Mora's "L'Homme nouveau," to the tune of the "Marseillaise" (Bibl. Nat., Paris).

Plate 23. Costumes for Barrault's Compagnons de la femme and "for the artists." Ink and water color, by Machereau (Bibl. de l'Arsenal, Paris).

1833.

Je pars pour l'Orient. Sur les traces de BARRAULT, je vais au devant de la MÈRE, près de laquelle je puiserai une nouvelle vie.

Mais avant de quitter cette France qui retient le PÈRE captif, je dois un adieu à l'Occident, car lui aussi m'a fourni de grandes pensées religieuses, et je l'aime. Je lui laisse les chants que sous l'inspiration du PÈRE j'ai composés à Ménilmontant, et que mes frères et moi avons si souvent exécutés en face d'un public bienveillant et nombreux. Déja ces productions, d'une époque que nous avons traversée, appartiennent à l'histoire, et DIEU m'a donné de pressentir une musique nouvelle.

Habitués que nous sommes à donner ce que nous possédons, nous ne faisons pas de spéculations : Cette musique sera donc donnée à un prix très peu élevé; qu'on y songe pourtant, c'est le denier de l'artiste et de l'amateur au pèlerin que je demande en échange de mes œuvres; car le 22 mars nous mettrons à la voile.

L'ouvrage complet formera huit livraisons, comprenant ensemble vingt-deux morceaux.

PREMIÈRE LIVRAISON.	Prise d'Habit.
Appel.	Prière du PÈRE.
Salut.	Vᵉ LIVRAISON.
Danse des Astres.	Peuple fier! Peuple fort!
IIᵉ LIVRAISON.	Gloire à celui.
Prière du Matin.	Je ne veux plus être exploité.
Tout est mort.	VIᵉ LIVRAISON.
Au Peuple.	Avant et après le repas. (Nᵒ 2)
IIIᵉ LIVRAISON.	Femmes, levez-vous!
Prière du Soir.	Paris est là!
Soldats Ouvriers.	VIIᵉ LIVRAISON.
La Prison du PÈRE.	Valses pour le piano { Mes Amours (1ʳᵉ série.) Ménilmontant (2ᵉ série.)
IVᵉ LIVRAISON.	VIIIᵉ LIVRAISON.
Avant et après le repas. (Nᵒ 1)	Pensées à Ménilmontant pour le Piano.
Le nouveau Temple.	

Il se vendra 40 fr. Pour les souscripteurs dont les demandes arriveraient après la publication de la 4ᵉ livraison, le prix sera porté à 50 fr.

On souscrit :

A LYON, chez Mᵐᵉ Durval, libraire, place des Célestins;
MM. Nallez, rue Gentil, Fevrol, rue Clermont; Mazoyer, rue St-Pierre. } m. de m.
A MARSEILLE, chez M. Boisselot, marchand de musique.

A PARIS, chez M. Launer, boulevard Montmartre;
Pleyel, rue Grange-Batel.
Frère, pass. des Panoram.
Frey, place des Victoires;
Paccini, boulevard des Italiens;
Lemoine, rue des Fossés- } march. de musiq.

St-Germain-des-Prés;
Meissonnier, rue Dauphine;
Janet et Cotelle, rue Neuve-des-Petits-Champs;
Troupenas, éditeur de musique, rue St-Marc-Feydeau. } march. de musiq.

LA PREMIÈRE LIVRAISON PARAITRA LE 3 MARS.

Lyon, imp. de Perret.

FÉLICIEN **DAVID**, 𝕮ompagnon de la **FEMME**

Plate 24. Prospectus for David's Ménilmontant choruses (Bibl. de l'Arsenal, Paris).

Plate 25. Henri Reber, professor of harmony, ca. 1860 (photo Pierre Petit, Bibl. Nat., Paris).

Plate 26. Vinçard (*bottom row, third from right*) and other members of the Lice chansonnière in 1876. Photo by Pierre Petit (from Charles Coligny, et al., *La Chanson française*).

Plate 27. Félicien David (1850s?). Photo Nadar (Caisse nationale des monuments historiques, ©ARCH. PHOT./ S.P.A.D.E.M., Paris/V.A.G.A., New York, 1985).

present to disperse as quickly as possible, since Herr Enfantin and the others have been arrested in the rue Monsigny. In the rue Monsigny a party of National Guards and other soldiers are standing in formation. Everything gets locked up and now the trial will begin. They will have a difficult case, because the new jury, which no longer consists of the candidates of [liberal leader] Odilon Barrot, supports the ministry [of Auguste Casimir Périer] and has already given out several very harsh verdicts. My B-minor [Piano] Quartet, which is lying in the rue Monsigny, gets locked up as well; only the Adagio movement belongs to the *juste milieu,* all the others are *mouvement;* I shall eventually be obliged to play it before the jury. But seriously, I feel extraordinarily sorry for the Eichthals. Gustav [*sic*], who is in London, will probably have a tough case, and in the end it will become apparent that he has been the [Saint-Simonians'] chief dupe.[75]

Rodrigues's "disclosures" must indeed have shocked Mendelssohn greatly. He seems to have held to his resolve never again to visit the Saint-Simonians. He did continue to see Gustave d'Eichthal socially—he even went to the theater with him.[76] But his attitude toward Olinde Rodrigues and the movement now became firmly ironic and distant.

I've seen Rodrigues, the father, several times. He is in no way a Saint-Simonian, and the apostlehood of his son and of his daughter seems to give him little joy. A few days ago his daughter married the Saint-Simonian preacher [Henri] Baud in a simple civil exchange of vows, not with church, organ, benediction and that sort of outdated rubbish [*und dergleichen veraltetem Zeug*].[77]

On 19 February, about a month after the catastrophic visit from Olinde, Mendelssohn wrote a letter (in French) to the editor of *Le Globe* that marked the definitive close of his collision with the Saint-Simonian movement.

Monsieur,

My friend, M. Gustave d'Eichthal, undertook several days ago to ask you no longer to send me your newspaper *Le Globe,* since all my ideas are too opposed to all those which you espouse. In spite of this, I have continued to receive it since that time, and I am therefore writing to ask you yourself no longer to send me a newspaper whose sole aim is the propagation of your new religion, and which, since I have read it, has only served to alienate me from it [your religion] irrevocably.[78]

How is one to interpret the predominantly negative view of the Saint-Simonians that speaks from all these letters of Mendelssohn's? What, in particular, led him to feel this way? It may be helpful to start by examining one remark in the letter of 14 January that can be partly reinterpreted in a positive sense. Mendelssohn lists several essentially religious ideas of the Saint-Simonians with which he agrees, objecting only that these ideas are not at all novel: "universal brotherly love; disbelief in Hell, the devil, and damnation; the annihilation of egoism." I can find no satisfactory explanation for Mendelssohn's curious claim that these ideas "spring from nature [in Germany] and . . . prevail in every part of Christendom." True, Mendelssohn's own family, with its roots in the German Enlightenment, held firmly to such ideas as religious tolerance and public service, specific instances of two of the principles that Mendelssohn cites here (brotherly love, annihilation of egoism). But the Mendelssohns were hardly typical, as the young musician himself had discovered on many occasions. He cannot honestly have been convinced that religious superstition (belief in the devil) was entirely a thing of the past and that humanitarianism already existed everywhere and no longer needed to be preached. Perhaps he simply could not become accustomed to the Saint-Simonians' willingness to attack such problems head-on, even insolently; certainly no social or political movement back home in Prussia would have dared to do so.

The remaining negative remarks in the letter of 14 January, truly negative ones now, refer to two basic issues: the movement's views on the social role of art, and the movement's authoritarian tendencies. Mendelssohn attacks first the movement's aesthetic views as promulgated in what he calls "an appeal to all people by Olinde Rodrigues." The brochure in question is clearly the *Appel* that Rodrigues wrote in November 1831 to announce a fund-raising bond drive. The specific passage to which Mendelssohn must have been referring has been cited in Chapter 7; it contains the very phrases that annoyed him: about composing better than Rossini and Beethoven, painting better than Raphael and David, and building "temples of peace." Rodrigues's offhand attitude toward Beethoven must have been particularly distasteful.

The main idea Rodrigues was pushing in this passage was that—as Mendelssohn put it—artists should "henceforth devote their art to this religion." The Saint-Simonian leaders were particularly eager to find what we might call a "house composer," but they would no doubt have been happy to receive artistic support of a more modest or conventional nature—a benefit concert, for example, such as Berlioz seems to have been planning on their behalf in July 1831, or an oratorio or opera based on a libretto that even faintly echoed their sentiments. It is not inconceivable that Mendelssohn would have given a public performance or composed a piece in honor of a social movement. Indeed, in 1828 he had already written a "Humboldt" Cantata for a major gathering of scientists and doctors, and the text—using images not unlike those favored by the Saint-Simonians—conjured up visions of a blessed future in which men together harness the forces of nature to "shape and build the magnificent world." Nonetheless, the disrespectful tone in the Saint-Simonians' approaches to him—their condescending flattery that he complained of—would in itself have gone far toward souring any enthusiasm he might have felt.

This lack of respect toward artists was symptomatic of a more general authoritarian tendency that Mendelssohn noted during the meeting at which Olinde presided and which he found perhaps even more disturbing. The very existence in this religious movement of a few infallible Fathers, who gave orders to their subordinates, "praised and blamed them," and called on them to confess their errors, went so directly against Mendelssohn's individualistic, liberal-Lutheran ideals that he could not possibly have remained interested for long.

The final break, though, came for other reasons, which Mendelssohn hinted at in his second letter (22 January). Rodrigues, he wrote, made certain "disclosures" that so "shocked" him that he resolved never again to visit Rodrigues or "the other accomplices." This is harsh language. It suggests that Rodrigues, perhaps naïvely, had told Mendelssohn about the government's continuing attempt to prosecute the Saint-Simonians. (Indeed, matters were coming to a head; it was the very next morning that the troops shut down the movement's headquarters and lecture hall and confiscated their papers—Mendelssohn's Piano Quartet included!)

The other disclosure Rodrigues may have made and that would have been more than enough to occasion a violent reaction from Mendelssohn concerned sexual matters. The principle of the "rehabilitation of the flesh," despite its attractiveness to Liszt, David, Heine, and others, would surely have made him feel uneasy. (He was prudish about sex, and hedonism of any sort struck him as vaguely immoral.) Indeed, in recent months the movement had gone quite far in its interpretation of the principle; Duveyrier's article about the desirability of changing partners had appeared nine days before this last meeting between Mendelssohn and Rodrigues. What is more, several members of the movement were or had recently been involved in extramarital liaisons, including (as Rodrigues perhaps was beginning to suspect) Rodrigues's wife. What Mendelssohn would have thought of this we can only imagine, or perhaps—as seems likely—we do not need to imagine; we can read it in his letter of 22 January, the letter that documents the precise moment of impact in the collision between Mendelssohn and the Saint-Simonians.

Curiously, Mendelssohn came into contact again with Enfantin and his friends some ten years later. In 1842, Charles Duveyrier, desiring to establish himself as a librettist, wrote to Mendelssohn—who was by that point conductor of the Leipzig Gewandhaus Orchestra—to try to interest him in an opera libretto. On the face of it, he was making a perfectly reasonable gesture in proposing a collaboration with Mendelssohn. But the details and tone of his proposals reeked of the disrespect for art that Mendelssohn had objected to ten years earlier. Duveyrier at first suggested an opera on the life of the prophet

Muhammad, a subject that no doubt had for him the advantage of being both *religieux* and symbolic of the Saint-Simonians' continuing hope of cutting a canal through Suez to improve trade and international relations.[79] Mendelssohn replied that he was not interested; he wanted to write a more modest work, in three acts, for the German public.[80] Duveyrier assured him rather heavy-handedly that he understood "the political, moral, artistic, and religious reasons why Muhammad is more a Spanish or Italian subject than a German one," and he quickly came up with another suggestion: Schiller's *Jungfrau von Orléans,* whose heroine (Joan of Arc) embodies "patriotism, exaltation, simplicity, modesty."[81] Mendelssohn's response to Duveyrier's letter is not known.

A year later, Duveyrier, attempting to salvage the Joan-of-Arc project, wrote to suggest that the opera could stress the "marvelous" rather than the historical and that, in particular, the character Lionel could be transformed into "a true demon, a true amorous devil," citing the success of Scribe's libretto for Meyerbeer's *Robert le diable.*[82] Enfantin's close friend Arlès-Dufour also wrote, promising that—if Mendelssohn accepted the task—he would ask Enfantin's business associate Louis Jourdan to do the versification. Arlès-Dufour waxed poetic about the proposed subject: "Joan, the daughter of the people, she whom God raises above kings, princes and nobles"; Joan, who would be applauded not just by "the elite of a single city" but by "the people *en masse*" of all Europe. Furthermore, Arlès transmitted some comments of Enfantin, such as that "Joan would necessarily have an ecstatic vision of the future."[83] Mendelssohn must have been aghast at this onslaught of suggestions, instruction, and shards of Saint-Simonian philosophy, and nothing ever came of the project. Félicien David flourished under similar conditions; a stronger artistic personality could only have felt stifled.

In 1845, when David was making a concert tour of Europe conducting *Le Désert,* Mendelssohn—to his credit—received the young Frenchman with all possible kindness. David was preceded by letters of recommendation from Enfantin and from Duveyrier.[84] Enfantin closed his letter with "the feelings of religious admiration that are wished for you by this old friend of some good friends of your father," meaning the Rodrigues and d'Eichthal families.[85] Enfantin could not resist inserting, and underlining, a bit of the old dogma ("les sentiments de *religieuse* admiration"), but his main appeal was to Mendelssohn's sense of loyalty to family and social circle. There was no longer any use pretending. Enfantin recognized clearly enough that Mendelssohn, despite all efforts at converting him, had never been, and would never be "a raging Saint-Simonian."

BERLIOZ AND THE SAINT-SIMONIANS

When Enfantin wrote to Fournel on 26 October 1830 about the prominent figures who were "approaching" the movement (see the passage cited above in the section on Nourrit), he mentioned three musicians: two performers of high repute (Liszt and Nourrit) and one musician who was no performer at all, Hector Berlioz (1803–69). That he should have considered Berlioz an important "catch," and that he could refer to him by last name only and in one breath with Liszt and Nourrit, reveals how much this young composer's reputation had grown in recent months (especially after his winning the Prix de Rome in July). But the letter is even more important as the earliest testimony—however brief—of Berlioz's interest in the Saint-Simonians. Fortunately we also have a second and more detailed document of Berlioz's attraction, a letter that he himself addressed to Charles Duveyrier the following July. From these two letters, both of them rather neglected until recent years, we can extract the basic story of Berlioz's short-lived but passionate interest in the movement. For further clarification we must then draw on his other letters and writings, the history of the movement itself, and our knowledge of the Saint-Simonian activities of Nourrit, Liszt, Hiller, and Tajan-Rogé.[86]

Enfantin's letter, in its main lines, is perfectly straightforward. It indicates quite simply that Berlioz became interested in the movement in the days or weeks before 26 October 1830. Berlioz's letter to Duveyrier is a more detailed and puzzling document and requires substantially more explication. Berlioz wrote it on 28 July 1831, several months after arriving in Italy to fulfill the residency requirement of the Prix de Rome. The preceding December he had gained public acclaim with the premiere of the *Symphonie fantastique* and had won the hand of Camille Moke. In January 1831 he set out for Italy, where he received the news that his fiancée had married another man (Camille Pleyel). Furious, he headed back toward France to kill the faithless one and her husband (and to crown the slaughter with his own suicide), but he stopped at Nice and, after a period of rest, regained enough control to return to Rome. There he wrote the following lines to Duveyrier.

> My dear friend, or rather my dear father! Your words were not lost on me; the fervor and passion with which you preached the doctrine to me at first startled [*étonné*] rather than moved me; but in this case, as in all other things, one must let time act. Since I left you, new storms have broken over me; vileness and turpitude had plotted my undoing; as you have perhaps heard, Camille has married Pleyel, in spite of the strongest, most sacred bonds, to the detriment of her honor and reputation. But no more about that. Since my return to Rome I have met one *of us*, Cendrier the architect. We have often spoken of you and Saint-Simon. His cool, calm conviction made me think a lot. I read eagerly a stack of issues of the *Globe* which someone lent me recently, and my last doubts have been completely removed. In all that concerns *the political reorganization of Society* I am convinced today that Saint-Simon's plan is the only true and only complete one, but I must tell

you that my ideas have not changed a bit in all that concerns the supernatural [*le surhumain*], God, the soul, an afterlife, etc., etc. I suppose this does not need to prevent me from joining my hopes and efforts to yours for the betterment of the most numerous and poorest class, for the natural ordering of talents, and for the destruction of all kinds of privileges, which, hidden like vermin in the folds of the social body, have up to now paralyzed all efforts which attempt to provide a cure.

Write to me about this; I will at once answer you and let you know my ideas about the ways in which you can use me musically in the Great Work when I return to Paris. I can assure you that, until that moment, which I await with all my heart, I shall, as much as it is in my power, seek to spread among the Artists I frequent the conviction with which I am penetrated. Adieu,—I wait and hope![87]

The letter indicates that Berlioz had one or more conversations with Duveyrier toward the end of 1830 and that the last of them probably took place shortly before his departure for Italy (since Duveyrier appears to know about Berlioz's betrothal to Camille). Berlioz was "startled" (perhaps even repelled)[88] by Duveyrier's passionate attempts to convince him of the importance of the doctrine. Upon his return to Rome in June, though, Berlioz met the architect Alexis Cendrier (a fellow Prix de Rome recipient), whose calmer reasoning was more persuasive.[89] After reading "a stack of issues of the *Globe*," Berlioz took pen in hand to reestablish contact with Duveyrier, to announce his conversion, to offer his help as a musician when he returned to Paris, and to say that he would in the meantime spread the word among his artist friends. Berlioz made plain to Duveyrier his admiration for the Saint-Simonians' social doctrines but also his distaste for their new religion and specifically for their mystical metaphysics. (It seems that he had gotten wind of Enfantin's ideas on reincarnation, transmigration of souls, and the like, though these were not yet published.) And, perhaps significantly, he left unmentioned the movement's well-known views on the social and religious role of art.

Two other things about this letter are apparent. One is that for Berlioz, or anybody else in Italy in 1831, to write such (predominantly) favorable sentiments about the Saint-Simonians was a significant, even bold move; indeed, the letter was briefly intercepted by the Austrian censor (he made a copy and labeled it "lettre d'un Saint-Simonien"), as a result of which Metternich wrote a letter warning his ambassador in Rome not to let this dangerous musician enter Austrian territory.[90] The other thing is that Berlioz was writing to Duveyrier in a spontaneous burst of enthusiasm, perhaps,[91] but not without reflection. He took pains to express clearly and forcefully what he did not like in the doctrine, as well as what he did. But the letter also raises a number of questions, of which we shall treat four here: (1) How much earlier can we trace Berlioz's interest in the doctrine? (2) How did he come into contact with

Duveyrier or, more generally, with the Saint-Simonians? (3) What kind of musical assistance did Berlioz plan to offer the movement? (4) What became of his Saint-Simonian "conviction" in later months and years?

1. We have frustratingly few indications of Berlioz's social ideas in his early years. In one passage of his *Mémoires* he recalled that he used to discuss philosophy and religion with his teacher Lesueur and that they reached agreement only in their common admiration for Napoleon. Twice in early letters home he mentioned that numerous "ideas" were preoccupying him, but there is no reason to believe that either time he was necessarily referring to political and social ideas rather than, say, musical projects.[92] Only in the weeks after the July Revolution of 1830 (in which he took part briefly) did he begin to refer to politics, speaking proudly of the battle "for the conquest of our liberties." He wrote to his mother that he rarely engaged in political discussion although he had "quite a deeply-held political view"; this phrase in itself, however vague, suggests that his support of and participation in the Revolution was based on a wider concern for social progress and reform. In short, Berlioz was a young liberal—or perhaps left-liberal—of the July Revolution and thus potentially receptive to Saint-Simonian ideology, but before October 1830 there are no definite signs of contact between him and the movement or even of his interest in related ideas.

2. It was at this point, we recall, that Berlioz "approached" the movement. No matter how concretely or tentatively one interprets Enfantin's use of the verb *s'approcher*, it seems undeniable that in late October 1830 Berlioz's interest had already been kindled and he was in contact with one or more members or close associates.[93] Who or what sparked that interest and how was the contact made? Perhaps Duveyrier was already acting as representative. If so, the first meeting between the two would have been easily arranged, since Duveyrier had plentiful contacts in Parisian theatrical and literary circles. (His brother was the successful librettist Mélesville, whose *Zampa,* with music by Hérold, would bring him yet another shiny wreath the next year. Duveyrier himself would write his first libretto in 1834 and achieve co-immortality with Scribe in 1855 for Verdi's *Les Vêpres siciliennes.*) Also, Berlioz's close friend Ferdinand Hiller was being drawn to the movement sometime in 1830–31 (although not necessarily this early) and might have introduced him to Duveyrier or other members. Yet another possible intermediary was Dominique Tajan-Rogé, whom Berlioz had apparently known at the Conservatoire, who, as we have seen (Chapter 8), became actively associated with the movement in 1830 and who was to remain a faithful friend of Berlioz's in later years (Chapter 13).

Enfantin's letter also suggests that either Liszt or Nourrit might have served as intermediaries, for he writes "Listz [*sic*], Berlioz, Nourrit s'approchent de nous," as if they constituted a little group of three. Of course he may have just lumped them together because they were the three interested musicians of some renown. Indeed, Berlioz states in his *Mémoires* that he did not know Liszt until 4 December. But perhaps Berlioz was simplifying for effect, writing "Nous ne nous connaissions pas encore" (a vague enough phrase) when the truth was something like "we had never really got to know each other well until that night." Concerning Berlioz's early relationship with Nourrit there is even less documentation, but these two great Gluckists may certainly have met on a number of occasions.

The possibility also exists that Duveyrier was not involved at the beginning in any way. Enfantin indicated earlier in the same letter that Duveyrier had recently left on a mission to the provinces (or returned from one);[94] he thus may have been out of town during the beginning stages of Berlioz's contact with the Saint-Simonians. If this was the case, then perhaps Berlioz simply went off to a lecture or soiree with one of the four friends already cited, or with one of the many nonmusicians he must have known who, intrigued by the sect, had become active followers of their gatherings. Or perhaps Berlioz, having read something by or about the Saint-Simonians, took the initiative himself. In the end the question is relatively unimportant. One way or the other the contact was made, and by December Duveyrier was trying—rather too heatedly, it seems—to convince him of the importance of the doctrine and probably of the role an artist could play.

3. Soon after the talk (or talks) with Duveyrier, Berlioz traveled to Italy, had his crisis over Camille, returned to Rome, talked with Cendrier, read the *Globe,* and wrote the letter to his dear Saint-Simonian father in which he offered to let the movement "use me musically" upon his return to Paris. From these words of Berlioz's—"m'employer musicalement"—we can more or less safely assume that he was considering writing a piece of music to aid the Saint-Simonian cause in some way. (The alternatives were few; he was neither a performer nor, at this point, an experienced conductor.) But just what kind of piece may he have had in mind? It could well have been some kind of relatively simple choral music, possibly with passages for soloists, modeled after the hymns and songs of the French Revolution—something along the lines of what he himself had done in the men's choruses of the 1829 collection sub-sequently known as *Irlande* and would again do later in life in a number of occasional choruses bearing religious or "social" texts (notably the *Hymne pour la consécration du nouveau tabernacle, Le Temple universel,* and the *Chant des chemins de fers* [1846], whose text, with its cries of "Industrie!" was the most overtly Saint-Simonian of any that Berlioz set).

It is conceivable, though, that Berlioz was thinking of somehow publicly associating the Saint-Simonians with his projected dramatic oratorio, *Le Dernier Jour du monde,* whose plot he had sketched less than a month earlier in a letter to his friend Humbert Ferrand.[95] There are striking similarities between this scenario for *Le Dernier Jour* and the ideology of the Saint-Simonians; both envision a small band of prophets leading the attack on a depraved and vicious society ruled by a small, selfish class (or ruled, in Berlioz's version, by an insatiable tyrant living in the midst of gluttonous, Sardanapalan sensual excess). But the similarities, striking though they are, do not mean that Berlioz intended the oratorio as a votive offering to Saint-Simon, nor do they even necessarily show a direct "influence" of Saint-Simonian doctrine. More likely, the resemblance derives from the fact that Berlioz conceived *Le Dernier Jour* during the same period in which he was feeling an affinity with Saint-Simonian thought. Both the oratorio and the attraction to Saint-Simonism were nourished on Berlioz's own feeling of isolation in post-July France and especially in the musical world, his feeling of being an unheeded prophet of the true musical gods, in constant battle against academic sterility and Italianate superficiality. It is not by chance that Berlioz, in the same letter to Ferrand of 3 July 1831, used the Saint-Simonian catchword *industriel* (and underlined it) to castigate his fellow art and music students in Rome: "The air I share with the *industrials* of the Académie is unpleasant to my lungs; I am going where I can breathe a purer one [i.e., to Subiaco]."[96] His "approach" to Saint-Simonism was from its inception linked to the historical moment and to his personal situation.

4. Jacques Barzun, the great Berlioz scholar, has humorously remarked that Berlioz's espousal of the faith lasted "a short time—maybe half a day, maybe half an hour."[97] There is a good kernel of truth in this. After Berlioz sent off the letter to Duveyrier, he seems to have done little for the movement. We know for sure that his enthusiasm began to wane by the end of the year, if not earlier. He apparently still read the *Globe* for a time but did not like what he found in it, for in a letter to Hiller of 1 January 1832 he objected to an article which the paper had recently printed: "I had seen a review of your concert in the *Globe,* which gave you a rather good article, a bit philanthropico-mystical [*mezzo philanthropico-mystique*], and claims that you are a graduate of the Paris Conservatoire."[98] The passage that annoyed Berlioz was obviously the closing one, reproduced in Chapter 7. Berlioz must not have liked the vague exhortatory tone (too fervent, like Duveyrier), the insultingly superior attitude toward Beethoven and toward Rossini's *Barber,* and, perhaps most of all, the idea—basic to Saint-Simonian aesthetics—that composers need to find "an inspiring thought" if they expect to have an honored "place" in the society of the future. Berlioz must have felt as uncomfortable with these facile value judgments as Mendelssohn was when the Saint-Simonians loudly lamented that his great talents were going to waste. (Mendelssohn was, significantly enough, encountering the movement just at this same period—December 1831.) Berlioz sensed in the Hiller review and perhaps in other items in recent issues of the *Globe* that the movement was veering away from the concrete social concerns that he had spoken of in his letter to Duveyrier. And, true enough, the mystical strain he had always disliked was now in the ascendant and soon would take forms that Berlioz could hardly have imagined, much less supported, when writing his enthusiastic letter to Duveyrier in July 1831. Once Saint-

Simonism came to mean hierarchy, revelation, Ménilmontant, and the Female Messiah, not to speak of illegal (and reputedly immoral) activity, Berlioz had no more use for the movement.

But though it is probably true that Berlioz now dissociated himself totally from the movement—he evidently did not restore contact with Duveyrier when he returned to Paris in November 1832—it is also true that for many years he felt a lingering affection for parts of the doctrine and that his critical writings reflect aspects of Saint-Simonian aesthetics.[99] In particular, his view of Beethoven as a great humanitarian is—as Schrade has noted—couched in Saint-Simonian terms,[100] as is, to some extent, the musical utopia (Euphonia) described in his *Evenings with the Orchestra*.[101] His musical works, too, are rich in social and political overtones that deserve to be carefully sifted and examined.[102] But if an examination of influences such as these lies beyond the scope of this study, Berlioz's explicit statements about the movement can be documented rather simply.

Berlioz retained a basic sympathy for the Saint-Simonian ideal. This was not a question of personal involvement; the relationships he had with David, Duveyrier, Barrault, Louis Jourdan, and Michel Chevalier in later years were superficial and primarily professional in nature. (Duveyrier, in a letter to Berlioz of 17 December 1844, did try to turn Berlioz's rave review of *Le Désert* into a gesture of solidarity with Enfantin, but Berlioz was apparently not receptive.[103]) In his letters he even made occasional jokes about David's "infantile music" (*musique enfantine*—a pun on "Enfantin") and the cliquish behavior of "the former Saint-Simonians."[104] And a passage in the *Mémoires* reflects his lasting distaste for Enfantin's papal pretensions and the overheated rhetoric of his circle. (The young Berlioz, proselytizing for the cult of Gluck, of which he is "the pontiff," drags his friends to the Opéra and revives their lagging fervor "with sermons worthy of the Saint-Simonians."[105])

But the more positive side of his feelings shows up in a passage in *Les Grotesques de la musique,* one of the most touching in his prose works. Before the text proper, Berlioz inserts two imaginary letters, first a missive from the chorus members of the Opéra to him, then an "author's reply." In response to the complaints of the overworked *choristes,* Berlioz meditates on the Saint-Simonian vision of a world of fraternal love, where each would be placed and rewarded according to his ability—not, as Berlioz had so often been, held back and punished for that very ability—and where work would become a pleasure rather than a burden.[106] He begins with a melancholy conjugation. "Vous travaillez, je travaille, nous travaillons pour vivre": "You work, I work, we work in order to live; and you live, I live, we live in order to work. The Saint-Simonians claimed to know how to make work attractive; they kept the secret well; I can assure you, that kind of work is as unknown to me as it is to yourselves."[107] The passage is ironic but regretful, perhaps even a bit admiring.

The fraternal utopia was a dream . . . but a dream that Berlioz had shared for a time and could never completely forget.

A FORCE FOR CHANGE

One is naturally struck by the diversity in these six stories, but at a deeper level one sees common features as well. Most notable is the simple fact that all six musicians had close contact with the leading social movement of the day, had feelings about it ranging from moderately strong to intense, and acted on those feelings in various ways. We often are led to believe that the dominating factor in the life of the Romantic artist was his isolation, an isolation that was in part forced upon him (by the uncomprehending, philistine society in which he had the misfortune to live) and in part freely chosen (as a way of maintaining his independence and finding his own creative voice). Much less often do we hear mentioned a factor that was perhaps just as important: his need for group activity and for a feeling of community, his urge to identify with the larger society (or at least with segments of it) and to be accepted by it. True, we are accustomed to thinking of Romantic artists—perhaps especially those in Paris—as congregating in groups, schools, and "movements": the Delacroix circle, the Hugo circle, the poets of the *cénacles,* the academic architects, the composers of grand opera, the composer-pianists, the proponents of program music. But even in these cases we too often tend to focus on stylistic preferences and technical innovations (Delacroix's experiments with color; Hugo's departures from classical norms of diction and versification; Meyerbeer's deployment of massive vocal and orchestral forces; Berlioz's and Liszt's use of thematic transformation) rather than the urges and dreams that led to those stylistic choices and that not only bonded members of a group together but also bonded them to people active in the other arts, and to the world outside.

Even if we do take the "urges" seriously and try to take their measure, we may too hastily assume that they operated only on a subconscious level. Georg Knepler, for example, argues that musicians of stature are in general more aware of the political and social currents of the day than we think but cautions that they gain this awareness mainly in indirect ways and only rarely through reading or direct personal contact with the agents of social change.[108] Perhaps this warning is well taken for earlier centuries, or our own, but the evidence is beginning to accumulate that, during much of the nineteenth century, composers and other prominent musicians (such as Nourrit) were often deeply immersed—on a conscious if at times also deeply emotional level—in the events and concerns of the day. Beethoven apparently admired the ideas of Babeuf and other leading participants in the French Revolution, and Schumann, Verdi, Wagner, and even Offenbach were quite aware of shifting tensions on the social and political scenes.[109] Seen in this context, the Saint-Simonian interest of our six musicians seems no fluke but rather a particularly intense manifestation of a widespread trend toward greater involvement in the life of society.

Of course, the Saint-Simonian movement did not win any of the six over to "the cause." But it had done something perhaps more important: it had reached out to them at a time when they were searching, and had encouraged them to listen, to think, and to speak. Admittedly, the encouragement was not always presented in the quiet, tolerant, open-minded tone that some of them might have preferred. But stubborn dogmatism and overheated rhetoric can in their own way be surprisingly effective tools for jostling minds that have grown complacent, as the cases of Mendelssohn and Berlioz attest. In short, all six stories presented here testify to the movement's success at making itself—for a few years—a central factor in daily musical and artistic life, a catalyst for change, an agent for what we would today call "consciousness raising."

What is more, the consciousness being fostered was not purely a social one. The movement somehow managed to convey to these six musicians (and even more powerfully to David and the other "member" musicians) that art, too, must be transformed, must do more than amuse the privileged classes. There can be few precedents, especially in France (where the status of a musician was perhaps lower even than in England or Germany), for Liszt's remarkable essays on the demeaning social position of the artist or for Nourrit's willingness to proclaim his feelings about the need to restore musico-dramatic integrity and moral power to the operatic stage. Even Nourrit's headier visions, and Berlioz's, mark a new willingness on the part of musicians to take responsibility for their art and its relationship to its audience. Like the best teachers in any age, the Saint-Simonians caused many a musician to reflect on great matters—artistic and social—and to clarify his own position. It was not the least of their many achievements.

10

MUSIC AT THE MÉNILMONTANT RETREAT (1832)

THE ROLE OF MUSIC AT MÉNILMONTANT

The Retraite de Ménilmontant shared certain features with the *phalanstère,* the idealized communal settlement proposed by Fourier in his writings of the 1820s; unlike the *phalanstère,* though, the Retreat was never intended to be a lasting, self-sufficient, and relatively self-enclosed community.[1] More than the Fourierists and other groups of utopian socialists, the Saint-Simonians felt strongly that their mission required them to maintain constant contact with the larger society and its leading figures: men of state, captains of industry, and great movers of minds. Besides, the forty disciples could not be expected to submit themselves forever to a regime of celibacy and asceticism. Those who were married had been obliged to leave their beloved wives behind. (Cécile Fournel and Clorinde Rogé took the separation very hard but soon decided that they as well would devote themselves to the doctrine and the cause of women.) The move to Ménilmontant was a brilliant makeshift,[2] a move that would buy time, close the ranks, and serve as a "repudiation of all slanderous interpretations of the call for enfranchisement of women."[3]

On 22 April and succeeding days some forty members of the movement took up residence in the house, and Enfantin ordered the gates to the world closed until 1 June. Unlike at rue Monsigny, there were no domestics at the Ménilmontant Retreat; the disciples themselves planted, cooked, did laundry, and maintained the house and grounds. Enfantin's aim was to turn the forty disciples into apostles—to produce, as he put it, a "compact and unbreakable kernel" whose every act would lead, and lead others, toward "the new life." In order to create true apostles there was much work to be done, much learning, and much cultivation of ceremony and dogma. Enfantin explained to a doubting disciple:

> [For the *apostolic nature* to develop,] we first had to leave our Monsigny shell in which we were suffocating; next we had to leave behind us our habits of being in command and of being idle; to build our bodies through work and exercise, and our voices through singing, our ears through harmony; nourish

123

our spirits with knowledge of the *world,* help our children to see God in the HEAVENLY BODIES, on the surface of the globe and in its *entrails,* speak of MUSIC and ASTRONOMY, ARCHITECTURE and GEOGRAPHY, *poetry* and *geology.* From these things will come the *hymn,* the *temple,* and the *Genesis.*

Have you sometimes dreamed of those great words: *language, prayer, sacrifice, gospel, catechism, costumes, ceremonies?* All that cannot be invented on command, but it can all be prepared.[4]

Singing, music lessons, discussions about music, the creation of a new liturgy—all this was an integral part of Enfantin's plan from the start. Music was not just an "authorized distraction" at Ménilmontant, as d'Allemagne puts it,[5] but the prelude to a new universal religion, with its own rites and musical life. "Let the new art take shape," wrote Michel Chevalier: "Let POETRY, COSTUME, MUSIC be implanted in the apostles' work. Art is the lever with which we shall move the heart of humanity, i.e., the *women, artists,* and *proletarians.* Art will cause us to be *loved* and *admired;* our current works have more often brought us respect and esteem.[6]"

The music at Ménilmontant was the work of Félicien David. For years the Saint-Simonians (and Saint-Simon before them) had been pressing for a new cult in which music and the arts would serve a social role. The leaders had expended much energy attempting to solicit young, enthusiastic artists and musicians—Berlioz, Hiller, Mendelssohn, Liszt—to serve as priestly propagandists, but their searching was always in vain. With David's arrival, the search ended and the months and years of theorizing about the role of art quickly began to bear fruit. The existence of a Saint-Simonian composer now allowed and encouraged the movement to develop its own liturgy.

True, David did not act alone in the shaping of the music at Ménilmontant. Tajan-Rogé, assisted by Duveyrier and Lambert, helped him build a trained choir out of the engineers, journalists, former soldiers, and others who had chosen the life of an apostle. But Rogé and the others were not composers. The music that echoed in the garden of Ménilmontant during the first, secluded weeks, the music that later impressed the tens of thousands who came to view the public ceremonies, was David's.

How important his contribution was can be seen in the remarks of other members of the Retreat. In July, Michel Chevalier, describing life at Ménilmontant, wrote: "Singing holds a large place in our life. David and Roger [*sic*] are teaching us under the direction of Duveyrier. David has composed some excellent pieces of music which are sung in chorus."[7] Enfantin, looking back on the days of the Retreat, evoked the music with obvious affection: "And the songs so sweet of my David / Kept far [from us] all gloomy thoughts."[8] More vivid still are the words of one of the singers in the choir, Auguste Chevalier (younger brother of Michel):

> We all sang with feeling and ardor the pieces which David
> had made with feeling and ardor. We all felt our blood rise
> and our arteries beat loud when we struck up those religious
> hymns in which we asked the rich to love the poor, and the
> latter to await patiently the happiness which we were de-
> manding for them.[9]

Even the public came to consider the hymns of the Saint-Simonians one of
their most characteristic features. *Le Figaro,* in a satire on the breakup of the
Ménilmontant Retreat (December 1832), claimed that the Saint-Simonians had
stopped singing the glory of Enfantin and fraternity and were now singing
the praises of good cuisine.[10] Ten years later, and in a more sympathetic vein,
the socialist Louis Blanc could not discuss the apostles of Ménilmontant without
noting that David's pieces "served to exalt their souls while charming their
labors."[11] And the composer Hippolyte Chelard, in a comic opera first performed in 1844, twelve years after the Retreat, gave his ensemble of Saint-
Simonian women an *invocation à Saint-Simon* whose text is a lethal parody of
David's *Hymne à Saint-Simon* and the Ménilmontant choruses.[12]

The music was indeed, as we shall see, an essential component in *la vie de
Ménilmontant.* But it was also formed by that life. The pieces David wrote
during the months of collective living on the outskirts of Paris faithfully reflect
the growing and waning enthusiasm of the apostles, reaching a high point in
June and July with a large number of ceremonial choruses and then tapering
off when the continued existence of the Retreat was threatened by the public
trials of Enfantin, Duveyrier, and Chevalier in August and October. Toward
the end of the year David wrote simple chansons, or as simple as his artistic
ambitions permitted, trying to conform to the changing needs of a movement
that was being forced to give up its fancy ceremonies and look to the road.
The change from polyphonic choruses to solo chansons is all the more striking
since David's compositional technique (and no doubt the choral skill of the
apostles) was maturing just at the point when the Retreat began to collapse.
His choruses were becoming more varied, with more independence of voices,
more use of contrast between solo voices and the choral body. David's comparatively simple chansons from late 1832 have their merits. But his heart must
have been in the choruses, such as the *Ronde* or the *Danse des astres,* for, as we
shall see later, it was along these lines that his career was to develop. His art
and the desires of the movement completely coincided only for one year, 1832.
But it was a productive and fascinating year.

ORGANIZATION OF MUSICAL LIFE AT MÉNILMONTANT

The apostles at Ménilmontant were by no means a community of equals. The
younger or less experienced members were put in the care of older or more

reliable ones. David and the more musical, artistic, and literary of the young disciples were generally assigned to those "fathers" most interested in the arts. David, his friend Justus, and Rogé were among the charges of Duveyrier; Barrault was *père* to Bergier (who would write the text for David's *Appel*) and to the chansonnier Mercier; and Rousseau and Pouyat (also future text writers) were entrusted to d'Eichthal and Lambert, respectively.[13] (Duveyrier was probably something of an amateur musician[14] and certainly an eager, facile writer; at the Retreat he was known as "Charles, poète de Dieu." Barrault was a former professor of rhetoric and a brilliant public speaker. D'Eichthal was bred on music and classical literature, and Lambert had an absorbing fascination with questions of acoustics and harmony.)

Duveyrier was named *chef de musique;* this gave him the final responsibility for all musical activities. David does not seem to have resented Duveyrier's authority, but Rogé, a far more experienced musician than David, later admitted that he had been deeply bitter over Duveyrier's appointment.[15] Rogé should have been able to predict that, consistent with the aims of the Retreat, a member of the Collège would be chosen to oversee the development of the musical aspects of the new *culte*. Instead, he had naïvely construed the delegation of work according to "capacity" as meaning that Rogé himself would be put in charge of all musical activities.

Music at Ménilmontant consisted mainly of choral singing, the most basic (and cost- and time-effective) form of communal music making. In this regard the Retreat resembled many other religious and utopian communities of the nineteenth century (e.g., the Shakers and Harmonists in America). But, given the Saint-Simonians' particular attachment to the idea of using art as a "lever" to "stir the heart of humanity," it can scarcely be doubted that simple choral music was for them not just a necessity born of the peculiar situation at Ménilmontant but also a desirable first step in the development of a new universal musico-liturgical cult.

From the very first days of the Retreat, David and Rogé began organizing their choir. Stéphane Flachat reported to Holstein on 2 May: "David (the musician) and Rogé will teach us music. There are superb voices in the family, and I believe that soon we shall be singing very beautiful choruses."[16] Auguste Chevalier later recalled that only five of the twenty members of the choir had studied music before—and his five included David![17] By mid-July the choir involved, if we count David and Rogé, twenty-one members of the Retreat:

Dessus: Pol Justus, Auguste Chevalier, Auguste Broët, and Félix Tourneux.

First tenor: Jean Terson, Joseph Machereau, and Louis Désessarts.

Second tenor: Charles Lambert, René Holstein, and Antoine Ribes.

Bass: Charles Duveyrier, Antoine Ollivier, Achille Rousseau, Charles-Antoine Duguet, Jules Toché, Alexis Petit, Edouard Pouyat, Raymond Bonheur, and Alexandre Massol.[18]

An earlier list contains the names of three additional disciples who took part in the choir at least for a while,[19] giving a total of twenty-four of the forty *apostles,* an impressive figure that augured well for the *culte nouveau.*

Much of our information about the musical life of the Retreat comes from detailed accounts of important events that the movement published for propagandistic purposes during the course of 1832.[20] Although written, no doubt, under the close supervision of Enfantin and Chevalier,[21] they avoid rhetoric in favor of a detailed, almost stenographic chronicle of the day's events that is demonstrably reliable.[22] These accounts do not say much about the organization of rehearsals, but Auguste Chevalier states in his brief memoir that David accompanied the chorus at the piano while "the worthy and brave Roger [*sic*] ... taught us the [vocal] parts and directed the performance as a whole." Rogé may have done most of the recruiting and organizing, too.[23] How directly Duveyrier intervened in rehearsals, or even in the act of composition, cannot be known. But it seems likely that he supervised the writing of the texts (as we shall see below).

There were some instruments, too, at Ménilmontant. In addition to accompanying the choir at the piano, David probably improvised and played his own solo compositions. Strangely, Tajan-Rogé seems not to have played his cello, but d'Allemagne says that after the first weeks "some instruments (a horn and a trombone) were rented for accompanying the singing."[24] Presumably, the instruments were used to double the melody or a weaker lower voice, not to play independent lines. They might have been useful on occasions such as Talabot's funeral at Père-Lachaise Cemetery, when David could not bring his piano along. Brass instruments had other functions as well. The horn called the apostles to dinner and, as early as May, awakened them in the morning.[25] Later in the Retreat, Auguste Chevalier may have taken over these functions, for he reports that a gendarme guarding the house taught him to play the trumpet.

Although music played a large part in the life of Ménilmontant, there was much other work to be done as well. Most of the members of the family had a regular assignment. (Rogé and Justus, for example, seem to have tended the garden.) It is thus revealing of the high value placed on David's compositional and performing activities that he does not appear in any of the lists of various household "functions."[26] Apparently he was given free time to compose, much as the active propagandists were allowed to devote themselves to writing.[27] But David may also have made himself useful in ways that are unrecorded. We can safely infer that he improvised at the piano during meals and at other times, for he later announced for publication three sets of piano pieces written during the Retreat. Perhaps he also entertained his fellow disciples during their chores in the garden (we know that he brought the piano outdoors for various public ceremonies).

In addition, it is possible that David was assigned a humble nonmusical chore, namely shoemaking; that claim, for what it is worth, appears only in an obituary article on David.[28] But if David did learn to make a sturdy pair of shoes, it is unlikely that he enjoyed it. He would no doubt rather have been weeding the garden with his fellow sons of Duveyrier, for a desire to till the soil appears repeatedly in his later correspondence and he spent his last years tending a large yard of roses in Saint-Germain-en-Laye.

DAVID'S FIRST PIECES FOR MÉNILMONTANT; THE TAKING OF THE HABIT

David wrote three pieces during the few weeks that the members of the family spent in seclusion before they opened their gates again on 6 June. Each represents one of the three major types of composition that he would write over the coming months: (1) a strophic song with general ideological content, (2) a chorus set to a text that is either generally propagandistic (as in type 1) or keyed to an event in the daily ritual, and (3) a piece composed for one specific occasion. (The song type always uses rhymed verse; the other two types frequently use prose texts, rather like the motets of Catholic tradition, such as David had written in Aix.)

The first of these three pieces, the ideological song, is *Appel*. It is not a song in the sense of a *romance* or *mélodie* but a kind of highly developed chanson, with a more complex melody than one finds in the usual chanson tunes. The verse is set for solo voice (or unison choir) and piano, and the refrain expands to a full four-part setting. (This use of a choral refrain had a long tradition in France, dating back at least to the music of the French Revolution.[29] Berlioz used the same arrangement in several of his patriotic choruses.) In spite of the difficulties it poses to the amateur singer, *Appel* became one of the best-known musical numbers at the Retreat. The song was also one of the few Ménilmontant pieces to survive as an unaccompanied chanson during the dispersal of the Saint-Simonian missionaries into southern France. (See the publication history in Appendix D.2; *Appel* is reprinted below, Appendix E.2.)

▽ The text of *Appel* is by Bergier, a paving-stone laborer and former soldier who had taken part in the Saint-Simonian propaganda effort among the workers.[30] He took the apostolic habit on 6 June but is described as a "man of Paris" on 1 and 18 July, indicating that he had finally decided against life at Ménilmontant. The music is energetic, and even infectious in the refrain. At one point David's desire to reflect the idea of a passage from sorrow to hope led him to modulate to the minor and back ("Femmes, vos larmes [etc.] . . . un sort plus doux"). One would think that this passage, difficult enough to sing even with the harmony, must have proved quite a trial for the people who tried to learn *Appel* as an unaccompanied chanson. And yet *Appel* was an immediate and continuing popular success, an achievement that David would not
△ repeat until later in the year when he returned to writing this kind of chanson.

The first of the true choruses, and the first of David's pieces for daily, quasi-liturgical use (i.e., type 2), was the double composition *Avant le repas* and *Après le repas* (Appendix E.3). These settings were specifically designed to enhance the ritual significance of the daily meals. Michel Chevalier describes the biblical stateliness of these occasions.

> I wish I could have you witness one of the Ménilmontant dinners, which carry me away every time that I go there. . . . I would like to show you our Père, with his calm countenance, surrounded by his ten apostles, with the family to the right and left. I wish I could depict the beginnings of costumes and ritual, the music which opens and closes the meal, the tanned complexions, the physiognomies whose seriousness is increased by the majesty of a beard.[31]

Sometime during the Retreat, David wrote a second set of mealtime prayers (possibly to the same text), so the experiment of composing music to celebrate the events of daily life must have been thought a success.

Of the two sets of prayers, only the first can be reconstructed. Its text survives in ▽ two brochures published by the movement in 1832, and a musical setting that fits the text perfectly is found—with a totally different text—in David's collection *La Ruche harmonieuse* of some twenty years later. The reconstructed piece falls into two clear parts, each less than a minute long: an Andantino for before the meal and an Allegro vivace for after. Both parts begin and end in C but modulate widely in the middle. Sometimes this is quite effective, as when—in *Avant le repas*—David jumps suddenly from the key of E back to C for the words "Gloire à Dieu," a contrast heightened by the return of the opening barcarolle motive, now transformed into an assertive dotted figure. Similarly, the sequential passage in the middle of *Après le repas* gives a nice sense of directed motion (suggested perhaps by the text: "We shall give the world back that fruitful vigor"). But both passages then move on to hasty modulations (to A minor [?] and F major, respectively), which are immediately contradicted by the sudden appearance of the final tonic cadences in C major. It is interesting that both these ill-considered modulations coincide with lines addressed to Enfantin ("A vous, Père, merci" and "Père, Père"); in his music as in his life, David rather lost his head at the thought of his leader and spiritual father.

The choral writing in these pieces is skillful and sonorous, especially in the opening barcarolle-like phrases. (In the *Ruche* version, Charles Chaubet retexted this first section as an epithalamium; he was no doubt responding to the placid beauty of David's serenade-cum-hymn, and the choice of a wedding text is not even as un-Saint-Simonian as it may appear, for Chaubet speaks less of marriage than of sensual love, bliss, and flowers.) The chorus occasionally sings in unison at the beginnings of phrases and then expands satisfyingly into harmony; the chordal texture is also varied by a brief passage for the basses *soli*. David makes varied and effective use of inverted chords (recalling his *Hymne à Saint-Simon*) and brief patches of horn-call and pedal figures

(*Après*, mm. 4, 12) that will show up much more frequently and prominently in his later music. In *Avant le repas,* the melody at one point passes briefly to the second tenors and is then taken up by the basses *soli* as mentioned (mm. 7–8, 9–10). In contrast, *Après le repas* presents the melody entirely in the upper voice; perhaps because of this feature (and the partly rhymed text), *Après le repas,* in spite of its weak ending, was the only one of David's pieces associated with the daily ritual that became part of the chanson repertoire after the dispersal of the Retreat.

△ The other ceremonial chorus written before 6 June, *Le Retour du Père* (Appendix E.5), was written not for the daily ritual but for a specific event, the ceremony of 6 June itself. It is thus the first of David's "occasional" choruses (type 3). Enfantin had kept the forty disciples in seclusion with the intention that on 1 June the entire Saint-Simonian community and any interested observers would be invited to attend the ritual of the taking of the habit, whereby every worthy disciple would become an apostle. Because of rain, the ceremony was postponed until 6 June, and Enfantin decided to withdraw from his disciples on 3 June in order to settle some personal matters of his "past life" (and in order, one suspects, to return with great effect on the appointed day). He left instructions to guide the disciples in his absence, specifically calling for a new music worthy of apostles.

> Work, that all may be ready for my *return;* and MEDITATE upon
> our *future:* the NEW MAN is forming.
>   May GOD be IN you.
>   Charles! I want each of my children to have a *sound,* a WORD
> to SING the *glory of GOD* and his OWN *worth.*[32]

During the three days that Enfantin was away from Ménilmontant, the disciples cleaned the house and constructed ceremonial paths in the garden, and those who were in the choir learned a new piece for the occasion, *Le Retour du Père* (later known as *Salut*). Much of the day before Enfantin's return was spent rehearsing—as he had instructed—various solemn processions.[33] On 6 June Enfantin appeared before the assembled family and was greeted by the new piece, a chorus in praise of God and the new apostles (as Enfantin had requested) but even more so of Enfantin himself. The account suggests that Le Père was not displeased by this added emphasis:

> Le Père steps forth, slowly, his head bare. A severe majesty
> is upon his face.
>   He has barely appeared when a part of the family [i.e., the
> choir] greets him with the song:
>   Salut, Père, salut,
>   Salut et gloire à Dieu.
>   Le Père enters the circle of the Ménilmontant family, where
> those walking with him take a place. He casts his gaze silently
> upon it [the circle of disciples]. His children, from whom he

had been separated for three days, quiver with a joy that is keen, serious, exalted, and deep. A religious emotion can be seen on everyone's face and in everyone's bearing.[34]

David's chorus has nothing of the chanson about it. It is laid out in several sections ▽ that contrast in key and tempo and reflect the spirit of the various segments of the prose text. The opening (and closing) material, directly addressed to Le Père, is entitled "Acclamation" in the score and, after a unison fanfare ("Salut, Père, salut"), is written in strict chordal style, with the melody in the top voice. There follow a modulatory recitative, sung and accompanied in bare octaves, and a longer Vivace, mainly chordal but with some brief staggered entries of voice pairs, in praise of *le peuple* and *les femmes* (this last in the major mode). The music then changes to a majestic Andante in 3/4 (and C major) as the singers announce, ceremoniously and more or less chordally, their desire to wear the costume of an apostle (*l'homme nouveau*), and the piece concludes with a repeat of the "Acclamation." The harmony throughout is effective, with occasional modal features (lowered seventh degree in G minor and even G major: mm. 4 and 33 of the central section, beginning "Le peuple a faim") that seem to derive, as often also in Berlioz, from a predominant concern for melodic integrity.

In places the text is plainly occasional, and David—or one of the other Saint-Simonians—soon revised the text to make it appropriate to any occasion (e.g., "nous *portons* . . ." in place of "nous *attendons* l'habit nouveau"); the title of the piece was quickly replaced by one drawn from the opening words: *Salut.* Thus emended, the piece was performed on 17 and 18 July—at Enfantin's request—and many other times as well, including (Pellarin informs us) at the ceremonious entry of Le Père into the dining room each evening.[35] (One suspects that at times only the "Acclamation" was performed, since its music is simpler than that of the other sections and its text praises Le Père more directly.) The chorus even survived the dispersal of the Retreat, for it was included in one of the propagandistic songbooks of 1833 (see Appendix B.1). David later used the opening measures again ("Acclamation" and unison recitative, mm. 1–22) in his oratorio *Moïse au Sinaï,* at Enfantin's request (see Chapter 12), and he salvaged the rest for his *Ruche harmoniuese* collection by writing a new, much superior opening and closing section and having Charles Chaubet patch together a new text, *Le Chant des moissonneurs.*   △

The ceremony on 6 June was of course only secondarily important for Enfantin's return and David's chorus. The main event was the abolition of the former Saint-Simonian hierarchy through the taking of the habit. The habit in question included a loose blue jacket and, under that, a white vest that, because it fastened at the back, could only be donned with the aid of another, thus serving as a twice-daily reminder of the "sentiment of association."[36] The entire costume is visible to some extent in Machereau's cover engraving for some copies of David's choruses (plate 13) and more clearly in Bonheur's portrait of David done at Ménilmontant (frontispiece)[37] and numerous popular engravings of the apostles.[38] It was intended to serve as a visible sign of belief; when the apostles left the Retreat, it would announce their devotion to the cause of women and the people. A similar motivation had led the apostles to let their beards grow, an unusual practice at the time[39] and one that must have flattered their biblical pretensions, although in the public mind it seems only to have reinforced their image as either uncontrolled sensualists or ridiculous clowns.

Anyone who took the habit was making a firm commitment to the movement and to Enfantin. Le Père himself took pains to present the whole event as a transition between authoritarian and egalitarian relations within the movement. When Talabot, distributing the costumes at the ceremony, presented him with a velvet belt, he handed it back theatrically, saying, "I asked you for a *leather* belt, like that of my children, and I was right; this one does not suit me." Still decisions had to be made, and Enfantin kept on making them.

The most pressing question, of course, was who should henceforth serve as a representative of the movement, more specifically which of the disciples would be allowed to take the habit. In theory the movement welcomed anybody who expressed sufficient desire and felt ready to take on the responsibilities of apostleship. In practice, though, the decision rested with Enfantin, who had to judge whether the disciple had actually demonstrated those qualities of desire and readiness. Enfantin exercised this judgment in various ways. To begin with, those at the Retreat were already a hand-picked group; they had been invited to accompany Enfantin to Ménilmontant.[40] Even those who had for weeks been participating in the Retreat (or serving the movement in some equally valued function, such as the direction of one of the proselytization centers) could not be sure that Enfantin would welcome their continued presence on 6 June. And in fact, when that day came, Enfantin more or less told some (publicly) to get out or, in the case of Alexis Petit, to come back later.

It is revealing to compare Enfantin's brutal treatment of Caboche that afternoon with the unquestioning welcome that greeted David when each stepped forward, hoping to be raised to the rank of apostle. Caboche was one of the few disciples that day who was not seeking to enter the Retreat but to be permitted to continue working for the movement "out in the world."

> Le Père.—They are fighting in the Faubourg Saint-Antoine. *Caboche,* are you sure you have all the *strength,* all the *virtue* necessary to direct this center that I have entrusted to you and to show yourself in the midst of a fighting people?
> *Caboche.*—Yes, Père.
> Le Père.—I do not believe it, and I would prefer that you admit it publicly.
> *Caboche (after a moment of reflection).*—I would need a man with me.
> Le Père.—That is not the issue. I ask you once more if you believe yourself worthy of representing—at this moment, in the faubourg that you are directing, in the midst of an armed

people—the peace-loving family which announces what we announce.

   Caboche (hesitantly).—But . . . Père, it is not yet time.

   Le Père.—I am not asking you if the faubourg is ready but if you are ready.

   Caboche.—Not today, Père.

   Le Père.—You are suspended from your function. Your father *Hoart* will take special charge of directing that faubourg.

   Hoart.—Père, I will do so.

   Le Père.—*Justus.*

   Justus.—Père, I have often hesitated, and the family may sometimes have had doubts about me. But I have enough faith to bend my independence to the rule [of the Saint-Simonian order], and today I feel I can answer for myself.

   Le Père.—I was counting on it. . . . David, you have nothing outside that holds you back [*qui te retienne dans le monde*].

   David.—No, Père.

   (*Justus* and *David* take the habit.)[41]

David's apparent dependence on Justus in this passage did not long continue, but his laconic reply is completely characteristic of his unprepossessing, soft-spoken nature. There was also melancholy truth in David's two words. Whereas Duveyrier, d'Eichthal, Bonheur, and others had precious ties to family and friends outside (*dans le monde*) that sooner or later interfered with their devotion to Enfantin, David had nothing and nobody. Enfantin and the movement became his *nouveau monde*.

Among the others to take the habit on 6 June were several figures of interest to us: Duveyrier, Barrault, Bergier, Pouyat, and Achille Rousseau, all of whom had written or would soon write lyrics for David's choruses and chansons. The future chansonnier Jules Mercier also became an apostle that day, but Vinçard, later the leader of the chansonniers, kept his distance from the entire Ménilmontant adventure. Most interesting, perhaps, is the behavior of Rogé, who, when called upon, said he was not yet ready. "Père, having recently arrived among your children, I do not yet feel I have the strength necessary to take the apostolic habit. I would need to be more detached than I can be today from an affection for the old world. But I hope that I will [eventually] prove myself worthy of it."[42] To which Enfantin, perhaps pleased to demonstrate that the movement respected the individual's judgment (sometimes), replied, "You do well." We must wonder, though, what led Rogé to hesitate. It is not clear, for example, what he meant when he said that he had arrived but recently ("nouvellement"); as we have seen (Chapter 8), Rogé had attended meetings since 1830. Furthermore, he was one of the many Saint-Simonians (including Enfantin) who had legally placed his personal finances in the care of Olinde Rodrigues (presumably in late 1831).[43] He was thus less "newly arrived" than a number of other disciples, among them Félicien David. But several factors may well have caused him to hesitate: love and concern for Clorinde, bitterness over his lowly musical position at the Retreat, and perhaps, too, an instinctive dislike for Enfantin. Rogé must have overcome these feelings by the end of June, however, for in the account of the temple ceremony (1 July) his name is given in italics, the typographical distinction reserved for apostles.[44] Considering his major role in the training of the choir, it seems probable that he—unlike, for example, Alexis Petit—remained in residence (perhaps wearing civil dress) at Ménilmontant more or less continuously between 6 June and the date of his own *prise d'habit*.[45] (Apparently Rogé spent two evenings a week during this period doing musical propaganda work in Paris; see, below, his direction of the "Workers" at the Temple ceremony.)

The ceremony of 6 June concluded when the family, newly outfitted in their curious vests and led by Le Père, consecrated the garden by marching through it, singing David's *Appel*.

All of this had taken place against the sound of cannon fire, for nearby Saint-Merri was at the moment the scene of a workers' insurrection. The next day, Charles Lemonnier published a pamphlet explaining the Saint-Simonian position on the politics of the day: each party—republican, *juste-milieu*, and legitimist—has its laudable aims, but each wishes to exterminate the others. "We are RELIGIOUS, which is to say PEACEABLE and LOVING toward all *men*, all *classes*, all *parties*. We WANT improvement in the lot of everyone. . . . We think that violence is always fatal, always blasphemous."[46]

JULY: THE TEMPLE CEREMONIES AND TWO FUNERALS

During July, life at Ménilmontant clearly reached a high point in intensity. At the beginning of the month the apostles began to construct in one part of the garden an open-air "temple" for public sermons. Since 6 June the Retreat had opened its doors on Sundays and Wednesdays to curious and sympathetic members of the public.[47] Beginning with the ceremony of 1 July, the Retreat was open more or less continuously, and this added to the excitement of the forty disciples. After months of training, they were now greeting *le monde* as apostles, carrying out—in their beards and vests—the daily labors that were an object lesson in the dignity of physical labor and (more generally) in the rehabilitation of the flesh. The public came in hundreds, sometimes thousands, making these weeks among the most successful—at least numerically—in the whole history of Saint-Simonian propaganda. In the middle of the month, Edmond Talabot, one of Enfantin's favorite disciples (and designer of the apostolic habit), died of cholera in the arms of his fellow apostles; this provided the occasion for an outpouring of fraternal sentiments, for music and speeches, and for the first widely publicized Saint-Simonian funeral. July also saw the composition of that copious mass of speculative rhetoric called the *Livre nou-*

veau. At the end of the month the completed temple was consecrated, presumably with much ceremony, although in this case the details are not known.

All of this activity had its musical side. The combination of a large crowd of visitors, a choir now well trained, and several significant ceremonial occasions, allowed David the composer to unfold as never before or after in his entire career. No fewer than seven choruses are known to date from the month of July or shortly before, and, if none of them had the catchiness of *Appel,* the quality on the average was probably as high as it had been in the three pieces (or four if one counts each of the mealtime prayers) from May and June together.

David's first compositions during these midsummer days were choruses for the Cérémonie de l'Ouverture des Travaux du Temple of 1 July (repeated 8 July).[48] At this public ceremony the apostles, aided by a group of Saint-Simonians from Paris, began to carve steps and channels into a grassy knoll in the garden, creating a broad speaker's platform to serve as a new type of temple, in accordance with the leaders' habitual glorification of the (outdoor) religious theater of ancient Greece (plates 14, 17).[49] The ceremony that was built up around this event was certainly the most elaborate of the Retreat and the one in which music played the largest and most varied role. Indeed, a discussion of the music performed that day amounts to a narration of the entire ceremony.

The ceremony began at 2 P.M. when the family marched out to the garden, the choir leading, "arranged by section." Reaching the raised hill near the site for the temple, the family divided in two, the choir at the left facing the house and the rest on the right.

Chevalier and Fournel then brought Enfantin to the garden. As he approached, Bonheur announced simply, "LE PERE." The published account continues: "Immediately the family strikes up the *Salut.*" (Here as elsewhere little distinction is made between the choir and the family in musical matters; presumably it was the choir that struck up the *Salut* [*Le Retour du Père*] and the less musical members joined in as well as they could.) For the occasion Enfantin had decorated his shirtfront with the words "LE PERE," a touch that was soon incorporated into many illustrations and portraits of the leader, although Gustave d'Eichthal later noted in the margin of his copy of the temple account that he found this exhibition "tactless,"[50] no doubt because it went counter to the apostolic equality that Enfantin was so distinctly preaching.

After the performance of the *Salut,* Barrault, assisted by Rogé and Toché, brought forward a group of "Parisian Workers," consisting perhaps of members of the Saint-Simonian workers' choruses, which Rogé had formed in two areas of the city during May and June.[51] The workers, no doubt conducted by Rogé, sang a piece by Félicien David, *Le Nouveau Temple* (Appendix E.6), in which they offered their labor for one day a week: "Tous vos jours sont pour le peuple, / Nous vous offrons notre dimanche." During the course of the piece, the "Family" (i.e., the choir?) echoed approvingly and in four-part harmony the words of the workers ("Leur dimanche") and, at the end, the "Apostles" (the choir again?) repeated the whole melody, again in four-part harmony. Everyone joined in on the final refrain: "C'est le jour du peuple! / C'est le jour de Dieu!"

▽ Not surprisingly, in view of its occasional origin, this piece of music did not survive as a Saint-Simonian chanson after the breakup of the Retreat, but it seems to have received a prominent performance in Marseilles, to a new text, on the occasion of the departure of some of the Saint-Simonians for the Orient (see Chapter 12). Much later, David inserted this same chorus, with yet another text, into his *Christophe Colomb* (1847). This last version, the only one whose music survives, is a vigorous march, strongly accented and squarely phrased, which captures well the enthusiasm of the sun-drenched days of Ménilmontant when the work was first composed. One special touch: throughout

△ most of the four-part "Apostles" section the melody is given to the basses.

The temple ceremony continued with a long speech by Barrault on the activities of the Saint-Simonians, in particular justifying their Retreat as a means of learning simplicity and thus of finding their way to the people. During this most rhetorical speech, "David, placed at the side, performs chords and accompaniments on a piano at prearranged moments." Anyone who has heard recordings made a generation or two later by the great actors and orators (e.g., Sarah Bernhardt or Tolstoy) will easily imagine the fervent swing with which Barrault pronounced this inspirational harangue. It must have been an example of the *verbe rythmé* in all its glory. The published account states, "Barrault's speech was listened to contemplatively," and adds: "This mixture of speech and religious music greatly struck the audience." Even if only half true (there must surely have been some snickering), this description suggests that David's accompaniment gave resonance and depth to Barrault's cadenced, imaged, but still rather threadbare proclamations. A portion of the speech is reproduced below, complete with the descriptions of David's musical commentary that were published with it. This remarkably detailed transcript permits us to "attend" the ceremony ourselves and to "listen" to Barrault's rhetoric and David's simple but effective improvisations.[52]

Reprise des dernières mesures du chant de triomphe;	Sourds à leur promesse, Hors de cette route Glorieuse et sûre, Nous tournons à gauche, Et laissons à droite Nos amis qui grondent, S'étonnent, se taisent, Jetant la couronne Qu'ils tressaient d'avance,
Accompagnement avec sourdine.	Et dans la retraite Nous oubliant vite,

> Ainsi qu'on oublie
> Les morts dans leur tombe.

Une note.   SEULS

Nous sommes demeurés, ouvrant en vain la porte;
Nul d'entre eux ne répond aux voix qui les invitent.

Une note.   NUL.

Accord   GLOIRE À DIEU!
glorificateur.   Il a montré notre chemin
                                      A ceux qui ne le savaient pas;
                                      S'il s'écarte d'anciens amis,
                                      Il nous en conduit de nouveaux.

Même accord.
                                      Les *bourgeois* cherchaient nos salons;
                                      Le PEUPLE nous cherche au désert.
                                      Les *bourgeois* nous croyaient perdus,
                                      Le PEUPLE nous a retrouvés.

Même accord.
                                      Les *bourgeois* vantaient notre esprit;
                                      Le PEUPLE aimera notre coeur.
                                      Les *bourgeois* lisaient nos journaux.
                                      Le PEUPLE répète nos chants.
Même accord.   GLOIRE À DIEU!

C'est que le PEUPLE enfin commence à nous connaître.
Pour lui nous avions fait livres, journaux, discours;
Mais nous voulons par lui nous laisser voir nous-
    mêmes,
Et par lui nous laisser toucher nous-mêmes, NOUS!

Accompagnement   S'il regarde le ciel, le PEUPLE le croit vide;
plaintif.   S'il regarde la terre, il fléchit sous son poids
                        Sait-il d'où viendra le souffle
                        Qui relèvera son front?
                    Ah! l'espoir est en nous! nous saurons le lui rendre!

                    Le PEUPLE cependant, solide sur sa base,

Accompagnement   Est ferme et patient, mais l'ardeur est en nous!
ferme.   Pour forger le nouveau monde
                        Dieu mariera nos efforts;

                    L'apôtre est le marteau, mais le peuple est l'enclume!

137

(Apparently on other occasions David accompanied Duveyrier in recitations, but the results are not preserved.[53])

After Barrault's *parole*, the family performed another new piece by David, *Au travail*, whose music does not survive. At the final words *"au travail!"* the workers—Parisians and apostles—took their shovels, picks, and wheelbarrows and ceremoniously marched to the site of the temple, where they sang a new set of words to the tune of the *Appel*. (At the words "en nous donnant la main," each digger took a wheelbarrow driver by the hand.) They filled the wheelbarrows with dirt and marched to the pit where it was to be emptied; there they sang "in chorus" yet another new set of words to the tune of Appel and returned to the temple site for another load. "The work then continues until five o'clock," says the account, not specifying whether the songs continued to be sung with each and every load.

At 4:30 a table was prepared with dinner for the workers: bread and sliced meat, salad, and a mildly alcoholic punch. (Perhaps it was tea-based. Charles Pellarin later recalled that the apostles generally took tea at dinner "in order, as it was explained, to initiate the people into the use of exotic products."[54]) At 5:00 the horn was sounded to announce dinner, and the workers (seventy-two in number) set down their tools and took seats at the table. Before eating they rose to sing "in chorus" David's prayer *Avant le repas*, turning toward Enfantin "spontaneously" at the words "à vous, Père, merci." After the meal they sang *Après le repas* and set to work again until 7:30, when they assembled in the grove and sang the *Appel*. Then they mixed with the crowd until at 8:00 the horn announced the retreat and the onlookers left, "struck"—we are informed—by the ceremony, the costumes, and "those songs by which we are leading to [*préludons*] the new art, the pacifying art, the art that will be, in the hand of our FATHER, what the sword was in Muhammad's."

The account goes on to state that the number of people who visited the grounds during the course of the day was nearly five thousand; some two thousand observed the ceremonial meal at which David's prayers were performed. Michel Chevalier told the police that same day that similar numbers of people came every Sunday to hear the songs of the apostles and to view their simple meal. Another account claims that on certain Sundays nearly ten thousand people visited the garden.[55] Even allowing for some exaggeration, the figures give an idea of the large number of people who heard, in impressive surroundings, the Saint-Simonian choruses of Félicien David.

The following Sunday, 8 July, the entire ceremony was repeated "with the same songs and the same practices." At 4:00 in the afternoon, while the apostles and the men of Paris were busy at work, the commissar of police arrived with a hundred men from the First Regiment, armed with bayonets.[56] The *travaux* continued, the dinner was served, just as before (except that a few Saint-Simonian women were also invited to take part), and the work was taken up once more until Hoart, director of the project, "sounded the retreat" at 8:00.

The workers returned to the courtyard singing the *Appel,* and at 11:00 the gates were closed and the soldiers and the visitors who were still left in the rue de Ménilmontant went home.

The next day and thereafter the gates of the house were opened at 5:00 in the morning and "a great number of people came to witness our morning labors and our evening labors and songs." The National Guards from Belleville came on Wednesday 11 July, but they did not disrupt anything, and the account states that individual soldiers showed admiration and "sympathy" for what they had seen and the desire to return "in civil dress and as friends." The account also mentions that, of the soldiers who had come with the commissar on Sunday, several did in fact visit again on their own.[57]

These reports of numerous and sympathetic visitors may at first seem untrustworthy, coming as they do from the movement's own publications. But we have seen in Chapter 8 that other sources provide evidence of the Saint-Simonians' long-standing success in attracting large crowds. Even the caricatures and cynical jibes in *Le Figaro* and other papers give involuntary testimony to the popular appeal of the ceremonies, costumes, and songs of Ménilmontant.[58] Of course attracting a crowd was not enough. The disciples wanted to win the support of their onlookers, a more difficult and perhaps impossible task. Charles Pellarin, who was a member of the Retreat in late June and July, stated categorically in August that "the effect of the *travaux* and the monastic life of Ménilmontant upon those who came to visit the garden was nil, for they were more inclined to laugh at the eccentricity of the recluses than to imitate them. The people [working-class onlookers], in particular, watched with pity . . . as these former bourgeois worked up a heavy sweat for the purpose of raking dirt from one end of the yard to another."[59] But Pellarin wrote this shortly after making his angry break with the movement; no doubt he was accentuating the negative. A quite different response to the ceremonies—a response of delight and awe—is found in a letter to Alexis Petit from a man named Luce who was, or became soon thereafter, a spirited proponent of the movement in Dijon. Written the following year, 1833, these few but deeply sincere lines attest to the powerful effect that could be worked, on a mind inclined not to laugh, by the almost chemical interaction of the various ingredients of the Retreat: the peaceful setting, the philosophical discussions, the momentary isolation from "the world," the calm yet purposeful fraternal activity, and—not least—the music of David. Luce tells Petit that he has decided to write in spite of the fact that he is quite sure that Petit will not remember him. They talked one evening at Ménilmontant, perhaps during the very days of June and early July we have been studying.

> The sky was veiled by the shadows of night. . . . You did not know what was going on in my soul. I was transformed. As I went down [the hill and into the communal house], it seemed to me that my being was splitting apart, and, in the midst of

> the noise in the big hall, I neither saw nor heard a thing, unless
> it was—from time to time, as if in a far-off *mysterium* [esoteric
> religious ceremony]—the songs of David. My ears were buzz-
> ing and my heart was beating, but in a strange way.—Alexis,
> you will write to me, won't you?[60]

An epiphany of sorts, with David's music setting the mood.

Shortly before the temple ceremony, Alexis Petit finally took the habit and David wrote a piece for the occasion, *La Prise d'habit d'A. Petit,* to a text by Enfantin. The very title indicates that the movement gave exceptional prominence to Petit's acceptance of the habit, for David's choruses normally do not mention individuals other than the near-divine Saint-Simon and Enfantin. It is also significant that Le Père wrote the text. (Only one other David chorus, *La Prière du Père,* uses a text by Enfantin.) But most striking of all is the fact that, as Charles Lemonnier, a visiting *fidèle* from the provinces, records, "For the first time, LE PÈRE SANG. HIS VOICE WAS SWEET AND MAJESTIC."[61] The probable reason for all this special treatment is simply stated. Petit and his mother gave vast sums of money to the movement, some 250,000 francs, amounting in late 1832 to over forty-seven percent of all income from major gifts (excepting the contributions of Enfantin himself).[62] Unfortunately, the piece itself is lost, but we can get a feeling for it, and for the occasion, from the continuation of Lemonnier's account: "Alexis answered [Le Père]. *Lambert* and *Bruneau* took part in this sung dialogue, the former as [Alexis's] sponsor, the latter as his brother. After this, the whole chorus of *apostles* broke out in a quick, fervent, catchy song that made more than one heart beat and more than one tear flow in the astonished crowd which, quite unawares, was receiving Saint-Simonian life through all its senses . . . [as a result of] the costume, the deportment [*tenue*], and most of all the choruses."[63]

During early July, David composed two choruses that no doubt quickly became fixed items in the daily ritual: *Prière du matin* and *Prière du soir* (Appendix E.9–10). Two other choruses—*Tout est mort* and *Au peuple*—may also date from early July. These four numbers continue to use, with varying success, many of the stylistic procedures seen in the *Salut;* refreshingly, they also begin to vary the choral texture.

▽ The morning prayer is an undistinguished chorus with changes of tempo and other naïve attempts to reflect the changing imagery of the text (especially images of light and dark, e.g., hushed chords at the words "Les astres de la nuit s'évanouissent"). The more attractive evening prayer is notable for a lyrical middle section ("La nuit tombe et rappelle"), which David scored for a solo quartet. This was the first of his attempts since the *Hymne à Saint-Simon* to introduce variety into his choruses through extended interludes for solo voice or voices (cf. *Danse des astres, Le Sommeil de Paris,* and, in Chapter 12, *La Prison du Père*).

We do not know whether either *Tout est mort* or *Au peuple* was written with a particular occasion in mind, but the general ideological content of the texts would have been appropriate to any situation in which the Saint-Simonians confronted the public. *Tout est mort* is a through-composed piece, with several changes of tempo and material to reflect the moods of the text. David varies the texture by setting one voice (either the top or bottom) in opposition to the other three; at one point the responding voices enrich the texture by developing a melodic character of their own (contrary motion at beginning of page 7). In other respects, the music is rather weak; the modulations up or down a third have become a mannerism, and the material is repeated at unbearable length. Nonetheless David reused the music unchanged in his oratorio *Moïse au Sinaï* (see Chapter 13).

Au peuple is also one of the weaker Ménilmontant choruses, with the by now familiar modulatory oddities and lengthy repetitions. The writing for chorus is rather plain here except for brief passages for the basses alone, usually to fill out the end of a four-bar phrase. The work is in three musically distinct sections, reflecting the contrasts in the text. The first is a declamatory call to the people ("Peuple, Peuple! Savez-vous qui nous sommes?"); the second, a slower passage depicting the alienation of the workers ("sans amour entr'eux"); and the last, a bouncy and rather successful allegretto encouraging them to love each other "et vous deviendrez patients (bons, etc.) comme nous." The preachiness of the text is obvious, and Charles Chaubet performed a valuable service when, retexting the work for David's collection *La Ruche harmonieuse,* he composed a text—*Chant des travailleurs*—to be sung *by* the workers, not *at* them. △

After the temple ceremonies (and attendant confrontations with the "forces of order"), the next important event in the life of the apostles was the death of Edmond Talabot from cholera. Again music played an enormous role; Talabot's last hours, the wake, and the funeral were all embellished or intensified by the use of music, including some quickly written or improvised for the occasion.[64]

It was on Monday 16 July that Talabot, one of the most prominent of Enfantin's disciples, first became seriously ill. The evening, according to one witness, was proceeding in the normal fashion: "speech on women by Barraut [*sic*], to the people—supper—procession around the temple—gathering around Le Père—."[65] At 9 P.M. Enfantin was discussing Bouffard and Lemonnier's intended mission "into the world" when Tourneux and Pellarin interrupted him with the news that Talabot had contracted cholera. In spite of the combined attention of Pellarin and four other doctors, it was clear at 2 A.M. that the end was near. Enfantin came in and "judged that music would ease Talabot's suffering." The published account continues with a detailed list of the music which was performed.

> Immediately *David, Justus, Duveyrier* and *Rogé* got out of bed and came into the sitting room [next to Talabot's bedroom]. . . . There David performed the tunes which the family sings, and he improvised chords—some sad and lamenting, others gentle and hopeful. With *Justus, Duveyrier, Machereau,* and *Rogé, David*

141

sang the *Prière du matin; Justus, Machereau,* and *David* sang a nocturne composed by *David.*

Finally *Justus* repeated a tune from the mountains of the Limousin (Talabot's native land), a tune which Talabot loved a lot.

During this time, Talabot had appeared to fall asleep and had died in the arms of *Duguet.*

We are familiar by now with the "tunes" of the family that David probably played: *Appel, Salut,* the music from the temple ceremony, and so on. The *Prière du matin* has just been discussed above. And the nocturne that Justus, Machereau, and David sang was probably one of the three-voice nocturnes that, Saint-Etienne informs us, David had written in 1828–30.[66]

The Limousin tune that Justus sang to Talabot is one that, as we are later informed in the account, Talabot himself had taught to the choir: "Baisse-toi montagne, / Elève-toi vallon, / Pour me laisser voir / Ma Jeanneton." The only other musical novelty in the account of Talabot's death is David's improvisation. David apparently liked providing mood music in this fashion; he did much the same thing on later occasions.

Once the doctors confirmed the death of the apostle, Michel Chevalier roused the family, who gathered on the terrace and, though it was hardly 4 A.M., sang the *Prière du matin.* Enfantin then appeared, leading Talabot's brother Léon, who was bathed in tears. Enfantin, in sharp contrast, wore an almost ostentatious self-composure, as if to make clear that death should not be allowed to interfere with the serious work ahead. Turning to the apostles, he called upon them to help him be strong by singing him his piece, the *Salut.* The details of wording in this passage of the account communicate vividly Enfantin's masterful control—partly through a selective display of his own inner turmoil, partly through David's music—of the emotions and behavior of his disciples.

> On the face of Le Père was a severe calm that was repeated on the faces of the Family.
>
> When the Family had sung the morning prayer, Le Père cried in a loud voice, touched with emotion: "Children, I need your *salut* [i.e., greeting]."
>
> The Family sang the *salut,* then went down to the temple and worked until nine.

Without doubt the *Prière du matin* and *Salut* helped unite the community at an emotionally difficult moment. At the same time, though, this passage reveals again how successfully David's music bolstered Enfantin's own self-aggrandizement within the movement.

Later that same day, 17 July, Talabot's body—washed and dressed in the apostolic habit that he had helped to design—was placed on view in the house, and the local population was allowed to enter and file past. Appropriate music was not lacking.

> In the large room next to the sitting room, which had been separated from it by a simple gauze curtain, David was seated at a fortepiano. He played slow, sad, solemn chords. With him were *Rogé, Duveyrier, Justus, Holstein, Terson,* [who] from time to time sang some of the Family's songs, interspersed with some others that the ceremony had inspired.[67]

Here again we find David improvising appropriate background music in between ▽ performances of his choruses. One of the pieces that he apparently composed during Talabot's last hours or during the wake is preserved in manuscript at the Bibliothèque nationale; it bears the title "Morceau écrit pendant le choléra" and is followed by a fragmentary "Prière," perhaps also improvised on this occasion. One is naturally curious about the vocal pieces that were "inspired by the ceremony." The wording suggests strongly that David had spent the morning hours working up some new pieces, or arrangements, for the occasion. Perhaps this refers to *Il est mort* and the *Chant de vie,* both of which were performed at the funeral the next day. ▵

That night Rogé and others stood guard over the body. The next day, 18 July, the body was placed in a coffin at the door to the house where it could be seen by the large crowd in the garden. At 4 P.M. the family, arranged "in singing order," marched with the coffin to the temple site. (Here we note again the somewhat misleading practice of identifying the choir with the entire family.)

The family, the female Saint-Simonians, and the men of Paris formed a broad semicircle at the temple, facing the crowd of people who, informed by the newspapers of the hour of the procession, had come to join the cortège or to stand and gape. The choir then sang *Il est mort,* an arrangement of *Tout est mort* that introduced several specifically funereal passages of text and apparently replaced the lively coda in 3/4 ("plus d'esclavage") with a return to the stern opening. (*Tout est mort* is thus a chorus whose general propagandistic text was later altered to suit a special occasion; this is the reverse of the procedure by which *Le Retour du Père,* an occasional piece, became the *Salut,* an "all-purpose" one.)

The family then formed several lines and groups (one carrying a pick and shovel) and—accompanied by an immense crowd—marched silently to Père-Lachaise Cemetery with the coffin. At the grave the family divided into two groups: the choir at Enfantin's right, "in singing order," and "the nonsingers" at his left. (This time the account correctly distinguishes between the choir and the rest of the Ménilmontant family.) Enfantin instructed Barrault to tell the onlookers who Talabot had been. Barrault stepped to the edge of the grave, but before beginning, turned to the choir, saying, "Brothers, let us first greet Le Père and the people." The choir responded by singing the *Salut,* as they had the previous morning. One can easily imagine Enfantin's own performance during this homage; whatever the strong emotions seething in his soul—sincere grief, trepidation about the future, or relief and pleasure at this sign of deference from his "sons"—he must have remained unflinchingly severe in outward aspect. Once again, David's music, and Enfantin's self-control, had served to strengthen the authority of Le Père.

Barrault next delivered his eulogy for Talabot, mentioning how the apostle, in his last night, was "charmed by our religious songs which echoed softly in his ear." "Brothers," he cried in his best rhetorical fashion, "sing again that tune from his countryside which you learned from him, with which his family of birth rocked him in the cradle, and which his new family sang to him on his death bed." And the choir sang the Limousin folksong that Talabot had heard from the lips of Justus in those early morning hours.

Later during Barrault's eulogy, the choir performed David's *Chant de mort* again (i.e., *Il est mort*). When Barrault was finished, a *Chant de vie* was performed, consisting of the *Prière du matin* with new words appropriate to the occasion. Four of the apostles then took the pick and shovel—the very tools used for excavating the temple mound—and ceremoniously covered the coffin with dirt. (The account states with biblical momentousness: "And this act was another symbol of the rehabilitation of all work.") The family sang the *Prière du soir* and perhaps some other pieces, then took to the road.

The choir marched together as before and presumably led the singing that is reported in the account:

> And we came back to the house of Le PERE in Ménilmontant, singing the *Appel*. A crowd of men and women accompanied us. . . .
>
> On the way back, the crowd began, for the first time, to repeat our songs. They took up the refrain [of *Appel*] with us: "Gloire à Dieu!"

What, one may wonder, did the writer mean by "for the first time"? Presumably nothing more than "for the first time that day," for these accounts or chronicles rarely refer to events prior to the ones that they are reporting. (The phrase could, of course, also mean that none of the visitors at any of the previous Ménilmontant ceremonies had ever chimed in with the choir during any of David's catchy refrains; that, however, seems quite improbable.)

The month of July ended with two events, one long-awaited, the other unanticipated. The first of these, the inauguration of the temple, is unfortunately not the subject of a published account. It took place on 29 July before a "large public" and Enfantin had told the apostles to be "calm" on this important occasion.[68] A drawing by Machereau, reproduced on the cover of certain copies of David's choruses (plates 17–18), permits us to see what a ceremony at the finished temple must have been like. Barrault declaims, Chevalier surveys the crowd complacently, and a David of delicate build stands next to and a bit to the rear of a portly Enfantin, literally in his shadow, and ready to turn and conduct the choir members, who are arrayed more or less in a semicircle at the rear and sides of the platform. A very bourgeois public looks on, the ladies in wide-brimmed bonnets. Some children are playing quietly.

All looks well in this scene. In fact, though, the tensions in the Saint-Simonians' situation showed up very clearly the day after the inauguration of the temple. Bazard, the former leader who had made a bitter separation from Enfantin the previous November, had died suddenly, and the leaders, apostles, and a group of men and women from Paris decided to march out to Courtry for the funeral. Enfantin warned his disciples in advance to show calm and dignity in presenting themselves to the world, "to those who would judge us."[69] They carried propagandistic literature with them, perhaps expecting to distribute it to sympathetic souls along their route. What they met was beyond the power of the most persuasive brochures. First, the gendarmes of Bondy attempted to block their path, for rumor had it that the group was armed. After some explanations they were permitted to continue, and they began attracting a few curious men and women of Livry, who turned out to have only "confused ideas" about what the Saint-Simonians' aims were and apparently showed little capacity for being enlightened. Finally, after marching so long, they learned that the distressed Claire Bazard was asking them through her devoted friend Jules Lechevalier to turn back and so to spare her an encounter that, she felt, could only be "painful." Enfantin objected and tried to assert his former paternal authority over Jules, but he finally had no choice but to yield. On the way back to Ménilmontant the apostles twice sang David's *Appel,* and—pausing at an inn to eat—they struck up *Avant le repas* and the *Salut* (when Enfantin entered).[70] The singing may have helped raise their spirits a bit, but probably not as much as was needed. In one short day, the officials had greeted them with suspicion, the people with ignorance, and former comrades with rancor.[71] The halcyon days of summer were coming to an end and a tortured autumn lay ahead.

MUSIC DURING THE DECLINE OF THE RETREAT; UNDATABLE PIECES

When Enfantin said that the outside world wanted to judge the disciples, he was speaking literally. The movement had been the subject of drawn-out legal inquiries since late 1831, and everyone realized that soon the Saint-Simonians would have to defend themselves before their accusers.

Nobody could be sure of the outcome. Of the various charges, one, although unfair, was undeniably true: the movement had often held meetings of more than twenty persons in defiance of the repressive Article 291 of the penal code. As for the "immorality" that the prosecutors had found in certain

Saint-Simonian publications, all would depend on the court's definition of the term. One charge was patently absurd, that the leaders had committed fraud, appropriating for themselves large sums of money from their adherents' pockets and inheritances. In fact they had, if anything, gone into debt for the cause.

Unfortunately for the movement, although in part through their own miscalculations, the first trial (27–28 August) turned into something of a public circus. Enfantin and Chevalier decided to plead (unsuccessfully, as on previous occasions) that their movement was a religious one and thus exempt from the law of illegal assembly. The witnesses for the defense, some thirty-five members of the movement, stepped up one by one and refused to take the oath because it did not contain the words "before God and men." In a last desperate attempt to assert his superiority over the law, Enfantin began to stare charismatically at the judges and jury, a lesson, he insisted, in the important role of gestures and physical beauty in establishing—through the senses rather than the intellect—religious and affective relations between people. This "tried the patience . . . of even the most sympathetic portion of the audience."[72] The judges, for their part, reacted with undisguised hostility, sentenced Enfantin and Chevalier to a year in prison, and ordered "the so-called Saint-Simonian society" dissolved and its publications seized.

The newspapers quickly protested the government's repressive actions, but their cries came months too late. Irreparable harm had already been done (not least by the newspapers themselves) to a movement that depended more than most on its public image and on the support it could win among working people, solid citizens of the entrepreneurial class, artists, and men in government. By the time of the second trial (19 October), which acquitted the movement of the charges of fraud, the members had begun to leave the Retreat either on a daily basis to do propaganda work in the working-class *quartiers* or more permanently to establish new centers of activity south of Paris. The apostles who remained behind often launched their fellows on their way by parading with them, in costume, through the streets of Paris and singing Saint-Simonian chansons.[73] The rejoicing was real, and so were the insecurity and the disappointment. Ménilmontant died a slow death during these months, and the new phase of missionary wanderings was as yet disorganized and unfocused.

It is no doubt for these reasons that, compared with the large number of pieces David wrote for the movement during the month of July, his harvest during August, September, and October was relatively meager. During August, in fact, David apparently wrote only one piece, the *Ronde* ("Soldats, ouvriers, bourgeois"; Appendix E.14). Nothing is known about performances of this chorus, except that it must have caught on as a propaganda number, since a separate text sheet with twelve strophes was published by the end of the year (Appendix E.14a). The piece is certainly well suited to impromptu performance. It consists, as the title suggests, of a simple chain of dancelike tunes in rondo form: A B A C A coda. The musical phrases are simple four-bar units, and in general the upper voice presents a completely self-sufficient melody. The *Ronde* thus represents the turn to a more popular musical style than that which David had cultivated during June and July. As the government threatened the continued existence of the Retreat and the Saint-Simonians began to look to the outside world again, David resorted more frequently to the catchier style of the *Appel,* his first piece for Ménilmontant. Of course that piece was primarily a chanson (with a simple choral refrain), whereas the *Ronde* is for chorus throughout (and even makes brief use of antiphony between the topmost and the three lower voices). But, with the exception of a brief modulatory passage before the last statement of the refrain, the melody of the *Ronde* could easily be sung alone as a chanson, and apparently was.[74] (The work's simplicity and charm have also assured its survival into the twentieth century. It is the only one of David's choruses available on disc—see Appendix D.14.)

Although the anxiety over the forthcoming trial may have helped make August a musically unproductive month, the two trial days themselves (27–28 August) were filled with musical activities of some importance. On the day that the trial began, the Saint-Simonians, now the center of public attention as never before, marched on foot from the Retreat at the eastern edge of the city to the Court House in the center, and they set out singing the *Salut* (as Enfantin joined them from the house) and the first strophe of the *Appel.*[75] Marching through the city streets, they were greeted by "silence, curiosity, and signs of interest on the part of the ladies."[76] (Vinçard confirms this account but also records two incidents of antagonistic behavior.[77]) The onlookers were so numerous that the apostles were forced to leave their planned route and take side streets.[78] Neither the published account of the trial nor Vinçard's memoirs mention whether the apostles did any singing at the end of the first day of the trial (it lasted until 11:30 P.M., and the apostles marched all the way out to Ménilmontant to spend the night). But Vinçard states proudly that late in the second day, when the unhappy verdict was finally given, the apostles, "Le Père at the lead," and some hundred *fidèles* of Paris marched back through the crowds to Ménilmontant and, in spite of a torrential downpour, "sang with full voice the hymns of Félicien David!" Enfantin, deeply disturbed, finally gestured to them to cease. (Vinçard admits that the singing had been "a bit wild [*charivarique*]").[79] But the group burst forth again with the *Appel* when they crossed the city limits, and they arrived at the great house singing the *Salut.*[80] The music had helped bolster the morale of the shaken apostles and had brought their message, in a joyous and beautiful form, to the population of Paris. The new art was proving its worth.

In September David wrote three more pieces for the movement, each representing one of our aforementioned types: a chanson, a chorus to a general ideological text, and a chorus written for a specific occasion. It is worth noting that, though the second category had originally also included pieces for the daily ritual, in fact David wrote no pieces of this type after mid-July (unless the second set of mealtime prayers dates from this period). Clearly, the enthusiasm the disciples had felt during the early stages of their experiment in communal living was beginning to wane in the face of government hostility.

It is in this context that the *Danse des astres* (Appendix E.15) is best understood. The *Danse* is the piece David wrote in September for a specific occasion, but that occasion was not a significant public ceremony celebrating fraternity, labor, or some other part of the doctrine. It was an elementary astronomy lesson, given by Charles Lambert, with various apostles spinning and dancing the roles of sun, earth, and moon.[81] There may well be something characteristically Saint-Simonian in this demonstration, with its emphasis on learning through the mobilization of all the senses (a minor corollary of the doctrine of the rehabilitation of the flesh). And the subject matter—the heavenly bodies— had specifically been mentioned by Enfantin in April as one of the things that apostles needed to learn about. Admittedly, it all seems rather petty and "safe" after the grand controversial designs that the Saint-Simonians had sketched of a new social order. Yet this simple demonstration was the very thing to capture David's imagination, and the piece is among the best he ever wrote. (He must have known this, for he later expanded and orchestrated it.) In particular, the vocalise interlude for tenor solo which he wrote for himself to sing has a sweet and graceful lilt that David was later to apply in his comic operas. Berlioz, reviewing the orchestrated version in 1844, found the work "very fresh, and pretty in color," and Ernest Reyer praised it as a "composition filled with poetry and charm, a swirling and luminous *ronde.*"[82] Enfantin, too, seems to have retained a special affection for the piece. One day in 1833, as the early spring sun filled his prison room, his memory turned to David: "What sunlight! Oh yes, 'le ciel est beau, la terre est douce!' Do you remember, after the singing [i.e., the choral opening?], David modulating his pretty waltz of the stars?"[83]

The chanson that David wrote during September is *Peuple fier! peuple fort!* (Appendix E.16), a song of solidarity with the toiling masses. In spite of some difficulties that it poses for the singer, the song must have caught on, for its text was published several times during the months after Ménilmontant (Appendix E.16a).

▽ The music has the quality of a fanfare in places because of the arpeggiated melody and the dotted rhythm ("ton bras est fort"). After forty years, the impact of the "Marseillaise" was still being felt. (Compare the chansonniers' response to the great Revolutionary hymn, pp. 158-61.) In the second measure David uses a rather religious-sounding progression (4–3 suspension) that seems less appropriate to the cheery populism of the text; perhaps it reflects a bit too faithfully the movement's inability to leave their self-righteous obsession with ritual. (In 1848, possibly as a tribute to the February Revolution, David republished the song, with a new text and optional
△ choral parts for the refrain, as *Hymne à la fraternité.*[84])

The third piece written in September was the *Prière du Père,* a chorus on a text by Enfantin. It is not clear whether Enfantin specifically wrote the text for David to set, as he perhaps did for the *Prise d'habit,* or whether, as the title seems to suggest, David extracted the lines from the writings of the adored leader.

The style of the chorus is similar to that of the works from June to July. This is ▽ most obvious in the chordal-declamatory opening section and the descriptive descending figure on the word "soupir." *Priere du Père* is the only chorus written by David after July that does not have either prominent solo episodes (*Danse des astres, Prison*) or a light, tuneful quality (*Ronde*). In fact, it generally lacks melodic appeal but offers some compensation in the solidity and richness of the harmonic progressions (e.g., an internal pedal in the Allegro and a traditional but enormously effective cadential tonic pedal, to the words "Gloire à nous, gloire à Dieu"). The strongest extended passage is the solemn yet sweet Adagio addressed directly to Père Enfantin ("Père, c'est Dieu qui nous unit à vous"); its mood and its means were to recur the next year in some of David's pleas and prayers for the arrival of La Mère. △

Existing documents suggest that David may have composed no new pieces during the month of October. In certain ways, though, music did figure in events surrounding the second trial. Duveyrier and Lambert, who had been refused admittance to a defamatory satire, *Les Saint-Simoniens,* at Madame Saqui's theater on 15 October, announced through the newspapers that they would attend a performance of Meyerbeer's *Robert le diable* after the conclusion of the trial on Friday.[85] (Perhaps they chose Meyerbeer's opera in part because Adolphe Nourrit, who had created and who regularly sang the title role of Robert, was sympathetic to their views.) The visit, Enfantin felt, carried special significance because it was announced several days *before* the trial and thus indicated the Saint-Simonians' confidence in a victorious outcome.[86]

While ten of the apostles, conspicuously costumed, were making themselves visible at the Opéra[87] and others at Madame Saqui's—to which they had gained admittance after all[88]—the rest of the Saint-Simonians celebrated the favorable verdict in their own musical way. They moved to a restaurant on the Place du Châtelet and awaited Le Père. As he proceeded through the crowded streets, amid applause and cries of *vivat,* the disciples went to the open windows and welcomed him, of course, with David's *Salut.* The meal was preceded and interrupted by songs: *Appel, Ronde, Au peuple,* and the mealtime prayers. The account of the trial states that "the new song" *Peuple fier* was performed there for the first time. Actually it had been written the month before. Perhaps the anonymous writer was impressed because this was the first *public* performance of *Peuple fier.* If so, his attitude is revealing. The attention of the movement, for months centered on themselves, was now turned outward again, to the crowd that filled the square outside of the restaurant and listened to the proud and passionate songs of the faithful within. After the dinner, Enfantin, Barrault, and Holstein set out for Ménilmontant and were joined by some men who greeted Enfantin with the *Appel* and accompanied him, "still singing," all the way to Ménilmontant.[89] After the August trial, music had been a balm in defeat; now it helped the members give expression, however short-lived, to their joy and relief after a sorely needed legal victory.

In November David wrote another strophic chanson, *La Voix du peuple,* also known as "Je ne veux plus être exploité." (The music was published and even reviewed, but no copy has surfaced.) The fact that it was a chanson coincides with the general tendency of the movement during this period away from ritual and toward a more active proselytization *dans le monde.*

It was perhaps also during these slow autumn days that David gave music lessons to Justus and to Lambert. The Bibliothèque nationale possesses a sheaf of simple exercises in harmony and counterpoint, partly in David's hand, partly in that of Justus.[90] As for Lambert, there is an even more elementary music lesson preserved in his hand, a listing of the successive key areas of David's *Salut,* concluding with a warning: "hard to sing F-natural in the Andante because of the impression of the key of G."[91] Perhaps Lambert used these instructions to help train the chorus (or at least his fellow second tenors). He was quite interested in music; we have his copious philosophical and mathematical ruminations on the properties of scales and intervals and on the relationship between melody and harmony, dating perhaps from those speculative July evenings with Enfantin.[92] Later in life Lambert took up the study of music more seriously with Armand Chevé, the proponent of the Galinist system of numeric notation (a type of tonic sol-fa system). It must be said that his efforts at writing harmony were no more successful than his attempts to grasp it philosophically,[93] but Lambert's interest was no doubt sincere, and it is possible that he was the one who later interested Vinçard and David in the Galinist system.

There are a number of pieces that David wrote during the Ménilmontant Retreat but that we cannot date with greater precision. *Le Sommeil de Paris,* admired by Berlioz when David had it performed with *Le Désert* in 1844, was apparently a fully worked-out chorus with brief episodes for solo singers (perhaps a quartet, as in the *Prière du Soir*). Only the bass part survives. The piece opened by evoking the cries of grief and sadness rising from Paris, the sleeping giant; it closed by encouraging *le peuple* to hope in God and to await the dawning of "the day when all will be united." *Femmes, levez-vous* may have been either a chorus or a song; the music is lost. The rest are inconsequential piano pieces—waltzes and *Pensées*—the detritus, it seems, of months of improvisational noodling.[94]

THE DISPERSAL OF THE APOSTLES

During the last three months of 1833, the Retreat gradually dissolved. Knowing that he and Michel were to enter the walls of Sainte-Pélagie on 15 December,

Enfantin attempted to set the movement on a course that would enable it to survive, if not to thrive. To begin with, he publicly released his followers from his authority. Exploiting the messianic and feminist strains that had been developing in the movement, he stated that he would not be able to regain control until the female Messiah arrived and that his disciples must now go out into the world spreading the dogma (with an emphasis on issues touching *le peuple* and *la femme*) and searching for *La Femme-Messie.* This was a lot to ask, after so many months of sacrifice; Duveyrier, d'Eichthal, and others of the Ménilmontant forty chose instead to return, in civil dress, to their homes in Paris and try to pick up the pieces of their former lives. But many believers did respond to the call for a new proselytization effort, including some who had not been part of the Retreat. As early as 10 October, groups of apostles began heading southward, sometimes wearing new costumes and always buoyed by the songs of fellow *fidèles* who had come to see them off. Indeed, it was Enfantin's idea that the movement now needed to reach "artists, the people, and women" and that "costume and songs" would be the most effective "means of action."[95] And so the members of the various brigades sang—at the slightest opportunity, it seems. Jules Mercier and his fellow missionaries, for example, were well received when they sang to a crowd of over two hundred in a Melun inn, and, when imprisoned near Montercan—in part for singing—they cheerfully struck up their tunes in the jail![96]

By the middle of 1833 these missionaries had helped build additional support for the movement's ideas in a number of provincial centers of Saint-Simonian activity, such as Toulon, Dijon, and Castelnaudary.[97] A particularly active community (or family) formed in Lyons, the city that now served as the base of operations for further missions to the provinces, Algeria, and southern Germany. Barrault organized a special troop, the Compagnons de la femme (including Félicien David), to seek the female Messiah (La Mère) in the Orient, and for various reasons Enfantin and others later joined in this grand relocation. All of this, not least the musical activities of David, will be traced in Chapter 12.

During this time another group of Saint-Simonians was developing in Paris, one that consisted of working-class *fidèles,* very few of whom had participated in the activities at rue Monsigny, the Salle Taitbout, or Ménilmontant. Some no doubt had been won over by the vigorous proselytizing efforts in the popular quarters of the city; perhaps others joined spontaneously after hearing of the movement's declared intention to work for the good of the poorest and most numerous class. The Famille de Paris, as it came to be called, and its leader Vinçard now undertook the production of Saint-Simonian songs. The songsters that the missionaries brought to the provinces, and even those that were published in regional cities such as Nantes and Grenoble, contained few Ménilmontant pieces by David but many chansons composed by Vinçard and the working-class members of the Famille de Paris. This important body of songs, modeled in many ways on the political chansons of Béranger, became in the wandering years 1833–35 what David's choruses had been in 1832: the movement's chief and, as Enfantin had foreseen, most successful form of propaganda through art.

11

VINÇARD AND THE
SAINT-SIMONIAN
CHANSON

THE MUSICAL LIFE OF THE FAMILLE DE PARIS

Life in Paris for the Saint-Simonians during the year or so after the breakup of the Ménilmontant Retreat focused largely on the two imprisoned leaders and on the various disciples who were now moving "into the world." Shortly before entering prison with Enfantin, Chevalier called together the Saint-Simonians for a ceremony at the grave of Saint-Simon,[1] after which all apparently adjourned to rue Monsigny to celebrate this new stage of the Saint-Simonian adventure. It is significant that, as far as we know, this occasion featured several chansons,[2] including Vinçard's "L'Avenir est à nous," but probably no piece by David, and certainly not a new one. Although David had not yet left Paris, his music was already being replaced. Songwriters such as Vinçard, Mercier, and Mora now became the most active musical propagandists of the movement, writing relatively simple and short strophic songs in great quantity. More precisely, they wrote song *texts,* to be sung to preexisting and widely known tunes.

Chansons had several obvious advantages over "composed" pieces, such as the choruses of David. They could be sung with little preparation at gatherings of Saint-Simonians in Paris; they could be written in a short time in order to celebrate a particular occasion; and they could be published in cheap, handy formats (containing only the words and a brief tune indication) and then distributed by the handful to members and to interested observers.

All three of these tendencies can be seen in the chansons published by the movement (Appendix B). The practice of performing songs at gatherings of the faithful continued for several years after the reunion at Saint-Simon's grave—we have a set of four songs for one meeting in 1835, three for another in 1836. The inexpensive, popular orientation of many of these publications is clear from their format: most are small—in-12mo, 16mo, even 32mo—and many consist of only a single sheet.[3] As for the special occasions, we find song after song written in celebration of significant events: Enfantin's birthday, the anniversary of the temple ceremony, Rogé and Massol's return to Paris in autumn

153

of 1833, the departures for the Orient, and Vinçard's departure from Paris in 1836 for a tour of the Midi. The advantages of the chanson fit perfectly the needs of a movement that had turned into a loosely organized network of wandering proselytizers.

The wanderers were successful in spreading Saint-Simonian songs and propaganda throughout the country and beyond, and even more successful at drawing attention to themselves and getting involved in colorful and risky escapades. But the song texts that they carried on the road were not of their own devising. Most, aside from the few pieces of David's that remained in the repertory, were written by songwriters who stayed in Paris and formed part of what came to be known as the Famille de Paris, headed by the artisan and songwriter Jules Vinçard (1796–1879?; see plate 19).

The Famille de Paris consisted primarily of artisans and workers. There were of course other Saint-Simonians still in Paris, notably Duveyrier, the Pereires, and Chevalier, none of whom chose to go to Egypt (Enfantin did, after he was released from prison in August 1833).[4] But these socially favored individuals who remained in Paris took little part in the activities of the Famille de Paris. The Famille was far more an outgrowth of the *degré des industriels* (proselytization effort in the working-class neighborhoods) than of the rue Monsigny or the Ménilmontant Retreat.[5]

Despite their modest origins, the members of the Famille showed deep concern for Enfantin and his adventuresome apostles. In particular, a number of women took the lead in publishing chronicles of the various missions, notably *Le Livre des actes,* a compilation of letters and accounts by the missionaries themselves.[6] Letters from the "friends in the provinces, especially those located in Egypt," were also read aloud during the Tuesday-night gatherings of the Famille in Vinçard's shop.[7]

From time to time the Parisian family even became caught up in what can only be described as the madness of the Egyptian Mission, the most curious instance being the series of visits from "the lady in blue." This young woman asked the Saint-Simonians to gather at Ménilmontant early one cold morning. They arrived in large numbers, Vinçard later recalled, "but without great enthusiasm." When she appeared, dressed in blue robes, with white roses in her hair and a long blue veil hanging to the rear, they were stunned to hear her announce that she wished to become an apostle and was looking for a man capable of leading and defending her on her way to join Enfantin in Egypt. Vinçard and some others, distressed at having initially received her so coldly, struck up a song by Jules Mercier, the "Appel à la femme." ("Parmi nous, FEMME douce at chère, / Viens pacifier l'univers. . . ."[8]) A month later, she returned to collect her escort. A substantial crowd had gathered, including many non-Saint-Simonians. Of the few men who offered her their arm, she deemed all unworthy. During a third session her mother arrived to take her away. The daughter commanded the members of the audience to kneel before her mother, and most obeyed instantaneously. She then handed her veil to the startled Saint-Simonians and left, saying, "I yield to my mother. I go back into my tomb."[9]

This episode, which Vinçard himself recalls with some astonishment, was very much an exception. For the most part, the efforts of Vinçard's circle were modest, local, and eminently sensible. This was even true of their more symbolic activities, such as their 1836 New Year's gift to George Sand: a varied selection of practical and largely homemade objects and items of clothing, "in the name of Saint-Simon and as a tribute from his disciples to the most worthy woman."[10] Sand, characteristically, replied with a warm and frank letter, admitting her admiration for Saint-Simonism while insisting that the immediate future had greater need of republicanism. "The salvation of the world seems to me to rest upon us to destroy, upon you to rebuild."[11]

Although very different in character and composition from the wandering apostles, the members of the Famille de Paris were, in their own way, extremely active and imaginative in creating and spreading Saint-Simonian propaganda, especially through song. The public celebrations that provided the occasion for the composition of songs were usually organized by Vinçard's friend Julien Gallé (plate 21), who was always eager to find new opportunities and new ways to communicate the Saint-Simonian message.[12] Vinçard recalls that Gallé considered the departure of Jules Mercier and five other missionaries "a splendid opportunity to 'do some ritual' [*faire du culte*], as he used to say to us."[13] One of Gallé's effective schemes consisted of bringing a number of *fidèles* to a performance at the Panorama Dramatique. They took seats in various places throughout the hall, but during the intermissions they lifted their voices together in song, to the delight of the whole audience.[14]

Vinçard remarks that "our singing demonstrations were always a success."[15] Particularly successful were the processions in honor of the various returning missionaries. "The presence of these men in apostolic costume in our midst during our customary processions always drew a crowd of curious people. Some people were touched [by what they saw], followed us, joined us, and swelled our group." At Gallé's insistence, Vinçard wrote songs for three of these homecomings: "Le Grognard" (for Delas), "Nous voilà" (Rogé), and "Travailleur, chante" (Duguet).[16]

In the end, though, it is perhaps the Famille's hearty attempts at extravagant and luxurious entertainment that were most characteristic of the group and that reveal most sharply the difference between its members and the apostles who were now proving their devotion by marching through marshes and hostile towns. "The life of an apostle is harsh and severe," Achille Rousseau had proclaimed in the text of David's *Salut;* the life of the movement's working-class members was harsh and severe, too, but not by choice. Whereas the wandering apostles could glory in the austerity of their bread, water, and celibacy, the Parisian family heard Vinçard's chansons amid whatever sensual gratifications they could afford (within the limits of propriety). On Sunday, 6 October 1833, for example, Vinçard and two assistants organized in a room in the Prado one of a series of parties: "relaxations of our good proletarians, and compensation for the labors of the week." On this occasion they made a special effort "that the pleasures might be diverse. A modest contribution of 75 centimes procured the use of an appropriate hall, a good orchestra, and even some refreshments. The lively dancing was occasionally interrupted by beautiful religious songs written by Mercier and Vinçard."[17] The affair seems to have been more refined but no less pleasure-oriented than the average gluttonous and brawling banquet in a *goguette* (working-class song club).[18] Similarly, the celebration of Enfantin's birthday on 8 February 1834 combined "a simple meal," "beautiful songs," and "lively dancing"; the anonymous author of the published account, well versed in the doctrine of the rehabilitation of the flesh, added a note to Enfantin saying that the more than three hundred participants had turned their thoughts to him while enjoying "the pleasures which you have come to sanctify in the name of GOD."[19]

CHANSON TRADITION, BÉRANGER, AND THE WORK OF THE SAINT-SIMONIAN CHANSONNIERS

It is hard to find information about many of the movement's chansonniers. The earliest Saint-Simonian chanson—"La Loi de Dieu" (1831)—was written by a man named Lagache.[20] He was probably one of the working-class or artisan members (Vinçard refers to him as "one of our poets, friend Lagache").[21] As the movement became more deeply involved in missionary work in Paris and the provinces, Lagache was replaced by more prolific hands: Mora (or Morat), Charles Chevalier, Jules Mercier, Boissy, and Vinçard himself. Perhaps the most talented of these was Mercier,[22] but his contribution to the movement was cut short when, feeling unappreciated as a poet and rejected as a lover, he committed suicide in 1834.

For centuries the French had sustained a thriving tradition of writing songs on subjects of topical interest; the resulting repertoires extended from the naïve and charming sixteenth-century noels to the thousands of songs openly reviling the hated cardinal and minister Mazarin. More recently, the tradition had put forth one of its most splendid blossomings in the work of Pierre-Jean de Béranger (1780–1857), a member of the literarily inclined Caveau Moderne (named after Le Caveau, the distinguished, debonair song club of the mid-eighteenth century). Under the Bourbon Restoration, Béranger had devoted vivid and elegantly turned verses, not to traditional praise of wine, women, and song, but to bold and scarcely veiled attacks on the repressive policies of the government. The voice of the liberal and republican opposition, Béranger was jailed twice by the Bourbons but lived to see the regime overthrown and to see his works sung and read throughout the Western world.[23]

It is this tradition, and especially the example of Béranger, that served as a model for the Saint-Simonian chansonniers. Like their predecessors, the Saint-Simonians generally set their songs to well-known tunes and indicated the tune by a *timbre* (tune name) printed just under the title of the song. The *timbre* normally consisted of the title, or first line of the refrain, of the tune's original or best-known text. A person who did not happen to know the tune to which a particular *timbre* referred could easily look it up in Capelle's compendium of chanson tunes, *La Clé du Caveau.*

French chanson writers had long been interested in creating a vibrant interplay between their new text and the chosen tune, or between new text and old. Béranger, in particular, although his songs are generally treated purely as literary or political documents, was quite careful in his choice of tunes. (For example, he assigned a martial tune to a song about an army canteen woman, a barcarolle to a song that treats life as a journey in a boat, and a royalist tune—irony here—to several songs denouncing the repressive policies of King Charles X.[24]) The Saint-Simonians followed this practice, sometimes with great success. Mercier, for example, chose "Vive le roi, vive la France" (1816) as the tune for his "Le Règne du peuple."[25] This seemingly perverse choice of the quasi-official Bourbon hymn in fact served his purposes nicely, for it automatically called up in the listener's mind the original words—and with them memories of the misery and oppression of the Restoration years—as a silent gloss on Mercier's celebration of a more democratic future.

The Saint-Simonians willingly commented on the republican past as well. Vinçard, for example, rewrote the Revolutionary song "Ça ira" (see below), and Mercier apparently intended something similar when he chose to set "La Charte de Dieu" ("La liberté pour le Peuple et la Femme, / Bonheur pour tous, c'est la Charte de Dieu") to a song about "Les Trois Couleurs" (i.e., the Revolutionary tricolored flag). Indeed, the chosen *timbre* did not have to be political at all. Vinçard used one called "Ermite, bon ermite" to underline the apostles' hermitlike retreat from the world in his "Salut à Ménilmontant."[26]

Occasionally the Saint-Simonian text sheets and songsters identify the chosen tune by the title of Béranger's recent words rather than by the generally accepted *timbre*. In songwriting circles this was considered poor form, for it could mislead people who wanted to find the tune in the *Clé du Caveau* (Capelle prided himself on listing a tune only under the name or names that it had "properly" acquired in chanson tradition). But such a *faux timbre*, as it was called, reveals the overwhelming influence that Béranger had on the Saint-Simonian chansonniers—not surprisingly, since he shared many of their sentiments and even praised Saint-Simon and Enfantin in his song "Les Fous" (1832).[27] More specifically, it also suggests that the chansonnier and his listeners may have had part or all of a Béranger text in mind when composing, singing, or hearing a new Saint-Simonian chanson. Thus the anonymous "Les Saint-Simons sont de bons lurons" gives the *timbre* as "Les Gueux," a Béranger chanson whose tune was in fact properly known as "La première ronde du *Départ pour Saint-Malo.*"[28] The humorous application of the beloved Béranger song about some cheerful beggars ("Ils s'aiment entr'eux. / Vivent les gueux!") to the text "the Saint-Simons are jolly fellows" must have made the movement seem especially endearing to inhabitants of the poorer *quartiers.*

At other times the Saint-Simonian chansonniers, though using tunes that Béranger had also employed, gave the "correct" *timbre;* in these cases they were probably drawing less from Béranger than from chanson tradition generally. For example, Mercier's new text to "Les Trois Couleurs" and Vinçard's salute to the hermits of Ménilmontant, both discussed previously, clearly allude to the traditional texts, rather than to any of Béranger's texts for the same tunes. (He had written three for one, two for the other.) Indeed, a tune may have been used so frequently through the years, and in such varied ways, that it no longer had any fixed connotations whatever but remained in use simply because it was sturdy, singable, and well known. One of Béranger's favorite tunes was "A soixante ans il ne faut pas remettre"; he used it for no fewer than seven chansons on the most varied subjects. Mercier, too, appropriated the melody for one of his best pieces, "La Sainte Canaille" ("The Holy Rabble").

The Chansonniers, the "Marseillaise," and Later Generations

The Saint-Simonians' selection of songs differed from that of Béranger in one important respect: the Saint-Simonians made willing use of the two best-known songs of the French Revolution: the "Marseillaise" and "Ça ira." Of course, Béranger would not have dared to use either of these tunes before 1830, but even after the downfall of the Bourbon monarchy he continued to avoid them. Perhaps his deep respect for the "Marseillaise" and his friendship with its author and composer Rouget de Lisle prevented him from tampering with it.[29] As for "Ça ira," its refrain about stringing up the aristocrats ("Ça ira, les aristocrates on les pendra!") no doubt made it too violently republican for him to use either straight or satirically; it would have raised hackles on one side or the other of the political spectrum. Vinçard discovered exactly that when he set new words to it: "Ça viendra! espérance, persévérance! / Ça viendra! tout le monde un jour nous aimera." Vinçard tried to sing this song in late 1832 to a crowd at Charenton but, as he recalled later, the "fatal resemblance" to the old revolutionary song angered the crowd, which grew larger and more "ill-willed" by the minute, hurling epithets and then stones at the unsuspecting missionaries.[30] Vinçard does not say why the people were so furious. Perhaps some felt that these were impostors, appropriating and distorting the proud revolutionary heritage ("Jesuits in disguise," as some republicans in Grenoble had put it);[31] perhaps others feared the opposite: that these might be some kind of dangerous republicans or revolutionaries, reviving the old songs as a means of fostering insurrection. In truth, the Saint-Simonians considered themselves neither antirepublicans nor republicans reborn but rather social prophets of a new kind, who had transcended both republicanism and reaction. That is precisely what Vinçard was trying to express by consciously replacing "Ça ira" with "Ça viendra": the age of happiness *will come,* if only we forswear violence and adhere to the principles of patience and pacifism.

The attempts to rewrite the "Marseillaise" resulted in less distress, but they derived from a similar line of thought: in order to create a hymn appropriate to the new age of *association,* poets must seek an alternative to the militaristic and chauvinistic imagery of the "Marseillaise." The Saint-Simonians were apparently the first movement on the "left" to criticize the "Marseillaise";[32] they were certainly the loudest. On 11 September 1830, only six weeks after the July Revolution, Michel Chevalier complained in a long article in the *Organisateur* that the people had nothing to sing but "that hymn of blood, those atrocious curses" and that the lack of more uplifting songs was proof of "the impotence of liberal poetry ... for which the love of one's fellows [*l'amour social*] ... [is] a deadly poison." (This striking article was reprinted as one of the *Feuilles populaires* in May 1832.[33]) Barrault insisted in his sermon on art (1 May 1831) that the "Marseillaise," the people's only "song of victory and liberty," was inappropriate to the problems of society after the revolution, for it encouraged hatred and violence, and he lamented that poets had not taught the people any other hymns, any "words of love, peace, and hope."[34] Olinde Rodrigues asked on 27 November 1831, immediately after the Bazard schism: "When will I hear the people sing the hymn of peace—more electrifying than the awesome 'Marseillaise,' more joyful than the simple 'Parisienne?'"[35] And Henri Fournel expressed himself in similar terms in 1833.[36]

With all the leaders proclaiming the need for a new "Marseillaise," it is no surprise that a number of their followers rushed into the breach. At least three new texts for the "Marseillaise" were produced by the Saint-Simonian chansonniers: "Le Chant du travail" by Vidal and Bertu, "L'Homme nouveau" by Mora, and a "Marseillaise pacifique" of unknown authorship.[37]

The three new versions are spirited, if predictable. That of Vidal and Bertu begins:

> Allons, enfans de l'industrie,
> Voici venir des temps nouveaux;
> La sanguinaire tyrannie
> Ne fait plus flotter ses drapeaux.

Later strophes praise steam power and a "gentle, strong people" that, updating the injunction of Isaiah, beats its muskets into shining rails. Each strophe ends with the couplet: "Courage! mes amis, ensemble travaillons; / Marchons, [marchons,] que notre ardeur féconde nos sillons." Vidal and Bertu knew well how to turn the "Marseillaise" text and imagery to their own purposes. Indeed, the fourth stanza handily transforms Rouget de Lisle's familiar "Amour sacré de la patrie" into a paean to Love: "Amour sacré! flamme éternelle."[38]

Mora's version (plate 23), a more typical product of L'Année de la Mère (1833), traded vivid imagery for more abstract visions of a "happy future" and of equal rights for women, "the victim of customs and laws." It devoted a stanza to the imprisoned Enfantin and another to the steadfastness of his apostles in the face of the "enemies of SAINT-SIMONISM," ending each time with a rather sodden refrain whose prosody (the syllables *de* and l'hom*me* fall on long accented notes) is unfortunately typical of the whole: "Enfans du même DIEU, plus de servilité. / L'HOMME NOUVEAU chérit le PERE et sent sa dignité."

The third version, the anonymous "Marseillaise pacifique," is perhaps inferior in prosody even to Mora's "L'Homme nouveau" and suffers from a refrain that doesn't really rhyme: "Plus de sang!!! plus de sang!!! Humains, embrassez-vous, / Bientôt, [bientôt,] l'âge de DIEU va luire enfin pour tous." At times the call for world peace is powerfully expressed: "Oh, Earth! Inhuman discord has devoured your children long enough."[39] But, even at its best, the pacifist imagery of the text sits a bit strangely on Rouget de Lisle's stirring tune, with its unmistakably military allure.

Within a few short years these new "Marseillaises" were forgotten, along with the rest of the Saint-Simonian chansons. But even if the clamoring did not produce a lasting alternative to the traditional hymn, it may have encouraged other writers to try. Louis Festeau, a Fourierist chansonnier, composed a "Marseillaise de 1840."[40] In 1841, Lamartine, responding to the violent German nationalism of Nikolaus Becker's "Rheinlied," penned a call for cooperation and brotherhood that was Saint-Simonian in its imagery (on commerce: "These living boats whose soul is steam") and that, although not intended to be sung, bore the title "La Marseillaise de la paix."[41] In 1844, a particularly rich year, Mora used the tune again, Jean Journet wrote a Fourierist text for it ("La Marseillaise des travailleurs"), and Flora Tristan printed two proposed versions of a "Marseillaise de l'union ouvrière."[42] The Revolution of 1848 brought forth a competition for a new national hymn.[43] In Germany in the 1840s, Ferdinand Freiligrath composed two new texts for the "Marseillaise" tune, but these impetuous calls for armed rebellion ("Toward the silver fleets of property boldly aim the cannons' bore!")[44] would not have pleased Barrault and Rodrigues.

Indeed, the Saint-Simonians would have been pained by many of the political chansons of the 1840s and later—whether "Marseillaises" or not. In France the reactionary policies of the Guizot ministry gave rise to a new and very different generation of versifiers and songwriters: class-conscious, radical, more socialist than utopian, pointing the way toward the Revolution of 1848 and the Second Republic. (Among the best of these angry young *poètes-ouvriers* were Gustave Leroy and Louis Festeau.) Their energetic message—full of urgency, sarcasm, and foreboding—fused effortlessly with the sort of tunes that Béranger had used ten, twenty, and thirty years earlier—much better, it must be said, than had the more ameliorative message of the Saint-Simonians.

But the latters' yearning for a hymn that would celebrate *association universelle* was not entirely submerged by the new fighting spirit. Modified by the class-consciousness of the age, it shows up in the "Chant des ouvriers" (1846) of Pierre Dupont, which Baudelaire called "the 'Marseillaise' of labor," and, during the Paris Commune of 1870–71, in the "Internationale" of Parisian transport worker Eugène Pottier, set stirringly to music in 1881 by Pierre Degeyter and quickly adopted as a symbol of newfound strength by "the wretched of the earth" for a century or more thereafter.[45]

VINÇARD'S SONGS

We have seen that the Saint-Simonian chansonniers almost always used traditional chanson tunes, at times with conscious artistry. One of them, though, often wrote his own tunes: Jules Vinçard, generally known as Vinçard aîné.[46] Vinçard became during his long life one of the most respected figures in the French chanson movement, and he further established a place for himself in the annals of the chanson because of his detailed and perceptive *Mémoires épisodiques d'un vieux chansonnier saint-simonien.*

The son of a ruler maker and a laundress, Vinçard was persuaded by a friend in 1831 to attend some meetings of the Saint-Simonians. Although at first he thought their ideas dangerous, he was also impressed by their calm and assured delivery. He soon inscribed as a member and had some responsibility for the propaganda efforts in one of the working-class districts. He began to write Saint-Simonian songs and sang them to his cohorts in the Garde nationale during his term of service in 1832.[47] He had not joined the apostles in Ménilmontant because he disliked the shift in emphasis from social change to adoration of Le Père.[48] When he saw the martyrdom that Enfantin was suffering at the end of the year, he returned to the fold, wrote more songs, and participated musically in celebrating the *départs* and *retours* of the various missionary groups. In late 1833, after Enfantin and his circle left Paris for Egypt, Vinçard was acclaimed *pasteur* of the Famille de Paris, which gave him the responsibility for some quite wayward sheep. If the historians of Saint-Simonism had, during the past 150 years, paid as much attention to the working-class members as they did to the barons and bankers, the name of Vinçard might now loom as large as that of Enfantin.

For our present purposes, though, Vinçard is most interesting as the only Saint-Simonian chansonnier to have written his own melodies, and to have written them with fair regularity in spite of a total lack of musical training. His *Mémoires* contain few remarks on the musical side of his activity as chansonnier, but those remarks are quite informative. He says that he learned versification from Marchand, a fellow worker in his father's shop, who "gave me *bouts rimés* to fill,[49] and so, without being aware of it, I acquired the ability to express myself more or less well in verse, and more correctly anyway than I could have done in prose." Marchand also tried to get Vinçard to study grammar and music notation, but Vinçard did not have the necessary self-discipline.[50] Thus, although Vinçard began to attend the *goguettes* (working-class song clubs) in 1818 and write patriotic and political songs in conscious imitation of Béranger,[51] it was not until the 1850s that he learned how to write the tunes down.

> I generally did the tunes for my own songs. My great frustration was in notating the tunes. I [finally] had the idea of attending the courses of M. Emile Chevé, that devoted apostle of the numerical method, and, by the end of several months of study, I was able to write down immediately all the snatches [*réminiscences*] of tunes that passed through my mind.[52]

It appears that Vinçard, like most other chansonniers, could not accompany his own songs, for he never mentions an instrument, not even a guitar, in connection with his renditions. Only toward the end of his *Mémoires* does he speak of musical instruments—a violin and a piano—and the context of this passage suggests that he acquired them in middle life at the earliest.[53] It seems likely, though, that other people occasionally provided an accompaniment to his singing, especially when he performed indoors. Edgar Leon Newman points out that most of the goguettes "had a piano player to accompany the singers," and one imagines that the instrument was often to be found in the restaurants in which the Famille de Paris met. Even the more "old-fashioned" goguettes often used a guitar player or harpist, in apparent continuation of a centuries-old tradition of accompaniment on the lute or viol.[54]

It is not clear when or how Vinçard began to compose his own tunes. He does not seem to have been proud of the fact and certainly made no attempt to publicize it. In his first printed collections of chansons he simply gave no *timbre* for certain songs, a misleading step that prompted Béranger—to whom he had boldly sent a copy—to write back critizing him for being a snob: "It is not fitting for us verse makers to flaunt the desire to be read. If people do us that honor, fine, but let's not go chasing after it."[55] Vinçard must have been mortified that his modesty had been interpreted as grandiosity by the man he had taken as his model.

The next year (1835), at Enfantin's instigation, Vinçard finally went out to Passy to visit Béranger and offer him his latest chanson. Béranger at first teased Vinçard and the Saint-Simonian woman who, for symbolic reasons, had been asked to accompany him. Vinçard finally interrupted the poet's insinuations about free love, and the discussion turned to the presentation chanson. " 'To what tune do you sing these verses,' he asked. 'To a tune of my own [*de ma façon*], or rather to snatches of several other tunes that have stuck in my memory.'" Then, to close what Vinçard felt was already a disastrous meeting, Béranger offered detailed criticisms of Vinçard's song (e.g., feminine rhymes make a bad effect at the end of a strophe).[56]

Vinçard's statements about his tunes are more informative than they may at first appear. They indicate that he must often have started composing the words first and thereby found himself tempted (or forced) to cobble together a tune appropriate to the meter and substance of the text. This is the very opposite of Béranger's usual procedure, in which the traditional tune (and at times its text) played a role in the creation of the new words.

Of course, Vinçard was not the only chansonnier who began writing the words first. The *Clé du Caveau* contains a massive cross-index of its tunes according to *coupe* (meter and rhyme scheme), precisely intended to help songwriters find a tune for words they had written, or at least begun to write. But what is different about Vinçard is that, instead of searching for an appropriate tune in the *Clé du Caveau* index, he often made up a melody of his own.

It would be an error to think that the act of composing his tunes necessarily confers some kind of virtue on Vinçard. A published chanson, in order to be sung by others, must bear a known *timbre*, not an unhelpful indication such as "air de l'auteur des paroles." Indeed, of the forty-eight songs by Vinçard in his retrospective collection *Les Chants du travailleur* (1869), fifteen do bear a *timbre* indicating a well-known tune. But more than twice as many—thirty-three chansons—use melodies composed (or assembled) by Vinçard. Fortunately for us, in this collection Vinçard finally printed these tunes. (See the table below. For convenience this list includes as well the four other tunes published in Vinçard's collection; the words for three of them are not by Vinçard and the composer of the other is probably Musard, so all four will be excluded from discussion below. This explains, though, why Vinçard's thirty-three tunes bear numbers as high as thirty-seven.[57])

TABLE

Songs in Vinçard's *Chants du Travailleur* for which tunes are notated. Words are by Vinçard except nos. 9, 21, 22. CSS here indicates "Chant saint-simonien" or "Chanson saint-simonienne." The dates are as given by Vinçard; my corrections are in brackets.

1. Elan! (1840).
2. Le Sonneur de cloche (1860).
3. Aux pauvres gens (undated [by 1869]).
4. Aux goguettiers (1845).
5. L'Attente (1838).
6. Le Forgeron (1838).
7. La Paille et la poutre (1854).
8. La Poule aux oeufs d'or (1856).
9. La Loi de Dieu (CSS, words by Lagache, 1834 [1831?]).
10. Travailleur, chante (CSS, 1835).
11. Alerte! (or Appel, CSS, 1836).

12. Le Congrès de Paris (CSS, 1857).
13. Le Chant du travail (1855).
14. La Bonté (CSS, 1839).
15. Le Prolétaire (CSS, 1835).
16. Appel à la chanson (1856).
17. Le Brin d'herbe (1863).
18. Le Dix-neuvième Siècle (1842).
19. Accord (1837).
20. L'Homme a des travers (1868, tune by Musard).
21. La Prolétairienne (words by Corréard of Lyons, 1833).
22. A l'Orient (words by Félix Maynard, music by Henri Reber, 1834).
23. Le Départ: Apôtre, en avant! (CSS, 1834).
24. Invocation (1834).
25. Notre foi, notre vie (CSS, 1836).
26. Courage! (or L'Avenir est là, CSS 1836 [1835]).
27. Le Retour (or Le Grognard, CSS, 1835).
28. Place au peuple (1848).
29. Nous voilà (CSS, 1836).
30. En avant (1838).
31. Chantons la paix et donnons-nous la main (1843).
32. L'Oeuvre de Dieu (CSS, 1861).
33. La Poire est mûre (CSS, 1868).
34. La Ronde de Saint-Simon (1861).
35. Pendons la crémaillère (1862).
36. Souvenir au Père Enfantin (1865).
37. Affirmons-nous (CSS, 1868).

Not all of the thirty-three chansons with tunes by Vinçard are specifically labeled "Chant saint-simonien," but the sentiments and musical style are consistent throughout the songs. Indeed, Vinçard himself apparently considered most of his songs to be Saint-Simonian propaganda, whether or not the message was explicit; he states in his *Mémoires* that, after Enfantin and Chevalier were sentenced to prison, the antagonism of the public was so fierce that he was forced to disguise the Saint-Simonian ideas in his songs by "a triple veil of allusions to current politics."[58] A number of the pieces in *Les Chants du travailleur* (including four of those entitled "Chant saint-simonien") were actually written late in Vinçard's life, but again the style of the pieces is relatively consistent with that of the works from the 1830s and therefore they can all be considered as a group.

Most of Vinçard's tunes are of the type that Béranger most favored, with verses and refrain, the verse often hanging around the fifth degree of the scale. The melodies have much in common with standard chanson tunes in use at the time. But Vinçard's melodies, or melody compilations, have a rough-hewn, often asymmetrical character that sets them apart even from the less regular of the traditional chanson melodies. A few are constructed entirely of four- or eight-measure phrases, but more often there are expansions, particularly at the end of the refrain (an extra measure in song 15, four in song 5, six in song

29, eight in song 19, a two-measure interpolation in song 35 that delays and intensifies the cadential arrival of the song's motto). The structure can become even more free (five plus three plus five measures in the refrain of song 1— see Appendix C) and especially so in the verses (songs 10, 11, etc.).

The asymmetrical structure of Vinçard's tunes often derived from his unconventional verse structures. Enfantin complained of this in 1855:

> Your devilish songs have an irregularity of rhythm which forces you to make lines of very differing meters. This is an obstacle which prevents anyone other than you to sing them, to set them to different music, or to put yours into score for an accompanist. For example, your first eight lines [in *Chant du travail*—song 13] have seven, eight, eight, six, eight, six, seven, and six syllables. This is as anti-metrical as you can get. Still, it's first-rate and of the right stamp [*frappé au bon coin*]![59]

Vinçard reports that he took most of Enfantin's advice and that Béranger wrote to say how much he liked the result. (Indeed, the refrain as published is somewhat more regular than what Enfantin had seen.) Even so, Vinçard discovered at a gathering a year later that people had trouble singing this "Chant du travail" because the melody was too difficult.[60] His decision to let the words dominate and form the music shows its weakest aspect here.

In other respects the songs are more successful. The tunes are quite stable tonally, with a characteristic tendency to move toward the tonic minor, especially at the end of the verse just before the return (songs 6, 10, 13, 17, 19, 24, 28, 32). In song 29 (Appendix C) the shift to the minor is used to highlight the phrase "Désespoir, halte-là!" and in song 33 it is used to set up the shift back to the major at the statement of the Saint-Simonians' motto, drawn from Saint-Simon's dying words: "La poire est mûre" ("The pear is ripe, pluck it").

Unlike the usual chanson tune—which, however appropriate to a given text, still merely "carries" it—Vinçard's melody often reflects the meaning of the words in quite a specific way, either by echoing its images through dance rhythms (song 34—Appendix C) and church-bell and bugle-call figures (songs 2, 11, 12, 23) or by emphasizing one or more words through more abstract musical means such as cross-accents, patter treatment, or sudden changes or range and phrase length (song 34 again; also songs 2, 7, 28). These are of course some of the advantages that a chansonnier can have when he composes his own tunes, and they are features that Vinçard no doubt heightened when performing the songs.

Viewed purely as music, Vinçard's melodies are a mixed lot. Some are quite effective on their own (those in Appendix 3, plus songs 2, 3, 11, 15, 19, 36). Others, though, use awkward intervals or long-held notes that defy a clear harmonic interpretation and perhaps could only make sense if accompanied by an instrument (songs 10, 23, 25, 26). One cannot help wondering whether some of these features—the irregular phrase structure mentioned earlier and melodic turns that do not clarify the intended harmony, or the nearly two-octave range of the aforementioned "Chant du travail"—are the result of an attempt (probably unconscious and certainly unsuccessful) at imitating the more pretentious, more "bourgeois" melodies that professional musicians such as Meissonnier and Panseron were fond of composing to the verses of Béranger.[61]

This emulation of high-toned music (a natural result of the decline in the city of true, mainly rural, folk traditions)[62] appears even more strongly in a published arrangement, with choral refrain and piano accompaniment, of a Vinçard song, "Elan" (Appendix C).[63] The arranger, and in this he is quite possibly typical of the piano players who accompanied chansons in the go-guettes, seems to be trying to copy the "elegance" of the quadrilles and waltzes played almost nightly by Musard's and Valentino's orchestras. There is even a little science in the voice-leading of this piano part (concern to avoid doubling the melody, mm. 3, 11, 22–27), and the choral writing, complete with a cadential chromatic passing tone, is pure Wilhem. The regular harmonic cushion does counteract some of the roughness and eccentricity in Vinçard's melody, but it also obscures much of the verve of those bold ups and downs. Vinçard, like Béranger, may well have personally welcomed such fashionable accompani-ments, but the singer's own sturdy personality shines better unbedecked.

One exception to many of the remarks made earlier about Vinçard's rather asymmetrical melodies is "Le Brin d'herbe" (song 17—Appendix C) written around 1858, soon after Vinçard had settled in his country home in Saint-Maur. The song describes a clump of grass growing in the shade of a wall and asks with great social significance, "N'as-tu pas ta place au soleil?" ("Don't you have your place in the sun?") Perhaps because the subject is a little plant, Vinçard has lavished on it a lovely chanson in the style of the simpler senti-mental romances of the day, with their flowing melody, their decorative ap-poggiaturas and turns, their standard structure of four eight-bar phrases (plus in this case a brief coda), and their equally standard modulatory and thematic structure:

$$A \qquad A' \qquad B \qquad A''$$
$$I \rightarrow I \quad I \rightarrow V \quad V \qquad I$$

Hundreds of these things must have been written about roses covered with dewdrops. The socialist Vinçard wrote his about a clump of grass.

SURVIVAL OF THE WORKS OF DAVID DURING THE DISPERSAL

The distance is immense between the chansons of Vinçard and the choruses of David. Even in the song just examined, with its echoes of the "cultivated" music of the salon, and even in the songs with curious melodic leaps and surprising phrase structure, Vinçard's songs remain chansons—melodic inspirations that serve to transmit, and on occasion modestly interpret, a text—a far cry from most of David's compositions, with their harmonic and textural variety. But Vinçard was happy, even eager, to use material by David when it could suit the movement's purposes. He reports several occasions on which he and the Famille de Paris performed "the songs by David" in the streets as part of their ceremonies: for the departure of Jules Mercier and five other missionaries; on Sundays, walking back to Paris "in a grand procession" after the communal meal at Ménilmontant (this is confirmed by Suzanne Voilquin); and on 8 February 1833, Enfantin's birthday (a special "choral" performance of the *Salut* outside the walls of the prison).[64] This last occasion continued with more musical activity. The family marched to Ménilmontant singing, in alternation, David's *Appel* and Mercier's "L'Arche de Dieu." In the great house they set a bust of Saint-Simon on the mantel, Mercier sang his song "Le Père" to the portrait of Enfantin, Ferrand sang his "Le Temple de Dieu," and they marched out to the temple where Hoart led them in the *Appel,* Mercier spoke, and they sang *Peuple fier.*[65] This free mixture of rhetoric, ritual, chansons, and pieces composed at the Retreat by David (sung melody-only, one imagines) must have been typical of the movement's more ceremonial reunions in the years after the dispersal of the apostles.

Vinçard's description of another public performance gives the flavor of some of the more vigorous public manifestations.

> Another time, he [Gallé] had the idea of walking the bust of Saint-Simon through the streets of Paris, with all the pomp of a religious ritual. Upon a stretcher covered with a tapestry curtain we built a kind of altar and placed the bust upon it, surrounded by flowers and ribbons. Four of us, dressed in the apostolic costume with all its insignias, carried the stretcher, preceded and followed by the whole Family—men and women—singing in chorus the hymns of Félicien David.
>
> In this manner we went through or across the most heavily traveled streets of Paris. The crowd, struck speechless, stopped. Some people came up to us, asked questions, and ended up joining our demonstration.[66]

Vinçard also reports hearing "a tune by David" sung a few years later by a small knot of wealthy young *fidèles* in Marseilles. They had learned the tune from their leader, the impoverished tapestry weaver Julie Fanfernot,[67] who had, one gathers, learned it from Vinçard on an earlier occasion.[68]

With the exception of the *Salut,* neither Vinçard nor Suzanne Voilquin mentions by name the various *chants* or *airs* of David that they and their comrades performed. Hoart, in the account cited earlier, mentions the *Salut* and two of David's chansons with choral refrain: *Appel* and *Peuple fier.* As late as March 1834 the intrepid Castelnaudarians were preparing to sing "in the streets" these same three pieces plus *Je ne veux plus être exploité.*[69] And these four David numbers, plus two others (*Compagnonnage* and *Après le repas*) show up, sometimes repeatedly, in the song booklets of 1833–35.[70] All of this suggests strongly that David's more elaborate works disappeared quickly, whereas his chansons and the melodies of his simpler choruses continued to spread the word. (The one relatively difficult chorus in the list is Enfantin's piece, the *Salut;* perhaps its more polyphonic sections were often omitted.[71]) Tuneful songs fitted the needs of the splintered movement after 1832. This did not stop three musicians—David, Rogé, and a new recruit, Henri Reber—from trying to sustain the momentum that Ménilmontant had given to more elaborate composition. But the moment was no longer theirs.

PART FOUR
ECHOES

12

THE MUSICIANS
DURING THE DISPERSAL
AND THE EGYPTIAN
MISSION

DAVID AND HIS WORKS TRAVEL SOUTH

Of the many groups of "missionaries" that left Paris after the collapse of the Retreat, perhaps the most important was led by Barrault and included seventeen apostles, among them David. This group departed for Lyons on 15 December 1832, carrying a number of song sheets to distribute along the road (Appendix B.1). One of the travelers recalled soon after that "everywhere our songs, our costumes, Barrault's speeches, and the proletarian life which we were going to lead in Lyons stimulated eager interest in our favor—especially among the women."[1] Only in Nogent-sur-Seine were they threatened and attacked; everywhere else they were welcomed, feted, and given supplies for the road.[2]

It was Enfantin's intention that these and other apostles establish Lyons as the new center of Saint-Simonian activity. He felt that they needed to undergo a "wage-labor baptism"—by sharing the work, the bread, and the humble roof of the *prolétaires*—and he also wanted them to bring a message of calm and patience to the city's angry weavers and fearful bourgeois.[3] The baptism was easy to arrange, but exhausting: Toché worked as a laborer from 5 A.M. to 8 P.M. for 50 sous a day, and Rogé spent similar hours turning cranks and cutting screws.[4] Still, the apostles found the strength to give frequent lectures, though their message of calm only succeeded in making the city's elite even more nervous. (Police reports show that they were under constant surveillance; at one point the prefect even urged the mayor to forbid them—Rogé included—from lecturing.[5])

But many of the apostles were eager to go on to something else, and to some other place. For many of them that something, that somewhere, was what Frenchmen called the "Orient"—North Africa and the Near and Middle East. The region held great appeal for Enfantin and Barrault. Often in late 1831 and 1832 they had preached the future union of East and West. Enfantin, like Michel Chevalier, was particularly interested in the economic advantages of such a union. But there was a further attraction. The region was ancient and hallowed—the cradle of three world religions—and, most of all, myste-

171

riously different—a land of changeless tradition, impervious to Western rationality and concepts of progress and therefore perhaps more naturally attuned to the intuitive, emotional, prophetic vision that Enfantin was so eagerly developing. From this point of view, the East—backward but vital—was to the West as woman was to man.[6]

Barrault drew the consequences of this particular line of thought. He and his fellows had frequently proposed that Saint-Simonian propaganda be directed toward women (through the arts, especially the novel),[7] and as early as April 1832 he had entertained the analogous idea of proselytizing in the East. Now, only a month after arriving in Lyons, he fused the two images in a burning conviction that the female Messiah would appear before the end of 1833 in Constantinople. On his own authority he decided to dissolve the Saint-Simonian hierarchy. In its place he established a new and much smaller order, the Compagnons de la femme (or Femme), dedicated to advancing the cause of women's rights and, above all, to searching out the blessed lady in the eastern Mediterranean. Barrault announced all of this to Enfantin in a letter of 30 January 1833, emphasizing that the inspiration was his own and that a number of the *fidèles* most devoted to Enfantin had at first resisted Barrault's assertion of his "independent energy." Enfantin himself, as it happens, had by then developed some rather more practical Oriental schemes that he no doubt realized he could intertwine with those of Barrault. And so he approved the plan and told his correspondent to take charge of the "songs and costumes," to insist autocratically on celibacy and "strict discipline," and to have the Compagnons extend Enfantin's personal greeting to Byron's tomb, to the city of Jerusalem, and to every single Oriental woman that they met on their way. He concluded with words that David must have taken to heart: "To La MERE: the *chorus* of MORNING; to Le PERE: the *song* of EVENING and solitary meditation."[8]

Enfantin decided that the first twelve Compagnons should set forth from the port of Marseilles on 22 March (the vernal equinox). In the meantime, the apostles remained in Lyons, working, speaking about La Femme-Messie, and, as instructed, making music. The very day of their arrival in Lyons, Barrault had given a speech to a crowd of two thousand, and soon thereafter he "improvised" (as usual) at a banquet of working-class Saint-Simonians.[9] The apostles were visible in the wealthier quarters as well. "On certain evenings," Rogé recalled with a bit of class-conscious irony, "we removed our boots in the front hall of Mme Montgolfier, Mme Didier, Mme Duval, or other persons of 'distinction,' and we gave some musical *soirées* and *matinées* in full sight of the prefect and other leading lights of Lyons."[10] (Rogé did not choose these names haphazardly. Jenny Montgolfier, a talented pianist and friend of Liszt's, was a close acquaintance of Enfantin's trusted friend, the silk manufacturer Arlès-Dufour. Anaïs Saint-Didier and her husband seem to have befriended Félicien David in various ways, and the composer later dedicated piano pieces both to her and to Jenny Montgolfier. Finally, Mme S. Durval—if that is Rogé's "Mme Duval"—was the bookseller who undertook the publication of various Saint-Simonian pamphlets and of David's choruses and songs.) One performance of David's *Tout est mort* at Mme Montgolfier's ended in a particularly delicious victory for the apostles and their doctrine. David's piece includes the words "n'aimons que le peuple, il n'est pas aimé!"—words that must have disturbed the prefect, M. Gasparin, for he hastened to protest that he and his kind actually loved the people a great deal. "Yes," Rogé recalls having replied, "the people is loved the way the shepherd's master loves the flock: for its meat and wool!"[11]

Clorinde Rogé, in a letter to Enfantin, described a similar salon presentation that generated rather less acrimony. Although Clorinde was by now fiercely antagonistic to Barrault's self-serving interest in the cause of women and his unabashed courtship of people of wealth, even she was forced to admit that David's music was providing effective support for the proselytization effort.

> Last Sunday there was a *matinée musicale* at M. Saint-Didier's. The *haute bourgeoisie* was gathered there and anyone [else] who wanted could come. There were more than 200 people. Those gentlemen [the apostles] sang, and people listened to them in religious silence. The propaganda effort is going well in Lyons. The songs produce a great effect. Even the devout ladies call loudly for them.[12]

It was perhaps at a musical gathering of this type that the piano manufacturer Chavan decided to contribute a five-octave metal traveling piano for David's forthcoming sea voyage.

During his stay in Lyons David attempted to supply the movement with music appropriate to its diverse goals and activities. His letter to Enfantin on 9 January 1833 shows clearly his feeling that the "proletarian" effort required one type of music and the search for La Mère another.

> Whereas I shall give the workers inelegant but catchy songs [*chants rudes, mais entraînants*], I shall sing to the woman [i.e., La Mère] something sweet and full of desire and anticipation. She shall learn, through music, of your devotion, your love. I will tell her that you are calling her, waiting for her—that she should hurry, because you are suffering, Père, and you are suffering greatly because you love so greatly![13]

David in fact wrote one piece of each type while in Lyons: *Compagnonnage de la Femme* (a strophic chanson that was no doubt "inelegant"—i.e., simple—and "catchy") and, "sweet" and "full of desire," an elaborate chorus entitled *La Prison du Père*. Of the chanson all that remains is Barrault's text, but its widespread diffusion is evident in the numerous printings it received,[14] in various references to performances during 1833–34,[15] and perhaps most of all

173

in the fact that eleven years later the Fourierist chansonnier Jean Journet could simply use David's *Compagnonnage* as the *timbre* for a song of his own.[16]

Fortunately, the chorus that David wrote during these days in Lyons was published in score. Although less widely disseminated than the *Compagnonnage*, it deserves attention as the first of David's attempts to continue the Ménilmontant tradition during the period of "exile". In spite of his earnest desire to produce something of value to the movement in its new phase, David had some difficulty writing the piece. In a letter to Enfantin he admitted that his sexual longing gave him bouts of impatience and burning desire that he tried to still by focusing his thoughts on Enfantin's sufferings in prison and on how the woman he had left behind in Paris was unworthy of an apostle. ("I shall not drink from her cup.") Two further passages in his letter reveal in greater detail some of his hopeful intentions and some of the difficulties in his path.

> Good old Roger [*sic*] turns the wheel like a true demon. With what pleasure I embraced this good friend! The musical movement is halted a bit, since all the singers work from morning until evening. We can't [even] think of having the rehearsals which are indispensable to us. . . . We plan to give a *matinée musicale* at Mme Mongolfier's (a pianist in Lyons). There are supposed to be several artists and amateurs, and some ladies. We shall see the effect [it makes]. . . .
>
> Father Barrault gave me some poetry on the imprisonment of Le Père. I shall set to work on it, one of these days. Only it's quite annoying not to be able to work comfortably. M. de Saint-Didier has invited me to compose at his house, but that's no good for me. I'm always afraid that I'll be disturbed myself. I'll try to get a piano rented for me, and then I'll let myself go. I shall see your eyes fixed upon me, and in them I shall find new inspiration.[17]

David did finally compose a chorus using Barrault's text, *La Prison du Père,* but the difficulties of his situation left their mark on the music. Although the work is the biggest of David's Saint-Simonian choruses since the *Hymne à Saint-Simon* of January 1832, it is less satisfyingly worked out in nearly every regard.

▽ The attempt at grandeur is apparent from the very opening. David had often begun his choruses with a declamatory passage, and here the effect is heightened by the varied choral treatment, with brief solo passages for each of the four choral voices. The harmony is also more bold than in many of the Ménilmontant pieces and the text-music relationship is handled with unusual effectiveness. The passage "Peuple, peuple," for example, moves in sweet sixths over a static open-fifth pedal, a reflection of the Compagnons' idealized view of the people. David then makes a sudden shift up a major third to underscore the words "C'est lui" (Le Père). This is the same

Beethoven-inspired progression David had used in the *Hymne à Saint-Simon* to emphasize the word "Dieu." Truly Père Enfantin had in the intervening year assumed the role that was previously assigned to the heavenly Father!

There is a curious harmonic touch on p. 6 ("chants de paix et d'espoir") that does not seem justified by either musical or textual considerations. This is followed, however, by a well-handled modulation (pp. 7–8) from bright G major to somber F minor, an apt setting for the devastating revelation that Le Père, the savior of the world, is in prison.

Soon after, there are florid passages for several altos "soli" (reminiscent of the vocalise in the *Danse des astres*), and the piano part also breaks away at times from its usual role of doubling the chorus (especially at the bottom of p. 11). The passage for the altos is interrupted by spoken shouts of "Liberté" in which the audience was presumably asked to join (the words are labeled "Cris du peuple"). This may at first seem an imaginative, if crude, device to involve the unconverted, but it must be pointed out that the choice of the all-purpose slogan "Liberté" (as opposed to, say, "La Femme-Messie") was a fairly safe one for this little experiment in participatory propaganda.

The rest of the piece goes quickly downhill. The repetition of the altos' aria in the major is trite; the chromatic cadence at the bottom of page 10 queasy; and the up-tempo chordal conclusion pat and all too familiar from David's other choruses. The brief andante final cadence even has an unfortunate miscalculation: the sixth degree is held over a cadential V–I$_4^6$–V^7, producing a curious dominant ninth. In short, if David was hoping to produce a major piece in a new style, he did not succeed. On the purely technical level, *La Prison du Père* seems halfhearted, and the new "sweet" style seems little more than David's Ménilmontant style watered down with some pastoral moments and spineless melodies that occasionally sprout little decorative rosettes. $\triangle$

In spite of its weaknesses, David's *Prison* had its moment. Barrault reported back to Enfantin that "the piece that he [David] composed about your imprisonment has produced a great effect on everyone who has heard it."[18] Indeed, Clorinde Rogé reported that there was such great demand in Lyons for all David's Saint-Simonian pieces that the movement could make a lot of money if it had more printed copies to sell.[19]

David's musical productivity during this period was clearly not high, especially in comparison to his fluent production during 1832. Lack of privacy and a piano—his excuses to Enfantin—were surely not the only inhibiting factors. The movement was stagnating, waiting for sufficient organization and finances to be able to undertake the long-promised search for La Mère in the fabled lands of the East. On 22 February 1833 David announced the forthcoming publication of his choruses, chansons, and piano pieces, from the *Hymne à Saint-Simon* to the recent *La Prison du Père*. The prospectus (plate 25) is drenched with longing for the Orient. "I go toward La MÈRE, from whom I shall draw new life. . . . These products of a period which we have passed through already belong to history, and GOD has given me to discover [*pressentir*] a new music." Only when they reached Smyrna and Egypt would David's genius feel the impulse again.

David's total absorption in the forthcoming trip to Constantinople was typical of the feeling in Lyons. On 5 March Barrault sent a large mission (including Rogé) southward "to announce the great act of faith which was about to take place."[20] The missionaries terminated their baptismal employment and took to the road, distributing their leaflets, singing "our peaceful hymns," getting shouted at and pelted with stones, and lodging with friendly villagers and the fishermen of the Camargue.[21] The departure from Arles was particularly festive and, as Hoart described it in a letter to Enfantin, characteristically musical:

> PERE, our departure was worthy of your love and was an imposing spectacle of most religious character. Your sons, in the middle of the Rhône, on the deck of the ship, sang of your captivity and the coming of La MERE, and the people—men, women, and children, crowding along the bank—responded with shouts of joy, threw their hats in the air, and waved their arms.... During our meal of figs and almonds, we sang our songs and preached, in the presence of the fishermen and crew of 17 boats.[22]

Finally they headed toward Marseilles to attend the *départ pour l'Orient* of Barrault's men.

Marseilles was quickly becoming the third major center of the movement's activity in France, partly through the efforts of Auguste Colin and Louis Jourdan.[23] A false rumor of Barrault's arrival sent thousands of eager people out on the road to greet him. The adventuresome Compagnons finally arrived, wearing a special new costume that included a symbolic necklace and ring;[24] Rogé's troop joined them soon after, in time to take part in a festive ceremony the day before the ship was to set sail.[25]

This ceremony, as described in a Marseilles newspaper the next day, strongly resembled the ceremonies at Ménilmontant. The apostles sat at a table prepared with bread and wine and flanked by David's piano (in this case the metal one). The audience of four or five hundred young people, watching from long benches, went silent as Barrault, "with inspired glance and grave gestures," began to speak. "He proclaimed the Saint-Simonian mission.... [Then] he said, 'The mouth of man does not only speak to man,' and the singing began."

First the apostles sang the *Ronde,* a "hymn to peace and to the union of people," whose "lovely melody ... removed mocking ideas from every heart and cast impressions of mystery and contemplation into people's souls." Barrault then "analyzed" the text; repeating for emphasis the words of the refrain ("soyons unis, et nos travaux seront bénis"), "he seemed to be calling power to account for its persecution [of the powerless]." Next *La Prison du Père* was performed, with spoken remarks by Barrault at the end of each section. The "pleasantly modulated music" stirred the audience to enthusiasm, and the reporter was impressed—as the audiences at Ménilmontant had been—by Barrault's words and by their effective combination with David's music: "One would have guessed that he was reciting strophes by Tasso entirely accompanied by a harmonious interlude."

Two of Barrault's messages differed substantially from what he had preached in Paris and Ménilmontant. Gazing at the frugal meal spread before the apostles, he boldly proclaimed something the Saint-Simonians had often attempted to deny: " 'Our mission,' he said, 'is to give everybody an equal part in the feasts—everybody, the great and the small.' Universal applause greeted these words." Barrault, ever aware of his audience, must have known that this kind of egalitarian talk would be well received. (Were there many workers present?) To be fair, though, the egalitarian strain also ran strong among the Compagnons themselves, free now of the hierarchy that had once determined their every move and word.[26]

The other new message was of course that the Woman was in the East. Here, the reporter felt, Barrault's logic "lapsed a bit," but the inspired tone with which he pronounced the news made "a profound sensation." The choir performed *Compagnonnage de la Femme* with taste and "admirable precision," and the audience applauded the refrain: " '*Vive la femme. C'est l'ange de la liberté.*' "[27]

Barrault, perhaps recalling his earlier statement, invited everyone to share the apostles' modest repast—something the Saint-Simonians seem never to have done at Ménilmontant—and the crowd came forward "in the most orderly fashion." At the end of the meal the choir sang *Après le repas,* a piece "heavenly in its harmony." Barrault also pointed out David, who was seated at the piano, and announced that " 'this young man . . . [composed] these songs which have inspired such enthusiasm in you.' A voice from the people shouted, 'He's from Provence.' " At this, the applause became so wild that David wept. A fellow apostle stepped forward and dried his tears.[28]

The fact that David was, on this occasion, able to draw from the Compagnons creditable performances of four pieces, including the long and complicated *Prison du Père,* is indicative of the high priority that this group placed on musical propaganda. Indeed, they may well have sung even more than the four pieces mentioned. The *Salut,* for example, was almost obligatory on such occasions. (It had been performed at their farewell banquet in Lyons.[29]) And it seems unlikely that the singers could have sung only the *Après le repas* but not *Avant le repas.* In addition, there were two new pieces that—though impossible to date with precision—would have been particularly appropriate to the Marseilles banquet or other gatherings provoked by the departures for Egypt: a new David chorus, *Le Départ pour l'Orient,* and an adaptation entitled *Cantate composée en l'honneur du départ des Saint-Simoniens en Egypte.*

▽   The text of the first of these two pieces is lost, but the music can almost assuredly be identified with that of *Le Retour des proscrits,* published in *La Ruche harmonieuse,* 1853. It shows many of the features of the other Saint-Simonian choruses: simple chordal writing varied by unison passages and occasional independent motion in the topmost voice, organization of the piece into shortish sections (ten to thirty measures each) reflecting the feeling or imagery of particular lines of verse, hasty modulations and sentimental or *religioso* progressions (chromatic cadence before the *con fuoco,* limp IV^6–V–I cadence at "plainte amère,"[30] similar to m. 4 of *Tout est mort*), and a fondness for lengthy passages in 6/8 meter.

   The text of the *Cantate* is of unknown authorship. It survives in a scribbled copy and begins with what are obviously some new lyrics for David's *Le Nouveau Temple* ("Frères partez! Nous qui restons ayons courage . . .") and continues with a text that presumably fits another of the movement's tunes: "Compagnons au revoir aimez nous
△ et le peuple entendra notre parole. (Dieu bénit vos efforts.)"[31]

   As the farewell ceremony ended, the crowd took up a collection for the impoverished travelers (it amounted to 180 francs)[32] and then followed them to the port. Onlookers filled the streets and shouted greetings and encouragements; even the businessmen came out of the Stock Exchange to watch the procession. The port area was an anthill of activity. Boats of all sizes formed an escort around the Sardinian brig, renamed the "Clorinde" in honor of Mme Rogé. The crowd rushed onto the vessel, and Barrault consecrated it in the name of "God FATHER and MOTHER."[33] More details of the scene appear in a letter that Mme Durval (in Lyons) wrote to Alexis Petit (in Paris) a few days later.

> The Marseilles newspapers (notably *Le Messager*), and some private letters agree in saying that everything went admirably. They figure the number of onlookers at more than 20,000. The port—they say—was covered with boats which were decorated with streamers and which escorted the boat of the Compagnons de la FEMME, which could be distinguished because of the Saint-Simonian colors. The music produced an admirable effect and David, who wrote me on the 23rd from on board the Clorinde, a Sardinian vessel that is supposed to bring them to Constantinople, ends his letter: "Marseilles was superb yesterday—our music, too, and ourselves, too. Everything is going fine."[34]

In these words of David we hear pride and excitement, but most of all a sense of satisfaction and confidence in the future. The previous month he had announced that his Ménilmontant choruses already belonged to history, that his life was entering a new phase. Just as, entering the Retreat, he had admitted that there was nothing to hold him in the outer world, so there was now nothing to hold him to France. He was free to go to the Orient in search of La Mère, "a new life," and "a new music."

But before we embark with David, it would be best to finish following the activities of Rogé and a new recruit, Henri Reber, up to Rogé's own departure for the Orient in late 1834.

ROGÉ'S SUBSEQUENT ACTIVITY IN FRANCE; HENRI REBER

After they bade farewell to Barrault and his men in Marseilles, Rogé and his fellow missionaries continued on to Montpellier, Béziers, Carcassonne, and the Saint-Simonian city of Castelnaudary, then back north to Lyons by way of Albi, Rodez, Le Puy, and Saint-Etienne, singing as they went and drawing large crowds. In Narbonne, singing in the streets was forbidden, so the crowd followed the missionaries into the courtyard of the inn to hear the message. The young people of the town serenaded the Saint-Simonians in the evening with David's *Compagnonnage de la Femme* and then repeated their performance under the windows of the subprefect. One night, along the road near Arboras, where a Saint-Simonian, Decaen, ran a large factory, they struck up the *Compagnonnage* and men and women of all classes came running to greet them, from the foremen and their workers to fine ladies and their servants.[35]

On 16 May, shortly after returning to Lyons, Rogé led eight men out of Lyons to begin what they called an "art and work mission" ("art" meaning song and costume) in the eastern part of France.[36] A large crowd, consisting mainly of women Saint-Simonians, marched with them through the streets of Lyons to see them off; the women's presence, Hoart reported, "impressed respect and silence upon the incredulous throng [of onlookers]." Outside the city limits, they all joined together in a single banquet. The Compagnons sang their theme song, and the reality of one line—"Compagnons, il faut partir"—caused the women to burst into tears. The crowd, unwilling to let the Compagnons leave, continued down the road with them till dusk. Chancing upon a small country inn, they all squeezed in and sang and even danced excitedly to the tune of a violin (apparently played by Rogé). After further affectionate farewells, the Compagnons set out on the road, returned one last time singing *Compagnonnage*, then disappeared behind the mountain. "Never had the Family of Lyons had a finer day," added Hoart.[37]

From Lyons and Mâcon they traveled north to Chalon, Beaune, and Dijon, then southeast into the Juras. In Dijon they were welcomed into the heart of the city and gave a lecture at the Wauxhal which was well received except by a few republicans. In Auxonne the crowd was so large that the Saint-Simonians decided to sing their songs from the town's ramparts. When the authorities of Villefranche forbade them to preach within the city limits, they held forth from a knoll in the surrounding countryside. Indeed, the singing seems never to have stopped, and the missionaries were gratified to find in most cities enthusiastic women and even, on occasion, a sympathetic magistrate.[38] At Lons-le-Saunier they were surrounded by admiring throngs, invited to speak from the broad balcony of the Hôtel de l'Europe, and conducted at evening to a large park where the entire town—including a large contingent of workers—turned out to give solemn ear to the "new word" and to join in festive celebration. That day the impoverished missionaries also profited directly from the generous feelings of the inhabitants, selling brochures (including song-books, no doubt) for two, ten, twenty sous—whatever a person could pay. (Normally the publications were distributed at no cost whatever.[39]) With the resulting eighty francs in pocket they were able to move on through the mountains to Geneva and back to Lyons.[40]

While in Geneva, Rogé had received a letter from Tourneux in Smyrna transmitting Barrault's request for more men. Rogé returned to Lyons to organize this second group of travelers (including Reboul, Colin, Machereau, Tamisier, and Lamy—names that will recur),[41] and on 14 July, at a banquet in their honor, he picked up a violin and led the dancing.[42] On 7 August Rogé accompanied the men, briefly and with a heavy heart (for he would have liked to join them), onto the boat in Marseilles, where they all sang the "hymn of departure" (either David's *Départ pour l'orient* or the *Cantate composée en l'honneur du départ*) and exchanged tender and religious farewells.[43] The eight Compagnons then set sail for Alexandria, the French government having refused them passports for Smyrna. Again David's Ménilmontant choruses (sung in harmony!) and the colorful costumes served as proud marks of apostlehood:

> At sunrise and sunset our gay and harmonious religious songs, with their poetic composition and their melodious chords, made quite a contrast to the sad and monotonous Christian prayer, the raucous voices of the crew members and the insignificance of their facial features. Our costumes, bright and varied in color, provided an all the more striking effect since the others [the crew's costumes] were dark-hued and simple in shape.[44]

Perhaps immediately after seeing off this group in Marseilles, Rogé and Massol made a trip to Algiers. There they were prevented from giving any public lectures; they did what private preaching they could for two weeks and then returned to France.[45] This was one of a number of missions during 1833 that attempted with varying success to bring the word to Bavaria, Belgium, England, and the French provinces. All this scattered activity, even when immediately fruitful, lacked focus. When, on 1 August, the government released Enfantin from prison as a conciliatory gesture in commemoration of the July Revolution, the Saint-Simonians felt a new surge of energy. Le Père quickly resumed his authority over the apostles; he announced that the Saint-Simonians would now concentrate their energies on a mission to Egypt, and he set a rendezvous in Alexandria with many of them.

Rogé was among those who journeyed to Marseilles again to bid farewell to Enfantin and his men. On 22 September, the eve of the departure, they all slept on board ship and Rogé, Massol, Holstein, Ollivier, and Lambert sang Enfantin's beloved *Salut,* the *Appel, Peuple fier,* and Talabot's folksong. As Rogé and his fellows returned to shore the next day on a tugboat, Rogé led them in the *Appel* one last time.[46] (Rogé went to Marseilles yet again on 27 October to attend the departure of his wife Clorinde and Cécile Fournel.[47])

To those who were remaining in France Enfantin had left the imposing task of preparing a "peacemaking army of workers" and raising substantial funds to send it to Egypt once Enfantin and his engineers had cleared the way for the construction of a canal at Suez. Enfantin also wanted to bring artists and musicians to Egypt but not, as Napoleon had done, in order to examine, record, and collect materials of Egyptian culture. "Today," wrote Enfantin, "Egypt needs to be given a new life. It is our Western arts and pleasures that the East is demanding."[48]

While Hoart and Bruneau were entrusted with the larger task of organizing the brigade and its equipment, Enfantin instructed Rogé and Massol to take charge of the music and costumes.[49] "[Let Rogé prepare] good voices to respond to the cry that I will give forth from beyond the seas."[50] These inspiring words, however, were balanced with a warning clearly directed at Rogé and Massol, who seem to have been fearing (with good reason) that their part of the effort would be less well funded than Hoart and Bruneau's formation of the workers' corps. "Your missions are distinct; your means and resources will be just as much so. When you gather for a common project, let your love for ME always be among you, that you may be united, in spite of how you feel."[51]

Rogé, after seeing Enfantin off in Marseilles, traveled back to Paris and began to establish a chorus and band that he hoped would be able to inspire the canal laborers to joyful work, but he soon encountered problems of morale and of finances. As he explained in a letter to Enfantin, "ever since your departure, [most of the former sympathizers have been feeling] like a ship that a furious hurricane has tossed far, far away from the protective beacon." More bluntly, "faith in the accomplishment of your industrial work is conditional among some of them, . . . nonexistent among most."[52] Rogé told Enfantin that he felt he could count on a dozen men in Paris for his musicians' brigade and was planning to start giving them brass lessons "within a few days," but he needed money to rent instruments and halls and to pay several teachers.

> For an artist, his own willingness is not enough. A corps of artists cannot be scratched together at a moment's notice. It needs time and zeal—and money to prepare it and to organize

it in advance. But the faith is cooling down and there isn't
enough money. . . .

    PÈRE,

    Since long ago, glory is attached to your name and your
word is going to become omnipotent again. If you feel you
should protect my work, then—once again—protect it.[53]

This last sentence is revealing. It clearly states that the musicians' brigade was
very much Rogé's own project and even suggests that the idea had been his
from the beginning. Enfantin seems at this point to have considered Rogé's
corps d'artistes an admirable effort that must however remain marginal unless
and until the Egyptian venture as a whole became a flourishing success.

In spite of these problems, Rogé was soon able to organize a group of brass
players; at the celebration in honor of Enfantin's birthday, on 8 February 1834
(see Chapter 11), Rogé and his musicians were apparently present. The published account does not make clear whether they accompanied the dancing,
but it does state that, at the evening's end, "as we walked down the hill, the
musicians [presumably Rogé's] performed several symphonies."[54] (Perhaps
these "symphonies" were instrumental arrangements of the David choruses
that Rogé knew so well.)

By March 1834 the news had reached Egypt that Rogé's *musique de cuivre*
was on its feet[55] and David, who had been in Egypt, aimless, for several
months, felt sufficiently encouraged to start setting some Arab tunes for brass.[56]
Around the same time Enfantin wrote to Hoart and Bruneau (who had been
having no luck in raising funds or forming a workers' army), calling them to
join him in Egypt and to bring with them several other trained engineers.
Rogé and Massol had expected to be called at the same time, but instead
Enfantin offered them vague promises and bland encouragement.

> Rogé and Massol should continue their work. It will not be
> long before I ask for the music [to join me here], too. The
> Arabs do not march to work without it. (We have just seen
> ten thousand peasants come to dig a little canal in the area
> where the dams will be. The darabukka, the fife, and the ivory
> flute marched at the head.) They should get ready, as if they
> were leaving at the same time as you.[57]

Three months later the message was the same.

> Let Roger [*sic*] make his preparations, without as yet saying
> anything. I intend to write to him more specifically in a few
> days and to have decided then about several important things
> . . . [including] the instruments and instrumentalists that he
> should or should not bring. [But] he should take care of himself
> first. He is not in the habit of doing so, and he needs to learn
> that a bit. Most of all, he shouldn't become impatient—if my
> letter is late, it will [still] come in time.[58]

All these words were no doubt meant to hearten Rogé and to lessen the blow of Enfantin's repeated decision to delay the departure of the "army" (which was not materializing) and its music. Things were not going well in Egypt; the viceroy, Muhammad Ali, had already rejected Enfantin's plan for a Suez canal and proposed instead the construction of a dam across the Nile, and even that project was hindered by a lack of funds and by the viceroy's increasing indifference.

Disappointed but undaunted, Rogé continued to develop his forces, led them in concerts, and even, in David's absence, persuaded another young composer, Napoléon-Henri Reber (1807–80), to compose *A l'Orient,* a substantial piece for chorus and band in praise of the Mission d'Egypte. Vinçard gives a glowing report of the success of Rogé's *corps de musiciens,* specifically mentioning that Rogé recruited his instrumentalists and choristers from among "the workers of the Family" and that few if any already knew how to read music or to play. Vinçard adds that Reber's work "was performed with full orchestra in Salle Molière, Passage du Saumon, to the acclamations of everyone present."[59]

As the months passed, it became clear to the members of the music brigade that Enfantin was not in a position to call them to Egypt, and they began to lose interest. In July 1834 Enfantin began to worry, because Rogé was no longer writing and because even Clorinde, now in Egypt herself, knew only that her husband had assembled as many as forty brass players.[60] Enfantin was right to be concerned. In October he finally received a letter in which Rogé explained with much bitterness that the obvious failure of the Egyptian mission had forced him to give up in despair.

> I succeeded in getting [twenty-six instrumentalists][61] to per-
> form a number of pieces, such as: *Soldats, ouvriers, bourgeois*
> [i.e., David's *Ronde*], *Peuple, viens à nous* by Briouse, *Nous voilà*
> by Vinçard, *A l'Orient,* a magnificent industrial-emigration piece
> [by Reber]. . . .
>
> In addition, I had trained a choir of more than 60 voices,
> including 23 women. With these forces, I gave three concerts
> [*fêtes*] in different halls in Paris. They were quite lovely and
> they made a strong impression on the people who attended
> who were not part of the Family. But it was no longer possible
> for me to sustain any longer by myself the prodigious amount
> of activity [that this project had demanded of me for eight
> months]. . . . My health declined; I was forced to stop. . . . [Be-
> sides, the police have recently been empowered to prevent any
> kind of popular gathering. And the uncertainty about our de-
> parture] disenchanted many of my men. . . . I could no longer
> count on more than ten to depart with me. . . . Also, the monthly
> dues were not coming in very well anymore. . . .
>
> PÈRE, when you left me in France, I hoped to join you again
> soon with the flag of an industrial battalion, marching joyously

under the peaceful inspiration of vigorous and catchy music. The battalion is not ready; the music was. The one was easier to get than the other.[62]

In the same letter, Rogé had the pleasure of informing Enfantin of the new composer he had won for the movement. It is not known what first drew Henri Reber—the future professor of harmony at the Conservatoire—to the movement. He had given private harmony lessons to David in 1830 or 1831, but his involvement with the movement seems to have begun after David left France in 1833.[63] Perhaps Reber and Rogé knew each other from the Conservatoire or professional circles. In any case, the new *fidèle* seems not to have remained interested for long; his *A l'Orient,* with Rogé's and Vinçard's remarks about it, constitutes the only evidence of his participation.

A l'Orient, to a text of Félix Maynard, was scored for five-part mixed chorus, winds, brass, and drum. As Rogé proudly wrote in the aforementioned letter to Enfantin:

> It is the work of a young man [Reber] who has shared our faith since a little while ago and who loves you through me. It was impossible to grasp better than he did in his first attempt the transformation of the destructive regiment into a productive one. It's all there, it's admirable!! In the middle of the piece is a prayer that exhales the perfume of the purest and sweetest Christianity. The composer of this piece will have a quite glorious name in a few years. . . . David knew him. He will be pleased.[64]

Reber's *A l'Orient* was published in late 1834,[65] a privilege that had not been accorded any of David's Saint-Simonian choruses after *La Prison du Père.* The music itself—written largely in march rhythm—unfolds more spaciously, with more apparent self-confidence, than do the larger of David's Saint-Simonian choruses, yet Reber preserves, through his use of an essentially strophic form, a simplicity and practicality that had often escaped David in those large-scale choruses.

▽   Transitional material is entrusted to the accompanying brass, thus leaving the singers free to reenter with their well-rehearsed tune. To make things even easier, the verse in strophes 1, 2, 5, and 6 is sung by the high voices in unison, and only the refrains, plus the verse of strophe 3, are sung in harmony. In the middle of the work, directly following the third strophe, Reber introduces new, contrasting music: a recitative (for basses) speaking of the sea, a five-part invocation to Le Père, and the four-part a cappella prayer (by the men, on behalf of the mothers left behind) to which Rogé referred. This quite lovely prayer is continued in the minor by the women, with reduced brass accompaniment. After a restatement of the invocation, the orchestra enters with a passage that culminates in a great march and then leads back to the
△ opening tune for strophes 5 and 6.

The temptation is perhaps to overpraise the work, as Rogé did, on account of its undeniable professionalism. There is, however, one problem: the melodies do not flow and in fact are neither appealing nor especially singable. For this most basic aspect of composition the naïve David had a greater natural gift, one that would later bring him the sort of fame and affection that the craftsmanlike Reber would never know.

DAVID IN SMYRNA; PIANO PIECES AND CHORUSES

David, we recall, had set out for Constantinople on 23 March 1833, traveling with Barrault and ten others on a Sardinian brig newly renamed the *Clorinde.* The missionaries frequently spoke of their doctrine to the ship's mates, among whom was the young and sympathetic Garibaldi.[66] On 15 April they arrived, sought out modest lodgings, and began their program of saluting, in a loud voice and with bare head, every Oriental woman they encountered, whether rich or poor. People on the streets reacted with astonishment at this exhibition, as well as at the Compagnons' costume and their serious and military bearing.[67]

David naturally took an immediate interest in the atmosphere of the place and on the third day after their arrival set down a keyboard fantasy entitled *Le Harem.* This is the first of twenty-one piano pieces that David was to compose during his stay in the East. It contains many features that recur in those pieces and in David's exotic works in general, notably a free alternation of barbaric and idyllic moods.

The barbaric passages, here and elsewhere, are characterized by bare octaves and ▽ pounding chords, sudden juxtapositions or shifts of key, and preference for duple meter and minor mode. The idyllic passages are generally written in gentler 6/8 meter; they consist of flowing melodies that end weakly (by extending past the downbeat or by emphasizing the third or fifth degree rather than the root) and that are accompanied by static drone chords in a rocking barcarolle rhythm. David introduces into *Le Harem* several pianistically grateful variations on an *espressivo* modulatory passage, causing the form to ramble; also, the pianistic glitter occasionally pulls one back with a jolt into the drawing rooms of the Occident. But the barbaric/idyllic contrast is nonetheless sharp and telling. △

The idyllic passages no doubt were intended to represent the unfortunate women captives; David, perhaps consciously, avoided portraying them—after the fashion of Ingres—as sultry, heavy-lidded temptresses. For the Saint-Simonians and for David, as the harsh opening and the Beethovenian *furioso* (mm. 48–52) make amply clear, the harem was a monstrous social institution, a crime against womankind and humanity.[68]

From the Compagnons' very first day in Constantinople the government had expressed some uneasiness. On 20 April the strange visitors were arrested, incarcerated for three days, and then expelled from the city. They were forced to travel in a series of small boats (often in the hold) and never permitted to set foot on land, to learn their destination, or to eat properly. Finally, ten days later, they were deposited in Smyrna, where they settled in the French quarter.[69]

The nine remaining Saint-Simonians (for three—Carolus, Jans, and Rigaud—had soon decided to return to France or go separate ways)[70] enjoyed Smyrna's sun-drenched days and cool, clear nights.[71] One account states that the Compagnons purchased a donkey and a violin and that, with the piano on the donkey's back, David and Barrault, "who was rather talented," gave concerts throughout the city.[72] But for the most part they seem to have done no work, not even any missionizing. "Singing, contemplating, praying," recalled P. Granal a few years later in a series of newpaper articles, "were the occupations of all our days." They watched the sun set over the water from a café near the Pont des Caravanes, and they spent their days walking through the Greek, Turkish, and Jewish quarters of the city, or hiking out to the fabled Grottoes of Homer. They heard Greeks singing and playing their instruments; they listened to the Turkish muezzin; they heard a caravan arrive, bells jingling, and watched it unload by the light (and pungent odor) of resin torches; they marveled at the curious figures of the Jews; they admired the grace of the local women, smoked a water pipe, and saw Turks sitting in a drugged haze along the streets. In short, they drank in all the sights, smells, and—not least—sounds[73] of Smyrna like the European tourists they were. (They even took in a house boy and made frequent fun of him.)

David presumably went along on most of the group's little expeditions, but his name enters Granal's story only twice: once when Granal recalls David's violent hatred of mosquitoes (a trait of his Provençal childhood?) and, more significantly, when Granal mentions that David gave evening concerts on the balcony of the villa, seated at Chavan's metal piano. These informal concerts became so frequent and regular that David developed an adoring audience, consisting largely of young women.[74] David, in a letter to Urbain (who had left Smyrna with Barrault and three others sometime in May and gone to Alexandria), described these concerts, the lovely lady listeners, and the frustrations of being celibate in Smyrna.

> [If the piano] is the least bit inconstant, like its master, then the demands start coming, and entreaties on the part of the ladies. This amuses me. And since I give a concert every evening, the terraces fill up more and more with beautiful women. . . .
>
> . . . Anticipation [*attente*], anticipation, how hard you are! You, [Urbain,] are you quite content? At least the women of Alexandria wear veils. They are not at the window, pretty and full of desire. They don't throw flowers as you pass—a Satanic temptation that I've been experiencing recently. Oh, La Mère. I call to her quite often, both night and day. I fear that I may lose my voice from shouting.[75]

During the months that David spent in Smyrna, he composed four more piano pieces that, like *Le Harem,* were later published in 1836 as part of the *Mélodies orientales.* The first three—*Smyrne, A une Smyrniote,* and *Souvenir d'occident*—are lyrical character pieces that catch the relaxed aimlessness and melancholy charm of the Compagnons' stay in Smyrna. David's musical language and keyboard style here are not far removed from Mendelssohn and Schubert, but certain patches of experimental harmony—long-held pedal tones, chords sliding up and down chromatically, idiosyncratic uses of chord inversions (including fauxbourdon)—speak distinctly of the strange world into which David and his fellows had been cast, and echo faintly the idyllic passages of *Le Harem.* In the fourth piece, *L'Almée* (The Dancing Woman), the exotic element appears far more strongly, this time in its barbaric aspect: relentless repetition of a short rhythmic motive, hammering ostinato chords, sudden contrasts of forte and piano, even a rapid descending scale with the augmented second (typical of the Islamic mode *hidjaz*) that was to become such a standard feature of French "oriental" music (e.g., in the Bacchanale from *Samson et Dalila*). But whereas *Le Harem* was stern, *L'Almée* is lively and intriguing, and its contrasting episodes of Mendelssohnian lyricism supply a chaste sweetness that David's *pudeur* (and perhaps the Compagnons' idolization of women) forced him to substitute for the ripe, shameless allure that he so well described in his letter.

L'Almée is not only one of David's finest piano pieces but, with *Le Harem,* the seed of his life's work and, more generally, of the entire exotic strain in French music to our day. It is therefore not in Egypt, as writers have often stated, but already in Constantinople and Smyrna—the Smyrna of hashish, cafés, and dark, beckoning women—that David was first seduced by the Orient and intrigued by its atmosphere and its sounds. To understand the full meaning of David's "Hymne à la nuit," an aria from *Le Désert* of the most gentle and evanescent exotic character, it is helpful to have read Granal's poetic account of the "splendid nights" of the region, of how the Saint-Simonians, aboard the small boat that was bringing them to Smyrna, spoke softly of their distant homeland, prayed together, and then took their beds onto the deck and slept in the gentle air "under the friendly glance of the stars." David had come to the East as a missionary; he would leave it as a lover.

David seems not to have recognized the significance of his Oriental piano pieces at the time. In the letter that he wrote to Urbain from Smyrna, he did not mention them at all, but rather spoke of more choral pieces, which he was—to his regret—reduced to performing all by himself, apparently from the balcony:

> I am pretty frustrated [here]. I have given birth to several new children that I love a lot, but that I cannot see in all their splendor, i.e., adorned with the voices of my singers. *L'Attente de la Mère* has made a big effect. Mersane in particular adores

it. The neighbors, male and female, must love it, too. At least
it's not for lack of singing it to them.[76]

Four of these "new children" survive in whole or in part. Among David's
papers at the Bibliothèque nationale is a large bifolio in his own hand, containing the topmost ("alto") line to four pieces, presumably for four-part men's
chorus and piano (and, in one case, tenor solo). Three of these—*Prière* (called
L'Attente in David's letter), *Les Etoiles,* and what we may conjecturally call
Hymne à la Mère—were published, to different texts, later in David's career
and so can be reconstructed with little difficulty.[77]

These three choruses are all quite long. Not surprisingly, they resemble in
many ways the more substantial of the Ménilmontant choruses.

▽ First, they go through a series of tempo, meter, and key changes to reflect the
changing text. *Prière,* for example, contains a stern passage in C minor at the words
"Le monde est dans les fers" ("the world is in chains"), and the first twenty-two
measures of the same piece pass through six different tempo markings, an extension
of the declamatory openings that David had often favored during his stay at Ménilmontant. Second, the three pieces occasionally attempt, as did *Tout est mort* and *Danse
des astres,* to break away from strict chordal style. The long solo vocalise in *Les Etoiles*
is directly comparable to that in *Danse des astres* (and evidently composed for the same
singer, David himself), and *Prière* makes effective and practical use of unison singing,
especially in modulatory passages, as a contrast to more chordal textures at cadences.

Last, one notes again the makeshift harmonic setting, which at times produces
interesting and unusual progressions (fauxbourdon to open *Les Etoiles*) or refreshing
sonorities (such as the diminished seventh resolving to a downbeat V_2^4 in mm. 18–20
of the same piece or the passing dissonances in the first ten measures of *Prière*) but
which can also result in sudden and ill-prepared modulations (such as the leap into
and out of the mediant in mm. 22–28 of *Les Etoiles*)[78] or quirky cadences (I–V–v–I,
all over a tonic pedal, in *Prière,* mm. 18–20; David may have intended it as a half-
△ cadence, V–II–ii–V, in the key that follows).

In addition, the large Smyrna choruses give striking and repeated evidence
of David's stated desire to write something different and "sweet" in honor of
La Mère. David now develops further the idyllic tone found already in *La
Prison du Père* and *Le Harem.*

▽ *Prière* slips into andantino passages in flowing 6/8 meter three separate times, at
the words "Tournons nos âmes vers la Mère" and (more briefly) at "La Mère, la
Mère" and "Nous te prions, Dieu, donne-nous la Mère." The aforementioned vocalise
in *Les Etoiles* (at the words "Dansez, chantez, offrez à la Mère") is also an andantino
in 6/8, as is the "Belle, oh belle" passage from *Hymne à la Mère* (to be discussed
below).

These passages in 6/8 do not appear here for the first time in David's work. We
encountered at least one precedent in the vocalise section of *Danse des astres.* But a

comparison of the earlier vocalise with the one in *Les Étoiles*—both, incidentally, representing the singing of the stars and both accompanied by pedal-drenched repeated chords in the other voices and piano—shows that in the course of a single year David had moved from a kind of complacent salon style to a more mysterious one in which melodies may start regularly but never cadence on the tonic degree. The device is simple but effective, creating—in conjunction with the static harmonies—a mood of unceasing bliss. David seems to have viewed these unresolved phrase endings in *Les Étoiles* as exotic, for he subtitled the piece *orientale* and nothing else in it remotely suggests such a quality. (In the intentionally exotic "Hymne à la nuit" of *Le Désert* he would write a melody that similarly stresses the fifth degree at cadences; he does finally resolve, but on a weak beat.)

From the structural point of view, the avoidance of the tonic also allows David's music to flow unimpeded, a rare quality in his early works. The goal toward which the music is flowing is no more than a repetition of the tune in vi, then I, then ii, and finally a melodically weak cadence in I again. But perhaps precisely because the frame is simple, David manages to make us unaware that the frame is there at all. He remembers to precede each new key by a measure of its dominant seventh, and all works out well. The last statement, for variety's sake, is neatly reharmonized to provide its own transition into ii and then back to I, a rather eventful twist in this leisurely piece. One other imaginative touch is the transformation of another 6/8 episode into 3/8 (measure for measure), thus shifting from a gentle two-stress pattern to a quick three. ("Voici venir la plus belle des filles de Dieu" . . . "Chantons la plus belle des filles de Dieu."[79])

Of the three large choruses the *Hymne à la Mère* is the most intriguing from the point of view of the development of David's style. The opening two sections are rather backward-looking: rather tuneless successions of *accords plaqués* recalling the weakest of the Ménilmontant choruses. One suspects that David gradually lost interest in setting texts proclaiming "Gloire, salut" and the like; his first, in the *Hymne à Saint-Simon,* was his best. In contrast, the "Belle, oh belle comme l'ange" section (Appendix E.29) seems to have sprung from his melodious imagination uncoaxed. (It was apparently the first section of the work to be written.) At first it may seem to be just another example of La Mère music: a lyrical andantino, again in 6/8, with a touch of melodic chromaticism (on the word "beauté") to add to the sweetness of the portrait. But it also has certain features that make it distinctive: an achingly lovely minor-mode cadence in mm. 9–12 (David reused it in his song "Le Nuage" of 1846) and, most notably, the combination of an open-fifth pedal in the lower two voices and pentatonic horn-call writing in the upper two. What we have here is a piece that clearly combines the idyllic style with elements drawn from the pastoral tradition of Western music. David was often to resort to the resulting pastoral-idyllic style when portraying exotic lands in his *odes-symphonies* and operas.[80] Here is its origin, in a love song for La Mère. △

The fourth piece from the Smyrna days, a compact *Sérénade* in D, is preserved only in David's "alto" part, and there it is untexted (except for an occasional la-la-la). Like the Ménilmontant *Ronde,* it consists of a charming melody that returns refrain-like several times after episodes in which the texture is pleasantly varied (with, as in the *Ronde,* some held high notes in the top voice). The use of a lively 6/8 meter is also reminiscent of the *Ronde.* Judging by the top voice, this appears to have been one of the more attractive, if also one of the simpler, of David's Saint-Simonian choruses.

Some of these pieces composed in Smyrna did finally reach performance on repeated occasions once David arrived in Egypt. In the meantime, David sent a manuscript copy of the *Prière* to Rogé, who was still in Paris. Perhaps David was hoping that Rogé would perform the work[81] or that he or Clorinde would help get it published. (Clorinde had apparently served as engraver for some or all of the *Ménilmontant* series.[82]) Rogé was pleased at David's progress in compositional technique and, it seems, at his avoidance of certain crude and overinsistent aspects of the Ménilmontant style: "Nothing," he wrote to Enfantin, "can compare to the sweetness and delicacy of this piece. Never before did DAVID pour out his life [*sic*] so fully."[83] Rogé appreciated the new dreamy aroma that was entering David's music. The composer would most likely have claimed that he was capturing the sentiment of "anticipation of La Mère." But the scent that reached Rogé's longing nostrils was also laced with the perfume of the Orient. David, perhaps still unawares, had already begun to yield to the charm of the Orient, not only in his descriptive piano pieces but also in choruses that were still conceived as ideological works. He had begun an adventure that would change his life, his career, and his music.

David and Rogé in Egypt; Arrangements of Arab Tunes

Smyrna was never an intended goal of the Saint-Simonians, but it served as a temporary base of operations. A group led by Barrault, as we have seen, left for Alexandria in May; on 15 June Cognat and Granal departed for Beirut (to visit Lady Stanhope, the eccentric patroness of the Bedouins).[84] Barrault, who was having some success with his speeches in Alexandria,[85] wrote to Enfantin that he wanted David to come to Egypt, where "his piano and his vocal works [*chants*]" would produce a "favorable impression" as they had already done in Smyrna. (He also added: "I have had somebody write to France for some musicians to come join David."[86] He must have known, if only from David's letter to Urbain, of the composer's desire to be surrounded by singers.[87]) Barrault eventually returned to Smyrna to fetch David; together with Granal, they made their way to Egypt by a combination of sea and land, stopping in several places in Palestine: Jaffa, a Spanish convent in Ramla, and—fulfilling Enfantin's longstanding request—Jerusalem.[88]

Finally, they arrived in Egypt and were thrown back into the same atmosphere of hectic activity that had surrounded the Saint-Simonians in Paris, Ménilmontant, and Lyons.[89] Barrault gave lectures on art history,[90] Alric sculpted a bust of Muhammad Ali (a bold attempt, made with permission of the viceroy himself, to introduce Western-style graven images into Muslim society),[91] and others expounded in public the basic principles of the doctrine and the need for a canal through Suez. Everyone awaited Enfantin's arrival in Egypt and his completion of the necessary negotiations with Muhammad Ali.

David made some attempt to serve musically the rather unclear needs of the movement during these weeks. Lambert reported in his diary that the Saint-Simonians of Alexandria, under Barrault's direction, "organized three concerts in which some new pieces by David were sung before the elite of the population of Alexandria." The *Moniteur égyptien* wrote that the performances were received with great applause and admiration; the paper drew special attention to David's own expressive and pure singing and to the novelty of his compositions.[92] When Enfantin finally arrived by boat on 23 October, the disciples knew how to greet him: "David's piano was carried [to where the boat was docked], and the port of Alexandria reverberated with the new vocal works which his travels in the East have inspired in him."[93]

After this, we glimpse David only occasionally in the letters and writings of Saint-Simonians in Egypt. He appears in various places in Barrault's tow, or Granal's, or Lamy's, or he is spending weeks, perhaps months, in relaxed isolation with a few companions, as when Suzanne Voilquin found him, "our sweet nightingale of Ménilmontant," living in brotherly peace with Lamy and Maréchal in Cairo. (They introduced her to hashish, and her memoirs describe her visions and sensations in some detail.[94])

Two months after his arrival in Cairo, David wrote to his brother-in-law Pierre-Eugène Monge, instructing him to forward several hundred francs of his to Mme Durval for the publication of the music he was now writing in the Orient. "Do not imagine that I may need it some day. I will never need anything—either here or in France."[95] David still put his trust in the movement, although the movement was coming to have less and less to offer him—especially, as we shall see, from the financial point of view.

Musically, David now completed the shift in direction that he had begun on the terrace in Smyrna, writing piece after piece based on Arab melodies or descriptive of Egyptian scenes. (The nasty review of *Hymne à Saint-Simon, Peuple fier,* and *La Voix du peuple* that appeared in the *Revue musicale* and the *Allgemeine musikalische Zeitung* may have strengthened his desire to develop a new style.[96]) The piano pieces, when published in 1836 under the general title *Mélodies orientales,* were a commercial failure, but they formed the first step in the direction of *Le Désert* (1844) and the other works that were to bring David public acclaim and commercial success. (Indeed, the rage for *Le Désert* led several publishers to reissue the piano pieces in two collections entitled *Brises d'Orient* and *Les Minarets.*)

It would be an exaggeration to say that David's new exotic strain marked a break with the aesthetic "line" of the Saint-Simonian movement. In fact,

Enfantin seems to have changed his mind about the role of the arts in Saint-Simonian Egypt. Whereas he had once claimed that the Orient needed the arts of the West, now that he was on the scene he was proposing a dynamic synthesis: "We shall have as masters our Western memories, the taste of the Arabs, and our inspiration of the future."[97]

But it would be just as wrong to see David's interest in the exotic as a mere *result* of Enfantin's new ideas, for David had begun to develop his new style in Smyrna, while Le Père was still in France preaching the white man's artistic burden. Furthermore, unlike Enfantin's newfound interest in the native taste, David's savoring of the music of the Islamic world had nothing of the functional about it; he had found an untapped source of artistic material and he set about tapping it. His attitude was no doubt similar to that of the apostles who now chose to dress as Arabs and even to convert to Islam, or to that of Reboul, who decided soon after Enfantin's arrival that the time had come for an apostolate of absorption rather than of expansion: "After having taught, it was our turn to study and learn; after having spent, we needed to reacquire." Reboul was led to this regretful but liberating conclusion by his awareness that the Saint-Simonians could never hope to influence, much less transform, a country whose culture was new and foreign to them.[98] David would never have so doubted Le Père and the plans for an industrialized Egypt, but he certainly must have sensed that whatever kind of music he now wrote would of necessity be more or less irrelevant to a movement in circumstances that, as we shall soon see, were increasingly desperate and hardly conducive to the production of art. This left David the composer free to follow his own path, to absorb what appealed to him in the music of the cafés and the nomadic tribes and to cultivate an "oriental" style in which East met West in unprecedented vividness. That the exotic element in David's music would years later—in *Le Désert* (1844) and succeeding works—finally serve the interests of Saint-Simonian propaganda was something that David could not have foreseen in Smyrna and Egypt when he first snatched these Oriental breezes from the air and preserved them on paper.

Of David's musical activities in Egypt after the Alexandrian concerts of 1833 we know very little. He taught piano, and there is a charming story, perhaps apocryphal, that he eagerly accepted an invitation to visit, as music teacher, the viceroy's harem, only to find, once he arrived there, that he was expected to teach the eunuchs, who would then—behind closed doors—pass the wisdom on to their charges. (He turned around and left.) David must also have continued to play and sing, and his works apparently remained a constant feature of Saint-Simonian gatherings.[99]

David may, in addition, have participated in a concert given at a Capucin monastery in Alexandria one Saint Cecilia's Day. Granal, recalling the occasion in one of his articles in *Le Temps*, states that the orchestra was organized by an Egyptian seed and grain merchant and that a mass was performed by a mélange of singers: "Jews, Christians of all varieties, Muhammadans, and Saint-Simonians."[100] But if David did have a large role in this event—something more than simply singing in the tenor section—one imagines that Granal would have mentioned it.

As for the role of music in the Egyptian mission itself, it is hard to reconstruct an accurate picture of what happened, and even harder to imagine what might have happened if the mission had been more successful and lasted dozens of years instead of two and a half. The potential for frustration and homesickness was naturally high among these several dozen exiles. When the viceroy refused to lend his support to their canal project, even the faithful Henri Fournel could not resist complaining to Enfantin of the constant "inactivity,"[101] and he embarked for France soon after. Enfantin had to find some project for his followers, since the search for La Mère could hardly justify their continued presence in the Land of the Pharaohs. He thus agreed to offer their assistance to the viceroy's favored plan for a dam across the Nile. As elaborated by the French consul general Linant, it would make use of music to lift the spirits of the toiling laborers.

> The organization of the peace army is beginning. Linant has asked authorization to form a corps of 12,000 regular workers, enrolled, watched over, disciplined, dressed, fed, and housed, . . . composed of men and children, [marching] with music at the head, pickaxe and hatchet on their shoulders, compass and square at their sides, and meter stick in the hands of the officers and subofficers.[102]

Linant specifically requested that David prepare the music,[103] and, as we have seen in the previous subchapter, David actually set about arranging Arab tunes for band while Rogé in Paris trained brass and wind players who—he hoped—would soon be playing at the dam site. Apparently David's arrangements finally ended up as piano pieces in the *Mélodies orientales,* where we can recognize them not only by their dates of composition but by their continued use of the barbaric and idyllic styles first seen in *Le Harem* and *L'Almée* and by superscriptions in which David proudly identified several "airs arabes," some native drum rhythms ("le tarabouka"), and a boatsmen's song ("les rameurs").

Rogé's orchestra failed, and on 13 November 1834 he left for Egypt with a mere three apostles (plus Suzanne Voilquin). Rogé's almost solitary arrival was but one of many symptoms of impending failure and crisis in the Oriental mission. Another was the fact that when, on the previous 9 May, Enfantin had moved his quarters to the dam site, David had apparently not joined him there. The truth is that even on those occasions when David did leave his simple but comfortable lodgings to visit the project, his music could not have helped much. Enfantin's efforts were being undermined by the fact that numerous Egyptian workers were deserting the worksite (perhaps they were not being paid) and eventually by the appearance of a few cases of plague among the workers; finally the government took action and suspended all work on the dam.

The failure of the dam project and, even more, the rapid spread of the plague from Alexandria up the Nile to Cairo in December 1834 struck a harsh blow to an already weakened movement. The individual Saint-Simonians were forced to look to their own needs. Enfantin found a protector in Soliman-Pasha (the former French colonel Sève), whose palace soon became the center of new Saint-Simonian soirees. The Maréchal Marmont later recalled that the Saint-Simonians treated him there to "a concert and a little show that gave us much pleasure."[104] Most of the Saint-Simonians tried to make ends meet by teaching, practicing medicine, or serving in low-level goverment posts. Rogé and Yvon taught music at the cavalry school in Gizeh[105] during this difficult period, and it appears that the apostles who remained in Cairo often gathered chez Suzanne Voilquin, Rogé, or Lambert to make music and dance.[106] David, no doubt deeply disheartened, fell into a fallow period. From the abandonment of the dam project (14 December 1834) to his departure four months later, David seems to have produced but a single piece—a cantata (now lost) in honor of Muhammad Ali's son Ibrahim-Pasha—and even that was perhaps not newly composed. (Suzanne notes that it was written quickly for a reception at Soliman-Pasha's house; the piece was put into rehearsal, but the event was finally canceled because of the plague.[107]) Le Père, with obvious regret, encouraged David and Petit to leave Egypt, admitting that they had "nothing useful to do here" and would be, "in contrast, well placed in France."[108]

> David has soaked up enough Oriental sun to be drenched with it through and through, but no matter how much he has squeezed and twisted himself here, nothing has flowed out. I am relying on French hands; they will know how to press out of this pretty child [*gentil enfant*] the juice which he gathered here.[109]

As the plague worsened in early 1835, Enfantin decided to escape to safer territory in Upper Egypt.[110] Rogé, fortunately, was protected by being at Gizeh. David and some others did return to France. And a small number of dedicated apostles (among them, Suzanne and Clorinde) remained in Cairo, either in quarantine or actively fighting the spreading disease in the poorest quarters; some—including David's two former housemates—fell victim themselves.

Enfantin remained in his uplands retreat until 16 December 1835, when he returned to Cairo to resume charge of the tatters of a movement. There were still plans in the air: Clorinde wanted to found a girls' school, others wished to establish a polytechnic institute, a model farm, and so on. But the plague had been devastating and the morale of the members, already weakened by deaths and departures,[111] was further shaken by the ill favor with which Muhammad Ali—in part because of some shifts in international politics—was viewing these French people and their projects. In the course of 1836 Enfantin was gradually forced to recognize the failure of the Egyptian mission; every month more of the disciples left, and Enfantin himself boarded ship on 30 October 1836, closing forever a chapter in the history of the movement. He left behind some eight *fidèles* (among them Auguste Colin, future librettist of *Le Désert*) who preferred to keep working to improve the lot of the Egyptians. He also left a total of twelve more buried in that soil which they had hoped to see sprout with new life.

The regret of the departing Saint-Simonians was perhaps best expressed by P. Granal:

> I doubt that one can love deeply those places where one is perfectly happy. Sorrow impresses upon objects . . . a more secure and durable mark. . . . We had all come, animated by a common desire, dreaming of damming the rivers, of joining the seas, of making the desert fertile, of raising new cities. We considered ourselves scouts [*éclaireurs*], the vanguard of an immense army. But the time was not ripe, and it pleased God to give us as a tomb this land which we had chosen to be the theater of a new glory. The angel of death marked most of us, as it did long ago the eldest sons of the Egyptians.[112]

Thus withered the vision of 12,000 happy Egyptians singing at their work and marching to the tunes of a Saint-Simonian band.

13

1836–76:
THE MOVEMENT
IN DECLINE

DEBRIS OF A GREAT SHIPWRECK

When exactly did the Saint-Simonian movement go into decline? Some contemporaries and historians have placed the beginning of the end in 1833 with the ill-fated trip to the East; others, in late 1832 with the trials and the collapse of the Retreat;[1] and still others, yet a year earlier with the schisms of Bazard and Rodrigues. Indeed, some historians continue to look on the whole movement as an aberrant outgrowth—from its very inception—of the truly fertile ideas of Saint-Simon himself.[2] All would agree, though, that by 1836 the movement was definitely in eclipse, for even in its own terms it had now failed. No female Messiah, no Suez Canal, no Nile Dam, not even a school to bear the names of the twelve Saint-Simonian dead. Nothing remained of the movement but its members, and they were choosing different paths. Most returned to France, but a number of them stayed on in Egypt, moved deeper into the African continent (Reboul, Combes, and Tamisier), or wended their way to Syria and Constantinople. This last party included Clorinde and Rogé, heading northwards to Saint Petersburg.

The growing distance between the members was even more spiritual than physical. Among certain of the Saint-Simonians who returned to France (or who had never left) there broke out a dissension as rancorous as the fraternity of Ménilmontant had been sweet. Michel Chevalier embarked openly on a new career as journalist and economist (and, eventually, senator), publicly disavowing his Saint-Simonian past in an article in the *Journal des débats* of 6 January 1838. Barrault, after speaking at a *réunion* on 10 August 1835, withdrew from all public involvement, feeling that he had nothing more to say. Fournel had already admitted his error in private, and many of the returning missionaries were to do the same. Bitterness, anger, scorn, and even disgust were vented on Enfantin at a time when he sorely needed emotional support. His property, including the house in Ménilmontant, had been sold to lessen his debts, and a few of the faithful even raised a subscription in his behalf. But he refused to accept a normal job, such as a position in his friend Arlès-

Dufour's silk manufacture in Lyons, for he still hoped to gain the position of influence in international affairs that had eluded him as head of the movement. He wrote letters full of proposals and philosophy to heads of state, and finally Louis-Philippe sent him to Algeria as a subordinate member of the official Commission scientifique de l'Algérie; he remained there for nearly two years.[3]

The decline of the movement was accompanied by a collapse of the musical movement to which it had given birth. Several "marginal" figures (from the movement's point of view) soon distanced themselves from Enfantin and his admirers, or had indeed done so already: Reber never had any dealings with the Saint-Simonians after his one composition of 1834; Berlioz and perhaps Hiller, too, had lost their enthusiasm by the time of the move to Ménilmontant; and Liszt dissociated himself publicly from the Saint-Simonians in 1838, though he never ceased to admire many of their ideas. The tenor Nourrit, another continuing admirer, was acting erratically and would soon commit suicide, and the chansonnier Jules Mercier had already thrown himself into the Seine. Though other songwriters were still producing chansons in the mid-1830s, none but Vinçard was actually composing melodies.

The decline of the movement and of its musical component affected most deeply the three musicians who had been involved in it most deeply. David and Rogé were now forced to begin looking elsewhere for sources of daily bread and for opportunities to exercise their creative "capacity." Eventually, through much hard work and some suffering, they established themselves in the world of concert music and opera. Nonetheless, their experience with the Saint-Simonians had marked them for life and in quite contrasting ways, as an examination of their later activities will reveal.

It may be better, though, to look first at the movement's other leading musician, Vinçard. Unlike David and Rogé, he was not at all dependent on the movement financially, because he had never ceased making measuring sticks in his father's shop. But he, too, suffered for a time when Enfantin's overloaded ship ran aground on the rocks of reality. And he, too, remained devoted to the cause, in his own way, for the rest of his years.

VINÇARD'S ACTIVITIES AFTER 1835

Vinçard and his proletarian supporters in the Famille de Paris had admired and supported the Egyptian adventure, but they had never been closely involved in it, and so their spirit was less damaged by its failure. In fact Enfantin's return to France gave them a momentary new impulse, as can be seen in the production of occasional songs in 1836 (Appendix B.3). Vinçard went south in excitement to greet Le Père at Lyons. On his return to Paris, though, he found a letter from Enfantin warning Vinçard that it is very difficult to try to improve the world. "You are forever caught between people who love you almost too much and others who detest you, between heat and cold, and you end up getting ill from it." Vinçard recognized the truth of these words in the personal antagonisms that had been growing in the Paris family. He put an end to the *réunions*, reasoning that in any case they made no sense now that not only the other Saint-Simonians but Le Père himself had reentered *le monde*. In 1839, in order to salvage what remained of the family's fraternal spirit and to place it in the service of "the people's cause," he created a new Saint-Simonian journal, *La Ruche populaire, journal des ouvriers rédigé et publié par eux-mêmes* (*The People's Beehive*), which would express Saint-Simonian doctrine in prose, verse, and song (*Mémoires,* pp. 168–78).[4] It was here that Vinçard published, among other songs, his "Chantons la paix et donnons-nous la main," a fraternal rebuke to Félicien David for having joined in the current wave of anti-German feeling by setting Musset's jingoistic "Le Rhin allemand."[5] The journal also attracted Fourierists and revolutionary democrats, who came into unresolvable conflict with the founders; as a result, the journal folded after several years.

Undaunted, Vinçard founded a second journal, *L'Union,* in which he voiced— in song as well as prose—the demand for assured employment, higher salaries, and retirement pensions.[6] This program, typical of the "cooperative socialism" of the day, was far more modest than the full societal transformation formerly preached by the Saint-Simonians, but Vinçard no doubt considered it, in the words of historian Bernard H. Moss, "a practical and transitional form of utopia." (We may recall Vinçard's statement in his memoirs that during un-sympathetic times he found it necessary to present his Saint-Simonian ideas in veiled and moderated form.[7]) At various times in his life Vinçard also took an active role in the founding of mutual-aid societies, further evidence of his desire to find immediate, pragmatic solutions to the problems of the poorest and most numerous class—solutions that derived their very power from the principle of "association."

With the encouragement of his friends he next undertook a project that— he later realized—was "quite beyond" his abilities. He decided to write an *Histoire du travail et des travailleurs en France,* a work that would have a "moral aim" and that would recount the achievements "of all those who, by their genius and their persevering labors in the sciences, arts, and industry, had enriched the world with everything that gives it its grandeur, its glory, and its generative power." The word *travailleur* was thus used in its broadest sense, much as the word *producteur* had been used by Saint-Simon himself to include members of all three of society's main branches of activity. Vinçard compiled his chronicle almost entirely from specialized works by professional writers and historians; with financial assistance from Enfantin, he published the first two volumes, which included an account of the achievements of, among other "workers," the medieval composer Philippe de Vitry! Clearly Vinçard had cast his net too wide, and, when the book received only one review ("an unreadable work," wrote the *Revue des deux mondes*), he tossed the sketches for the succeeding volumes into the wastebasket and devoted his literary talents henceforth to the production of chansons (pp. 205–13).

Vinçard had made an immediate success when he first appeared at the Lice chansonnière as a songwriter and singer (ca. 1839), and there is ample evidence that he and a number of like-minded artisan chansonniers gradually transformed this old liberal-nationalist goguette into an outpost of Saint-Simonian doctrine and the annual Lice songster into a propaganda vehicle. Although Vinçard regretted in his *Mémoires* that he never made any converts (p. 214), Edgar Leon Newman has shown that the social questions which the Saint-Simonian chansonniers raised did encourage other *licéens,* as they punningly called themselves, to abandon the traditional praise of wine and military glory for questions of social and economic reform. All too soon the Saint-Simonians were being attacked not only by the more conservative *licéens,* who resented the politicization of "these places made for pleasure," but also by the radical democrats, who wished to move faster than their self-appointed preachers and who ridiculed Vinçard's double message of progress and peace as "Marchons! mais ne bougeons jamais!" (March, but don't budge!).[8] Vinçard found that he could not always defend the Saint-Simonian principles against the practical day-to-day questions of the more activist workers, and he had to content himself with the fact that one of them, Chanu, delighted in hearing "the fraternal songs of Ménilmontant" (pp. 216, 224). David's songs were obviously beginning to acquire a nostalgic patina, having passed from relevance to sentimentality in a mere seven years.

Vinçard also brought his "propaganda in song" to a singing club called L'Enfer, where he became friendly with some republicans in the vain hope of drawing them away from their secret societies. The club eventually attracted students and bourgeois republicans, and it was only a matter of time before the police stormed one of the meetings and dissolved the organization (pp. 232–34).

The last years of the July Monarchy brought an increasing demand for social and electoral reform. The goguettes featured songs of social criticism by another Saint-Simonian, Lachambeaudie (converted in Lyons in 1832),[9] and the carpenter Rolly. Vinçard himself attended democratic meetings, while continuing to participate in what he later called the "quite innocent works" of the Saint-Simonians (p. 234). Perhaps it was at least somewhat gratifying for Vinçard to see the growth of the Fourierist movement during these years. Despite some major differences, the disciples of Fourier did share many of the Saint-Simonian aims. Furthermore, their most prominent songwriter, Jean Journet, clearly modeled his songs partly on those of the Saint-Simonians, using the "Marseillaise" and David's *Compagnonnage de la Femme,* in addition to the expected tunes associated with texts by Béranger or Pierre Dupont, e.g., "Les Gueux." In fact, Journet took the Saint-Simonians' reworking of the "Marseillaise" even further by boldly setting new words to a number of songs associated with the Revolution and the Empire: "Le Chant du départ," "Les Girondins," "Les Trois Couleurs," "Partant pour la Syrie," and "Veillons au salut de l'Empire."[10]

When Vinçard's father died in 1846, the son sold the ruler factory and all its tools, retaining only the right to sell rulers in a little shop that barely paid the family's food and rent. When the February Revolution of 1848 sent rich people scurrying from the city and left workers on the street without jobs, Vinçard became employed as a printer by the short-lived *ateliers nationaux* (pp. 238–47). At a meeting of former Saint-Simonians at Rodrigues's house, he did his best to convince them that the time was ripe to make a public restatement of the principles of the doctrine. The matter was dropped when only one person agreed to sign such a document—the wealthiest (and in that sense most secure) of them all, Isaac Pereire (pp. 257–59).

Life after the revolution was difficult. Vinçard's wife kept the shop running, and he looked for work elsewhere. When he applied for jobs in the enterprises of various successful Saint-Simonians, several turned him down, afraid that his proselytizing would "demoralize" the other employees (pp. 249–50). Vinçard's attempt to run for election as a "republican" delegate was undermined by the barely disguised Saint-Simonian doctrine he continued to espouse. Louis Jourdan finally gave him a clerical job on a short-lived newspaper he had founded; next, Duveyrier (who in 1848 had briefly employed him in a company of his that attempted to centralize the placing of advertising in the major Paris newspapers [p. 252]) welcomed him on the staff of *Le Crédit,* which struggled for a year and folded. Disappointed, Vinçard reopened the ruler factory and joined a new singing club, Le Lycée (the pun again), which, however, closed as an indirect result of the 1851 insurrection. (It reopened in 1855, with Vinçard again participating.) He continued to write songs and sing them at reunions and anniversaries of the Saint-Simonian family, devoting three to his friend Gallé's founding of a mutual-aid society in Colombes (pp. 261–72).

It had been Vinçard's lifelong desire to settle in the country; in 1857 he finally yielded and bought a plot of land in Saint-Maur-les-Fossés near his friend and fellow chansonnier Boissy. On 3 May Enfantin and "the principal members of the Family" came out to the new house to sanctify it with a fraternal banquet. For a while Vinçard continued to produce his measuring sticks in Saint-Maur, but Enfantin and others wanted to see him free to pursue more "religious" work. To begin with, Enfantin insisted on reimbursing him the 3,000 francs that he had spent for the house. Then Enfantin, Duveyrier, Arlès-Dufour, and others began a campaign to persuade Vinçard to accept a pension from them in exchange for organizing a mutual-aid society for all the former members of the Saint-Simonian family. (One Marxist historian has noted pointedly the change in his friends' attitude: "His peaceful socialism no longer scared anyone, now that the people's torment [the Revolution of 1848] had passed."[11]) This project had long been Vinçard's dream and he had in fact already begun it in a small way. Arlès finally convinced him to accept, Henri Fournel was named president, and "Les Amis de la famille" was officially constituted on 27 July 1861 (pp. 291–307). The annual reports of the "Amis" for the first few years give names and addresses of those who contributed to the society's charity.[12]

The pension left Vinçard freer than ever to compose and sing for the family gatherings. Enfantin continued to request his favorites, especially "Le Travail." The song "L'Oeuvre de Dieu" was inspired by Enfantin's last major philosophical work, *La Vie éternelle*, and (like "Le Travail") it incorporated suggestions from Le Père; Vinçard presented the song to him on his birthday, 8 February 1862. It was one of Vinçard's last happy moments; the following December his devoted wife died and, broken with sorrow, he fled Saint-Maur that very night and took up lodgings with his old friend Ducatel in Paris (pp. 307–14). His *Mémoires* stop here, but we know that he continued to take part in the formation of various mutual-aid and cooperative societies, not least by publishing a periodical on the subject, *La Mutualité* (Brussels, 1865).[13]

Although his activities since the 1840s had been mainly oriented toward these rather modest local efforts, he insisted to the last on his identity as a Saint-Simonian. When in 1869 he published a retrospective collection of chansons by himself and others, he proudly subtitled many of his lyrics—including some recent efforts—"Chant saint-simonien." In 1879 he recounted his lifetime of Saint-Simonian involvement in the *Mémoires épisodiques d'un vieux chansonnier saint-simonien:* memoirs, one notes, not of a "former" (*ancien*) Saint-Simonian, just an "old" one. A photo taken in his last years (plate 26) lets us see this "vieux chansonnier": he is grinning with satisfaction and looking hearty, with a full head of hair and full beard, both gone pure white. The accompanying biography calls him "dean of the Lice [chansonnière]," praises him as "perhaps the first to give to the chanson a truly social mission," and notes that he remains "a good and vigorous walker, a joyous table companion, and a merry singer."[14] Clearly he was considered a model chansonnier; even more notably, he was that rare example of an individual who, while preserving high and at times unfashionable ideals of international cooperation and social justice, never ceased to "cultivate his garden": to work in smaller and more practical ways for the improvement of life here and now.

DAVID'S ISOLATION AND FIRST STEPS TOWARD A CAREER

When David and Henri Granal left Egypt around April 1835, they were among the first Saint-Simonians to depart. Actually, David, unlike most of the others, had been invited to stay and could even have achieved some status and financial security. As he wrote to his friend Sylvain Saint-Etienne on 11 May, "I was offered a very lucrative position which would in time have taken on great importance. I refused because I would have had to obligate myself to stay for an indefinite period of time. That was not my aim."[15] In Egypt David would probably have been expected to teach piano or perhaps to direct the viceroy's band, much as Giuseppe Donizetti (brother of the opera composer) was doing in Constantinople.[16] But David sought fulfillment as a composer, something that the viceroy could not provide, as the same letter to Saint-Etienne makes clear:

> Two years in the Orient, that is all that was necessary for me to gather the inspirations there that I was searching for. I return to sing of the Orient in France. You can imagine that I need a great theater and great poet [Duveyrier]. I run to him. We shall do something brand new. How can you think that I might settle in Egypt? It is still a child as far as art is concerned. And, besides, Muhammad Ali is too preoccupied with material interests to think of anything *artistic*. So people believed I was the pasha's chief composer. With or without the fancy title, that's what I was in reality. Because in his states there are hardly any [composers] at all.[17]

David would learn through hard personal experience that Paris was not necessarily any more welcoming to self-styled "artistic" geniuses than the Egypt of Muhammad Ali.

David had taken the land route from Cairo to Beirut, abandoning his possessions, which were at the home of a friend in plague-ridden Alexandria. It was with special regret, as he admitted to Saint-Etienne, that in Cairo he had bid farewell to his portable piano. "It had given shelter to all my emotions during my travels."[18] But he wrote enthusiastically about the trip through Gaza and Palestine, and about the music he had gathered in nearly three years abroad:

> Oh, my friend, what a beautiful trip, especially for an artist! What places, what cities fertile with great memories. . . . That's the kind of thing that can inspire you. And then those various peoples, with their magnificent and grandiose costume, their language—sometimes harsh and guttural, sometimes soft and harmonious. And their simple and original songs. I am bringing back a great quantity of them.[19]

David arrived in Marseilles around 19 June 1835. He had to be completely outfitted and was waiting for money, but he took advantage of the delay to play his new Oriental piano pieces in the salons of the piano manufacturer Boisselot.[20] In Marseilles he met a friend from Lyons, Théodore de Seynes, and David held him spellbound with his stories of the East. David recognized the reason: "It's because the Orient over there is so different from the one that people invent here."[21] De Seynes's and Boisselot's interest in hearing David's Oriental tales and tunes may have confirmed his suspicion that there was a certain distinction in being the first composer to have visited Egypt. From now on David had a new mission—to sing of the East, the "real" East, to Western audiences.

This did not mean that David had abandoned his faith. In a passage that deserves to be quoted at length, David wrote proudly of his plans for a grand collaboration with the man who had been his artistic *père* at the Retreat and, no less proudly, of his continued adherence to Saint-Simonian principles.

> You can imagine how impatient I am to be in Paris, where *Duveyrier* is waiting for me. . . . He is already very well known in Paris by his poetic verve. He was at Ménilmontant with me. In Paris they called him "The Poet of God," a name he very well lived up to. Recently he gave a drama full of beauties at the [Théâtre de la] Porte Saint-Martin, and it had some success. In my opinion he is the man who suits me best for an original creation. He knows me. And I know him. Our souls have met, and you will see that they will produce something powerful.
>
> It seems that you believe me to be an *ex-Saint-Simonian*. How can you believe that I am so fickle [*léger*]? You clearly do not know that *Saint-Simonism* has given me an entirely new life. You do not know what vast things this religion contains and how an artist can find in it new and grand inspirations.
>
> I have never had doubts about the future of my religion. Only the means may vary. Thus, time is not a matter that in any way weakens my faith.
>
> Perhaps you felt that the name "Saint-Simonian" would do me harm in the minds of my acquaintances [in Aix]. If so, you were right to say that I am no longer one. But when I stop there [on my way to Paris] I will not hide. Besides, I still carry the sign of the Saint-Simonian. You will see me with a beard and long hair. . . . I do, though, wear regular clothes.
>
> Nonetheless, I laugh at whatever those *legitimist, Christian* or what-have-they gentlemen may say. Again, I will not hide my opinions if someone asks me for them.[22]

The proposed collaboration with Duveyrier may well have sprung from the eager brain of Père Enfantin. Various letters show him encouraging Duveyrier, David, Urbain, and Barrault to join their efforts in a theatrical venture.[23] He specifically mentioned that Duveyrier was working on an "Egyptian play" and said he considered it one of the "good signs on the horizon" for the movement.[24] Perhaps Enfantin hoped that David would turn his authentic Egyptian tunes to profit by writing simple, quasi-authentic incidental music for this play; maybe he even envisioned more elaborate solos, choruses, and orchestral numbers. In truth David could have filled the task well, as his Egyptian piano pieces show, and a theatrical collaboration with Duveyrier would have brought him public and critical attention (as well as much-needed practical experience). It might even have spared him the years of obscurity and frustration that lay ahead and that would only be broken in 1844 by the success of *Le Désert*.

As it turned out, after David reached Paris, there was no more talk of a theatrical collaboration. The times were different now. The Saint-Simonians were no longer a unified group, they no longer felt obligated to assist each other, and many were now primarily concerned with acquiring a position for themselves *dans le monde*. Duveyrier had stayed in Paris during the Egyptian mission, giving him something of a head start in this pursuit of career, wealth, and recognition. Already in February 1834—only months after Enfantin's release from prison—he had cowritten a vaudeville with his brother Mélesville, and in 1835 and 1836 he collaborated on scripts for three opéras-comiques. He did not seem to feel that there was any contradiction between his ideas and his actions. Indeed, the Saint-Simonian leaders had never seen a virtue in poverty and anonymity; they had always reasoned that money and power would have a "moral power" when placed in (their) religious hands. How it was earned was not a matter of great significance.

David, in contrast, held a sternly critical view of the boulevard theaters and opéra-comique. He had taken the Saint-Simonian critique of bourgeois culture more deeply to heart than had Duveyrier, with the result that he now had more difficulty adjusting to the requirements of the marketplace. To Saint-Etienne he complained that he was not made for "intrigue" and "conventional music."

> You will cite the names of Meyerbeer and others who are greatly applauded. . . . But, *mon cher*, he had 40,000 francs in income to help him push his *Robert* [*le diable*]. As for those gentlemen of the Opéra-Comique, I do not know if they have made concessions to the public. I prefer to think not. In which case, they were made for it, for its pleasure. Well, I am not made for it. I am well aware of that. I am too severe, too religious for it.[25]

If David was still too religious for the public, he was also too religious for the public's darling that Duveyrier was becoming.

Duveyrier, for his part, cannot be blamed for losing interest in David. Although the young composer had been of undoubted value to the movement, he was still but twenty-five years old, totally inexperienced in practical matters, and largely self-taught. Nobody could have predicted that he would accomplish great things *dans le monde*. Rogé, for example, was astonished years later when he heard that David was writing a Desert Symphony, recalling that in 1835 (when he last saw him) David "was so completely inexperienced that he had not read a single [orchestral] score of the masters" and restricted himself to "fresh, dreamy melodies" accompanied by "simple and good harmonies (for luckily his training in harmony had been good)."[26] The apathy of the musical public when the *Mélodies orientales* were published in 1836 must have done nothing to raise David in the estimation of Duveyrier. A number of more established theater composers, including Piccini, Béancourt, and Montfort, were available to the former "Poet of God." His brother Mélesville's connections would soon lead Duveyrier's career onward and upward, reaching its peak in a collaboration with Scribe for the Paris Opéra: *Le Duc d'Albe* (intended for Donizetti and later successfully reworked for Verdi under the title *Les Vêpres siciliennes*).

Enfantin in fact, once the "Egyptian play" was abandoned, began pushing Duveyrier along this very path, urging that he devote himself to something more significant than vaudevilles, comic operas, and ballet scenarios.

> Think of [the soprano] Mlle Falcon and the great [tenor] Duprez! Are *Robert le diable* and *La Juive* plots [*aventures*] beyond your power of invention? ... But for God's sake have them sing things that move people's hearts, like [Gluck's] *Armide, Alceste,* and *Orphée,* and are not merely a lovely exercise for their voices, as *La Chatte* is for the graces of Mlle Esser [sic].
> . . . Nature is singing, dramatic, loving, like Beethoven, Weber (whom you love)—like the way you were [reciting verses accompanied by David] at the piano during our first days at Ménilmontant, the way you were [so eloquent] at the Court of Assizes [during the trial in August 1832], which makes Gustave [d'Eichthal?] think that you ought to do tragedies. . . .
> . . . Here is what should distinguish you from Lavigne [Casimir Delavigne], Hugo, and Dumas: you are not the author of any coterie, of any party. You want what is for everybody's good.[27]

It is not known whether Enfantin intended that David should contribute the music for this great never-to-be-written work, the Saint-Simonians' definitive response to the superficialities of French grand opera. He too may have already given up his hopes for David by 1837. But one thing is clear: in this letter we hear the voice of the man who had pressed for a David-Duveyrier collaboration in 1835 and who probably encouraged David to think of himself as "religious" and "severe."

David's distress after his arrival in Paris must have been intense. Not only had his comrades lost interest in him and the public rejected his *Mélodies orientales,* but the entire stock of unsold copies of those pieces was destroyed by fire soon after their publication in 1836. David went into partial seclusion for several years, developing his compositional skills by writing works in the Austro-German manner: "I am working on some symphonies—slowly, because it is no small task. If you knew the symphonies of the great *Beethoven*

[sic], you would see that I am right to be scrupulous in my labor.[28]" Rogé probably exaggerated in saying that David had never studied a score of the masters. But David was clearly realizing now how much he still had to learn; Azevedo reports that during the years after his return to France David submitted the Beethoven Third and Fourth Symphonies to an "assiduous meditation" in all their details.[29]

Between 1836 and 1844 David wrote three symphonies, two brass nonets (apparently unrelated to the arrangements of Arab songs which he had made for Rogé's musicians in 1834), some chamber music, and a number of short piano pieces and songs. He was trying valiantly to establish himself as a composer—in the most varied genres—but none of his former companions was doing much to help him. Only five years earlier, shortly after arriving in Egypt, David had announced to his brother-in-law that he would never need anything again, whether in Egypt or in France.[30] Now, though, he was obliged to write time and again to Saint-Etienne with various requests relating to money. "I don't see any way to get out of [financial] difficulties. I repeat, there is nobody here who can help me."[31] Many of his closest friends in the movement did not have the means to help. More upsetting, those who did were no longer interested in helping.[32]

At least one of David's Saint-Simonian friends, Félix Tourneux, did stand by him. Tourneux had been a member of David's chorus at Ménilmontant, a Compagnon de la femme in Smyrna, and a member of the Egyptian mission. On his return to France, he seems to have taken a violent dislike to Enfantin[33] and never had much to do with the movement again. For several years, beginning in August 1837, David lived in Igny (near Palaiseau) with Tourneux and his wife Emma, "who, despite their straitened circumstances, give me generous hospitality."[34] The Tourneux themselves stayed at Igny only during the warm months, but David remained there pretty much the whole year round, studying, composing, and tending the garden.[35] Gardening was a joy to which he would often return later in life. It also had a spiritual and social significance for this apostle of Ménilmontant. In one letter from Igny he reminded Saint-Etienne of the importance of combining physical and mental labor and recommended the writings of Fourier, "especially the *Treatise on Agriculture and Domestic Association*. In it are contained the salvation of society and humanity's path to happiness."[36] David's reference to Fourier suggests that his mind was as active at Igny as his hands and pen and also that he was not afraid to look beyond the immediate circle of Saint-Simonians for his intellectual nourishment.[37] Fourier's desire to restore the nobility and pleasure of manual labor may have appealed to David because of his early memories of life in rural Provence or because the Saint-Simonians, too, had preached the "rehabilitation" of manual labor (though not nearly in so much detail as Fourier). Years later David was to remain a modest supporter of the Fourierists, contributing five francs to the publication of Jean Journet's *Poésies et chants harmoniens.*[38]

In 1841 David moved back to Paris to live with his brother Charles, who was a professional trombonist and sometime painter.[39] Once again he attempted to conquer the musical world. He had some musical friends in Paris—Xavier Boisselot, the violinist Armingaud and two singers (Wartel and Amat) who were performing his songs—and he slowly acquired piano students and publishing contracts for his songs, notably with Schlesinger.[40] But David was not content with the modest success of a salon composer.[41] He wanted to make his mark with something big and preferably something new. He had often talked grandly of arranging a concert of his works or of composing an opera for one of the Paris theaters. In 1838 he had managed to get his Symphony in F performed at Valentino's excellent and low-priced popular concerts, and the next year two movements of his Nonetto in F had been played by the cornettist Forestier and other skilled players under Musard's direction.[42] But the plans for a full concert of his own works, analogous to the concerts that had made Berlioz's reputation in 1830 and 1832, always fell through. As for the opera, there was talk of his being invited to set two librettos: one by Mélesville, the other, on an Oriental subject, by Royer and Rouget.[43] But neither of these projects ever materialized either.

The darkness and isolation of these years must have seemed unbearable; David's years with the Saint-Simonians had accustomed him to a great deal of favorable attention, frequent performances, and a feeling of belonging. Even at his most hopeless, though, he managed to avoid prolonged self-doubt, blaming instead the social situation in which he was trapped. Looking around him, he saw composer after composer writing music that was "cold, colorless, like our century," and he wondered honestly whether there might simply be no place for him in the musical world as it was then constituted.

> I almost have a desire not to compose anymore. In order to believe in myself, I would need to hear my works and to see an audience forcefully impressed. And [even] that would not satisfy me completely. I would like to see art have a social mission, and today it is far from having it. What is the final result of all the products of art today, except to amuse some people who have nothing else to do? And if only it did amuse them, but they yawn as they listen to you. Miserable century, which no longer has any belief, or rather which has but one: money. And which lowers everything to that. Today, more than ever, society is one big con game [*flouerie*] in which everyone tries to trick his neighbor. It is an organized war in everything, whether industry, science, or art.[44]

"Le Désert" and David's Tour of Germany

David's thoughts on the social mission of art no doubt found little sympathy with the various librettists who were proposed as his collaborators. Finally, however, he came into renewed contact with a young writer who shared his concerns and many of his experiences. The writer was Auguste Colin, and the work that resulted from this collaboration was *Le Désert*. Colin, a leading Saint-Simonian from Marseilles, had been in the group of missionaries that Rogé dispatched to Egypt in late 1833 and was among the few who stayed on there for several years when the others left in 1836. In Egypt and then in France, Colin developed an active career as journalist and writer (in part on Egyptian matters). More important, he had strong ideas on the mission of art. In 1834, in a letter to the black Saint-Simonian and would-be poet Thomas Urbain, he had expressed at great length his views on the proper form and content of Saint-Simonian art. One point in particular seems to have remained with him when, ten years later, he wrote the text of *Le Désert*. "It seems to me that, in our manner of feeling love, our raptures must be calmer, more generous, more religious. In your love scenes [in your poem], I see too exclusively two individuals. I do not see the society enough. And yet, as you know, there is no true love outside of a social milieu."[45]

In Colin's text for *Le Désert* the "social milieu" was clearly defined by the almost unremitting focus on the Arab people (represented by male chorus) rather than on individuals. (Of the three solo numbers, all for tenor, only one deals primarily with love; it is sung by a character never named or encountered again, and his beloved is apparently not with him.) The basic premise of the work—a caravan moving across the desert, stopping for the night, then moving on—led naturally to depictions of the wonders of nature: the endless sands, a desert storm, the starry night, a majestic sunrise. (Barrault had called on artists in 1831 to depict some of these very "riches of nature."[46]) The scenario also invited the insertion of musical passages rich in local color. And, not least, Colin's text explicitly contrasted the freedom and vigor of life in the desert with the paleness of urban society.[47] David must have found all of this uncommonly appealing. It permitted him to exploit the Oriental vein, transmit a social message, and, in the descriptive passages, fulfill his longstanding desire to sing of "the *beautiful* and the *good*."[48] In fact, the text of *Le Désert* was so well fitted to David's needs and tastes that it seems more than likely that he had a role in shaping it himself. The plainly Oriental numbers—the muezzin's chant, for example, and the two orchestral dances ("Fantasia arabe" and "Danse des almées")—were no doubt included at his request; the "Hymne à la nuit" already existed;[49] and the "Rêverie du soir" is based on the first of the *Mélodies orientales*.[50]

Some populist tendencies in the wording of the text did not escape observers of the day, and Colin was obliged to defend himself, much as Hugo had done during the battle over *Hernani* in 1830.[51] The music, too, had a certain populist appeal. In the choral movements David returned to the chordal style (and the all-male forces) that had characterized his pieces for Ménilmontant. The spoken narration (over held chords in the low strings) was clearly a gesture toward direct communication with the audience, and the Oriental numbers for orchestra or for tenor and orchestra were not only appealingly novel in melody and rhythm but clothed in effective instrumental colors that won the praise of listeners as diverse as Hector Berlioz and Temistocle Solera, Verdi's librettist.[52] As for the central image of a desert caravan, the audience cannot have missed in it an allusion to the Saint-Simonian mission to Egypt. Less obvious, perhaps, was the Saint-Simonian origin of the narration-over-chords. David was very proud of this feature, feeling that it transformed his vocal-orchestral work into the first example of an entirely new genre, to which he gave an entirely new name: *ode-symphonie*.[53] But it should not take away from David's achievement to suggest that he had, with Barrault and with Duveyrier, combined music and spoken text twelve years earlier at Ménilmontant.[54]

Le Désert was the first major work of David's since 1833 to be written in collaboration with a Saint-Simonian and to show Saint-Simonian influence in its essential conception and, to some extent, in the details of the composition. Perhaps because of the strong Saint-Simonian echoes in the piece or because of pressure from Colin, several of the leading Saint-Simonians began to take interest again shortly before the premiere. Michel Chevalier, by now somewhat reconciled with Enfantin, helped David get permission to put on his concert at the Salle du Conservatoire,[55] no mean feat, as Berlioz well knew. According to one report, Chevalier also raised 1,200 francs for David.[56] Enfantin himself apparently set up a letter campaign before the premiere, inviting various well-known figures to attend. Enfantin's invitation to the worker-poet Savinien Lapointe specifically stressed David's Saint-Simonian credentials, and similar letters went out to the anticlerical historian Edgar Quinet, the novelist Eugène Sue, and no doubt dozens of other notables.[57] Enfantin even wrote to Saint Petersburg to invite Rogé.[58]

The premiere took place on 8 December 1844, and it was an immense success. The Saint-Simonians were eager to claim the success as their own, especially since the concert also included *Chant du soir* and *Le Sommeil de Paris,* retexted versions of, respectively, the Ménilmontant choruses *Danse des astres* and (apparently) *Paris est là.*[59] Duveyrier wrote an excessively warm letter to Berlioz thanking him for his favorable review of the concert. (He had actually tried to visit him personally but resorted to a written note when the critic happened not to be at home.) Duveyrier's larger aim was clearly to draw Berlioz into the Enfantin circle, and in that—as we have seen in Chapter 9—he was manifestly unsuccessful.

Duveyrier was the first to take action, but the privilege, and burden, of exploiting the success of *Le Désert* finally fell to Enfantin and his friend Arlès-

Dufour. The burden was not light. David, totally inexperienced in business matters, had sold to the publisher Escudier the rights not only to *Le Désert* but to all his works *in aeternam* ... and for a total of 1,200 francs! (David would soon earn this amount in a single concert.) Fortunately, Enfantin and Duveyrier were able to get this disgraceful contract annulled, and they also helped steer David through a number of other legal disagreements—with Colin, with theater managers, and with unscrupulous publishers—that resulted from the sudden and enormous success of David's *ode-symphonie*.[60]

Enfantin was now as personally concerned and protective of David as if the composer were his own son. This is hardly surprising; David's past activities would have been enough reason for Enfantin to feel pride and responsibility for the musician's current exploits. But, in addition, Enfantin had plans that David could serve. Still longing to make his debut in the world of diplomacy, Enfantin arranged to make a trip to Germany and Austria; his arrival would be announced by performances of *Le Désert* under David's own direction. Since his current plan was, once again, a Suez Canal, *Le Désert* would be the perfect eye-and-ear-catcher. As he himself put it as the time, David's purpose in traveling through Germany was "to make people there love Egypt."[61]

In a short time, David's affairs were totally in the hands of the Saint-Simonians, especially Enfantin's assistant Louis Jourdan. Félix and Emma Tourneux seem to have resisted this development and perhaps, more generally, David's increasing subordination to Enfantin's will. Enfantin responded with vicious personal insults that angered Félix and Emma but wounded the sensitive David:

> You have cast slurs on a man and woman who did not deserve it—friends who have long loved me as a brother and who have been hospitable to me for such a long time. . . . Félix may have acted inconsiderately toward you, but he never had the intentions which you attribute to him. Emma, in spite of her violent and quick-tempered character, has always been a noble soul. Ah, I have received a wound from which I shall never be healed. . . . My life is poisoned forever.[62]

David nonetheless chose to make the trip to Germany, as Enfantin wished. His letter of explanation to Emma reveals the continuing depth of his social commitment (and, incidentally, of Emma's antagonism toward Enfantin).

> I have sounded my heart for a long time. In it I have found the same affection for you and Félix, in spite of the unfair suppositions that you both have made about me. But I also have great love for Le Père. I cannot forget that he has always loved me like a son. If you have loved me like a brother, he bore [*enfanté*] me into new life, and Félix himself cannot have forgotten that. My greatest sorrow will be to have been the innocent cause of such great suffering for you two, and to

have been forced by you, [Emma,] to choose either Le Père or you two, instead of us all blending together in a holy love. . . .

I began my career as an artist with work to benefit society [*par une oeuvre sociale*]. I have always suffered for not having continued it. Now the moment has come. It may be that I am not strong enough for this work, but God will take my efforts into account. My destiny is to march with Le Père, in whom I have always had faith.[63]

Enfantin kept delaying his own departure, but he did everything in his power to pave the way for David. In a personal letter to Mendelssohn in Frankfurt, Enfantin explained that David was, "of all the men who have given me filial affection, the one who always was and is the most my son. He is the Benjamin of that family of which you know and love several members."[64] When David finally arrived in Frankfurt, he was received cordially by Mendelssohn. Meyerbeer, in Berlin, did much more, arranging a performance of *Le Désert* at court in Potsdam. (The royal family enjoyed the work more than did some public audiences elsewhere on David's journey.)[65] David also mentioned in letters that he spent several pleasant days in the company of Ferdinand Hiller and was well treated in Leipzig by the great violinist Ferdinand David (no relation).

The men in Paris were not happy sending alone into central Europe this musical representative of their Suez Canal schemes. Letters of introduction were important, but hardly sufficient. David, as they had learned, was naïve, erratic in judgment, and a total stranger to diplomacy. Arlès-Dufour therefore instructed his wife's nephew Dufour-Féronce to keep the scatter-brained composer on schedule. It was Dufour who introduced David to the leading literary and musical figures in Leipzig,[66] and it is no doubt thanks to young Dufour that the trip to Germany turned out as successfully as it did. Even with Dufour's guidance, David managed to depart for the forthcoming concert in Berlin without the scores and parts for *Le Désert*.[67]

Moïse au Sinaï, Christophe Colomb, AND *L'Eden*

David no doubt had his own reasons for making the trip—most of all, the desire to advance his renown and to be acclaimed by German audiences for works that in his own mind had drawn great inspiration from the German masters.[68] But there can be no doubt that the strongest single force in David's career during this period was Enfantin and that the latter's strongest motivation was a desire to publicize the Canal. Perhaps Enfantin had even given David the idea of writing an Arab (ode-) symphony in the first place, just as, years before, he had tried to get Duveyrier and David to collaborate on a theatrical work set in Egypt. About David's next work, an oratorio entitled *Moïse au Sinaï,* there is no doubt

211

whatever; from the outset it was planned as propaganda. The Saint-Simonians had often compared their leaders to Moses,[69] but the analogy was much more telling now that Enfantin was boldly proclaiming (again) his intention to lead the world to—of all places—Sinai. And the message of the new oratorio—the importance of moving jointly toward a goal (the Promised Land)—must have seemed even more promising for propaganda purposes than was the more meandering action of *Le Désert*. Enfantin undertook to write the libretto and persistently urged David, still touring in Germany, to get working on the music.

> I recommend that you push Moses along, too. The Suez business is going better and better here. There is no chance that I will not be going to Germany soon on its behalf. Everything is preparing marvelously for it, and Moses must come with us. . . .
>
> I advise Dufour . . . [to remember] that you are at this moment doing the Suez affair in Germany, just as much as he is himself, and consequently your travels, your presence, your music, all your actions should be incorporated into the aim of your Religious life. . . . Yes, dear friend, think of David carrying *Moses* in him, the *Moses* who is pushing *Israel* to the *promised land*. Show this to Dufour and walk firmly, both of you, along the line that leads to Suez.[70]

Two weeks later, Enfantin reminded the composer that *Moïse* should be his main concern. "Your success in Leipzig, though I value it enormously, is worth less to me than the good words of calm, confidence, and hope that you give me. It is also not worth as much as the fervor which I see you applying to your Sinai work, . . . that holy prelude to our Suez Mass."[71]

Enfantin even undertook to advise David on the musical composition of the work, particularly requesting that David insert his favorite Ménilmontant chorus, the *Salut* (with new words, of course). He also wanted David to follow it with a magnificent finale, which he was only too happy to sketch for his obedient disciple.

> It seems to me that immediately after the last "Gloire à Dieu" [of the *Salut*], there should be a joyful transition leading to a chorus beginning with children's voices, merry and feeling the gaiety (the opposite of the Christian choirboy) and starting off the general dance, which the first and second tenors next take up, then the women, then the *tutti*. Perhaps Moses himself, like the musician, poet, and dancer David, should set them in motion, one after the other. For that, dear friend, I feel that we would need to be side by side, you at your piano, me with pen in hand.[72]

A month later, he elaborated his plan for a vast peroration.

I still insist on the *Salut,* but it should end with something else, and I would like that something else to be an instrumental and *then* vocal crescendo, such as has never been heard before—*apocalyptic,* but an apocalypse of joy. The reverse of your "Entrée au désert" [part 1 of *Le Désert*], i.e., the opposite of immensity and eternity: the point, the moment, the fact, the present, the instantaneous, the wild religious dance [*la Chahut Religieuse*], the Dance of David—before the ark, upon the altar, before the God of grace and power, the God of beautiful, good, and frisky flesh [*chair belle et bonne et fringuante*]. And meanwhile the masons build the Temple, the engineers dig the canal, the blacksmiths beat the iron, the children peal with laughter, the women sing, and all nature—Sun, Earth, and Heaven—is in joy.[73]

Was ever a composer badgered by a patron more persistently (and pretentiously) than David by his Saint-Simonian Father?

Fortunately or unfortunately for David, Enfantin was not in the end able to break away from his business commitments to come to Germany and, although he at first tried to have Louis Jourdan write the remaining verses of the libretto, the task finally fell to David's faithful friend Sylvain Saint-Etienne. Enfantin was clearly losing interest in the work, as successes of a more practical nature began claiming his attention. He was put in charge of consolidating the three railroad lines that covered the stretch from Paris to Marseilles, and named secretary general of the Paris-Lyons line.[74] Even more promising was the foundation in 1846 of the Société d'études pour le canal de Suez, consisting of engineers from England, France, and Germany and Austria and supported financially by the Chambers of Commerce of Trieste, Venice, Lyons, and Prague, by Austrian Lloyd, and so on.[75] With both of these projects coming so suddenly to fruition, Enfantin must have realized that he had no need for propagandistic oratorios, and *Moïse au Sinaï* dropped quickly from its position as a first-priority project.[76] Enfantin continued to encourage David and Saint-Etienne to finish *Moïse,* but the project was now all theirs.

The oratorio failed dreadfully when performed in Paris on 8 March 1846 and was given rarely thereafter. The anonymous critic of the *Revue et gazette musicale* quite fairly noted that the chorus "Israël, Israël" used the music (and indeed much of the text) of the lengthy *Tout est mort* of Ménilmontant days. (Now it is "the yoke of Pharaoh" rather than "the life of an apostle" that is "harsh and severe"; the biblical setting allows "the people" to suffer here in exactly the same words as before.) The critic, however, did not mention the briefer snippet from *Salut* that David had, in apparent deference to Enfantin's wishes, decided to retain as the first twenty-two measures of "La Terre promise." ("Père, salut" easily became "Terre, salut," and, in a direct transferral of traits from Enfantin to Moses, the music of "Vous nous avez dit: travaillez, travaillez" received the text "Mais Moïse a crié: liberté, liberté!") Both of the borrowed numbers are distinctly inferior to much else in the score.

Several months after beginning *Moïse* David had decided to add "a plaintive romance sung by a woman" in order to "reduce a bit the monotony of such a serious subject."[77] His instincts were right. It was the only moment that the critic of the *Revue et gazette* praised even coolly ("rather pretty"). For the rest, the critic concluded that David had overshot himself,[78] and Berlioz, on tour in Prague, heard the bad news and reacted the same way: "What an idea—to try to climb Sinai when one is short-winded and to wish to carry the tables of the law when one does not have a strong arm! . . . This subject did not suit him at all."[79] David had of course been led down the path of pretension by Enfantin, but that was little consolation. Unlike *Le Désert,* a success in which the prominent Saint-Simonians were glad to bask, *Moïse* was a failure, and it hurt only the composer and his devoted friend Sylvain.

David had meanwhile begun a third major work that was in truth rather more appropriate to his modest but real descriptive and lyrical gifts and was as a result quite a success with both audiences and critics. *Christophe Colomb* (1847), like *Le Désert,* was an *ode-symphonie* and contained passages of narration, solos, choruses, and orchestral movements. David took advantage of the opportunity for local color—some Spanish ballads, a dance of savages, a lullaby sung by an Indian mother, and also a storm scene. (David attempted to depict the latter realistically, taking as inspiration the coastal storms he had observed at Dieppe.[80]) The Saint-Simonian element is still very stong in the work. As in *Le Désert,* the emphasis on nature seems a sort of belated response to Barrault's *appels.*[81] As in *Moïse,* the leader is a thinly veiled Enfantin and the effortful journey (toward the New World) represents the Saint-Simonian call for a new society. (Duveyrier had, in fact, already cast Enfantin as Columbus in 1832.[82]) Indeed, Columbus is allowed to encounter resistance from his sailors (in part 3: "La Révolte") and then to regain their loyalty by his "unshakable sense of mission"—a fantasy that must have appealed to the rejected leader in Enfantin.[83] But there is a more specific allusion in the work that no doubt remained hidden to all but the closest circle. The Saint-Simonians had made use of one of David's Ménilmontant choruses, *Le Nouveau Temple,* as a cantata in 1833 in celebration of the departure to the Eastern regions. Now David used the same music, in its entirety, with yet a new set of words to represent the departure of Columbus and his crew to the unknown regions of the West. The connection between Columbus's adventure and the search for La Femme was no doubt present in David's own mind and would have been obvious to a number of the Saint-Simonians in the audience.[84] The critics, however, did not take David to task this time for reusing old material; perhaps the composer had learned not to advertise his borrowings. (David may later have mentioned the retexting to Azevedo, since the latter mentions it in his biography.) In addition, there is—as we have seen in Chapter 12—a second Saint-Simonian chorus in the work; it is the "Choeur des génies de l'océan," an arrangement of *Les Etoiles,* the orientale that David wrote in Smyrna and dedicated to La Mère.

During the next five or so years David's relations with Enfantin seem to have remained cool. Enfantin's loss of interest during the completion of *Moïse* was no doubt intensified by the devastating failure of the work. Perhaps Enfantin was pleased by the success of *Christophe Colomb,* but David's reputation was soon damaged again by the failure of *L'Eden* in 1848. (This all-too-innocent oratorio on life in the Garden of Eden before the Fall was perhaps a casualty of the turbulent political fever of the moment.[85])

There was also a more personal source of tension between David and the Enfantin circle: the professional ambitions of David's friend Sylvain Saint-Etienne. Enfantin had been violently opposed to Saint-Etienne's desire to manage David's affairs in 1845, the year of the German tour. Enfantin repeatedly accused him of total incompetence in business matters and, worse, of not understanding the Saint-Simonian faith.[86] Arlès-Dufour even described him to Enfantin as "a terribly spineless creature [*emplâtre*] who will create lots of trouble and annoyance in David's future."[87] Saint-Etienne defended himself in relentlessly long letters to Enfantin, until Le Père was forced to cry out to David in mock horror, "The astonishing correspondence that we are producing on this subject will be no less marvelous to posterity than your music itself."[88]

DAVID AND SAINT-ETIENNE; DAVID'S OPERAS; RETIREMENT

Friendship won out and Saint-Etienne joined the composer in Germany. He quickly became David's librettist, completing, as we have seen, Enfantin's text for *Moïse* and later writing the libretto of *Christophe Colomb* (in collaboration with his friend Charles Chaubet and the experienced librettist Joseph Méry). He also took advantage of David's fame to establish himself as a music publisher in Paris during the late 1840s and 1850s, but his success was undermined by the fact that the works for which demand was great—*Christophe Colomb* and *La Perle du Brésil*—went to bigger publishers, and he was left with the unsuccessful oratorios *Moïse* and *L'Eden,* some minor piano pieces, and the scores of David's three purely instrumental symphonies. Saint-Etienne even took the hopeless risk of republishing the Ménilmontant choruses (in a collection entitled *La Ruche harmonieuse,* the original texts being replaced by neutral ones from the pen of Chaubet) and six motets that David had written at Aix before he entered the Paris Conservatoire.[89] Without a single hot item, Saint-Etienne was eventually forced to close up shop.[90]

Enfantin was still proud of David and spoke warmly of him in an open letter to Lamartine after the 1848 Revolution.[91] But in general Le Père and his friends were less in evidence in David's life during the late 1840s and early 1850s than earlier or, indeed, later. The Saint-Simonians had helped David mount his first success in 1844; it was Saint-Etienne who was by his side—although not always helping—when he achieved his second, the aforementioned opéra-comique *La Perle du Brésil* (1851). And the work, not surprisingly, is almost devoid of Saint-Simonian echoes. (Or, to put it another way, the Saint-Simonian echoes are no stronger than in many operas of the day by composers unaffiliated with the movement.[92])

David's career had long been heading toward the stage; the critics had predicted it,[93] and he had wanted it himself since his student days. After one abortive effort (incidental music for *Le Jugement dernier*), he succeeded in getting *La Perle du Brésil* accepted for the first season of the Opéra national (Seveste's company, soon renamed the Théâtre lyrique). The librettist, the successful playwright Joseph Gabriel, was apparently first introduced to David by Saint-Etienne,[94] and Saint-Etienne's name actually appears as colibrettist. (David and Gabriel tried to prevent this, since Sylvain had contributed so little to the work,[95] but the insistent friend won out.)

The opera was a great success in spite of an inadequate cast. (It was performed sixty-eight times during its first three years and another seventy-six times in 1858–64.[96]) David must have felt encouraged in his aspirations. He decided to attempt a grand opera now, based on the substantial and unperformed *Jugement dernier* music. The negotiations dragged on, and librettists came and went. David, finding himself in financial trouble, finally turned to Enfantin and Arlès-Dufour, who between them lent him a total of 20,000 francs during the years 1854–59. (Enfantin calculated at one point that, counting from 1835, David had received between 100,000 and 120,000 francs from his friends.[97]) In addition, they opened a subscription in 1857 to free David from "worrying about his daily bread and to permit him to devote himself in full freedom of mind and heart to the work of his calling."[98] The subscribers included, aside from Enfantin and Arlès-Dufour (at an additional 10,000 francs each), Jenny Montgolfier, Lemonnier, Bröet, Holstein, A(uguste?) Chevalier, Duveyrier, and various intimates of Enfantin and Arlès. The total sum fell far short of the 60,000 franc goal: 32,400, or only 12,400 if one discounts the contributions of the two organizers.[99]

David reworked and reworked his opera. The title of the work went through a number of changes, and even the story was altered so drastically that it finally left no place for the Last Judgment music. Through all this time, David had little income and depended on the loans from his friends. Fortunately, David's money was managed by the capable Arlès-Dufour, now not only a silk merchant but a major financier. David had ways of thanking his friends. His piano trios were performed at Boisselot's home with Enfantin in attendance, and David dedicated the D-minor Trio to Arlès-Dufour (who had, in addition to his other favors, arranged several performances of the trios in Lyons).[100] By 1858 Enfantin and his circle had completely readopted David as their musical protégé ("spokesman" would now be too strong a word). When *La Perle* was revived that year at the Théâtre lyrique, they attended proudly and loudly, to the consternation of Berlioz. "All the former Saint-Simonians were there," he reported to his sister. "They made a grotesque success for him."[101]

No doubt they were particularly willing to help David now, because they realized what an honor and opportunity it would soon be for him when his grand opera, now titled *Herculanum,* was mounted at the Paris Opéra, possibly the world's most prestigious theater. The honor, of course, was also theirs (though the work itself had few identifiable Saint-Simonian traits), and perhaps the opportunity as well. There are strong indications that Térence Hadot, the "colibrettist" (with Méry) of the *Herculanum* libretto, had contributed little to the text and had in fact been introduced into the project only weeks before the first performance so that he could draw a share of the profits that should rightly have gone to the authors of the original *Jugement dernier* drama, Gabriel and Mirecourt.[102] Hadot was a civil servant at Chateaudun (Eure et Loire), a close friend of Enfantin and David who had contributed or raised money to support Le Père after his return to France in 1836,[103] who had borrowed money at one time or another from both of them, and who had often opened his house to David when the composer wanted to get into the country to relax and do some gardening; David would later name him executor of his will.[104]

When *Herculanum* was finally about to open, David had his chance to show his gratitude to Enfantin and the rest for all their attention and support. The members of the circle were all naturally expecting to receive tickets for the premiere of the opera whose completion they had so generously underwritten. David, ever unworldly, did nothing whatever for them. Enfantin and Jenny Montgolfier were hurt that David did not reserve them boxes, and Aglaé Mathieu (née Saint-Hilaire) could not even purchase a ticket at the box office, since the performance was sold out.[105]

Enfantin tried to persuade his friends to forgive David's erratic behavior, arguing that he was a "sick person," but Arlès-Dufour was furious and insisted now that David totally repay him his money.[106] Arlès made clear to the childlike David that he was legally and morally bound to return the loans to the other subscribers as well, especially since the work was becoming a financial success. (The composer had received 10,000 francs from the publisher for his share in the score, quite aside from performance royalites.[107]) Arlès-Dufour drafted the form letter of reimbursement that went out to the subscribers over David's signature, and the banker could not help sighing to Enfantin that he was glad to be getting rid of the "financial tutelage of David."[108]

Arlès-Dufour was furious on one other point. The two richest Saint-Simonians were without doubt the Pereire brothers, by now major competitors of the Rothschilds in the financing of railroads and industry. And yet, complained Arlès-Dufour, the Pereires refused to contribute (at all or in sufficient amounts) to the David subscription or to Enfantin's scheme for a Saint-Simonian archive. "From the moment that the two Pereires did not understand that they ought to, between them, do three of four times more than us, the plan[s] should have been aborted."[109] But the Pereires had in fact done something more, giving David an annual pension of 1,200 francs,[110] and perhaps for this reason David dedicated the score of *Herculanum* to them rather than to Enfantin or Arlès-Dufour. (Isaac Pereire must have been moved by the dedication, for he purchased the original manuscript from David's heir after the composer's death.[111]) David's friendship with the Pereires is reflected in Azevedo's biography of 1863, which makes prominent mention of the Pereires' devotion to the composer but does not say a word about Enfantin or Arlès-Dufour. Isaac Pereire also received the dedication of David's last opera, *Le Saphir,* and in 1873 David published *Henriette,* "Valse composé pour sa jeune amie Henriette Pereire."[112]

Although David never dedicated a single work to Enfantin (if one excepts the Ménilmontant choruses in his honor), the personal bond was surely deep, to the point that David remained one of the few Saint-Simonians to follow the example of Le Père and never marry.[113] Visitors to his home and flower garden often heard him assert that "his entire happiness is in work and in a few select friendships, and that, outside of his art, he has remained the same as before: full of faith in Saint-Simon and in the divine mission of Enfantin."[114] Even in David's last days, as we shall see, it was the spirit of Enfantin, by then twelve years dead, that haunted the failing musician.

In the meantime he continued his musical career. *Lalla-Roukh* (1862) was a great success—100 performances in the first year—but *La Captive* had to be withdrawn in rehearsal in 1864. *Le Saphir* was a relative failure the next year, and David never again wrote for the stage. Enfantin's death in 1864 may have been too much for him, but he also complained about the singers of the day—their "bleating and lack of rhythm."[115] His social ideas, barely discernible in these operas, showed up in his active patronage of the Galin-Pâris-Chevé singing method. Based on tonic sol-fa principles, the Galinist system had raised the hackles of many French musicians trained in the tradition of fixed-do *solfège*.[116] But David, perhaps more aware of the musical needs and limitations of the untutored multitude, decided to support this practical effort at "spreading the art and science of music among the popular masses."[117] His attempt in 1864 to organize a regular symphony orchestra and concert hall, echoing Berlioz's effort at a Grande Société philharmonique (1850), may also have had a social component.[118] David seems to have given up most of these activities in the late 1860s, although he continued to conduct concerts, mainly of his own works, and he made an exhausting and unprofitable journey to Saint Petersburg to hear *Herculanum* at the Court Opera.[119]

David's social ideals remained firm to the end. In 1870, just after the proclamation of the Republic on 4 September, David could hardly contain his joy at this new step toward "universal brotherhood." In March 1871, when the workers established a people's government—the Commune—and Paris became the scene once again of a bloody clash of arms, David recoiled in horror, reacting just as the Saint-Simonians had reacted in 1830 and 1848:

> There is one thing that I am certain about: France is pregnant with new destinies for the entire world. She will again undertake the painful experiment of this [social] reorganization, as in 1789. After the enfranchisement of the third estate and the rise of the bourgeoisie must infallibly come the emancipation of the proletariat. That is the law of progress. But it is deplorable that this should proceed by violent means. Brute force cannot found anything lasting. It brings on a fatal reaction. That is why I do not believe in an immediate realization, this time either, of the reforms that are to be accomplished in society. The ideas of *association* and solidarity will have to filter bit by bit into [people's] ideas. . . . We must resign ourselves and try to console ourselves by casting our eyes toward the future. My own consolation and glory will be to have laid the peaceful paths for it by being part of the Saint-Simonian school.[120]

David, who had always been physically frail, spent his declining years mainly at spas and in the country house of Mme Tastet, widow of his friend Tyrtée Tastet, several of whose poems he had set to music. (He must have been very close to Tastet for he once approached Isaac Pereire on his friend's behalf, although normally he hesitated to make such request of the Pereires.[121]) Louis Jourdan reports that David kept, to the end of his days, a large portrait of Enfantin above the piano in his "little house [in Paris] in the rue la Rochefoucauld." One day his old maid Marie Martin came out to Saint-Germain-en-Laye to bring him his mail and reported a bizarre incident: an owl had flown into the living room at night and perched on the frame of the portrait, staring with enormous eyes and spreading its wings. David, hearing this story, paused before speaking. "It is the announcement of my death. It is Enfantin calling me." The next day his condition worsened alarmingly, and he died on 29 August 1876, two days before the twelfth anniversary of Enfantin's own death.[122]

The newspapers hastened to publish glowing eulogies of the little man, stressing his honors and titles: Membre de l'Institut, Officier de la Légion d'honneur, and so forth. David himself, in his last will and testament, had emphasized instead his quiet but firm devotion to the Saint-Simonism of his youth: "I die in the Saint-Simonian faith which has been my life since the age of 22 by making me truly religious and to which I owe everything good that I have been able to do or produce. Consequently I desire that there be at my burial no use of Catholic ritual."[123] One last ironic twist to the story of David's involvement with the Saint-Simonians is that this desire of his for a funeral without priests led to the resignation of Prime Minister Jules Dufaure. Tensions within the government were running high in the years 1875-77 (and eventually led to a crisis over the balance of power between President MacMahon and the Chamber of Deputies). David, as a member of the Legion of Honor, was entitled to a military honor guard at his funeral, but when the officer in command learned that the ceremony was to be a civil one, he instructed the soldiers to turn back before they reached the grave. The Chamber of Peers later reprimanded the minister of war for this lack of respect to a member of the Legion, and the prime minister resigned in solidarity with his minister. The monarchist and republican newspapers went at each other's throats over the affair, and David's own modest dream of a better world for mankind was left behind in a storm of partisan debate.[124]

ROGÉ IN SAINT PETERSBURG AND PARIS; FRIENDSHIP WITH BERLIOZ

Whereas David remained close to Enfantin personally, Rogé slowly withdrew. The disappointment that he had felt at Ménilmontant and later in Paris intensified when he joined Enfantin at the site of the proposed Nile Dam in December 1834. Years later Clorinde reminded Enfantin that on that occasion he had hurt Rogé both "by your manner and by your words."[125] Rogé had already been feeling that he was not appreciated in the movement; now he knew that even Le Père held him in disdain. This confrontation in Egypt must have given the decisive impulse to the bitter anti-Enfantinism that later found expression in the musician's letters and memoirs.

Rogé, Clorinde, P. Granal, and Massol left Cairo by river, taking with them the portable piano that David had left behind. When they arrived in Alexandria (9 May 1836), Auguste Colin informed them that their friend Ollivier had just died. They washed the corpse and arranged a simple funeral. At the end of the month, the four boarded ship for Smyrna but were forced ashore at Beirut. They eventually reached Turkey without Granal (who had left them at Cyprus for Marseilles) but accompanied by a former sympathizer, Charles Emmanuel. After some adventures in Constantinople, the travelers parted ways. The Rogés headed north and finally reached Saint Petersburg in very cold weather ($-34°$C/ $-30°$F), without the piano, which they had lent to the Dutch consul to Odessa for the musical training of his child.[126] Two or three winters later the piano caught up with them. By then it had little strength left except in its lower register, no surprise considering the shock it had once received when dropped sidelong by an Egyptian baggage-carrier, not to speak of the changes of climate it had undergone.[127]

Rogé, meanwhile, had secured a position as cellist (possibly first-chair)[128] in the Imperial Opera at Saint Petersburg. (He also tried for a year to make the round of the salons but was paid poorly in rubles and generously in rudeness.[129]) Being in the orchestra gave him the pleasurable opportunity of renewing in 1847 his friendship with a visiting guest conductor, his (as he recalled in his memoirs) "old friend" Hector Berlioz: "that friend of our fair youth . . . a composer born with a horror of the vulgar, the trivial [*faridondaine*], and the commonplace in all matters."[130] Berlioz, too, valued the encounter and spoke flatteringly of Rogé in his own memoirs. "[In the orchestra] I had rediscovered a fellow countryman, the fine cellist Tajan-Rogé, a true and warm-hearted artist who assisted me with all his soul."[131] During these months together they became trusting, jesting friends, as several unusually frank letters from the following year attest.[132]

One exchange is of particular interest, for it indicates how strongly Rogé still held to his belief in the rights of women and the dignity of the working class. In Saint Petersburg Berlioz fell in love with a youngish singer from the Opera chorus who had been forced by poverty to sew corsets at her sister's shop. Berlioz not only had a wife and child back in Paris but was traveling with his mistress, Marie Recio (a singer herself). Nonetheless, he managed to spend secret and, as he put it, "innocent" hours with the Russian singer, and they parted with promises to write. When Berlioz did not receive the expected letter from her in Berlin, he recruited Rogé to forward a letter to her—with all possible discretion—and send back her reply. Rogé did as he was asked, but reproached Berlioz for being embarrassed about the affair and, in particular, for writing in this tone of shame to Rogé of all people, to whom a *dame des choeurs* was no less worthy than "any countess from the Faubourg Saint-Germain" (an allusion to Liszt's mistress, Marie d'Agoult). "Can you still be so unfamiliar with my ideas and those of my fellows [*celles des nôtres*] that you could write me, *me,* such a letter? . . . That is a bit much, after more than fifteen years of propaganda."

Rogé took the opportunity to remind Berlioz of his continuing devotion to Saint-Simonian ideals. "I had beside me an adviser [David's piano] to encourage my conduct, a guide that you do not know, that you have not wished to know despite all the noise that it has made throughout the world." And in one pointed sentence he identified the essential difference between his talented friend and himself—the composer's egocentric existence and lack of social concern: "But what good is all this to you who, aside from music and love, seem to be indifferent to everything?"

To this letter Berlioz wrote a humble, even apologetic reply, thanking Rogé for his "kindness" and his "indulgence for the afflictions of others." "Excuse the silly jokes in my first letter. I am so constantly surrounded by people with vulgar and narrow opinions, that it never occurs to me that there are also a few, rare upright and free spirits such as yours." Soon Berlioz would prove by his actions the respect and admiration for Rogé that he expressed in these unusual lines.

In the exchange of letters just quoted Rogé seems to be suggesting that Berlioz had long known of Rogé's Saint-Simonian ideas and that through the years Berlioz had remained as impervious to them as Rogé had remained faithful. The first point is of interest, since it suggests that Rogé may have attempted to convert Berlioz many years before. The second point is not quite accurate, for, as we know, Berlioz—although never deeply involved—had in fact not been able to resist the lure of the doctrine in late 1830 and 1831. Perhaps Enfantin and Duveyrier never bothered to tell Rogé of the letter that Berlioz had written from Italy in July 1831.

Rogé's remarks to Berlioz about his own uninterrupted Saint-Simonian involvement are also somewhat misleading. Though his ideas on women and the workers did remain relatively fixed, he had traveled a good distance from Enfantin in more than the geographical sense. From the time he left Egypt, he did not correspond with the leader until 1844 when Enfantin himself took pen in hand to invite the cellist to David's forthcoming concert featuring the premiere of *Le Désert*. Rogé responded in a long, fascinating letter that shows clearly how antagonistic he had become, in only eight years, to Le Père, to the hierarchic and messianic aspects of the movement, and to the growing tendency of certain of the leaders—among them Duveyrier—to rejoin the hectic chase after worldly success and riches.

Rogé's basic message to Enfantin in the letter was that he had no desire "to shake your hand" at David's concert:

> Well, well! A concert given by David, with all his old baggage, at the Ecole Royale de Musique [the Conservatoire]. . . . The bourgeois will no doubt applaud these graceful, naïve, and touching melodies. If some word or other [of the text] begins to put a mocking smile on his lips or to irritate slightly his peace of mind, the music (I mean David's) will calm him quite soon and he will think he heard wrong. Besides, what does he care about a thing that dates back twelve years? Twelve years! "Tout est mort [Everything is dead]," he will say with the chorus, and he will be amused, because above all he wants to be amused. . . . What a pitiful thing this concert and show will be. The public, curious and skeptical, would irritate me. The voices, all men's, would make me sadder than would an opera in which none of the violins had an E string [the highest string].

By 1844 it was Rogé's bitter pleasure to be preaching the equality of the sexes to Enfantin himself.

Openly flaunting his disenchantment with the former leader, Rogé closed with a sarcastic request for an invitation to the banquet table. "If you happen to find a way for me to make lots of money, please let me know immediately."[133] He was in fact deeply concerned about his finances and would have welcomed any offer, even from Enfantin, that allowed him to leave Saint Petersburg.[134]

He finally returned to France after the 1848 Revolution, as disappointed as Vinçard that the Saint-Simonian leaders had not made a gesture in support of the Second Republic.[135] From that time on, through coups-d'état and wars, his life story can be briefly told as a series of projects: skirmishes (often ill-fated) in the long fight for good music or for social reform.

In late 1849 Rogé attended meetings of socialist schoolmasters (*instituteurs*) at the home of Pauline Roland and became friendly with the revolutionary socialist Gustave Lefrançais. (Perhaps he was partly responsible for Roland's and Lefrançais's decision to require, as part of their pathbreaking curricular proposals for the nation's schools, music study at all age levels.[136]) He also began to involve himself in musical life again. In the Bibliothèque de l'Arsenal there is a copy of a program for the Fête commémorative (11 July 1850) of the Société internationale des artistes and Union fraternelle des artistes français et étrangers. The festival consisted of an art exhibition and a concert conducted by Panseron, voice professor of the Conservatoire and "president of the musical section of the Society." Tajan-Rogé was one of two vice-presidents; the "founder and manager" was David's old hot-headed friend Pol (now Paul) Justus.[137]

In 1850 Rogé joined Berlioz and Léon Kreutzer in another attempt at organizing an orchestra, the Grande Société philharmonique de Paris. Characteristically, Rogé undertook the preparation of the statutes of the Society. (He based the statues on those prepared, in large part by himself, for Habeneck's Conservatoire Concerts of the late 1820s. No doubt at Berlioz's request, the new document tempers a bit the strikingly democratic provisions of the earlier one, stressing instead the need for regular attendance at rehearsals and concerts.[138]) From the beginning the Society was rife with dissension, fostered mainly by the Society's chorusmaster, Dietsch, who felt strongly that the concerts should include fewer works by Berlioz and more by Dietsch. Tajan-Rogé took Berlioz's side at the meetings of the administrative committee and was rewarded with successive promotions to deputy secretary, member of the committee, and finally vice-president. In this last capacity he replaced Berlioz during the composer's brief trip to London in 1851.[139]

The Société philharmonique ceased operating in late 1851, and Rogé seems to have joined Berlioz in a four-month concert trip to London in mid-1852.[140] Back in France at the end of the year, he collaborated on another project that barely lasted a year, the music journal *L'Avenir musical.* There is some evidence that he was one of the main contributors to the journal. The first issue, notably, contains a front-page editorial on the glorious progress of modern music, one of Rogé's favorite notions, and gives as an example of great promise in the art David's *Le Désert.* (Rogé's attitude toward David had become more favorable since his return to France.[141]) On the second page much is made of Henri Reber, the composer whom Rogé had "discovered" for the Saint-Simonians in 1834.[142]

After this, Rogé disappears for a few years, but we know that by early 1855 he was one of the several French musicians making a living (of sorts) in the orchestra pit of the New Orleans opera house. (Berlioz wrote to thank him for sending a six-column *feuilleton* from the New World. The letter also indicates that Clorinde and their daughter had remained in Paris and that Rogé had brought with him a number of little bottles for certain "business projects."[143]) In May 1856, after touring the East Coast as cellist with a roving opera company, Rogé was in New York and gave two public talks on the arts in America. These fascinating documents were printed the next year, first as articles and then, with a dedication to Berlioz, as a small book (favorably reviewed by the dedicatee in the *Journal des débats*).[144] Rogé, back in France, wrote glowingly of a plan—in which Félicien David was involved—for a new music school, L'Ecole Beethoven.[145]

Around this same time Clorinde died,[146] but Rogé continued with his various projects. In 1862 he organized a subscription for the publication of *Les Ouvriers de Paris* by Vinçard's nephew Pierre. The prospectus, quite possibly by Rogé, praises the author's concern for "the lot of the most numerous, most useful, and most unfortunate classes."[147] In the same year he published a brochure attacking Fétis for certain anti-Saint-Simonian statements in the "David" article of the new *Biographie universelle* and for his oft-stated belief that music evolves historically but does not by any means progress.[148]

In 1864 Rogé formed the Première Union de crédit mutuel, another in the series of mutual-aid societies spawned by the Saint-Simonian experience.[149] His lawyers in this effort were the Saint-Simonian Charles Lemonnier and Rogé's own son-in-law Henri Brisson—a prominent journalist who became one of the leading political figures of the Third Republic (he served as president of the Chamber of Deputies beginning in 1881). Rogé's association with Brisson, and also with Antonin Dubost, another leading spokesman for the republican opposition during the Second Empire (and future president of the Senate in the Third Republic), gives further evidence of a commitment to the welfare of the working classes.[150]

Again there is a gap of a few years; it may be that Rogé was hard at work on his last testament: the memoirs of his life as a Saint-Simonian. In 1872, Rogé was invited to the Conservatoire—his old school—to give a speech (later published) in memory of the great violinist Baillot.[151] Finally in 1876 he published the *Mémoires d'un piano,* prefacing it with several Saint-Simonian slogans and boldly dedicating it to the workers and women of the world and to "la Jeunesse militante de 1876."[152] With this last phrase Rogé introduced a new element, appropriate to a more violent and less innocent age than the early years of the July Monarchy. Rogé had lived through the bloody months of the Paris Commune and realized—whether or not he was ever truly resigned to it is unclear from his letters—that the pacifism of his youth had little place in the "day of the revolver."[153] He died two years later—perhaps a *jeune militant* of seventy-five years, but still one of the last and most devoted of the Compagnons de la femme.

The Saint-Simonian piano, we are informed, had been in the possession of a friend of Rogé's outside of Paris when the Prussian army invaded in 1871. It was gone when the troops withdrew.[154]

14

THE CHALLENGE OF
THE SAINT–SIMONIAN
MUSICAL EFFORT

"None of those who passed through Saint-Simonism, or who brushed up against it, went away unchanged."[1] When the essayist Sainte-Beuve wrote these words in 1852, he was referring mainly to the large number of prominent literary and political figures who carried Saint-Simonian ideas into their own life's work: men and women such as Chevalier, Carnot, Pierre Leroux, and Guéroult (all four of whom had been members), Sainte-Beuve himself, Vigny, Balzac, Pauline Roland, Louis Blanc, Heine, and even the Englishmen Carlyle and Mill (both of whom had corresponded at length with leaders of the movement).

Sainte-Beuve's words can be applied with equal justice to the musicians. Those who "passed through" the heart of the movement—Vinçard, David, and Tajan-Rogé—were marked by the experience for the rest of their days. No matter where the winds of fate blew them, the ideas and values that they had absorbed continued to find expression in their musical careers, in their social and political involvements, and even in their affective relationships.[2]

As for the seven musicians who merely "brushed up against" the Saint-Simonians, they too were affected by what they saw and heard. Liszt and Mendelssohn seem to have responded the most intensely, but the others as well—Berlioz, Hiller, Nourrit, Reber, and even the cautious Fromental Halévy—were fascinated beyond simple curiosity. Reber confessed as much by composing a piece in celebration of the Saint-Simonian mission to the East. And most of the seven continued later in life to esteem the movement, its leaders, and certain aspects of its teachings.

The impact on these two groups of musicians has been demonstrated at some length in the preceding chapters. But to focus exclusively on what Saint-Simonism meant to the individuals (whether musicians or not) who had been in the movement or on its fringes is to miss a crucial point. For, as historians have long recognized, Saint-Simonian ideas and concerns, in part transmitted by these same individuals, exerted a remarkable influence on the lives of large numbers of people who had never even heard of Saint-Simon or his apostles.

Long after the members of the movement had gone their separate ways, and long after the last of them had died, their ideas lived on—though in various, often conflicting interpretations—in the work of influential philosophers, economists, leaders of government, industry, and various political movements, and, not least, aestheticians and creative artists, including musicians. Whereas Saint-Simon had been ignored during his lifetime and his disciples had been hounded and ridiculed, Saint-Simonian doctrines now took root.

It may be helpful to reduce the varieties of Saint-Simonian influence on the modern world to two large categories. Certain aspects of Saint-Simonian thought are very much with us, for they have taken concrete form in present-day institutions and practices. In contrast, certain other aspects have inspired and continue to inspire protests against the status quo. These two great streams of Saint-Simonian influence—one might tag them the stream of "accomplishment" and the stream of "challenge"—derive to some extent from a split between the two main groups of Saint-Simonians: what Walch calls the "right wing," including Chevalier and the Pereires, and the "opposition," including Leroux, Carnot, Reynaud, and Charton.[3] And these two streams can be seen not only in the area of social thought generally but also, as we shall discuss a bit later, in specific regard to music.

Of all the basic Saint-Simonian doctrines, perhaps the most immediately influential was the idea that national health rests on productivity, especially industrial productivity. Within decades of the movement's collapse, France saw the rise of new banks geared—as England's and Belgium's had been for some time—to providing the capital necessary for building the two basic tools of a modern industrial economy: factories and railroads. The prestige that Napoleon III willingly granted to the heads of industry and to such symbolic events as the Exposition of 1855 contrasts strikingly with the insulting attitudes shown at times toward the entrepreneurial class by the Bourbons and Louis-Philippe. Even more essential was the progressive widening of the franchise to include more men of "made" wealth and, as a result, proportionally fewer of the noble landowners whom Saint-Simon had castigated as comfort-loving parasites.

These are developments on a very large scale. How much can we attribute them to the "influence" of the Saint-Simonians? A good deal, in some cases. Arlès-Dufour and the Pereire brothers were among the major builders of the nation's banks, factories, and railroads; Chevalier and the Pereires were plainly instrumental in bringing about the Anglo-French Commercial Treaty of 1860; and it is generally agreed that Enfantin kept alive for decades the idea of the Suez Canal, until it was taken out of his hands rather ungraciously by de Lesseps and his international sponsors in the 1860s.[4] Less easily documented are the wider and perhaps more significant influences that historian Theodore Zeldin has in mind when he concludes that certain doctrines "ceased to bear the specific imprint of Saint-Simonianism because everybody came to believe in them."[5] Many of the daring goals that the Saint-Simonians had proclaimed around 1830 were in subsequent decades adopted, not by "everybody," to be sure, but certainly by mainstream politicians and social thinkers in France and elsewhere. As Sainte-Beuve noted at the time, the so-called utopians "have changed . . . [and] become practical," but "the public [has changed] perhaps more."[6]

The net result of this absorption of Saint-Simonian thought is that we today are, to some extent, living in a world governed by the disciples' sacred principle of association (cooperation). Many of the features of modern life that we take for granted, such as health-care and unemployment benefits, compulsory labor-management contract negotiations, and international arms-reduction talks, are the very kinds of things the Saint-Simonians were hoping to implant in this antagonism-ridden world and for which they might justly take a distant bit of credit. As the philosopher Jean Lacroix has argued, "the modernity of Saint-Simon [and the Saint-Simonians] lies not in the fact that we are still discussing the same themes but that we are carrying them into practice. . . . Today, Saint-Simon has, in part, won out."[7]

But there was that other stream of social thought (and action) that derived from Saint-Simon: the stream of challenge, represented by social reformers, labor organizers, and revolutionaries. Angry dissenters and sowers of discord—these may at first glance seem the very antithesis of the apostles of Ménil-montant, with their unshakable belief in patience, nonviolence, and *association*. But these impatient newcomers (including Louis Blanc and Karl Marx) simply read their Saint-Simon from a different perspective, focusing on the parable of 1819, with its coolly witty contrast between the do-nothing aristocrats and those who produce goods. Marx and Engels, for example, admired the *Globe*'s "critiques of existing conditions, especially economic," and the movement's proposed "practical social reforms" (such as the abolition of inherited wealth).[8] Engels even wrote that Saint-Simon was "among the greatest minds of all time"[9] and insisted that in Saint-Simon's writings "one can find the seed of nearly all the ideas—other than purely economic ones—of later socialists."[10] In a classic instance of Hegelian *Aufhebung*, Marx and Engels, by rendering socialism "scientific," destroyed the "utopian" socialism of the Saint-Simonians and at the same time preserved it; they gave it new life by transforming it beyond recognition.

Perhaps as a result, present-day historians within the Marxist tradition tend to view the Saint-Simonians as heralds, not of our own age (Lacroix's view, and Zeldin's), but of a better future toward which mankind—and more precisely the working class—is yet struggling. The noted historian Maurice Agulhon, for example, contends that the greatness of the Saint-Simonians derived from two things: their preaching of the "socialist aim" to members of the working class, and their willingness to pose a number of vexing but essential questions, such as "the forms that the new ethics should take, the problem of women, the problem of the organization of the world in peace time, . . . [and the question of] whether one must always move through a complete seizure of state power in order to install justice." "The Saint-Simonians," Agulhon stresses, "did not always give answers that we would judge to be the best," but at least they were the first to confront and explore publicly some of the most important issues "which we today still rack our brains about."[11]

If views of the Saint-Simonians' contribution vary so widely, there can be no simple, definitive judgement about the long-range significance of the "artistic" and "musical" parts of that contribution. It may be well to start with some influences that are beyond debate. There can be no doubt, for example, that David, in *Le Désert* and other works directly inspired by the Egyptian mission, created almost single-handedly an eager interest in non-Western music among music lovers and professional musicians of the day.[12] But, however important this development may have been in its own right, in the context of the Saint-Simonians' concerns it was quite marginal.

More central to those concerns was a vision of the artist as priest or prophet. From this vision derived the concept of the politically committed or socially radical artist (or writer) that flourished later in the century and persists even today.[13] In part, this transmission of ideas was effected by the Marxists and social reformers mentioned earlier—the more distant heirs to the Saint-Simonian tradition. But we should not ignore the continuing impact of people who themselves had been part of or been in direct contact with the movement. (Pierre Leroux, for example, after leaving the movement, became an influential spokesman for—and in some cases spiritual father to—such socially conscious writers as George Sand and Victor Hugo.[14])

The same was true for music. The ideal of music as a noble, moralizing, "social" art was kept alive not only by the social movements of the mid-century (as we shall see), but also by musicians who had been active members of the Saint-Simonian movement or at least fascinated observers. The ideal found rich and varied expression in the later work and pronouncements of Nourrit, Halévy, David, Vinçard, and Rogé, but most of all Liszt. His settings of religious and political texts embodied this ideal in relatively pure form, but of more far-ranging impact on later composers was his insistence that instrumental music, too, must have a poetic vision or message if it is to rise above the level of simple entertainment. This morally charged view of art, particularly favored by Liszt's Saint-Simonian guide Barrault, became the basis of Liszt's concept of program music, as manifested in his stirring and inspirational piano cycles (notably the *Années de pèlerinage, Consolations,* and *Harmonies poétiques et religieuses*) and his symphonic poems and dramatic symphonies (such as *Les Préludes,* after Lamartine, or the "Faust" and "Dante" symphonies).[15] And Liszt's programmatic works, as is well known, helped give birth to Wagner's epic-symphonic operas, in which the poetic or social idea is never a surface decoration (as sometimes in Liszt) but the "fertilizing seed" (Wagner's term) from which the whole work grows.[16] In the process the composer became more than just a *Tonsetzer* (a craftsman who combines sounds); he became a true *Tondichter:* a poet who could convey, through music, urgent and heartfelt messages about such matters as the seductiveness of power or the need for cultural regeneration and (on the personal level) for the restoration of psychological and emotional wholeness. This "tone-poet" soon exercised such a weighty social and spiritual mission that he became nothing less than a "poet-priest" (Wagner's own term, from *Religion and Art,* 1880). And this almost sublime figure—the "grandson," we might say, of Barrault's "artist-priest"— exerted in his turn an enormous and diverse influence on Wagner's contemporaries and on modernist and other later movements in music, art, literature, and even politics.[17]

Wagner's (and "Wagnerism's") debt to the Saint-Simonians and other early socialists has long been recognized.[18] Less well known are many other ways in which the Saint-Simonians influenced, or provided a model for, later musical practices. Indeed, it is possible to trace, once again, two broad "streams": the one modest and easily contained; the other turbulent, problematic, yet rich in unharnessed energy. Like Lacroix, we can emphasize the ways in which the Saint-Simonians' ideals have already been realized. For example, taking a clue from David's own later activities, and Tajan-Rogé's, we can point to the vast increase in musical literacy: the Orphéon movement of the 1850s and 1860s, the public-school singing movement in modern Hungary and elsewhere, the rise of civic orchestras, and the wide dissemination of musical culture made possible by the advent of recordings and the broadcast media. The Saint-Simonians would be pleased and proud to learn of the progress that has undoubtedly been made in these areas.

But so would many of their contemporaries, including liberals, such as the composer Halévy, and even other social reformers, such as Owen and Bentham. The difference is that the Saint-Simonians, however pleased at such signs of progress, would not be at all satisfied. Though they were eager (like Saint-Simon before them) to make the arts more accessible to the masses, they rejected views that more or less stopped there, such as Bentham's view that the arts should function as an after-hours distraction for the workers.[19] Instead, they had directed music and its sister arts to enter as active participants into the struggle for social reform. They demanded that music sing forth the ideals (including diligence and patience) toward which society should be striving and that it draw people's attention to what one of them called society's "hideous sore[s]" (such as prostitution and social parasitism).[20] This proposed use of music to foster socially progressive behavior in the masses of listeners was one of the things that antagonized Mendelssohn and Berlioz during their brief contact with the movement, but it appealed strongly to Liszt and Adolphe Nourrit and to the musicians who were members of the movement. When Félicien David spoke of his desire to devote his life to "une oeuvre sociale" and later recalled with gratitude how the Saint-Simonians, and Enfantin in particular, had "given birth to me anew,"[21] he was referring to this musical mission, one that for him transcended the modest efforts of a Wilhem, Mainzer, or (in our own century) Kodály. The choral works and chansons that he composed for the movement, taken together with Reber's piece and the large body of songs by the movement's *chansonniers,* constitute a serious, varied, and extended effort—one of the first in Europe since the collapse of churchly authority—at creating a *musique sociale:* a music that points the way toward the future instead of adapting itself comfortably to the needs of the present, a music that presents its listeners with an inspiration for new activity, not a placid after-dinner diversion.

Since the 1830s, efforts of this sort have become a major feature of musical and social life in Europe and America (and no doubt elsewhere). Most often they have consisted not of new music (the path chosen by David, Reber, and Vinçard) but of new texts matched to simple, familiar tunes (the traditional path of Béranger, also adhered to by Mercier and most of the other Saint-Simonian songwriters). For a century and a half the advantages of this type of chanson (or political "folk song," as it has become known in America) have remained potent: no other propagandistic musical genre is as quickly produced, as easily taught to a crowd, as readily adapted to changing circumstances, and as cheaply distributed. As a result, almost every important political or social movement in Europe or America has produced an eager and often very able spokesperson in song: from Pierre Dupont, Gustave Leroy, various Fourierists, Freiligrath in Germany, and Pottier during the Paris Commune, to the song-writers of the Russian Revolution, Joe Hill of the Wobblies, and the ardent folk singers of the Spanish Civil War, of the American civil rights movement, and (most recently) of the international anti-nuclear and women's liberation movements. Of course, only a few of these songwriters were or are familiar with the songs of the Saint-Simonians. But it can be shown that many (if perhaps not all) of these repertoires belong to a single coherent tradition, each new repertoire having been to some extent inspired by or even modeled on one or more previous ones. For example, many of the folk and protest songs of Pete Seeger, Bob Dylan, and others in the 1960s clearly derive from the labor songs of the Depression, and similar modeling can be demonstrated in the successive early stages of the socialist movement in nineteenth-century France. Movements on the right, too, have borrowed from this democratic and socialist song tradition; the Nazis lifted whole tunes and texts, sometimes changing but a few words.[22] For better or for worse, music has often fulfilled the role envisioned by Barrault and others, spreading social messages beyond the reach of the most impassioned prose.

Music can, of course, carry messages in various directions. If the examples just cited were produced by people who were to varying degrees outside of power (including the Nazis during their early years), there are just as many examples of music being harnessed by ruling elites. And these insiders often had access to the full resources of established musical institutions, as can be seen in the massive celebratory cantatas produced by Berlioz (*Le Temple universel*), Verdi (*Inno delle nazioni*), Parry, and others for international exhibitions and royal jubilees, or the nationalist symphonic poems, operas, and ballets that continue to proliferate in our own day.[23] In the process, music can at times become very much part of the way things are—the stream of "accomplishment"—rather than instigating people to think of other ways things might be. This is not necessarily regrettable. (Certain existing societies, most of us would agree, do have at least a few praiseworthy features!) But it cannot be denied that most societies, whatever their virtues, strongly resist reform; and music can become part of that resistance.

For example, the very sorts of musical organizations that, as mentioned earlier, are widely viewed as progressive, in that they enable people of the middle and lower classes to make and enjoy music, may in a larger societal sense be quite reactionary. One particularly clear case is the growth of amateur choral societies in late-nineteenth-century France and England. Working under the protection of church and government, these societies amounted to what Arthur Jacobs (writing about England) has astutely described as a massive musical movement of "anti-radical and conservative" character, "a manifestation of the idea that ordinary people could be led to moral improvement within the existing society by the ennobling cultivation of the arts."[24] Similarly, some of the most authoritarian nations in our own century—the Soviet Union, Nazi Germany at its height, and the People's Republic of China—have made conscious, systematic use of music to engender positive sentiments (some might say docility) toward the government of "the people."[25] Indeed, in almost all countries, our own not excepted, there has probably been more military, patriotic, and other government-ordained music making in the present century than in any previous one. Many generations after Saint-Simon urged that the trumpets ring out in favor of acts of "civil courage," those instruments persist in blaring forth—to the ears of millions, thanks to the mass media—their age-old message of battlefield glory. As the Saint-Simonians recognized, music's service to society—which they saw as natural, desirable, and indeed unavoidable—can be a force for good but also for ill.

There are other dangers as well. An artist, in his desire to serve, to please, or—as in some recent cases—to save his own skin, may feel tempted (or compelled) to compromise his standards of personal loyalty or public conduct. He may also end up compromising his artistic principles, as Shostakovich quite consciously did (if the memoirs published under his name can be trusted) when, under pressure from the commissars, he gave his Fifth Symphony a finale full of "triumphant," "pro-people" bombast.[26] These are the very kinds of dangers that were sensed by Stendhal, Mendelssohn, and others who resisted the Saint-Simonian *appels aux artistes;* it is sad but true that in the intervening years some of the most unfortunate tendencies in these appeals have been carried into practice—including the nightmare (described by Barrault himself) of art being "entombed . . . under the first stone of [a political] monument."[27]

But, while it is easy to emphasize the dangers, it is perhaps harder, at least for Westerners in the 1980s, to understand or even imagine the possible advantages. Broadening one's style so that it can be understood by larger audiences does not necessarily entail a lowering of standards. We need only think of the many wonderful pieces of music written to be played by amateur performers or to be heard by untutored mass audiences: utilitarian choral works (Berlioz, Liszt, Brahms), pieces for children (Hindemith, Weill, Orff, Britten, Maxwell Davies), even scores for films or the Broadway stage (Prokofiev, Copland, Walton, Bernstein). And it is not hard to find similarly distinguished examples among works written to bear messages of national aspiration or political conviction, from the Hungarian works of Liszt and the Risorgimento-inspired choral scenes in Verdi's operas to the Brecht-Eisler "Kampflieder" and Schoenberg's *Survivor from Warsaw*. All these composers must have experienced what Copland, looking back on his own activities of the Depression and World War II years, calls "the heady wine of suddenly feeling ourselves . . . needed as never before." And all of them tried in these "social" works—as Copland did—to compose "in a way that would satisfy both our collaborators and ourselves."[28]

Of course the dynamic balance between "satisfying ourselves" and "satisfying our collaborators" (a group that might be helpfully understood to include also the intended performers and listeners) is not always as easy to achieve as Copland implies. For example, Henze and other politically left-wing members of today's musical avant-garde find themselves caught between the irreconcilable demands of their ideology and their chosen musical style. Indeed, the difficulties that these composers face have given rise to some very heated debates about whether it is ever really possible for *musique engagée* ("music of commitment"—the currently fashionable term) to fulfill its social function without sacrificing aesthetic integrity.[29] But it is obviously prejudicial to let such a debate hinge on the few most problematic cases, when—as we have seen—there is a whole varied body of socially committed music from the past and present, much of which has been ignored entirely since its own day or at least has not been considered in this kind of context. The music of the Saint-Simonians is one such forgotten repertoire, and—in its best moments, such as David's *Hymne à Saint-Simon* and *Ronde*—it makes many of the objections to *musique engagée* seem hopelessly academic.[30]

To be sure, it would be irresponsible to suggest today, as Léon Halévy and Barrault did, that direct involvement in progressive social struggle is a necessary precondition for greatness in the arts. Just as there are many types of creative personalities (something that the Saint-Simonians, with their passion for generalizing and schematizing, preferred to overlook), so there are many different paths to greatness. Though some composers today might welcome wholeheartedly the chance to "serve" a cause in their music, others might find the whole prospect threatening in the extreme. And with good reason. We know much more than people did in 1830 about the pitfalls and even terrors that in certain situations may await a musician who steps into the public arena.

But if we can no longer be naïve, we should not fall into the opposite error of hopeless cynicism, rejecting as a mirage the idea that art can draw strength from being integrated into the larger human enterprise. True, an artist, by withdrawing into a private world, may avoid certain risks, but he thereby exposes himself to others—in particular, to the risk of becoming irrelevant to all but a handful of the members of his society. And what is perceived as irrelevant may quickly come to seem expendable. Though the phenomenon of the artist's withdrawal was barely out of its infancy in 1830, the Saint-Simonians were quick to notice it and warn of its dangers. As it happens, many musicians today are beginning to regret their isolation and the fact that, as composer-conductor Lukas Foss has put it, "nobody seems to look forward [any more] to the composer's next work."[31] "The composer," Foss concludes— and we might well add: the performer, the scholar—"needs the nourishment of society needing him."[32] Perhaps the Saint-Simonians' message of *association,* and the musical effort which both embodied and propagated that message, may serve us all as a timely reminder of some other ways that music—as also individuals and nations—can live and thrive.

APPENDIX A

SAINT-SIMON, ROUGET DE LISLE, AND THE "PREMIER CHANT DES INDUSTRIELS"

The friendship between Rouget de Lisle and Saint-Simon dated back many years, perhaps to the period of the French Revolution.[1] According to the most authentic surviving account, that of Joannis Guigard, it was the poet-musician who suggested to the social philosopher—presumably around 1820—that music might be able to serve as a "means of action" in the latter's scheme for the renewal of society.[2] By this, Guigard states, Rouget de Lisle meant that music could accomplish three things: stimulate the workers' and artisans' sense of beauty, add variety to their lives, and bolster their spirits. Saint-Simon no doubt responded with enthusiasm; all three of these functions had already found some sort of echo in his own writings on the arts. But how to put these ideas into practice? Probably any pleasant musical experience—even a rather passive one, such as listening to a band concert at twilight—could serve the first two functions cited: bringing variety and beauty into the life of a worker. In contrast, bolstering his spirits—or, as Guigard words it, "encouraging and supporting the artisan during the long hours of his [work] day"—would presumably require a very special musical experience, an active one that would explicitly direct his feelings toward the joy of *association* and his thoughts toward the value of industry and labor. That is precisely the sort of music which had been suggested in Saint-Simon's description of music in the parks (1819), and that is precisely what Rouget de Lisle now produced: a song, to be sung by the workers in chorus (thus developing their feelings of cooperation, however subliminally), to a text that limned the achievements of industry and the *industriels* (thus raising their consciousness in a quite explicit way). The song is indeed called "Premier Chant des industriels"; it is reproduced here in its fullest version—for voice, three-part men's chorus, and piano.

Though it was Rouget de Lisle who took the original initiative in suggesting a practical collaboration between Saint-Simon and himself, the resulting song was evidently written to very detailed specifications from Saint-Simon. The text specifically glorifies the latter's most faithful supporter, the woolens merchant Guillaume-Louis Ternaux, and it was first performed, by Ternaux's workers and others, at the merchant's estate in Saint-Ouen. In 1818 Ternaux had been elected a member of the Chamber of Deputies, defeating the novelist and liberal publicist Benjamin Constant. Ternaux soon became a respected speaker on matters concerning the budget and industry, devoting special effort toward establishing an "industrial" party independent of both the repressive royalists and the "left" (liberal and republican) opposition. Such a plan was of course far milder than the thoroughgoing social transformation Saint-Simon was urging; he could not help but feel that Ternaux was still mired in hopeless liberal preconceptions. Still, he considered Ternaux a major ally. He more or less dedicated to Ternaux his major prose work of 1821, *Du système industriel*. Indeed, that fat treatise is best understood as barely disguised propaganda for Ternaux's "industrial" party.[3] And—to make the connection crystal clear—he published Rouget de Lisle's song (melody and words only) as an appendix to the work.[4]

In that same appendix Saint-Simon added his own remarks about the song, as discussed in Chapter 4 above. Most interesting is the way he dealt with what was the obvious anomaly of the text: the words spoke mainly of the virtues of industry and the industrial class as a whole ("The hundred thousand arms of industry . . . fertilize our plains") but shifted suddenly in the last strophe to specific praise of one individual ("Ternaux, you are the true noble . . . you who created goods and cultivate them in order to spread them around to others"). This startling invocation had not gone unnoticed. As Saint-Simon frankly admitted, "some members of industry [e.g., other prominent businessmen?] seem to have been pained to see the name of the Ternaux honored [*consacré*] in the song." Saint-Simon countered with a little historical background: the homage was directed not at Ternaux the man but at Ternaux's refusal to accept the title of baron—a "courageous and philosophical action by which he drew attention to the birth of the industrial order of things."

The incident to which Saint-Simon was alluding was indeed a striking one. In 1821 the government, in one of its increasingly numerous reactionary gestures, granted a certain worried nobleman assurance that his father's and grandfather's involvement in commerce would in no way be allowed to diminish his aristocratic status and prerogatives. Ternaux objected eloquently that the ministers, by even accepting the aristocrat's concern as valid, had shown unmistakable disdain for the productive classes, and he announced that he consequently could not accept the title of baron (recently offered him by the king, in the wake of the Exposition industrielle of 1819).[5]

This may well have been an occasion worth celebrating, but the use of Ternaux's name in the "Premier Chant"—surrounded by a kind of halo—trivialized the song's message and tied the piece too plainly to specific events of 1821. Rouget de Lisle, in his own publication of the song (reprinted here), wisely replaced Ternaux by the *industriels* as a class—"Friends, we are the true nobles!" (Indeed, that version possibly preceded Saint-Simon's "Ternaux" version, though it was not published until four years later. Its title, by the way, omits the perhaps polemical "Premier."[6])

The significance of Rouget de Lisle's song and of its performance by the workers has been stated in various ways. Frank Manuel views the Saint-Ouen performance as a "striking symbolic act in illustration of the natural unity of all industrials as Saint-Simon conceived it, the commonality of workers and entrepreneurial chiefs," and he even points out that all three classes of *producteurs* were "joined in a mass public demonstration [that day] . . . the artist, the industrial and his workers, and the philosopher 'founder of the industrial doctrine' [i.e., the *savant*]."[7] Guigard, writing in the *Almanach des orphéons*, preferred to view the whole episode as a glorious anticipation of the Orphéon, Wilhem's lay-choral-society movement, and he urged all *orphéonistes* to perform Rouget de Lisle's song, "the primordial cause of their institution," on the songwriter's birthday.[8] Some writers, focusing on the song (and its upbeat dotted rhythms) rather than its performance, have viewed the song as a kind of second "Marseillaise" and compared and contrasted the two songs in terms of their content (war vs. peace) or their musical or literary quality (the "Marseillaise" usually wins).[9]

Whatever its other merits, though, the "Premier Chant des industriels" must certainly be regarded as the practial culmination of Saint-Simon's aesthetic writings until that point. It combines the praise of great individuals suggested in the *Lettres* of 1803 with the more daring suggestion of 1819 that the arts—especially music—might engender in people good feelings about themselves and about the important work they do.

Looking forward, the song must also be regarded as the first piece in the Saint-Simonian musical repertory. Henri Fournel recognized this when he listed the song prominently as the first of the "morceaux de musique composés sous l'inspiration du Saint-Simonisme."[10] This reference—the only mention of the song in the writings of Saint-Simon's disciples—suggests that the movement's leaders were at least somewhat familiar with the song, its origin, and the story of its performance by the factory workers. (In fact, they could hardly have been unaware of the song, in its "Ternaux" version, since it had been published in one of the master's major works.)

To say that the piece was the first in the repertory, though, should not imply that it was part of the *active* repertory of the disciples of Saint-Simon. In fact there is no evidence that the piece was performed by the Saint-Simonians, on any occasion, whether for internal or external consumption. Similarly, there is no evidence that the movement's musicians and chansonniers, however well they may have known it, took the "Premier Chant des industriels" as a model for their own songs. This is unfortunate, for Rouget de Lisle's tune—though not a perfect gem—has flow and forward drive, a clear tonal and formal structure that allows it to be learned and sung easily without accompaniment, and an appealing directness in its language, elements lacking in some of Vinçard's songs and David's choruses. Most of all, the idea of using music and words, not to tell the people "who we [the enlightened few] are," but to involve them directly in singing about themselves, could have formed the basis for an insidiously effective musical propaganda effort and counteracted the Saint-Simonians' tendency to praise their own virtue and thereby to reduce themselves to objects of curiosity and derision.

Rouget de Lisle, "Chant des industriels" (1821)

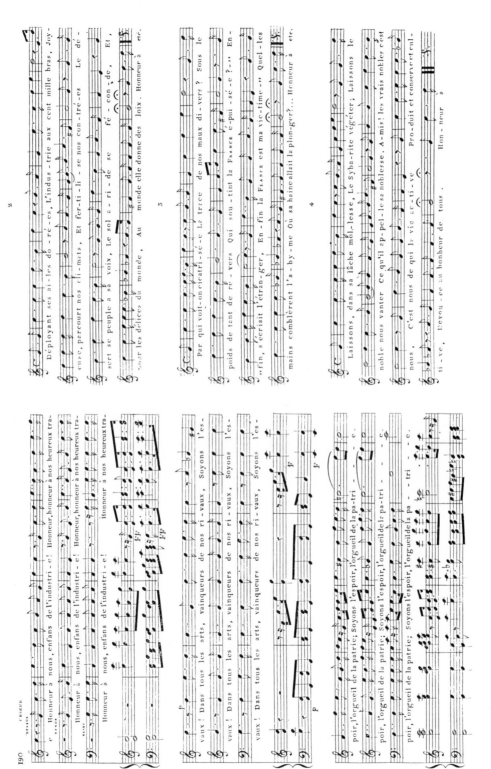

APPENDIX B

SELECTED LISTS OF SAINT–SIMONIAN CHANSONS

1. PROPAGANDISTIC PUBLICATIONS OF LATE 1832 AND 1833
CONTAINING SONG TEXTS
(INCLUDING TUNE INDICATIONS WHEN PRESENT)[1]

Chant[s] Saint-Simonien[s] (Paris)—BNImp 8°Z 8129/16-22; separate copies of no. 7 in
   BHVP 5 (see Appendix B.2), BNImp Ye 51461.
This publication consists of seven songs published together but each on a separate
leaf or (in the case of *Peuple fier*) bifolio. Taken together they form a kind of unbound
songster, but no doubt they were often distributed singly, as the survival of individual
copies of song no. 7 attests. Songs nos. 1, 4, 5, and 6 are headed "Chant Saint-
Simonien"; song 2 is headed "Aux Saint-Simoniens." All bear the printer's mark
"Paris.—Imprimerie de Carpentier-Méricourt, Rue Traînée, no. 15, près S.-Eustache."
Fournel, in the volume of his own collection (volume r) that contains the complete
set of seven, describes them as follows: "[item no.] 16. *Sept Chants,* ou Chansons Saint-
Simoniennes, destinées à être distribuées sur la route par les missionnaires qui partaient
pour Lyon. Décembre 1832. 15 pages."
   1. [Anon.:] Les Saint-Simons. Air: Les Gueux.
   2. [Anon.:] Aux Saint-Simoniens. Nous sommes les vôtres. Air: La Catacoua.
   3. [Anon.:] V'là ce que veul'ent les Saint-Simoniens. Air: Une Vestale.
   4. David [and Bergier]: Appel.
   5. Vinçard: Nouvelle profession de foi d'un libéral. Air: Dans un grenier
      qu'on est bien à vingt ans.
   6. David and Rousseau: Peuple fier! Peuple fort!
   7. David and Rousseau: Je ne veux plus être exploité.

Chants saint-simoniens (Grenoble)—BNImp Ld ¹⁹⁰170.
   Chants saint-simoniens. Grenoble: Imprimerie de J.-L. Barnet, rue St-André N° 4,
   [1833]. In-8°.
      1. [David, Apôtre, Compagnon de la Femme, and] Rousseau, Apôtre: Le
         Peuple. Ses travaux. Patience du peuple.
      2. Bergier, ouvrier, Saint-Simonien: L'Appel au peuple.
      3. Vinçard, ouvrier, Saint-Simonien: L'Avenir est à nous.
      4. Prose declaration by G. Biard, Apôtre, Compagnon de la Femme.

Dialogues saint-simoniens—BNImp 8°Z 8131 (36).

T. [Jean Terson], *Dialogues saint-simoniens . . . Le Prolétaire et le bourgeois*. Bordeaux: Imp. de P. Coudert, 1833. 12 pp., in-8°. The dialogue begins with the full text of Vinçard's "L'Avenir est à nous."

Foi nouvelle (Bordeaux)—BNImp 8°Z 8131 (35).

Bertu and Vidal. *Foi nouvelle: Omnibus saint-simonien*. Bordeaux: Imp. de Ch. Lawalle neveu, 1833. 16 pp., in-8°. The pamphlet ends with the following song texts:
1. Vidal and Bertu: Le Chant du travail. Air de la Marseillaise.
2. Béranger: Les Fous. Air du Magistrat irréprochable.

Foi nouvelle (Nantes)—BNImp 8°Z 8131 (33).

Foi nouvelle. Nantes: Imp. de Victor Mangin, 1833. 8 pp., in-12mo.
1. One-page introduction to the Saint-Simonians.
2. Vinçard: L'Avenir [est à nous].
3. David and Bergier: Appel.
4. [Anon.:] Les Saint-Simons. Air: Les Gueux. ("Les Saint-Simons / Sont de bons lurons.")
5. David and Rousseau: Peuple fier, peuple fort (7 strophes).
6. David and Rousseau: Je ne veux plus être exploité (3 strophes).

Foi nouvelle (Saint-Pons)—BNImp 8°Z 8131 (34).

C.-F. Bertu. *Foi nouvelle: Discours de prise d'habit*. Saint-Pons: Imp. de J. Franc, 1833. 12 pp., in-8°. The pamphlet ends with the following texts:
1. Vidal: L'Avenir [est à nous]. Air du Chant du Midi.
2. Vidal and Bertu: Le Chant du travail. Air de la Marseillaise.
3. [David and] Barrault: Le Compagnonage de la Femme (3 strophes).
4. Béranger: Les Fous. Air du Magistrat irréprochable.

Mercier—BN 8°Z 8131 (37); BNImp Ye 47435; *BHVP* 5 (see Appendix B.2).

Jules Mercier. *Dieu, le peuple et la femme*. [Paris]: Imp. de Carpentier-Méricourt, 1833. 12 pp., in-8°. A poem followed by four songs:
1. Le Chant du poète. Air: Zampa. Lyon, 24 août 1833.
2. Hymne à la gloire. Air: Remplis ton verre vide. Lyon, 7 septembre 1833.
3. La Charte de Dieu. Air: Des trois couleurs. Colonges, près Dijon, 5 juin 1833.
4. Le Règne du peuple. Air: Vive le roi, vive le [sic] France. Joigny, 24 juin 1833.

Chansonnier saint-simonien.
1. Mercier: Le Peuple a faim!
2. Mora [or Morat]: L'Homme nouveau. Air de la Marseillaise.
3. Mercier: La Sainte Canaille. Air: A soixante ans, il ne faut pas remettre.
4. Mercier: Le Père.
5. Vinçard: L'Avenir est à nous.

6. Mercier: A la Femme. Air de la Varsovienne.

7. Les Fous. Extrait des oeuvres de M. de Béranger. Air du Magistrat irréprochable.

Nouveaux Chants saint-simoniens.[2]

1. Vinçard: Ça viendra. Air: Allons, mettons-nous en train.

2. Mercier: L'Arche de Dieu. Air: Gai, gai, marions-nous!

3. Mercier: Les Gens de bien. Air du Carillonneur de Béranger.

4. Jules Mercier: Les Pélerins. Air de Fiorella.

5. Vinçard: Les Compagnons de la Femme. Air: Tendres échos errans dans ce vallon.

6. Jules Mercier: A l'Orient.

7. David and Barrault: Après le repas.

8. David and Rousseau: Le Retour du Père, 6 juin 1832.

2. OTHER COLLECTIONS OF SAINT-SIMONIAN CHANSONS (THREE OR MORE CHANSONS)[3]

Appel—BNImp. Rés. Ye 3484.
 Vinçard, Jules. *Appel.* Paris, Imp. de Herhan, [1836?]. 8 pp., in-32mo.

*Ars 7803/21-36, 55-57, 7804/15. Loose song sheets.

*BHVP 5—Bibliothèque historique de la ville de Paris, shelf no. 18832, *Recueil de pièces sur les saint-simoniennes* [*sic*], vol. 5.

Boissy—BHVP 31685.
 Boissy, [A. L.] *Poésies saint-simoniennes et phalanstériennes.* Paris: A. Patay, 1881. 128 pp., in-24mo.

Chansons de Vinçard—BNImp Ye 56366.
 Vinçard, Jules. *Chansons de Vinçard.* [Paris]: chez l'auteur . . . et . . . chez Pierre Vinçard, n.d. [1850s?]. 36 pp., in-8°.

Chants du travailleur—copy in Library of Congress (Washington, D.C.).
 Vinçard, Jules, ed. *Les Chants du travailleur.* Paris: Librairie des sciences sociales, 1869. 283 pp., in-8°. See the table on pp. 163–64 and Appendix C.

Foi nouvelle (1835)—BNImp Rés Ye 4012; *BHVP 5*.
 Vinçard, Jules, ed.[?] *Foi nouvelle: Chants et chansons, premier cahier.* Paris: Johanneau, 1835. 96 pp., in-32mo. No second *cahier* was published.

*Recueil—BN Ye 7185.
 Recueil de chansons (binder's collection).

Rodrigues—BNImp 8°Z 8082; Ye 32315.
  Rodrigues, Olinde, ed. *Poésies sociales des ouvriers*. Paris: Paulin, 1841. 527 pp., in-8°.

Soirée—BNImp 8°Z 8133 (10); *BHVP 5* (see above); BNImp Ye 52260.
  Soirée du 8 novembre 1835. [Paris]: impr. de A. Everat, n.d. 16 pp., in-8°.

Vinçard (1833)—BNImp Rés Ye 5001.
  Vinçard, Jules. *Foi nouvelle: Chants de Vinçard (1831–1832–1833)*. Paris: Johanneau, n.d. 32 pp., in-32ᵐᵒ.

3. Single Chansons Referring to Special Occasions[4]

Vinçard: L'Apôtre / A Barrault, A Rigaud, A Hoart. In *Vinçard (1833), Foi nouvelle (1835)*, and *Chants du travailleur*.

Vinçard: 1ᵉʳ Départ pour l'orient / A Barrault. In *Vinçard (1833), Foi nouvelle (1835)*, and in a separate in-4° publication (under the title "Aux Compagnons de la Femme," BNImp Ye 5000).

Vinçard: A revoir. / Au Père. In *Vinçard (1833)* and *Foi nouvelle (1835)*.

Vinçard: 2ᵉ Départ pour l'orient. In *Vinçard (1833)* and *Foi nouvelle (1835)*.

P. Maynard: L'Avenir est beau / A Rogé et Massol / . . . / Ces couplets furent chantés par Maynard et Pelletan, à la suite d'un déjeuner qu'ils offrirent à Rogé et Massol lors de leur rentrée à Paris, en automne 1833. In *Foi nouvelle (1835)* and *Chants du travailleur*.

Vinçard: Le Départ / Dédié à Rogé. In *Foi nouvelle (1835)* and *Chants du travailleur*.

Vinçard: Le Retour / Dédié à Delas. In *Foi nouvelle (1835)* and *Chants du travailleur*.

Vinçard: L'Avenir est là, / Chant d'espoir, / Offert à Barrault et à Duguet, / Par Vinçard. / Ile Saint-Denis, Dimanche 5 Juillet 1835, 3ᵐᵉ Anniversaire de / l'Ouverture des Travaux du Temple. In-fol., BNImp Rés. Ye 1149; Ars 7803/33. Also in *Chants du travailleur* (entitled "Courage").

Boissy: Pour l'anniversaire du Père Enfantin [no year given]. In *Boissy*.

Vinçard: Fête du Père / 8, 10 & 14 Février 1836 / Salut à Ménil-Montant, / Offert à Augustine Curie / par Vinçard. In *Chants du travailleur* and (as a separate in-4° publication) in *BHVP 5*.

Boissy: Foi nouvelle / Le Dimanche 24 Avril 1836, Vinçard a quitté Paris pour aller faire, à / Lyon et à Marseille, une Tournée Industrielle et Pastorale. La Famille lui a fait une Conduite d'Honneur, et Boissy lui a offert ce Chant. Ars 7803/21.

Vinçard: Foi nouvelle / 1760–1836 / 17 octobre / Chant d'anniversaire [Saint-Simon's birthday]. In *Appel*.

Vinçard: Le Sonneur de cloche, / A propos de la fondation d'une Société de Secours Mutuels [. . .] 1860. In *Chants du travailleur*.

Vinçard: La Poule aux oeux [sic] d'or. / A mon ami J. Gallé, / A propos de son oeuvre de bienfaisance à Colombes [. . .] 1856. In *Chants du travailleur*.

Vinçard: Souvenir au Père Enfantin [. . .] 1865. In *Chants du travailleur*.

Vinçard: Que sont-ils devenus? / 8 février 1867. / Jour anniversaire de la naissance du Père Enfantin. In *Chants du travailleur*.

4. SETS OF SONGS SUNG AT (AND IN SOME CASES WRITTEN FOR) PARTICULAR "RÉUNIONS"

14 December 1832
   1. Mercier: A la femme. In *Foi nouvelle (1835)* and (as a separate sheet) in *Recueil* and Ars 7803/25.
   2. Mora: Le Rêve de Morat. Single song sheet, in Ars 7803/24.
   3. Vinçard: L'Avenir est à nous. ("Chantée pour la première fois le 14 décembre 1832, à la rue Monsigny," according to Fournel in 1837.) In *Vinçard (1833), Foi nouvelle (1835), Vinçard Chants,* and (as a separate publication) in Ars 7803/28.

8 November 1835 (all texts in *Soirée*)
   1. [Vinçard]:[5] Puissance, aux femmes.
   2. Boissy: L'Oisiveté, à Victor Considérant.
   3. Mercier and Boissy: Le Prolétaire en 1835.
   4. Vinçard: Anniversaire de la naissance du PERE. Noël saint-simonien.

17 August 1836 (all texts in *Appel*)
   1. Vinçard: Appel (à mon ami Julien Gallé). Also in *Foi nouvelle (1835)*.
   2. [Anon.:] Foi nouvelle / 1760–1836 / 17 octobre / Chant d'anniversaire.
   3. Ponty?: A la trinité nouvelle / S-S. E. F. [i.e. Saint-Simon, Enfantin and Fourier].

APPENDIX C
FIVE SONGS
BY VINÇARD

1. Vinçard aîné, "Elan!" (1840), with piano accompaniment by an unidentified musician

LE BRIN D'HERBE.

(Air : de l'auteur des paroles.

Pe - tit brin d'her - be so - li - tai - re
Qui crois au pied de ce vieux mur,
Quel im - pé - né - tra - ble mys - tè - re
T'a fait naître en ce coin obs - cur?
Pour - quoi, tout com - me le grand chê - ne,
Com - me la ro - se au teint ver - meil,
Sur la col - line ou dans la plai - ne,
N'as - tu pas ta place au so - leil ?
N'as - tu pas ta place au so - leil ?

17. Vinçard aîné, "Le Brin d'herbe" (1863)

LE RETOUR.

Air : de l'auteur des paroles.

Place au gro - gnard De pro - lé - tai - -
re, Lui seul sait fai - - re, En vrai flam-
- bard, Res - pec - ter notre é - ten - dard. A -
- mis, ou-vrons nos rangs, Et que du fond de
l'à - me Sé - e - chap - pent dé - li - rants Nos
chants persé - vé-rants. Voi - ci l'affran-chis - seur Du
peuple et de la fem - me, Le fier dé - mo - lis -
- seur De tout joug op - pres - seur.

27. Vinçard aîné, "Le Retour" (1835)

LA RONDE DE SAINT-SIMON.

AIR : de l'auteur des paroles.

34. Vinçard aîné, "La Ronde de Saint-Simon" (1861)

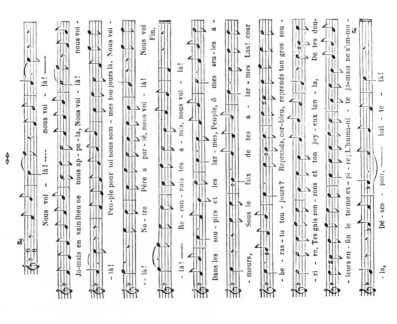

NOUS VOILA!

AIR : de l'auteur des paroles.

29. Vinçard aîné, "Nous voilà" (1836)

APPENDIX D
CATALOG OF SAINT–SIMONIAN WORKS BY FÉLICIEN DAVID AND HENRI REBER

1. Félicien David, *Hymne à Saint-Simon*.[1]

> Composed in Paris, January 1832.
>
> For mixed chorus SATB (sometimes divided SSATTB), "alto" and "Coryphée" solos (both for high tenor?), and piano.
>
> Text by Raymond Bonheur.
>
> The score was published in the *Ménilmontant* series (although the piece was not composed at Ménilmontant); a copy survives in BNMus.[2] The date is given by Fournel.[3]

It is not known for what occasion, if any, the chorus was written. It may conceivably have been performed at rue Monsigny or the Salle Taitbout. There is no record of any performance at Ménilmontant either. Although David could easily have arranged the choral parts for men only, the Ménilmontant singers would no doubt have found the piece impractically long and elaborate.

The author of the words was the painter Raymond Bonheur (? –1849), better known today as the father of Rosa Bonheur (whose landscapes with cattle are a standard fixture of French museums). Raymond Bonheur painted the only portrait of David from this period, the one that shows the musician in Saint-Simonian costume, with the harp of his biblical namesake decorating the front of his tunic (see frontispiece and Chapter 10). David does not seem to have been particularly friendly with Bonheur, and they never collaborated again.

The first word of the text is of course not "Groire" (see Appendix E.1) but "Gloire."

2. Félicien David, *Appel* (and *Les Apôtres au travail*).

> Composed at Ménilmontant, late April or May 1832.
>
> For voice (and men's chorus TTBB in the refrain) and piano.
>
> Text by Bergier, "ouvrier carreleur" (paving-stone worker).
>
> The score was published in the *Ménilmontant* series; copies survive in BNMus, BHVP, Thiers.
>
> Also published (without the piano accompaniment) in a special octavo format (see below); copy survives in BNImp 8°Z 8129/8.

The text alone was published in *6 juin 1832, Chant[s] saint-simonien[s] (Paris), Foi nouvelle (Nantes),* and *Chants saint-simoniens (Grenoble).*[4]

Additional strophes to the same tune (entitled *Les Apôtres au travail*) were published in *Travaux de Temple.*

There is a curious second musical source for this chorus, an inexpensive octavo printing ([Paris?]: n.p., [1832 or 1833?]) of the full vocal parts (solo—or unison—for the verse, and four-part harmony for the refrain) but with no accompaniment. This unusual format suggests that the effort was made to teach the harmony in the refrain to the crowds of visitors at Ménilmontant or to sympathizers in Paris and the provinces.

There is one important textual change between the first printing of the text and all later versions (including the score and the voice-only sheet). Originally the Saint-Simonians were called "apôtres d'un Dieu de liberté pour vous"; this was soon emended to "apôtres d'un Dieu de paix, d'amour pour vous." The movement's desire to replace the divisive political parties with a pacifist religion of brotherly love could not be made clearer than in this self-censorship of the word *liberté,* with its accumulated overtones of republicanism and revolution.

Performances of *Appel* and *Prière du matin* were included in an internationally syndicated series produced by the French Radio (*Masterworks from France*); a tape recording is preserved in the Columbia University Library.

> Text of "Les Apôtres au travail":
>> Quand notre père nous appelle
>> Et nous crie: "Enfants, travaillons!"
>> Prenons la brouette et la pelle,
>> Serrons nos rangs, et commençons!
>> En nos chants que la gaîté brille,
>> Nous travaillons en nous donnant la main.
>> L'humanité sera notre famille,
>> Et l'univers notre jardin!
>>> Gloire à Dieu!
>>
>> Allons, bourgeois et prolétaires,
>> Le travail nous a faits égaux.
>> Ensemble remuant la terre
>> Montrons à tous l'homme nouveau!
>> Notre temple au toit de charmille
>> Doit recevoir un jour le genre humain
>> L'humanité sera notre famille
>> Et l'univers notre jardin!
>>> Gloire à Dieu!

3, 4. Félicien David, *Avant et après le repas,* nos. 1 and 2 (two different settings of—presumably—the same texts).
> Composed at Ménilmontant—setting no. 1 in late April or May 1832, setting no. 2 probably later in 1832.
> Presumably for men's chorus TTBB and (optional) piano.[5]

Text by Emile Barrault.

The scores of both settings were announced in the *Ménilmontant* series. No. 1 was published but no copy survives; no. 2 was never published.

The music of one of the settings (almost certainly no. 1) is preserved—but without piano—as *Epithalame* (text by Charles Chaubet, published as piece no. 2 in *La Ruche harmonieuse*).

The text alone was published in *6 juin 1832* and *Travaux du Temple. Après le repas* was also published in *Nouveaux chants saint-simoniens.*

David's prospectus for the *Ménilmontant* series mentions two separate pieces, each called *Avant et après le repas* and further distinguished as "no. 1" and "no. 2." If we assume that the numbers reflect the order of composition, then no. 1 dates from the beginning of the Ménilmontant Retreat and must have used the text by Barrault that survives in the brochures cited above. The fact that David gave the second set of prayers the same title as the first suggests strongly that it used the same texts. The *Epithalame* fits these words of Barrault easily (with only a few adjustments of rhythm); see Appendix E. Since only the first set was published at the time, it seems likely that *Epithalame* is a retexting of this rather than of the unpublished second set. The original piano part, lacking in *Epithalame,* presumably doubled the voices.

5. Félicien David, *Le Retour du Père* or *Salut.*

Composed at Ménilmontant, late May or early June 1832.

For men's chorus TTBB and optional piano.

Text by (René-)Achille Rousseau (and Charles Duveyrier?).

The score was published in the *Ménilmontant* series; copies survive in BNMus, BHVP, and Thiers.

The text alone was published in *6 juin 1832, Travaux du Temple,* and *Nouveaux chants saint-simoniens.*

The music reappears, with new texts, in two works. The introductory "Salut, Père, salut" becomes the opening of the chorus "La Terre promise" in *Moïse au Sinaï* ("Salut, terre, saint lieu"; reprinted without accompaniment as no. 18 in *La Ruche harmonieuse*). The rest of *Le Retour du Père,* outfitted with a new opening section which also returns as a coda, becomes *Le Chant des moissonneurs* (text by Charles Chaubet, no. 27 in *La Ruche harmonieuse*).

The date of 6 June which Fournel gives is the date of the first performance. Obviously it was written at least slightly in advance; the question is how much. Azevedo says six days,[6] thus dating it back to the postponement of the ceremony on 1 June. Since Enfantin did not leave the Retreat until 3 June, it is possible that David was informed in advance of Enfantin's plan.

The version in the temple account (*Travaux du Temple*), in addition to eliminating certain specifically occasional phrases, contains a last stanza that is greatly expanded over the first version. (The temple account also refers to the piece indirectly as the

Salut, a nickname that seems to have stuck.) The published score has a coda using the longer last stanza, but, perhaps through an oversight, it otherwise preserves the early version of the text (and the original title).

Regarding the authorship of the text, there is a somewhat confusing reference in a letter that Talabot wrote the day before the ceremony: "[La famille] ouvrira le cercle pour le recevoir et chantera dans cette position, salut, Père, salut et gloire à Dieu! Les chanteurs se mettront ensuite en place et feront entendre le chant nouveau de David, Rousseau et Duveyrier."[7] Assuming that "Salut, Père, salut" (*Le Retour du Père*) and the "chant nouveau" are one and the same, Duveyrier's name should probably be added to that of Rousseau as coauthor of the text. It is perhaps typical of the leaders' heavy supervision of their artist-sons that a text which was nominally composed by Rousseau may in fact have been written in part by Père Duveyrier.

6. Félicien David, *Le Nouveau Temple* or *Chant de l'ouverture des travaux du Temple.*
      Composed at Ménilmontant, late June 1832.
      For two men's choruses (one unison [?], one TTBB), presumably
        with piano.
      Text by Emile Barrault.
      The score was published in the *Ménilmontant* series; no copy
        survives.
      The text alone was published in *Travaux du Temple.*
      The music is preserved in David's *Christophe Colomb* (see below).
      A new text was devised for this chorus in 1833 or 1834. See entry
        26 below: *Cantate composée en l'honneur du départ.*

Only the second title appears at the head of the text in the temple account, and no author is mentioned. David and Fournel, in their lists, mention a chorus, *Le Nouveau Temple* (text by Barrault), which is surely the same piece, since Fournel's date (June 1832) coincides and the title is not only appropriate to the ceremony but present in the first lines of text ("Vous commencez le nouveau temple").

The music survives, with orchestral accompaniment, in David's *Christophe Colomb.* (Azevedo first pointed this out, and the original text in fact fits the *Colomb* music, with a few emendations—see below. The restored version of the piece in Appendix E is based on the piano-vocal score.) In *Colomb* the music serves as a dialogue between Columbus and the sailors ("Amis fidèles"). Dramatically, roles are somewhat reversed, for Columbus takes the vocal line that the workers once sang (presumably in unison), and the sailors—although dramatically analogous to the workers—sing (in four-part harmony) the music of the Saint-Simonian family.

It is conceivable that the music for the workers was originally written in four-part harmony also and that David reduced it to a solo for Columbus; it is also conceivable that the family's music was not originally written in harmony. But both possibilities are unlikely. The alternation of unison and four-part chorus was a natural choice for the forces available; the "Ouvriers" were a mixed group of Saint-Simonians from all walks of life who must have had barely enough rehearsal time to master even a single musical line, whereas the "Famille" was largely, and perhaps wholly, made up of members of David's Ménilmontant choir, a regular performing body with plenty of time to be coached for the event and to learn four separate vocal parts.

The text as given in *Travaux* (the only source) is not quite complete. A few words or phrases given once need to be sung twice in the musical setting. (Also, as in piece 3, a few note values have to be adjusted.) More importantly, two phrases of text are missing but, thanks to parallel constructions and the surviving text for piece 26, can be easily inferred: "Nous sommes prêts" (mm. 5-6) and "Ce jour est à nous/vous" in mm. 16-17. Finally, two problems arise from the text sheet's assigning of various lines not only to "Les Ouvriers" and "La Famille" but also to "Les Apôtres" and "Tous." I have taken "Tous" to mean simply that in the relevant measures (mm. 16-18, 32-34) the workers join with the four-part chorus, even though in the *Colomb* version their part (i.e., Columbus's) has rests. (The music they must sing is obvious: a repetition of mm. 14-16.) It is less clear why the text sheet asks for "La Famille" to alternate with the workers in the first half but for "Les Apôtres" (not "La Famille") to sing the second half. I have assumed in the present edition that the two names refer to one and the same body of singers (David's choir), and that the distinction is merely an editorial slip. But the possibility exists that not two but three differently constituted choral groups performed.

7. Félicien David, *Au travail.*

        Composed at Ménilmontant, late June 1832.

        Presumably for voice (or men's chorus) and piano.

        Text by an unknown author.

        The music is lost.

        The text alone was published in *Travaux du Temple.*

The music was never published (or even announced for publication), but David may well have reused it later. As for the forces, the piece is called a "chant" in the temple account; this is probably an imprecise usage (as in the *Chant de l'ouverture*), but it might possibly indicate that the work was a song (one vocal line) rather than a chorus.

Text of "Au travail":
Au travail!
Le soleil
Nous sourit,
Et le peuple
Est avec nous;
Dieu bénit
Nos travaux.

Que l'on sache
En tous lieux
Qu'ici s'élève
Un autel
A la paix
Universelle.

Au travail!
Le soleil
Nous sourit,
Et le peuple
Est avec nous,
Commençons
Le nouveau temple.

Au travail!

8. Félicien David, *La Prise d'habit d'A. Petit.*
> Composed at Ménilmontant, late June 1832.
> Apparently for one or more solo voices, men's chorus, and piano (see Chapter 10).
> Text by B.-P. Enfantin.
> The score was published in the *Ménilmontant* series, but no copy survives.

Fournel apparently possessed a published copy which is now lost. The full published title of the piece is given in his list; David called it simply *Prise d'habit* in the prospectus. Fournel places the work in July, but Petit became an apostle in late June.

9. Félicien David, *Prière du soir.*
> Composed at Ménilmontant, late June or early July 1832.
> For men's chorus TTBB, solo quartet TTBB, and (optional) piano.
> Text by Gustave d'Eichthal.
> The score was published in the *Ménilmontant* series; copies survive in BNMus, BHVP, Thiers.
> The text alone was published in *Mort de Talabot.*
> The music reappears as *Le Départ des marins* (text by Charles Chaubet, no. 4 in *La Ruche harmonieuse*).

Fournel dates the piece in July, and in fact the text first appears in the account of Talabot's funeral (18 July). The piece, however, was certainly in the Saint-Simonian repertory before that date; the first lines suggest that the *Prière du soir* was written as part of the public ceremonies involved with the building of the temple: "Adieu peuple. / Dis à la ville / Qu'ici travaillent / Des hommes qui t'aiment." Although the piece is not mentioned in the account of the temple ceremonies themselves (1 and 8 July), the description (appended to the same account) of the activities on 9 July and subsequent days states that large numbers of people came to hear, among other things, "nos chants du soir." If we are correct in concluding that the piece was performed in these first days of July, then it may have been written in late June or even earlier.

The version of the text in the account of Talabot's funeral is missing the first section (up to the beginning of the passage for solo voices). Presumably it was decided to drop the opening lines (quoted above) as inappropriate to the situation.

The published score neglects to mention the author of the text; the text is attributed to d'Eichthal in Fournel's unpublished bibliography and in a handwritten note on the copy of the published score in the Bibliothèque Thiers (formerly in the possession of Cécile Fournel, later of Gustave d'Eichthal himself).

10. Félicien David, *Prière du matin* and *Chant de vie*.
>   *Prière du matin* composed at Ménilmontant, early July 1832.
>   For men's chorus TTBB and (optional) piano.
>   Text (of *Prière du matin*) by Emile Barrault.
>   The score (of *Prière du matin*) was published in the *Ménilmontant* series; copies survive in BNMus, BHVP, Thiers.
>   The text alone (of *Chant de vie*) was published in *Mort de Talabot*.
>   The music reappears as *Le Reveil du jour* (text by Charles Chaubet, no. 7 in *La Ruche harmonieuse*).

We know nothing of the origin of this piece. It was written in July, according to Fournel, and must have been part of the choir's repertory by 16 July (see the description of Talabot's death in Chapter 10). A second (and inept) text for it, apparently cobbled together on short order for Talabot's funeral, was entitled *Chant de vie:*

> Cherchons la lumière nouvelle;
> Les ombres de la mort s'évanouissent.
> Dieu! Dieu! tu nous rends le jour.
> Pour nous c'est l'espérance;
> Pour lui c'est le travail.
>   PÈRE!
> Votre enfant vous aime.
>   FRÈRES!
> Il nous tend la main.
> Salut! salut! à l'homme nouveau:
> Dieu l'appelle au travail!
> Dieu lui rend la vie.

For a recording of the *Prière du matin,* see piece 2.

11. Félicien David, *Tout est mort* (*La Mort et l'espérance*) and *Chant de mort* ("Il est mort").
>   *Tout est mort* composed at Ménilmontant, early July (?) 1832.
>   For men's chorus TTBB and (optional) piano.
>   Text (of *Tout est mort*) by Charles Duveyrier.
>   The score (of *Tout est mort*) was published in the *Ménilmontant* series; copies survive in BNMus, BHVP, Thiers.
>   The text alone (of *Chant de mort*) was published in *Mort de Talabot;* that of *Tout est mort* was published in Tajan-Rogé's *Mémoires d'un piano* (see Chapter 12).
>   The music reappears with orchestral accompaniment as the mixed chorus "Les Hébreux dans le désert" ("Israël, Israël") in David's *Moïse au Sinaï.* This version then appears in a setting for men's chorus TTBB, but with no accompaniment, in *La Ruche harmonieuse* (no. 20).

Tout est mort is apparently the earlier version, and the only one that David intended to be preserved. Fournel dates it in July, and we can probably date it to the first half of the month, for, when Talabot died on 17 July, David and his singers quickly worked up a version of the chorus with a specifically funereal text, entitled *Chant de mort*. The published words of *Chant de mort* reveal that the music was preserved nearly intact except for the lively 3/4 coda ("plus d'esclavage"), which was replaced with a more appropriate return to the stern opening. It is not known who made the textual and musical changes—perhaps David and Duveyrier together.

Autograph MS parts for *Tout est mort* (tenor I and bass only) exist in BNMus MS 1812 a-b. They are entitled *La Mort et l'espérance;* presumably this was the original title, but the work was published and always cited by its first words.

Text of "Tout est mort":
 Tout est mort, tout est mort.
 Nous avons Dieu pour nous.
 Tout est mort, tout est mort.
 Faisons toutes choses nouvelles.

 La vie de l'apôtre est rude et sévère,
 Comme le vieux monde où Dieu l'a jeté.
 Grand Dieu prenez soin de ceux qui nous aiment.
 N'aimons que le peuple, il n'est pas aimé.

 [First stanza is repeated.]

 Nous avons tout donné, tout quitté pour toi.
 Peuple! nous avons tout donné, tout quitté pour toi.
 Et que sont les dangers, les douleurs, la misère,
 Quand on sauve le monde.

 Plus d'esclavage, imitez-nous.
 Espoir, espoir, les temps sont proches.
 Paix et bonheur seront pour tous.
 Paix et bonheur.

Text of "Chant de mort":
 Il est mort! il est mort!
 La nuit voile son front.
 Il est mort! il est mort!
 Cherchons la lumière nouvelle.

 La vie de l'apôtre est rude et sévère,
 Comme le vieux monde où Dieu l'a jeté.
 Grand Dieu! comme lui n'aimons que le peuple!
 N'aimons que le peuple, il n'est pas aimé!

 [First stanza is repeated.]

Il avait tout donné, tout quitté, tout donné,
Tout pour toi! Peuple! peuple!

Il est mort! il est mort!

12. Félicien David, *Au peuple.*
     Composed at Ménilmontant, July 1832.
     For men's chorus TTBB and (optional) piano.
     Text by Charles Duveyrier.
     Score published in the *Ménilmontant* series; copies survive in
       BNMus, Thiers.
     The music reappears as *Le Chant des travailleurs* (text by Charles
       Chaubet, no. 1 in *La Ruche harmonieuse*).
The date is not certain. Fournel gives merely "July," but it is possible that the piece
was performed on 16 July (see Chapter 10, note 65) and was thus composed in the
first half of the month.

Peuple, peuple, savez-vous qui nous sommes?
Comme vous bourgeois, ouvriers,
Vos compagnons d'école et de chantiers,
Unis pour vous unir, donnant tout entier au Père
Que Dieu donne à tout le monde.

Père, pourquoi votre bonne nouvelle
Les trouve-t-elle sans amour et sans foi?
Ils sont si malheureux.
Tout les abandonne:
Travail, repos, gloire et bonheur.
Sans foi, sans amour entr'eux,
Ils n'ont d'espoir en personne.

Aimez-vous, aimez-vous.
Prenez foi les uns dans les autres.
Aimez-vous, aimez-vous,
Et vous serez patients comme nous.
Notre espoir deviendra le vôtre.
Vous deviendrez bons comme nous.
Aimez-vous, aimez-vous
Et joignez vos efforts aux nôtres.
Vous serez forts et vaincrez avec nous.
Suivez-nous, suivez les apôtres.
Notre Dieu fait justice à tous.

13. Félicien David, *Morceau écrit pendant le choléra* and *Prière.*
     Possibly composed at Ménilmontant on 17 July 1832.
     For piano.
     The music survives in David's autograph (BNMus MS 1830,
       fol. 1).

It is the titles of these pieces, in David's own hand, which suggest that they were composed in connection with the death of Talabot. The first piece is complete; the opening measures of *Prière* follow it in the MS. No other source is known for either work and David did not announce them in the *Ménilmontant* series (unless he intended them to serve as part of the set of *Pensées,* now lost—see item 22).

14. Félicien David, *Ronde.*
        Composed at Ménilmontant, August 1832.
        For men's chorus TTBB and (optional) piano.
        Text by Edouard Pouyat.
        The score was published in the Ménilmontant series; copies sur-
           vive in BNMus, BHVP, Thiers, Ars.
        The text alone was published in 1832 as a separate sheet (contain-
           ing twelve strophes) entitled simply *Chant saint-simonien* (copies
           in *Recueil,* Ars 7803/31, 57, and *BHVP 5*), reprinted with an at-
           tribution to Lagache in *Foi nouvelle (1835).*
        The music reappears as *Ronde des vendanges* (text by Charles
           Chaubet, no. 5 of *La Ruche harmonieuse*).
We do not know when the piece was first performed (the date derives from Fournel). The general ideological nature of the text, though, suggests that it was not written for a particular ceremony. The piece may have been an important item in the repertory during the closing months of 1832, since a separate text sheet was published for it before the end of the year. (The sheet is already listed in Fournel's published bibliography, which restricts itself to publications before 1833.) This text sheet also makes clear that the chorus was performed as a chanson, since the publication of texts without music was normally used only for chansons. The text sheet offers, chansonlike, a full dozen verses for the *Ronde* (as opposed to three in the score). The *Ronde* has been republished many times since David's death, in new choral arrangements and with new texts, and is available on disc.[8]

The poet of the *Ronde,* Edouard Pouyat, is a neglected figure in discussions of the Saint-Simonian movement. At the habit ceremony of 6 June, Enfantin accepted him as an apostle with the warning: "Tu es ici l'un des plus jeunes; mais ta vie est ici. Ajoute seulement à ta figure plus de gravité; elle sied à l'habit que tu vas prendre." Pouyat published in 1833 an idiosyncratic work of fiction mixed with reminiscences, entitled *Caliban.* In the late 1830s he became a regular literary critic for the heavily Saint-Simonian newspaper *Le Temps.*

15. Félicien David, *La Danse des astres.*
        Composed at Ménilmontant, September 1832.
        For men's chorus TTBB, solo tenor (or violin, or cello) and
           piano.
        Text by Charles Duveyrier and (René-)Achille Rousseau.
        The score was published in the *Ménilmontant* series; copies survive
           in BNMus, BHVP, Thiers.
        The music, orchestrated and expanded, reappears as *Chant du soir*
           (text by Sylvain Saint-Etienne, published 1846 with piano and

1867 with orchestra). Saint-Etienne arranged *Chant du soir* (presumably with David's permission) for children's chorus (SSA), soprano solo, and piano (*Hymne au Créateur,* published 1847).

16. Félicien David, *Peuple fier! peuple fort!* or *Le Peuple.*
     Composed at Ménilmontant, September 1832.
     For voice and piano (and, possibly, men's chorus TTBB).
     Text by (René-)Achille Rousseau.
     Score published in the *Ménilmontant* series; a copy survives in BNMus.
     Text alone published as two separate text sheets: one in-quarto entitled *Le Peuple. / Chanson Religieuse,* copies in Ars 7803/222, 75 and BHVP 5; the other in-octavo entitled *Chant saint-simonien. / Peuple fier! Peuple fort!,* copy in BNImp Ye 51462.
     Text alone published also in *Procès (octobre)* (reprinted in *OSSE* 47:548–49), *Foi nouvelle (Nantes), Chants saint-simoniens (Grenoble),* and *Foi nouvelle (1835).*
     The music reappears, with significant revisions in both piano and vocal parts, as *Hymne à la fraternité* (words by A. Colin) (Paris: J. Meissonier, [1848]).

The date comes from Fournel, although the account of the second trial claims that the piece was first performed the night of 19 October (see Chapter 10). Rousseau himself presumably entitled the piece *Le Peuple,* the title that appears on one of the separate text sheets and in the Grenoble songster. The latter also groups three strophes together under the heading "Ses travaux" and another three under "Patience du peuple."

An engraver's error: there should be a natural sign before the D in "Je suis au Père."

It is possible that a four-part choral refrain—such as appears in the 1848 reworking—was composed for the original version as well, though excluded from the published score (for economic reasons, perhaps, or for fear of discouraging impromptu performances).

17. Félicien David, *Prière du Père.*
     Composed at Ménilmontant, September 1832.
     For men's chorus TTBB and (optional) piano.
     Text by B.-P. Enfantin.
     The score was published in the *Ménilmontant* series; a copy survives in BNMus.
     The music reappears as *Hymne à Dieu (Foyer de la charité)* (text by Charles Chaubet, no. 21 in *La Ruche harmonieuse*).

> Grand Dieu, source inépuisable de vie.
> Que suis-je en ce monde qui m'environne?
> Un point dans l'immensité, un moment dans l'éternité,
> Un soupir de l'universelle vie.
> Mais toi, tu es l'immensité, la vie.

Monde des mondes, gloire à moi!
Etre des êtres, gloire à toi!
Je vis, je veux, je vis, je veux.
Père, tu m'aimes, gloire à moi!

Père, c'est Dieu qui nous unit à vous.
Peuple, c'est lui qui nous dévoue à toi (c'est Dieu).
Terre, c'est lui qui t'a fiancée à nous.
Soleil, c'est lui qui nous attache à toi
Et qui te lie à tous les mondes.

Que suis-je? Un point dans l'immensité.
Je suis un monde. Un moment dans l'éternité.
Je vis, je veux.
Je suis un soupir de l'universelle vie.

Je t'aime aussi, je t'aime.
Je le veux, je le veux.
Gloire à moi, gloire à toi, gloire à nous!
Gloire à Dieu!

18. Félicien David, *La Voix du peuple* ("Je ne veux plus être exploité").
    Composed at Ménilmontant, November 1832.
    For voice and piano.
    Text by (René-)Achille Rousseau.
    The score was published in the *Ménilmontant* series but no copies
        survive.
    The text alone was published as an octavo text sheet (BNImp Ye
        51461, another copy in *BHVP 5*) and in *Chant[s] saint-simon-
        ien[s], Foi nouvelle (Nantes).*
Fournel and Mme Mathieu both possessed copies of the published score, but I have
not been able to locate them (see Note on Sources).
    The title of the piece, *La Voix du peuple,* derives from the lines "Et moi le peuple,
/ Je suis la voix de Dieu," an elaboration of the well-known motto "Vox populi vox
dei." A contemporary reviewer (see Chapter 12, n.97) indicated that it was, like *Peuple
fier,* a strophic chanson, presumably with piano (he uses the word "romance"), and
opined that it was "bien accentué" and melodically smoother than *Peuple fier.* It was
taken up into the movement's chanson repertoire (using the first line as title).

Je ne veux plus être exploité.
Je ne veux plus être trompé,
Je ne veux plus d'oisiveté
Et je ne veux plus de révolte.
    Le juste Dieu,
    Dieu n'en veut plus aussi,
    Et moi le peuple,
    Et moi le peuple,
    Je suis la voix de Dieu:
    La voix de Dieu, entendez-vous!

Assez j'ai vécu de douleur,
Je suis fort et bon travailleur.
Je ne veux plus de mes haillons,
Je ne veux plus de mes misères.
    Le juste Dieu, etc.

Pour mes filles je veux l'honneur,
Je veux l'honneur et la santé,
Je veux respect pour leur beauté,
J'ai soif d'honneur, j'ai soif de gloire.
    Le juste Dieu, etc.

19. Félicien David, *Femmes, levez-vous.*
    Composed at Ménilmontant, 1832.
    Forces unknown.
    Text by an unknown author.
    The music and text are lost.
    The score was announced for publication in the *Ménilmontant* se-
       ries but never appeared.

20. Félicien David, *Le Sommeil de Paris* or *Paris est là.*
    Composed at Ménilmontant, 1832.
    Probably for men's chorus TTBB, solo quartet TTBB, and piano.
    Text by an unknown author.
    The music and text are lost, except for an autograph bass part in
       the Moldenhauer Archive, Northwestern University Music Li-
       brary. The score was announced for publication in the *Ménil-
       montant* series but never appeared.

Paris est là is the title used by David and Fournel. What must have been the correct title, *Le Sommeil de Paris,* is given at the head of the only surviving source, a four-page bass part. (The informal title derives from the words that end the first section: "Paris est là qui dort. . . .'") In this source David has carefully crossed out every appearance of the Saint-Simonian slogan word *peuple,* replacing it with the more neutral *monde.* This suggests that the bass part dates from 1832 or 1833 but was used again at a later performance, after the movement's decline—most likely at David's concert of 8 December 1844, which included a performance of *Sommeil* with orchestral accompaniment.

Berlioz, reviewing the concert, had kind words for the harmony, rhythm, and vocal and orchestral scoring of this piece. He also described it as a "grand morceau avec choeur, solos et orchestre";[10] unless the piece was greatly altered for the concert (and Saint-Etienne implies that it was not),[11] the "solos" in question were probably passages for a solo group (quartet?) within the chorus. (The surviving bass part contains several phrases marked "solo," but they are clearly not solo melodies. They recall instead the bass's role in the solo quartet section of *Prière du soir.*) There is also a ten-measure pause after the first section—perhaps the occasion for a true solo in some other voice.

Paix, écoutons.

Quand la nuit se répand sur Paris,

Ecoutons le géant qui s'endort murmurant,

Ecoutons l'hymne saint, chant de vie et de mort,

Ecoutons ce concert de Paris qui s'éteint.

Paris s'éteint, Paris s'endort.

Dieu, quelle voix monte et prie, s'enfle et crie

Vers le ciel, sourd, froid, muet,

Voix de mort, hymne grinçant et discordant,

Voix de deuil et de douleur:

C'est que Paris est là qui dort;

Cette voix qui la nuit se répand sur Paris,

Cette voix qui supplie et qui crie et maudit,

C'est le chant des douleurs, c'est le choeur de la nuit.

Paris est là! Paris est là!

Entends leur voix, père.

Il a crié vers toi; il a jeté ses cris.

En toi le peuple [changed to *monde*] espère,

Vers toi dans sa misère

Il a jeté ses cris.

Espoir, peuple [monde], Dieu qui voit ta misère,

Dieu notre père, Dieu te délivrera.

Entends leur cri, père.

Ils ont crié vers toi.

Entends les cris du peuple [monde].

Entends, il souffre et implore.

Espoir, le jour viendra.

Espoir, peuple [monde], espère, peuple [monde], courage.

Dieu veut que sur terre

Le bonheur soit pour tous.

Espère, car voici venir le jour où tous seront unis.

Peuple [monde], espère, car voici venir

Les temps heureux pour tous.

21. Félicien David, Waltzes for piano.

 Composed at Ménilmontant, 1832.

 Publication of two series of waltzes was announced in the prospectus to the *Ménilmontant* series; apparently only the first
appeared.

 A copy of the first series survives in BNMus; also a manuscript of
Désir: MS 1826 (dated 3 December 1847).

David announced two sets of waltzes, the first "série" entitled *Mes amours,* the second
Ménilmontant. The set that did reach publication is labeled "first series" but combines
the titles of the two sets: MENILMONTANT / mes Amours / Pour / Le FORTE-
PIANO / Par / FELICIEN DAVID / 1ère. Série. . . (Lyons: Mme Durval, [1833]).

This first set contains eleven waltzes, all with titles referring to emotional states or relationships between individuals: *Insouciance, Mélancolie, Désir, Impatience, Causerie, Transports, Je t'en prie, Bonheur, Jalousie, Rupture, Réconciliation.*

David reprinted four pieces from this first set later in life under different titles. *Bonheur* became *L'Allemande* (no. 2 of *Deux Bluettes*—published by Meissonier, 1850); *Insouciance* became *La Bergeronette* (Saint-Etienne, 1853); and *Désir* and *Je t'en prie* became, respectively, *Carmina* and *Flavia,* published together as *Les Deux Amies,* deux pensées mélodiques (Saint-Etienne, 1854). In all four cases David expanded the waltzes by adding a contrasting middle section and then repeating the original waltz in its entirety. It is conceivable that pieces from the lost second series of Ménilmontant waltzes eventually reached publication in the same manner.

22. Félicien David, *Pensées* for piano.
>   Composed at Ménilmontant, 1832.
>   MS of first piece: BNMus MS 1830, fol. 2.

The *Pensées* are another set of piano pieces that David announced in his prospectus. With the exception of the first, which exists in MS, they have all disappeared, or were perhaps published later without reference to Ménilmontant. Two possible such belated publications are the *Pensée* (published in 1845 by the Bureau central de musique, but no copy survives) and *La Pensée* (no. 3 of the *Trois mélodies-valses*—Heugel, 1851). The latter was published separately in England as *Pensée fugitive* (copy in the British Library, London).

23. Félicien David, *La Prison du Père.*
>   Composed in Lyons, January 1833.
>   For men's chorus TTBB and piano.
>   Text by Emile Barrault.
>   The score was published in the *Ménilmontant* series (although it was not in fact composed at Ménilmontant); copies survive in BNMus, Thiers.
>   The music reappears as *Paix et bonheur* (text by Charles Chaubet, no. 3 of *La Ruche harmonieuse*).

The place and year (as well as David's new rank of "Compagnon de la *Femme*") appear at the head of the score. The rhythm in the right hand at the bottom of p. 11 should be notated with four thirty-second notes (not sixty-fourths).

>   Peuple, entends notre voix.
>   Femmes, prêtez l'oreille.
>   Dieu nous a séparé d'un Père,
>   Et nous fils dévoués, nous redisons sa gloire.
>   Ecoutez nos chants.
>
>   Peuple, peuple, sais-tu qui nous envoie
>   A tes ateliers, à tes fêtes?
>   C'est lui.
>   Pour tes rudes travaux
>   Il arme nos bras pacifiques.

C'est lui qui pour toi nous inspire
Chants de paix et d'espoir.
C'est le Père, le Père en prison.

Pour un sexe encore esclave
Il cria "Liberté!"
(*Cris du peuple:* "Liberté")
Femmes, voilà son crime
Et les verroux l'en punissent.

Femmes, aimez le Père
Dieu, tu nous en sépare,
Mais tu nous le rendras
Par la main de la Mère,
Triomphant et béni,
Par le peuple et les femmes.

24. Félicien David, *Compagnonnage de la Femme.*
> Composed in Lyons (?), January–March 1833.
> Presumably for voice and piano, perhaps with choral refrain.
> Text by Emile Barrault.
> The music was never announced for publication and does not
> survive.
> The text was published as a separate sheet three times in Castel-
> naudary (twice in French and once in the local dialect—see
> Fournel's revised list). Yet another text sheet, printed in Lyons,
> exists in BNImp Ye 55472/344 and contains six strophes.
> The text is also included in *Foi nouvelle (Saint-Pons)* (three
> strophes) and *Foi nouvelle (1835)* (six strophes).

The stanza and refrain structure of the text clearly indicates that this piece was a chanson (or a very chansonlike chorus). It must have been written between late January (founding of the Compagnons) and 22 March (the departure of David and Barrault for the Orient).

> 1. Peuple, rends hommage à la FEMME,
> Et change tes cris en concerts!
> Ne maudis plus un joug infâme;
> Sa main détachera tes fers.
> Douce, majestueuse et belle,
> Elle fait bénir sa bonté;
> Et la paix marche devant elle;
> C'est l'ange de la liberté!
>> Compagnons de la FEMME,
>> Si sa voix nous réclame,
>> De coeur, de bras et d'âme
>> Soyons prêts!
>> Que nul effort ne coûte:
>> De fleurs semons sa route

> Et que la terre écoute
> Ses chants de paix!

2. Voici la fin de ta souffrance!
   Tes rois étaient d'ingrats tuteurs:
   Ils déshéritaient ton enfance,
   Et s'engraissaient de tes sueurs.
   Peuple, tu n'avais point de MERE,
   Et tu souffrais sans être plaint;
   DIEU prend pitié de ta misère,
   Et tu ne seras plus orphelin!
   > Compagnons de la FEMME, etc.

3. Partis! c'est l'heure de la trève;
   La FEMME paraît dans vos camps;
   Ah! loin, loin de vous votre glaive!
   Embrassez-vous, fiers combattants.
   Prompte à désarmer l'indigence,
   En bonne mère, entre ses fils,
   C'est elle qui tient la balance,
   Et les frères vivent unis.
   > Compagnons de la FEMME, etc.

4. Plus de sang, de haine et de guerre!
   L'atelier est un champ d'honneur;
   Le travail embellit la terre;
   La gloire attend le travailleur.
   Peuple, relève enfin la tête
   De la poussière du chantier;
   La FEMME t'invite à la fête
   Et sa main te tresse un laurier.
   > Compagnons de la FEMME, etc.

5. Ah! bientôt cet astre sans tâche
   Doit te faire un nouveau destin;
   Du bonheur que l'ombre te cache
   Va, l'horizon est moins lointain.
   La FEMME, au milieu de l'orage,
   Luit comme l'étoile des mers;
   Ses feux te montrent le rivage,
   Des cieux amis et des flots clairs!
   > Compagnons de la FEMME, etc.

6. Peuple, apprends à bénir la MERE!
   Le PERE est captif en prison,
   Et toi, captif dans ta misère;
   Ensemble invoquons tous son nom.
   C'est l'heure de la délivrance;

Prison! rendez lui son époux!
Enfin la liberté commence;
La FEMME nous a sauvés tous!
    Compagnons de la FEMME, etc.

25. Félicien David, *Le Départ pour l'Orient.*
    Composed in Lyons (possibly completed in Marseilles), March
      1833.
    Probably for men's chorus TTBB and (optional) piano.
    The text, by an unknown author, is largely lost.
    The music survives (presumably) as *Le Retour des proscrits* (text by
      Charles Chaubet, no. 8 in *La Ruche harmonieuse*).

David, writing to the Lyons pianist Jenny Montgolfier in March 1833, stated that he wanted to "composer un nouveau choeur pour le départ."[12] Twelve years later, Saint-Didier (another supporter of David in Lyons—see Chapter 12) sent Sylvain Saint-Etienne a stack of David's unpublished choruses, including one that Saint-Etienne had not previously seen, "le choeur le *Départ pour l'Orient.*"[13] Were it not for these two letters, the piece would be entirely unknown to us. (It was not included or even announced in the *Ménilmontant* series, because it was composed *after* David made up the prospectus of 22 February.) But once we know to look for such a piece, it is easily found. Of the eleven choruses in *La Ruche harmonieuse* that have texts by Charles Chaubet, ten can be shown to derive from known Saint-Simonian choruses of 1832–33. The eleventh is the *Retour des proscrits*. A glance at the text, which (as so often with the Chaubet retextings) can be expected to preserve some phrases of the original Saint-Simonian text, is sufficient to place the work in March 1833, the month of the Compagnons' departure for the Orient. There is talk of exiles, and of people (no doubt Enfantin, in the original version) being enchained alone, "sous la voûte des prisons." In clear reference to the departure of the Compagnons for the Orient, the text continues: "ils restent [originally 'il reste'?] et nous partons, oui seuls, nous partons." The final words, "Dieu donne enfin la terre," make no sense in context. Obviously the line was originally something like "Dieu, donne enfin *la Mère,*" and Chaubet adapted it as best he could. ("Père" became "Terre" when David and his friends turned the *Salut* into a chorus for *Moïse au Sinaï.*)

   The musical style and choral writing also speak for a date of 1832–33. Perhaps the original words will yet turn up to confirm what already seems a near certainty: that *Le Retour des proscrits* preserves the music (and some words) of the last piece that David wrote for the movement before embarking for the Orient.

    Text of "Le Retour des proscrits":
        Proscrits, le Ciel nous rappelle;
        Aux feux de l'aube nouvelle,
        Sur l'onde riante et belle
        Nous voguons
        Vers les rivages prospères
        Où sont les toits de nos pères.
        Nous retournons,

Oui, nous volons dans les bras de nos frères
Vers les riants vallons,
Les vallons tutélaires
Et prospères
De nos pères.

Ah! trop d'infortunés
A l'exil condamnés
Sont encore enchaînés
Sous la voûte des prisons.
Hélas, ils sont seuls.
Ils restent et nous partons.
Oui, seuls, nous partons!

Rayon divin, un jour pur nous éclaire.
Dieu donne enfin la terre,
A notre coeur si chère;
Plus de plainte amère,
Plus de douleurs,
Aux bras des travailleurs
Dieu donne enfin la terre.
Oui, Dieu donne enfin la terre.

26. Félicien David, *Cantate composée en l'honneur du départ des St. Simoniens en Egypte.* This was not a new work by David but a retexting of *Le Nouveau Temple,* followed by other material (apparently a retexting of a Saint-Simonian chanson). For a fuller discussion of this *pièce d'occasion,* see the discussion in Chapter 12. The entire text is given below, as preserved in a page handwritten by Charles Lambert, Ars 7803/50. This, the sole source for the work, is written on stationery with the letterhead "Religion saint-simonienne" and is transcribed below. Some periods, commas, and capital letters have been added, but the ellipsis points and dashes are all original; they indicate breaks between musical phrases rather than omissions of material.

Frères partez . . . Nous qui restons ayons courage . . . . nous sommes forts forts [sic]. Et vous voulez toucher [prêcher?] à tous que nos jours sont pour le peuple. (Nous attendrons avec courage) (bis) . . . (le grand jour du peuple le grand jour de dieu) (bis).
Compagnons au revoir aimez nous et le peuple entendra notre parole. (Dieu bénit vos efforts) (bis)—. . . . que l'on sâche en tous lieux qu'ici se lève l'étendard de la paix universelle (bis). —Au revoir — aimez-nous et le peuple ira vers vous. Dieu bénit vos efforts — commencez, commencez la vie errante. Compagnons au revoir bon courage, espérez (Dieu bénit vos efforts) (bis) (au revoir) (bis).

27. Félicien David, *Prière* or *L'Attente de la Mère*.

    Presumably for men's chorus TTBB and (optional) piano.

    Composed in Constantinople and Smyrna, ca. April–June 1833.

    Text by Thomas Urbain.[14]

    An autograph MS containing the "alto" voice part for this and the three following works survives in BNMus W8, 19.

    A version of this piece for TTBB a cappella (perhaps identical to the voice parts of the original) is found, with a new text, in *La Ruche harmonieuse* (as no. 6, *Les Statues de Prométhée*, text by Charles Chaubet). The first tenor part is identical to the 1833 "alto" part.

The title of the piece, *Prière,* is given in the surviving "alto" part. David mentions what appears to be the same piece by the title *L'Attente* in his letter to Urbain of 12 June 1833, cited in Chapter 12. The identity of the two pieces is confirmed by an editorial remark in the *Livre des actes* (p. 234) about "la prière à la MERE, que David a composée à Smyrne, sous le titre *L'Attente.*" (The prayer is actually addressed, though, to *God* and speaks *about* La Mère.) Tajan-Rogé in a letter praising the piece (see Chapter 12) gives additional information about its composition: "PERE, David m'a écrit et m'a adressé une prière à la MERE, commencée à Constantinople et finie à Smyrne."[15]

        Les temps sont accomplis.
        Tout s'agite pour la bonne nouvelle.
        Le monde est prêt.

        Tournons nos coeurs vers la Mère.
        Elle entend nos chants d'attente et d'espoir.
        Prions, prions.

        Le monde est dans les fers;
        Les femmes, sans amour.
        Le peuple crie.
        Qui viendra le sauver?
        La Mère!

        Dans son coeur est l'amour
        Pour ses fils, pour ses filles.
        Dans sa main est la paix
        Pour le monde,
        La paix et le bonheur.

        Nous te prions, Dieu,
        Pour guérir nos douleurs,
        Pour épanouir nos joies,
        Donne-nous la Mère,
        L'épouse pour nous,
        La mère pour le monde,
        La Mère.

28. Félicien David, *Les Etoiles* or *La Nuit: à la Mère (orientale)*.
  Probably for men's chorus TTBB, tenor solo, and piano.
  Composed in Smyrna, April–June 1833.
  Text by P. Granal.[16]
  Text and music of the 1833 version survive only in the aforementioned "alto" part, BNMus W8, 19.
  The music reappears with a new text as the "Choeur des génies de l'océan" in David's *Christophe Colomb* (1847), set for chorus TTBB, tenor solo, and orchestra. The first tenor part in the chorus is identical to the 1833 "alto" part.

The piece is called *Les Etoiles (orientale)* in the "alto" part discussed above. David, in his letter to Urbain of 12 June 1833, refers to what is presumably the same piece as *La Nuit: à la Mère (orientale)*.

> La nuit descend des montagnes.
> Les étoiles, ses compagnes, se pressent au rendez-vous
> Comme un choeur qui se déroule.
> Ecoutons leurs chants si doux.
>
> Elles commencent leurs danses en rond.
> Les voilà qui se balancent,
> Leur couronne au front.
> Les voilà.
>
> Dansez, chantez, offrez à la Mère
> Pour prière et pour encens
> Vos danses et vos chants.
> Voici venir la plus belle des filles de Dieu.
> La terre l'attend, l'appelle.
> On l'attend aux cieux.
> La la ra la, la la ra la... [under solo tenor vocalise].
>
> Chantons, dansons, offrons à la Mère
> Pour prière et pour encens
> Nos danses et nos chants.
> O Mère! entends!
>
> Entends, entends la voix des étoiles.
> Ecarte les sombres voiles qui te cachent à nos yeux.
> Chasse la foudre qui gronde.
> Oh! viens exaucer, Mère, nos voeux.
> Pour nous point de chants, de danses.
> Nos nuits et nos jours—
> Sans toi dans le silence
> Sans toi dans la souffrance—
> Hélas! s'écoulent sans amour.
> Prions, offrons à la Mère
> Pour prière et pour encens
> Nos coeurs, nos coeurs souffrants.

29. Félicien David, *Hymne à la Mère* (hypothetical title), including the section "Belle, oh belle comme l'ange."

> Probably for men's chorus TTBB and (optional) piano.
>
> Composed in Smyrna?, April–June 1833?
>
> The text, possibly by Emile Barrault, is lost except for the words of the "Belle, oh belle" passage.
>
> For "Belle, oh belle," the music (of the topmost voice) and the text survive in the aforementioned "alto" part (BNMus W8, 19). The piece is entitled "Fragment."
>
> What is presumably the music of the entire piece survives, in a version for TTBB a cappella (presumably identical to the voice parts of the original) and with a partly new text by Charles Chaubet, in *La Ruche harmonieuse* (no. 10, *Hymne à la nature*).

Our knowledge of this piece is based solely on the two musical sources: a fragment from (presumably) 1833 and a complete piece published in 1851 and containing as one of its four sections the music of the fragment, minimally adjusted to accommodate different words ("O nature immortelle"). A likely hypothesis is that the fragment was composed slightly earlier than the other sections and around the same time as the rest of the pieces in the "alto" bifolio (mid-1833). It is also conceivable that the whole piece was written before David left France, and only a fragment was retained for performance with the Smyrna pieces. The slight possibility also exists that only the fragment is from 1833 and the other three sections were written years later. Speaking against this is the fact that almost all Chaubet's other textings in *Ruche* are of music entirely written in 1832–33 (see piece 25 above; a partial exception is piece 5); in addition, Chaubet's text seems to preserve large chunks of La Mère phraseology ("shining queen") and the musical style clearly places it with the other Saint-Simonian choruses.

The version given in Appendix E is essentially the music of the *Ruche* version adjusted to fit the earlier text, after the model of the surviving top voice. Measure numbers refer only to the "Belle" section, not to the *Hymne* as a whole. Two peculiarities: Bass, m. 12, beat 4 is *f* in *Ruche*, but *d* works better (cf. m. 10). And the text refers repeatedly to "Dieu bonne" rather than "Dieu bon"; this usage is characteristic of Saint-Simonian writings during the search for the Mother (it appears in the *Livre des actes*, passage quoted in d'Ivray, *Aventure*, 126). Cf. "Dieu mère" in piece 31.

> Text of Hymne à la nature:
>
> > O nature souveraine,
> > Des humains brillante reine,
> > Salut! gloire, salut!
> > Saint et sublime ouvrage,
> > Où Dieu mit son image,
> > Reçois des coeurs le doux tribut!
> > Gloire, salut!
> >
> > L'ombre du Ciel dévoilé
> > Te forme un dais étoilé,

Mais il s'efface,
Et dans l'espace
On voit éclore
La blonde aurore.
Salut! salut au soleil nouveau.
Salut! salut au divin flambeau,
Sur les mers si beau.

Cieux, ondes, fleurs,
Enivrez nos coeurs;
Travail et plaisirs,
Voilà nos désirs.
Nature, au bonheur
Admets tes enfants;
Au champ du labeur
Rends-les triomphants.

O nature immortelle,
Le Dieu de beauté
Et de majesté
Te rendit bien belle!
Soleils d'or épars
Aux vallons des Cieux,
Feux,
Eclairs radieux:
Vous êtes ses brillants regards!
O nature immortelle (etc.)
Dans la voix de nos bois,
Dans les bruits de nos nuits,
Dans l'écho
Du coteau,
Toi qui sais murmurer,
Chanter, soupirer,

Nature, entends nos voeux
Et rends-nous heureux!
Cieux, ondes, fleurs (etc.)

30. Félicien David, *Sérénade.*
    For TTBB and piano?
    Composed in Smyrna?, April–June 1833?
    Text by an unknown author (if indeed it ever did receive a text).
    The "alto" voice survives in the part sheet mentioned previously
        (BNMus W8, 19).
The tentative date corresponds to that of the two longer and datable pieces preserved
in the same source. The *Sérénade* may of course have been composed earlier, but the
fact that it was copied down almost entirely without text suggests that the piece was
a recent one, still untexted.

31. Henri Reber, *A l'Orient!*

> Composed in March 1834 (?).
>
> For mixed chorus, piccolo, 3 clarinets, 3 keyed trumpets, 2 valve trumpets, 4 trumpets, 2 horns, 2 ophicleides, trombones, and drum.
>
> Text by Félix Maynard.
>
> Published in Paris by Richault and in Lyons by Mme S. Durval, 1834. The basic tune (top voice only) was published in Vinçard's *Chants du travailleur* (1869), transposed from E flat to D, along with the words of strophes 1–3, 5, and 6. Dated "1834."
>
> Copy survives in the Collection Joseph Pierre. MS score in BNMus Ms. 11,217 (dated, erroneously, "Mars 1833").
>
> Text only published in *Foi nouvelle (1835).*

The published score, "luxeuesement éditée," bears a dedication from the authors to D. Rogé. The one surviving printed copy is in the Collection Joseph Pierre, a major George Sand collection that is currently inaccessible to scholars. It bears the following autograph dedication: "A George Sand. Au nom des chanteuses et des chanteurs de la soirée du 24 octobre 1834. D. Rogé." (All information about the published score from Marix-Spire, *Romantiques,* 469–70.) The words are given below as they appear in Reber's autograph score and Vinçard's *Chants.* Variants in the latter are indicated in brackets.

> 1. *Full Chorus:*
>
>   A l'Orient, à l'Orient, à l'Orient,
>   Majestueuse et solennelle
>   La voix du Père nous appelle,
>   A l'Orient, à l'Orient,
>   Majestueuse et solennelle
>   La voix du Père nous appelle,
>   A l'Orient, marchons, marchons à l'Orient.
>   Frères, prenez vos rangs, déroulons à la brise
>   L'oriflamme des travailleurs,
>   Suivons ses brillantes couleurs,
>   Qui marchent en avant vers la terre promise.
>   Sonnez clairons, sonnez le départ dans les airs;
>   Notre drapeau n'a plus assez du ciel de France,
>   Des minarets d'Egypte il faut qu'il se balance:
>   Sentinelle de paix aux yeux de l'univers.
>   A l'Orient, etc.
>
> 2. Et les peuples diront, à notre allure franche,
>   *Où marchent ces nouveaux soldats?*
>   Et les peuples suivront nos pas
>   Et s'en viendront grossir notre sainte avalanche.
>   Vieux monde, éveille-toi; qu'au bruit de nos clairons
>   Tombe dans ses fossés ta robe de murailles,
>   Pour payer le pain noir du pauvre qui travaille

Nous voulons monnayer l'airain de tes canons.
>A l'Orient, etc.

3. *Men:*

Et les femmes aussi qui disent: nous en sommes!
>Et qui s'attachent [se prennent] à nos bras,
>Et qui, pour marcher notre pas,

Revêtent [Attachent] à leur pieds les sandales des hommes.
Femmes, venez, venez, l'Orient est à vous,
Vos voix nous soutiendront, gracieuses et pures,
Vos baisers sont puissants à guérir nos blessures.
Dieu mère en vos souris donne un sourire à tous.
>A l'Orient, etc.

4. *Basses:*

Halte! voici la mer....Aux bords de ses rivages
>L'émotion a pris nos coeurs.
>N'ayons pas honte de nos pleurs;

Les larmes iront bien à nos mâles visages.
Frères, dans la douleur épanchons nos regrets
Pour la mère patrie et les beaux lieux d'enfance.
Prions la dernière heure aux rivages de France.
Oui, frères, prions tous, reviendrons-nous jamais[?]

Full chorus:
Père! la route est longue et les railleurs sont forts.
O pour nous prémunir contre ceux du dehors
Que ton puissant regard plane sur la famille,
Qu'il brille à l'Orient comme l'étoile brille.
Père! la route est longue et les railleurs sont forts.

Men:
Mon Dieu! fais que les pleurs que nous versent nos mères
Tarissent pendant leur sommeil.
Avec nos plus beaux jours fais leur des jours prospères
Et que leur main nous bénisse au reveil.

Women:
Et ceux qui nous ont mis la couronne d'épine,
Nous ne l'ôterons pas pour la mettre à leurs fronts.
Dieu seul nous donnera celle qu'il nous destine:
Bonheur et paix à tous! Hommes! nous vous aimons.

Full chorus:
Père! la route est longue (etc.)

5. Nos pères étaient grands, quand soldats intrépides,
>Ayant du sang à leurs mousquets,
>Ils se parlaient de leurs hauts faits,

Et vainqueurs prenaient l'ombre au pied des Pyramides.
Et nous aussi là-bas! nous aurons des grandeurs,
Des gloires, des hauts faits à remplir notre vie;
Nous serons grands comme eux, soldats de l'industrie,
Ne versant pas comme eux du sang, mais des sueurs.
[Ne versant pas de sang, mais versant nos sueurs.]
    A l'Orient, etc.

6. Alors ils nous verront en travailleurs agiles
    Avec nos lanières de fer
    Dompter les sables du désert,
Et comme des palmiers croîtront partout des villes,
Et le sol revêtu des fleurs de nos guérets,
Comme un riche divan de pourpre triomphale,
Sera dans l'avenir, la couche nuptiale,
Où deux mondes viendront s'épouser dans la paix.
    A l'Orient, etc.

32. Félicien David, arrangements of Arab tunes for brass and wind instruments
(and drum).
    Composition begun ca. February 1834.
    Possibly taken up again ca. May 1835.
    The music is lost.
David began arranging Arab airs for band with the intention that the band that Rogé
was training in France would soon arrive and play them as an inspiration for the
workers on the projected Suez Canal and Nile dam. (See Chapter 12.) The failure of
both projects no doubt led David to give up the musical arrangements.

While in quarantine in Italy on his way back from Egypt, he wrote Saint-Etienne
of his intention to publish "tous à la fois" his arrangements of Arab tunes for piano
and for band ("musique militaire").[17] But the band pieces never did get published in
that form. Soon after David returned to France, he published twenty-two pieces for
piano, entitled *Mélodies orientales* (see entry 34). Perhaps several of these are equivalent
to the pieces for band. (It is conceivable that others ended up in the instrumental
movements of David's *Le Désert*, 1844, or in the unpublished *Souvenir d'orient* for
orchestra, now in the Northwestern University Music Library Moldenhauer Archive.)

33. Félicien David, Cantata in honor of Ibrahim-Pasha.
    Composed (or compiled) in Cairo, early 1835.
    For men's chorus and piano?
    Text by one of the Saint-Simonian missionaries?
    Score and text do not survive.
The sole mention of this piece is in Voilquin's *Souvenirs,* chap. 24. (See Chapter 12
above.) Since she says it was "improvise[d]" (written quickly), it may have been based
on some earlier piece, such as the *Hymne à Saint-Simon.*

34. Félicien David, *Mélodies orientales.*

      Composed in Constantinople, Smyrna, Cairo, and Alexandria, and perhaps in France, 1833–35.

      Twenty-two pieces for piano, in seven livraisons.

      Published in Paris by Pacini, 1836. Prospectus reprinted in Prod'homme, "Félicien David," 123–24, and Locke, "Music and the Saint-Simonians," 690.

      Livraisons 1–6 were republished in 1845 as *Brises d'Orient* (Paris: Bureau central de musique; Mainz: Schott). Livraison 7 was republished in 1845 as *Les Minarets* (Paris: Bureau central de musique). The 1845 Paris editions were reissued by F. Gauvin after David's death.

      Copies of the various Paris editions survive in BNMus, except for *Mélodies orientales,* livraisons 5 and 6. Livraison 5 exists in the Bibliothèque Inguimbertine, Carpentras.

The complete *Mélodies orientales* will be reprinted in a forthcoming edition by Da Capo Press (New York), with a critical introduction by the present author. That introduction will also give details on the differences among the various editions. (Some of the titles are changed and the 1845/1880 Paris edition omits the first piece and reorders some of the remaining pieces. The omitted piece was published separately in 1845 as *Rêverie du soir*—the title of a movement from *Le Désert* based on the same Arab tune.)

Many of the *Mélodies* were dedicated to Saint-Simonian friends ("B," "C," and "H": presumably Barrault, Colin, and either Henri Granal or Hoart) or to people who had befriended David in Lyons and Marseilles (Théodore de Seynes, Jenny Montgolfier, and Anaïs Saint-Didier).

APPENDIX E
SELECTED SAINT–SIMONIAN WORKS BY FÉLICIEN DAVID

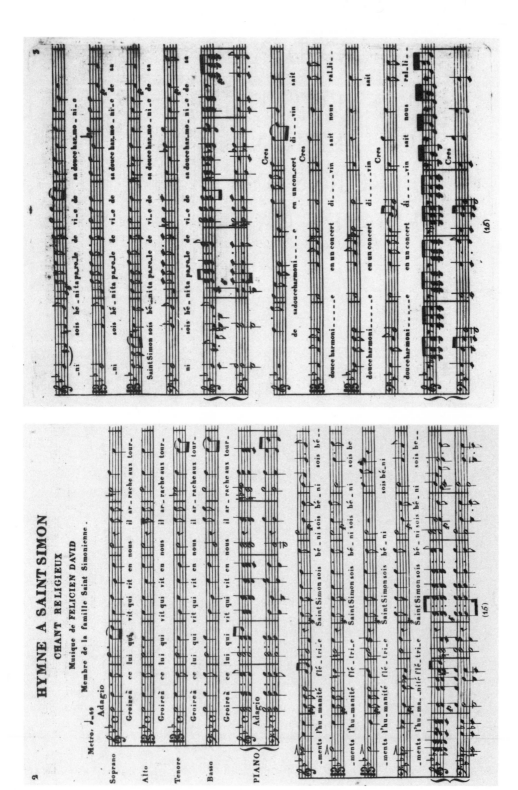

1. Félicien David, *Hymne à Saint-Simon* (text by Raymond Bonheur)

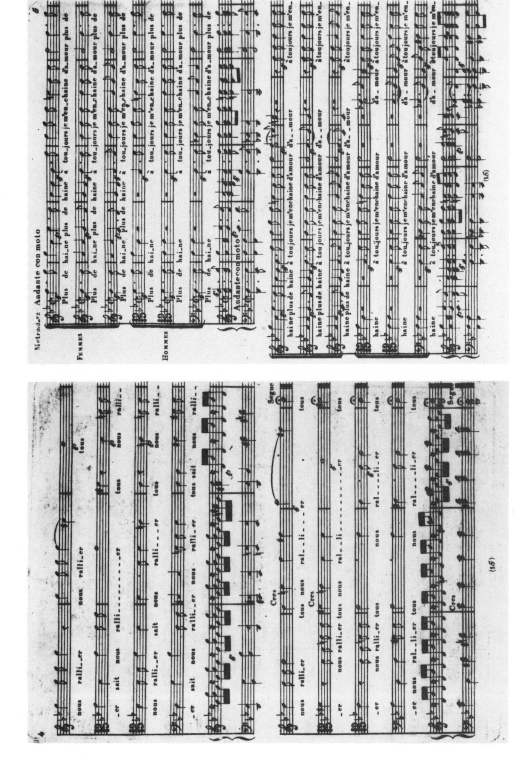

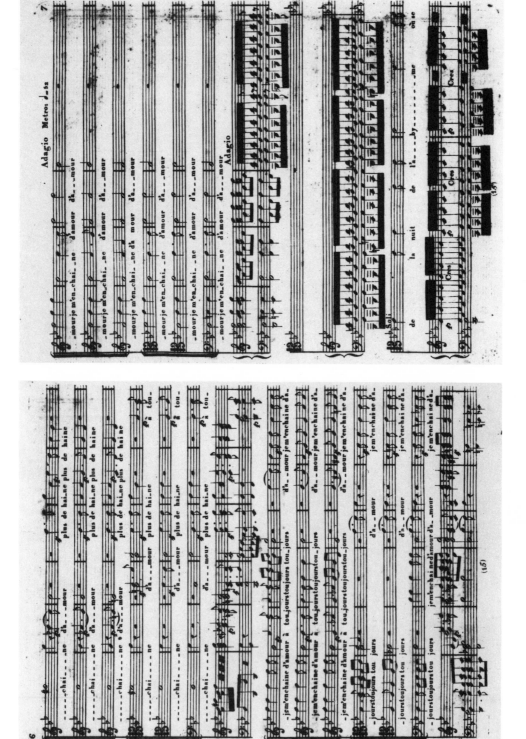

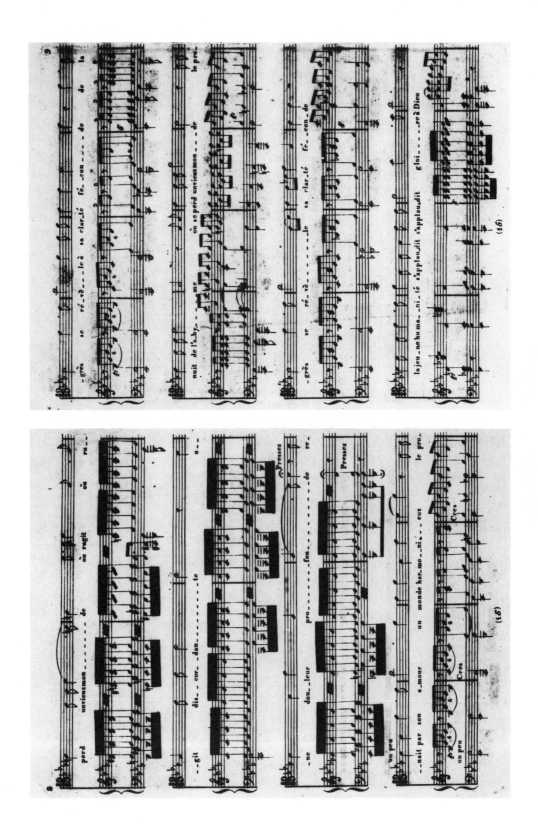

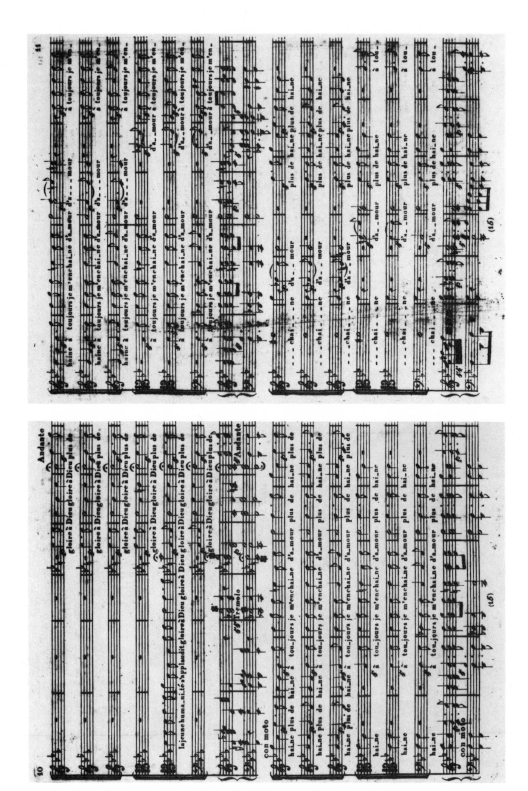

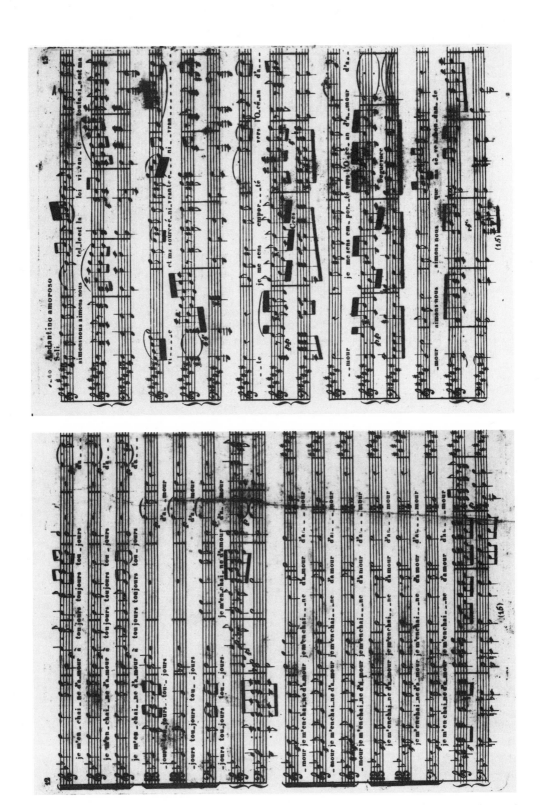

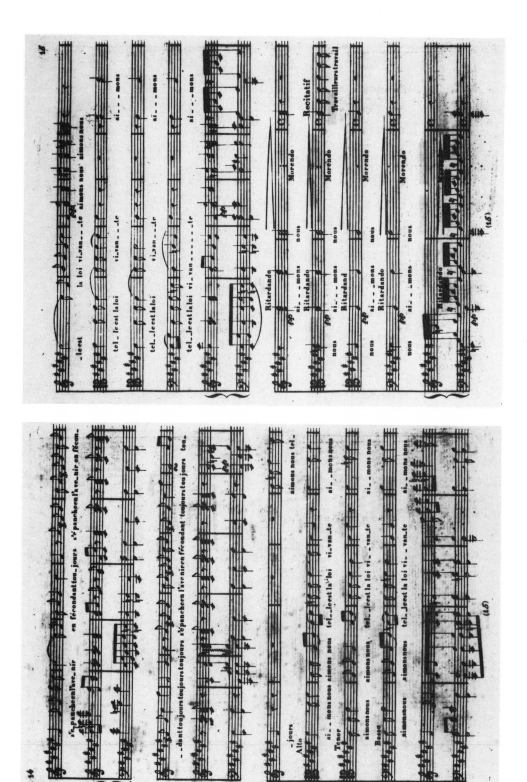

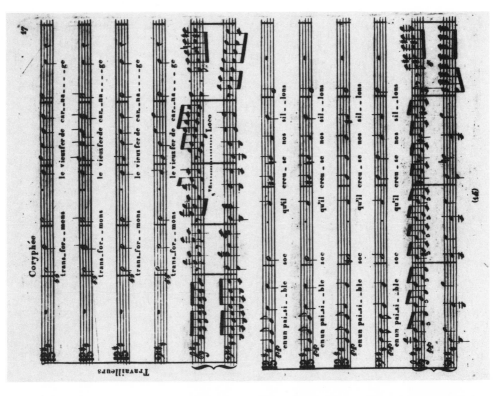
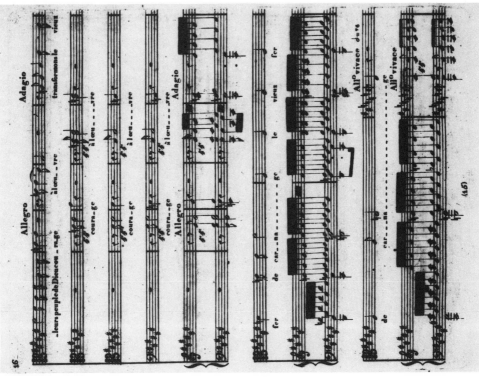

18
en unpaisi_ble soc qui creuse nos sil_lons plus dedroits oppres_
8va
Loco
_seurs plus dehai_ne sau_va - - - - - - - - ge plus dedroits oppres_
(15)

19
_seurs plus de hai_ne sau_va - - - - - - - - geplusdedroits oppresseursplusdehai_ _ne sau_
- - - va - - - - ge honneur hon- - - neur aux travailleurs
honneur honneur honneur honneur aux travailleurs
honneur honneuraux travailleurs
(15)

20
à nos saints ba_tail_lons honneur honneur
à nos saints ba_tail_lons à nos saints batail_lons
à nos saints ba_tail_lons à nos saints batail_lons
à nos saints ba_tail_lons à nos saints batail_lons
plus dedroitsoppresseursplusdehainesau _ va_ _ _ _ _ _ geplusdehai_ _ne sau_ _ _ va_ _ _
Cres
plusdedroits oppresseurs plus dehai_nesau_va_ge de hai_ _ne sau_ _ _ va_ _ _
Cres
plusdedroits oppresseurs plus dehai_nesau_va_ge de hai_ _ne sau_ _ _ va_ _ _
Cres
plusdedroits oppresseurs plus dehai_nesau_va_ ge de hai_ _ne sau_ _ _ va_ _ _
Cres
(15)

21
ge honneur hon _ _ neur aux travailleurs à nossaints batail_
ge honneur honneur honneur honneur aux travailleurs à nos saints batail
ge honneur honneur aux travailleurs à nos saints batail
ge honneur honneur aux travailleurs à nos saints batail
lons honneur honneur honneur aux travail _
_lons à nos saints bataillons honneur
_lons à nos saints bataillons honneur
_lons à nos saints bataillons honneur
(15)

22
Adagio
leurs à nossaints bataillons hon _ _neur honneur à nossaints bataillons honneurhon_ _
honneur à nossaints bataillons honneur à nossaints bataillons
honneur à nossaintsbataillons honneur à nossaints bataillons
honneur à nossaintsbataillons honneur à nossaints bataillons
Adagio
Adagio
gloireà ce_lui qui vit qui vit en nous il ar_ _rache auxtour_mens l'hu_
_ _neur à ce_lui qui vit qui vit en nous il ar_ _racheauxtour_mens l'hu_
gloire à ce_lui qui vit qui vit en nous il ar_ _racheauxtour_mens l'hu_
gloireà ce_lui qui vit qui vit en nous il ar_ _racheauxtour_mens l'hu_
Adagio
(15)

23
_ma_nite flé_ _tri_e Saint Simon soit bé_ _ni soit bé_ _ni sois bé_ _
_ma_nite flé_ _tri_e Saint Simon soit bé_ _ni soit bé_ _ni sois bé_ _
_ma_ni te flé_ _tri_e Saint Simon soit bé_ _ni sois béni
_ma_ _ _ni te flé_ _tri_e Saint Simon soit bé_ _ni soit bé_ _ni sois bé_ _
_ _ni sois bé_ni ta paro_le de vie de sadouceharmo_ni_e
_ _ni sois bé_ni ta paro_le de vie de sadouceharmo_ni_e de sa
Saint Simon sois bé_ni ta paro_le de vie de sadouceharmo_ni_e de sa
_ _ni sois bé_ni ta paro_le de vie de sadouceharmo_ni_e de sa
15

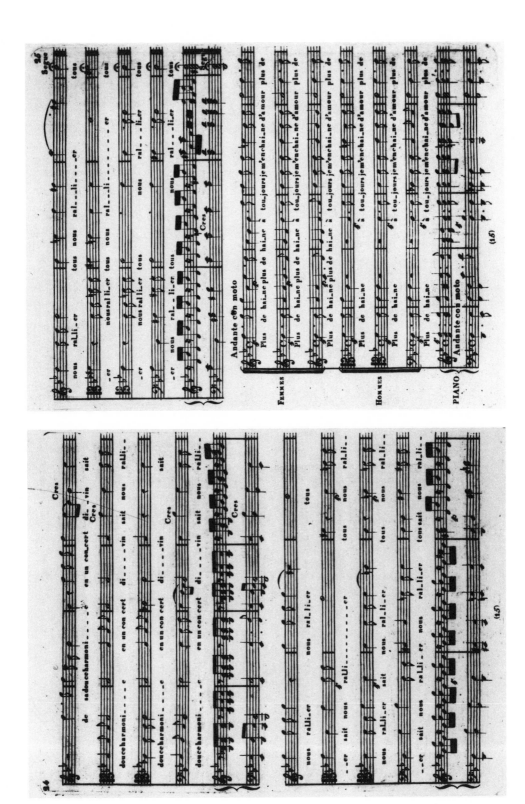

haine plus de hai_ne à toujours je m'enchaine d'amour d'a_ _mour à toujours je m'en_
haine plus de hai_ne à toujours je m'enchaine d'amour d'a_ _mour à toujours je m'en_
haine plus de hai_ne à toujours je m'enchaine d'amour d'a_ _mour à toujours je m'en_
haine à toujours je m'enchaine d'amour d'a_ mour à toujours je m'en_
haine à toujours je m'enchaine d'amour d'a_ mour à toujours je m'en_
haine à toujours je m'enchaine d'amour d'a_ mour à toujours je m'en_
- - - _chai_ _ _ne d'a_ _mour plus de hai_ne plus de haine
- - - _chai_ _ _ne d'a_ _mour plus de hai_ne plus de haine
- - - _chai_ _ _ne d'a_ _mour plus de hai_ne plus de haine
- - - _chai_ _ _ne d'a_ _mour plus de hai_ne à tou_
- - - _chai_ _ _ne d'a_ _mour plus de haine à tou_ _
- - - _chai_ _ _ne d'a_ _mour plus de hai_ne à tou_ _
(15)

je m'en_chai_ne d'a_mour à tou_jours tou_jours tou_jours d'a - - -
je m'en_chai_ne d'a_mour à tou_jours tou_jours tou_jours d'a - - -
je m'en_chai_ne d'a_mour à tou_jours tou_jours tou_jours d'a - - -
jours toujours tou _jours d'a_ _ _mour
jours toujours tou _jours d'a_ _ _mour
jours toujours tou _jours je m'en chai_ne d'amour d'a_ _ _mour
_mour je m'en_chai_ne d'a_mour je m'en_chai_ _ _ne d'a_mour d'a_ _ _ _mour
_mour je m'en_chai_ne d'a_mour je m'en_chai_ _ _ne d'a_mour d'a_ _ _ _mour
_mour je m'en_chai_ne d'a_mour je m'en_chai_ _ _ne d'a_mour d'a_ _ _ _mour
je m'en_chai_ne d'a_mour je m'en_chai_ _ _ne d'a_mour d'a_ _ _ _mour
je m'en_chai_ne d'a_mour je m'en_chai_ _ _ne d'a_mour d'a_ _ _ mour
je m'en_chai_ne d'a_mour je m'en_chai_ _ _ne d'a_mour d'a_ _ _ mour
(15)

2. Félicien David, *Appel* (text by Bergier, "ouvrier carreleur")

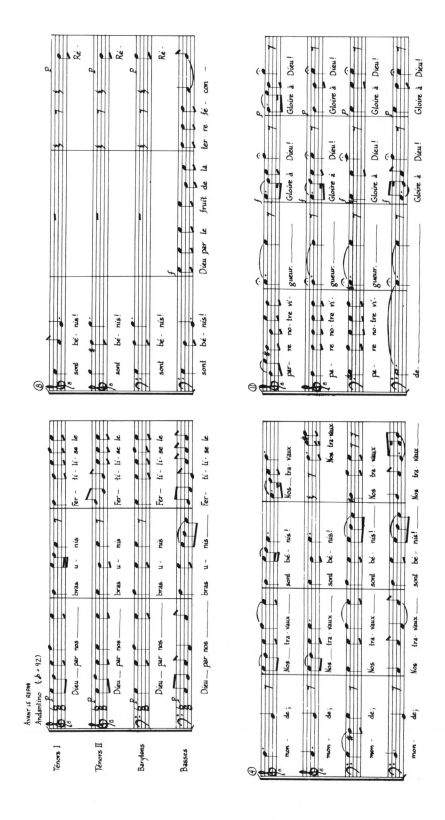

3. Félicien David, *Avant et après le repas* (text by Emile Barrault)

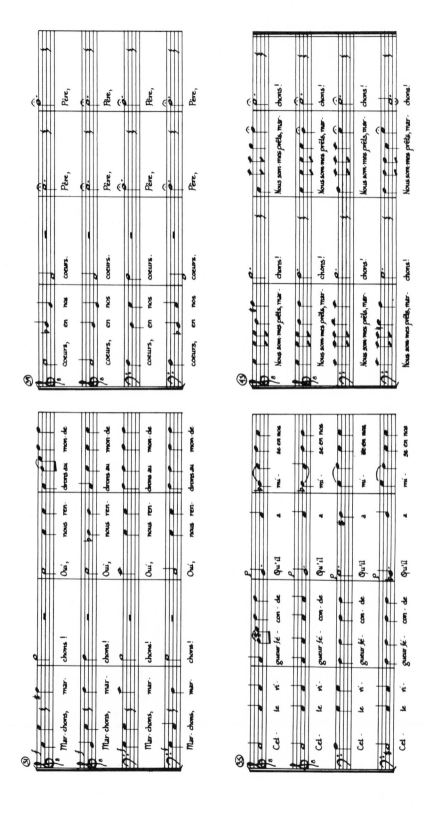

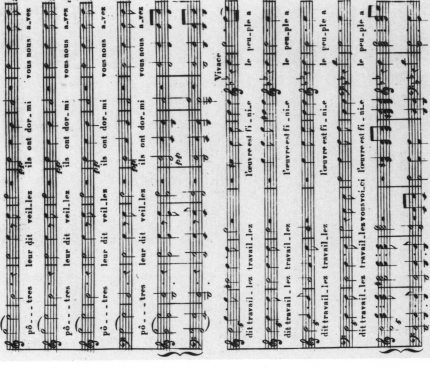

5. Félicien David, *Le Retour du Père* or *Salut* (text by Achille Rousseau)

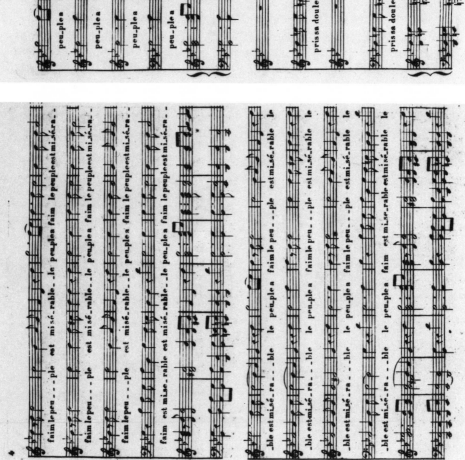

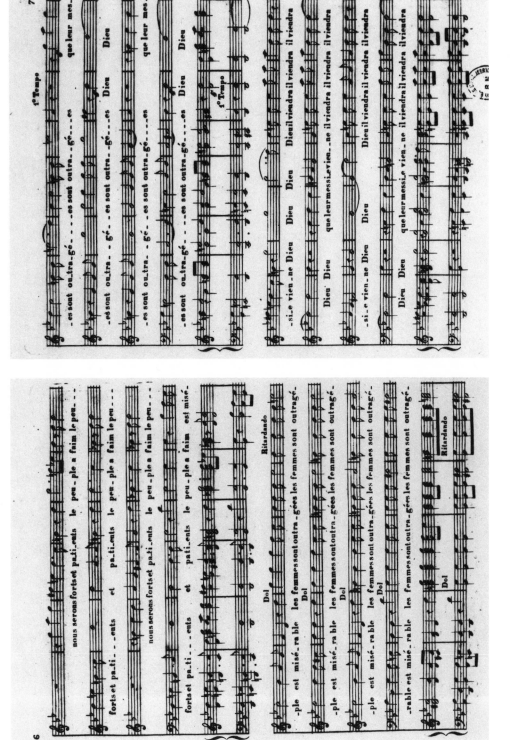

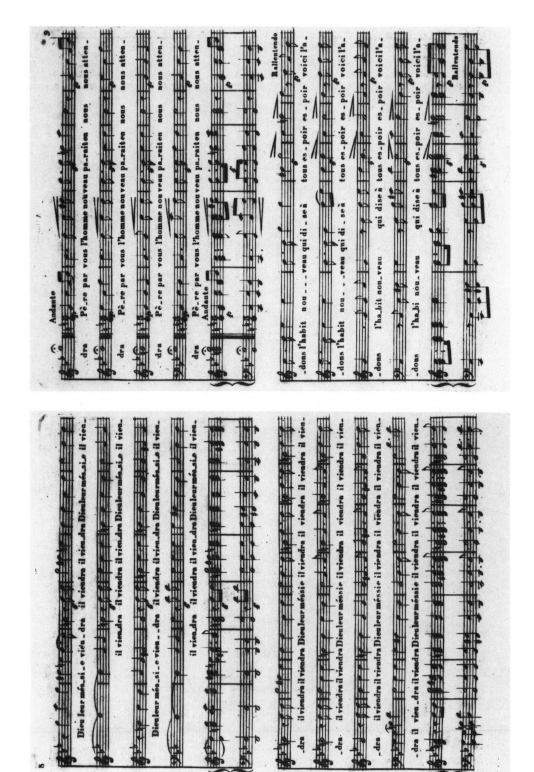

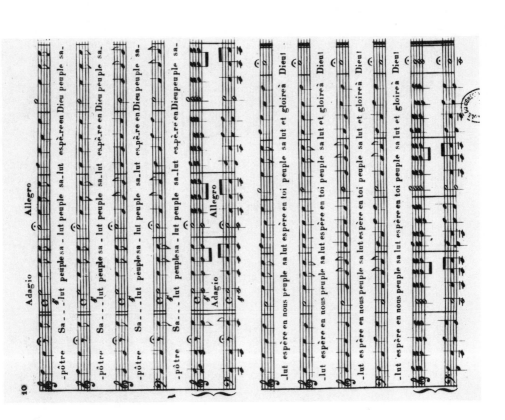

6. Félicien David, *Le Nouveau Temple* or *Chant de l'ouverture des travaux du Temple*
(text by Emile Barrault)

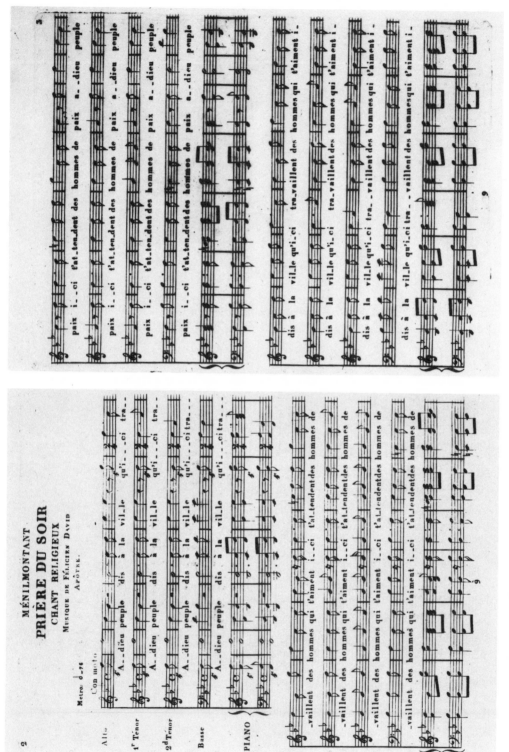

9. Félicien David, *Prière du soir* (text by Gustave d'Eichthal)

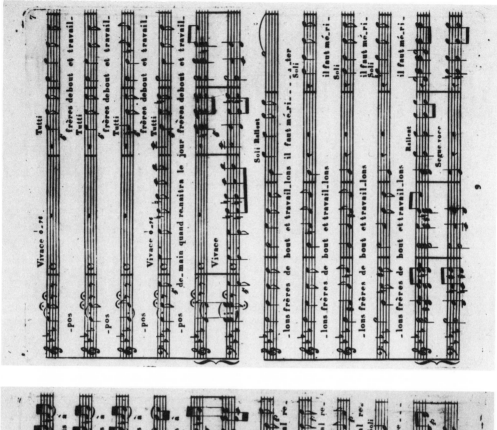
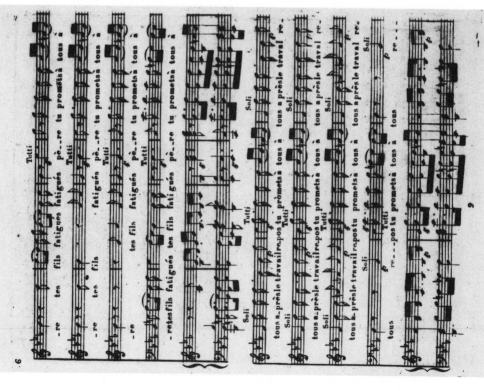

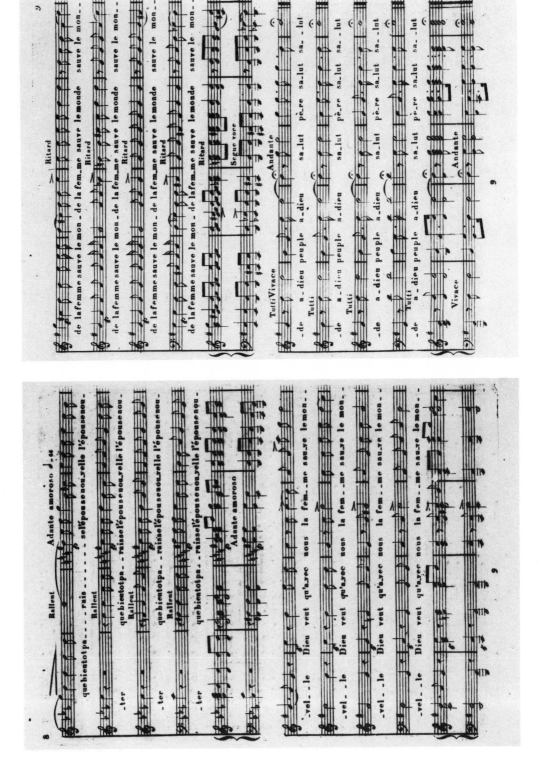

10. Félicien David, *Prière du matin* (text by Emile Barrault)

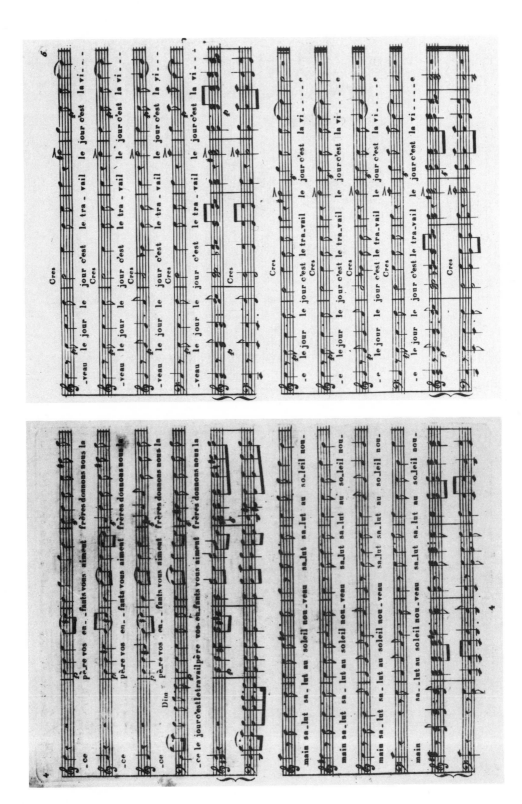

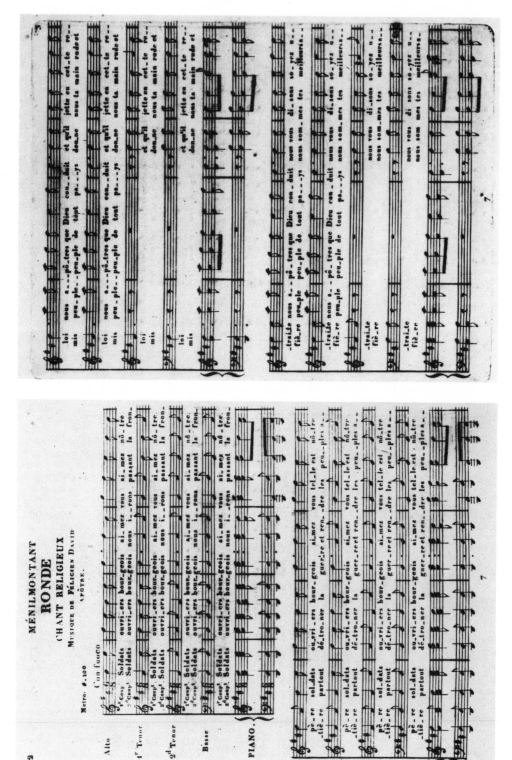

14. Félicien David, *Ronde* (text by Edouard Pouyat)

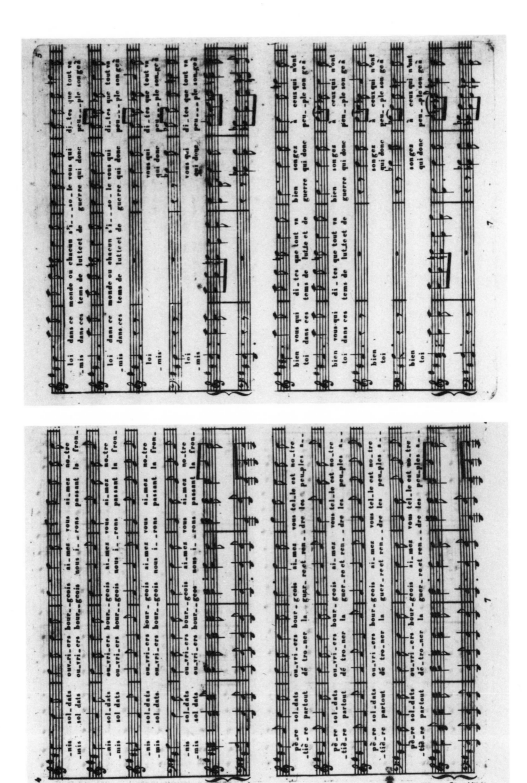

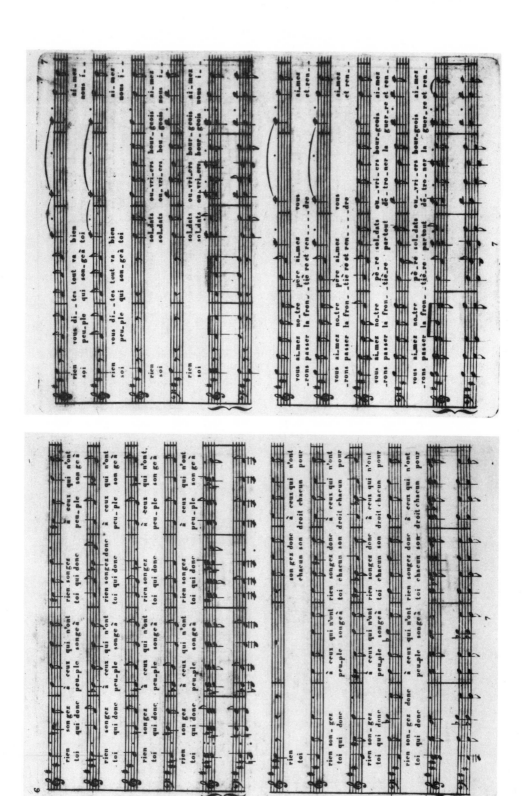

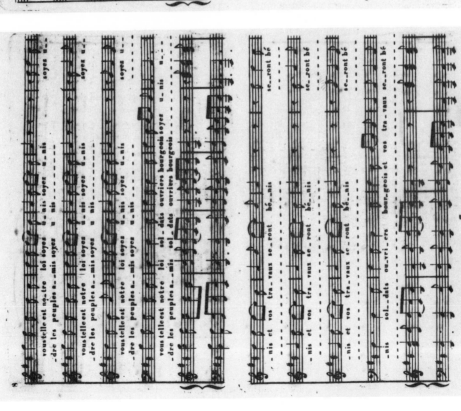

3.e c.t

Soldats ouvriers bourgeois,
Nous venons affranchir la femme
Nous venlons briser le joug
Qui pesait sur sa dignité.
Femme, femme nos cris d'espoir
N'éveillent-ils pas ton ame;
A nos cris de liberté
Répondras-tu pas liberté.
Soldats..... (comme 1er & pre vers)
Faudra-t-il tous montrer les maux
Qui naissent de votre éclavage
Long tems il les fallut souffrir
Il faut aujourd'hui en finir   (Bis)
Il faut, femmes en finir   (Bis)
Il faut aujourd'hui en finir   (Bis)
    (Alto) Aujourd'hui en finir
Soldats ouvriers bourgeois
Nous venons affranchir la femme
(Alto) (Du joug
(Nous voulons briser le joug
Qui pesait sur sa dignité.
Soyez unis..... etc

7

CHANT SAINT-SIMONIEN.

Soldats, ouvriers, bourgeois,
Aimez-nous, aimez notre Père ;
Soldats, ouvriers, bourgeois,
Aimez-vous, voilà notre loi.

Mille cris partout répétés
Viennent assiéger notre asile,
Et calmes et le front tranquille,
Nous leur répondons : *Écoutez !*

   Soldats, etc.

Ils ont dit : Armons-nous contre eux
De mandats et de baïonnettes,
Et nous, chantant l'hymne des fêtes,
Nous annonçons des jours heureux.

   Soldats, etc.

Qui peut arrêter notre ardeur ?
Devant des juges qu'on nous traîne,
Pendant qu'on forge notre chaîne,
Nous répétons toujours en chœur :

   Soldats, etc.

Notre crime c'est de vouloir
Affranchir le peuple et la femme ;
C'est de sentir au fond de l'âme
Et leurs douleurs et leur espoir.

   Soldats, etc.

Quand le peuple expire de faim,
Que sa grande voix nous appelle,
Pouvons-nous lui crier : Rebelle,
Attends encor jusqu'à demain.

   Soldats, etc.

Nous l'avons pressé de s'unir,
Et sur son immense bannière,
Au milieu de flots de lumière,
Nous avons écrit *l'Avenir.*

   Soldats, etc.

La femme criait : Malheur !
Mon front pâlit par la souffrance.
Dans une froide indifférence,
Devions-nous fermer notre cœur.

   Soldats, etc.

Non, non, notre Père a parlé ;
Le doigt posé sur la blessure,
Par sa bouche hardie et sûre,
Le remède fut révélé.

   Soldats, etc.

D'une éclatante vérité,
Qui fait rougir et qui réveille,
Nous avons frappé leur oreille ;
Ils ont dit : *Immoralité !*

   Soldats, etc.

Comme une autre langue de feu,
Cette parole de lumière
Dans les palais, dans la chaumière,
Descendra sur l'aile de Dieu.

   Soldats, etc.

Elle ira, grandissant encor,
Résonner par toute la terre
Et fera rouler notre sphère
Au sein d'un éternel accord.

   Soldats, etc.

Peuple ! le temple s'est ouvert :
Qu'aux accents de ta foi profonde,
Sur le vaste orchestre du monde,
S'élève un sublime concert.

   Soldats, ouvriers, bourgeois,
   Aimez-nous, aimez notre Père ;
   Soldats, ouvriers, bourgeois,
   Aimez-vous, voilà notre loi.

IMPRIMERIE DE DAVID,
boulevart Poissonnière, n. 4 bis.

14a. Alternative text for *Ronde,* by Lagache

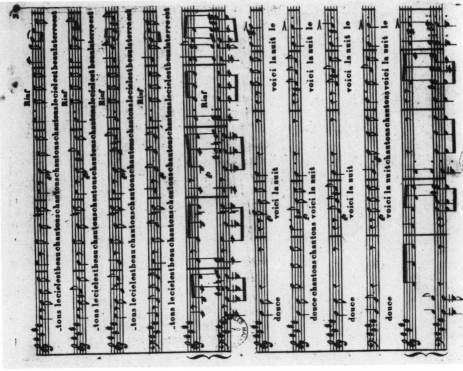

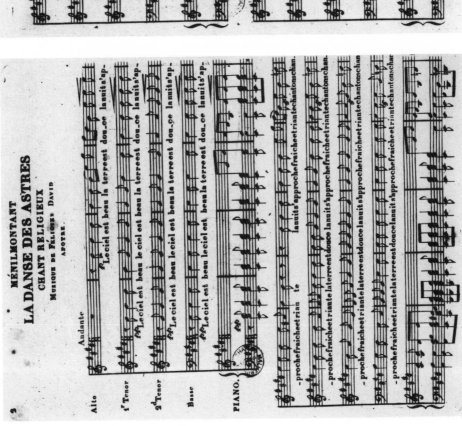

15. Félicien David, *La Danse des astres* (text by Charles Duveyrier and Achille Rousseau)

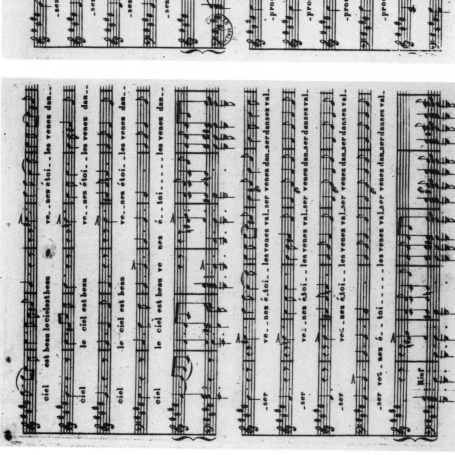

6
-toiles chantons chantons voici la nuit chantons chantons chantons chantons
-toiles chantons chantons voici la nuit chantons chantons chantons chantons
-toiles chantons chantons voici la nuit chantons chantons chantons chantons
-toiles chantons chantons voici la nuit chantons chantons chantons chantons
VALSE
voici la nuit fraiche, levez vous é - toi - les, rompu de fa - ti - gue
voici la nuit fraiche, levez vous é - toi - les, rompu de fa - ti - gue
voici la nuit fraiche, levez vous é - toi - les, rompu de fa - ti - gue
voici la nuit fraiche, levez vous é - toi - les, rompu de fa - ti - gue
Violon ou voix ad libitum
Violoncelle.
VALSE

7
le peuple se couche les étoiles valsent les planè-tes tournent
le peuple se couche les étoiles valsent les planè-tes tournent
le peuple se couche les étoiles valsent les planè-tes tournent
le peuple se couche les étoiles valsent les planè-tes tournent
quand pourras-tu peu-ple danser et val-ser? a moi qui suis peu-ple
quand pourras-tu peu-ple danser et val-ser? a moi qui suis peu-ple
quand pourras-tu peu-ple danser et val-ser? a moi qui suis peu-ple
quand pourras-tu peu-ple danser et val-ser? a moi qui suis peu-ple

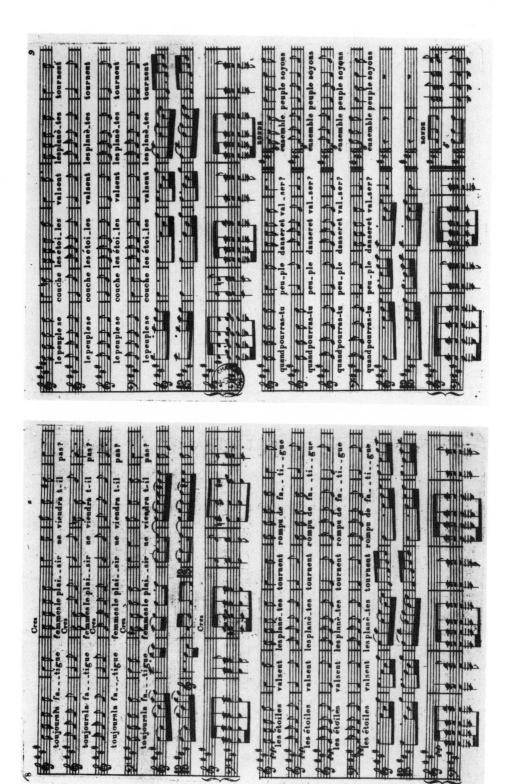

10
frèresnous sommes peu_.ple. avecnous lajoiel'espé_rance et
frèresnous sommes peu_.ple. avecnous lajoiel'espé_rance et
frèresnous sommes peu_.ple. avecnous lajoiel'espé_rance et le cou.
frèresnoussommes peu_ _ _ _ _ _ _ple. avecnous lajoiel'espé_rance et le cou.
lecoura_ge avectoi peuple avectoipeupleunis chantons chantonsdan.
lecoura_ge avectoi peuple avectoi peupleunis chantons chantonsdan.
_ra_ _ _ _ _ _ ge avectoi peuple avectoi peupleunis chantons chantons dan.
_ra_ _ _ _ _ _ _ge a_vec toi peu_ple u_nis chantons chantons dan.

11
_sonschantonsdan sons dansons_en ron_ depeuplevoi ci letemsheureuxoul'hy_ver
sonschantonsdan sonsdansons en ron depeuplevoi ci letemsheureuxoul'hy_ver
sons chantonsdan sonsdansons en ron depeuplevoi ci letemsheureuxoul'hy_ver
_sonschantonsdan sonsdansons en ron_depeuplevoici letemsheureuxoul'hy_ver
aurases plaisirqui te con_so_ _le rontensembleunisnousdan_se_ronsespère
aurases plaisirqui te con_so_ _le rontensembleunisnousdan_se_ronsespère
aura ses plaisirqui te con_so_ _le rontensemble unisnousdan_se_ronsespère
aurases plaisirqui te con_so_ _le rontensemble unisnousdan_se_ronsespère

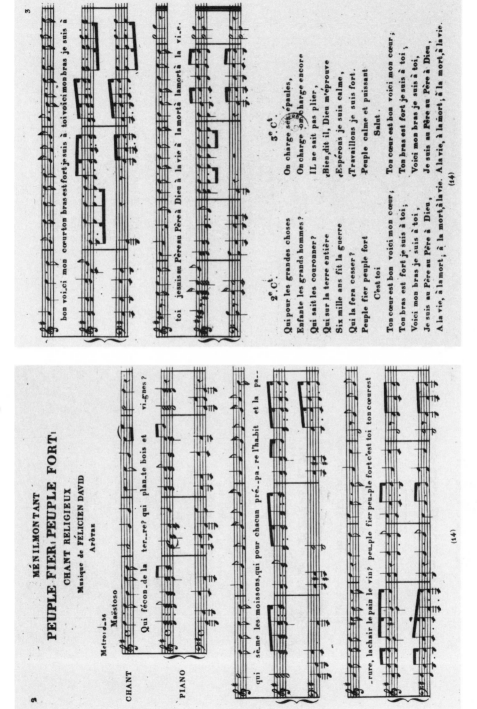

16. Félicien David, *Peuple fier! peuple fort!* or *Le Peuple* (text by Achille Rousseau)

7 CHANTS SAINT-SIMONIENS.

Nous TRAVAILLONS par nos *chants*, nos *écrits*,
notre *parole*, nos *actes* :
A la gloire du PÈRE,
A la venue de la MÈRE,
Car le salut du PEUPLE en dépend.

LE PEUPLE.

Travaux.

Qui féconde la terre ;
Qui plante bois et vignes ,
Qui sème les moissons ,
Qui pour chacun prépare
L'habit et la parure
La chair, le pain, le vin ?
Peuple fier, peuple fort
C'est toi.

Ton cœur est bon, voici mon cœur ;
Ton bras est fort, je suis à toi ;
Voici mon bras ; je suis à toi,
Je suis au Père, au Père, à Dieu,
A la vie, à la mort, à la mort, à la vie.

Qui des flancs de la terre
Tire le grès, le marbre,
L'or, le plomb et le fer ,
Qui fait sa face belle
En la parant de villes ,

(2)

De chars et de vaisseaux ?
Peuple fier, peuple fort,
C'est toi.
Ton cœur est bon, voici mon cœur , etc.

Qui pour les grandes choses
Enfante les grands hommes ?
Qui sait les couronner ,
Qui sur la terre entière
Six mille ans fit la guerre !
Qui la fera cesser ?
Peuple fier, peuple fort
C'est toi.
Ton cœur est bon, voici mon cœur, etc.

Patience du Peuple.

On charge ses épaules ,
On charge, on charge encore ;
Il ne sait pas plier :
Bon, dit-il, Dieu m'éprouve,
Espérons avec calme ;
Travaillons, je suis fort ;
Peuple calme et puissant,
Salut.
Ton cœur est bon, voici mon cœur , etc.

Oui, répète le peuple,
Travaillons et qu'importe,
Oisifs et vagabonds ,
Ma force leur pardonne ,
Un oisif n'est pas homme
C'est un chétif enfant.
Peuple calme et puissant
Salut.
Ton cœur est bon, voici mon cœur, etc.

Dieu veut que je travaille ,
C'est que Dieu m'a fait homme.

16a. Songster pages with additional text for *Peuple fier* (Achille Rousseau)

Je nourris les enfans,
A quiconque travaille
Dieu promet récompense.
J'attends en travaillant.
Peuple calme et puissant,
     Salut,
Ton cœur est bon, voici mon cœur;
Ton bras est fort, je suis à toi;
Voici mon bras, je suis à toi,
Je suis au Père, au Père, à Dieu, à la vie.
A la vie, à la mort; à la mort, à la vie.

       ROUSSEAU, *Apôtre.*

L'APPEL AU PEUPLE.

PEUPLE, si notre voix réclame,
C'est pour toi, pour ta dignité.
Par nous les vertus de ton âme
Jailliront de l'obscurité.
FEMMES ! vos larmes sont les nôtres,
Mais espérez un sort plus doux.
Femmes, peuple, aimez les apôtres
D'un Dieu de paix, d'amour pour vous.
    Gloire à Dieu !
    Gloire à Dieu !
    Gloire à Dieu !
    Gloire à Dieu !

En disant à l'homme de guerre,
Ton fer, il le faut déposer;
A l'avenir tout adversaire
Sera vaincu par un baiser.

29. Félicien David, "Belle, oh belle comme l'ange" from *Hymne à la Mère* (text by Emile Barrault)

nous, Dieu bonne en-tends-nous, Dieu bon - ne en- tends-nous, Dieu bon - ne,

nous, Dieu bonne en-tends-nous, Dieu bon - ne en — tends-nous, Dieu

nous, Dieu bonne en-tends-nous, Dieu bon - ne en — tends- nous, Dieu

nous, Dieu bonne en-tends-nous, Dieu bon - ne en — tends-nous, Dieu

bon - ne en — tends-nous! Belle, oh bel - le __, Belle, oh bel - le com-me l'an —

bon - ne en — tends-nous! Belle, oh bel-le com-me l'an —

bon - ne en — tends-nous! Belle, oh bel-le com-me l'an —

bon — ne en — tends-nous! Belle, oh bel - le com-me l'an —

ge Du Dieu de beau-té, Du Dieu de beau-té, _____ Pa - raî - tra l'é - pou -

ge Du Dieu du beau-té, Du Dieu de beau-té, Pa - raî - tra l'é - pou -

ge Du Dieu du beau-té, Du Dieu de beau-té, Pa - raî - tra l'é - pou -

ge Du Dieu du beau-té, Du Dieu de beau-té, Pa - raî - tra l'é - pou -

se; Dieu bon - ne en-tends- nous, Dieu bon-ne en-tends nous, Dieu bon-ne en-tends-

se; Dieu bon-ne en-tends- nous, Dieu bon-ne en-tends nous, Dieu bon-ne en - tends-

se; Dieu bon - ne en-tends- nous, Dieu bonne en - tends-nous, Dieu bon-ne en - tends-

se; Dieu bon - ne en - tends- nous, Dieu bon-ne en-tends-nous, Dieu bon-ne en - tends-

nous, Dieu bon-ne en-tends-nous, Dieu bonne en-tends-nous, Dieu bonne en-tends- nous!

those that emphasize "social unity and shared normative systems" (*Dictionary,* 651). Saint-Simon and his disciples adopted the former view when describing present-day society and the latter when limning the organic society of the future and its art.

13. In 1958 Iggers explicitly used such terms as "propaganda," "tools of the state," and "political control" to assert a relationship between the role of art in Saint-Simonism and in the "modern totalitarian state" (*Cult of Authority,* 158; cf. his Introduction to *Doctrine,* xliv–xlv). By 1972 he came to feel hesitant about "using the term 'totalitarianism' " to link these two very different phenomena (Preface to the Second Edition, *Doctrine,* vi–vii).

14. For some related misunderstandings of Saint-Simon's doctrine of art as a means of social control, see Chapter 5 below (Constant and Stendhal) and Leroy, *Socialisme,* 114. On the positive meaning of "propaganda" in the nineteenth century, see Corcoran, *Before Marx,* 22–23 n.19.

15. Wellek, *Modern Criticism* 3:29. Hunt argues that "art for art's sake" was rather an extension of the "social" thrust than a reaction against it (*Socialisme,* 339–46); cf. Hauser, *Social History of Art* 3:192–96.

16. Saint-Simon, *Nouveau Christianisme,* in *OSSE* 23:116–17, 166–67 (the quotation).

17. Ibid., in *OSSE* 23:138–39.

18. Ibid., in *OSSE* 23:160–62. Translation based on Markham, *Saint-Simon,* 103–4.

19. Manuel, *New World,* 145, 335. Regarding Plato's influence on all later utopians, see Manuel and Manuel, *Utopian Thought,* 104–12. For Plato's writings on music and society, see Andrew Barker, ed., *Greek Musical Writings,* vol. 1 (Cambridge: Cambridge University Press, 1984), 124–69.

20. Abrams, *Mirror and the Lamp,* 14–21. The eighteenth-century connection is discussed briefly by Bénichou (*Temps,* 248–60, 277).

21. Quotations from Abrams, *Mirror and the Lamp,* 14 (Sidney) and 19 (Johnson); Wellek, *Modern Criticism* 1:21 (Molière); Rousseau, *Lettre à d'Alembert,* 181–83; William Weber, "The Contemporaneity of Eighteenth-Century Musical Taste," *Musical Quarterly* 70 (1984):191 (Weedon).

22. It is almost entirely ignored by Wellek (*Modern Criticism*); Hauser treats it with some seriousness, though briefly, in *Social History of Art* 3:143–63.

23. Elizabeth Gilmore Holt, ed., *A Documentary History of Art,* vol. 3 (New York: Doubleday and Co., Anchor Books, 1966), 190–91, 265–71, and pl. 30.

24. Iggers, *Cult of Authority,* 39; Manuel, *Prophets,* 115–18.

25. *Lettres d'un habitant de Genève à ses contemporains* (1802–3), in *OSSE* 15:51–52. There were two editions: Geneva (addressed "à l'humanité)", 1802; and Paris, 1803. (Fournel, *Bibliographie,* 11–12; *OSSE* 15:7–10; Manuel, *New World,* 61, 379–80.)

26. *Cult of Authority,* 169.

27. Donakowski, *Muse,* 33–75; David Lloyd Dowd, *Pageant-Master of the Republic: Jacques-Louis David and the French Revolution* (Lincoln: University of Nebraska Press, 1948); *New Grove Dictionary,* s.v. "Revolutionary hymn"; Ringer, "Barthélemy." On Saint-Simon's intimate knowledge of the Revolutionary theophilanthropic cults, see Manuel, *New World,* 123–25, and the discussions listed in Walch, *Bibliographie,* 46–48.

28. *Nouveau Christianisme,* in *OSSE* 23:162.

29. Hunt, *Socialisme,* 19.

CHAPTER 4

1. *Nouveau Christianisme,* in *OSSE* 23:177–80; "Dialogue" (from *Opinions littéraires*), in *OSSE* 39:248; Thibert, *Rôle social,* 12.

2. *Lettres d'un habitant de Genève,* in *OSSE* 15:11.

3. Manuel, *New World,* 13–14.

4. Manuel, *Prophets,* 113–14.

5. L. Halévy, "Souvenirs"; Hubbard, *Saint-Simon,* 7–29; biography in *OSSE* 1:1–21; Dondo, *French Faust,* 5–89; and Manuel, *New World,* 9–58.

6. The following five paragraphs are based mainly on statements from Saint-Simon himself in Halévy, *Souvenirs,* 526–28; ibid., ed. Brunet, 167–68; and Hubbard, *Saint-Simon,* 34–37.

7. Mme de Bawr, *Souvenirs,* 21–33 (Grétry), 49–53 (Garat), 244–55 (theater), 304–5 (Mme Gail), and briefer comments passim; and idem, *Histoire de la musique,* 255–56 (Grétry and Roze). The composer Boïeldieu and the singer Elleviou also taught her and assisted her efforts at

composition (Dondo, *French Faust,* 89–96, citing Elise Gagne, *Mme de Bawr,* 10–11, 22–23).

8. Halévy, "Souvenirs," 528; ibid., ed. Brunet, 168.

9. Thibert, *Rôle social,* 7–8.

10. Ibid., 10.

11. Halévy, "Souvenirs," 535; ibid., ed. Brunet, 171.

12. Ibid., 528; ibid; ed. Brunet, 168.

13. *Lettres,* in *OSSE* 15:11–13.

14. Ibid., in *OSSE* 15:12–13, 24.

15. Ibid., in *OSSE* 15:12–14.

16. Ibid., in *OSSE* 15:13–14.

17. Ibid., in *OSSE* 15:47.

18. Manuel, *Prophets,* 124–29.

19. *Lettres,* in *OSSE* 15:21–22.

20. Manuel, *Prophets,* 118 (the quotation), 109–110.

21. Manuel, *New World,* 94–109.

22. *Catéchisme des industriels* (1823–24), in *OSSE* 37:3–4; also 38:4.

23. Saint-Simon's debt to liberal economics is demonstrated in Briscoe, *Saint-Simonism,* 11–120; on his disciples' increasingly vehement critique of the privileged classes and championing of the *prolétaires,* see ibid., 121–285, and idem, "Unfinished Revolution."

24. Subscription list in *OSSE* 19:6–7.

25. *Catéchisme,* in *OSSE* 37:3–4.

26. *L'Industrie; ou, Discussions politiques . . .* (1817) 2:54, cited in Leroy, *Socialisme,* 108.

27. Parable ("Premier extrait de l'*Organisateur*"), in *OSSE* 20:21–22.

28. *L'Organisateur,* first installment (December 1819), in *OSSE* 20:52–53. Translation based on that in Manuel, *New World,* 315.

29. Manuel, *New World,* 315.

30. *L'Organisateur* (December 1819). See note 28 above.

31. Ibid., in *OSSE* 20:51. Manuel suggests (*Prophets,* 122) that one can already see here the artist moving into a favored role of "original inventor" and the scientists reduced to "emendator." (Bénichou makes the same point—*Temps,* 258.)

32. Ibid., in *OSSE* 20:52–54.

33. Ibid., in *OSSE* 20:52–53.

34. Manuel, *New World,* 292–93, 337–38; the quotation is from *Opinions littéraires* (1825).

35. *Opinions littéraires,* in *OSSE* 39:246–48. (The passage was surely approved by Saint-Simon, even if not written by him.)

36. Manuel, *New World,* 206–14.

37. On the "revolt of the subscribers," which began in 1817, see Manuel, *New World,* 199–205 (but also Gouhier's contrasting view, cited by Manuel on 215); and Dautry, *Saint-Simon,* 32–36, 136–37 (unpublished autobiographical fragment). The quotation from the parable is in *OSSE* 20:24.

38. *Saint-Simon,* 113.

39. *Opinions littéraires,* in *OSSE* 39:131–32; cf. *Lettres* (1802): "TOUS LES HOMMES TRAVAILLERONT" (in *OSSE* 15:55; see also 15:57–58).

40. As Saint-Simon later realized—*Opinions littéraires,* in *OSSE* 39:248.

41. Manuel, *New World,* 325–43.

42. Ibid., 344–47. Rodrigues's interest in "social" literature is seen in his anthology, *Poésies sociales* (1844); Halévy's, in the "Dialogue" (see Chapter 5 below).

43. Manuel, *New World,* 348–63; on Rodrigues's contribution, see pp. 346 and 353, also *OSSE* 23:12.

44. *Nouveau Christianisme,* in *OSSE* 23:173 (cf. 23:109).

45. Ibid., in *OSSE* 23:177–80. The passage is couched in what, the context makes clear, is a misleading use of the past tense ("J'ai dû d'abord m'adresser aux riches . . ."); this corrects Manuel, *Prophets,* 140.

46. Ibid., in *OSSE* 23:185–86.

CHAPTER 5

1. The authorship of the "Dialogue" has been a matter of some dispute. Halévy seems to have been the main author and editor (Hubbard, *Saint-Simon,* 101–2), but Saint-Simon also had a part in it (as Comte heard it said—Manuel, *New World,* 338—and Halévy himself admitted—"Souvenirs," 539). In 1833 Fournel cited Rodrigues, not Saint-Simon, as Halévy's collaborator (*Bibliographie,* 59, carried over into *OSSE* 23:11; the attribution to Rodrigues alone in *OSSE* 39:199 is either a slip or a willful attempt to mislead). We may conclude that the "Dialogue" is a free reworking (mainly by Halévy?) of discussions among all three: Halévy (represented by the *Artiste*), Saint-Simon (*Savant*), and Rodrigues (*Industriel*). (Bénichou, among others, discredits as "late"—which

it isn't, since it first appears in 1833—the claim that Rodrigues had a part in the work [*Temps*, 260, 288, 319].)

2. Hunt, *Socialisme*, 19; Iggers, *Cult of Authority*, 174–75.

3. Saint-Simon originally intended *Nouveau Christianisme* for inclusion in the *Opinions* but decided that separate publication would give it greater weight (Manuel, *New World*, 353).

4. Lambert's notes, Ars 7804, cited in Thibert, *Rôle social*, 16; *OSSE* 24:76, cited in Hunt, *Socialisme*, 21. Cf. Bénichou, *Temps*, pp. 276–77.

5. See Hunt, *Socialisme*, 21–27, and Charléty, *Saint-Simonisme*, bk. 2, chap. 1, pt. 1, pp. 61–67.

6. "Dialogue," in *OSSE* 39:205.

7. Ibid., in *OSSE* 39:206, 210–11.

8. Ibid., in *OSSE* 39:212–13, 215–16. The word for lead is *diriger*.

9. Ibid., in *OSSE* 39:220–25. The last of these phrases reads: "Quand les arts suivent le mouvement des esprits."

10. Hunt, *Socialisme*, 11.

11. *Du système industriel*, pt. 1 (1821), in *OSSE* 22:78–79.

12. Hunt, *Socialisme*, 12.

13. On the Romantic genius, see *Dictionary of the History of Ideas*, s.v. "Romanticism in Literature" and "Genius, Musical." Saint-Simon's glimpse of the artistic genius is in *OSSE* 15:14: "His place . . . [is] above all other men, even those who are invested with the highest authority."

14. "Dialogue," in *OSSE* 39:225; 223–25.

15. *OSSE* 20:52–53; 22:78–79.

16. "Dialogue," in *OSSE* 39:212–13.

17. Leroy, *Socialisme*, 114.

18. "Dialogue," in *OSSE* 39:210–11.

19. Hauser, *Social History of Art* 3:196–207.

20. All unidentified quotations in this paragraph and the three following paragraphs come from articles in *Le Producteur*, vols. 1–2 (1825–26), as cited in Thibert, *Rôle social*, 21–24; cf. Fournel, *Bibliographie*, 35–38.

21. Cf. another statement by Halévy, *Producteur* 1:74–83, cited in Hunt, *Socialisme*, 22; also a much later version of the same thought: "The Soviet writer is an engineer of human souls"—Stalin at the Eighteenth Party Conference, Moscow, 10 March 1939, cited in Rena Moisenko, *Realist Music: 25 Soviet Composers*, (London: Meridian Books, 1944), [5].

22. *Producteur* 2:60 (Garnier), in Charléty, *Saint-Simonisme*, bk. 1, chap. 1, pt. 2, p. 41.

23. See Chapter 3. For a rare "utilitarian" remark on art by Saint-Simon, see "De l'organisation sociale," in *OSSE* 39:131–32.

24. Thibert, *Rôle social*, 24; and Hunt, *Socialisme*, 23–24. Cf. Stendhal, *D'un nouveau complot contre les industriels*, in Stendhal, *Mélanges de littérature*, vol. 2, ed. Henri Martineau (Paris: Le Divan, 1933), and—for his later views—Fernand Rude, "Stendhal et les Saint-Simoniens," *Economies et Sociétés* 4, no. 6 [June 1970]:1121–47.

25. *Producteur* 2:185, cited in Hunt, *Socialisme*, 22.

26. Lambert's notes, Ars 7804, cited in Thibert, *Rôle social*, 16.

27. Ars 7643, cited in Thibert, *Rôle social*, 24, and in *OSSE* 1:171.

28. Enfantin, prospectus to vol. 3 of *Le Producteur*, in Thibert, *Rôle social*, 24, and in *OSSE* 1:172. Cf. Bénichou, *Temps*, 276.

29. [Philippe Buchez], "Quelques réflexions sur la littérature et les beaux-arts," *Producteur* 4, no. 2 (August 1826):189–211. (Buchez's authorship is stated in Fournel, *Bibliographie*, 54.) Citation from p. 204.

30. Hunt, *Socialisme*, 20, 24.

CHAPTER 6

1. Hunt, *Socialisme*, 24–27, and Charléty, *Saint-Simonisme*, bk. 1, pt. 1, pp. 51–67.

2. *OSSE* 3:229, 21.

3. Enfantin, letters of 1829 (Ars 7643, 7644), cited in Thibert, *Rôle social*, 28; cf. *OSSE* 2:158, 160. Cf. *Organisateur*, 24 June 1830. A full 1,500 copies were published (the first edition of the *Doctrine* was only a bit larger: 2,000 copies), and there was some interest in republishing it in 1833 (Fournel, *Bibliographie*, 65–66, 90–91). It was also issued in Belgium, in a volume entitled *Religion saint-simonienne* (1831).

4. It appeared in *Le Globe* the next day. An additional 1,000 copies were run off in brochure form. "L'Art" was also included in *Religion saint-simonienne. Recueil de prédications*, vol. 1, of which 3,000 copies were published in March 1832. (Fournel, *Bibliographie*, 81, 86.) Full text also in *OSSE* 44:160–90. Citations hereafter are to the *Recueil de prédications* volume, which—like *OSSE*—shears the sermon of its subtitle.

5. In fact a footnote in the *Doctrine* referred readers to Barrault's *Aux artistes* for more details (*OSSE* 42:108).

6. *Doctrine,* 2d year, in OSSE 42: 155–56.

7. *Doctrine,* 1st year, ed. and trans. Iggers, 154. Iggers based his annotations freely on those in the French edition of C. Bouglé and Elie Halévy. I have revised Iggers's translations in spots and restored the authors' rhetorical use of italics and small capitals (following the text in *OSSE,* vols. 41–42).

8. *Doctrine,* ed. Iggers, 155.

9. Ibid., 156.

10. Ibid., 213.

11. Ibid., 16.

12. Ibid., 18.

13. "Rational argument can only convince, whereas feelings [*sensations*] persuade and stir to action [*entraînent*]" ("Dialogue," in *OSSE* 39:207).

14. Ibid., 157.

15. Barrault, *Aux artistes,* 84. Théophile Gautier keenly parodied Barrault's kerygmatic excesses in the preface to *Mademoiselle Maupin.*

16. Thibert, *Rôle social,* 33; Hunt, *Socialisme,* 34; Schrade, *Beethoven,* 103; Marix-Spire, *Romantiques,* 329; Perényi, *Liszt,* 101–2.

17. Barrault, *Aux artistes,* 77–79; cf. 20–22.

18. For examples in music criticism, see Cambini on Beethoven (Schrade, *Beethoven,* 3), Berlioz on Beethoven (*Mémoires* and *A travers chants,* in Schrade, *Beethoven,* 40, 56–57, 103–4), and Schumann's oft-cited judgment of the young Brahms.

19. Goethe and Shelley of course gave us the most notable examples, which in turn inspired musical works from, among others, Schubert and Liszt. Fauré's *Prométhée* is based more directly on Aeschylus.

20. Bénichou, *Temps,* 291–92, who notes similar constructions in Barrault's sermon on sacerdocy and in the *tableau synoptique* (see note 23).

21. *Doctrine de Saint-Simon,* 2d year (1829–30), in *OSSE* 42:355–56. This text, from the tenth session, was first published in *L'Organisateur* on 13 May 1830. Its significance was appreciated by Thibert (*Rôle social,* 37).

22. *L'Organisateur,* in Iggers, *Cult of Authority,* 102. I have used the (presumably) original

French word *culte* in place of Iggers's "cult."

23. Tableau synoptique, February 1831, reproduced in d'Allemagne, *Saint-Simoniens,* following p. 96. The definition of the artist is borrowed bodily from the second paragraph of Bazard's clarification, cited in note 21.

CHAPTER 7

1. *Doctrine,* ed. Iggers, 15–20; see the passages quoted in Chapter 6 and below.

2. "Dialogue," in *OSSE* 39:221–25.

3. Barrault, *Aux artistes,* 35–36. (On the chant reform, see *New Grove Dictionary,* s.v. "Plain chant" II; 9–10.) The following pages are based almost solely on *Aux artistes;* references will henceforth be given in the text.

4. Barrault's aesthetics here were surely also influenced by Romantic neomedievalism.

5. Barrault, *Aux artistes,* 64; *Doctrine,* ed. Iggers, 19; Barrault, "L'Art," 507–9 (referring to Lamartine, Hugo, and Byron, though not by name). The desire to avoid negativism is apparent in *Doctrine,* ed. Iggers, 17 (*OSSE* 42:110).

6. *Doctrine,* ed. Iggers, 17–20. Cf. Bénichou, *Temps,* 295.

7. For Rousseau's disgust with the theater of his day and for his proposed alternative (simple rural festivals in honor of virtue and filled with "public joy"), see his *Lettre à d'Alembert*—quotation from pp. 181–82 (260–62 in the 1758 ed.).

8. Enfantin agreed: "The Christian temples are deserted; the playhouses are filled with the faithful.... It is by the regenerated *actor* that the Christian will be saved." (Fourth *enseignement* to his disciples, 3 December 1831, *OSSE* 14:123.) Cf. Barrault's description of the new temple in *Livre nouveau* (d'Allemagne, *Saint-Simoniens,* 305).

9. Elsewhere the Saint-Simonians argued that music was in a healthier state because its essence is "harmony," and that (as Fourier also argued) it could thus serve as a model for society. ([Barrault?], "Discours sur les beaux-arts," in *L'Organisateur,* 2d year, no. 19 [25 December 1830]:149; cf. Fulcher, "Music and the Communal Order," 27–33, and Beecher and Bienvenu, eds., *Utopian Vision,* 260.)

10. Barrault, *Aux artistes,* 70–71; regarding concerts, cf. 17–19 (art museums are "cata-

combs" filled with a distracting jumble of objects torn out of their social context).

11. *Le Globe,* 26 September 1831, in Iggers, *Cult of Authority,* 178.

12. *Doctrine,* ed. Iggers, 256, and *OSSE* 42:110. The sixteenth session was one of three written by Enfantin and read publicly by him rather than by Bazard (Fournel, *Bibliographie,* 70). Enfantin admired Rossini's freedom (in contrast to Cherubini's strict counterpoint)—*OSSE* 25:131.

13. *Doctrine,* ed. Iggers, sixteenth session, 257. The full paragraph (*OSSE* 42:111–12) goes on to imagine that the women in the audience have come for the coronation of "the most loving [woman] . . . who has the greatest power over hearts. . . . There she is, the Sibyl of our own day." This passage caused rumors that Maria Malibran had become a Saint-Simonian priestess (see Chapter 8). It is also an intriguing foretaste of the cult of the female Messiah of 1833.

14. See p. 205.

15. Enfantin to Thérèse Nugues, [September 1829], *OSSE* 2:81–82. Enfantin to Charles Lambert, 23 July 1834, *OSSE* 29:224. Cf. Iggers, *Cult of Authority,* 124; and Fulcher, "Music and the Communal Order," 31.

16. Note the two strands of critical individualism isolated here, apparently modeled after the two currents the Saint-Simonians saw in contemporary literature: elegy and satire.

17. Enfantin to Thérèse Nugues, 4 April 1833, in *OSSE* 29:20–21. Thérèse had written to Enfantin that Paris was a "lieu de perdition."

18. *Le Globe* lamented the fact that such gifted musicians such as Paganini, the child guitarist Jules Regondi, and the four Koella brothers were forced to serve as "sublime buffoons" and playthings of the *oisifs* (articles of 29 March, 4 and 29 April 1831, cited in Hunt, *Socialisme,* 56 and 349).

19. On the sociology of musical life in Paris (including Mme Girardin's views), see Weber, *Music and the Middle Class,* 19–29, 53–61, 69–75.

20. *Cérémonie du 27 novembre,* 11, also in *OSSE* 4:203–39. The entire text was first published in *Le Globe* on 28 November and later included in the *Prédications,* vol. 2 (reprinted in *OSSE,* vol. 45). Rodrigues's speech was also pub-

lished separately—in a run of 10,000 copies—as *Religion saint-simonienne: Appel* (Paris: Bureau du Globe, 1831). (Cf. Fournel, *Bibliographie,* 83, 89–90.)

21. On Vinçard and the other Saint-Simonian songwriters, see Chapters 11 (which cites the Chevalier and Barrault passages) and 13.

22. Cf. the word *combinaisons:* Brian Primmer, *The Berlioz Style* (Oxford: Oxford University Press, 1973), 1–14, and Barrault, *Aux artistes,* 15–19 (the passage on architecture cited earlier).

23. See Chapter 9.

24. David to Saint-Etienne, 15 April 1831, BNMus lettre autographe 66. Berlioz was in Italy at the time of Habeneck's performance, but his admiration for the Ninth (which he knew from reading the score) and for Beethoven more generally was of course enormous. (See *Correspondance générale,* 1:229, 2:159, and the libretto of *Lélio,* not to mention the music of *Harold en Italie* and *Roméo et Juliette.*)

25. Barrault, "L'Art," 495. Compare this to the long passage quoted earlier from Barrault's *Aux artistes,* 77–79.

26. *Cérémonie du 27 novembre,* 16–18.

27. *Le Globe,* 7 December 1831.

28. On women, see the end of Chapter 8. On reincarnation, see Enfantin's letter to Duveyrier, 21 June 1830 but not published until 1834 (excerpts in d'Allemagne, *Saint-Simoniens,* 251–54).

29. *Livre nouveau,* in d'Allemagne, *Saint-Simoniens,* 304–5. The complete *Livre nouveau* materials have never been published.

30. Ibid. (on "new poetry").

31. *Livre nouveau,* in d'Allemagne, *Saint-Simoniens,* 307–8.

32. Ibid., 305.

33. "La Ville nouvelle," 318, 325, 238–29, 342, 332.

34. Charléty, *Saint-Simonisme,* bk. 2, chap. 4, pt. 3, p. 195.

35. Lambert to Enfantin, September 1834, in Charléty, *Saint-Simonisme,* 194.

CHAPTER 8

1. The following discussion of the Saint-Simonian religion and its hierarchy is based pri-

marily on Charléty, *Saint-Simonisme,* bk. 2, chap. 1, pp. 61–78.

2. Enfantin to Rességuier, 29 January 1831, in *OSSE* 3:92.

3. Ibid.

4. Transcript of the *réunion générale* of 19 November 1831, in *OSSE* 4:173–76.

5. Claire Bazard to Bazard and Enfantin, late December 1830, and Enfantin's comments thereon (1832 and 1833), in *OSSE* 3:72–74.

6. Enfantin to Rességuier, 28 October 1830, in *OSSE* 3:52.

7. Edouard Charton, *Mémoires d'un prédicateur saint-simonien,* in Charléty, *Saint-Simonisme,* bk. 2, chap. 1, pt. 2, pp. 71–72.

8. *OSSE* 3:39–42.

9. Charléty, *Saint-Simonisme,* bk, 2, chap. 2, pt. 2, pp. 89–91.

10. Ibid., bk, 2, chap. 1, pt. 2, pp. 70–71. On the missions, see also ibid., bk. 2, chap. 2, pt. 3, pp. 92–94, and Briscoe, *Saint-Simonism,* 310–51 (quotation from p. 338).

11. Ibid., bk. 2, chap. 3, pt. 1, p. 123; *OSSE* 8:110.

12. D'Allemagne, *Saint-Simoniens,* 350; an entire pocket-size (in-18mo) *Calendrier S.-S.* [*sic*] for 1833 was actually published and distributed.

13. *OSSE* 1:123–26.

14. *OSSE* 1:179–80.

15. Account in Enfantin's hand, 25 February [1831?], in *OSSE* 4:114–16.

16. *OSSE* 4:111–13. Her name, like her mother's, was Claire.

17. Mendelssohn refers to the civil nuptials of Henri Baud and Olinde Rodrigues's sister—see Chapter 9.

18. *OSSE* 3:21 (letter misdated?), 25, 49, 52, 55. Briscoe refers to "audiences of two to three thousand" at Salle Taitbout (*Saint-Simonism,* 304).

19. Fournel, *Bibliographie,* 86–90.

20. Louis Blanc, *Histoire de dix ans* 2:105–6.

21. See Enfantin's remarks, in *OSSE* 2:173, 3:229.

22. Ceremony of 27 November 1831, in *OSSE* 4:224–32 (briefly cited in Chapter 7, p. 64).

23. Charléty, *Saint-Simonisme,* bk. 2, chap. 3, pt. 1, p. 124. The number of members in the third degree comes from d'Eichthal's list, June 1831 (ibid., bk. 2, chap. 1, pt. 2, p. 78). Suzanne

Voilquin gives a similar arrangement (*Souvenirs,* chap. 7, p. 111).

24. *OSSE* 3:52.

25. Börne, *Briefe aus Paris,* letter 65 (30 December 1831), in his *Sämtliche Schriften* 3:428–29.

26. *OSSE* 3:55, 57, 86; 4:62, 75–80. Cf. Voilquin, *Souvenirs,* chap. 7, p. 110.

27. *OSSE* 2:156. Egbert's guess that this architect Henri was Charles Léopold Henry (*Social Radicalism,* 763) is strengthened by the existence of a rental agreement between a Charles Léopold Elie Henry and the owners of a house, 2 place Sorbonne (Salle de l'Athénée), permitting him to set up a platform and amphitheater in it (Ars 7819/178, with other papers concerning Saint-Simonian halls and buildings of 1830–31). Regular lectures at the Athénée were announced in the *Globe* on 24 January 1831 (*OSSE* 3:86). Egbert gives Charles Léopold Henry's dates as 1796–1885; he should not be confused with the physiologist Charles Henry, whose ideas on universal harmony influenced the painter Seurat (Egbert, *Social Radicalism,* 250). "Our" Henri/Henry became briefly a member of the Collège after Rodrigues's schism (*OSSE* 5:246).

28. Summary of a report of Carnot and Dugied, directors of *enseignement,* read 16 August 1831, summary printed in the *Globe* in the first days of September (*OSSE* 4:43, 75–80, citation from p. 79).

29. See Charton, *Mémoires,* cited in Charléty, *Saint-Simonisme,* bk. 2, chap. 1, pt. 2, p. 73.

30. Blanc, *Histoire de dix ans* 2:106.

31. Charton, *Mémoires,* in d'Allemagne, *Saint-Simoniens,* 116.

32. Börne, *Briefe aus Paris,* letter 74 (10 February 1832), in *Sämtliche Schriften* 3:520–21, 5:168. For his earlier remarks, see 3:39 (regarding his banker's son, presumably Olinde Rodrigues), 428–34, 504, and 5:135, 166; also Butler, *Saint-Simonian Religion,* 67–69.

33. Charton, *Mémoires,* in d'Allemagne, *Saint-Simoniens,* 116. The anonymous caricature is reproduced by d'Allemagne on the facing page.

34. Claire Bazard to Aglaé Saint-Hilaire, 12 July [1830], Ars 7608. I have not been able to identify the "pauvre prussien."

35. Carnot, *Saint-Simonisme,* 25–26. Besides the piano, mentioned here, the Saint-Simonians apparently had at 6 rue Monsigny a violin,

"harmonica" (glass harmonica, or harmonium?), and some walnut music stands (see sale of furnishings, in d'Allemagne, *Saint-Simoniens*, opp. p. 244).

36. Fraser, "Saint-Simonism," 86. On the Malibran story, which involves Liszt as well, see my article "Liszt's Saint-Simonian Adventure," 126n. D'Ortigue, in an article that seems to be the only source about the Malibran concert, simply says that Liszt and Malibran gave a concert "in the Saint-Simonians' hall, rue Taitbout." Perhaps they rented or borrowed the hall for a few hours. Indeed, when the Saint-Simonians first began using it in 1830 they referred to it as "la salle de *concert* de la rue Taitbout" (*L'Organisateur*, 1st year, no. 11 [30 October 1830]:[81]). A few years later it was regularly used for chamber concerts (Joël-Marie Fauquet, "La Musique de chambre à Paris dans les années 1830," in Bloom, *Music in Paris*).

37. *OSSE* 3:49; fuller text in Chapter 9, p. 98.

38. Fétis, *Biographie universelle*, supplement, s.v. "Delsarte, François." This report has been repeated in later reference books but is not mentioned in the official biography by Angélique Arnaud (*François del Sarte, ses découvertes en esthétique, sa science, sa méthode* [Paris: Ch. Delagrave, 1882]). Of course Delsarte may well have attended soirées or lectures and absorbed the doctrine; Arnaud, perhaps significantly, quotes from Béranger's tribute to Saint-Simon, Enfantin, and Fourier, "Les Fous" ("On les persécute . . ."), and applies it to Delsarte. Arnaud herself shows utopian socialist influence in her novels (Hunt, *Socialisme*, esp. 152); Thibert even tags her a "Saint-Simonian author" (*Rôle social*, 50).

39. In 1826 Cherubini purchased a frame for "le tableau d'Enfantin." This was not a portrait of Père Enfantin (as scholars have so far assumed) but a sepia drawing by a certain A. Enfantin. (The error started with Maurice Quatrelles l'Epine, *Cherubini [1760–1842]: Notes et documents inédits* [Lille: Imprimerie Lefebvre-Ducrocq, 1913], 9, 98; on p. 81 he himself published the drawing, correctly labeled!)

40. He generally signed letters "D. Rogé" and used "D. Tajan-Rogé" for publications. His first name appears only rarely, as in a legal document cited in Chapter 13 below or in the account of the August 1832 trial (in *OSSE* 47:42–47). I shall often refer to Tajan-Rogé and his wife Clorinde Rogé as "Rogé" and "Clorinde," following their own usage.

41. D. Tajan-Rogé, *Hommage à la mémoire de Baillot*, 4. The Archives nationales preserve "une demande d'admission de Tajan-Rogé à l'Ecole royale de Musique pour l'année 1817–1818" (0³ 1801, dossier III, no. 658; information kindly transmitted by Jean Favier). Rogé apparently did not complete the Conservatoire training, for he is not mentioned among the laureates in Constant Pierre, *Le Conservatoire national de musique et de déclamation* (Paris: Imprimerie nationale, 1900). (It seems unlikely that he finished but won no prize.)

42. The *Almanach des spectacles* lists Rogé among the cellists of the Théâtre du vaudeville orchestra in the issues dated 1822–24 (spelled Roger) and of the Opéra-Comique orchestra in those of 1825–31 (Rogé). Since a given issue of the *Almanach* refers to the previous year's situation, Rogé may have left the Opéra-Comique sometime in 1831, perhaps to devote himself more regularly to Saint-Simonian meetings and propaganda.

43. This, the only known "social" activity of his pre-Saint-Simonian days, is also the best documented episode of his early life. Antoine Elwart records that Tajan-Rogé was present on 24 March 1828 at the first meeting of the founding members. After the statutes were read, Habeneck thanked him for "the very personal role he played in the drawing up of the Rules [later] amended by the Provisory Committee" (*Société*, 68–69).

44. This time sequence is given both by Clorinde (in the letter quoted immediately below) and by Rogé in his "Mme Clorinde." D'Eichthal, in a list of the seventy-nine members of the Saint-Simonian family (June 1831), included Rogé in the largest and lowest group (*membres du troisième degré*—Charléty, *Saint-Simonisme*, bk. 2, chap. 1, pt. 2, p. 78).

45. Letter from Clorinde Rogé to Enfantin, Paris, 23 June 1845 (Ars 7776/52).

46. Even as late as the first trial (27 August 1832), Rogé was being described as one of the movement's three *novices* (with Casimir Cayol and Thomas Urbain—*OSSE* 47:43, 45).

47. For a short introduction to the life and works of David, see Macdonald's article in the *New Grove Dictionary of Music and Musicians* or my "Notice biographique sur Félicien David." Hagan's recent *Félicien David* is the closest thing we have to a full-length portrait. (See also Hagan's *French Musical Criticism,* 282–314.) All the earlier biographies are quite brief, but several carry some authority. Saint-Etienne, David's close friend, wrote the first of these, stressing David's years in Aix. Mirecourt's mixes authentic details with fictional dialogue. Azevedo seems to have written his in close collaboration with David himself. Brancour's, although based in large part on the other three, treats the music in somewhat greater detail.

48. David to Sylvain Saint-Etienne, 15 April and 12 August 1831 (BNMus lettres autogr. 66, 67). Justus's age is given in *OSSE* 47:44.

49. Azevedo, *Félicien David,* 39–41.

50. Ibid. Donakowski isolates the Saint Ambrose reference from the other three and gives it a fanciful interpretation (*Muse,* 181).

It is curious to learn from a letter of David's (11 May 1835, to Saint-Etienne, BNMus lettre autogr. 69) that another young Saint-Simonian, Casimir Cayol, was also a friend of Saint-Etienne's. Perhaps either Cayol or David encouraged the other to join.

51. David to Saint-Etienne, 15 December 1830 and 12 August 1831 (BNMus lettres autogr. 65, 67).

52. Or at the home of the Saint-Simonian physician Léon Simon, where some of the musicians lodged (d'Allemagne, *Saint-Simoniens,* 106).

53. Or the father-mother: "il m'a enfanté à la vie nouvelle" (see Chapter 13). David's own parents, by the way, were worldly people, though of modest means. His father Charles Nicolas David was a goldsmith who had lived for a time in Saint-Domingue (Haiti); chased back to France by the "Revolution of the Blacks," he married Marie-Anne Françoise Arquier, daughter of the head of the Marseilles goldsmiths' guild. (Genealogical information kindly provided by Jacques Kryn and Mme A. Deniau-Treppo, supplemented by statements in Saint-Etienne, *Félicien David,* Azevedo, *Félicien David,* and Jacquème, "Félicien David.")

54. David to Sylvain Saint-Etienne, 29 Oc-

tober 1831 (BNMus lettre autogr. 68). Actually David last mentions his Conservatoire classes in lettre autogr. 67 (12 August 1831), so perhaps he dropped out of classes sometime in late summer or fall of 1831. This is also suggested by Azevedo's statement: "sorti du Conservatoire aux vacances [summer vacation] de 1831, Félicien David n'a reçu d'enseignement régulier de la composition que pendant dix-huit mois" (*Félicien David,* 36). Alfred de Beauchesne, for many years the chief administrator of the Conservatoire, noted (BNMus W 24, 165) that David was admitted on 18 December 1830 and left on 1 October 1832. This suggests that David either neglected to withdraw officially in late 1831 or perhaps hesitated to do so until it became clear to him that his future lay with the Saint-Simonians. (Beauchesne penned this brief biographical note in his autograph album as commentary to a musical quotation written by David on 25 February 1846 and signed "à Mr. Alfred de Beauchesne, Souvenir du Conservatoire / Félicien David.")

55. In December the tailor Frison asked payment for Justus's "pantalon bleu 3me degré," and in January he listed David as the recipient of "un habit bleu 3me degré" (Ars 7819/188).

56. One reference does put him in the "atelier de peinture," perhaps as a beleaguered assistant to Raymond. (Raymond was instructed to decorate the walls with frescos and inspirational sayings [d'Allemagne, *Saint-Simoniens,* 276; Thibert, *Rôle social,* 44].) Perhaps it was for his artistic talent that he was invited to participate in some of the *Livre nouveau* sessions (see d'Allemagne, *Saint-Simoniens,* 304–7). A few years later Justus lithographed a portrait of George Sand and ran off 200 copies "for the [Saint-Simonian] proletarians" (George Sand to Adolphe Guéroult, [ca. 20 October 1835,] in George Sand, *Correspondance* 3:73).

57. *Liberté, Femmes!!!* (Lyon: Mme S. Durval, 1833). On Justus's conversion to Saint-Simonism, see *OSSE* 7:181–82. On his temper tantrums while a member of Cayol's brigade, see Ars 7624/14, 17. On his "tenacious" character and love of propaganda work, see Vinçard, *Mémoires,* 461–70; cf. his letters ([1850?], Ars 7630/148, 149), concerning two later brochures of his.

58. These motets (plus a miniature *quatuor*

concertant) were formerly in the Cathedral.

59. Azevedo, *Félicien David,* 18–19. They apparently did not, though, perform operas, as Donakowski implies (*Muse,* 81).

60. David to Saint-Etienne, 15 December 1830 (BNMus lettre autogr. 65).

61. David to Saint-Etienne, 12 August 1831 (BNMus lettre autogr. 67).

62. David to Saint-Etienne, 15 April 1831 (BNMus lettre autogr. 66).

63. David to Saint-Etienne, 12 August 1831 (BNMus lettre autogr. 67).

64. Azevedo, *Félicien David,* 39–40. Azevedo states that during this early period he heard about David's activities in the movement directly from someone "who was a kind and tender sister to me" and who died at the age of twenty-six. (I cannot identify this witness.) Georges Weill wrote that Azevedo had himself been a Saint-Simonian (*Ecole saint-simonienne,* 121). But perhaps he confused Alexis Azevedo with Jules Azévedo, one of several Jews who were "on the periphery of the movement.... [He] attended some early meetings." (Barrie M. Ratcliffe, "Some Jewish Problems in the Early Careers of Emile and Isaac Pereire," *Jewish Social Studies* 34 [1972]:202.)

65. One was attended by some five hundred people (Butler, *Heinrich Heine,* 114).

66. David to Saint-Etienne, BNMus lettres autogr. 84, 85, 89 (1838–41).

67. These clefs and other details suggest that the "altos" in the SATB passages may also have been high tenors, i.e., STTB.

68. David and Bonheur may have drawn the word from Revolutionary or Masonic musical traditions. Méhul and Gossec, among others, had made use of "Choryphée" to indicate the solo performer of a verse or declamatory passage. (Examples in Pierre, *Musique.*) In *Le Déluge,* a Masonic funeral cantata by François Giroust (1737–99), the part labeled "Choryphée" was to be taken by a *basse chantante* (Cotte, *Musique maçonnique,* 97). Berlioz applied the term to the bass soloist in Beethoven's Ninth Symphony. (Article of 1838, incorporated in *A travers chants* (1862), ed. Léon Guichard [Paris: Gründ, 1971], 71, 76.)

69. The apparent echoes of Mendelssohn and Schubert—and, at *segue voce* on p. 13, of the first movements of Haydn's Symphony no. 86

(written for Paris) or Mozart's D-Minor Piano Concerto—do not so much indicate a direct influence (David could hardly have known much Mendelssohn and Schubert yet) as a successful absorption of current "serious" musical style.

70. He did propose, though, in the *Lettres* of 1802, that women be permitted to vote (and even to be nominated) for the future Council of Newton.

71. Charléty, *Saint-Simonisme,* bk, 2, chap. 2, pt. 5, pp. 115–20; see also Louvancour, *De Saint-Simon à Fourier.*

72. Beecher and Bienvenu, *Utopian Vision,* 54–64, 329–58, 367–95.

73. Enfantin to Thérèse Nugues, 15 November 1828, in *OSSE* 25:99–100.

74. *Doctrine,* ed. Iggers, sixth session, 85.

75. Charléty, *Saint-Simonisme,* bk, 2, chap. 3, pt. 1, p. 126. Much of the information on the following pages derives from Charléty, *Saint-Simonisme,* pp. 121–36; *OSSE* 4:118–38; or Manuel, *Prophets,* 151–55.

76. Letter in *OSSE* 4:118–25.

77. Enfantin to his mother, August 1831, in *OSSE* 27:195–6.

78. Ibid., in *OSSE* 27:197–201.

79. See Butler, *Heinrich Heine* and *Saint-Simonian Religion.* For Liszt's insistence that "rehabilitation of the flesh" should not be interpreted as a crude "emancipation" (i.e., sexual license), see Chapter 9, p. 105.

80. He had already in 1829–30 dreamed of a new sibyl, although in obscure terms. (The passage on ladies at the opera, *Doctrine,* ed. Iggers, sixteenth session, 257; Charléty, *Saint-Simonisme,* bk. 2, chap. 3, pt. 1, pp. 128–29.)

81. *OSSE* 4:145, 158; 27:192.

82. Enfantin to his mother, August 1831, in *OSSE* 27:197, 201–2. For further discussion of this whole matter, see Briscoe, *"Enfantinisme."*

83. Note on marriage and divorce, read to the Collège on 17 October 1831, in *OSSE* 4:126–35.

84. *OSSE* 4:138–54.

85. An editors' remark, in *OSSE* 4:155. Cf. *OSSE* 6:20–34. On Enfantin's success at holding onto the sources of power—disciples, propaganda vehicles, provincial missions—see d'Allemagne, *Saint-Simoniens,* 224–27, and Briscoe, *"Enfantinisme."*

86. *OSSE* 4:198–204.

87. *OSSE* 4:197–201.

88. *OSSE* 4:239. Reynaud was still angry at this "hypocrisy" a year later (Charléty, *Saint-Simonisme,* bk. 2, chap. 3, pt. 1, p. 135).

89. *OSSE* 4:214 (Rodrigues) and 230 (Barrault); Robert J. Bezucha, The *Lyon Uprising of 1834* (Cambridge: Harvard University Press, 1974), 60, 115–16; Briscoe, *Saint-Simonism,* 351–54; Fernand Rude, *Les Révoltes des canuts (novembre 1831–avril 1834)* (Paris: Librairie François Maspéro, 1982), 74–75, 78–85; Rude, *Insurrection,* 206–7, 267–73, 346, 671–74, 697–710.

90. *OSSE* 47:5. (This volume contains the accounts of the two trials and of the preliminary investigations.)

91. *OSSE* 47:14–16, 21–25.

92. Charléty, in fact, concludes that the accusation under Article 291 was a mere pretext, a legal way to discredit the Saint-Simonians (*Saint-Simonisme,* bk. 2, chap. 3, pt. 5, pp. 156–58).

93. Editors' note, *OSSE* 5:224.

94. Charléty, *Saint-Simonisme,* bk. 2, chap. 3, pt. 5, p. 157.

95. Duveyrier, "De la femme," *Le Globe,* 12 January 1832, in Charléty, *Saint-Simonisme,* bk. 2, chap. 3, pt. 3, p. 146; full text in *OSSE* 47:135–52.

96. *OSSE* 4:207 (Enfantin's words, 1831, without "direct"), 5:242 (Rodrigues's words, after the second schism).

97. On the "Rente," which consisted, in theory, of investments rather than outright contributions to the movement, see Charléty, *Saint-Simonisme,* bk. 2, chap. 3, pt. 4, pp. 152–53; *OSSE* 47:21–25; the paragraph in Chapter 9, p. 98; and Ratcliffe, "*Saint-Simonism,*" 492–93.

98. D'Allemagne, *Saint-Simoniens,* 243–44; cf. Charléty, *Saint-Simonisme,* bk. 2, chap. 3, pt. 4, pp. 150–54. James B. Briscoe informs me that Claire Bazard (presumably not the mother but the daughter) had an affair with Margerin (a *père du Collège*). In general, the story of personal relations within the movement remains to be written.

99. *OSSE* 5:240–43, 6:41–48.

CHAPTER 9

1. Perényi, *Liszt,* 101–2.

2. Léon Halévy, *F. Halévy,* 17. The reference to Halévy's term at the Théâtre italien allows us to place these gatherings in the years 1826–29. His first work for the Opéra (a ballet) was in 1830.

3. Mina Curtiss, *Bizet and his World* (New York: Alfred A. Knopf, 1958), 237. Léonie's brother Hippolyte Rodrigues-Henriques was an amateur composer (ibid., p. 252).

4. Letter from Enfantin to David, [Paris,] 8 August 1845 (Ars 7616/80^v–81), also published in J.-G. Prod'homme, ed., "Correspondance," 77.

5. See Mina Curtiss, "Fromental Halévy," *Musical Quarterly* 39 (1953):196–214, and Wolff, "Halévy."

6. Léon Halévy's paraphrase, in *F. Halévy,* 57.

7. From the description of the approach to be taken in all the articles (*Encyclopédie: Procès-verbaux* [n.p., n.d.], 24, copy in Ars 7860/2).

8. For example, Littré and Viollet-le-Duc were members of the editorial committee (*Procès-verbaux*).

9. Chevalier's words, *Procès-verbaux,* 9.

10. Léon Halévy, *F. Halévy,* 67–68.

11. F. Halévy, galley proof entitled *Musique* (n.p., n.d.), reprinted in full in Locke, "Music and the Saint-Simonians," 135–37, from the copy preserved in Ars 7860/18.

12. Even a more modest concept of art's impact on society—the "utilitarian" one favored by many architects and designers (see Chapter 3)—was explicitly rejected by Halévy and his fellow academicians. See his report "Les Arts et l'industrie," a response to proposals of Léon de Laborde, in F. Halévy, *Souvenirs et portraits: Etudes sur les beaux-arts* (Paris: Michel Lévy Frères, 1861), summarized in Wolff, "Halévy," 699–700.

13. Undated extracts from Nourrit's letters, cited in Boutet de Monvel, *Adolphe Nourrit,* 79–80.

14. Quicherat, *Adolphe Nourrit* 1:325.

15. Berlioz to his father, 11 May 1839, in Berlioz, *Correspondance générale* 2:555.

16. Quicherat, *Adolphe Nourrit* 2:345–70. Boutet de Monvel, *Adolphe Nourrit,* 73–85. Blaze de Bury mentions Saint-Simon in a list of the thinkers on whom Nourrit "s'enivrait," alongside Spinoza, George Sand, de Maistre,

Lamennais, Plato, and Descartes (*Musiciens contemporains,* 228–29).

17. Nourrit's letters fill an entire volume in Quicherat, but only a small number come from the years before 1835 (*Adolphe Nourrit,* vol. 3).

18. "Adolphe Nourrit était fort entouré" (Carnot, *Saint-Simonisme,* 26); see Chapter 8.

19. Enfantin to Fournel, 26 October 1830, in *OSSE* 3:49.

20. See Chevalier's remarks on the *emprunt, OSSE* 47:21–25.

21. Ars 7819/1, 9, 186, 187. Cf. Ratcliffe, "Saint-Simonism," 492–93. Another indication of Nourrit's liberal tendencies is a receipt (Ars 7817/121) showing that he had owned a share in Pierre Leroux's *Le Globe.* (He was required to sell it to the Saint-Simonians when they took over the newspaper.)

22. Boutet de Monvel, *Adolphe Nourrit,* 78.

23. From a letter of Nourrit's, printed posthumously (and apparently without date) in *Le Monde illustré* (26 December 1863), in which the singer humorously criticized the prevailing social prejudice against actors and proudly identified himself with his lesser-known brothers of the stage (letter reprinted in Quicherat, *Adolphe Nourrit* 3:10–14).

24. Letter of 10 February 1836, in Quicherat, *Adolphe Nourrit* 3:14–15.

25. Letter to Théodore Anne, Lyons, 19 July 1837, in Quicherat, *Adolphe Nourrit* 3:55–56.

26. That, at least, was the reason he himself gave earlier in the letter just quoted.

27. *Courrier de Lyon,* 31 March 1829 [recte: 1839], cited in Boutet de Monvel, *Adolphe Nourrit,* 82–83. Cf. C. A. Paravey to Jules Janin, in Mergier-Bordeix (pseud.), ed., *Jules Janin: 735 Lettres à sa femme,* 3 vols. (Paris: C. Klincksieck, 1973–79) 2:569.

28. Boutet de Monvel, *Adolphe Nourrit,* 83.

29. Comtesse [Marie] d'Agoult, *Mémoires,* 99–102 (diary entry, Lyons, 31 July 1837).

30. Both Blaze de Bury (*Musiciens contemporains,* 234–35) and Ernest Legouvé (*Soixante ans* 1:131) present Nourrit's vision of himself, an "apostle" with a "mission," as the unfortunate chimera of a generous but weak character. Berlioz's view (cited earlier) is only slightly less condescending.

31. Even the recent and praiseworthy biography by Alan Walker treats the Saint-Si-

monian connection briefly and perpetuates a few traditional misconceptions (*Franz Liszt* 1:152–54). By far the most accurate and detailed view of Liszt's philosophical and political activities during the early years is given by Marix-Spire (*Romantiques,* 419–68), whose findings are summarized by Perényi (*Liszt,* 98–109). More recently, Bénichou has offered insightful readings of one important body of evidence, the Liszt (or Liszt-d'Agoult) articles of 1835–41 (*Temps,* 417–22).

The present subchapter is a revised and much abbreviated version of my article "Liszt's Saint-Simonian Adventure."

32. Ramann, *Franz Liszt* 1:151–61. This account is itself based in large part on two earlier sources: a biographical article by Joseph d'Ortigue and Schilling's *Franz Liszt,* 106–12 and 264–65.

33. Similarly, Bénichou astutely notes that in Liszt's writings "the humanitarian ideology" derives from "the principle of the priestly artist" instead of the reverse (as was the case in writings of other "humanitarians")—*Temps,* 418.

34. Guy de Pourtalès surely errs in suggesting that it was Félicien David who led Liszt to the Saint-Simonians (*La Vie de Franz Liszt* [Paris: Gallimard, 1927], 41–42), a claim repeated elsewhere. David did not become involved until the end of 1831, a year later than Liszt. Humphrey Searle names the violist Urhan as intermediary (*New Grove Dictionary,* s.v. "Liszt"), perhaps misremembering Marix-Spire, *Romantiques,* 426–28. Also, Alan Walker's recent statement that Liszt "immersed himself in Saint-Simon's early *Lettres d'un habitant de Genève* (1803)" (*Franz Liszt* 1:152) is not confirmed by any evidence I have seen. Liszt, as we shall see, was attracted more strongly to the movement's *later* writings.

35. Vier, *Comtesse d'Agoult* 1:156, 378.

36. D'Agoult, *Mémoires,* 26. In her 1846 novel *Nélida* she offered a more penetrating description (or is it a caricature?) of "Guermann Régnier's" (i.e., Liszt's) attraction to Saint-Simonism, stressing that the movement flattered the arrogance ("caressa l'orgueil") of the age's bright and handsome young men but also that Guermann, through this contact, soon came to a "keen, morbid awareness of social in-

equality" (cited in Vier, *Comtesse d'Agoult* 1:378). Cf. Ernest Newman, *The Man Liszt* (London: Cassell, 1934), 124–45.

37. He almost surely did not, however, accompany the soprano Maria Malibran in a benefit concert for the Saint-Simonians. (See Chapter 8.)

38. Undated letter ("Croissy, mardi matin"), perhaps from late 1833 (d'Agoult-Liszt, *Correspondance* 1:54).

39. Liszt to d'Agoult, undated (early 1834?), *Correspondance* 1:63.

40. Eugène Rodrigues, *Lettres sur la religion et le politique,* summarized in Vier, *Comtesse d'Agoult* 1:156.

41. Fraser, "Saint-Simonism," 107. D'Agoult-Liszt, *Correspondance* 1:54.

42. 27 June 1835, Geneva, in Marix-Spire, *Romantiques,* 611; he lent her, too, his copy of Eugène's *Lettres* and asked for her reaction. (Liszt's reading of the *Prédications* on the journey to Basel is confirmed by a diary entry for 2 June—mentioned by Maria Párkai-Eckhardt in her corrigenda [available on request from the American Liszt Society] to her "Diary of a Wayfarer" article cited below.) Marix-Spire (pp. 469–70) gives Liszt credit for bringing George Sand to a positive estimation of the Saint-Simonians in late 1835 (Sand: "I continue . . . to place them, in a sense, above all else").

43. Diary entry for 22 June transcribed (but inadequately interpreted) in Maria P[árkai-]Eckhardt, "Diary of a Wayfarer: The Wanderings of Franz Liszt and Marie d'Agoult in Switzerland, June–July 1835," *Journal of the American Liszt Society* 11 (June 1982):10–17; 12 (December 1982):1, 182–83. Vier erroneously read the same diary entry as implying that Liszt and the countess had heard a sermon on incredulity in a church in Switzerland and found it rather Saint-Simonian in content! (Vier, *Countesse d'Agoult* 1:180.)

44. "L'Incrédulité" (28 November 1830), in *Religion Saint-Simonienne: Recueil de prédications,* vol. 1 (March 1832), reprinted in *OSSE* 43:94–121.

45. This note on marriage and divorce (*OSSE* 4:126–35) was actually composed by Olinde Rodrigues as an attempted compromise between the ideas of Enfantin and those of Ba-

zard. (For Enfantin's serious but unchaste views, see Chapter 8 above.)

46. Liszt to Sand, (autumn 1835,) in Marix-Spire, *Romantiques,* 466, 614.

47. Liszt to d'Agoult, (late April?) 1836, in *Correspondance* 1:144, 170.

48. Vier, *Comtesse d'Agoult* 1:234; d'Agoult, *Mémoires,* 100–102 (cf. Vier, *Comtesse d'Agoult* 1:271). Additional remarks of interest by Liszt or Mme d'Agoult are in their *Correspondance* 2:20, 100, 310, 395, 416.

49. "De la situation des artistes et de leur condition dans la société," *Gazette musicale* 2 (1835), nos. 18–20, 30, 35, 50, rpr. in Liszt, *Pages romantiques,* 32–33.

50. "Lettres confidentielles," no. 2, in *Revue et gazette musicale* 5, no. 5 (4 February 1838):42.

51. "Lettres d'un bachelier-ès-musique," no. 7 (to Heinrich Heine), *Revue et gazette musicale,* 8 July 1838, in Liszt, *Pages romantiques,* 199, 202–3.

52. Schilling, *Franz Liszt,* 106–12 and 264–65 (Liszt's corrections).

53. Letter from Liszt to the publisher Heinrich Brockhaus (publisher of the *Conversations-Lexikon*), 22 March 1853, in *Briefe* 1:133–34.

54. Letter dated 6 December 1863, in Liszt, *Briefe* 3:169. (His emphases.)

55. Marginal notes in the copy of Ramann's *Franz Liszt* (1:154) now in the Liszt-Museum, Weimar (Ramann-Bibliothek, no. 225).

56. Letter of 15 March 1880, in *Briefwechsel zwischen Franz Liszt und Carl Alexander Grossherzog von Sachsen,* ed. La Mara [Marie Lipsius] (Leipzig: Breitkopf und Härtel, 1909), 183; Liszt to Princess Carolyne, 6 September 1885, *Briefe* 7:428–29.

57. "Lyon" was excised when Liszt later reworked the *Album* as *Années de pèlerinage* I, but has recently been revived on recordings. (See Alexander Main, "Liszt's *Lyon:* Music and the Social Conscience," *19th-Century Music* 4 [1980–81]:228–43.) The male choruses can be heard on Hungaroton SLPX 11765.

58. Bénichou—perhaps unaware of these facts—unfairly accuses Liszt of rarely putting his humanitarian ideas into practice (*Temps,* 422).

59. From a passage in one of Hiller's letters "from late in his life" that appeared in an article by L. Bischoff in the *Rheinische Musikzeitung* 3

(1852):937–38, as cited in Sietz, *Aus Ferdinand Hillers Briefwechsel* 1:23–24. Hiller's political passion led him to enlist (with Nourrit) in the National Guard in 1830 (Sietz, *Briefwechsel* 1:11).

60. The connection conjectured here derives from the fact that Börne discusses Hiller's plans (and his unfortunate adoption of slick, pretentious Parisian manners) one paragraph later in this same letter, as if they had spent the evening together at 6 rue Monsigny. (Letter 385 to Jeannette Wohl, 10 February 1832, in *Sämtliche Schriften* 5:168–69. The version published at the time as letter 74 of Börne's *Briefe aus Paris—Sämtliche Schriften* 3:521–22—eliminated Hiller's name and truncated the remarks concerning him.)

61. *Le Globe*, 7 December 1831. (Text of the closing *appel* is on p. 65 above.)

62. Leipzig, 25 July 1845, Ars 7710/16 (also printed in Prod'homme, *"Correspondance,"* 76).

63. "Maxime DuCamp," *Erinnerungsblätter* (Cologne: M. DuMont-Schauberg, 1884), 144.

64. Charléty, *Saint-Simonisme*, bk. 4, chap. 3, pt. 3, p. 325.

65. Eric Werner was the first to make substantial use of many of the original letters. His account of Mendelssohn's months in Paris (*Mendelssohn*, 185–89) is still unsurpassed, but it deals with the Saint-Simonian episode only very briefly.

The present section is a much abbreviated version of my article "Mendelssohn's Collision with the Saint-Simonians." The original texts of all unpublished or incompletely published letters translated here will be found in that article or in Locke, "Music and the Saint-Simonians," 157–59, 162–65.

66. Mendelssohn to his father Abraham, 21 February 1832, in *Briefe*, 248. All page references to the *Briefe* are to the "Erster Theil," a republication (differently paginated) of the *Reisebriefe* (1862). I have based my translations of letters from the *Briefe* on those of Lady Wallace.

67. Mendelssohn to his sister Fanny Hensel, 2 September 1831 (*Briefe*, 200).

68. Mendelssohn to Fanny Hensel, 20 April 1825 (Sebastian Hensel, *Die Familie Mendelssohn*, 18th ed. [Leipzig: Insel-Verlag, 1924] 1:167–69). Cf. letters of 2 September 1831 (Auber is "commonplace and trivial"), 15 Feb-

ruary 1832 (Paris's "fashionable music" has not changed in seven years), and 21 February 1832 ("mediocre music" gets performed and extolled)—*Briefe*, 200, 243, 249.

69. Mendelssohn to his father, 11 December 1831 (unpublished, New York Public Library). Hiller recalled his early friendship with Mendelssohn in *Felix Mendelssohn-Bartholdy: Briefe und Erinnerungen*, 2d ed. (Cologne: M. Du Mont-Schauberg, 1878). On Gustave d'Eichthal's stay in Berlin, see Barrie M. Ratcliffe, "Saint-Simonism," 489–90.

70. Letter of 11 December 1831, just cited.

71. Ibid.

72. E.g., letters of 19 December 1831 (*Briefe*, 217), 20 December 1831 (*Briefwechsel mit Legationsrat Karl Klingemann* [Essen: G. D. Baedeker, 1909], 88–89), and 11 January 1832 (*Briefe*, 227).

73. Mendelssohn to Karl Immermann, 11 January 1832 (*Briefe*, 227–28).

74. Mendelssohn to his family, 14 January 1832 (Bodleian Library; incompletely published in *Briefe*, 232–33).

75. Mendelssohn to his family, 21 [recte 22 or 21–22] January 1832 (Bodleian Library; incompletely published in *Briefe*, 235–36). "Justemilieu" was a term used to refer to *political* moderates, i.e., supporters of Louis-Philippe; "mouvement"—which Mendelssohn humorously equated here with *allegro*—meant liberal or progressive, e.g., the opposition leader Adolphe Thiers.

76. Unpublished letters in the New York Public Library: 29 February 1832, to his father, 2 April 1832, to his brother Paul, and 11 April 1832, to his sister Rebecka.

77. Felix Mendelssohn to his father, 13 February 1832 (unpublished, New York Public Library).

78. Mendelssohn to Michel Chevalier, 19 February 1832, Ars 7759/38. (Incompletely published in d'Allemagne, *Saint-Simoniens*, 182.)

79. Duveyrier to Arlès-Dufour, 18 August 1842, forwarded to Mendelssohn by the latter with a friendly cover letter, 26 August 1842 (Green Books, Bodleian Library).

80. Mendelssohn's letter to Duveyrier (13 October 1842) is lost, but his objections are clear from passages in Duveyrier's letters back to him, 28 November 1842 and 6 November

1843 (Green Books, Bodleian Library).

81. Duveyrier's letter, just cited, of 28 November 1842.

82. Duveyrier to Mendelssohn of 6 November 1843, cited above.

83. Arlès-Dufour to Mendelssohn, 3 November 1843 (Green Books, Bodleian Library).

84. Duveyrier to Mendelssohn, 7 May 1845 (Green Books, Bodleian Library).

85. Enfantin to Mendelssohn, 7 May 1845 (Green Books, Bodleian Library). His emphasis. He also reminded Mendelssohn that he had met the composer (and his father) in 1822 (in Switzerland?) and the composer again in 1825 "chez Rodrigues."

86. My "Autour de la lettre"—of which the present subchapter is a greatly abbreviated and revised version—contains the original French text of most of the passages cited in the following pages. Enfantin's remark about Berlioz, though published around 1870 (in *OSSE* 3:49), has until now been noticed only by scholars specially interested in the Saint-Simonians (d'Allemagne, *Saint-Simoniens,* 116; Thibert, *Rôle social,* 54; Hunt, *Socialisme,* 54; and Schrade, *Beethoven in France,* 90), not by students of Berlioz.

87. The letter is now lost; its text, though, is preserved in two incomplete but complementary sources and was first reconstructed in 1972 by Pierre Citron—Berlioz, *Correspondance générale* 1:476–79. Of the various incomplete publications of the letter, three contain valuable discussions: Barzun, *Berlioz* 1:136, Espiau de la Maëstre, "Berlioz, Metternich et le Saint-Simonisme," and John Crabbe, *Hector Berlioz: Rational Romatic* (New York: Taplinger Publishing Co., 1980), 25, 42–49, 56.

88. Compare Berlioz's nightmare about an orator "who clamps you to the drawing-room mantelpiece in order to saturate you with his doctrine" (*Evenings,* Sixteenth Evening, 190).

89. Cendrier appears from his letters in the Arsenal (esp. to Gustave d'Eichthal, 17 June 1833, Ars 13747/84) to have shared certain characteristics with Berlioz: a quick wit, occasional poetic outbursts, a longing for community and "a noble aim," and a distaste for the life of a "galley slave" in Paris (a reference to his impending career as a staff architect).

90. Espiau de la Maëstre, "Berlioz, Metter-

nich et le Saint-Simonisme," 66.

91. Even Berlioz's language has taken on a Saint-Simonian tinge. Compare his description of privileges ("cachés comme la vermine dans les derniers replis du corps social") with Paul Rochette's castigation of inheritance: "une lèpre hideuse s'attachant à toutes les affections de famille pour les fausser" (*Le Globe,* 13 January 1832, in *OSSE* 6:40).

92. *Correspondance* générale 1:154 (to Nanci—cf. 1:229 to E. Rocher) and 1:317 (to Adèle).

93. He did not, however, attend the propaganda sessions for artists run by the architect Henry; these took place in 1831, when Berlioz was in Italy. (This corrects a statement in Egbert, *Social Radicalism,* 149, which derived from an unfortunate ambiguity in Hunt, *Socialisme,* 50.)

94. "Jules Lechevalier est à Bordeaux, l'autre Chevalier [Michel] à Limoges; Duveyrier ne fait que d'arriver; Lebreton prépare Nantes . . ." (*OSSE* 3:46; cf. 2:183, 192–93; also Thibert, *Rôle Social,* 40n).

95. 3 July 1831, *Correspondance générale* 1:467–68; cf. 1:520.

96. *Correspondance générale,* 1:467.

97. "Paris in 1830," in Bloom, *Music in Paris.*

98. *Correspondance générale* 1:516.

99. Hagan, *French Musical Criticism,* offers suggestive parallels between Saint-Simonian attitudes and the music journalism of Berlioz and certain contemporaries.

100. Schrade, *Beethoven in France,* 91. There is an astonishing parallel between Barrault's image of the artist winging through the heavens and Berlioz's oft-cited descriptions of Beethoven as an eagle of the Andes (from the *Mémoires* and from *A travers chants,* in Schrade, *Beethoven,* 40, 56–57, 103–4). But surely the eagle metaphor was a commonplace by Berlioz's day; see Chapter 6 n.18 above.

101. Twenty-Fifth Evening, 258–97. No doubt this tale, first published in 1844, draws from other utopian traditions as well, but the centrally placed pipe organ seems to have been modeled on the organs in the *Livre nouveau* or Duveyrier's "Ville nouvelle," the Song of Praise and the Hymn of Night suggest that Berlioz knew (about?) David's choruses, and the particular mix of authoritarian and democratic forms of governance (and the elitist selectivity

according to "intelligence or musical culture") recalls passages in many Saint-Simonian writings, beginning with the *Lettres* of 1802.

102. Rey Longyear finds a specific echo of Saint-Simonian *association* in Berlioz's portrayal (both musical and dramatic) of Dido's peaceable, laboring kingdom (act 3 of *Les Troyens*)—"Political and Social Criticism in French Opera, 1827–1920," in Robert L. Weaver, gen. ed., *Essays on the Music of J. S. Bach and Other Divers Subjects: A Tribute to Gerhard Herz* (Louisville: University of Louisville, 1981), 248–49. Hermann Hofer finds similar echoes in this and other Berlioz works—"Pour une lecture politique des livrets de Berlioz," *Festival Berlioz: Berlioz, biographie et autobiographie: Actes du colloque 1980* ([Lyons]: n.p., [1981]), 52–55.

103. *Correspondance générale* 3:209–10. There is no evidence that Berlioz appreciated, much less carried out, Duveyrier's suggestion that he "ought to go see [Enfantin]."

104. "Musique enfantine" appears in a disheartened polemic on how time had faded *Le Désert* (letter to Adolphe Samuel, 16 October 1855, in *Le Ménéstrel* 15 [8 June 1879]:225–27). Berlioz complained of "les ex-Saint-Simonniens" in a letter regarding David's *Perle du Brésil* (see Chapter 13).

105. *Mémoires* 1:105 (chap. 15).

106. Actually, Berlioz's emphasis on "attractive work" in the following passage suggests that he may have been thinking in part of the Fourierists as well as of the Saint-Simonians—or that the two groups had become fused together in his mind. Fourier: "The common people will derive so much pleasure and stimulation from work in the societary state [the Fourierist utopia] that they will refuse to leave their jobs to attend balls and spectacles scheduled during work periods" (*Utopian Vision*, 274; cf. 27–53, 271–328).

107. *Grotesques*, 25.

108. Knepler, *Geschichte als Weg zum Musikverständnis*, section 3.3.1.3, pp. 489–92 (1977 ed.).

109. See, for example, Frida Knight, *Beethoven and the Age of Revolution* (London: Lawrence and Wishart, 1973); Maynard Solomon, "Beethoven's 'Magazin der Kunst,'" *Nineteenth-Century Music* 8 (1983–84): 199–208; and Knepler's own *Karl Kraus liest Offenbach* (Berlin, GDR: Henschelverlag, 1984), 18–84.

CHAPTER 10

1. Enfantin to Capella, 30 April 1833 (i.e., 1832), Ars 15032/34 (manuscript copy), reprinted (without date) in *OSSE* 7:21. Enfantin originally intended the Retreat to last only three months. (Letter to S. Flachat, 20 April 1832, in *OSSE* 6:229.) Cf. Barrault's disparagement of "petty" experiments in communal living, 4 December 1832, *OSSE* 5:15.

The opening pages of this chapter are based on the account given in Charléty, *Saint-Simonisme*, bk. 2, chapt. 4, pt. 1, pp. 161–68.

2. "Ménilmontant will cost us little"—Enfantin to S. Flachat, 20 April 1832, in *OSSE* 6:228.

3. Remark of the editors, *OSSE* 7:2, confirmed by Enfantin's letters throughout *OSSE*, vol. 7.

4. This and the two brief preceding quotations come from Enfantin's letter to Capella (see note 1), *OSSE* 7:23. (I have incorporated some textual details from the manuscript copy.)

5. D'Allemagne, *Saint-Simoniens*, 276.

6. M. Chevalier to Albert Brisbane, the future Fourierist leader, 20 May 1832, Ars 7646, fol. 96, cited in *OSSE* 7:35–36.

7. M. Chevalier to Eugène (?), 2 July 1832, Ars 7814/36, with additional remarks on the need for a new *culte*.

8. Poetry of Enfantin (from Barrault's personal papers), Ars 7811/15.

9. "Exposé sommaire de mes fonctions à Ménil-Montant," *Le Cabinet de lecture*, no. 129 (4 January 1833):9–10. All references to A. Chevalier's recollections in the following account are drawn from these pages.

10. "Les Saint-Simoniens en voyage," *Le Figaro*, 25 December 1832, 2–3. The article, after reviving the old accusation (already disproven in court) that the Saint-Simonian leaders had opened the purses of their disciples, discusses the voyage of Barrault and his followers from Paris. At Troyes they found an excellent dinner and they sang "not in honor of God, the Word, the sun, neither to the glory of Enfantin, nor of sociable vests [a snide reference to the apostles' costume at Ménilmontant], nor of equality and fraternity—they sang to the glory of the chef in Troyes." Barrault supposedly led the

disciples in "a gastronomic hymn, to the tune of *Veillons au salut de l'empire*" (the official hymn of the Napoleonic Empire), with the refrain "Voici du potage délicieux" ("This soup is delicious"). Barrault gave a discourse between the fruit and cheese courses, and the chef was so touched by it all that "they promised him a place as dishwasher in the city of the future" (an allusion to Duveyrier's *La Ville nouvelle*).

A few days later *Le Figaro* commented with mock regret that the Saint-Simonians ought not to have given up their life of seclusion, since fashionable people were beginning to copy them. "Before long every family would have been singing canticles after dinner. It would have been marvelous" (31 December 1832, 2).

11. Louis Blanc, *Histoire de dix ans* 3:322.

12. *La Guerre aux hommes; ou, Les Faux Saint-Simoniens*, opéra-comique in 4 acts. In order to trick some women who are on strike against marriage, a group of men decide to disguise themselves as Saint-Simonians. The women's *invocation* is in act 2: "Grand Saint-Simon, veillez sur nous, protégez-nous. Votre secours ici devient bien nécessaire. Chaque soir après ma prière ponctuelle et recueillie, l'esprit tout rempli de sermons, [etc.] . . . Jusque là c'est bien mais en songe vient un joli et blond fantôme qui se met à me sermonner. . . ." (Information and text excerpts kindly provided by M. Elizabeth C. Bartlet, who located and examined for me the short score with French and German texts, in the Deutsche Staatsbibliothek, Mus. MS. autogr. 27¹. The full score, with German text only, *Die Seekadetten, oder die Emancipation der Frauen*, is autogr. 27.) The work seems never to have been performed in French; it received its premiere in the Weimar Hoftheater on 3 May 1844 under the title *Die Seekadetten, oder Nieder mit den Männern* (libretto by Sondershausen).

13. List in letter from Stéphane Flachat to Holstein, 2 May 1832, Ars 7727, in *OSSE* 6:245.

14. Duveyrier's brother Mélesville was an occasional composer as well as a successful librettist, and it seems unlikely that Baron Duveyrier would not have provided his younger son, too, with a proper musical education.

15. Rogé to Enfantin, 25 September 1834: "I owe it to my habits of self-denial [*abnégation*]

and modesty that at Ménilmontant I saw Duveyrier named director of music, no doubt by virtue of the 'placement according to aptitudes'" (Ars 7776/66). Rogé's allusion to the Saint-Simonians' motto is drenched in irony.

16. S. Flachat to Holstein, 2 May 1832, Ars 7727, in *OSSE* 6:244–45.

17. The five probably included Justus, Duveyrier, and Lambert. David mentioned Justus's musical talent to Saint-Etienne the year before (12 August 1831, BNMus lettre autogr. 67). Lambert seems to have had at least some grasp of solfège and modulation. (See p. 150.)

18. The original list (containing mainly last names only) appears on p. 8 of the account of Talabot's funeral (see n. 20 below). First names have been restored here (see note to Index).

19. The list is identical to that given above except that Auguste Chevalier and Alexis Petit are not yet in the chorus, and Edmond Talabot sings *dessus*, Franconie second tenor, and Emile Barrault bass. (Archives Alfred Pereire, cited in d'Allemagne, *Saint-Simoniens,* 276. The voice ranges in this list are actually labeled *Haute contre, Premier ténor, Ténor,* and *Basse.* David's scores usually call the top voice *Alto.*) Most of the changes in the chorus can be easily explained. A. Chevalier had perhaps been shy about joining the chorus (see the note on his recruitment below), and Petit withdrew from Ménilmontant on 6 June and presumably stayed away until he was ready to become an apostle. As for Talabot, he appears to have been a faithful member of the chorus until he contracted cholera and died (16–17 July). Franconie, after leaving the chorus, eventually left the Retreat altogether. (He had already had doubts on 6 June and declined temporarily to take the habit.)

20. There are six such accounts, all rich in song texts and information about musical activities.

1. *Retraite de Ménilmontant: 6 juin 1832* (Paris: Everat, [1832]), 12 pp., copy in BNImp 8°Z 8129/3. This brochure, hereafter referred to as *6 juin 1832,* consists of two sections: "Parole du PERE," dated 3 June 1832, and "Chants." The first section only is reprinted in *OSSE* 7:75–79, where it is dated 2 June. This brochure was presumably printed in advance for distribution at the ceremony of 6 June. It is not to be confused

with the following, the published account of the ceremony.

2. *Retraite de Ménilmontant: [Prise d'habit, 6 juin 1832]*, 18 pp., copy in BNImp 8°Z 8129/5. Hereafter referred to as *Prise d'habit;* the full text is reprinted in *OSSE* 7:94–115.

3. *Retraite de Ménilmontant: Cérémonie du dimanche 1er juillet, et récit de ce qui s'est passé les jours suivans: Ouverture des Travaux du Temple,* 27 pp., copies in BNImp 8°Z 8129/7, 1830/3. Hereafter referred to as *Travaux du Temple* or the temple account; the main body of the text is reproduced with some omissions in *OSSE* 7:134–59 and the closing pages (concerning the "following days") are reprinted in *OSSE* 47:30–40.

4. *Mort de Talabot,* 24 pp., copy in BNImp 8°Z 8129/9. The text of this brochure, the account of Talabot's funeral, is reproduced, greatly abridged, in *OSSE* 7:166–75.

5. *Religion saint-simonienne: Procès en la Cour d'assises de la Seine les 27 et 38 août 1832,* 405 pp., portraits. Another edition, presumably identical except for a differently worded cover and title page, was published by B. Warée aîné, copy in BNImp Ld¹⁹⁰159. Hereafter referred to as *Procès (août);* reprinted partially in *OSSE* 7:197–256 and entirely in *OSSE* 47:5–537.

6. *Religion saint-simonienne: Procès en Police correctionnelle le 19 Octobre 1832,* 105 pp., portraits. Hereafter referred to as *Procès (octobre);* reprinted partially in *OSSE* 8:100–109, entirely in *OSSE* 47:539–604.

21. For example, a surviving copy of a letter of Enfantin's (possibly in Michel Chevalier's hand) relating the events of 1 July 1832 (Ars 7814/31) appears to have served as one of the sources for *Travaux du Temple.* (It cannot have been copied from the publication, for the text of a David chorus in the letter is a bit more accurate.) The letter is immediately followed in the archives by a sketch (also in Chevalier's hand?) of the layout of the garden: *Temple, gazon,* etc. (Ars 7814/32).

22. The accuracy of the information in these accounts was tacitly accepted at the time and has never, to my knowledge, been challenged. Much of it is confirmed and little of it contradicted by reports in the daily newspapers or indeed by confidential police reports (cf. the reports in Walch, *Chevalier,* 27–29, and the Saint-Simonian versions of the same events, in *OSSE,* vols. 7, 47). In his memoirs, Dr. Charles Pellarin, who had spent six disenchanting weeks at Ménilmontant, quotes whole paragraphs and pages from these and other of the movement's official accounts, clearly considering them a fatally accurate depiction of the follies of Ménilmontant. His only objections are that the authors, including Enfantin himself, repeatedly described Le Père in adulatory language ("calm," "majestic"), and that in one case they reported Enfantin as saying something that Pellarin—who was present—does not recall having heard (*Souvenirs,* 135, 134).

23. Auguste Chevalier recalled that it was Rogé who overheard him singing David's *Salut* one day and grabbed him for the chorus. The task of copying—they probably sang from parts rather than full scores—may have been shared among the musically literate. (The one incomplete set of parts that survives is in David's hand; see Appendix D.11, *Tout est mort.*)

24. D'Allemagne, *Saint-Simoniens,* 276, apparently drawing on the memorandum cited above from the Archives Alfred Pereire (see note 19).

25. M. Chevalier to Brisbane, 20 May 1832, Ars 7646, fol. 96, in *OSSE* 7:37. For the call to dinner, see the temple ceremonies, below. Cf. d'Allemagne, *Saint-Simoniens,* opp. p. 392.

26. One list is given by Stéphane Flachat in his letter to Holstein, 2 May 1832, Ars 7727, cited in *OSSE* 6:243–44. A second appears in a four-page leaflet by Léon Cognet (or Cogniet), *Les Apôtres à Ménilmontant* (Lyons: Imprimerie de Charvin, [1832]), dated 19 [recte 9] July 1832; this list was clearly used as the basis for a well-known anonymous engraving of the apostles and was reprinted in Charléty (*Saint-Simonisme,* 165–66) and d'Allemagne (*Saint-Simoniens,* 273—d'Allemagne also reproduces the engraving). A third list appeared in a letter of Michel Chevalier to Humann, July 1832, Ars 7641, fol. 265, cited in d'Allemagne, *Saint-Simoniens,* 273. David figures in none of these lists (except in Flachat's, as a musician—passage quoted earlier). All the lists are incomplete. Rogé and Justus tend the garden in the second; in the third, Justus washes dishes and Rogé is not mentioned.

27. Similarly, Justus must have spent much time helping Bonheur and Talabot design the Saint-Simonian outfits and perhaps doing decorative artwork. Talabot, who seems to have succeeded Duveyrier as *père* to Justus, wrote on 5 June: "Justus worked all day in the painting studio" as his share of the *manoeuvre.* (Talabot to Chevalier, Barrault, and Fournel, in *OSSE* 7:92.)

28. Unidentified newspaper clipping (ca. September 1876) in the David dossier, Musée Arbaud, Aix-en-Provence.

29. Pierre, *Musique,* gives the music for twenty-seven Revolutionary hymns in the form "solos avec refrain de choeur," works such as Lesueur's *Hymne du IX Thermidor.* Many of the forty-six "solos" and works for larger forces (e.g., chorus, solos, and orchestra) are also strophic with refrains (or with choral refrains, in the case of the works with larger forces). "Solo" in this sort of repertoire means—according to Pierre—"pour voix seule ou plusieurs voix à l'unisson" (p. 561), the performing forces presumably varying according to the situation.

30. "Degré des industriels.—Instruction pour la propagation," in *OSSE* 6:115.

31. M. Chevalier to Brisbane, 20 May 1832, Ars 7646, fol. 96, in *OSSE* 7:38.

32. "Parole du Père," in *6 juin 1832,* 6.

33. Talabot to M. Chevalier, Barrault and Fournel, 5 June 1832, in *OSSE* 7:90–93. Talabot complained (ibid., 7:91) that some members of the family skipped rehearsals. Pellarin, who resided at Ménilmontant from 23 June to 10 August, quickly became disgusted with these "vain and grotesque parades"—including what he calls "*le cercle du Père*" (perhaps what can be seen in plate 13)—and the "endless" rehearsing (*Souvenirs,* 132, 135, 141–43, 177).

34. *Prise d'habit,* 4.

35. Pellarin, *Souvenirs,* 132. This was often, he says, the only time of day that Enfantin was seen by the bulk of his disciples.

36. Enfantin's words, in *Prise d'habit,* 12. The remainder of the present section is based on this account.

37. The painting, inscribed on the back "Portrait de F. David peint à Ménilmontant en 1832 par Raymond Bonheur / P. Enfantin," was given to the Musée municipal de Saint-Ger-main-en-Laye by David's dear friend and heir Mme Tastet and her daughter Mme Jourdan. Cf. Charléty, *Saint-Simonisme,* opp. p. 344.

38. Many such engravings, some sympathetic and some satirical, are reproduced in d'Allemagne, *Saint-Simoniens* (after originals in Ars).

39. An "unknown" practice, according to a memorandum, apparently by Gustave d'Eichthal, in *OSSE* 7:83.

40. Rogé, for example, was proud to have been asked. It should be added, though, that certain others—such as Félix de la Maillauderie and the future industrialist Capella—were also invited to join, but they refused because they could not share (or even comprehend) the enthusiasm.

41. *Prise d'habit,* 9, 14–15. Ellipsis points (indicating pauses) are in original.

42. *Prise d'habit,* 14.

43. Ars 7814/21, 22.

44. *Travaux du Temple,* 3 and 13n.

45. Indeed, Pellarin records that several members of the Retreat, including himself and Massol, never did take the habit, but only wore the leather belt over their usual clothes (*Souvenirs,* 139).

46. *Les Saint-Simoniens!!!,* in *OSSE* 7:115–23. Quotation from p. 116.

47. See the note "Convocation du 1er juin" appended to the reprint of a *Globe* article on the "Marseillaise" by Michel Chevalier: *Religion saint-simonienne: La Marseillaise* ([Paris]: Imprimerie d'Everat, [1832]).

48. The following pages, covering events of 1–11 July, are based on the official published account, *Travaux du Temple,* and all unidentified quotations are drawn from that brochure.

49. On the need for a new religious theater and on Attic tragedy (especially the chorus), see Chapter 7; Thibert, *Rôle Social,* 30; d'Allemagne, *Saint-Simoniens,* 276, 318; and *Doctrine,* ed. Iggers, 1st session, pp. 17, 20.

50. *Livres saint-simoniens* (binder's collection), vol. 3, no. 3, in Bibliothèque Thiers.

51. D'Allemagne, *Saint-Simoniens,* 312 (passage entitled, rather grandly, "Création du groupe symphonique"). D'Allemagne adds: "Some rehearsals took place in May and June, Wednesdays at 8 P.M. (69 boulevard de la Contrescarpe) for the Faubourg Saint-Antoine and

Thursdays at 8 P.M. in the Salle de l'Athénée." I have seen no other evidence of this modest but significant undertaking.

52. *Travaux du Temple,* 5–11 (the quotation comes from pp. 6–7), reprinted entire in Locke, "Music and the Saint-Simonians," 207–14, and summarized in Thibert, *Rôle Social,* 42–43.

53. Thibert, *Rôle Social,* 47.

54. Pellarin, *Souvenirs,* 132. Pellarin also states that at evening meals in the great house the crowd watched through the windows.

55. *Procès (août),* in *OSSE* 47:29.

56. *Travaux du Temple,* 25.

57. This kind of contact did not perhaps last long, though, for the police became increasingly obstructive during the following weeks. A permanent guard was set up in front of the house to intercept all incoming and outgoing "communication." To facilitate the surveillance, the prosecutor arranged to have three garden doors locked shut (*Procès [août],* in *OSSE* 47:41). All of this harassment was of doubtful legality, to be sure, but it was probably effective in isolating the apostles from much of their intended public. The soldier in charge, by the way, was a "former trumpeter" (ibid.); no doubt it was he that taught Auguste Chevalier to play. (See the beginning of the present chapter.)

58. See this chapter, nn. 10, 38.

59. Pellarin to his friend Foucaut, (August 1832), in Pellarin, *Souvenirs,* 142.

60. Luce to Alexis Petit (with concluding remarks by Luce's "frère" Michaud [i.e., his Saint-Simonian brother]), Dijon, 12 February 1833 (Ars 15031/244). In the same letter, Luce asked to buy copies of "the [set of] waltz[es] and other pieces of music," and Michaud thanked Petit for sending some music.

61. *Lettre de Lemonnier à Toussaint à Castelnaudary,* 25 June 1832 (pub. 1832), in Thibert, *Rôle Social,* 41–42.

62. Enfantin to his father, 20 October 1832, in *OSSE* 8:110. For other estimates of the Petits' contributions and of those of Henri Fournel and Gustave d'Eichthal (possibly as high as 150,000 francs apiece over the years), see Briscoe, *Saint-Simonism,* 292–93.

63. *Lemonnier à Toussaint,* in Thibert, *Rôle Social,* 41–42.

64. The following pages on Talabot's death and funeral are based on the official published account, *Mort de Talabot.* All unidentified quotations are drawn from that brochure.

65. Anonymous MS chronicle of the day's events, Ars 7825/6. (The phrase "au peuple" may possibly refer instead to a performance of David's chorus *Au peuple.*)

66. Saint-Etienne, *Félicien David,* 12–13. Perhaps the nocturne they sang was "Douleur et joie," "Heure du soir," or "Hymne à l'harmonie"; all three were later published by David in *La Ruche harmonieuse.*

67. This passage seems somewhat mangled in the published account. A period follows "*Justus,*" and then a new quasi-sentence begins: "*Holstein, Terson,* disaient par intervalle. . . ." I conjecture instead a comma and a missing "qui."

68. Enfantin's comments about the inauguration, spoken at a memorial service for Bazard the next day and quoted in the official account of the funeral, in *OSSE* 7:180–88. The description below of events relating to the funeral is based on this same account.

69. Pellarin later did not recall Enfantin saying this (*Souvenirs,* 134).

70. Notes on the trip back by P. Rochette, Ars 7776/13–17.

71. Pellarin was distressed by Enfantin's behavior toward Jules and returned with his faith "badly shaken"; he left the Retreat, and the movement, eleven days later (*Souvenirs,* 135–36).

72. Pellarin, *Souvenirs,* 181.

73. E.g., the *départ* of Machereau et al., 10 November 1832 (*OSSE* 8:171); on the chansons, see Chapter 11.

74. The text sheet of *Ronde,* mentioned earlier, is one of eleven sheets listed by Fournel under the heading "Chansons saint-simoniennes" and in fact all but the *Ronde* are true chansons by Vinçard and others (*Bibliographie,* 1833 ed., 122).

75. *Procès (août),* in *OSSE* 47:48–49.

76. Ibid., 47:360.

77. Vinçard, *Mémoires,* 68.

78. *Procès (août),* in *OSSE* 47:50.

79. Vinçard, *Mémoires,* 72.

80. *Procès (août),* in *OSSE* 47:511.

81. Azevedo relates the episode in *Félicien David,* 44–45.

82. Berlioz, "Le Concert de M. David: *Le Désert,*" in *Musique,* ed. Hallays, 224, and Reyer,

Notice sur Félicien David (Paris: Firmin-Didot et Cie, 1877), p. 3 (information kindly supplied by Elizabeth Lamberton).

83. Enfantin to Aglaé Saint-Hilaire, 6 April 1833, in *OSSE* 29:22.

84. The text states: "La France ... n'a plus de roi. . . . A tous travail et liberté." A copy in the Bibliothèque Inguimbertine, Carpentras (no. 1991/1) bears a more explicit handwritten note: "composé à l'occasion de la Révolution de février 1848."

85. Correspondance, *Le Figaro,* 17 October 1832, 3.

86. Enfantin to Thérèse Nugues, 2 [recte ca. 25?] October 1832, in *OSSE* 8:118.

87. Duveyrier, d'Eichthal, Lambert, Rigaud, Duguet, Ollivier, Rogé, David, Urbain, and Retouret (*Procès [octobre],* in *OSSE* 47:550). See also Hagan, *French Musical Criticism,* 232.

88. Enfantin to his father, 20 October 1832, in *OSSE* 8:110.

89. The preceding sentences are based on *Procès (octobre)* in *OSSE* 47:547–49.

90. BNMus MS 1829. The manuscript bears a hesitant cover note by librarian Charles Malherbe, "Le reste est de son élève Pol. J...t (?)." This note apparently was transferred from a wrapper now lost, for Justus's name appears nowhere on the pages.

91. Ars 7865/8.

92. Ars 7856/1–7, 9–19. In 7856/9 he indulges in a typically Saint-Simonian dichotomy, linking melody to "egoism" and paganism and harmony to "association" and Christianity. "The living form is the progressive union of these [two] forms." (Cf. *Livre nouveau* in Chapter 7 above.) He also suggest that the ear responds to the "spirit" and the eye to "matter," an extension perhaps of the Romantic notion that music, because nonrepresentational, is the art of feelings.

93. Lambert's harmony exercises, Ars 7858/2–4; the middle of these three contains parallel fifths in a progression from V to vi!

94. An anecdote relates that Duveyrier asked David (at Ménilmontant?) to write a symphony on the motto "To each according to his capacity..." (Brancour, *Félicien David,* 21n, citing no source).

95. D'Allemagne, *Saint-Simoniens,* 317–18;

quotes from letters of Enfantin, 24 and 26 October 1832.

96. Mercier to Gallé, 30 April 1833, in *Livre des actes,* 33–36.

97. Voilquin, *Souvenirs,* chaps. 10–18, including vivid depictions of Luce, Arlès-Dufour, Mme Durval, and many other provincial sympathizers. See also Agulhon, *Ville ouvrière,* [199]–265; Jean Vidalenc, "Les Techniques de la propagande saint-simonienne à la fin de 1831," *Archives de la sociologie des religions* 10 (1960):3–20; and Puech, "Saint-Simoniens."

CHAPTER 11

1. It is presumably to this occasion that item H 26 in Fournel's *Bibliographie* refers: "Invitation pour le jour des Morts; en date du 12 Décembre 1832."

2. See Appendix B for lists of the various Saint-Simonian songsters and of the chansons associated with specific meetings and reunions. (I use the word "songster" to mean a collection of three or more poems intended to be sung and usually containing references to the names of the tunes that the songwriter had in mind when he wrote the words—definition adapted from Irving Lowens, *A Bibliography of Songsters Printed in America before 1821* [Worcester: American Antiquarian Society, 1976].)

3. Appendix B does not completely reveal this; for reasons of space, it eliminates most publications of one or two songs, notably those that are listed by author in the published *Catalogue des imprimés* of the Bibliothèque nationale. Some of these, and also some of the songsters (*Chansons de Vinçard; Mercier; Foi nouvelle (1835); Soirée*), are included in the Hachette microfiche series *Les Saint-Simoniens.*

4. D'Eichthal, too, declined to make the voyage; after reconciling with his family, he spent some time on his own in Italy.

5. On the Famille and its various members (*lingères, menuisiers,* and so forth), see Vinçard, *Mémoires;* Voilquin, *Souvenirs,* chap. 8; and Elhadad's insightful introduction to the Voilquin.

6. *Foi nouvelle. Livre des actes, publié par les femmes,* henceforth referred to as *Livre des actes.* (The eleven livraisons of this "book," published between 15 July 1833 and 20 February 1834, are paginated consecutively.) Much of

the material from *Livre des actes* to be cited below can also be found, in whole or in part, in *OSSE,* vol. 9.

7. Vinçard, *Mémoires,* 153–55.

8. Song reprinted in *Foi nouvelle (1835)* and *Chants du travailleur* (see Appendix B.2).

9. Vinçard, *Mémoires,* 119–23. (Vinçard notes that four former members of the Ménilmontant Retreat [including Rogé] were present at the second appearance of "la dame bleue" but did not offer her their services.) Cf. Ars 7825/22.

10. Justus's words (the *étrennes à George Sand* were his idea), in Vinçard, *Mémoires,* 126.

11. George Sand's letter, in Vinçard, *Mémoires,* 130. Cf. George Sand, *Correspondance* 3:73, and Marix-Spire, *Romantiques,* 469.

12. Vinçard, *Mémoires,* 75.

13. Ibid., 76.

14. Ibid., 115–16.

15. Ibid., 116.

16. Ibid., 113–14.

17. *Livre des actes,* 137, in *OSSE* 9:134–35; cf. *OSSE* 9:238.

18. See Joseph Landragin's description, *Les Mystères de la goguette dévoilés* (Paris: chez l'auteur, 1845), 5, 8–14, in Newman, "Politics and Song in a Paris Goguette."

19. *Livre des actes,* in *OSSE* 9:214–15; cf. Voilquin, *Souvenirs,* chap. 8, pp. 124, 136–37.

20. Dated 1831 in Fournel, *Bibliographie,* 123, and (revised version) item I/xi. The song is printed in Vinçard, ed., *Chants du travailleur,* 66, where it is dated 1834. The song also appeared in Vinçard's collection *Foi nouvelle 1835* (see Appendix B.2) and is reprinted in *OSSE* 8:172–73.

21. Vinçard, *Mémoires,* 77–78, referring to a second Lagache poem, "Le Temple de Dieu" (published anonymously—copies in *BHVP* 5 and Ars 7803/29—see Appendix B.2). Lagache also wrote twelve new stanzas for David's *Ronde* ("Soldats, ouvriers, bourgeois")—Appendix E.14a.

22. So thinks Brochon (*Pamphlet,* 24).

23. The history of the French chanson is perhaps too large ever to be written. Vernillat and Barbier give a fine overview, weighted toward the political, in their eight-volume anthology *Histoire de France par les chansons* and its companion record album. On Béranger,

the Saint-Simonians, and related developments, see Touchard's *Béranger,* Brochon's anthologies *Béranger* and *Pamphlet,* and Brécy's *Florilège.*

24. For details see my article "Music of the French Chanson."

25. This is the fourth item in Mercier's songster of 1833 (see Appendix B.1).

26. Vinçard, ed., *Chants du travailleur,* 206.

27. On Béranger's relations with the Saint-Simonians and on "Les Fous," see Locke, "Music and the Saint-Simonians," [iv–v], 250–54.

28. Capelle described it as an *air ancien* that had been altered several times (*Clé,* 246).

29. Béranger, "Préface de l'auteur: 1833," in *Les Chansons de P.-J. de Béranger,* xiii; and Touchard, *Béranger.*

30. Vinçard, *Mémoires,* 85–86. The occasion for the march to Charenton was the departure of Mercier and five other missionaries. When Vinçard printed the chanson in *Nouveaux Chants saint-simoniens* (see Appendix B.1), he wisely recommended a different timbre: "Allons, mettons-nous en train" (*Clé,* no. 1072 or possibly 1437).

31. Briscoe, *Saint-Simonism,* 327.

32. Information kindly supplied by Frédéric Robert.

33. [Michel Chevalier], *Religion saint-simonienne: La Marseillaise* ([Paris]: Imprimerie d'Everat, [1832]), 4. According to Thibert (*Rôle social,* 32), an article in the *Globe* of 28 July 1830 (i.e., the second day of the Revolution) entitled "Fêtes officielles" had already voiced the same concern.

34. Barrault, "L'Art," 494–95.

35. *Cérémonie du 27 novembre,* 11. "La Parisienne" was the most popular battle hymn of the July Revolution; the jaunty tune was erroneously thought to be by Auber.

36. Fournel to Arlès-Dufour, ca. September 1833, in *Livre des actes,* reprinted in *OSSE* 9:95–96.

37. Possibly written by or for Casimir Cayol's brigade; see letters from Cayol to Chevalier, [20 December 1832] and 27 December 1832 (Ars 7624/25, 26).

38. Barrault singled out this stanza by Rouget de Lisle as being particularly religious (sermon of 28 November 1830, in *OSSE* 43:99–100).

39. "Marseillaise pacifique," in *L'Homme nouveau* (prospectus) (Lyons: Mme Durval, [1833]), BNImp 8°Z 8132/25.

40. It does not, though, fit the "Marseillaise" tune (information kindly provided by Frédéric Robert).

41. [Alphonse de] Lamartine, "La Marseillaise de la paix," in *Méditations poétiques, Nouvelles Méditations poétiques suivies de poésies diverses,* ed. Marius-François Guyard (Paris: Le Livre de poche, 1969), 407–11, 494.

42. Mora's "Le Goguettier réformateur" appeared in Vinçard's publication *L'Union,* vol. 1, no. 2 (October 1844); information kindly supplied by Edgar Leon Newman. Marie-Christine Marquat, "Jean Journet (1799–1861): L'Homme et l'oeuvre," thèse de troisième cycle, Université de la Sorbonne nouvelle (Paris III), 1978:343. Flora Tristan, *Union ouvrière* (Paris and Lyons, 1844; reprint, Paris: EDHIS, 1967), 120–29. Tristan gives two new chansons (neither one of which follows the meter of the "Marseillaise") and the winning musical setting (by A. Thys, who was a Mason, according to Cotte, *Musique maçonnique,* 219). The poète-ouvrier Charles Poncy declined to write a chanson but offered a poem ("L'Union: Au peuple"), noting modestly that Vinçard would have done it better. (On Tristan's competition, see J.-L. Puech, *Flora Tristan, sa vie, son oeuvre* [Paris, 1925], 156, briefly summarized in Thibert, *Rôle social,* 32.)

43. Félicien David was one of the judges and Pauline Viardot won a bronze medal (George Sand, *Correspondance* 8:359–60).

44. From "Vor der Fahrt," the first poem in *Ça ira* (1846). The other poem is "Reveille," 1849. (*Freiligraths Werke,* ed. Paul Zaunert, 2 vols. [Leipzig and Vienna: Bibliographisches Institut, 1912] 1:354–56, 2:47–48.)

45. On French political song after the utopian socialists, see Vernillat and Barbier, *Histoire,* vols. 6–8; Brochon, *Pamphlet;* and Brécy, *Florilège.*

46. Suzanne Voilquin gives his first name as Louis (*Souvenirs,* chap. 38, p. 396). "Luc" is given in some modern sources.

47. Vinçard, *Mémoires,* 140.

48. Ibid., 60. Since the following few pages are derived almost solely from the *Mémoires,* page references will be given in the text.

49. A traditional exercise, often used for competitions in singing clubs. The aim is to compose a chanson (on any subject) that incorporates a predetermined series of final rhyming syllables (line "stubs"). See for example "Concours de bout rimés," *Almanach des musiciens de l'avenir,* ed. A. de Gasparini, 2 vols. (Paris: Librairie du Petit Journal, 1867–68) 2:18–23, or Pellarin, *Souvenirs,* 104.

50. Vinçard, *Mémoires,* 20–24.

51. Ibid., 24–25, 29.

52. Ibid., 266–67.

53. Ibid., 312. He does mention using this piano to help him write the tunes to four of his songs (ibid., 299).

54. Newman, "Politics and Song in a Paris Goguette," drawing on [Eugène Imbert], *La Goguette et les goguettiers, étude parisienne,* 3d ed. (Paris: n.p., 1873), 15. See also Guy Erismann, *Histoire de la chanson* (Paris: P. Waleffe, 1967), 70.

55. Vinçard, *Mémoires,* 136 (letter of 24 September 1834).

56. Ibid., 138–52.

57. The tune to song 20 actually carries the same timbre as most of the others: "Air de l'auteur des paroles." The printed text, though, contradicts this: "Air final du quadrille le Meunier d'Auteil (Musard)." For songs 9 (by Lagache) and 21 (Corréard) there is no timbre in either the music or the printed text. For no. 22 (by F. Maynard), the music is by Reber; see Chapter 12. I am presuming that all the rest have texts by Vinçard (even song 26, which credits no author at all) and that he used his own tunes in the five songs (10–12, 23–24) that carry no timbre, not just in those labeled "Air de l'auteur des paroles."

All thirty-seven tunes listed here are reprinted (and erroneously numbered 1–21, 30–45) in Locke, "Music and the Saint-Simonians," app. 4, pp. 413–52, and app. 5, p. 690. Nos. 1, 17, 27, 29, and 34 are reprinted in Appendix C below.

58. Vinçard, *Mémoires,* 94.

59. Enfantin to Vinçard, 3 November 1855, in Vinçard, *Mémoires,* 283–84. Cf. letter of Enfantin (recipient unknown), 25 August 1857, Ars 15032/146 (claiming that songs can do more than did all the sermons given by Barrault and others in 1831).

60. Vinçard to Enfantin, 11 February 1856, Ars 7804/18.

61. See examples 2, 5, and 8 in my "Music of the French Chanson."

62. See E. J. Hobsbawm, *The Age of Revolution: 1789–1848* (New York: New American Library, 1962), chap. 14 ("The Arts," esp. 323–26).

63. Vinçard, *Elan,* Publications du *Sabbat musical* 3 (Paris: au Bureau du *Sabbat Musical,* [1841]). The accompaniment may be by Auguste Vincent, who is credited with the rather similar piano part for another Vinçard song, *Chant du travail* (Paris: Ch. Killian, [1856]); also, the *Elan* title page was engraved by "A.V."

The accompanied *Elan* was also published (in the same year) in Rodrigues's *Poésies sociales,* 363–70. The melody is the first in Vinçard's *Chants du travailleur.*

64. Voilquin, *Souvenirs,* chap. 8, pp. 136–37; Vinçard, *Mémoires,* 80, 90, 91. The French phrase, "en choeur," does not, in Vinçard's usage, imply singing in harmony—merely many people singing a tune together. (Cf. ibid., 119, where the song in question is a chanson of Mercier and the performance hurriedly struck up.)

65. Hoart to Enfantin, 3 March 1833, in *OSSE* 8:222–24.

66. Vinçard, *Mémoires,* 116.

67. Ibid., 165.

68. He had once sung "some stanzas of our habitual songs" at dinner while visiting a working-class *phalanstère* (Vinçard's word) run by Fanfernot near Rambouillet (ibid., 158–60).

69. [Gabriel or Marie Antoine] Toussaint to Alexis Petit, [March 1834], Ars 15031/966. The occasion was the impending arrival of four missionaries. Rousseau and Biard, when departing for Lyons (28 November 1832), received instructions to "chanter beaucoup les trois chansons de David" and to retext them as necessary (d'Allemagne, *Saint-Simoniens,* 326).

70. See the 1833 songsters (Appendix B.1) and *Foi nouvelle [1835]* (Appendix B.2).

71. Gallé tried (with what success?) to organize a benefit concert for the Mission d'orient, featuring performances of *Salut, Ronde,* and *La Prison du Père* (letter of July [?] 1833, Ars 7728/5).

CHAPTER 12

1. Jules Toché, in [Tajan-Rogé], *Mémoires d'un piano,* 51.

2. [Tajan-Rogé], *Mémoires d'un piano,* 51–52, based on a letter of 1873 from Amable Lemaître (to Rogé?).

3. *Ménilmontant, le 23 novembre 1832: A Lyon!* (Paris: imprimerie de E. Duverger, [1832]), 1, 2, 5.

4. [Tajan-Rogé], *Mémoires d'un piano,* 53, 12.

5. Dossiers I², Archives municipales de Lyon, cited in J. Gaumont, *Histoire générale de la coopération en France,* 2 vols. (Paris: Fédération nationale des coopératives de consommation, 1923–24) 1:123–24; cf. Rude, *Insurrection,* 268, 697–99.

6. Charléty, *Saint-Simonisme,* bk. 3, chap. 1, pp. 206–7. See also Chevalier's *Système méditerranéen,* summary in *OSSE* 6:55–96, and Barrault's sermons in *OSSE* 45:392–416, 421–73.

7. See Chevalier's remarks (cited at the beginning of Chapter 10) or Enfantin's (24 January 1832, in *OSSE* 17:27).

8. *1833; ou, l'année de la Mère: Janvier* (Lyons: S. Durval, [1833]) contains both letters. Enfantin's is dated 26 January, and Barrault's 30 January. I have discussed them in the text in reverse order because Enfantin admitted in his letter that he was not initiating the idea of an Oriental voyage but approving a plan that Barrault had presented in April and again in June of the previous year. (Cf. d'Allemagne, *Saint-Simoniens,* 313–15.)

9. *L'Homme nouveau ou le messager du bonheur,* no. 1 (14 July [1833]):1–2.

10. [Tajan-Rogé], *Mémoires d'un piano,* 15.

11. Ibid.

12. 5 February 1833, Ars 7624/42.

13. David to Enfantin, 9 January 1833, Ars 7647, fol. 422, in Prod'homme, "Félicien David," 120. Prod'homme's transcriptions are sometimes faulty; my translations rely primarily on the manuscripts (see corrected transcriptions in "Music and the Saint-Simonians," chap. 7).

14. Fournel lists three printings, one in "patois" (revised edition of the *Bibliographie,* item I/xi).

15. See Hoart's report of performances of *Compagnonnage* and *Ronde* during the Mission du Midi, Ars 7647/273, cited in Marquat, "Jour-

net," 63–64, and the references to various performances in the present chapter.

16. Marquat, "Journet," 342. Journet and his family lived in Villefranche and were ardent Saint-Simonians. Around 1832 they may well have been in close contact with Toussaint and the other Saint-Simonians in nearby Castelnaudary (ibid., 49–55, 60–61).

17. David to Enfantin, 9 January 1833 (as cited above). David indicated earlier in the letter that in his first weeks in Lyons he had waged "a heated battle against wrong notes" among "my gallant proletarians."

18. 22 February 1833, Ars 7647, fol. 123ᵛ, in Prod'homme, "Félicien David," 120. A letter of David's to Jenny Montgolfier of ca. March 1833 refers to its first public performance, at the Rotonde (Saffroy catalogue 62 [February 1969], item numbered [6122] and 5).

19. Clorinde Rogé to Aglaé Saint-Hilaire, 15 February 1833, Ars 7624/42. She asks Aglaé (who is in Paris) to tell M. Chabanis to send as many copies of David's pieces as he can.

20. *Mission du Midi*, 7.

21. *Mission du Midi*. [Tajan-Rogé], *Mémoires d'un piano*, 29–32, 48–61. *Livre des actes*, 21–33.

22. Hoart to Enfantin, 4 April 1833, in *Livre des actes*, 24–25.

23. [Tajan-Rogé], *Mémoires d'un piano*, 55. On 17 June of the previous year Colin wrote to Ollivier to request copies of David's *L'Appel au peuple* and *Le Retour du Père;* the music, he added, was making the movement go forward (Ars 13739/149). Marseilles declined in importance as quickly as it had risen (Vinçard, *Mémoires,* 157).

24. Costume, necklace, ring: d'Allemagne, *Saint-Simoniens,* 347–50, 354–56, 371–72, and drawing opp. 368.

25. [Tajan-Rogé], *Mémoires d'un piano*, 58–60. Rogé's figure, twenty thousand, is surely an exaggeration.

26. Lambert's diary, Ars 7751/10, fol. 8r (14 October 1833); see also Ars 7624/23.

27. The newpaper report does not actually cite the title of this piece (or indeed of the others), but David's *Compagnonnage de la Femme* includes the words "C'est l'ange de la liberté" (quoted in the report). "Vive la femme," curiously, is not in the text. Perhaps the Compagnons shouted it.

28. "Banquet saint-simonien," *Le Sémaphore de Marseille* (22 March 1833), reprinted in *L'Homme nouveau,* no. 1:3–5.

29. On 17 February (d'Allemagne, *Saint-Simoniens,* 371).

30. Compare what Beethoven makes of IV⁶–I in the closing pages of the *Missa Solemnis.*

31. Ars 7803/50. Since the text is in Lambert's hand and Lambert was not, to my knowledge, present in Marseilles in March, it is conceivable that the *Cantate* was first sung in September for the *départ* of Enfantin, Lambert, and others.

32. List of contributions in Barrault's hand, Ars 14697/32. "Granal aîné" (P. Granal?) contributed the largest amount: 2,000 francs.

33. [Tajan-Rogé], *Mémoires d'un piano,* 60–62.

34. 28 March 1833, Ars 15031/259.

35. [Tajan-Rogé], *Mémoires d'un piano,* 30–32, based on the full account, *Mission du Midi.* See also letter to Enfantin, 30 April 1833, in *Livre des actes,* 21, 33.

36. [Tajan-Rogé], *Mémoires d'un piano,* 33–44. See also Hoart's letter to Enfantin, 30 April 1833, in *Livre des actes,* 32.

37. Hoart to Enfantin, dated "Saint-Simon Emile Barrault [i.e., Monday, 24] juin 1833," in *Livre des actes,* 40. The dates of this and other letters have been "translated" with the help of the *Calendrier S.-S. 1833.*

38. *Mission de l'Est.*

39. Azevedo, *Félicien David,* 49.

40. [Tajan-Rogé], *Mémoires d'un piano,* 44–48, based on the full account, *Mission de l'Est.* See also *Livre des actes,* 120–36.

41. Reboul's journal was first identified and published by G. D. Zioutos in "Cahiers inédits." Reboul implies (ibid., 30) that this second group of Compagnons, after seeing the first twelve off in Marseilles, stopped singing and proselytizing and restricted their apostolate to manual labor until Barrault called them to the East. Tamisier—one of the movement's obscure figures—later became involved with a publication called *La Critique musicale* (Ars 7630/230–31) and—unless this was a different Tamisier—became a Fourierist (*Almanach social 1840*).

42. "Chroniques lyonnaises," *L'Homme nouveau,* nos. 2–4 (August 1833):37–38.

43. Letter of Toussaint (ca. September 1833),

in *Livre des actes,* 92; letter from Tajan-Rogé to Enfantin, dated "Lyon, Barrault, Jean Reynaud [i.e., Thursday, 11 (no month)] 1833," in *Livre des actes,* 89–90.

44. Reboul's account, in Zioutos, "Cahiers inédits," 30–32.

45. [Tajan-Rogé], *Mémoires d'un piano,* 63–66, 76–78.

46. Hoart to Cécile Fournel, 24 September 1833, in *Livre des actes,* 99; see also Lambert to his sister Sophie, 1 November 1833, in *OSSE* 9:142 (reprinted from *Livre des actes*).

47. *Livre des actes,* 117–20. On their way to Marseilles the two women had stopped in Toulon to see some Saint-Simonians and ended up singing the movement's tunes by the sea to a large crowd (Weill, *L'Ecole saint-simonienne,* 174).

48. Enfantin, *Le PERE aux capitaines Hoart et Bruneau, à Rogé et Massol,* in *OSSE* 9:104. Alexis Petit approached Ingres and other artists about joining the mission but was rebuffed (d'Allemagne, *Saint-Simoniens,* 416–17).

49. Ibid., in *OSSE* 9:100.

50. Enfantin to Bruneau, 8 August 1833, in *OSSE* 9:61.

51. Enfantin, *Aux capitaines . . . ,* in *OSSE* 9:101.

52. Letter dated "Paris, décembre; Bazard, le Père; année la Mère" [Wednesday, 18 December 1833], Ars 7776/65. A few months earlier Rogé had complained of anarchy in the movement and had expressed longing for the Daughter of God (letter to Lambert, 1 August 1833, Ars 7624/100, copy in 7647, fol. 134ᵛ).

53. Letter of [18 December 1833] just cited.

54. From the account in *Livre des actes,* cited in *OSSE* 9:215. The writer also reports that, "thanks to the efforts of Rogé, whose tireless devotion overcomes all difficulties, instrumentalists are rehearsing."

55. Enfantin to Hoart and Bruneau, 19 March 1834, in *OSSE* 29:120.

56. Ibid. "David is busy arranging Arab tunes for brass band. I will have them sent as soon as some are ready, so that Rogé can have his musicians learn them."

57. Enfantin to Hoart and Bruneau, March 1834, in *OSSE* 9:208.

58. Enfantin to Aglaé Saint-Hilaire, 17 June 1834, in *OSSE* 29:208.

59. *Mémoires,* 114–15.

60. Enfantin to Aglaé Saint-Hilaire, [ca. July 1834], in *OSSE* 9:235.

61. Rogé has just listed these: three each of clarinets, keyed trumpets, valved trumpets, ophicleides, and trombones, four "ordinary trumpets," four horns, a piccolo, and a drum.

62. 25 September 1834, Ars 7776/66. (Rogé refers to a previous letter to Enfantin, now lost, perhaps from August 1834.) The present letter covers six closely written pages—one loose folio and bifolio—and begins *in medias res.* Apparently the opening sheet (beginning the first bifolio) was torn off. The pages that survive include quite angry remarks about Rogé's subordination to Duveyrier at Ménilmontant, about Hoart's assumption of the major glory for a "mission d'art" that Rogé had organized—the Mission de l'Est?—and about Michel Chevalier's description of Rogé (to Arlès-Dufour) as a fat fellow notable for his large and vigorous shoulders. Rogé sublimates his anger, blaming himself for being timid and unassertive (in contrast to those who had the "advantage of a glorious past").

In a postcript to this letter, dated 10 October, Rogé welcomes the news that he is being called to Egypt after all and says that he is sending the letter anyway as a faithful record of his recent life and development.

63. That, anyway, seems to be implied by Rogé's remarks cited below. One complication: Reber's piece is dated March 1833 in the manuscript. One must assume that the correct date is March 1834; if not, David and Enfantin would certainly have long known of Reber's interest. The later date also coincides with the establishment of Rogé's chorus and band.

64. Tajan-Rogé to Enfantin, 25 September 1834, Ars 7776/66.

65. The only known copy of this edition is currently inaccessible (see Appendix D.31). The source for the present description is Reber's manuscript, BNMus MS 11217.

66. An account of this inspiring encounter (from Dumas's *Mémoires de Garibaldi*) is cited in *OSSE* 9:25–26.

67. Barrault to Enfantin, 16 April 1833, printed in both *L'Homme nouveau,* no. 1 (13 July [1833]):6–8, and *Livre des actes,* 17–20.

68. On Clorinde's plans to educate the women of the harem in Egypt, approved by

the Viceroy and his son but never carried out, see her letter to Enfantin, 20 June 1845, Ars 7776/52.

69. Barrault to Enfantin, 19 May 1833, in *Livre des actes,* 48–50, and summary of a letter from Tourneux (ca. May 1833), in *Livre des actes,* 20. The brevity of the Compagnons' stay in Constantinople and the antagonism of the officials make it extremely unlikely that David heard the court orchestra, newly reorganized by Giuseppe Donizetti. This corrects a recent statement by Gültekin Oransay ("Orientalismus in der Musik: Hörprogramm," in Siegfried Wichman, ed., *Weltkulturen und moderne Kunst* [Munich: Verlag Bruckmann, (1972)], 154).

70. Barrault to Enfantin, 9 May 1833, in *Livre des actes,* 50.

71. The following account of the stay in Smyrna's derives—except as otherwise noted—from "Smyrne," a series of three articles published by P. Granal in *Le Temps* on 25 September, 30 September, and 10 October 1837. This newspaper is unrelated to its better-known namesake of later in the century; its editor was Adolphe Guéroult, trusted friend of Enfantin and others in the movement.

72. Charles de Varenne's brief biography of David (apparently based on an interview), in *Diogène,* no. 35 (19 April 1857), clipping in BNMus iconographie David no. 36.

73. Gradenwitz ("Félicien David," 485) speculates that David may have heard some Oriental music (of a sort) already in 1832 when he, d'Eichthal, Barrault, and others made a symbolic visit to a synagogue in Paris on the High Holy Days. But historian Barrie M. Ratcliffe suggests (in a kind personal letter to me) that they probably visited the central Paris synagogue, which followed Ashkenazic (Central European) traditions rather than Sephardic (Mediterranean). The cantor at the central synagogue was Elie Halévy, the father of Léon Halévy and of the composer Fromental Halévy. Concerning this visit, and a preceding one by d'Eichthal and Barrault alone, see a manuscript note of d'Eichthal (6 March 1836, in Ars 14390) and d'Eichthal's remarks in the anonymous article "Un Souvenir de Lambert-Bey," *Archives israélites* 25 (1864):211–15. The former source is summarized but inadvertently dated 1832 in Barrie M. Ratcliffe's excellent

article "Saint-Simonism," 496.

74. See Granal's article of 30 September 1837. The description of David as a "new Orpheus" serenading the "barbarian peoples" with unfamiliar sounds (cited in Gradenwitz, "Félicien David," 477) is not from Granal but from Saint-Etienne's inaccurate summary (*Félicien David,* 20). David in fact lived in the French quarter, and his immediate neighbor was a Mr. Cramer (according to the letter to Urbain cited directly below).

75. David to Urbain, 12 June 1833, Ars 13739/202.

76. Ibid. Mersane was perhaps an inhabitant of the French quarter; he was certainly not one of the Compagnons.

77. The *Prière* was retexted by Charles Chaubet as *Les Statues de Prométhée* (no. 6 in *La Ruche harmonieuse*), the first two sections (introduction and vocalise) of *Les Etoiles* (called "*La Nuit: à la Mère:* orientale" in David's letter) reappear with new words as the "Choeur des génies de l'océan" in David's *Christophe Colomb,* and a briefer piece in praise of La Mère—it is entitled simply *Fragment* and begins "Belle, oh belle comme l'ange"—was evidently soon included in a longer piece that I shall call *Hymne à la Mère* and that survives with a new text by Charles Chaubet as *Hymne à la nature* (*Ruche,* no. 10). Details in Appendix D.27-30.

78. Retexted in *Christophe Colomb* as "à l'hymne montant des ondes."

79. Passage omitted in *Christophe Colomb.*

80. Discussed in my "New View" and "Exotic Techniques."

81. Anaïs Saint-Didier performed a "jolie Prière" of David's in Enfantin's presence when the leader passed through Lyons en route to Egypt (*OSSE* 30:118); but the piece entitled *Prière* is not well suited to solo performance.

82. Clorinde, while in Lyons, informed Aglaé Saint-Hilaire: "I am now engraving the new piece, *La Prison du Père.*" Perhaps the earlier choruses had been engraved by a certain Mlle Charlotte: Clorinde asked Aglaé in the same letter to look in a big red box or else in Mlle Charlotte's "engraving drawer" for some manuscripts that David wanted (the two series of Ménilmontant waltzes). Letter of 15 February 1833, Ars 7624/42.

83. Letter dated "Lyon, Barrault, Jean Rey-

naud 1833 [Thursday, 11 (no month)] 1833," in *Livre des actes,* 90.

84. Barrault to Enfantin, 6 July 1833, in *Livre des actes,* 94.

85. Casimir Cayol, "Voyage au Caire," *L'Homme nouveau,* nos. 2–4 [August 1833]: 18ff.

86. Barrault to Enfantin, 6 July 1833, in *Livre des actes,* 94.

87. Rogé, in dispatching the desired men, several of them singers, seemed mainly concerned about the composer's health: "Lamy in Smyrna will be a great help to David's delicate chest." Letter to Enfantin dated "Lyon, Barrault, Jean Reynaud [Thursday, 11 (no month)]," in *Livre des actes,* 90.

88. A letter from Alric to a friend in Strasbourg (18 October 1833) indicates that on his arrival in Alexandria he found "our singers" (the men sent by Rogé) and Barrault, "who had traveled to Jaffa and Jerusalem with *David.*" (In *Livre des actes,* 202–6.) Alric does not mention Granal, but Azevedo repeatedly includes him, making a party of three (*Félicien David,* 54–57). Eventually ten of the original twelve (all but Jans and Carolus) did reach Egypt—see *OSSE* 12:13–14 and letters printed in *OSSE,* vols. 9, 10.

89. The historical background in the following pages on Egypt derives mainly from Fakkar, *Sociologie,* 217–29, and from Fakkar's main source, *OSSE,* vols. 9–10. Cf. Jean-Marie Carré, *Voyageurs et écrivains français en Egypte,* 2 vols. (Cairo: Imprimerie de l'Institut français d'archéologie orientale, 1932) 1:257–73; and Voilquin, *Souvenirs,* chaps. 20–35 (with revealing glimpses of Clorinde Rogé, Colin, and many others).

90. The *Moniteur égyptien* (26 November 1833, reprinted in *Livre des actes,* 210–11), reporting on Barrault's first lesson, found itself overwhelmed in spite of itself. Reboul gives further confirmation of the "astonishment" and "admiration" with which Barrault was received by the "European society" of Alexandria (in Zioutos, "Cahiers inédits," 36).

91. See P. Granal, "Choubrah et le buste du Pacha," *Le Temps,* 31 January 1838.

92. Lambert's dairy, Ars 7829, quoted in d'Allemagne, *Saint-Simoniens,* 379. *Moniteur* article of 28 September 1833, translated with some comment as "Aus der neuen ägyptischen Zeitung," *Allgemeine musikalische Zeitung,* vol. 37, col. 80. The information in both sources is confirmed by Alric's letter to a friend in Strasbourg, 18 October 1833, in *Livre des actes,* 202–6. Reboul notes that these concerts were arranged "by the leading lights of this port city" (in Zioutos, "Cahiers inédits," 36). Barrault gives the dates of the concerts: 25 September and 7 and 16 October 1833 (annotated calendar, Ars 14697).

Lambert, in a letter to his sister (1 November 1833), said that the "new vocal works of David generally pleased people" (from *Livre des actes,* as reprinted in part in *OSSE* 9:148). This letter of Lambert's was reprinted in *Le Temps,* where F. J. Fétis read it and expressed distress that such concerts of Western music might eventually replace the music indigenous to Egypt. Fétis quoted a second sentence from Lambert's letter: "David, with his piano and his delicious music, continues to be the charm of all the gatherings, and he has conquered everyone for us." He then went on to regret that David, "a capable musician" but young and inexperienced, had allowed his superiors to force him into mounting these concerts single-handedly, as composer, "vocal forces," and "instrumental forces" all in one. ([Fétis], "Concerts en Egypte," *Revue musicale* 8, no. 5 [2 February 1834]:36–38.) The editor of the *Livre des actes* replied that if Fétis had seen a copy of David's *Prière* he would have taken David's efforts more seriously (p. 234). Fétis was of course not completely accurate in his facts and surmises; David did have singers at his disposal in Egypt, and he hardly needed to be forced into taking on the multiple but gratifying roles of composer, accompanist, and tenor soloist.

93. Letters of 30 November 1833 (by Lambert and Fournel?), in *Livre des actes,* 206. Reboul specifies that on Sunday, 27 October, three days after Enfantin's arrival in port, the Saint-Simonians dined on board and celebrated with a soirée musicale, to which "some friends from the city" were also invited (in Zioutos, "Cahiers inédits," 37–38).

94. Ars 7751-11 (Lambert's diary, Alexandria, 24 October 1833); Ars 7828 (Fournel's diary, Old Cairo, 10 January 1834); Ars 7730/38 (letter from P. Granal to Lamy, Abou Zabel,

11 November 1834); Suzanne Voilquin, *Souvenirs,* chaps. 22–23, esp. pp. 248, 253–54. Cf. Enfantin's letters in *OSSE* 29:160 (David's impacted wisdom tooth) and 29:120 (David's and Urbain's yearning for *La Femme* and *les femmes*).

95. BNMus lettre autogr. 3, Cairo, 17 January 1833 [i.e., 1834], published in Julian Tiersot, *Lettres de musiciens écrites en français* 1:220–21. David spells the name Monge*s*, but family and legal documents more often give it without an *s*.

96. *Revue musicale* 7, no. 41 (9 November 1833):339–40 (signed B....), summarized in *Allgemeine musikalische Zeitung* 35, no. 50 (11 December 1833), col. 841, as follows: "The words are quite bad and the music is bizarre and without melodic appeal." Perhaps David was goaded as well by the strong words of his former teacher Fétis (cited in n. 92).

97. Letter to Hoart and Bruneau, March 1834, in *OSSE* 29:211–12. Enfantin is here specifically referring to the architecture of the city he wishes to found near the Nile dam. Cf. *OSSE* 30:221–22 (whether to dam the Nile by throwing in one of the pyramids).

98. In Zioutos, "Cahiers inédits," 38–40. Reboul also mentions (p. 34) that when he and his companions arrived at their lodgings in Alexandria they were brought two things: water and a "chalumeau" (presumably a wind instrument such as a *mizmār* or *sittawiyya*).

99. Rogé to Lamy, Maréchal, and Alric, "dimanche" (November 1834?), Ars 7776/68, in Prod'homme, "Félicien David," 123. Rogé informs them that David's *Prison du Père* will not, after all, be sung at the General's.

100. "Les Mélomanes d'Alexandrie," *Le Temps,* 14 February 1838.

101. Fournel's diary, 17 February 1834, Ars 7828/11.

102. Ars 7618, fol. 77, in Fakkar, *Sociologie,* 227.

103. Enfantin to Aglaé Saint-Hilaire, 17 June 1834: "I have succeeded in getting them to demand music for our workers. At first they asked for crude native music. Linant, who loves David greatly, made this demand [for something more European] largely in order to have a reason to keep David here" (in *OSSE* 29:207–8).

104. Auguste Frédéric Louis Viesse de Mar-

mont, *Voyage en Hongrie-Transylvanie, . . . en Syrie et en Egypte,* 5 vols. (Paris, 1837–38) 3:368 (reprinted in *OSSE* 9:60). Cf. Voilquin, *Souvenirs,* chap. 24, pp. 261–63. (This Maréchal Marmont was the infamous duc de Raguse who had led the Bourbon attempt to quell the Revolution of 1830.)

105. Salaries for such jobs amounted to 800–1,000 piastres monthly, modest but enough for comfort "if you can live without a harem, slaves, eunuchs, etc." (Enfantin to Aglaé Saint-Hilaire, 22 February 1835, in *OSSE* 10:77; Enfantin to Duguet and Petit, 7 May 1834, in *OSSE* 29:158.) Perhaps the teaching jobs were acquired through Soliman-Pasha, who served as inspector general of schools (*OSSE* 30:175).

106. Voilquin, *Souvenirs,* chap. 26, p. 277 ("Gondret chantait des morceaux d'opéra" at Dr. Dussap's); Fakkar, *Sociologie,* 230. Gradenwitz quotes a German account of musical evenings chez Clorinde Rogé that is surely overstated but indicative of the energy that she and Tajan-Rogé brought to these entertainments ("Félicien David," 474). A letter of Enfantin's gives further details about the participants in these musical and theatrical undertakings at Soliman-Pasha's home (which is probably where many of these events in fact took place, since Enfantin, Lambert, and Clorinde all seem to have been among his houseguests at some point during the months of plague). Enfantin first lists what appear to be the four best musicians (David, Rogé, Yvon, and the chemist Gondret); then what appear to be four additional singers (Machereau, Lamy, Maréchal, and Urbain); and finally four writers and artists. (Letter to Duguet, 28 December 1834, in *OSSE* 10:68. See also *OSSE* 30:54.) Fakkar also states that Robaudy (*sic*) was a musician, perhaps an error deriving from the fact that Georges de Robaudi, a merchant with strong Saint-Simonian sympathies, had provided lodgings for David in early 1834 (see David's letter to Monge, cited above, and also *OSSE* 9:224).

107. Voilquin, *Souvenirs,* chap. 24, pp. 266–67.

108. Enfantin to his father, [February 1835], in *OSSE* 30:71.

109. Enfantin to Aglaé Saint-Hilaire, 22 February 1835, in *OSSE* 10:76–77. Cf. Thibert, *Rôle social,* 48.

110. There he enjoyed the companionship of the unfortunate former director of the Paris Opéra, Lubbert (see *OSSE* 10:81, 83, 84).

111. Enfantin's close friend Hoart died while being lulled to sleep by "les chants du prolétaire" (David's hymns?)—Enfantin to Arlès-Dufour, Barrage du Nil, 25 October 1835, in *OSSE* 30:164.

112. "La Peste d'Egypte," *Le Temps,* 22 December 1837.

CHAPTER 13

1. This was clearly the opinion of Alexis Cendrier. In his letter to Gustave d'Eichthal, 17 June 1833 (Ars 13747/84), he used the phrase "débris d'un grand naufrage" (whence the title of this section) to describe himself and his correspondent. Cf. Pellarin, *Souvenirs,* 153–54, 177.

2. See Jean Dautry's introduction to his *Saint-Simon,* 8–9. Regarding Dautry's views, see Manuel, *New World,* 4. (Editions sociales—Dautry's publisher—is operated by the French Communist Party.)

3. Charléty, *Saint-Simonisme,* bk. 3, chap. 3. On Barrault, see Henri-René d'Allemagne, *Prosper Enfantin et les grandes entreprises du xixe siècle* (Paris: Gründ, 1935), 19.

4. The following pages are almost solely derived from Vinçard's *Mémoires.* Page citations will be given in the text.

5. After Nikolaus Becker stung French pride with his "Der deutsche Rhein" ("Sie sollen ihn nimmer haben / Den freien deutschen Rhein"), Musset's venomous reply ("Nous l'avons eu, votre Rhin allemand") made the round of the salons in settings by Loïsa Puget and then David (see David to Saint-Etienne, 27 November 1841, BNMus lettre autogr. 90). David's setting has a martial refrain for chorus. "Chantons la paix," Vinçard's contribution to the battle of verses was plainly subtitled "à propos du Rhin allemand de M. Alfred de Musset, dédiée à l'auteur de la musique, M. Félicien David." (*La Ruche populaire,* December 1842, pp. 118–19; information kindly supplied by Edgar Leon Newman. Friedrich Hirth erroneously states that David wrote the music for Vinçard's text [Heine, *Briefe* 6:161].) Vinçard, confusingly, later changed the subtitle of his chanson to "A propos d'un chant intitulé / Le

Rhin Allemand / Poésie de M. Lamartine" and dated the song 1843 (*Chants du travailleur,* 246–48).

6. On the *Ruche* and *Union* see Georges Weill, "Les Journaux ouvriers à Paris (1830–1870)," *Revue d'histoire moderne et contemporaine* 9 (1907):94.

7. Bernard H. Moss, *The Socialism of Skilled Workers: The Origins of the French Labor Movement* (Berkeley: University of California Press, 1976), 36; Vinçard, *Mémoires,* 94 (cited in Chapter 11, p. 164).

8. Newman, "Politics and Song in a Paris Goguette." Vinçard's songs first appeared in the *Lice chansonnière* yearbooks (Paris: various publishers) in vols. 6–7 (1839–40) and continued through 1845. The earliest are patriotic songs but the Saint-Simonian message becomes obvious in 1842 (vol. 9) with "Ramons tous à bord" (air du *Bravo*). These songsters were published in runs of 500 or 1,000, occasionally more; *La Ruche populaire* also printed 500 copies of each issue. Even if one adds the additional separate copies that Vinçard published of his songs (1,000 of *Appel* in 1840, 3,000 of its reissue as *Appel aux travailleurs* in 1849—AN F¹⁸*II 27, F¹⁸ 157), the total is far short of the mass circulation that Béranger's work enjoyed. (Facts and figures kindly provided by Professor Newman.)

9. On the working-class song and fable writer Pierre Lachambeaudie (1806–72), see Brochon, *Pamphlet,* 176–77. His Saint-Simonian past has been somewhat exaggerated. On 16 May 1833, at the last moment, he decided not to leave Lyons with Rogé and the other Compagnons, and he took off the costume. (Rogé to Enfantin, in *Livre des actes,* 89.) I have seen no evidence that he had been at Ménilmontant in 1832.

10. Marquat, "Journet," 342–43. Boissy wrote both Saint-Simonian and Fourierist songs.

11. Remark of Pierre Brochon in *Pamphlet,* 25.

12. Ars 7860/22–32. A letter from Duveyrier to Gustave d'Eichthal, 29 August 1860, indicates that Michel Chevalier had joined Fournel, Duveyrier, and others in establishing the Amis (Ars 13752/175). A copy of the statutes of the society is among Lemonnier's papers (Ars 7861/375 [Brochure 17]).

Among the Membres honoraires (i.e., those contributing 24 fr. a year) were Cendrier, Chevalier, Duveyrier, Ducamp, David, Enfantin, Fournel, Gallé, Guéroult, Henry, Jourdan, the Pereires, George Sand, and Urbain. Among the Membres participants (1 fr. 50 per month) were Boissy, Lachambeaudie *père* and *fils,* Mora, Rousseau, and Pierre Vinçard.

13. "Jules Vinçard," in Maitron, *Dictionnaire* 3:512–13. In 1866 Vinçard assumed editorship of another periodical, *La Nouvelle Gazette des abonnés, journal pour rien* (four issues appeared).

14. Coligny, *Chanson française,* photo opp. p. 233, text p. 250.

15. Lettre autogr. 69, 11 May 1835 "à bord de la Madona di Grazia" (written at sea between Livorno and Genoa). The David letters in BNMus will here be referred to simply as "Lettre autogr." followed by the number. All such letters are addressed to Sylvain Saint-Etienne unless otherwise indicated.

16. Giuseppe Donizetti (1788–1856) was invited by the sultan in 1832 (some sources say as early as 1828) to direct the Turkish military bands. He spent the rest of his life in Turkey and was richly rewarded for outfitting the bands with Western instruments and a modern repertoire.

17. Lettre autogr. 69 (cited earlier). See the letter to his brother-in-law Monge, also dated 11 May (Genoa), in the David dossier of the Musée Arbaud (Aix-en-Provence).

18. Lettre autogr. 69. The story about David's piano being destroyed by a band of Arabs (spread by journalists and repeated in Gradenwitz, "Félicien David," 480, and elsewhere) is thus a fiction.

19. Lettre autogr. 69.

20. Lettre autogr. 70, 24 June 1835 (from Marseilles); Saint-Etienne, *Félicien David,* 21.

21. Quotation from Lettre autogr. 71, 3 July 1835; cf. Lettre autogr. 70 (Tuesday, [no day] July 1835). David also writes (letter 71) that de Seynes composed words for a piece of his, *Promenade sur le Nil,* in which "the boatsmen's refrain is a very pretty Arab tune"; this song, surely a vocal adaptation of the piano piece of the same name (the first of the *Mélodies orientales*), is lost. David probably used it more or less unchanged as "Rêverie du soir," although perhaps with new words by Colin.

De Seynes also gave David money (Arlès-Dufour to Enfantin, 24 April 1845, Ars 7665, in Prod'homme, "Félicien David," 239) and David dedicated one of the *Mélodies orientales* to him (*Sous la tente*).

22. Lettre autogr. 71, 3 July 1835.

23. Enfantin to Urbain, Karnak, [August 1835], in *OSSE* 30:115; cf. Enfantin to Lambert, Thebes, 7 August 1835, in *OSSE* 10:36–46, 140–49.

24. Enfantin to Lambert, letter just cited.

25. Lettre autogr. 73, 24 July 1836. Saint-Etienne, in quoting this letter (in *Félicien David,* 23–24), compresses this particular passage to avoid mention of Meyerbeer and interpolates before it three sentences (beginning "Tu me parles de la gloire") from Lettre autogr. 67, 12 August 1831.

26. Rogé to Enfantin, 12 November 1844, Ars 7630/216.

27. Enfantin to Duveyrier, 25 November 1837, Ars 7667/48, fols. 2' and 3'. In the middle, Enfantin refers to the new ballet *La Chatte métamorphosée en femme,* starring Fanny Elssler, for which Duveyrier had written the "stupid and trivial" libretto (Ivor Guest, *The Romantic Ballet in Paris* [Middletown: Wesleyan University Press, 1966], 165–67, 268–69).

28. Lettre autogr. 73, 24 July 1836.

29. Azevedo also says that these scores were lent to David by Boisselot (*Félicien David,* 65–66).

30. Lettre autogr. 3, 17 January 1833 [1834], cited in Chapter 12, p. 191.

31. Lettre autogr. 83, 30 November 1838. The requests begin in 1836 with Lettre autogr. 73. These are by no means begging letters, though. David wanted Saint-Etienne to help sell his music or to remind his sister Clémentine of various sums that were owed him from family inheritances or from the sale of his linens.

32. One report states that David was supported (to what extent?) by d'Eichthal's brother Adolphe between 1835 and 1844. (Mme André Gedalge, *Les Gloires musicales du monde* [Paris: Librairie Gedalge, 1898], 355.)

33. Tourneux to Charles Duguet, 18 April 1837, curtly refusing to subscribe to the *liste civile* for Enfantin (Ars 15032/17).

34. Lettre autogr. 88, 21 May 1840. The first letter from Igny is number 78 (4 August 1837).

Several other letters are postmarked Saint-Maur (73, 24 July 1836), Antony (79 and 82), or Montrouge (83 and 84).

35. Azevedo, *Félicien David,* 66–67.

36. Lettre autogr. 86, 29 August 1839.

37. Tourneux may have introduced David to Fourier's writings; the former had shown an interest in Fourierism as early as March 1832 (*OSSE* 6:96). Among other Saint-Simonians to be attracted to Fourierism during the late 1830s were Abel Transon, Jules Lechevalier, and Auguste Colin, the future librettist of *Le Désert.* (Colin's name appears as one of the "principaux artistes et travailleurs appartenant à l'Ecole sociétaire" in the Fourierist *Almanach social,* 185.)

38. Première série (Paris, chez tous les marchands de nouveautés, 1851). In-12mo, 24 pp. Information kindly supplied by Marie-Christine Marquat.

39. Lettre autogr. 89, 14 June 1841.

40. Azevedo, *Félicien David,* 68–71.

41. Saint-Etienne, *Félicien David,* 26.

42. Azevedo, *Félicien David,* 68.

43. Lettres autogr. 85, 18 April 1839, and 86, 29 August 1839; cf. Lettre autogr. 81, 18 July 1838, his despairing response to Saint-Etienne's uninvited (and impractical) offer to write him a libretto.

44. Lettre autogr. 87, 8 December 1837. Cf. Lettre autogr. 89, 14 June 1841.

45. Colin to Urbain, 1 June 1834, Ars 13739/200. (See the similar exhortation—perhaps also from Colin's pen—in *1833, ou l'année de la Mère. Juillet* [Toulon: imprimerie de Canquoin, 1834], p. 60, cited in Zioutos, "Cahiers inédits," p. 26.) Ironically, Colin objects that Urbain's emphasis on local color—desert, Nile, palms, and dancing girls—is fit only for the taste of the idle class. It was of course the local color in *Le Désert*—admittedly more David's contribution than Colin's—that would make the work an astonishing success as its premiere.

46. "L'Art," in *Recueil de prédications* 1:509 (passage cited) and 498–502 (the pre-Christian artist's vivid portrayal of sun, stars, and "stormy sands").

47. Already in 1827 Colin had attacked the meanness of life in Paris: "This guilty city / In which the vices of the century absorb the virtues" (*La Corbiériade; ou, le Triomphe des moines,* poème héroï-comique en cinq chants, quoted in Pierre Citron, *La Poésie de Paris dans la littérature française de Rousseau à Baudelaire* [Paris: Les Editions de minuit, 1961] 1:196–97).

48. Lettre autogr. 89, 14 June 1841.

49. Azevedo informs us that the song was written while David was living in the countryside, to words by "M. Cogniat," presumably Jacques Cognat, who wrote texts for David's songs *Le Bédouin* and *L'Egyptienne,* published respectively in 1839 and 1842. Cognat was, as Azevedo rightly says, "one of his travel companions in Egypt" and therefore a Saint-Simonian (*Félicien David,* 72, 74). Whether Colin's text for the "Hymne à la nuit" preserves any of Cognat's original verses is not known. Brancour, apparently misunderstanding Azevedo, wrote that the piece was originally written in Egypt (*Félicien David,* 43).

50. See the note concerning de Seynes in the previous section. For a discussion of this and other Arab melodies in David's *Désert,* see my "Exotic Techniques" and "A New View." Brancour (*Félicien David,* 47) incorrectly stated that the "Rêverie du soir" was written for Ménilmontant, no doubt confusing the piece with *Chant du soir* (originally *Danse des astres*). David, to my knowledge, reused no Ménilmontant music in *Le Désert.* (This also corrects Donakowski, *Muse,* 183.)

51. Colin's letter to the *National* is reprinted in *France musicale* 7, no. 52 (29 December 1844):382–83.

52. Berlioz, "Le Concert de M. David," in *Musique,* ed. Hallays. Solera, in a published letter to Escudier, declared that he was particularly moved by David's sunrise (*France musicale* 8, no. 26 [29 June 1845]:205). He and Verdi followed David's example soon after by including an impressive sunrise in their opera *Attila.* (Solera also translated the libretto of *Le Désert* for the F. Lucca edition of the vocal score.)

53. Later David proudly (and rightly) claimed "l'innovation de l'ode-symphonie" as one of his qualifications for a seat in the Académie des beaux-arts (letter to Fiorentino [October–November 1853], New York Public Library). On the term "ode-symphonie," *Le Désert,* and David's three other large works of the 1840s, see Reinisch, *Oratorium,* 75–76,

139–82, 200–213, 299–311, 325–34, 432–39.

54. That it had been anticipated in some ways by "melodramas" of Benda, Beethoven, Berlioz, and others was hardly mentioned at the time, not even by Berlioz.

55. Letter to G. Delavigne, 6 December 1843 (BNMus Rés 2000[1]). Michel, at least, had acted without pressure from Colin, since, when he transmitted David's request for the Salle, the concert was still scheduled for 17 December 1843. *Le Désert* was only composed (and Colin involved) later, after David had been refused the hall at his first request and again for 21 April 1844. (See David's Lettre autogr. 4 to Auber, 1 March 1844, printed in Tiersot, *Lettres* 2:221; also Azevedo, *Félicien David,* 74.)

56. Brief biography of David by Charles de la Varenne, *Diogène,* no. 35 (19 April 1857).

57. Enfantin to Lapointe, 2 December 1844, in Tiersot, *Lettres* 2:222. See Ars 7616, fol. 61 for copies of Quinet's and Sue's letters of regret to Enfantin; Quinet speaks of David as "your glorious disciple."

58. Tajan-Rogé's reply to Enfantin, Saint Petersburg, 12 November 1844, Ars 7630/216.

59. Duveyrier expressed pleasure that these "vocal works which we once performed at Ménilmontant before a few friends and the crowd of children of the people" were now being acclaimed by the critics and the concert-going public. His attitude is symptomatic of the movement's progressive abandonment of "the people" and courtship of the bourgeoisie. (Letters to Charles Lambert and Plichon, both dated 1 January 1844 [1845], Ars 7720/174, 175.)

60. See the correspondence published by Prod'homme ("Félicien David," 229–40). *La France musicale* and other music journals were filled with articles on David's legal troubles.

61. From Enfantin's own list (1845) giving the current status of the various Saint-Simonians who had been in Egypt, in *OSSE* 12:13–15.

62. Letter from David to Enfantin, [1845], Ars 7710/11, also in Prod'homme, "Correspondance," 69–70. (Prod'homme incorrectly identifies Emma.) Enfantin later made light of David's "little sorrows" to Arlès-Dufour (2 July 1845, copy in Ars 7616, fol. 76, also in Prod'homme, "Correspondance," 73) and Arlès-Dufour in turn spoke of Emma as a "harpy" (letter to Enfantin, 6 June 1845, in

Prod'homme, "Félicien David," 249). The transcriptions of these and other letters published in this article of Prod'homme's are wildly inaccurate and even at times nonsensical; the present translations have been checked against the original manuscripts in nearly all cases. (My revised transcriptions are in "Music and the Saint-Simonians," chap. 8.)

63. David to Emma Tourneux, [1845], from an unsigned copy, Ars 7710/10, apparently sent by David to Enfantin with letter 7710/11 cited above.

64. Enfantin to Mendelssohn, 7 May 1845, Bodleian Library, Green Book XXI/168. Duveyrier also wrote to Mendelssohn on David's behalf (same date, Green Book XXI/170). See also Mme Kiéné's letter to Mendelssohn (24 June 1845, Green Book XXI/232) thanking him for receiving David so kindly. She was a friend of Enfantin's (see her letters to him in Ars 7755) and she no doubt remembered Mendelssohn from his stay in Paris in 1816, when her daughter Marie Bigot had given him piano instruction.

Heine, apparently on request, wrote a hearty letter of introduction for David and Enfantin to his faithful friend and fellow Young German Heinrich Laube in Leipzig (5 May 1845). He followed it with a more truthful private letter (24 May) saying that he in fact hardly knew David and not mentioning Enfantin at all, except perhaps indirectly in an ironic reference to the current craze for railway shares. (Heine, *Briefe* 3:23, 25; 6:16.) Enfantin also recommended David to Schletter (Hans Michel Schletterer?) on 3 May 1845 (Heine, *Briefe* 6:16).

65. Gradenwitz, "Félicien David," 496–97.

66. Including Ferdinand David, as mentioned above. David to Enfantin, 30 May 1845, Ars 7710/15, in Prod'homme, "Correspondance," 68.

67. Arlès-Dufour to Enfantin, 6 May and 26 May 1845, Ars 7665, in Prod'homme, "Félicien David," 240.

68. The Symphony in E-flat in particular— Sylvain Saint-Etienne, "Sur l'anniversaire du 8 décembre," *La France musicale,* 9, no. 3 (18 January 1846):21–22.

69. For example, Delaporte in 1832 (Charléty, *Saint-Simonisme,* bk. 4, chap. 3, pt. 3, p.

324). Cf. Olinde Rodrigues's call for a marble statue of "the Moses of peace" (in his speech of 27 November 1831; see Chapter 7) and d'Eichthal's proposal in 1848, two years after David's oratorio, that a statue of Moses be erected in the Place de la Concorde as the symbol of a religious democracy (d'Allemagne, *Enfantin*, 114).

70. Enfantin to David, 24 June 1845, copy in Ars 7617/72–73, in Prod'homme, "Correspondance," 70–71.

71. Enfantin to David, 3 July 1845, copy in Ars 7617, fols. 76–77, in Prod'homme, "Correspondance," 74.

72. Ibid.

73. Enfantin to David, 8 August 1845, copy in Ars 7616, fols. 80'–81, in Prod'homme, "Correspondance," 70–71.

74. It is surely to his railroad schemes that he refers already in the letter of 8 August quoted above, for on 27 August he speaks of "these damned railroads" that keep him tied to Paris (copy in Ars 7616, fols. 87'–88, in Prod'homme, "Correspondance," 82).

75. Charléty, *Saint-Simonisme*, bk. 4, chap. 1.

76. Enfantin even admitted to David, almost without regret, that he had neglected to put certain notices in the paper, no doubt regarding David's tour or the forthcoming premiere of *Moïse* (18 October 1845, copy in Ars 7617, fol. 98–98', unpublished).

77. David to Enfantin, Baden, early September 1845, Ars 7710, in Prod'homme, "Correspondance," 86.

78. "Académie royale de musique. Moïse au Sinaï. Oratorio de Félicien David," *Revue et gazette musicale* 13, no. 13 (29 March 1846):97–99. (Article signed***.)

79. Berlioz to d'Ortigue, Prague, 16 April [1846], in *Correspondance générale*, 3:336.

80. Lettre autogr. 113, 18 August 1846.

81. "L'Art," 499 ("the foaming waves of the Ocean").

82. "La Ville nouvelle," 322. Also in 1832, Fournel had declared, "the founder of the new era . . . needs to have the confident audacity of Christopher Columbus" (*OSSE* 6:159), and Enfantin had spoken of Paris as "the birthplace of the new world" (*OSSE* 6:224). Barrault had used the image of sailing to the new world in

Aux artistes (passage cited in Chapter 6); cf. Barrault, "L'Art," 497.

83. The apt characterization of Columbus is Reinisch's, though he tries to connect it (vainly) to some specific "crisis of leadership" among the Saint-Simonians in the mid-1840s (*Oratorium*, 172). Interestingly, David inserted a similar revolt of the followers into *Moïse* ("Ronde du veau d'or") when he revised it in 1847 (*Oratorium*, 326–28).

84. The connection would have been even clearer if David had kept Saint-Etienne's first version of the "Amis fidèles" text (in BNMus Ms 1082), which echoes the words "Voici nos bras" of the original Ménilmontant chorus.

85. For David's own responses to the February Revolution, see pp. 148 and 352n.43.

86. Enfantin to David, 28 August 1845, copy in Ars 7616, fols. 87'–88, in Prod'homme, "Correspondance," p. 84, and 23 September 1845, copy in Ars 7616/95–95', unpublished. Saint-Etienne began his letters to Enfantin with "Monsieur," changed to "Cher Père" in 1846, then to "Mon cher Monsieur" in 1853–54, and finally back to "Cher Père" in 1855 (letters in Ars 7779).

87. Arlès-Dufour to Enfantin, 23 April 1845, Ars 7665, in Prod'homme, "Félicien David," 238.

88. Enfantin to David, 23 September 1845, cited above.

89. Saint-Etienne to Enfantin, 10 October 1854, Ars 7779/20, in Prod'homme, "Félicien David," 266.

90. According to Hopkinson's catalog of French music publishers, the firm disappeared in 1856 and reappeared again in 1867, but it seems that few if any Saint-Etienne publications actually originated in the later period.

91. Lithographed letter from Enfantin to Lamartine, 15 September 1849 (Ars 15032/36 and Ars 7670), a defense of the Saint-Simonians against attacks in "several passages in your seventh *Conseil au peuple*." Cf. d'Allemagne, *Enfantin*, 145–46.

92. Hagan (*Félicien David*) finds much more that is specifically Saint-Simonian in these works than I do.

93. H. W. [Henri Blaze], *Revue des deux mondes*, n.s., 14 (1846):145–46.

94. Saint-Etienne to Enfantin, 10 October 1854, Ars 7779/20, in Prod'homme, "Félicien David," 266, 268.

95. Lettre autogr. 162 (to Gabriel, ca. 1851). David later expressed to Sylvain his annoyance at "that stupid dialogue by Gabriel" (Lettre autogr. 150, 20 September 1859).

96. T. J. Walsh, *Second Empire Opera: The Théâtre Lyrique, Paris: 1851–1870* (London: John Calder, 1981), 16–17, 300. On David's operas, see Morton Jay Achter, *Félicien David, Ambroise Thomas, and French Opéra Lyrique 1850–1870* (Ann Arbor: University Microfilms, 1972), and Hagan, *Félicien David.*

97. Enfantin to Arlès-Dufour, 25 March 1857, Ars 7665 bis, cited in d'Allemagne, *Enfantin,* 183.

98. Lithographed subscription letter in the hand of Arlès-Dufour, March 1857, copies in Ars 7686/194 and 7688/26–32.

99. D'Allemagne, *Enfantin,* 183.

100. Arlès-Dufour to Enfantin, 26 December 1857, 12 [January 1858], and 3 March 1858, Ars 7686/69, 76, 86.

101. Hector Berlioz to Adèle Suat, 11 March 1858, Collection Chapot. Berlioz also complained that the score itself was "a curious specimen of stupid music [*la musique bête*], which [David] thinks is simple music." (On "the stupid style," see *Evenings,* Sixteenth Evening, pp. 188–90.)

102. See the incriminating exchange of letters in Mirecourt's *Félicien David,* 3d ed., 47–63.

103. *OSSE* 10:206–7.

104. Letters from Térence Hadot to Enfantin from the years 1846–50, Ars 7630/134–49, partially published in Prod'homme, "Félicien David," 262–63, and a letter from David to Léonie Hadot (ca. 1851?) owned by the town of Cadenet (Vaucluse). Berlioz, no doubt well informed, reviewed the *Herculanum* libretto in terms implying that its sole author was Méry (*Journal des débats,* 12 March 1859). One letter of Hadot's (6 November 1848, Ars 7630/137) suggests that he may have received a share of *L'Eden* as well. David, in his late years, dedicated to Hadot the String Quartet in D minor (unpublished, BNMus 1799).

105. Arlès-Dufour to Enfantin, 28 February 1859 and 3 March 1859, Ars 7686/175, 178.

D'Allemagne (*Enfantin,* 183) offers further details.

106. Arlès-Dufour to Enfantin, 3 March (as above) and Tuesday [23? March 1859], Ars 7686/178, 184.

107. D'Allemagne says 15,000 (*Enfantin,* 183).

108. Arlès-Dufour to David, 4 May 1859, copy in Ars 7686/192; Arlès-Dufour's drafts, with David's corrections, of the letter to subscribers, Ars 7686/197, 198; and Arlès-Dufour to Enfantin, 22 and 28 May 1859, Ars 7686/195, 196.

109. Arlès-Dufour to Enfantin, 12 March 1859, Ars 7686/179.

110. As of February 1858 (Azevedo, *Félicien David,* 89). According to Barrie M. Ratcliffe, the date of 1858 is confirmed by the Pereires' wills (in the Archives Pereire).

111. Lettre autogr. 64 (in the David folder) from A. Le Marquand to J.-B. Weckerlin, 15 July 1879. A score, presumably the same one, is now located in the Nydahl Collection (Stiftelsen musikkulturens främjande, Stockholm).

112. Presumably a granddaughter of Emile or Isaac.

113. David's devotion seems also to have allowed no sympathy for those who had sided against Enfantin in the Bazard schism. He was "very much taken aback" one day when he heard Legouvé praise the character of Jean Reynaud. (Edouard Charton to d'Eichthal, 4 July 1863, in David Albert Griffiths, *Jean Reynaud: Encyclopédiste de l'époque romantique d'après sa correspondance inédite* [Paris: Marcel Rivière, 1965], 12–13.)

114. Brief biography of David by Charles de la Varenne, in *Diogène,* no. 35 (19 April 1857).

115. Lettre autogr. 9 to M. Vizentini, n.d. (after 1865).

116. See, for example, Berlioz's heated letter to Stéphen de la Madelaine, 1 December 1861, in my "New Letters of Berlioz," 77, 83. Cf. Sidney Kleinman's *La Solmisation mobile de J. J. Rousseau à John Curwen* (Paris: Heugel, 1974).

117. Azevedo's words, in his *Félicien David,* 89. One of David's tasks as an official member of the Committee of Patronage is recorded in a brochure, "Ecole Galin-Paris-Chevé: Visite d'inspection (sur invitation publique) . . . 20

Février 1861" (Paris: imp. de L. Tinterlin, 1861). The president of the committee, the comte de Morny, had been the protector of the Hadots in the *Herculanum* affair (Mirecourt, *Félicien David*, 49).

118. Little is known of this abortive effort, which receives the praise of Pougin (in the supplement to Fétis, *Biographie universelle*, s.v. "David") and of Ernest Reyer (*Notes de musique* [Paris: Charpentier, 1875], 297). In 1851 David had conducted concerts of the Union musicale.

119. Another undocumented episode in David's life. See his letter to Mme Magnus from Saint Petersburg, [1866], in the Musée Arbaud, Aix-en-Provence. A letter of his to the emperor of Russia was published incompletely in catalog 19 (June 1929) of Librairie Simon Kra and again in catalog 24 (May 1931).

120. David to Mme Magnus, [September 1870], beginning "je voulais vous ecrire," and 12 April [1871], both in the Musée Arbaud, Aix-en-Provence. Victor Considérant, the Fourierist leader, similarly urged (in 1848) that the masses were not yet ready for power (Zeldin, *France: 1848–1945* 1:443).

121. David to Pereire, n.d., letter on display at the David Centenary Exhibition, Cadenet, 1976 (property of M. Martin). Compare David's letter to Saint-Etienne, n.d., regarding a favor that Colin wished of the Pereires (Lettre autogr. 42). David asked favors for Tastet and for Térence Hadot of another correspondent (possibly a Mme de Villeneuve) in letters now in the Bibliothèque Méjanes, Aix-en-Provence.

122. From Louis Jourdan's account of David's last days, quoted in Brancour, *Félicien David*, 104, 107.

123. Preserved in the papers of the notary Yver, Minutier central (Paris), étude XVII, 1383, no. 205. Reproduced with permission of the successor notary, Jean-Marie Bellet.

124. The basic facts are stated in the (unsigned) David article of the *Grand Larousse encyclopédique* (1960). See the vituperative article in the *Mercure aptésien* for 10 September 1876, which cites other choice opinions from the daily press.

125. Letter from Clorinde Rogé to Enfantin, 20 June 1845, Ars 7776/52. (Cf. Enfantin's hearty letter of recommendation for Rogé, 15 December 1834, in *OSSE* 30:54.) Part of the problem was the recurrent mutual and apparently unfulfilled attraction between Clorinde and Enfantin. See her long letter, just cited, as well as those of 1845, 1848, 1857 (Ars 7776/53–60; excerpts in d'Ivray, *Adventure*, 145–52, 213–15).

126. [Tajan-Rogé], *Mémoires d'un piano*, 168–81, 192–278. Cf. P. Granal to Charles Lambert, Alexandria, 25 May 1836, Ars 7730/48.

127. [Tajan-Rogé], *Mémoires d'un piano*, 281, 172–73.

128. Maitron, *Dictionnaire* 3:427.

129. Letter from Tajan-Rogé to Enfantin, Saint Petersburg, 12 November 1844, Ars 7630/216.

130. From Tajan-Rogé's account of his friendship with Berlioz in 1847–48, including the text of several letters, in Rogé's *Mémoires d'un piano*, 284–95. (He deletes Berlioz's name throughout, as well as his own, mainly to pique the reader's curiosity.)

131. Berlioz, *Mémoires*, chap. 55, vol. 2, p. 257.

132. Berlioz's letter of 10 November 1847 (from Berlin), Rogé's reply of December 1847 (he does not specify the date) and Berlioz's answer of 1 January 1848 are given in full (as far as the sources allow) by Citron (Berlioz, *Correspondance générale* 3:460–64, 478–81, 479–98). Rogé's own revealing commentary on the letters, in his *Mémoires*, has never been reprinted in its entirety; it makes clear that Rogé's "counselor" and "guide" (see the passage cited in the text below) was the much-traveled portable piano.

133. Rogé to Enfantin, Saint Petersburg, 12 November 1844, Ars 7630/216. Another indication of Rogé's changed attitude toward his Saint-Simonian past is his negative reaction to visits from Suzanne Voilquin and Charles Duveyrier (*Mémoires d'un piano*, 281–84). But cf. Voilquin, *Mémoires*, 111–16, 150, 251, 276, 297–98, 303.

134. Rogé had bemoaned his situation earlier in the letter to Enfantin. Berlioz, in his letter to Rogé of 10 November 1847, refers to the latter's "extreme desire to leave" Saint Petersburg (*Correspondance générale* 3:460–64).

135. [Tajan-Rogé], *Mémoires d'un piano,* 299, 295.

136. Maitron, *Dictionnaire* 3:427; "Programme d'enseignement de l'association fraternelle des instituteurs, institutrices et professeurs socialistes," in Lefrançais, *Souvenirs d'un révolutionnaire,* ed. Jan Cerny (Paris: Société encyclopédique française and Editions de la tête de feuilles, 1972), 463–91. Perhaps Rogé was introduced to Proudhonist thought as well, through his close friend and fellow "Egyptian" Massol (reminiscences of Rogé's son-in-law Henri Brisson, in Iouda Tchernoff, *Le Parti républicain au coup d'état et sous le second empire* [Paris: A. Pedone, 1906], 308–9).

137. Ars 7860/48. The program states that the Société was founded in Paris on 6 July 1849.

138. *Grande Société philharmonique de Paris: Statuts et règlements de la Société fondée en 1850* (Paris: Imprimerie Dondey-Dupré, [1850]). Cf. Elwart, *Société,* 69–84.

139. On the Société, see Adolphe Boschot, *La Crépuscule d'un romantique* (Paris: Plon, 1913), chap. 4, pp. 229–59.

140. Berlioz to Lecourt, Paris, 22 June 1852, in *Correspondance inédite,* 365.

141. See the comments on a David piano trio in his report on the Ecole Beethoven (see below) and on *Le Désert* in his *Mémoires d'un piano,* 159–61.

142. Pougin states that Rogé "had taken part in putting out the journal *L'Avenir musical* (1853)." (Fétis, ed., *Biographie universelle,* Supplement 2:561.) In all the issues of *L'Avenir musical,* Rogé is mentioned by name but once: at the end of his review, "Opéra italien: Concert de M. Emile Prudent" (2, no. 9 [3 March 1853]). The references to David and Reber are in the first issue (November 1852), pp. 1–2. The journal also published an extract from Berlioz's *Soirées de l'orchestre,* perhaps through the intervention of Rogé ("Un Piano fantastique" in 1, no. 4 [1 January 1853]:1).

143. Letter from Berlioz to Rogé, Paris, 2 March 1855 (Berlioz, *Correspondance inédite,* 220–23).

144. "Les Beaux-Arts aux Etats-Unis d'Amérique: Arts plastiques (1856)" and "Les Beaux-Arts aux Etats-Unis d'Amérique: Etat général de la musique et de l'opéra lyrique,

suite et fin," *La Revue philosophique et religieuse* 6 (1857):347–51, 473–502, reprinted with an added preface (Paris: Bestel, 1857). Berlioz spoke of Rogé's book as "this pungent pamphlet, burning with great love of the beautiful and quite well written by M. Tajan-Rogé, one of our fine cellists" (*Journal des débats,* 26 April 1857). Among the other contributors to the *Revue philosophique* we recognize the names of five Saint-Simonians or sympathizers: Guépin (of Nantes), Lemonnier, A. Massol, Lambert, and Louis Jourdan. Jourdan, in "La Doctrine saint-simonienne," comments on a new edition of the *Doctrine* (3 [May 1855]:181–94).

145. Rogé's article on the Ecole Beethoven (*Revue philosophique* 9 [December 1857–January 1858]:153–55) is entitled simply "Beaux-Arts" and includes an ironic account of Berlioz's controversy about Beethoven with Marie Bernard-Gjertz and Louis Veuillot.

146. D. Tajan-Rogé, "Mme Clorinde."

147. Copy in Ars 7860/36.

148. D. Tajan-Rogé, *Fausses Notes.*

149. A blank copy of the statutes, dated 21 April 1864, is preserved as Ars 7861/381 (Brochure 17). (Item 382 is the cover letter to Lemonnier, 26 November 1864.) Rogé was to be the "délégué" and "mandataire spécial" of all the members.

150. Rogé's relationship to Brisson and Dubost (whom he called in 1872 "mon excellent ami, homme de bien, et chaud patriote") is reported by Tiersot in Berlioz, *Musicien errant,* 202. Brisson, like Rogé, contributed to the *Revue philosophique* (an article on Blanc's *Histoire de dix ans:* vol. 9 [December 1857–January 1858]). Elsewhere he also penned a favorable but strongly socialistic obituary of Enfantin (*Le Temps,* 10 September 1864).

151. Tajan-Rogé, *Baillot.*

152. *Mémoires d'un piano,* [v]. One should not forget the volcanic political situation in 1876, discussed earlier in reference to David's funeral.

153. Tajan-Rogé to Ismayl (formerly Thomas) Urbain, 14 January [no year: 1871–78 are possible], Ars 13739/47.

154. [Tajan-Rogé], *Mémoires d'un piano,* 301. The date of Rogé's death—March 1878—and his age are given in the supplement to Fétis's *Biographie universelle.*

CHAPTER 14

1. Sainte-Beuve (referring to journalist Adolphe Guéroult), in his *Nouveaux Lundis* (Paris: Michel Lévy frères, 1865) 4:146.

2. See Vinçard's admiring and appreciative remarks on his wife (*Mémoires*, 248, 310–15); and Tajan-Rogé's on his ("Mme Clorinde"). Though David never married, his continuing devotion to old comrades and "fathers" testifies to the staying power of bonds forged within the movement.

3. Walch, *Chevalier*, 61n.

4. D'Allemagne, *Enfantin;* Charléty, *Saint-Simonisme*, bk. 4, chaps. 1, 3; Walch, *Chevalier,* 56–57, 72–76. Some excessive claims on this score (e.g., Markham, in *Saint-Simon*, xli) are deflated in Barrie M. Ratcliffe, "Anglo-French."

5. Zeldin, *France: 1848–1945* 1:438.

6. Sainte-Beuve, *Nouveaux Lundis* 4:146.

7. Lacroix, "Idées religieuses," 711.

8. Marx-Engels, *Die deutsche Ideologie*, in *Werke* 3:495.

9. Engels, *Der deutsche Bauernkrieg*, in *Werke* 7:541; cf. 19:188.

10. Engels, *Anti-Dühring*, in *Werke* 20:242, passage repeated in *Werke* 19:196. The absorption of Saint-Simonian ideas by Marxism is treated briefly at the end of Chapter 2 above and at length in Manuel and Manuel, *Utopian Thought* (and, indeed, in most other major studies of the historical development of socialism). See also Corcoran, *Before Marx*, 1–29.

11. Maurice Agulhon, "Les Saint-Simoniens," 1–2.

12. David's music served as an inspirational model for the "Orientalist" work or views of, among others, the composer Delibes, the critic Stassov, and the ethnomusicologist Salvador-Daniel—see Locke, "New View."

13. Egbert, *Social Radicalism*, 119–23.

14. Charlton, *Secular Religions*, 82–87; D. O. Evans, *Le Socialisme romantique: Pierre Leroux et ses contemporains* (Paris: Marcel Rivière, 1948).

15. Franz Liszt, "Berlioz and His 'Harold' Symphony" (1855), excerpts in W. Oliver Strunk, ed. and trans., *Source Readings in Music History* (New York: W. W. Norton, 1950), 846–73. On *Les Préludes* (whose connection to Lamartine has sometimes been questioned), see Alexander Main's defense in "Liszt after

Lamartine: 'Les Préludes,' " *Music and Letters* 60 (1979):133–48.

16. "On Franz Liszt's Symphonic Poems" (1857), in *Richard Wagner's Prose Works*, trans. William Ashton Ellis (London, 1891) 3:235–54; Frank W. Glass, *The Fertilizing Seed: Wagner's Concept of the Poetic Intent* (Ann Arbor: UMI Research Press, 1983); Carl Dahlhaus, *Die Musik des 19. Jahrhunderts* (Wiesbaden: Akademische Verlagsgesellschaft Athenaion and Laaber: Laaber-Verlag, 1980), 159–70, 197–98.

17. Carl E. Schorske, *Fin-de-siècle Vienna: Politics and Culture* (New York: Random House, Vintage Books, 1981), esp. 68–72; William McGrath, *Dionysian Art and Populist Politics in Austria* (New Haven: Yale University Press, 1974) esp. [85]–162; Eric Eugène, *Les Idées politiques de Richard Wagner et leur influence sur l'idéologie allemande, 1870–1945* (Paris: Les Publications universitaires, 1978); Peter Viereck, *Metapolitics: The Roots of the Nazi Mind* (New York: Capricorn Books, 1965); David C. Large and William Weber, eds., *Wagnerism in European Culture and Politics* (Ithaca: Cornell University Press, 1984); Léon Guichard, *La Musique et les lettres en France au temps du Wagnérisme* (Paris: Les Presses universitaires du France, 1963); and Raymond Furness, *Wagner and Literature* (Manchester: Manchester University Press, 1982).

18. Ernest Newman, *The Life of Richard Wagner*, 4 vols. (rpr. Cambridge: Cambridge University Press, 1976) 1:163–72, 491–500; 2:3–17, 34–103; Hans Mayer, *Richard Wagner: Mitwelt und Nachwelt* (Stuttgart and Zurich: Belser Verlag, [1978], esp. 12–13, [31]–39, 73–87, [158]–69; Maurice Boucher, *Les Idées politiques de Richard Wagner* (Paris: Aubier Montaigne, 1947), 42–44; Maxime Leroy, *Les Premiers Amis français de Wagner* (Paris: Albin Michel, 1925), 125–34; and Egbert, *Social Radicalism*, esp. 57, 215–16, 240–41, 256, 440, 594–600.

19. "Dialogue," in *OSSE* 39:237.

20. Paul Rochette in 1832, see Chapter 9 n.91.

21. Félicien David to Sylvain Saint-Etienne (1835); David to Félix and Emma Tourneux (1845); and David's last will and testament—fuller citations in Chapter 13.

22. On the American repertoire, see Serge Denisoff, *Great Day Coming: Folk Music and the*

American Left (Urbana: University of Illinois Press, [1971]). On the nineteenth-century French repertoire, see my "Music of the French Chanson." On the Nazis' lifting of democratic and socialist *Arbeiterlieder,* see Werner Fuhr, *Proletarische Musik in Deutschland, 1928–1933* (Göppingen: Verlag Alfred Kümmerle, 1977), 250–56 (including a table of "stolen" songs in an S. A. songbook of 1933). Cf. ibid., 219–20.

23. I am thinking of works as varied as (to name some artful, complex examples) Falla's ballet *The Three Cornered Hat,* the operas of Kokkonen and Sallinen, and the African Suite for orchestra by Nigerian composer Fela Sowande. (On the Finnish operas, see Andrew Porter's article in the *New Yorker,* 16 May 1983; on Sowande's and other African "third-stream" works, see Ashenafi Kebede, *Roots of Black Music* (Englewood Cliffs: Prentice-Hall, 1982), 117–24.

24. "Postscript" in Jacobs, ed., *Choral Music,* 3d printing (Baltimore: Penquin Books, 1969), 392. Cf. Jane Fulcher, "The Orphéon Societies: 'Music for the Workers' in Second-Empire France," *International Review of the Aesthetics and Sociology of Music* 10 (1979):47–56.

25. "What is called 'Socialist Realism' is without doubt more Saint-Simonian than Marxist" (Jean Lacroix, "Idées religieuses," 710.)

26. *Testimony: The Memoirs of Dmitri Shostakovich as Related to . . . Solomon Volkov* (New York: Harper and Row, 1979), 183–84, 265–66.

27. Barrault, "L'Art," 495.

28. Copland, *The New Music, 1900–1960,* rev. (New York: W. W. Norton, 1968), 161–62.

29. See the thoughtful discussion of Nono and Henze in Ernst H. Flammer, *Politisch engagierte Musik als kompositorisches Problem* (Baden-Baden: Verlag Valentin Koerner, 1981) and of Rzewski in John Rockwell, *All American Music* (New York: Alfred A. Knopf, 1983), 84–95, 249–50, 254–55. Flammer also summarizes much of the literature on "musique engagée" (pp. 258–98). On an earlier case—Eisler—see Hermann Danuser's probing article "Hans Eisler: Zur wechselhaften Wirkungsgeschichte engagierter Musik," in Carl Dahlhaus, ed., *Die Wiener Schule heute* (Mainz: Schott, 1983), 87–104.

30. See my article "Musique engagée?" It is revealing of the prejudices of the debaters—including such respected figures as Stuckenschmidt and Dahlhaus—that they sometimes use simple chansons, marches, and the like as proof that *musique engagée* can never be of much artistic value (Flammer, *Politisch engagierte Musik,* 10–11, 265–66, 270).

31. Arthur Satz, "[Interview with] Lukas Foss," *High Fidelity/Musical America* 31, no. 1 (January 1981):6. A desire for greater "relevance" and "activism" in musical scholarship is expressed repeatedly in the symposium *Musicology in the 1980s,* ed. D. K. Holoman and Claude Palisca (New York: Da Capo Press, 1982); see esp. pp. 28–30, 127–29.

APPENDIX A

1. Hubbard states (authoritatively but vaguely) that Rouget de Lisle "was long on intimate terms with Saint-Simon" (*Saint-Simon,* 88). Perhaps they met (or met again) through the efforts of Saint-Simon's associate Humann (a financier and later minister of finance); on Rouget de Lisle's relations with Humann, see Leconte, *Rouget de Lisle,* 163–68. (Humann's son later ran away from home and was briefly given refuge by the Saint-Simonians.) Perhaps Ternaux was another intermediary; on his salon, see Guigard, "Rouget de Lisle," 118.

2. Guigard, "Rouget de Lisle," 118. This forgotten article offers the most complete discussion that I have found of the collaboration between Rouget de Lisle and Saint-Simon. I have not been able to determine from whom Guigard—a librarian at BNImp and an outspoken republican (Maitron, *Dictionnaire* 6:266)—got his information. But all later accounts—including those by Gindre de Mancy (père), Stéphen Leroy, and Frank Manuel—ultimately derive from Guigard's article.

3. On Ternaux's politics, see Leroy, "Ternaux," 29–34; on Saint-Simon and Ternaux, see Dautry, *Saint-Simon,* 34–37. Dautry suggests that Saint-Simon may have been influenced in this musical experiment by Owen's activities in Scotland (as reported by Alexandre Laborde).

4. Saint-Simon, *Du système industriel,* seconde partie, 209–13 (the song's text and Saint-Simon's comments) and the following pp. [1]–4 (words and music of the song). This version offers a melodic variant for "La force et l'erreur

détrônées: Quelques efforts" (G d d e f e d d e e-flat e-flat d c—the G is in the octave beginning with middle C and the other notes are in the next octave higher) and in the refrain resolves the G-sharp to G rather than A. The first variant sensibly eases the song's wide range; the second also makes the tune simpler to sing, though it may be an error (the G-sharp is not respelled A-flat as one would expect, nor is the resolution note—G—given a natural sign). Saint-Simon's version states that "le refrain se répète en choeur." It is unclear whether this means unison singing or four-part harmony.

5. Leroy, "Ternaux," 29–34.

6. Rouget de Lisle, *Cinquante chants français* (1825); reprinted with corrections (version reprinted here) in his *Quarante-huit chants français* (possibly 1830) (*Rouget de Lisle: Son oeuvre, sa vie* [Paris: Librairie Ch. Delagrave, 1892], 272 and [on dating the collections] 273). Elsewhere Tiersot mentions a surviving autograph of the song (presumably only the words)—*Lettres* 1:173.

7. Manuel, *New World,* 256.

8. Guigard, "Rouget de Lisle," 119.

9. Ibid., 116; Dautry, *Saint-Simon,* 137.

10. Fournel, *Bibliographie,* 1837 revision, item K. Indeed, Fournel refers in a footnote to its publication in *Système industriel* (in the 1833 version of the *Bibliographie* as well—p. 123).

APPENDIX B

1. Each publication is described as follows: First a shortened title (used for references in Appendix D), then locations of copies, a fuller citation, and a list of the songs and *timbres*. Authors' names have been standardized.

2. I have not seen copies of the last two songsters: *Chansonnier saint-simonien* and *Nouveaux Chants saint-simoniens.* Their contents suggest strongly that they belong to the year 1833; I thus identify the first with the following: "Chansonnier saint-simonien; in-12 de 1/2 feuille, imp. de Sétier. A Paris, chez Adolphe R., rue de Grenelle-Saint-Honoré, 29." (Mentioned in Brivois, *Bibliographie,* p. 43, as containing Béranger's *Les Fous.*) A copy of the second collection seems to be in BNImp Ye 54104; the first two pages (including shelf number) can be seen in the *Saint-Simoniens* mi-

crofiches. Both songsters are transcribed in full by Fraser, "Saint-Simonism and Music," app., i–xx. Her statement "contained in *Religion saint-simonienne—Correspondance,* Paris: 1831" presumably means that the copy she saw was *bound together* with a copy of that book. The songsters cannot possibly date from 1831 or even 1832.

3. Publications are described as in Appendix B.1, except that no list of songs is given. It should be added that many publications of one or two songs are listed by author in the published BNImp catalog or can be found in the collections of separate pieces indicated here by an asterisk.

4. Certain songs survive in text sheets bearing a specific date that cannot be related to a particular ceremony or occasion. See the four songs in *Mercier,* one by Charles Chevalier (for 23 November 1834) in Ars 7803/36, and several by Vinçard (for dates in 1854–55) in BNImp Ye 54103.

5. Vinçard's name is handwritten into the BN and BHVP copies. The timbre suggests original music: "Musique de mademoiselle Fanny." The same may be true of "Les Trois Jours de Paris" in *Vinçard (1833):* "Musique de M. Fourcy."

APPENDIX D

1. The present Appendix offers information about all the works written by David between January 1832 and mid-1835. The sole Saint-Simonian work by Reber is included in its chronological place (no. 31). Selected pieces discussed here can be found in Appendix E.

2. The *Ménilmontant* series of scores was published in 1832–33 and in erratic fashion. Surviving copies bear any one of three different title pages (plates 12–13, 17) or even just a blank title page. (The title page shown in Plate 13 was originally designed for *Appel* only and carried that title—and David's rank of "membre" rather than "apôtre." See photo in Brécy, *Florilège,* 40.) Many of the copies contain one or the other of the following (engraved) legends, often at the head of the first page of music: "Se vend à Paris rue Monsigny N°6 / Et chez les principaux Marchands de Musique" (wording may vary slightly), or "à PARIS et à LYON / Chez tous les Marchands de Mu-

sique." Copies may bear tax stamps, the florid signature of D. Tajan-Rogé, or the stamped initials S. D. [Mme S. Durval]. For more information on the publishing history of the series, see Note on Sources and Locke, "Music and the Saint-Simonians," 454–58.

3. The word "Fournel" in the present Appendix refers to the (unpublished) 1837 version of Fournel's *Bibliographie*. David's prospectus (see pieces 3 and 4) is reproduced as plate 24 above.

4. Full references for the brochures known in this or later entries as *6 juin 1832, Prise d'habit, Travaux du Temple, Mort de Talabot, Le Procès (octobre)* are given in Chapter 10 n.20. All other abbreviated titles in this Appendix refer to the various song publications in Appendix B.2 and B.2.

5. Most of the piano accompaniments published in the *Ménilmontant* series merely double the voices; they must have been omitted when the apostles sang the choruses in the streets, and David himself omitted them when he republished most of the choruses in *La Ruche harmonieuse*. Indeed, one of the 1833 publications (*Le Retour du Père*) bears the marking "Piano ad libitum." The accompaniments will thus be indicated here as (with a few exceptions) optional.

6. Azevedo, *Félicien David*, 44. He actually says that the chorus learned it in six days and (incorrectly) that Enfantin was absent for six days.

7. Talabot to Chevalier et al., 5 June 1832, in *OSSE* 7:91.

8. Arrangements for two, three, or four voices by Charles Magner (*Ronde des vendanges*, 1894), by Henri Radiguer (*Ronde des Saint-Simoniens*, 1926 and 1937), and by Marcel Lamarre (*Ronde des Saint-Simoniens*, 1949)—see Robert, "Cultes," 565, and Brécy, *Florilège*, 41–44. (Robert states erroneously that the *Ronde* was not published with the other Ménilmontant choruses.) Radiguer's arrangement of the *Ronde*

is reprinted by Brécy and is performed by the Chorale populaire de Paris on a small disc entitled *Chants de la liberté français:* Le Chant du monde label, no. LDy4171. Radiguer's new text seriously distorts the Saint-Simonian message (see Locke, "Music of the French Chanson," n. 8). I am told that the *Ronde* (in Radiguer's version?) has frequently been used in French television broadcasts and sung in socialist youth groups.

9. For other uses of the slogan "Paris est là" (as a rhetorical symbol of the great task of proselytization that lay ahead), see Barrault's speech of 6 June 1832 (in *Travaux du temple*, or Locke, "Music and the Saint-Simonians," 212) and Hoart's letter of Enfantin, 15 December 1833 (Ars 7619, fol. 25, in d'Allemagne, *Saint-Simoniens*, 388).

10. Saint-Etienne, *Félicien David*, 19.

11. "Le Concert de M. David," in *Musique*, ed. Hallays, 225.

12. David to Mme [Jenny] Montgolfier, March 1833, quoted in Saffroy auction catalogue 62 [February 1969], lot [6122], item 5.

13. Saint-Etienne to Enfantin, 29 May 1845, Ars 7779, in Prod'homme, "Félicien David," 247.

14. According to an inventory that Barrault made of his own papers (Ars 14697/8). He listed the piece as *Chant d'attente* (and later indicated that the item—a manuscript score?—was missing).

15. Letter dated "Lyon, Barrault, Jean Reynaud [Thursday, 11 (July?)]," in *Livre des actes*, 90.

16. According to David's letter to Urbain, 12 June 1833, Ars 13739/202. Barrault, in his inventory, mentions a *Prière à la Mère* of David's with words by himself (Ars 14697/8). This could also be "Belle, oh belle" (see below) or some other piece. Like the *Chant d'attente*, it was removed from his papers before they entered the Arsenal.

17. 11 May 1835, BNMus Lettre autogr. 69.

NOTE ON SOURCES

It has long been known that the Saint-Simonians at Ménilmontant used music to "charm their labors" (as Louis Blanc put it). But anyone who wanted to know more about the Saint-Simonians' use of music, or about their thoughts on music or their contacts with prominent musicians, would have had a hard time of it. Many books—including the valuable and often splendid works of Charléty, Weill, Thibert, Hunt, Manuel, Iggers, Egbert, and Bénichou—do, it is true, discuss the movement's general aesthetic theories, but they refer only briefly, where at all, to its views on music or its own musical activities, and sometimes even those references are misleading. Similarly, the writers on Liszt, Berlioz, and Félicien David who have dealt with the relationship of their subject to the Saint-Simonians have tended to repeat a stock set of facts—or legends.

I wanted more—and more accurate—information, so I went begin hunting down the primary sources. Fortunately, many of the movement's publications regarding music and the arts, such as Barrault's sermon of 1 May 1831, had been reprinted—though sometimes incompletely—in *OSSE* (the forty-seven-volume *Oeuvres*—see Bibliography). Many of David's letters to Enfantin had been published—though with woeful inaccuracies—by Prod'homme. D'Allemagne had even published one chorus by David in facsimile (*Appel*). In addition, Frédéric Robert had looked at several of the original scores of the choruses and had described them briefly and enthusiastically. And Lorna D. Fraser, a master's student at Yale, had taken a good look at some Saint-Simonian chansons and at the allusions to Saint-Simonian ideas in Liszt's published essays and letters. These all gave me encouraging indications of what might be found if I could get to Paris. I got there, only to discover that the surviving documentation of the movement's activities (including manuscript letters and rare printed materials) is massive, and not always easy to survey. Now that I have done battle with these materials over a period of years, I suspect it may be helpful to the reader—and to future scholars—to comment briefly on the sources of information that proved most helpful.

Of the various large collections of Saint-Simonian materials that can now be consulted in public libraries (see Abbreviations), that of Henri Fournel (BNImp) is particularly well organized. His indispensable *Bibliographie saint-simonienne,* published in 1833, was originally intended as a list of his own holdings. For several years thereafter, though, he continued to expand and reorganize his collection. Fortunately, he revised the *Bibliographie* and brought it up to date in around 1837. This second edition, which corresponds closely to Fournel's volumes now in BNImp, was never published, but a manuscript copy survives (BNImp Rés pZ 1217); it provides uniquely full information on the publishing history of the movement's chansons and choruses.[1]

Alas, the music volume of Fournel's collection (volume K in his unpublished bibliography) became detached from the rest at some point and cannot now be located. Of the surviving copies of David's choruses—in Thiers, Ars, BHVP, and especially BNMus—some were still uncataloged in 1974–75 and had to be hunted down by indirect means (e.g., entry registers and abandoned shelf numberings).[2] I still have not located two David choruses that I know were published. (Aglaé Mathieu and Fournel both owned copies of *La Voix du peuple*,[3] and Fournel owned a copy of *La Prise d'habit d'A. Petit*.[4]) In addition, there remain another nine pieces for which I have recovered only a single voice part (first tenor or bass), or the words, or the title. (Details are given in Appendix D.)

Fortunately, the "losts" are outnumbered by the "founds." The sixteen pieces by David (or sets of pieces) for which I have discovered complete versions dating from the years 1832–35 and the six pieces that can be easily reconstructed (David reused them later in life, disguising their music with new text) give a gratifyingly full picture of the music that the movement inspired and was inspired by. Add to this the precious indications about the circumstances of musical performance—in rare brochures (see especially Chapter 10, n. 20), in the published memoirs, neglected until now, of "lesser" members of the movement (e.g., Pellarin, Tajan-Rogé, and A. Chevalier, all unmentioned in Walch's comprehensive *Bibliographie*), and in unpublished correspondence now at the Bibliothèque de l'Arsenal—and the music can begin to be set into proper context. As for the "nonmember" musicians, such as Liszt, Berlioz, and Mendelssohn, enough letters and public statements survive to allow us to sketch their Saint-Simonian involvement in surprising detail.

The present book is based—sometimes loosely—on my doctoral dissertation, "Music and the Saint-Simonians." It is longer in some parts (especially Part Two, much of which is new) and shorter in others. Much of what was pruned will not be missed, but I do regret being forced by the economics of book publishing to eliminate (1) the full French texts of passages quoted from unpublished or exceedingly rare sources, such as propagandistic brochures, and (2) the scores of certain pieces composed for the movement. I have tried to compensate by providing (1) the original French wording of any crucial phrases not easily translated and (2) full information for (and even descriptions of) all the musical works in the Saint-Simonian repertoire, not just those printed here. And of course the dissertation is available to those who wish or need to consult it.

I should add that translations in the present book are mine unless otherwise indicated and that, on those occasions when my own source is one of the movement's original publications (rather than *OSSE*, in which the texts are silently "normalized"), I preserve as much as possible the frequent and often symbolic use of italics and small and large capitals. In the transcriptions in Appendixes D and E, I modernize word endings (e.g., enfans), accents, and (sparingly, and only for clarity) punctuation and capitalization.

1. The relevant sections from Fournel's 1833 and 1837 versions are transcribed in their entirety in Locke, "Music and the Saint-Simonians," app. 2. The main volumes of Fournel's collection (containing octavos and smaller formats) are shelved consecutively from 8ºZ 8113 (volume a) to 8135 (volume x, not identical to that in Fournel's published *Bibliographie*). The surrounding volumes are likewise from Fournel's library and contain some Saint-Simonian items. (Manuscript letters attached to his unpublished revised edition of the *Bibliographie* help explain the travels of the collection until it became "Don 216170" at the library.) Also shelved as a unit is Fournel's quarto series, containing extensive runs of the movement's periodicals.

An independently assembled collection of Saint-Simonian publications is shelved in BNImp under the prefix Ld[190]; see the listings in the library's published *Catalogue de l'histoire de France.* BNArs possesses an (unpublished) catalog of its own Saint-Simonian books and brochures as well as a detailed listing (Inventaire Boussard) of its Saint-Simonian manuscripts, including letters. For the latter, the brief listings in vols. 43 and 50 of the *Catalogue général des manuscrits des bibliothèques publiques de France* provide a handy, though not error-free, overview. See also Walch, *Bibliographie,* 20–31.

2. Only the copies in Ars are still uncataloged; they can be found in box 2040bis. (A few copies which were still in the Conservatoire library were finally transferred to BNMus in 1974.)

3. Lists of papers donated by Mme Mathieu to the Saint-Simonian archive (Ars 7858/1 and 7811/28) mention the twelve pieces that comprised *livraisons* 1, 2, 3, and 5 of the *Ménilmontant* series. (See plate 24.) One of these choruses, *La Voix du peuple,* exists in no other copy. Unfortunately, none of Mme Mathieu's twelve pieces has surfaced at the Arsenal.

4. Also two other "lost" choruses from *livraison* 4, *Avant et après le repas* [no. 1] and *Le Nouveau Temple;* these can, however, be reconstructed.

BIBLIOGRAPHY

This is primarily a list of all sources that are cited by shortened title in the notes. (A small number of works that, though not cited, were found useful have also been included. Many other items of possible interest to readers are listed in the works of Fournel, Charléty, Walch [1967], Fakkar, and Briscoe cited below.) Manuscripts, newspaper articles, and other documentary items cited in the text (e.g., materials in the Fonds Enfantin of the Bibliothèque de l'Arsenal) are omitted, as are most of the song sheets, songsters, and scores listed in the Appendixes.

Abrams, Meyer H. *The Mirror and the Lamp.* Oxford University Press, 1953.

Agoult, Comtesse [Marie] d'. *Mémoires (1833–1854).* Edited by Daniel Ollivier. Paris: Calmann-Lévy, 1927.

Agoult, Comtesse [Marie] d', and Franz Liszt. *Correspondance de Liszt et de la Comtesse d'Agoult.* 2d ed. Edited by Daniel Ollivier. Paris: Bernard Grasset, 1933–34.

Agulhon, Maurice. "Les Saint-Simoniens." Introductory article in the catalog of *Les Saint-Simoniens 1825–1834* (q.v.).

————. *Une Ville ouvrière au temps du socialisme utopique: Toulon de 1815 à 1851.* Paris: Mouton, 1970.

Allemagne, Henri-René d'. *Prosper Enfantin et les grandes entreprises du xix*ᵉ *siècle.* Paris: Gründ, 1935.

————. *Les Saint-Simoniens: 1827–1837.* Paris: Gründ, 1930.

Almanach social pour l'année 1840. Paris: Librairie sociale, 1840.

Azevedo, Alexis. *Félicien David: Coup d'oeil sur sa vie et son oeuvre.* Paris: Heugel, 1863.

Baker, Keith M. *Condorcet: From Natural Philosophy to Social Mathematics.* Chicago: University of Chicago Press, 1975.

Barrault, Emile. "L'Art." In *Religion saint-simonienne. Recueil de prédications* 1:491–511. 2 vols. Paris: Everat, 1832.

————. *Aux artistes. Du passé et de l'avenir des beaux-arts. (Doctrine de Saint-Simon).* Paris: Alexandre Mesnier, 1830.

Barzun, Jacques. *Berlioz and the Romantic Century.* 3d ed. New York: Columbia University Press, 1969.

Bawr, Mme de [née Alexandrine-Sophie Goury de Champgrand]. *Histoire de la musique.* Unnumbered volume of the *Encyclopédie des dames.* Paris: Audot, 1823.

————. *Mes souvenirs.* Paris: Pasard, 1853.

Beecher, Jonathan, and Richard Bienvenu, eds. and trans. *The Utopian Vision of Charles Fourier: Selected Works on Work, Love, and Passionate Attraction.* Boston: Beacon Press, 1971.

Bénichou, Paul. *Le Temps des prophètes: Doctrines de l'âge romantique.* Paris: Gallimard, 1977.

Béranger, Pierre-Jean de. *Chansons de P.-J. de Béranger 1815–1834 contenant les dix chansons* . . . . Paris: Garnier frères, n.d.

――――. *Oeuvres posthumes de Béranger: Dernières Chansons 1834 à 1851: Ma biographie avec un appendice* . . . . Paris: Garnier frères, n.d.

Bérat, Frédéric, ed. *Musique des chansons de Béranger: Airs notés anciens et modernes . . . augmentée de la musique des chansons publiées en 1847 et de quatre airs par Halévy, Gounod et Mme Mainvieille-Fodor.* 8th ed. Paris: Perrotin, 1861.

Berlioz, Hector. *Correspondance générale.* Edited by Pierre Citron et al. 4 vols. to date. Paris: Flammarion, 1972–.

――――. *Correspondance inédite, 1819–1868.* Edited by Daniel Bernard. 3d rev. ed. Paris: Calmann-Lévy, 1896.

――――. *Evenings with the Orchestra.* 1852. Translated by Jacques Barzun. Chicago: University of Chicago Press, 1956.

――――. *Les Grotesques de la musique.* 1859. Edited by Léon Guichard. Paris: Gründ, 1969.

――――. *Mémoires.* 1870. Introduced by Pierre Citron. 2 vols. Paris: Garnier-Flammarion, 1969.

――――. *The Memoirs of Hector Berlioz.* Translated and edited by David Cairns. Corrected edition. New York: W. W. Norton, 1975.

――――. *Le Musicien errant (1842–1852).* Edited by Julien Tiersot. Paris: Calmann-Lévy, 1919.

――――. *La Musique et les musiciens.* Edited by André Hallays. Paris: Calmann-Lévy, [1903].

Blanc, Louis. *Révolution française. Histoire de dix ans, 1830–1840.* 9th ed. 5 vols. Paris: Pagnerre, [1867?].

Blaze de Bury [Henri Blaze]. *Musiciens contemporains.* Paris: Michel Lévy, 1856.

Bloom, Peter A. *François-Joseph Fétis and the "Revue musicale" (1827–1835).* Ann Arbor: University Microfilms, 1972.

――――, ed. *Music in Paris in the 1830s: La Musique à Paris dans les années 1830.* La Vie musicale en France au xixᵉ siècle, vol. 9. New York: Pendragon Press, forthcoming.

Börne, Ludwig. *Sämtliche Schriften.* Edited by Inge Rippman and Peter Rippman. 5 vols. Düsseldorf: Joseph Melzer, 1964–68.

Booth, Arthur John. *Saint-Simon and Saint-Simonism.* London: Longmans, 1871.

Bouglé, C., and Elie Halévy. See *Doctrine de Saint-Simon.*

Boutet de Monvel, Etienne. *Un Artiste d'autrefois: Adolphe Nourrit, sa vie et sa correspondance.* Paris: Plon-Nourrit, 1903.

Brancour, René. *Félicien David.* Paris: Henri Laurens, [1909].

Brécy, Robert. *Florilège de la chanson révolutionnaire de 1789 au front populaire.* N.p.: Editions Hier et Demain, 1978.

Briscoe, James Bland. *Saint-Simonism and the Origins of Socialism in France, 1816–1832.* Ann Arbor: University Microfilms, 1980.

――――. "*Enfantinisme,* Feminism, and the Crisis of Saint-Simonism." Forthcoming.

――――. "The Unfinished Revolution: The Saint-Simonians and the Social Question."

In *Proceedings of the Fourteenth Consortium on Revolutionary Europe*. Forthcoming.

Brivois, Jules. *Bibliographie de l'oeuvre de P.-J. de Béranger.* Paris: L. Conquet, 1876.

Brochon, Pierre. *La Chanson française: Béranger et son temps.* Paris: Editions sociales, 1956.

———. *La Chanson française: Le Pamphlet du pauvre du socialisme utopique à la Révolution de 1848.* Paris: Editions sociales, 1957.

Bulciolu, Maria Teresa. *L'Ecole saint-simonienne et la femme.* Pisa: Goliardica, 1980.

Butler, Eliza Marian. *Heinrich Heine.* New York: Philosophical Library, 1957.

———. *The Saint-Simonian Religion in Germany: A Study of the Young German Movement.* Cambridge: Cambridge University Press, 1926.

Calendrier S.-S. [sic] 1833. [Paris]: Imprimerie de Carpentier-Méricourt, 1833.

Capelle, Pierre, ed. *La Clé du Caveau.* 4th ed. Paris: A. Cotelle, 1847.

Carlisle, Robert. "Saint-Simonian Radicalism: A Definition and a Direction." *French Historical Studies* 5(1968):430–45.

Carnot, Hippolyte. *Sur le Saint-Simonisme: Lecture faite à l'Académie des sciences morales et politiques.* Paris: Alphonse Picard, 1887.

Cérémonie du 27 novembre [1831]. See *Religion saint-simonienne.*

Charléty, Sébastien. *Histoire du Saint-Simonisme (1825–64).* 2d ed. Paris: P. Hartmann, 1931. The 1st and 3d eds. are paginated differently and the latter (a paperback) omits the notes. The organization by book, chapter, and part, though, is essentially the same.

Charlton, D. G. *Secular Religions in France, 1815–1870.* Oxford: Oxford University Press, 1963.

Chevalier, Auguste. "Exposé sommaire de mes fonctions à Ménil-Montant." *Le Cabinet de lecture,* no. 129 (4 January 1833), pp. 9–10.

Cobban, Alfred. *A History of Modern France.* Rev. and enl. ed. 3 vols. London: Jonathan Cape, 1962–65.

Coligny, Charles, Alfred Leconte, and Sylvain Saint-Etienne. *La Chanson française.* Paris: Michel Lévy frères, 1876.

Collin [Auguste Colin]; [Dominique Tajan-]Rogé; Maréchal; Charpin; and Lamy. *1833 ou l'année de le Mère, Juillet: Mission de l'est.* Toulon: imprimerie et lithographie de Canquoin, 1834.

Corcoran, Paul E., ed. *Before Marx: Socialism and Communism in France, 1830–48.* New York: St. Martin's Press, 1983.

Cotte, Roger. *La Musique maçonnique et ses musiciens.* Bibliothèque internationale d'études maçonniques, no. 1. Braine-le-comte, Belgium: Edition du Baucens, 1975.

Dautry, Jean, ed. *Saint-Simon: Textes choisis.* Paris: Editions sociales, 1951.

David, Félicien. *Christophe Colomb.* Ode-symphonie (1847). Reduction for voices and piano by A. de Garaudé. Paris: E. Gérard, [1863]. Reprint with added German text, Vienna: H. F. Müller, [1863].

———. *Ménilmontant.* Choruses and piano pieces. Paris: 6 rue Monsigny, and Lyons: [Mme S. Durval], 1832–33.

———. *La Ruche harmonieuse.* Thirty men's choruses. Paris: Sylvain Saint-Etienne, ca. 1854.

Démar, Claire. *Textes sur l'affranchissement des femmes (1832–1833).* Edited by Valentin Pelosse. Paris: Payot, 1974.

Doctrine de Saint-Simon: Exposition, première année, 1829. Edited by C. Bouglé and Elie Halévy. Paris: Marcel Rivière, 1924.

The Doctrine of Saint-Simon: An Exposition, First Year, 1828–1829. Edited and translated by George G. Iggers. 2d ed. New York: Schocken Books, 1972.

Donakowski, Conrad. *A Muse for the Masses: Ritual and Music in an Age of Democratic Revolution, 1770–1870.* Chicago: University of Chicago Press, 1977.

Dondo, Mathurin. *The French Faust: Henri de Saint-Simon.* New York: Philosophical Library, 1955.

Duveyrier, Charles. "La Ville nouvelle; ou, le Paris des Saint-Simoniens." In *Paris; ou, le Livre des cent et un* 8 (October 1832):315–44. (Also in *OSSE* 8:65–93.)

Egbert, Donald Drew. *Social Radicalism and the Arts.* New York: Alfred A. Knopf, 1970.

Elwart, Antoine. *Histoire de la Société des concerts du Conservatoire impérial de musique.* 2d ed. Paris: Librairie Castel, 1864.

Enfantin, Barthélemy-Prosper. See *Oeuvres* and Corcoran.

Espiau de la Maëstre, André. "Berlioz, Metternich et le Saint-Simonisme." *Revue musicale,* special issue 233: *Hector Berlioz: 1803–1869* (1956):65–78.

Evans, D. O. *Social Romanticism in France.* Oxford: Oxford University Press, 1951.

Fakkar, Rouchdi. *Sociologie, socialisme et internationalisme prémarxistes: L'Influence de Saint-Simon.* Neuchâtel: Delachaux & Niestlé, 1968.

Fétis, François-Joseph. *Biographie universelle des musiciens et bibliographie générale de la musique.* 2d ed. 10 vols. Includes 2 supplemental vols. edited by Arthur Pougin. 1873–80. Reprint. Brussels: Culture et Civilisation, 1963.

Foi nouvelle: Livre des actes, publié par les femmes. 11 issues, paginated consecutively. Lyons: Mme S. Durval, 1833–34.

Fournel, Henri. *Bibliographie saint-simonienne de 1802 au 31 décembre 1832.* Paris: Johanneau, 1833. Revised version, unpublished, in BNImp Rés pZ 1217. See Note on Sources.

Fraser, Lorna D. "Saint-Simonism and Music." Master's thesis, Yale University, 1948.

Fulcher, Jane. "Music and the Communal Order: The Vision of Utopian Socialism in France." *Current Musicology* 27 (1979):27–35.

Gouhier, Henri. *La Jeunesse d'Auguste Comte et la formation du positivisme.* 3 vols. Paris: Librairie philosophique J. Vrin, 1936–41; vols. 2–3, rev., 1964–70.

Gradenwitz, Peter. "Félicien David (1810–1876) and French Romantic Orientalism." *Musical Quarterly* 62 (1976):471–506.

Granal, P. "Variétés. Smyrne." *Le Temps,* 25 September 1837.

———. "Variétés. Smyrne. Le Pont des Caravanes.—Natchio." *Le Temps,* 30 September 1837.

———. "Variétés. Smyrne. Les Grottes d'Homère." *Le Temps,* 10 October 1837.

Guigard, Joannis. "Rouget de Lisle." *Almanach des orphéons* 2 (1864):109–19.

Hagan, Dorothy Veinus. *Félicien David, 1810–1876: A Composer and a Cause.* Syracuse: Syracuse University Press, 1985.

———. *French Musical Criticism between the Revolutions, 1830–1848.* Ann Arbor: University Microfilms, 1965.

Halévy, Léon. *F. Halévy: Sa vie et ses oeuvres.* 2d rev. ed. Paris: Heugel, 1863.

———. "Souvenirs de Saint-Simon." *La France littéraire: Politique, science, beaux-arts* 1 (March 1832):521–46. (Also abridged and edited by Georges Brunet. *Revue d'histoire économique et sociale,* no. 12 [1925]:166–76.)

Haraszti, Emile. *Franz Liszt*. Paris: A. and J. Picard, 1967.

———. "Franz Liszt—Author Despite Himself: The History of a Mystification." *Musical Quarterly* 33 (1947):490–516.

Hauser, Arnold. *The Social History of Art*. 4 vols. New York: Random House, Vintage Books, [1957–58].

Heine, Heinrich. *Briefe*. Edited by Friedrich Hirth. 6 vols. Mainz: Florian Kupferberg, 1950–51.

———. *Zeitungsberichte über Musik und Malerei*. Edited by Michael Mann. Frankfurt: Insel-Verlag, 1964.

Hiller, Ferdinand. *Aus dem Tonleben unserer Zeit: Gelegentliches*. 2 vols. Leipzig: Hermann Mendelssohn, 1868.

L'Homme nouveau; ou, le Messager du bonheur. Lyons: Mme S. Durval, 1833. Prospectus; no. 1 (14 July [1833]); and nos. 2–4 (August 1833, bound as one).

Hubbard, G. *Saint-Simon: Sa vie et ses travaux, suivi de fragments* . . . . Paris: Guillamin, 1857. Hubbard's "Life" draws on notes gathered by Olinde Rodrigues and was approved by the latter (p. 2).

Hunt, Herbert L. *Le Socialisme et le romantisme en France: Etude de la presse socialiste de 1830 à 1848*. Oxford: Clarendon Press, 1935.

Iggers, George G. *The Cult of Authority: The Political Philosophy of the Saint-Simonians, a Chapter in the Intellectual History of Totalitarianism*. The Hague: Martinus Nijhoff, 1958. See also *Doctrine of Saint-Simon*.

Ionescu, Ghiţa, ed. *The Political Thought of Saint-Simon*. With selections from Saint-Simon's writings translated by Valence Ionescu. London: Oxford University Press, 1976.

Ivray, Jehan d'. *L'Aventure saint-simonienne et les femmes*. Paris: Librairie Félix Alcan, 1928.

Jacquème, C. "Félicien David." In *Histoire de Cadenet* 4:517–41. Marseilles: Imprimerie de la S^{te} du "Petit Marseillais" (Samat et Cie), 1925.

Knepler, Georg. *Geschichte als Weg zum Musikverständnis*. Leipzig: Philipp Reclam jun., 1977; 2d. ed., rev., 1982.

———. *Musikgeschichte des neunzehnten Jahrhunderts*. 2 vols. to date. Berlin, DDR: Henschelverlag, 1961–.

Lacroix, Jean. "Les Idées religieuses de Saint-Simon." *Economie et sociétés* 4, no. 4 (April 1970):693–713.

Leconte, Alfred. *Rouget de Lisle: Sa vie, ses oeuvres, la Marseillaise*. Paris: Librairies-Imprimeries réunies, 1892.

Legouvé, Ernest. *Soixante ans de souvenirs*. 2 vols. Paris: P. J. Hetzel, 1886.

Leroy, Maxime. *Le Socialisme des producteurs: Henri de Saint-Simon*. Paris: Marcel Rivière, 1924.

Leroy, Stéphen. "Ternaux, Rouget de Lisle et Saint-Simon." *Bulletin de la Société grayloise d'émulation* 6 (1903):17–40.

Liefde, Carel Lodewijk de. *Le Saint-Simonisme dans la poésie entre 1825 et 1865*. Haarlem: drukkerij "Amicitia," 1927.

Liszt, Franz. *Franz Liszts Briefe*. Edited by La Mara [Marie Lipsius]. 8 vols. Leipzig: Breitkopf und Härtel, 1893–1904.

————. *Pages romantiques* [i.e., essays by Liszt]. Edited by Jean Chantavoine. Paris: Félix Alcan, 1912.

————. See also Agoult, Comtesse [Marie] d'.

Livre des actes. See *Foi nouvelle.*

Locke, Ralph P. "Autour de la lettre à Duveyrier: Berlioz et les Saint-Simoniens." *Revue de musicologie* 63 (1977):55–77 and 64 (1978):387. An expanded version, in English, is in preparation.

————. "Exotic Techniques and Their Meaning in the Music of Félicien David." M.A. thesis, University of Chicago, 1974.

————. "Liszt's Saint-Simonian Adventure." *Nineteenth-Century Music* 4 (1980–81): 209–27 and 5 (1981–82):281.

————. "Mendelssohn's Collision with the Saint-Simonians." In *Mendelssohn and Schumann: Essays on Their Music and Its Context,* 109–22, 176–80. Edited by Jon Finson and R. Larry Todd. Durham: Duke University Press, 1984.

————. "Music and the Saint-Simonians: The Involvement of Félicien David and Other Musicians in a Utopian Socialist Movement." Ph.D. dissertation, University of Chicago, 1980.

————. "The Music of the French Chanson, 1810–50." In Bloom, *Music in Paris* (q.v.).

————. "Musique engagée? The Experience of the Saint-Simonians at Ménilmontant." In *La Musique et le rite, sacré et profane. Actes du 13ᵉ Congrès de la SIM* [Société internationale de musicologie]. Edited by Marc Honegger. 2 vols. Strasbourg: Association des publications près les Universités de Strasbourg, forthcoming.

————. "New Letters of Berlioz." *Nineteenth-Century Music* 1 (1977):55–77. Reprinted with an addendum in *Berlioz Society Newsletter,* no. 102 (Winter 1978–79):2–20, and no. 103 (Spring 1979):2.

————. "A New View of Musical Exoticism: The Case of Félicien David." Paper presented at the annual meeting of the American Musicological Society, Los Angeles, Calif., November 1975. Forthcoming as an article.

————. "Notice biographique sur Félicien David." In *Célébration centenaire de la mort de Félicien David.* Cadenet: n.p., 1976.

Louvancour, Henri. *De Henri de Saint-Simon à Fourier: Etude sur le socialisme romantique français de 1830.* Chartres: Durand, 1913.

Macdonald, Hugh, and Ralph P. Locke. "Félicien David." In *New Grove Dictionary of Music and Musicians.* London: Macmillan, 1980.

Maitron, Jean, ed. *Dictionnaire biographique du mouvement ouvrier français.* 21 vols. to date. Paris: Les Editions ouvrières, 1964–.

Manuel, Frank E. *The New World of Henri Saint-Simon.* Cambridge: Harvard University Press, 1956.

————. *The Prophets of Paris.* Cambridge: Harvard University Press, 1962.

Manuel, Frank E., and Fritzie P. Manuel. *Utopian Thought in the Western World.* Cambridge: Belknap Press, 1979.

Marix-Spire, Thérèse. *Les Romantiques et la musique: Le Cas George Sand. 1804–1838.* Paris: Nouvelles Editions latines, 1954.

Markham, F. M. H., ed. and trans. *Henri de Saint-Simon: Social Organization, The Science of Man, and Other Writings.* New York: Harper and Row, Harper Torchbooks, 1964. (First published in 1952 as *Selected Writings.*)

Marquat, Marie-Christine. "Jean Journet (1799–1861): L'Homme et l'oeuvre." Thèse de troisième cycle, Université de la Sorbonne nouvelle (Paris III), 1978. Typewritten.

Marx, Karl, and Friedrich Engels. *Werke*. Vols. 3, 7, 19, 20. Berlin, GDR: Dietz Verlag, 1960–62.

Mendelssohn, Felix. *Briefe aus den Jahren 1830 bis 1847*. Edited by Paul Mendelssohn Bartholdy and Carl Mendelssohn Bartholdy. 6th ed. Leipzig: Hermann Mendelssohn, 1889.

————. *Letters from Italy and Switzerland*. Translated by Lady Wallace. Boston: Oliver Ditson, [ca. 1863].

1833 [Mil huit cent trente-trois] ou, l'année de la Mère: Mission du Midi. Lyons: Mme S. Durval, [1833].

Mirecourt, Eugène de. *Félicien David*. Paris: Librairie des contemporains, 3d rev. ed., 1869.

Mission de l'Est. See Collin.

Mission du Midi. See *1833 [Mil huit cent trente-trois]*.

Mort de Talabot. Paris: Everat, [1832].

Moses, Claire Goldberg. *French Feminism in the Nineteenth Century*. Albany: State University of New York Press, 1984.

Needham, H. H. *Le Développement de l'esthétique sociologigue en France et en Angleterre au XIXe siècle*. Paris: Librairie ancienne Honoré Champion, 1926.

Newman, Edgar Leon. "Politics and Song in a Paris Goguette: The Lice chansonnière, 1830–1848." In his book *Voices from Below: The French Worker Poets of the July Monarchy and the Spirit of Revolution*. Forthcoming.

Oeuvres de Saint-Simon et d'Enfantin [and of other Saint-Simonians]. 47 vols. Paris: E. Dentu, 1865–78; reprint ed., Aalen: Otto Zeller, 1963–64. Vols. 1–13 are the two "Notices historiques": a brief one on Saint-Simon (based on the biography by G. Hubbard) and a massive one on Enfantin and the Saint-Simonians (apparently by Laurent de l'Ardèche).

Ortigue, Joseph d'. "Etudes biographiques I: Franz Listz [*sic*]." *Gazette Musicale* 2, no. 24 (14 June 1835):197–204.

Pellarin, Charles. *Souvenirs anecdotiques: Médecine navale, Saint-Simonisme, chouannerie*. Paris: Librairie des sciences sociales, 1868.

Perényi, Eleanor. *Liszt: The Artist as Romantic Hero*. Boston and Toronto: Little, Brown and Company, Atlantic Monthly Press, 1974.

Perroux, François, and Schuhl, Pierre-Maxime, eds. *Saint-Simon et pari pour l'industrie: xixe–xxe siècles*. Published in *Economies et sociétés: Cahiers de l'Institut de Science économique appliquée*, vols. 4, nos. 4, 6, 10 (April, June, October 1970); vol. 5, no. 7 (July 1971); and vol. 7, no. 1 (January 1973).

Pierre, Constant. *Musique des fêtes et cérémonies de la Révolution française* .... Paris: Imprimerie Nationale, 1899.

Prise d'habit. See *Retraite de Ménilmontant*.

Procès (août). See *Religion saint-simonienne*.

Procès (octobre). See *Religion saint-simonienne*.

Prod'homme, J.-G. "Correspondance inédite de Félicien David et du Père Enfantin (1845)." *Mercure de France* (1 May 1910):67–86.

———. "Félicien David d'après sa correspondance inédite et celle de ses amis (1832–1864)." *Mercure musical et S.I.M.* 3 (1907):105–25, 229–75.

Puech, Jules L. "Les Saint-Simoniens daus l'Aude (1833)." *Révolution de 1848: Revue* 26 (March 1929–February 1930):276–306.

Quicherat, L. *Adolphe Nourrit: Sa vie, son talent, son caractère, sa correspondance.* 3 vols. Paris: L. Hachette, 1867.

Ramann, Lina. *Franz Liszt als Künstler und Mensch.* 2 vols. in 3. Leipzig: Breitkopf und Härtel, 1880–94.

Ratcliffe, Barrie M. "The Anglo-French Commercial Treaty of 1860." In *Great Britain and Her World, 1750–1914: Essays in Honour of W. O. Henderson,* ed. Barrie M. Ratcliffe, 125–51. Manchester: Manchester University Press, 1975.

———. "Saint-Simonism and Messianism: The Case of Gustave d'Eichthal." *French Historical Studies* 9, no. 3 (Spring 1976):484–502.

Reinisch, Frank. *Das französische Oratorium von 1840 bis 1870.* Kölner Beiträge zur Musikforschung, no. 123. Regensburg: Gustav Bosse Verlag, 1982.

Religion saint-simonienne: Cérémonie du 27 novembre [1831]. Paris: impr. de Giraudet, 1831.

Religion saint-simonienne: Procès en la Cour d'Assises de la Seine les 27 et 28 août 1832. Paris: Librairie saint-simonienne, 1832.

Religion saint-simonienne: Procès en Police correctionnelle le 19 octobre 1832. Paris: Librairie saint-simonienne, 1832.

Retraite de Ménilmontant: Cérémonie du dimanche 1er juillet, et récit de ce qui s'est passé les jours suivans: Ouverture des Travaux du Temple. Paris: Everat, [1832].

Retraite de Ménilmontant: [Prise d'habit, 6 juin 1832]. Paris: Everat, [1832].

Retraite de Ménilmontant: 6 juin 1832. Paris: Everat, [1832].

Ringer, Alexander L. "J.-J. Barthélemy and Musical Utopia in Revolutionary France." *Journal of the History of Ideas* 22 (1961):355–68.

Robert, Frédéric. "Les Cultes révolutionnaires." In *Encyclopédie des musiques sacrées,* 2:564–65. Edited by Jacques Porte. 5 vols. Paris: Editions Labergie, 1968–70.

Rodrigues, [Benjamin-] Olinde, ed. *Poésies sociales des ouvriers.* Paris: Paulin, 1841.

Rouget de Lisle, Claude Joseph. "Chant des industriels." Corrected version in *Quarante-huit Chants français,* 188–91. Paris, Schlesinger, [ca. 1830]. (Song first published in *Cinquante chants français,* 202–5. N.p., [1825].)

Rousseau, Jean-Jacques. *Lettre à Mr d'Alembert sur les spectacles* (1758). Edited by M. Fuchs. Lille: Librairie Girard, and Geneva: Librairie Droz, 1948.

Rude, Fernand. *L'Insurrection lyonnaise de novembre 1831: Le Mouvement ouvrier à Lyon de 1827–1832.* 2d ed. Paris: Editions anthropos, 1969.

Saint-Etienne, Sylvain. *Biographie de Félicien David.* Marseilles: Imprimerie de Marius Olive, 1845.

Saint-Simon, Claude Henri de Rouvroy, comte de. *Du système industriel,* pt. 2. Paris: Veuve Porthmann, 1821.

———. See also Dautry, Ionescu, Markham, *Oeuvres,* and Taylor.

Les Saint-Simoniens 1825–1834. Paris: Microéditions Hachette, 1977. Microfiche series of many of the movement's own publications; the songs (texts only, plus David's *Appel*) are on four fiches, order no. 6974. Also distributed by Clearwater Publishing Co., New York.

Sand, George. *Correspondance.* Edited by Georges Lubin. Paris: Garnier, 1964–.

Schrade, Leo. *Beethoven in France: The Growth of an Idea.* New Haven: Yale University Press, 1942; reprint, New York: Da Capo Press, 1978.

Schilling, Gustav. *Franz Liszt.* Stuttgart: A. Stoppani, 1844.

Sewell, William H., Jr. *Work and Revolution in France: The Language of Labor from the Old Regime to 1848.* Cambridge: Cambridge University Press, 1980.

Sietz, Reinhold, ed. *Aus Ferdinand Hillers Briefwechsel: Beiträge zu einer Biographie Ferdinand Hillers.* 7 vols. Beiträge zur rheinischen Musikgeschichte, vols. 28, 48, 56, 60, 65, 70, 92. Cologne: Arno Volk Verlag, 1958–70.

6 juin 1832. See *Retraite de Ménilmontant.*

Tajan-Rogé, D[ominique]. *(A M. F. Fétis) Fausses Notes: Les Anabaptistes et M. Félicien David: Le Saint-Simonisme et la musique.* Paris: E. Dentu, 1862.

———. *Hommage à la mémoire de Baillot.* Paris: Armand Le Chevalier, 1872.

———. "Nécrologie: Obsèques de Mme Clorinde." *Revue philosophique et religieuse* 8 (August–November 1857):312–18.

[Tajan-Rogé, Dominique.] *Mémoires d'un piano . . . .* Paris: imprimerie J. Cusset, 1876.

Talmon, J. L. *Political Messianism: The Romantic Phase.* London: Secker and Warburg, 1960.

Taylor, Keith, ed. and trans. *Henri Saint-Simon (1760–1825): Selected Writings on Science, Technology and Social Organization.* New York: Holmes and Meier, 1975.

Thibert, Marguerite. *Le Féminisme dans le socialisme français de 1830 à 1850.* Paris: Marcel Giard, 1926.

———. *Le Rôle social de l'art d'après les Saint-Simoniens.* Paris: Librairie des sciences économiques et sociales Marcel Rivière, 1927.

Tiersot, Julien, ed. *Lettres de musiciens écrites en français.* 2 vols. Turin, Milan, Paris: Bocca frères, 1924–36.

Touchard, Jean. *La Gloire de Béranger.* Paris: Armand Colin, 1968.

Travaux du Temple. See *Retraite de Ménilmontant.*

Vernillat, France, and Pierre Barbier, eds. *Histoire de France par les chansons.* 8 vols. Paris: Gallimard, 1956–61. Also companion four-record album (Le Chant du monde LDX 74461/64).

Vier, Jacques. *La Comtesse d'Agoult et son temps.* 6 vols. Paris: Armand Colin, 1955–63.

Vinçard, Jules [or Luc] [pseud. Vinçard aîné]. *Les Chants du travailleur.* Paris: Librairie des sciences sociales, 1869.

———. *Histoire du travail et des travailleurs en France.* 2 vols. Paris: P. Vinçard, 1845–46.

———. *Mémoires épisodiques d'un vieux chansonnier saint-simonien.* Paris: E. Dentu, 1878.

Voilquin, Suzanne. *Mémoires d'une Saint-Simonienne en Russie (1839–1846).* Edited by Maïté Albistur and Daniel Armogathe. Paris: Editions des femmes, 1977 [recte ca. 1979?].

———. *Souvenirs d'une fille du peuple; ou, La Saint-Simonienne en Egypte.* [Abridgement and] introduction by Lydia Elhadad. Paris: François Maspéro, 1978. First published pseudonymously [Mme Suzanne V***]. Paris: E. Sauzet, 1866.

Walch, Jean. *Bibliographie saint-simonienne.* Paris: J. Vrin, 1967.

———. *Michel Chevalier: Economiste saint simonien, 1806–1879.* Paris: J. Vrin, 1975.

Walker, Alan. *Franz Liszt.* Vol. 1: *The Virtuoso Years: 1811–1847.* New York: Alfred A. Knopf, 1983.

Weber, William. *Music and the Middle Class: The Social Structure of Concert Life in London, Paris and Vienna.* London: Crooms Helm, 1975.

Weill, Georges. *L'Ecole saint-simonienne: Son histoire, son influence jusqu'à nos jours.* Paris: F. Alcan, 1896.

————. *Un Precurseur du socialisme: Saint-Simon et ses oeuvres.* Paris: Perrin, 1894.

Wellek, René. *A History of Modern Criticism.* 4 vols. New Haven: Yale University Press, 1955–65.

Werner, Eric. *Mendelssohn: A New Image of the Composer and His Age.* Translated by Dika Newlin. Glencoe, Ill.: Free Press, 1963.

Wolff, Hellmuth Christian. "Halévy als Kunst- und Musikschriftsteller." In *Musicae scientiae collectanea: Festschrift Karl Gustav Fellerer . . . ,* edited by Heinrich Hüschen, 697–706. Cologne: Arno-Volk-Verlag, 1973.

Wright, Gordon. *France in Modern Times: 1760 to the Present.* Chicago: Rand McNally, 1960.

Zeldin, Theodore. *France: 1848–1945.* 2 vols. Oxford: Oxford University Press, 1973–77.

Zioutos, G. D. "Le Saint-Simonisme hors de France: Quelques cahiers inédits sur l'expédition à l'Egypte." *Revue d'histoire économique et sociale* 31 (1953):23–49.

INDEX

Members of the Saint-Simonian movement were generally referred to by their first or last name, but not both. I have attempted to reconstruct as many of their full names as possible, relying on lists produced by the movement (especially *Procès* [*août*], in *OSSE* 47:43–47, and Enfantin's retrospective list of 1845, in *OSSE* 12:13–15) as well as Maitron, *Dictionnaire*.

Provinces. *See under* Saint-Simonian
movement
"Prussian, poor," 81
Public festivals, 32, 56
Public works projects, 32–33, 42–43
Puget, Loïsa, 359n.5

Quatremère de Quincy, Antoine-
Chrysostome, 16
Quinet, Edgar, 209

Railroads, 94, 213, 217, 227, 362n.64
Ramann, Lina, 101–3, 105
Raphael Sanzio, 54, 61, 109, 112
Raymond. *See* Bonheur
Reber, Napoléon-Henri: and David and
Rogé, 184, 223; and the Saint-Simonians,
3, 82, 121–22, 164, 179, 183–85, 197, 223,
226, 230, 274–76
Reboul, 180, 196
Récio, Marie, 221
"Recreational" view of art. *See under* Social
role of art
Redern, Sigismund Ehrenreich, Graf von, 6,
29
Reformation, 53. *See also* Luther;
Protestantism
Régondi, Jules (guitarist), 335n.18
Renaissance, 21, 53
Republic, Second, 223
Republic, Third, 219–20, 224
Republicanism, 157, 158, 199, 200, 220, 224,
236, 252. *See also* Political parties
Rességuier, Jules, comte de, 74
Restoration, Bourbon, 157, 227
Retouret, Moïse, 350n.87
Revolution, American, 6
Revolution, French, 121, 157, 235; civic
religions, 22; music of, 42, 118, 128, 157,
199–200, 339n.68; Saint-Simon and, 6, 22,
331n.27
Revolution of 1830 (July Revolution), 9, 60,
117, 134, 159, 358n.104
Revolution of 1848 (February Revolution),
149, 160, 200, 215, 222, 350n.84
Reyer, Ernest, 148, 365n.118
Reynaud, Jean, 91, 92, 227, 364n.113
Rhetoric, 19, 21, 32, 41, 43, 56
Ribes, Antoine, 126
Rigaud, Adolphe, 350n.87
Rituals. *See under* Ménilmontant; Saint-
Simonian movement
Robaudi, Georges de, 358n.106
Robert le diable (Meyerbeer), 97, 98, 114, 149,
204, 205

Robespierre, 22
Rochette, Paul, 344n.91
Rodrigues, Eugène, 8, 51, 72, 102–3, 342n.42
Rodrigues, Mme (wife of Olinde), 93, 113
Rodrigues, (Benjamin-)Olinde: *Appel,* 60–63,
66, 91, 109, 112, 362n.69; Börne on,
336n.32; and F. Halévy, 95; and Henry
(Henri), 78; later activities, 200; leaves
movement, 11, 63, 93, 196; on the
"Marseillaise," 159; and Mendelssohn,
108–11, 113; on music, 60–63, 64; and
Saint-Simon, 7, 8, 35, 93; as Saint-
Simonian leader, 7, 8, 73, 91; on sex and
marriage, 89, 104; as singer, 81
Rodrigues family, 95, 108, 111, 114, 340n.3,
344n.85
Rogé. *See* Tajan-Rogé
Rogé, Clorinde, 83, 123, 133, 173, 178, 181,
183, 194, 196, 220, 224, 226, 357n.89,
365n.125; as music engraver, 190
Roland, Pauline, 223, 226
Rolly (carpenter), 199
Romances (salon songs), 116. *See also* David:
songs
Romanticism, 20, 21, 39, 41, 43, 50, 56, 57,
64, 66, 121, 334n.4, 350n.92
Rome, ancient, 17, 42, 46
Rossini, Gioachino, 58–59, 61–63, 64, 65, 97,
106, 109, 112, 119, 335n.12
Rouen, Pierre Isidore, 7
Rouget (librettist), 207
Rouget de Lisle, Claude-Joseph: "Chant des
industriels," 33–34, 62, 235–37; "La
Marseillaise," 60–61, 148, 158–61, 199,
237; and Saint-Simon, 26, 33–34, 235–37
Rousseau, (René-)Achille, 126, 133, 155,
260, 261, 262, 359n.12
Rousseau, Jean-Jacques, 21, 56
Royal Academy of Science, 29
Royer, Alphonse, 207
Roze, Nicolas, 25
Rubini, Giovanni Battista, 59
Ruche populaire, La, 198
Russia, 15, 196, 209, 218, 220–22, 231, 232,
333n.21
Rzewski, Frederic, 368n.29

Saint-Chéron, Alexandre, 75
Saint-Cricq, Caroline, 102
Saint-Didier (husband of Anaïs), 172, 173,
174, 268
Saint-Didier, Anaïs, 172–73, 277, 356n.81
Sainte-Beuve, Charles-Augustin de, 9, 98,
226, 227